**Andrew Stewart**
**Pearson Marvin Macek**
**Adelheid Gealt**
**Irma B. Jaffe**

# Art *of the* Western World
## Study Guide

*to accompany*

A College Television Course and Prime-Time Television Series Produced by

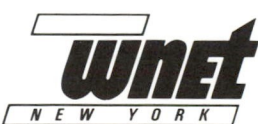
NEW YORK

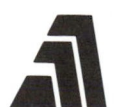 Major Funding from
**The Annenberg/CPB Project**

Corporate Funding by
Movado Watch Corporation

**McGraw-Hill, Inc.**

New York  St. Louis  San Francisco  Auckland  Bogotá  Caracas  Lisbon
London  Madrid  Mexico  Milan  Montreal  New Delhi
San Juan  Singapore  Sydney  Tokyo  Toronto

Art of the Western World Study Guide

89 KPKP 99

ISBN 0-07-557405-5

This book was set in Garamond Light by Ruttle, Shaw & Wetherill, Inc.
The editors were Niels Aaboe, Christopher Rogers, Edna Shalev, and Bob Greiner;
the designer was Leon Bolognese;
the cover designers were C. R. Russell–C. Helfet;
the production manager was Della R. Mancuso.

Excerpt from "Burnt Norton" in *Four Quartets,* copyright © 1943 by T. S. Eliot and renewed 1971 by Esme Valerie Eliot, reprinted by permission of Harcourt Brace Jovanovich, Inc.

Cover Illustration: Diego Velázquez. *Las Meninas,* 1656. The Prado, Madrid. Photo: Courtesy of Art Resource, New York.

Major funding for "Art of the Western World" is provided by the Annenberg/CPB Project.

Corporate funding for "Art of the Western World" is provided by Movado Watch Corporation.

Additional funding is provided by The Rosalind P. Walter Foundation, The Cowles Charitable Trust, The Lemberg Foundation, The Charles Evans Hughes Memorial Foundation, and public television stations.

**Library of Congress Cataloging-in-Publication Data**

Art of the Western world study guide.
　　(An Annenberg/CPB project/Alfred A. Knopf, New York)
　　"A college television course and prime-time
　　television series produced by WNET/New York."
　　Bibliography: p.
　　1. Art.　　I. Stewart, Andrew F.　　II. WNET
(Television station: New York, N.Y.)　　III. Art
of the Western World (Television program)
IV. Series: Annenberg/CPB project (New York, N.Y.)
N5300.A686 1989　　　　700　　　　89–2316
ISBN 0–07–557405-5

# ABOUT THE AUTHORS

**Andrew Stewart** is a scholar of classical art and archeology who teaches at the University of California, Berkeley. He is the author of several publications, including a forthcoming work on Greek sculpture.

**Pearson Marvin Macek** is an art historian who teaches at Lafayette College in Easton, Pennsylvania. A museum professional for several years, she recently received her doctorate from the University of Michigan where she specialized in English Gothic art.

**Adelheid Gealt** is Interim Director of the Indiana University Art Museum in Bloomington, Indiana. A specialist in Italian art, she has a particular interest in drawings and recently published to critical acclaim *Domenico Tiepolo: The Punchinello Drawings*.

**Irma B. Jaffe** is Professor Emeritus of art history at Fordham University in New York. She is a scholar of American art and has written on a wide range of topics in this area, including *John Trumbull: Patriot-Artist of the American Revolution* and a major monograph on Joseph Stella.

# ACKNOWLEDGMENTS

**Staff for *Art of the Western World* Television Course**

**Editorial Team for Printed Materials: WNET/New York**

Tim Gunn, *Project Coordinator*
Robert Miller, *Project Director*
Beatrice Rehl, *Project Manager and Editor*
Natasha Mostert, *Production Assistant*

**Television Production Team: WNET/New York**

*Executive Producer:* Perry Miller Adato
*Series Producers:* Tony Cash, Andrew Snell
*Coordinating Producer:* Gail Jansen
*Associate Producer:* Jane Alexander

**Educational Advisory Panel:**

Phyllis Bober
*Bryn Mawr College*

Eugene Brancolini
*Indiana University*

Karen Connolly
*Fairfield University*

Philip Eliasoph
*Fairfield University*

John Murphy
*Rockland Community College*

Richard Stapleford
*Hunter College, City University of New York*

**Editorial Team: Alfred A. Knopf, Inc.**

Roth Wilkofsky
*Publisher, Humanities*

Christopher Rogers
*History Editor*

Della R. Mancuso
*Production*

Niels Aaboe
*Associate Editor*

Bob Greiner
*Editorial Supervisor*

# CONTENTS

# INTRODUCTION

Welcome to *Art of the Western World*. The television course this Study Guide accompanies is one of a continuing series of such courses developed for public television. It is devoted to that most fundamental of all human activities, the production of art. Long before cultures have written languages, recorded history, and rudimentary technology, cultures have art. Art gives expression to the beliefs, the hopes, and the fears of the people who created it. It is shaped by the culture that produced it and shapes it in return. Today, art has nearly as many definitions as there are artists producing it. Perhaps one of the most memorable definitions comes from Picasso, who once called art a lie that told the truth. In this paradoxical statement, Picasso alluded to the magical ability of art to transcend the materials from which it was made to take on new and different meanings. Picasso also brought home the capacity of art to embody paradoxes of all kinds. Opposites of every description are reconciled in the magical realms of art, and the study of art means coming to terms with every sort of visual and intellectual paradox.

Art is, of course, one of the highest means by which the human mind and soul can express itself. It is the means by which humanity comes to terms with its own paradoxical condition. Made of flesh and unalterably mortal, humanity has the capacity to perceive, if not to understand, the immaterial and the eternal. Through art, time can stand still, the spiritual can be made real, and the real can be ennobled.

Perched on the start of a new century, we can look back on a long and glorious tradition of Western art. Contemporary ideas about art were shaped fairly recently. Reacting against accepted notions about the nature of art and the purposes it should serve, artists in the late 1860s declared that art had only one function and that was art. We now take this idea about art for granted, and therefore we have to be reminded that the bulk of what was produced by Western artists from roughly 1000 B.C. to about one hundred years ago, had purposes other than pure art.

Art served religion, it served kings and princes, families, cities, and organizations. It embodied beliefs, it made histories, legends, myths, and stories that were the common cultural coin of the day visible to all. These images were occasionally regarded as art, but they more often than not had another function. Today art serves only one master: art. That view, which was radical about a hundred years ago, is now commonplace. Today we tend to view art as the inspired but personal vision of an individual genius, whose creativity enables him or her to give artistic form and expression to some aspect of his or her experience. We do not always expect to understand this expression, nor do we question the right of the artist not to communicate in universally understandable terms.

Despite the gulfs that sometimes exist between us and art, the interest in it has never been greater. Visitors flock to museums in record numbers; they look, they buy postcards, books, and reproductions and they take nourishment from the long and vast visual culture to which they are heir. Art has now come to be viewed as belonging to all, speaking no more directly to one viewer than another. Museums, that product of the egalitarian system of the eighteenth century, gave birth to this idea, which has flowered and flourished in the present day as never before.

Yet the history of Western art is as complex and diverse as the many countries, periods, and artists that produced it. This *Art of the Western World Study Guide* is intended to help you understand in depth and greater detail the developments of three thousand years of Western art. Beginning with the civilizations of ancient Greece, nine programs take you from the earliest monuments of Greek antiquity to the art of the present day.

This Study Guide is an essential component in your educational experience. It will serve as the principal link between you, the television programs, and the textbooks. The Study Guide will not only prepare you for each of the nine programs you will see, but it will also discuss in depth the concepts and the cultural, philosophical, and historical contexts out of which artistic monuments have emerged. The Study Guide will explain to you why and how works of art are part of their time, for whom they were made, and the functions they served. And it will give you a basic idea about what makes them exceptional as well as typical.

Only certain key monuments have been selected for discussion in order that they can be examined in detail. The information provided in the Study Guide is intended to complement and embellish what can be learned from certain key textbooks, H. W. Janson's *History of Art* and H. Gardner's *Art Through the Ages*.

## Course Goals

By using the Study Guide, the textbook, the optional slides, and the video programs, you will learn to:

- Become sensitive to various periods, mediums, and subjects in art
- Become aware of artists' styles and begin to appreciate how and why art changes over time as well as sometimes within an artist's career
- Understand the relationship between the form a particular art work takes and its function and, on a broader level, understand some basic historical and societal conditions that produced particular artistic monuments
- Appreciate the changing relationship between artist and patron and gain an appreciation of the different kinds of patrons that have supported artists over time
- Gain a fundamental appreciation for the differences in materials, techniques, and subjects and learn to understand how these basic elements of art affect style
- Understand the fundamental conceptual framework that underlays the production of Western art from its origins with the ancient Greeks to the present day

## How to Use this Study Guide

First read the Learning Objectives at the beginning of each unit. Then watch the one-hour television program keeping in mind the outline that the summary has provided and look for the concepts and ideas it has prepared you to see.

Then turn back to the Study Guide and read the unit related to the program. That unit will provide a detailed discussion of the key monuments you have seen, giving the cultural, historical, intellectual, and physical circumstances for their creation. A section with textbook references, study questions, glossary, biographical notes, and bibliography at the end of each unit will enable you to inform yourself more deeply and provide a structure for your studies and learning. You can combine and recombine the themes and ideas you have learned to suit your interests and inclinations. References to the key textbooks will outline what corresponding chapters in those texts cover.

In some cases, however, the monument discussed is not illustrated in the textbook and reference is made to another book in which the image can be found with its plate number cited. Your instructor will place these additional books on a special "reserve reading" shelf in the library so that you will have easy access to them. A slide of every monument that we will be examining in depth will also be found in an *Art of the Western World* slide set, which will be put in a reserved reading shelf or in a media lab for your use. You will be expected to study these images and learn them thoroughly.

Note that while figure references are made to Janson's *History of Art,* Third Edition, 1986 (designated "J"), and Gardner's *Art Through the Ages,* Eighth Edition, 1986 (designated "G"), you are *not* responsible for reading both textbooks. Your instructor will tell you which one he or she has selected as the textbook for this course. We

have included additional references to Honour and Fleming's *The Visual Arts: A History.*

Read the appropriate chapter referenced in the selected textbook. These chapters will amplify and place into broader context the materials you have experienced in both the television programs and the Study Guide. These authors will, from their own vantage point, help you to see, understand, and appreciate the complex and challenging ideas that underlay the production of Western Art.

### Be Sure To

Obtain your own personal copy of the Study Guide. It is your vital link with the rest of the course. Take notes if you feel it helps you to grasp the many ideas and information each program contains. Write down questions about things you do not understand. Write down your own observations about the objects you see. Try to describe them in your own words. Try to remember an object again when the program has ended. Consider drawing it, however crudely, and consider as you make your "copy" some of the important ideas it contains. Think of its properties—its materials, its expression, its condition, its subject. Think about what makes it art.

Visit your nearest art museum and try to find other examples from the period you have just studied. See if you can detect similarities or differences in ideas discussed in the program. Keep notes on artists or monuments you find particularly interesting. Keep track of where they are. Work steadily and do not fall behind. There is sufficient material in this course to give you the framework for a lifetime's enjoyment of art. But if you wait too long, you will never absorb it in the period of your course work. Art must be absorbed slowly and savored.

Use your Study Guide. Go back and re-read relevant texts and reconsider what you have read. You are on the first step to a lifelong assembly of images and ideas which will sustain you and enrich you to the very end of your days. Each time you confront a new work of art, what you already know will shape your experience, and what you are seeing will affect it anew. Works of art that you come to know well will be old friends, never seen quite the same way twice. As you change, so will they. Art is a mirror in which you see and learn about yourself. The study of science, a famed scholar noted, is a step in the direction of knowledge; the study of art (as with all humanities) is a step in the direction of wisdom. The materials contained in this program may guide you in the direction of wisdom and will provide you with great pleasure and beauty along the way.

*Andrew Stewart*
*Pearson Marvin Macek*
*Adelheid Gealt*
*Irma B. Jaffe*

# Art *of the* Western World

## Study Guide

# The Classical World

## Greece and Rome

## Learning Objectives

Greece and Rome are seminal to the Western tradition in the visual arts, just as they are to Western literature, music, philosophy, and science. Yet their achievements, though extraordinary, are by no means the only reason why this survey of Western art begins with them. Just as importantly, their architecture, painting, and sculpture make a worthy overture to this enterprise because they display a particularly close and clear-cut relationship with the central concerns of the cultures that created them. Since the main tendency of contemporary thinking about art is to see it as a manifestation of cultural symbolism, where better to begin than here?

This unit begins with the destruction of the Bronze Age kingdoms in the twelfth century B.C., tracing the revival of Greek art in the developing city-state or *polis*-society of the Geometric and Archaic periods (ca. 900–700 and ca. 700–480 B.C.). An account of the culmination of this process in the fifth century, after the repulse of the Persian invasions of 490 and 480, focuses on Athens and her great temple, the Parthenon (447-432 B.C.), whose architecture and sculpture are treated in detail. Then follows the late classical period of the fourth century, setting the stage for the conquests of Alexander (336–323 B.C.) and the greatly expanded horizons, both political and artistic, of the Hellenistic age (323–30 B.C.). Our attention then shifts to the Roman republic, which from around 200 B.C. increasingly dominated the Mediterranean, plundering the East of its wealth and its art, but succumbed to internal conflict in the first century. Roman imperial art is introduced via the monuments of the first emperor, Augustus, who put an end to the Civil Wars in 30 and ruled until A.D. 14, and is analysed in detail in the case of Hadrian's Pantheon, built between A.D. 117 and 128. The survey continues with a discussion of the transformation of Roman art during the political, religious, and social crises of the third and fourth centuries, and ends with the fall of Rome to the Visigoths in A.D. 410.

Throughout this unit, we shall be focusing on a number of interrelated issues: analysis of style and content; the role of the client or patron; and the wider political and social context. The individual work of art will remain in the foreground throughout: this is art history, not political or social history illustrated by art. The objectives will be twofold: to be able to analyze the work of art both as an autonomous object, a unique creation of human hands and mind, and to see it in relation to the culture which brought it to be and which is registered, directly or indirectly, in its form. In this enterprise, certain terms and concepts will assume key importance: among institutions, the Greek *polis* or city-state, and the Roman notion of *imperium,* or supreme executive power; Greek values such as *arete* (personal excellence) and *sophrosyne* (the self-knowledge that begets a measured self-restraint), and their opposite, *hybris* or arrogance; Roman values such as *gravitas* (seriousness) and *constantia* (endurance), and the *auctoritas* or personal authority that results when one cultivates them; and art-historical terms such as *iconography,* the "what" of an image, not to mention the numerous technical terms for architectural members, sculptural types, and so on.

In particular, you should note that the term "classical" is used in a somewhat more restrictive sense in the following pages than is implied by the title of this unit. In conformity with current art-historical and archaeological practice, it will refer only to the art which was produced in Greece during the fifth and fourth centuries, and which served as a standard for all subsequent periods of ancient art; the terms "classicizing" or "neo-classical" are used to describe works of these later periods that in some way try to re-create this style. All these terms, and others, are listed and further explained in the glossary that follows the main text.

In this unit, you will learn to:

- Understand the meaning of humanism and its impact on the visual arts of Greece and Rome.
- Appreciate the differences between Greek and Roman art, and how humanism served different purposes in the art of each civilization.

- Know the basic elements of classical architecture and be able to distinguish between the three Orders.
- Understand the fundamental formal and structural principles that enabled artists to create convincing renditions of the human figure in sculpture and painting.
- Understand the social context and the philosophical and political values that conditioned Greek and Roman art.
- Be aware of the vital contributions to architecture and engineering made by the Romans and the technical achievements that made these possible.

So much for introductions. It is time to turn to the art itself.

## Part 1
## THE ART OF ANCIENT GREECE

## Beginnings (ca. 1200–700 B.C.)

"We sit," Sokrates once observed, "like frogs around a pond." Greece is not a large country, and the Aegean not a large sea. Yet high mountains and often rough water encouraged political and social fragmentation among a people that had always naturally been individualistic and competitive. Though a strong sense of ethnic unity seems to have survived the long "Dark Age" after the collapse of Mycenaean civilization in the twelfth century B.C., very little else did. What emerged from nearly four centuries of isolation, insecurity, and impoverishment (both material and cultural) was a self-reliant, male-dominated society obsessed with personal prowess and personal excellence (Greek: *arete*). In Homer's *Iliad* and *Odyssey*, largely a product of these very years and the "Bible of the Greeks" until the end of antiquity, *arete* means being stronger than your rivals (otherwise they will kill or enslave you), and being honored and recognized as such. Achilles withdrew from the siege of Troy because in taking Briseis from him, Agamemnon "did no honor to the best of the Achaeans." All this, in turn, helped both to generate what has aptly been called the Greek contest society, and to focus attention on the self and its attributes: its autonomy, strength, physical beauty, youth, and so on.

In the eighth century, for reasons we may never fully understand, the scattered Dark Age communities began to coalesce into larger units. These *poleis* or city-states immediately began to manifest a quite extraordinary dynamism, as population pressures forced them to send colonies overseas, to Sicily, Italy, North Africa, and the Black Sea. Simultaneously, their citizens began to com-

pete for honors and power, often overthrowing their aristocratic rulers and creating oligarchies or popular dictatorships, and instituting aggression against other *poleis*. Physically, a typical *polis* incorporated four main features: a wall for defense; an open space or *agora* where citizens could meet, talk, buy, and sell; a sanctuary to its protecting divinity, often sited on a citadel or *akropolis;* and a cemetery or *necropolis,* usually situated outside the main gate. Soon, all could be, and were, embellished by works of architecture, sculpture, and/or painting, as appropriate.

It is not surprising that Greek monumental art as we know it begins in earnest in these very years. Dark Age arts are few and usually portable: painted vases, some clay and bronze figurines, and the occasional piece of jewelry comprise almost the entire inventory of the period (**G 5.1, 5.12**). Suddenly, however, the eighth and early seventh centuries saw the revival of monumental architecture (in the form of large temples), the beginnings of monumental sculpture, the re-introduction of figure-drawing, and the first steps in pictorial narrative (**J 135–137, 144; G 5.2–5.3; H&F 4.1–4.2**). Though the exact origin of each of these genres is intensely problematic, the coincidence cannot be fortuitous. It must owe at least as much to the burgeoning need for self-registration on the part of *polis* and individual alike, as to influences from abroad, where the Greeks had begun to trade with the Near East around 800, and with Egypt around 660. The functions of the objects are manifold but divide quite neatly into the two spheres of sacred and secular: thus, while temples were houses for the gods, sculpture could embellish both sanctuary and grave, and vases could be votive offerings, gifts for the dead, and ornaments for the home.

This art, like the culture that produced it, was individual, experimental, and dogmatic. Individual, because it was made by individuals competing for commissions or markets, and continually refining their styles in order to do so effectively. Experimental, because this involved constant experiment with new forms, new techniques, new ways of looking at the world, new attempts to capture that most elusive of all qualities, beauty. And dogmatic, because each new solution automatically rendered its predecessors obsolete. Thrown back on their own resources, the Greeks focused on man and his doings, seeking out the typical and general in nature, to bring order to the otherwise chaotic flux of life, "to know what patterns govern mankind," as one archaic poet put it. The assertion that "man is the measure of all things" may have been first voiced by a fifth-century philosopher, but as an unspoken creed it pervades Greek art right from the very beginning. The artist's signature, an innovation of the late eighth century, not only embraces all of these traits in a single gesture, but connects him, via the use of the "ethnic" ("so-and-so the Athenian, Corinthian, or whatever, made this") firmly with his roots in the *polis*.

# From Archaic to Classic (ca. 700–440 B.C.)

Of the various genres and types, none exemplifies these characteristics more clearly than the *kouros* or nude striding male **(J 145–146; G 5.15, 5.16; H&F 4.9)**. Apparently borrowed from Egypt around 650, the type soon became popular for both funerary and votive use, and, furnished with appropriate attributes, for statues of the gods as well. The material is almost always marble, and the Egyptian kilt was immediately removed to display the body in all its naked glory, swiftly establishing the male nude as the central genre in Greek sculpture. The back-pillar was also abandoned, the stone removed from between the limbs, and the weight of the torso distributed equally between the two legs. This last trait is part and parcel of what is often called the "law of frontality," implying not only that the statue directly confronts the viewer, but that its frontal view dominates all others and that from this angle it is perfectly symmetrical about its central axis. All this transformed what had been a kind of quasi-iconic ultra-high relief into a fully autonomous, three-dimensional simulacrum of a naked man, smiling and confident in this own *arete,* striding towards the observer and invading his space in a quite direct way.

Independence, then, is the keynote from the start. Indeed, whereas Egyptian striding males hardly differ from each other in either anatomy or proportions **(J 55, 66; G 3.3, 3.44; H&F 2.28–2.29),** *kouroi* manifest some quite startling variations according to locale and sculptor. Thus, Naxians like youths who are slim and svelte; Parians prefer them robust and barrel-chested; Samians go for rounded, opulent forms; Boeotians enjoy sheer brute strength. All tend to stylize anatomy, but in different ways, producing a myriad of patterns or *schemata* that seek to pin down the shifting flux of existence. At Athens in particular, male beauty is equated with a kind of crystal-clear articulation of parts, leading to a quest for anatomical exactitude that by the beginning of the fifth century was to call into question the entire archaic notion of *schemata* as satisfactory descriptions of the world—but this is to anticipate.

Egyptian sculpture was proportioned according to a grid system, drawn on the block before carving commenced, that mandated twenty-one squares from feet to hairline, with intermediate features falling at fixed points **(G 3.4; H&F 2.30).** Some early *kouros*-sculptors adopted this grid but, characteristically, never without modifying it in some way: the New York *kouros,* for example, uses it in the vertical dimension only, narrowing the shoulders, waist, and hips by a full square. Others experimented with their own systems, seeking by trial and error to discover the right proportions for the perfect man. In this way what had begun as a convenient design aid eventually came to signify far more: a personal quest for ideal beauty (and thus *arete*) itself, soon identified with the pure sciences of

abstract mathematics and plane geometry. Statues of women, or *korai,* follow the same path, but less rigorously and with far more likelihood of being seduced by the purely decorative delights of pretty clothing, jewelry, and coiffure **(J 144, 149–151, clpl 15; G 5.14, 5.17, 5.18; H&F 4.6, 4.8).**

The notion that beauty means the correct proportioning of parts is fundamental to the other monumental art form of Archaic Greece, namely architecture. Greek temples **(J 153, 159–167; G 5.20–5.27; H&F 4.17)** can be defined as abstract sculpture in a landscape: unlike their Bronze-Age predecessors and their contemporaries in the Near East, but like the *kouroi,* they are free-standing, and manifest a high degree of cohesion between interior and exterior, a precise articulation of parts, and an orderly relationship between those parts based on mathematically worked-out proportions. Also unprecedented in Greece or anywhere else was their openness to the public: priests were elected officials of the polis, sacrifices took place in the open (on altars placed before the temple façade), and access to the interior and its cult image was normally unrestricted. One wonders if the colonnade, a feature that was both uniquely Greek and standard for their temples from the start, might not have been invented with this particular function in mind. For whereas the temples of Egypt and the Near East were exclusive affairs, and built like fortresses **(J 74–77; G 3.26–3.27, etc.; H&F 2.12–2.13, 3.8–3.10),** the colonnade mediates between temple and worshipper, creating a kind of twilight zone that both defines the temple against its surroundings, and yet invites entry and exploration by those outside.

The origins of the two main architectural styles or Orders (Doric and Ionic; **J 159; G 5.21; H&F 4.15–4.20)** are much disputed: Mycenaean survivals, borrowings from the Near East, and native traditions in timber all contributed something, though with so much lost or destroyed it is usually hard to know precisely what. What is clear, however, is that their aesthetics are quite different, based on quite different conceptions of proportion, articulation, embellishment, and space.

The Doric Order **(J 159, 161–167; G 5.22–5.26; H&F 4.15–4.17)** was so called because it was at home in the Doric-speaking Peloponnese, whence it soon spread to the Dorian colonies in the West, to Athens, and to the Aegean islands. A massive, compact, severely formalized construction of horizontals and verticals, it admits embellishment only between main structural members, and as a kind of final cadence on the points of the gable. Balance is all-important, as the eye first scans the firm foundation of the three-stepped platform or *krepis,* then is led upward by the fluted columns, is diverted laterally again by the lintel or *entablature* with its frieze's rhythmic beat of triglyphs and metopes, then led up once more via the vertical bars of the triglyphs themselves, then presented with a coda in the form of the heavy horizontal and raking cornices of the triangular gable. Finally, the culminating embellishments or *akroteria* on the gable-points focus the energy so generated, and disperse it into space.

The Ionic Order **(J 159; G 5.27; H&F 4.18–4.20)** was the creation of the Ionic-speaking cities of the eastern Aegean. While still adhering firmly to the rectilinear post-and-lintel system, it was far more flexible than the Doric in both plan and elevation. Ionic temples ranged from the tiny to the enormous, sometimes reaching over three hundred feet in length and sixty feet or more in height. They were also spatially more adventurous, often doubling the colonnade or even (on the façades) tripling it, spacing the columns further apart, opting for deep, columnar porches that greatly increase the interpenetration of exterior and interior, and last but not least, stretching the columns themselves to a height of up to ten times their lower diameter, as opposed to around five times for Doric. In addition, they admitted embellishment almost anywhere, using fine fluting, faceting, and delicate moldings to create a glittering shadow-play over the entire surface of the building.

Finally, while Doric developed a strong tradition of carefully framed narrative sculpture, filling pediments and metopes with scenes of divine prowess or divinely sanctioned heroic enterprise, Ionic used sculpture like a molding **(J 152–157; G 5.27–5.32; H&F 4.18–4.20).** Genre scenes of processions, dances, and sacrifices accompanied the spectator as he walked through the colonnade, winding around the bases of the columns themselves, while guardian animals watched him from architraves and capitals high above. Only towards the end of the sixth century, at Delphi, does Ionic develop what was later to become its most characteristic feature, the sculptured narrative frieze **(J 154–155; G 5.27–5.28; H&F 4.19).** Against the heavyweight Doric all around them, the little treasuries erected by the Ionian states perhaps looked too frivolous by comparison, and this may have been an effort to even the odds.

By this time, narrative had become the staple of another art form, painted pottery **(J 137–143, clpls 13–14; G 5.4–5.11; H&F 4.13).** Tens of thousands of these vases survive, but still represent only a minuscule fraction of what once existed—one percent or (probably) less. So intensive was the production, and (after an interlude when animals captured the painters' imaginations: **H&F 4.4)** so single-minded the concentration upon narrative, that E. H. Gombrich has even argued that the compulsion to narrate heroic myth, to *make present* its events to the eye, is what fuelled the unique "advance to naturalism" that is such a striking feature of Greek art of all kinds. Yet powerful as this thesis may be, it will be apparent from the remarks that opened this chapter that there is a wider context to be considered. For Greek narrative is but one element of Greek anthropocentrism, that concentration upon man and his doings which is absolutely central to their culture.

The subject matter of these vase-paintings has aroused attention in other quarters too. As a recent book notes, "In the case of society dominated by men who sequester their wives and daughters, denigrate the female role in reproduction, erect monuments to the male genitalia, have sex with the sons of their peers, sponsor public whorehouses, create a mythology of rape, and engage in rampant saber-rattling, it is not inappropriate to refer to the reign of the phallus. Classical Athens was such a society" (Eva Keuls, *The Reign of the Phallus,* p. 1). Feminist perspectives on Greek society are still rare, but in this case there is no denying the author's central point that Greek society, and Greek art, are sexist to the core. From the Greeks' worship of the naked male body in sculpture to the countless scenes in their vase-painting that are either explicitly sexual (heroic and divine rapes, orgies, satyrs molesting maenads: **H&F 4.35)** or implicitly so (fights with Amazons, Dionysiac revels, symposia, and so on: **J 140; G 5.10–5.11)**, the theme of male dominance overrides all others. Greek homosexuality is also tied in here, since narcissism and voyeurism are very obvious components of their cult of nudity, in art as in life.

Thus a feminist critic familiar with Freud's theory of the male castration complex would explain the archaic Greek fascination with the Gorgon as an obsession with the *vagina dentata,* and therefore a tacit acknowledgment of its powers. Aside from the hundreds of representations of the Perseus myth **(J 137; G 5.4)**, Gorgons' heads were regularly used as centerpieces on temple pediments **(cf. J 152–153 and G 5.29)**, and as embellishments for drinking vessels: in both cases the purpose was to shock, to avert evil by confronting it with the most horrific image the Greek imagination could dream up. Such a critic would also note the frequency with which Greeks stab at female breasts and genitalia in Amazonomachies, and the almost complete avoidance of representations of those genitalia themselves, even in scenes of explicit sex.

On a more sophisticated level, s/he might consider the way in which, even as the *kouroi* tend to a more organic, holistic rendering of the body, the late archaic *korai* become loaded with detail **(J 151 and clpl 15; G 5.16, 5.18; H&F 4.8).** Imported from Ionia, this trend is very common throughout late archaic art; yet even so, a persistent critic might argue that so distinct a parting of the ways in these two genres is an early example of that persistent dichotomy between masculine/generalizing and feminine/particularizing that became a commonplace of Greek and Roman thinking (and thereby of our own) about literature, philosophy, and art. At the least, to see these sculptors as seduced by particulars as soon as they essayed the portrayal of women would certainly offer a new perspective on the universal judgment of those (chiefly male) historians of ancient sculpture that, in the words of one of them, "artistically, the *kouros* had been moving on the right track while the *kore* had been led into a bypath" (Rhys Carpenter, *Greek Sculpture,* p. 55). As will appear, Hellenistic art is also an art of detail, and it too has suffered from exactly the same scholarly prejudice over the years.

Again following the ancients themselves, these same historians usually reserve their highest praise for the classical style, whose creations are the very apotheosis of consistency, economy, clarity, and the subordination of part to whole. The work that is universally held to mark the transition is the so-called "Kritian Boy" from the Akropolis, carved between the Persian invasion of Attica and defeat at Marathon in 490, and their massive assault on Greece and subsequent sack of Athens in 480 **(J 178; G 5.19; H&F 4.10).**

The "Kritian Boy," so-called because of his resemblance to Roman copies of the tyrannicide Harmodios by the sculptors Kritios and Nesiotes, is a work of almost evangelistic sobriety. Disdaining the archaic smile, he fails to replace it with anything more than a blank look. As Martin Robertson has remarked, this "vacant regard . . . is the vice of classical seriousness, as the simper is of archaic gaiety" (A *History of Greek Art,* p. 176). His originality lies not so much in his expression (the smile had been eschewed before) but in his pose. For the first time, the *kouros* schema is abandoned for a "musing pose," where one leg relaxes, the hip above it drops, the abdominal muscles respond to the movement, and the head turns to one side. Released from the sleepwalking stride of the *kouros,* and an organism rather than a mechanism, the statue now lives and breathes. His action locates him in time and space, inviting the spectator to ask *why* he is musing, and thereby immediately places him within an imagined narrative framework: assuming that (like others of his kind) he is a boy-victor at the games, one may see him as mentally gearing up for the contest, or as pondering his triumph after it.

This abrupt and thoroughgoing replacement of the archaic style by the classical around 480, perhaps the most rapid and momentous change ever witnessed by Western art, has inevitably led to much speculation about causes. In general, scholars have tended to divide into two separate camps according to whether they see it as a phenomenon largely or entirely internal to the art itself (formalists), or whether they admit external social, political, or intellectual factors into the debate (contextualists). If one takes a position such as that outlined at the beginning of this unit, that art is a form of cultural symbolism, the answer cannot be in doubt, and to be fair, few have taken the exclusively formalist path. The upheaval must reflect, on the one hand, a certain dissatisfaction with the archaic style as a medium of expression, and on the other, a distinct appreciation of the expressive superiority of the classical.

In other words, it represents the simultaneous recognition that archaic pattern-making leads only to endless elaboration, not to a more coherent ordering of reality; that its increasing artificiality forces the artist away from his goal of making man and his deeds persuasively present to the spectator; and that its intense concentration upon surface phenomena inhibits articulation of what differentiates man from the beasts, namely his ability to think and reflect. The classical, on the other hand, easily fulfills all these functions. Selective, economical, and committed to generalizing from nature rather than finding schematized substitutes for it, it simultaneously re-establishes hierarchies of significance, persuades the spectator by its verisimilitude, and enables the artist to combine postures and gestures from the everyday body language of the Greeks with facial expressions that are literally empty vessels, waiting to acquire character and soul from their context.

As to the "musing pose," this speaks to a new ethical ideal, increasingly promoted by the poets: *sophrosyne.* Aptly defined as "the self-knowledge that begets a measured self-restraint," this new ideal of moderation, of "nothing to excess," as the Apolline maxim of Delphi had it, quickly replaces the self-assertive machismo of the archaic. This is now condemned as *hybris,* or arrogance, inviting divine *nemesis,* or retribution. If politics are anywhere apropos, it is here: the miraculous defeat of the Persian and Carthaginian invasions in 490/480 was seen as their *nemesis* for such excessive ambition, powerfully reinforcing this emerging value system. Perhaps, then, we can hazard that the mass success of the new ideal in the tragedies of Aischylos, the odes of Pindar, and the visual arts immediately after 480 was a direct consequence of what many undoubtedly viewed as a powerful and timely validation by the Olympians themselves. For in this respect not only the "musing pose" but even the classical style itself, with its deliberately measured and restrained vocabulary, is a very definite exercise in *sophrosyne,* in contrast to the formal "excesses" of the archaic.

Monuments like the Delphi Charioteer, the sculptures of the temple of Zeus at Olympia, the recently discovered bronze warriors from Riace Marina, and the vases of the Niobid, Penthesilea, and Pistoxenos painters typify this early or "Severe" phase of the classical, which lasts until about 450 **(J 180–183; G 5.33–5.41, 63; H&F 4.22–4.23, 4.29).** Its full maturity, however, was to come in the next generation, with the work of the sculptors Polykleitos and Pheidias.

Polykleitos of Argos worked in bronze. His acknowledged masterpiece was a six-and-a-half-foot study of a young man carrying a large spear, the Doryphoros **(J 179; G 5.61; H&F 4.31).** Hints in the ancient authors suggest that the subject was actually Achilles, but its original location and purpose remain unknown. The Doryphoros, which Polykleitos accompanied with a manifesto, represents the summit of idealism in Greek sculpture. Its claim to absolute perfection found many adherents in antiquity, who followed Polykleitos's precepts "like a law" (Pliny), and through their agency, its influence upon later Western art has been incalculable. The wellspring of the academic tradition in the visual arts, it incorporated a comprehensive scheme of mathematical proportions that related every part to every other and to the whole, and was composed in a way that grouped these parts visually by pairs, balancing tense and relaxed muscles, weight-bearing and free limbs in a series of contrapuntally organized cross-relationships through the body. Standard practice for sculptors thereafter, this highly integrated form of composition is generally known as *contrapposto,* a name coined after its revival in the Italian Renaissance.

Finally, Polykleitos re-designed the musculature of the body itself. Sensitive to the fact that the abandonment of the archaic for a more lifelike and vivid style had inevitably led to a certain loss of distance, of monumentality, he not only strengthened the musculature all round, but completely re-worked the focal point of the entire composition, the torso. Heavy, prominent pectorals were now balanced by equally heavy flank muscles, linked by an accentuated costal arch and median line, and articulated by deep transitions from the smaller, more mobile muscles around and between. The resulting construction is truly architectural in character, like a Doric temple come to life. "A brilliant solution to the conflicting demands of naturalism and monumentality . . . on the one hand it blatantly advertises both increased anatomical knowledge and skill in naturalistic representation . . . on the other it combines these with an ingenious system of selective emphasis which endows the human frame with a powerful and monumental structure" (C. H. Hallett, "The Origins of the Classical Style in Sculpture," p. 82).

Yet this was not all: determined that his figure should be a paradigm of Greek values for all time, Polykleitos made it the incarnation of the Mean. Thus its physique was intermediate between fat and thin, its pose between movement and rest, its age between youth and maturity, even the poise of its head between undue self-assertiveness (*hybris*) and undue reticence: it is *sophrosyne* personified.

The classical Greek search for harmony and order so brilliantly exemplified by the Doryphoros extended throughout all spheres of art, with incalculable effects upon the subsequent history of Western art and thought. In fact, what is probably their most enduring legacy to the modern world, the grid plan for cities, was a product of these very years. Though evidence of rudimentary grids can be found as far back as the eighth century, the devastation of the Persian Wars gave a golden opportunity to a young visionary, Hippodamos of Miletos, to try out his theories in practice. His native town, totally destroyed by the Persians in 494, was rebuilt on the grid system around 470, and shortly thereafter Hippodamos was hired by the Athenians to rebuild their port of Piraeus: here, the ancient blocks still survive in the wide boulevards and high-rises of the modern town. To him, town planning was only but a part of a unified theory of the *polis.* His treatise on the subject discussed not only the grid as such, but also an ideal constitution which separated the city into sacred, public, and private districts, and its people into artisans, warriors, and farmers. We last hear of him in connection with the foundation of the Athenian colony of Thurii in Italy in 445. His system now spanned

the Greek world, and was soon to spread far beyond **(G 5.91, 5.95, 6.21, etc.; H&F 5.22).**

## Periklean Athens and the Peloponnesian War (ca. 460–404 B.C.)

When the Athenians returned to their shattered city after the Persians had been expelled from Greece in 479, their first actions were to rebuild its walls and to induce the Greeks of the Aegean islands and the coast of Asia Minor to join an alliance (the Delian League) that would carry the war into Persian territory. Within two decades, Athens so dominated her allies that she had effectively converted the League into her own empire, and in 454 she was able to remove its treasury (replenished by annual contributions from every state) from Delos to the Akropolis. Dissenters among the allies were ruthlessly suppressed, and Sparta and the other mainland states kept at bay in a series of daring naval and land campaigns. Now a radical democracy, the city was guided by a succession of elected leaders of extraordinary brilliance: Themistokles, Aristeides, Kimon, and finally Perikles.

Yet for all this, when Perikles' long period of ascendancy began in the 450s, the focus of Athenian religious life, the Akropolis **(J 168; G 5.42–5.43; H&F 4.16),** was still in ruins. Kimon and others had begun to rebuild the Agora and its civic buildings, erecting colonnaded halls or *stoas* and other structures to house the democracy's magistrates, councils, and courts. Yet an attempt by Perikles himself to use the conclusion of peace with Persia around 465 to convene a Panhellenic congress on the rebuilding of the devastated shrines had been universally snubbed. The problem was that before expelling the Persians, the Greek allies had sworn "never to rebuild the temples burned and sacked by the barbarians, but to leave them forever in ruins as a memorial to the impiety of the despoilers," and some kind of consensus was required if the oath was to be set aside.

In 449 Perikles tried again, but now took a rather different tack. First, despite some opposition, he secured the Athenian Assembly's approval for a motion to use League funds for the rebuilding. Next, he sited the new temples to one side of the old, ruined ones, so that technically the oath remained intact. Mere altars, and shrines unfinished and so not yet dedicated when the Persians arrived, were apparently not a problem. Thus, while the Erechtheion was carefully situated alongside the ruins of the Old Temple of Athena, the new temple of Athena Nike could be placed directly above the goddess's archaic altar on the western spur of the Akropolis, and the jewel of the entire ensemble, the Parthenon, built over the platform of a great temple to Athena whose construction had been rudely interrupted at an early stage by the invasion **(J 166–168, 186–188; G 5.42–5.45; H&F 4.15, 4.16, 4.18–4.20).**

And so the buildings arose, as imposing in their sheer size as they were inimitable in the grace of their outlines, since the artists strove to excel themselves in the beauty of their workmanship. And yet the most wonderful thing about them was the speed with which they were completed. Each of them, men supposed, would take many generations to build, but in fact the entire project was carried through in the high summer of one man's administration. . . . The director and overseer of the whole project was Pheidias, although there were various great architects and artists employed on the individual buildings. For example, Kallikrates and Iktinos were the architects of the Parthenon . . . , [and] Mnesikles of the Propylaia . . . , while it was Pheidias who directed the making of the great golden image of Athena, and his name is duly inscribed upon the marble stele as its creator.—*Plutarch*

Although eloquent, persuasive, and our major source for the Periklean building program, Plutarch's account is not unproblematic. Written five hundred years after the event, it compresses the chronology somewhat: though the Parthenon and Propylaea (begun in 447 and 438, respectively) were completed in 432, well before Perikles died in 429, the temple of Athena Nike was not finished till around 420, and the Erechtheion not till 406, a mere two years before Athens' surrender to Sparta and her allies terminated the building program forever. Yet though the historian can be forgiven for this and for his omission of the Parthenon's third architect, one Karpion (known from another source), his remark about the supervisory role of Pheidias is less easy to understand, and may be a complete anachronism.

Not only is the title Plutarch gives to Pheidias inappropriate, for it properly describes an inspector of Athens'

subject allies, but not even the inscribed building accounts name him in this—or any other—capacity. Jealous of its own supervisory role, the Athenian democracy would certainly have been extremely reluctant to grant such sweeping and open-ended powers to anyone; rather, it preferred annually rotating supervisors, who are named in the accounts, and executive committees like the three architects of the Parthenon itself. Most likely, then, Plutarch was projecting the practice of his own times back into the fifth century. So though the sculptor must have exerted a powerful influence upon his contemporaries, his involvement with the program as a whole (if historical at all) was probably quite informal. Yet as regards the Parthenon itself, someone must have planned the sculptures. Both unprecedentedly complex and achieving a high degree of stylistic unity by the time of Pheidias's exile on embezzlement charges in 438, the ensemble demands a director. If not him, then who?

Conceived as a votive offering to Athena for Athens' successes against Persia, the Parthenon certainly performed other, less obvious functions as well. Offering arguments for Athens' own claims to cultural and political hegemony, it also made a patriotic display of popular Attic myth, proclaimed Athens' special relationship with the gods, insinuated the benefits to be had from Perikles' leadership, and furnished a fine exhibition of Athenian skill and mastery of beauty. It was also a treasury, for not only was some of the tribute of the Delian League probably stored in its rear room, but the Athena's golden drapery (weighing almost 2,500 pounds) could be removed and melted down in time of need, provided that it were replaced later. Viewed in this light, the decision to

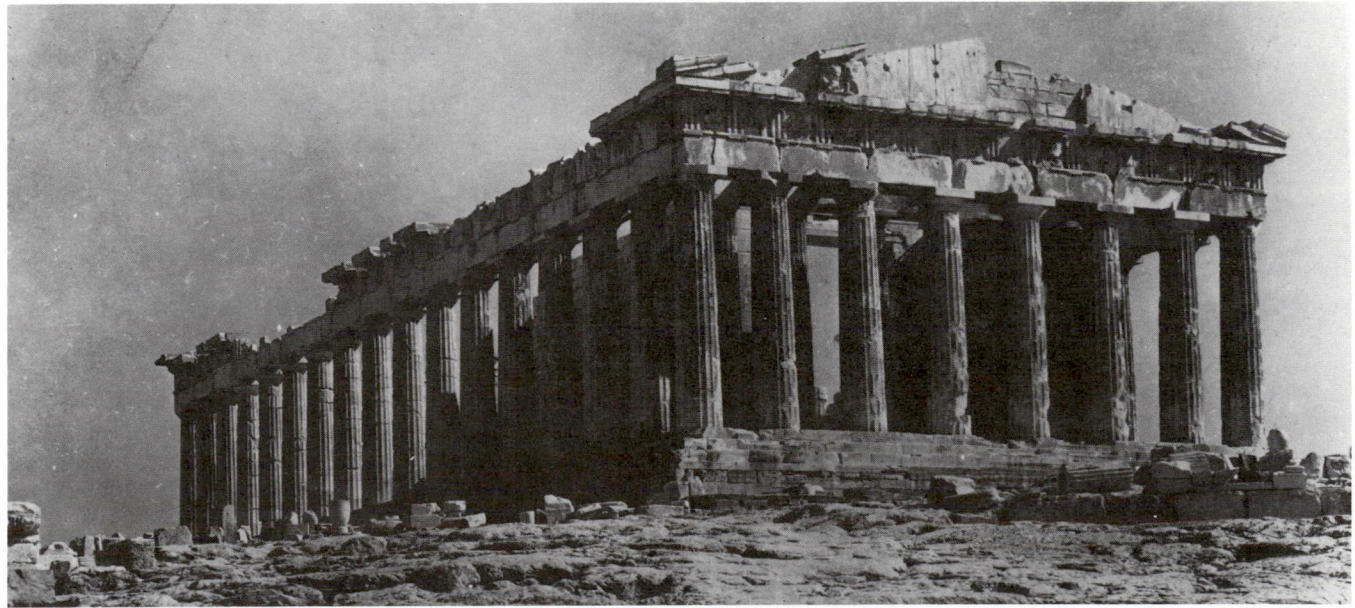

The Parthenon, West Façade, 447–432 B.C., Athens. (ART RESOURCE, NEW YORK)

build it entirely of marble, to lavish special care on its sculptures, to incorporate the Ionian feature of a carved continuous frieze around the *cella* or cult room, and to move the carved metopes from their normal position above the interior porches to the exterior, just like a treasury, becomes perfectly explicable. This temple was to be Athens' showcase, fusing the Doric and Ionic traditions, and proclaiming the city as the "education to Greece" of Perikles' dreams **(J 166–168, 186–188; G 5.42–5.52; H&F 4.15–4.16, 4.24–4.26).**

Usually treated as a "model" or typical Greek temple, the Parthenon is thus a highly idiosyncratic building, the product of specific and short-lived political circumstances that were unique to Athens herself. Though certain of its innovations, like the use of the Ionic frieze, were imitated in other Periklean buildings, it was too big, too expensive, and too unorthodox to inspire any lasting tradition. Rather, it set a standard in all sorts of ways. An almost inexhaustible reservoir of ideas, it marks a true watershed in the development of Greek art. To this extent, all subsequent Greek architects and sculptors stand in its shadow, and (whether they acknowledge it or not) are indebted to its achievements.

Architecturally, it constitutes the definitive statement of classic Doric. Built entirely of marble (a rarity in Greek architecture), and proportioned using a repeated series of 9:4 ratios (length: breadth, width: height of the façades, etc.), it is 228 feet long and 101 feet wide, with 17 columns on the flanks and 8 on the façades. The entablature is lighter than normal (less than one-third of the column height), imparting a new sense of grace to the exterior. A second, slightly smaller row of columns, re-used from the temple burnt by the Persians, is placed behind the façade columns to form a free-standing porch, supporting the figured Ionic frieze that runs round the entire *cella.* The *cella,* in turn, was designed specifically to show off Pheidias's great golden image of Athena Parthenos: not only was the internal colonnade placed so as to make the central aisle almost 35 feet wide, but windows were included on either side of the great east door, and a gallery ran around the inside at the level of the interior colonnade's intermediate architrave.

Yet this is not all: then as now, the building was renowned for its refinements. Many were not new, but never before or after were they to be applied so profusely or so delicately. The stylobate and entablatures rise just under 2 and 4 inches towards the center of the fronts and flanks, respectively (1 in 450/750), and the columns incline just over 2 inches inward (1 in 150), with a double angle contraction at the corners to reduce the progressive elongation of the metopes necessitated by the need to place the final triglyph not directly above the last column-axis, but right at the corner of the frieze. Meanwhile, the faces of the capitals, horizontal cornice, antefixes, akroteria, and the figures on the Ionic frieze lean slightly outwards, presumably to counteract the effects of perspective, and the columns both taper and are given a

slight curve or *entasis* of barely more than two-thirds of an inch (1 in 450) as they rise. The labor required to achieve these effects was prodigious, and the precision of the cutting extraordinary for a craft that lacked all but the most rudimentary methods of measurement: every one of the hundreds of blocks involved had to be individually cut on the bias, and in addition each column-drum had to taper and curve as well. None of the curves is an arc of a circle: all are hyperbolas or parabolas.

The question naturally arises: why? Ancient theorists, again writing hundreds of years after the fact, saw the entire operation as an attempt to counteract certain optical illusions, particularly a tendency for long horizontal lines to sag, for long vertical ones to look concave against the sky, and for upper elements to appear to be falling backwards. Yet not only is modern perceptual psychology dubious as to the existence of these alleged illusions, but the solutions recommended by these ancient authors have little in common with what actually appears on the Parthenon. Rather, one should seek a positive purpose for its special characteristics. What they do is to increase the compactness of the building, and to invest it with a sense of elasticity and life: it braces itself and flexes as a human figure would, to take the tremendous weight of its entablature and roof. In this respect, the Parthenon is the classic statement of the essentially sculptural nature of Greek architecture. It is the Doryphoros translated into the idiom of abstraction.

As to the sculptures themselves, these are usually discussed in the order in which they were carved: first the metopes (447–442), then the frieze (442–438), then the pediments (438–432); the cult statue usually comes last, although it was finished just before Pheidias's exile in 438. Yet this sequence is purely arbitrary, based upon the peculiar work schedule of the Doric temple whereby the colonnade was built first, then the *cella* erected inside it. A more satisfactory approach is to consider the sculptures in the order in which the ancient spectator would encounter them, beginning with the pediments and metopes, then moving on to the frieze, and ending with the cult statue. For as will appear, the subject matter of the sculptures expounds the generation and fulfillment of a world order, envisaged as occurring in exactly this sequence.

The pediments **(J 186–187; G 546–548; H&F 4.26)** showed the birth of Athena (east) and her contest with Poseidon for tutelage of the land of Attica (west). Almost ninety feet across, and crowded with figures that reached a full twelve feet high in the center, these dramatized the central event of each tableau by charting its electrifying effect upon a crowd of spectators. On the east pediment, the news of Athena's birth spreads like a shock wave to the wings. Except for a few scattered fragments the center is lost, but on the left, Artemis runs to talk with Persephone, her drapery sweeping in great curves behind her; Persephone turns to greet her, but her mother Demeter has yet to respond. Dionysos, the last figure, remains oblivious, toasting the dawn, as the Chariot of the Sun emerges in the corner from the rim of Ocean. On the right, the messenger may have been Apollo; Hestia turns to acknowledge him, but Dione and her daughter Aphrodite have yet to notice. Aphrodite herself is an extraordinarily voluptuous figure, reclining full-length upon a coverlet, her drapery not merely modelling the body through its spiralling folds, but teasingly emphasizing the curves of her breasts, belly, and thighs. Finally, in the corner, the exhausted team of the Chariot of the Moon plunges wearily below the horizon to take its rest.

On the west, the figures are better preserved, and drawings made by Jacques Carrey before the devastating explosion of a Turkish powder-magazine in the building in 1687 enable almost the entire composition to be reconstructed. The race to take possession climaxes at the center: Athena creates the olive tree, beating Poseidon by a hairsbreadth as he prepares to plunge his trident into the ground. Meanwhile, their teams of supporters rein in their chariots, and the two royal families of prehistoric Athens watch from the wings. Finally, the gods of Athens' two rivers, the Ilissos and Kephissos, occupy the corners. Once again, drapery and modelling are now used not merely to represent the exterior forms of the figures, but to describe their essential natures and characters: with his mighty, swelling muscles, Poseidon is the pounding sea, while Iris streaks through the air with drapery like scudding clouds, and Ilissos reclines with undulant flesh and a cloak that cascades off his shoulder like a waterfall.

From these two mighty epiphanies of divine power the spectator's eye would then pass to the metopes, ninety-two in all, encircling the entire building **(G 5.49–5.51; H&F 4.24)**. Here he would encounter the familiar world of the heroes, battling hybris and barbarism. Four themes were represented: the repulse of the Amazons, the sack of Troy (both now accepted as metaphors for the defeat of the Persians), the battle with the Centaurs, and the extermination of the Giants. The first and third acquired additional point in the local setting because they featured the Attic hero of heroes, Theseus. Unfortunately, only the Centauromachy is reasonably well-preserved.

Whereas the Amazons, Trojans, and Giants all represent external threats to civilization and order, the Centaurs (as half-horse and half-caveman) symbolize the barbarian within, the irrational and uncivilized that dwells in us all. Crazed with drink, they fight with anything to hand, and often succeed in overpowering their human foes. For the Lapiths, victory is hard won, achieved only through total control of mind and body, through *sophrosyne* once more. Thus, while some cave in before the violence of the Centaurs' assault, or grapple manfully with them in a series of complex wrestling-holds, others succeed in gaining the upper hand through superior technique and self-discipline. In what is certainly the *tour de force* of the series, South 27, the Lapith spreads commandingly over the entire face of the metope as he plunges his spear into

the small of the Centaur's back. Perfect in body, in total control of himself and of his enemy, hardly even exerting himself for the final blow, he is *sophrosyne* personified. To emphasize this, and to isolate him further from his enemy, his cloak hangs in great catenary folds behind him, static and immobile, suspending him in space like some kind of icon of eternal triumph.

In the frieze, the sculptor makes it clear that contemporary Athenians have now collectively attained that *sophrosyne* formerly vouchsafed to only this select few **(J 188; G. 5.49, 5.52; H&F 4.25)**. The style is highly uniform, achieving a clarity, consistency, vivaciousness, and beauty that is unmatched in classical sculpture. A full 520 feet long, and about four-fifths preserved, the frieze would come into view only as the spectator approached the building for a closer look. Encircling the top of the *cella* wall, and visible intermittently between the columns, it showed a great procession, presumably that which was held to honor Athena on her birthday, as a part of the Panathenaic festival. Following the spectator's path as he moved from the entrance of the precinct on the west to the great door of the temple itself on the east, it split into two streams at the southwest corner, one following the major route across the west front and along the north side, the other the minor one along the south side. Both converged on the east above the great door.

The cavalry is the backbone of the procession. On the west we see them making ready in the Kerameikos, then for a full two-thirds of the north and south sides galloping at full speed along the Panathenaic Way that crossed the city. Next come chariots, engaged in an ancient contest that involved the soldier aboard jumping on and off while the vehicle was still moving. And finally, the foot procession: sacrificial animals, musicians, acolytes. Receiving them all are the twelve Olympians, seated in two groups on either side of the building's central axis, which is occupied by five figures: two attendants, Athena's priestess, and the High Priest of Athens, who receives Athena's annual gift of a new robe from a little girl. While many problems of interpretation remain, the general sense is clear, and, despite doubts by some, one must conclude that the intention is to stress the piety of *contemporary* Athenians toward their guardian goddess. This, at least, is the impression created by the rendering of the figures themselves, as with heads bowed in reverence, or raised in triumphant exhilaration, they urge their ponies on, cajole the recalcitrant oxen, and at last assemble at their goal.

Finally, the spectator would enter the great door of the temple to behold the goddess herself. Fronted by a shallow pool of water inserted to humidify the building, she stood almost forty feet high, a colossus of gold and ivory molded around a cedar-wood core. Today, only later copies at reduced scale remain, but together with the literary sources they enable us to reconstruct the statue almost in its entirety. Fully armed and extending a six-foot Victory towards the entrance, she was both lavishly bejeweled, and surrounded by many of the sagas that embellished the exterior of the temple. Thus, her sandals showed Lapiths fighting Centaurs, and the Amazonomachy and Gigantomachy were embossed on the outside and inside of her shield, respectively. On the base was the creation of the first woman, Pandora ("All-gifts"), on her aegis and the boss of her shield were golden Gorgoneia, and on her helmet were Pegasoi and griffins, guardians of the gold of the North.

This array of "revelatory" iconography both amplified and defined the power of the goddess in a completely novel way, and also mediated between her and the observer, who was able to relate to them more directly through their familiar subject-matter and more human scale. The message, then, is that Athena *is* Athens; not only Zeus's favorite daughter, she stands for all that is best in her chosen city. The promise is clear.

The Parthenon stood untouched for rather over a century. In 295, however, the tyrant Lachares stole the statue's gold, which was replaced with gold leaf, and at some time in the Roman period a devastating fire swept the interior. Whether the Parthenon was destroyed is not clear: if so, the statue recorded by late antique authors must have been a replacement. In the fifth century A.D. the building was converted into a Christian church, and many of the metopes were defaced. As already mentioned, a devastating blow occurred in 1687, when the Turkish magazine inside blew up, destroying the *cella,* the east pediment, and much of the southern colonnade, and throwing many of the pedimental figures to the ground. In 1801, Lord Elgin removed many of the surviving marbles to the England, where they were eventually purchased by the British Museum. Air pollution has further damaged much of what remains, a severe earthquake in 1982 opened large cracks in the east front. A program of conservation and restoration was begun in 1977, but despite impressive results in certain areas, has yet to find any solution to the pollution problem. The next few years will be critical: assaulted by bigotry, fire, explosion, and earthquake, and stripped of her "Elgin Marbles," but still standing nevertheless, still radiating the power and self-confidence of Athens at her zenith, the Parthenon may yet succumb to the most insidious enemy of all.

To return to the fifth century B.C. As soon as the Parthenon's fabric was finished in 438, work began on the great gateway to the Akropolis, the Propylaea **(J 168–171; G 5.42–5.44, 5.53; H&F 4.16, 4.18).** Faced with a sloping site, the architect Mnesikles cleverly adapted his design to the terrain, orienting his building to provide a stunning three-quarter view of the Parthenon as one emerged from its eastern hall—though ironically, its full effect could never be appreciated in antiquity, because of other monuments already in the way. The Doric Order of the Propylaea also neatly complemented the Parthenon's own, using exactly the same proportions, but at two-thirds scale. In 431 the outbreak of war with Sparta

and her allies, the so-called Peloponnesian War, compelled a temporary halt in building, but by 425 the temple of Athena Nike was rising on its bastion to the west of the Propylaea, and shortly thereafter was surrounded with an exquisitely carved parapet, an allegorical version of the Parthenon frieze that showed winged Victories bringing thank-offerings to Athena **(J 171, 189; G 5.42–5.44, 5.54, 5.59; H&F 4.16, 4.18, 4.19).** Finally, that most unorthodox and exquisitely detailed of all Greek temples, the Erechtheion, was built on the northern side of the Akropolis **(J 174; G 5.42–5.44, 5.55–5.57; H&F 4.16, 4.20).** Designed to house numerous cults, it became to the Ionic Order what the Parthenon was already to the Doric: a storehouse of inspiration for generations to come. Now replaced by modern copies, its graceful but sturdy caryatids are a perfect foil for the Parthenon's massive Doric columns a hundred yards to the south across the Panathenaic Way.

When the Erechtheion was completed in 406, Athens was going down in defeat, slowly but surely. Within a year, the fleet was destroyed, the empire was liberated, and the campfires of the Spartans were burning outside the walls. Famine soon set in, and the city surrendered in April, 404. Fortunately, the penalties demanded by the Peloponnesians were relatively light, but with the treasury exhausted, the empire gone, and the cream of her manpower dead, a dream had been shattered, and would never revive.

## The Fourth Century

The fourth century witnessed a search for new values, new accommodations with the Gods. Personal deities like the healing god Asklepios came into favor, as men sought consolation from the cares of the world. From around 400, Asklepios's prime sanctuary at Epidauros was the scene of a large-scale building program, comprising temples, stoas, healing facilities, a stadium, and magnificent theater **(J 173, 176–177; G 5.73, 5.89–5.90; H&F 4.38–4.39).** Taking its cue from the achievements of Periclean Athens, Epidaurian architecture is highly innovative.

The most original of the Epidaurian architects was Polykleitos, presumably a descendant of the great fifth-century sculptor. Also a mathematical genius, he designed both the tholos, or round temple, and the theater.  Though the tholos's exact function is unclear, its contribution to architectural history was certainly profound. To avoid the cage-like impression that would have resulted from a conventionally proportioned Doric exterior, Polykleitos both increased the spacing between the columns and made them much thinner than usual. Almost seven times their lower diameter in height, they taper gracefully to neat, compact capitals, and are surmounted by a frieze with carved libation-bowls in the metopes. An acanthus ornament interrupted by lion's-head gargoyles ran along the roof gutter, and a great floral openwork akroterion surmounted the peak of the conical roof.

This richness of effect multiplied as one passed between the columns to the interior. The ceiling coffers were delicately carved with acanthus and lilies, the door fringed with rosettes, the floor given a complex spiral pattern of alternating black-and-white marble blocks, and the *cella* lined with fourteen columns in the new, foliated Corinthian Order **(J 173; G 5.73; H&F 4.39).** Invented around 400, and used already at Epidauros and Delphi as interior embellishment, Corinthian was a subspecies of Ionic. Only the capital is different: bell-shaped, it is fringed with acanthus leaves from which spring twelve spirals, four supporting the corners of the square abacus above, and eight more, paired and surmounted by a flower, between them. This design set the tone for the Corinthian style for the rest of antiquity.

The theater is also a classic statement of its genre, brilliantly proportioned and given an added refinement **(J 176–177; G 5.89–5.90; H&F 4.38).** Greek theater auditoriums are not semicircular but add an extra "wedge" on each side, making them actually three-fifths of a circle. Yet instead of continuing the circle of the auditorium through the extra "wedge" as usual, Polykleitos opened it out somewhat at this point, lengthening the radius of the last two "wedges" on each side so that the center of their arcs is displaced some fifteen feet from the true center of the main part of the auditorium. This not only made for better viewing from these seats, but helped to catch more sound from the stage, and opened out the gangways between the stage and the auditorium, improving traffic flow. A simple idea, but brilliantly practical, and aesthetically pleasing too.

The fourth century was the great age of panel and easel painting in Greece, but all the works of such masters as Zeuxis, Parrhasios, Nikias, Apelles, and Protogenes are lost. Texts, versions on Pompeian walls, and echoes in mosaics, in tomb frescoes, and on vases do a little to fill the gap, and show that by the end of the century a full command of the techniques of illusion, including chiaro-scuro and various kinds of perspective, had been achieved **(cf. J 192 and clpl 21; G 5.98, 6.38; H&F 5.7, 5.12, 5.23).**

Sculpture responds to this situation in various ways. The most "pictorial" of fourth-century sculptors, Prax-iteles of Athens, was also the most successful. Subtly exploiting the gentle play of light on softly polished marble, he was particularly in demand for studies of the love goddess, Aphrodite, and her son Eros. His Aphrodite at Knidos was the first fully nude statue of the goddess ever, and inaugurated a genre, the female nude, that has become central to Western art **(J 197; H&F 4.33).** The logic of his approach was simple: as the sculptors of the Parthenon had realized, the essence of the love goddess was her body **(J 187; G 5.48; H&F 4.26),** and since the sculptor's job was to reveal essences, her body must be revealed. Unfortunately, the original has long perished, and Roman copies give only a crude idea of its subtle and seductive loveliness.

The Hermes and infant Dionysos found at Olympia in 1877 **(J 198; G 5.65–5.66; H&F 4.34)** and ascribed to him by an ancient traveller might fill the gap, if only the attribution were correct. Unfortunately, this seems not to be the case: although the style is broadly Praxitelean, the technique is post-classical, as are the sandals Hermes wears. A date in the third century now seems the most likely, and is further suggested by the dreamy, other-worldly treatment of the subject. Totally self-sufficient and remote from the cares of men, the two recall the untroubled, passive, self-absorbed gods of the Hellenistic philosopher Epikouros (341–271 B.C.). Praxiteles' work was continued by his sons and grandsons, and perhaps the Hermes' author was one of these.

Here Dionysos is still a baby, but when grown he was to become a formidable force indeed, as powerful in his sphere as Aphrodite was in hers. His cult also made great strides during the century, as men sought closer commun-ion with the divine. In antiquity, the period's *tour-de-force* of Dionysiac sculpture was generally acknowledged to be the Parian sculptor Skopas's study of one of his maenads, now known only in a small-scale but high-quality replica in Dresden. Once shouldering a young kid, soon to be torn limb from limb in the grisly ritual of *sparagmos,* she twists this way and that in the rhythm of the dance. Sucked in by the vortex of her movement, caught up in the fervor of the ritual, the spectator vicariously participates in her ecstasy, and in doing so, meets the god. Here, Dionysos is all the more potent because unseen; he compels our credence, our submission to his will. This, Skopas is saying, is the true nature of the divine: not the rational, benign deities of Periklean Athens, but a world of unimaginable power that runs by its own logic and is ignored at one's peril.

Other sculptors and painters turned to portraiture, a revealing index of the individualism of the age. Most successful of these was Lysippos of Sikyon, who became court sculptor to the Macedonian prince Alexander in the 340s, just when Alexander's father, Philip, succeeded in establishing hegemony over the mainland Greek cities. Inheriting Philip's crown and ambitions, the young Alex-ander invaded Persia in 334, and in a series of lightning campaigns conquered the entire empire to the borders of India **(J 213, 275, clpl 21; G 6.38; H&F 5.1–5.3, 5.23).** Though Lysippos's bronzes are all lost, texts, copies **(J 200; G 5.70),** and an athlete by one of his pupils in the J. Paul Getty Museum in Malibu **(G 5.71)** show that his aim was to idealize his subjects while maintaining an illusion of objectivity. Working from life, he paid the utmost attention to details but increased the apparent height of his subjects by slimming down the body and reducing the size of the head. Whereas Polykleitos had aimed at an ideal based on a priori notions of the perfect man, he sought to capture Alexander's extraordinary charisma by manipulating truth to enhance his subject's physical and psychological appeal.

A marble Alexander in the Getty Museum shows him

in a slightly different light, as a reincarnation of the outgoing and ideally beautiful young Athenians of the Parthenon frieze. By casting him in the role of heir to Athens' imperial legacy, this sculptor (probably himself an Athenian) seeks to domesticate the otherwise alien and immensely powerful Macedonian, whose kingdom was not racially Greek and had only become Hellenized a few generations previously. Yet while essentially conservative in this respect, in others he seems to have been quite radical. For not only does his Alexander gaze with longing toward far horizons, transcending at a stroke the parochial limitations of the *polis,* but numerous other fragments found with the head indicate that it belonged to but one figure in a larger ensemble. This, it seems, included at least two divinities and a sacrificial group, represented at smaller scale. Possibly, then, it was a very early example of the practice of ruler-worship, inaugurated by Alexander himself in 324, and popular with his successors, Roman emperors included.

When Alexander died in 323, aged only 33, a power struggle ensued among his generals. Now but pawns in a titanic struggle for world domination, the Greek *poleis* were relics of a past that had disappeared for good. In this respect, as in the fields of art and literature, the classical period was over, and the Hellenistic had begun.

## The Hellenistic World (323–30 B.C.)

It took almost fifty years for the situation to stabilize. When the dust settled, the descendants of three of the generals, Ptolemy, Seleukos, and Antigonos, emerged with the lion's share of the spoils. Ptolemaic Egypt was the richest and most dynamic of the kingdoms; its capital, Alexandria, was a mecca for artists and intellectuals of all kinds, and well deserved its reputation as "Queen of the Mediterranean." Seleukid Syria, larger and more diffuse, nominally ruled from the Aegean to the Indus, though it was too heterogeneous and vast for proper control: Pergamon in the West and Baktria (Afghanistan) in the East soon broke away and charted an independent course. Antigonid Macedon, though cruelly drained of manpower and resources by Alexander, maintained a precarious hegemony over the reluctant cities of the Greek mainland. And finally, the West, never conquered by Alexander, was dominated by the tyrants of Syracuse, who managed to keep the Carthaginians at bay, but not the Romans, who ruled the whole area by 210.

Cut adrift from the cosy traditions of the city-states, at the call of a heterogeneous and far-flung clientele, proud of its glorious past yet deeply anxious to serve the present, Hellenistic art is a complex, difficult, and yet rewarding field of study. Not unjustly, the period has been called the first modern one in the history of art: protean, fragmented, self-conscious, often experimental, occasionally perverse, and sometimes deeply reactionary, it arouses strong emotions in critics accustomed to the reassuring certainties of the archaic or classical.

Though trends spread quickly, and in some cases it is therefore warranted to speak of a Hellenistic *koine* or "commonwealth," the art of the three main centers, Athens, Alexandria, and Pergamon, exhibits some striking differences in style and approach. Predictably, the Athenians were the most conservative, determined to compensate for their loss of political power by pressing their claims to be the "education to Greece" of Perikles' dreams. Courted by tradition-hungry individuals, cities, and kingdoms, Athenian sculptors produced portraits for them in discreetly modernized classical styles, and neoclassic images of the gods. The famous Aphrodite from Melos, produced by a classicizing sculptor from Asia Minor, shows how far the fashion had spread by the later Hellenistic period (**G 5–83; H&F 5.6**).

Athens herself benefited greatly from all this, as these same clients lavished funds upon her to demonstrate their cultural sophistication, and to upstage their political rivals. Turning her into a showcase of civic architecture, they donated theaters, gymnasia, stoas, and temples, some of which survive today. Thus the magnificent Stoa of Attalos that, reconstructed as a museum in the 1950s, again dominates the Agora and regularizes its formerly open east side, was given by King Attalos II of Pergamon around 150; as a youth, he had studied philosophy in the city. Doric below and Ionic above, it uses the distinctive Pergamene palm-capital for the interior order of its upper story. Indeed, the whole notion of a two-storied stoa is itself distinctively Pergamene, and in this case the choice made good sense, for the upper gallery could serve as a grandstand for spectators during festivals like the Panathenaia. A second major donation that still survives, at least in part, is the giant temple of Olympian Zeus given by King Antiochos IV of Syria around 170 (**H&F 5.20**). The earliest example of an *exterior* Corinthian Order in monumental temple architecture, it also represents the "classic" stage in the refinement of the Corinthian capital.

Alexandrian art is less easy to characterize, since the ancient city itself (laid out, like so many other Hellenistic foundations, on the Hippodamian system) is almost completely destroyed. One wishes that something had remained of its magnificent palaces, parks, library, and Mouseion (the world's first university), but all is lost. While its large-scale sculpture shows an increasing accommodation to the native style, and the Ptolemies were also active in building and embellishing temples strictly in that style, its other arts are more distinctive. In sculpture, thousands of small-scale genre studies (**J 209; H&F 5.9**) and grotesques in bronze or (most often) terracotta testify to a very bourgeois interest in low-life subjects. Replicated in Alexandrian poetry, and occasionally translated to large scale (**G 5.84**), these are often cruel and sometimes explicitly racist, poking fun at the poor and the deformed, and at the native Egyptians and blacks. Yet artistically, they are often of high quality, boldly and adventurously modeled. Both repellent and fascinating, the entire corpus deserves more attention than it has received.

In particular, though, Alexandria was the center of the luxury arts: jewelry, vessels in precious metals and rare stones, ivories, cameos, and eventually even blown glass. The very few pieces that survive intact are widely scattered: some have surfaced in Italy and France, and one splendid agate drinking vessel in the form of a gazelle's head even made it as far as China, where it was recently discovered in a tomb of the eighth century A.D. Exotic animals, complex allegories, and erotica are this industry's stock-in-trade. Glass blowing was discovered around 50 B.C. and swiftly conquered the Mediterranean; some of the finest products were made under Roman rule (cf. J 281 and clpl 23; G 6.34) and rank among the most elegant and refined to be found anywhere before Venetian glass of the seventeenth and eighteenth centuries.

Pergamon also developed a highly distinctive art, the so-called "baroque" (J 205; G 5.78–5.79; H&F 5.17–5.19). Actually an outgrowth of trends visible in Asia Minor as early as the fourth century, this style catered to a specifically Asian Greek taste for highly contrived rhetoric and emotional excitation. Local music, oratory, and poetry also tended this way, seeking to "sway the souls" of their audience through exaggeration, surprise, and other devices. Aiming to make their city the cultural center of Asia, the Pergamene kings adorned its magnificent Akropolis with terrace upon terrace of plazas, sanctuaries, and palaces, grouped around a stunningly sited theater like the spokes of a wheel (G 5.96–5.97; H&F 5.18). Each terrace had a particular part to play: the uppermost held an arsenal and the palaces; the next supported the Library; then came the sanctuary of Athena Bringer of Victory, embellished with mighty bronze groups celebrating Pergamene successes against invading Celts (J 201; G 5.77; H&F 5.17), Syrians, and Macedonians; and finally the terrace of the so-called "Great Altar," perhaps dedicated to the city's legendary founder, Telephos.

The sculptures of the "Great Altar," carved around 170, represent the definitive statement of the Pergamene baroque (J 203–205; G 5.78–5.79; H&F 5.19). The Battle of the Gods and Giants around the podium was meticulously planned, and carved by a team imported from all over the Greek world. Intended as a universal affirmation of the triumph of order over chaos, the reliefs range over the entire cosmos from Ocean to Aither, from East to West, from Hades to Olympos. All known sculptural styles are harnessed to proclaim the message; quotes from the Parthenon, suitably updated, are juxtaposed with others from the fourth century and from Pergamene art itself. A barrage of textures and forms assaults the senses, as the protagonists fight with every weapon imaginable. Gods are superhumanly muscular, goddesses stunningly beautiful, Giants monstrous hybrids. As highly contrived visual rhetoric, the frieze exploits every avenue of technique, overwhelming the spectator with an art that both vaunts

its supreme command of realistic detail and simultaneously declares its status as supreme contrivance: a teasing duality that suspends the spectator cunningly between the two poles of truth and fiction, and never lets one forget the sculptor's mastery. Meanwhile, around the interior, a second frieze chronicled the life and exploits of Telephos himself, against a landscape setting that progressively unfolded as the spectator walked around.

Both these friezes were highly influential. The Gigantomachy sparked a long series of imitations, most famous of which is the Laokoon by the Rhodians Hagesandros, Athanodoros, and Polydoros (J 207; G 5.80; H&F 5.46). Its date is disputed, and may belong as late as the Roman Empire. Rediscovered in 1506, and immediately recognized as the summit of pathos in sculpture, it profoundly influenced Michelangelo and was a major source for the Italian seventeenth-century baroque (J 612, 618, 649, 695–703; G 17.21, 19.23, etc; H&F 11.24–11.26, 13.1–13.5, 13.12, 13.14–13.16). As for the Telephos frieze, its "continuous" method of narrative representation, whereby the protagonists appear again and again within the continuously unfolding landscape setting, was enthusiastically taken up by the Romans (Trajan's column is their most sophisticated essay in this vein; J 265; G 6.64–6.65; H&F 5.55) and thence found its way into Medieval art, the Bayeux Tapestry being perhaps the best-known example of the genre (J 416; G 9.35; H&F 9.19).

The "Great Altar," like many of the monuments of the Pergamene Akropolis, was built at a time of great upheaval. In 197, the Romans had smashed the Macedonian army, and in 191–188 defeated the Syrians too, dictating settlements thereafter that seriously truncated the two kingdoms and rewarded Rome's allies, the Pergamenes included. The famous winged Victory of Samothrace (J 206; G 5.76; H&F 5.15), a *tour de force* of the baroque style, may be a monument to these events; it was probably set up by the Rhodians, yet another state allied to Rome. Henceforth, the center of gravity of the Mediterranean world was to shift inexorably westward, and we must follow it too.

---

## Part 2
# THE ART OF REPUBLICAN AND IMPERIAL ROME

## From Village to World Empire (ca. 753–31 B.C.)

For much of its early history, Rome was a province of Etruria. An enigmatic people who established themselves in northern Italy early in the first millennium B.C., the

Etruscans were voracious consumers of Greek art, and by around 600 B.C. had developed their own distinctive architecture, painting, and sculpture (**J 215–225; G 6.1–6.13; H&F 4.56–4.67**). As we know from scattered remains and texts, the earliest Roman art was of this kind: temples on podia, with deep porches, columns molded top and bottom in the so-called Tuscan style, light, wooden entablatures, and massive, overhanging roofs with sculpture placed along the ridge-poles (**J 221–222; G 6.1; H&F 4.63–4.64**). Because the marble deposits at Carrara were not discovered until the first century B.C., the sculpture is in bronze or terracotta; it borrows heavily from Greek archaic styles but tends towards exaggeration and emphasis of details, which now strain against the whole in a way that often produces work of great expressive power (**J 222, clpl 19; G 6.8–6.9; H&F 4.63–4.66**).

The Romans expelled the last member of their Etruscan royal dynasty in 510, and thenceforth the word "king" was execrated in Rome. A republic was instituted that in effect entrenched the power of the upper class or *patricians* by limiting access to office to them alone. To lessen the risk of tyranny, the leading magistrates or *consuls* only served for one year, were elected in pairs (each man having the right of veto over the other), and were answerable to the main body of the patricians, the Senate, for their actions. Two concepts were of central importance: *imperium* or supreme executive authority, which had to be conferred legally to be valid, and the *mos maiorum* or custom, which acted as legal precedent, and had to be consulted before any legislative, executive, or judicial action could be taken.

This highly conservative constitution was well-suited to a people who valued *gravitas* or seriousness above all other virtues, and made much of their capacity for endurance (*constantia*), their own dignity (*dignitas*), candor (*simplicitas*), and personal authority (*auctoritas*). Whereas Greek culture is essentially a youth culture, and actually worshiped youth in the form of the god Apollo, the Romans regarded forty as the prime of life, valued maturity above all, and scorned frivolities like personal beauty. Their personal names are often highly unflattering: Crassus = "fatso," Naso = "bignose," Caesar = "hairy," and so on. Down-to-earth and supremely practical, they had no real concept of life after death and regarded the survival of one's name and reputation (*fama*) as essential. Hence realistic portraiture quickly became their leading art form. By 158 the Forum was so crowded with portraits (in chariots, on horseback, or standing nude, in armor, or in a toga) that the censors removed all that were not authorized by popular or senatorial decree.

As one would expect, the lower or *plebeian* class deeply resented their exclusion from power, and the oppression and exploitation it inevitably engendered. The fifth and fourth centuries brought increasing agitation for plebeian rights, often verging on civil war. Yet by the early third century the plebeians were eligible to hold all important offices and were theoretically supreme in the state. In practice, however, the result had merely been to extend the ruling class somewhat, as both elements essentially subscribed to the same set of conservative values, and election to high office generally depended upon consensus and always upon the possession of substantial property.

During this period, and despite their internal troubles, the Romans had managed to extend their *imperium* over their neighbors to such a degree that by 264 all peninsular Italy was under their control. This process inevitably brought them into contact with the other great power in the region, the North African city of Carthage, whose empire included western Sicily, Corsica, Sardinia, and the Spanish coast. The two came to blows in 264, and war raged between them for most of the next sixty years. After Hannibal devastated Italy but failed to shake the Roman alliance, the Romans invaded Africa, decisively defeated the Carthaginian army in 202, and dictated a humiliating peace that deprived Carthage of all her overseas possessions.

This history repeated itself during the next fifty years, as Roman armies intervened in Greece and the East, eventually destroying Macedon and expelling the Syrians from Asia Minor; Carthage herself was finally disposed of in 146. The last king of Pergamon willed his realm to Rome in 133, and after a series of devastating wars with king Mithradates of Pontus (in northern Asia Minor), the Romans annexed most of Asia and Syria in 64, leaving Ptolemaic Egypt, increasingly enfeebled, as the only independent Hellenistic kingdom. Its brief revival under Kleopatra was brusquely terminated when Augustus defeated her and Mark Antony at Actium in 31, and with their suicide and the Roman occupation of Alexandria a year later, the *imperium* now spanned the Mediterranean.

As the triumphs mounted and the rivers of loot poured into Rome, year after golden year, the effect upon what had been a relatively simple peasant culture was traumatic. Later Roman historians, writing with the advantage of hindsight, saw the masses of Greek statues and paintings, the piles of precious metalwork, the luxurious furniture, the delicate textiles, and last but not least the mountains of hard cash, as the canker that corrupted the morals of a once-thrifty and virtuous people, and led to the eventual ruination of the republic itself. The tidal wave of Hellenization simply swamped the native traditions: Greek statues now replaced the Etruscan-style terracottas in Roman temples, the Greek Orders became fashionable in architecture, and Greek taste prevailed in all aspects of public and domestic life.

Social strains also increased, as thousands of veterans had to be settled, populist politicians took advantage of the situation, and Senate and people found themselves increasingly at odds. In portraiture, realism turns to *verism,* a style that by exaggerating the effects of age upon the face seeks to turn it into a map of hard-won experience (cf. J 254–255; G 6.14–6.15; H&F 5.49). Insinuating the subject's possession of the old Roman virtues of *gravitas, constantia,* and the like, a verist portrait presents him as a rock of stability in a disintegrating world.

To get away from the growing stresses of the capital, Roman aristocrats began building themselves sumptuous holiday villas in the country or by the sea (the Bay of Naples was the favorite location), embellishing them with Doric, Ionic, and Corinthian colonnades and filling them with Greek sculpture, painting, furniture, and tableware (J 247, 275–283; G 6.24–6.40; H&F 5.23–5.30). The J. Paul Getty Museum in Malibu is a re-creation of one such villa, and gives an excellent impression of the luxury of republican Rome at its height. Original works of art were bought if possible, but if not, one could always get copies (J 179, 184, 197, 199–200; G 5.38, 5.61, 5.70, 5.84–5.86; H&F 4.30–4.33, 5.4–5.5), which were now turned out by the hundreds from workshops largely manned by Greek slaves. Traveling ateliers of painter-decorators could be hired to fresco one's walls with replicas of Greek classic paintings framed within grandiose architectural schemes (J 277; G 6.32–6.33, etc.; H&F 5.25), and professional gardeners laid out elaborate formal gardens and ornamental pools. An art market sprang up with all the features (both good and bad) familiar in our own time: auctions, connoisseurs, dealers, agents, scouts, restorers, historians, as well as robberies, extortion, inflated prices, and fakes of all kinds.

Faced with these conflicting pressures, public building swiftly began to take on a hybrid character. The sanctuary of Fortuna at Praeneste and the Tabularium at Rome, both begun during the brief, pro-senatorial dictatorship of the reactionary L. Cornelius Sulla (82–79), exemplify this uneasy situation (J 230–232; G 6.18–6.20; H&F 5.32–5.33). Both utilize the Greek Orders as window dressing, as a veneer for an architecture characterized by rigid symmetry and based on the new medium of concrete and its very un-Greek, curvilinear forms of arch, vault, and dome (G 6.54). This veneer of Greek culture is a transparent attempt to civilize buildings that manipulate both environment and observer in a quite militaristic way. The buildings dominate their surroundings, overpowering them with grandiose evocations of senatorial *auctoritas.* The Sanctuary of Fortuna at Praeneste (J 230–232; G 6.18–6.20; H&F 5.32–5.33) was dedicated to Sulla's guardian goddess (his nickname was Felix, "the lucky"). With terrace upon terrace culminating in a semicircular theater and topped by a gigantic bronze statue of the goddess standing on a globe, it dominated both his colony of veterans there and the countryside around. The Tabularium, where all the state and senatorial records were kept, dominates the Roman Forum itself. Together, they herald the advent of a concept of architecture as a mechanism of social control.

## Augustan Rome (31 B.C.–A.D. 14)

Fifty years later, in one of those violent oscillations characteristic of an art that is super-sensitive to the winds of political change, the issue of consistency was settled decisively in favor of the Greeks—for a while. Proclaiming his new "Golden Age" after twenty years of civil war had almost torn the state apart, Augustus chose Greek classicism as the basis for the official style of a Rome reborn. And in this enterprise, architecture, sculpture, and the minor arts all had their parts to play, no less than did the poetry of the regime's chief apologist, Vergil, and the prose of its chief historian, Livy. Rational, measured, and authoritative, this new classicism suggested both that stability and harmony had returned at last, after generations of disintegration and chaos, and that under the wise guidance of her new *princeps* (first citizen), Rome had at last assumed her predestined place as heir to the greatness of Periklean Athens.

"I found Rome a city of brick, and left it a city of marble," boasted Augustus in his testament, the *Res Gestae* or "Achievements." Marble, not concrete: Augustan architecture completely eschews concrete vaulting, returning to a strict post-and-lintel system for all public buildings. Augustan architects not only exploited the newly discovered quarries at Carrara to the utmost but also imported marble from all over the Mediterranean: brilliantly colored marbles from Spain, North Africa, and Asia Minor, and pure crystalline white ones from Greece. In his most ambitious complex, the Forum Augusti and accompanying temple of Mars Ultor ("Avenger"—i.e., of the murderers of his adoptive father, Caesar), the aim is not merely richness of effect, but to demonstrate that the resources of the world were now at Rome's disposal (J 233; G 6.47). The Corinthian Order is used throughout for exteriors, and the detailing quotes Attic precedents like the Erechtheion and the temple of Olympian Zeus extensively. The manipulative planning of late republican ensembles is of course retained, and even the details often acquire totalitarian overtones. We learn from the Augustan writer Vitruvius, for example, that the copies of the Erechtheion caryatids (J 174; G 5.57; H&F 4.20) that lined the attic story of the Forum's colonnade were "symbols of eternal subjection." This is imperialist despotism with a human face.

Augustus's twin themes of peace and stability at home and imperialist expansion abroad, summed up in the *Res Gestae* and reiterated *ad nauseam* by his court poets, were precisely exemplified in a statue that is often considered the most important of all Roman portraits, the Augustus from Primaporta (J 256–257; G 6.57, 6.67; H&F 5.47). Quoting the pose of the Doryphoros (J 179; G 5.61; H&F 4.31) as if to herald the emperor himself as the new paradigm of classicism, and accompanied by a little Eros that signals his clan's descent from the goddess Venus, it shows him about to address the people. He wears the cloak of a general, and his breastplate carries a scene that demonstrates that Rome is now so powerful that her enemies bend before her without a fight. Between 53 B.C. and his accession in 31, three Roman armies had lost their standards to the Parthians, who a century before had conquered the eastern half of the Seleukid empire, modern Iran and Iraq. In 20, Augustus took advantage of a Parthian domestic dispute to induce them to withdraw from Armenia and to return the standards. The lull was only temporary, but perfectly vindicated his policy of "peace through strength." Accordingly, on the breastplate, we see the standards being returned, with submissive barbarians and Apollo and Diana (patrons of the Golden Age) to left and right, a nursing Italia surrounded by symbols of prosperity below, and the rising Sun, Jupiter, and Aurora (goddess of the dawn of the new age), above. The reminiscences of the Parthenon's east pediment were surely not lost upon the statue's audience, many of whom (if wealthy) would have visited Athens, ever a magnet for those with any pretensions to culture.

Augustus's constitutional position was vague, cloaked in a variety of republican forms, and buttressed by the claim that every aspect of his *imperium* had a republican precedent. This was true—except that whereas his predecessors had held first one office, then another, he exercised this *imperium* all at once. The Primaporta statue carefully maintains this constitutional façade, for the Parthian coup had been carried out with the civil and military powers of proconsular *imperium* voted him by the senate in 23; the *Ara Pacis Augustae,* or Altar of Augustan Peace, dedicated eleven years later, is more disingenuous, evoking the Parthenon frieze to show Rome as one big happy family, celebrating Augustus's triumphant return to Rome after establishing peace in the western provinces **(J 258–261; G 6.58–6.60; H&F 5.50).** Suggestively, it was sited to the north of the city center on the Campus Martius, the area dedicated to the war god, Mars.

While on the Parthenon frieze **(J 188, 260; G 5.52; H&F 4.25)** no citizen of Athens was singled out, here every figure is a portrait. Yet as in portraiture in the round, the members of the imperial clan all model themselves closely on Augustus and his wife, Livia, stressing both their solidarity and the supposedly ecumenical nature of the new order: a nice three-cornered balance of Greek precedent, republican sentiment, and political reality. Meanwhile, scenes from Roman history and allegories of Roman prosperity occupy the short sides, and the luxuriant vegetation below, inhabited by Apollo's bird, the swan, proclaims the fruits of the Golden Age once more.

Recent excavation in the basements of the houses around the Ara Pacis has revealed that is was but a part of a much grander scheme. It was surrounded to the east and north by parkland, and a great piazza was laid out to the west. This piazza was then turned into a huge sundial by setting letters of bronze into its pavement and erecting an obelisk brought from Egypt at the center of its southern side. The obelisk still survives but has been transported to another location in Rome. The inscription on its base celebrates Augustus's annexation of Egypt to the Empire in 30. On the autumn equinox, Augustus's birthday, the shadow from the obelisk would have pointed straight toward the Ara Pacis, creating in effect a gigantic horoscope which signaled his unification of East and West, and establishment of universal peace. At right angles to this line of destiny, several hundred yards away to the north, stood the emperor's enormous mausoleum, completing the cosmic cycle of events that, through him, had brought peace and unity to the world.

## From Tiberius to Domitian: The Consolidation of Empire (A.D. 14–96)

Augustan classicism continued to be the official Roman style for about forty years; yet when Nero came to power in A.D. 54 it was soon clear that here was a *princeps* with very different ideas. The great fire of 64 gave him the opportunity he craved: to turn the center of Rome into his personal estate. The area bounded by the Esquiline, Palatine, and Caelian hills became a park, connected to the Forum by a great colonnade that terminated in a 100-foot-high statue of the Emperor himself. Pavilions were scattered through the landscape, a lake was dug in the middle, and a sumptuous villa, the Golden House, was built on the slopes of the Esquiline above.

Now buried under Trajan's baths, this villa represented the first serious experiment with the curvilinear architecture of arches, vaults, and domes since the republic. In its great rotunda, sixty feet across and domed in concrete **(G 6.49–6.50; H&F 5.39),** Nero's architects Severus and Celer created a true architecture of space, placing the room at the focus of a series of interlocking vistas that expand one's horizons, continually opening up new prospects as one moves around it. This is probably not the main banqueting hall described by Nero's biographer Suetonius, which "constantly revolved day and night like the heavens," but even in its denuded state, stripped of its mosaics, its paintings, and its costly veneers, it gives some idea of the new paths Roman imperial architecture was now exploring. When Nero surveyed his new possession and remarked that he could now at last live like a human being, he jettisoned the last vestiges of the Augustan principate: Rome, he was declaring, was his personal estate, and let no one stand in his way.

Nero was assassinated in 68, and his successors took the hint: though some, like Domitian (81–96), were equally ruthless, none was as blatant a despot as he. Nero's statue was converted to an Apollo, and his great park was built over. Its lake became the site of the Colosseum, the mightiest of all Roman circuses and the prototype for all sports stadiums throughout the world **(J**

**235–237; G 6.45–6.46; H&F 5.36–5.38).** Significantly, though, the Golden House itself was only abandoned after Domitian had built himself an even bigger and more sumptuous palace on the Palatine. With its huge vaulted banqueting hall where the emperor could recline in a gigantic semi-domed apse, the focus of attention of all present, this marks the early maturity of a specifically Roman imperial architecture: "the very geometry of sovereignty," in W. L. MacDonald's felicitous phrase. The embellishment of the capital itself continued uninterrupted, as each new reign brought more temples, arches, fora, basilicas, circuses, theaters, baths, aqueducts, and bridges, all cast in the same majestic, imperial style **(J 233, 238–241; G 6.47–6.48, 6.55–6.56; H&F 5.40–5.44, 5.53–5.55, 5.60–5.62).**

Meanwhile, the consolidation of the empire proceeded apace. By A.D. 100 a network of superbly built roads and bridges linked every province with Rome, enabling rapid transmission of information and swift response to crisis. New cities were founded, and old ones re-planned, usually by combining the Hippodamian grid plan with that evolved by the Romans for their legionary camps. Square and surrounded with a wall and ditch, these were always neatly quartered by two main streets, the north-south *cardo* and the east-west *decumanus* **(G. 6.44).** They have survived from Jordan to Scotland, Algeria to Germany, either in lonely ruin or as the basis for many a modern town. Aqueducts supplied water to these cities from afar **(J 234; G 6.43; H&F 5.35);** like the bridges, they uniformly utilized the new architecture of arches, either in rough-hewn stone or brick-faced concrete, enabling them to span deep gorges and broad rivers with ease. Enlivened by a sparing use of ornament, and sometimes still in use today, they bear silent witness to the benefits of the *imperium,* remaining among the most attractive features of Rome's imperial legacy. If the arch has a meaning of its own in such a context, it is as a symbol of unity and concord, of the far-flung span of the *Pax Romana.*

In general, the provincial elites welcomed imperial rule, for it guaranteed them continued respite from endless local wars, and reprieve from the arbitrary exactions of the grasping officials of the republic. Accordingly, one is not surprised to find the building types and styles of the capital eagerly imitated by provincial notables anxious to establish their own reputations as public benefactors and friends of Rome. By the end of the first century A.D. one could travel from Spain to Jordan, from Germany to Algeria, and find essentially the same architecture wherever one went **(J 245–246, 249–251; H&F 5.58–5.59).** Porticoes, fora, theaters, circuses, temples, basilicas, and baths all accepted the same imperial style with only minor regional variations, using grandiose combinations of the three Greek Orders together with arches, vaults, and domes, not to mention sumptuous marble veneer.

In such a context, sculpture was now firmly relegated to the status of ornament, and the still mainly Greek workshops churned out an endless series of copies and versions of the Greek classical masterpieces to meet the ever-growing demand **(J 179, 184, 197, 199–200; G 5.38, 5.61, 5.70, 5.84–5.86; H&F 4.30–4.33, 5.4–5.5, 5.10).** Read in this light, these famous lines of Vergil take on new meaning:

> Let others better mold the running mass
> Of metals, and inform the breathing brass,
> And soften into flesh a marble face . . .
> But Rome! 'tis thine alone, with awful sway,
> To rule mankind, and make the world obey.

> (tr. JOHN DRYDEN)

Together, then, Roman imperial architecture and sculpture perform a fourfold function. Taking their cue from the capital itself, they rhetorically assert and re-assert the power of Rome throughout the Empire, the common Greco-Roman culture of East and West, the willing acquiescence of the provinces in Roman rule, and the solidarity and permanence of the imperium. Unprecedented in its scope and thoroughness, this unique program remains unequaled in human history. True, the architectural revolution of the twentieth century has spread the symbol of American capitalism, the skyscraper, over the entire face of the globe, but here motivations and effects are both more limited and rather different, and the representational arts have almost no part to play.

As to portraiture, while the local worthies continued to people their piazzas and sanctuaries with statues of relatives, friends, benefactors, and political allies, the emperor's image dominated all **(J 266–270; G 6.67, 6.69, 6.71–6.74; H&F 5.47, 5.52).** Whether it was erected in the city square or in its own shrine, was in armor, togate, or nude, was life-size or super-colossal, its message—conveyed by the uniform head types authorized by the emperor himself and specially disseminated from the capital—was the same: it was upon the emperor that the *Pax Romana* depended, and it was to him and him alone that one's ultimate allegiance was owed. Omnipresent, he was also by implication omniscient, informed of everything by his provincial administration, and omnipotent, possessed of unimaginable power with which to enforce his will.

## Imperial Summer: From Nerva to Marcus Aurelius (A.D. 96–180)

The reigns of the "five good emperors," Nerva, Trajan, Hadrian, Antoninus Pius, and Marcus Aurelius **(J 268–269; G 6.71–6.72; H&F 5.52)** represent the high summer of the Empire. Wars were few and limited, good government prevailed in the provinces, the treasury was full, and policies were liberal. Trajan's column, bearing the largest and most complete example of Roman imperial relief sculpture to have survived, offers the classic

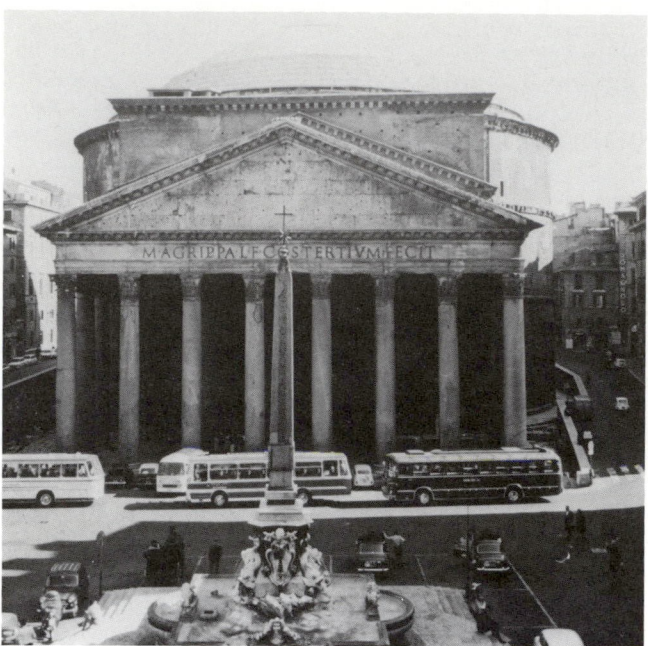

The Pantheon, Exterior. A.D. 125, Rome.
(SCALA/ART RESOURCE, NEW YORK)

statement of the aims and achievements of these men **(J 265; G 6.65–6.66; H&F 5.55).** A masterpiece of the "continuous" narrative style first encountered on the Telephos frieze of the so-called Great Altar of Pergamon, it celebrates Trajan's addition of Dacia (modern Rumania) to the empire. Substituting a rich and exact realism of detail for the mythological narrative of its Greek predecessor, it chronicles Roman expansion in a way that exactly echoes Vergil's injunction, penned over a century before, that they should "spare the conquered, but crush the proud."

The column's counterpart in architecture is Hadrian's Pantheon, or [building of] All the Gods **(J 238–241; G 6.51–6.53; H&F 5.42–5.44).** Begun in 117, and dedicated in 126–128, it stood on the site of an earlier Pantheon erected by Augustus's lieutenant, Agrippa, as a part of the great plan for the Campus Martius that also included the Ara Pacis, the sundial and obelisk, and Augustus's mausoleum. The form of this earlier building is not precisely known, but recent research suggests that it may have been a circular court entered by a colonnaded porch. If so, Hadrian not only borrowed the essentials of Agrippa's plan for his own, but may have allowed Agrippa's name to remain on the new building because he wished to acknowledge this. It is tempting to speculate that some of the new Pantheon's symbolism was present in Agrippa's too, but as we shall see, this symbolism is itself problematic, and in any case little more can be said until these new studies are published.

The Pantheon owes its remarkable preservation largely to the decision in 609 to consecrate it as a church,

Sancta Maria ad Martyres, and to periodic renewals of the metal covering of its roof after the original gilded bronze tiles were robbed by the Byzantine Emperor Constans II in 663. Dilapidation of the buildings around it, the Tiber floods, and the collapse of Rome's public services after the fall of the Empire caused the ground around it to rise, covering the lower steps of its portico, and depriving it of the visually firm foundation that these provided. Originally, too, it was approached by way of a great rectangular colonnaded court in the Corinthian Order, with a triumphal arch at its center. This arrangement, now lost under the surrounding houses and streets, was borrowed from Augustus's Forum, whose symbolism of universal domination set a clear precedent for the Pantheon's own.

Dominating this court at its northern end, very much as the temple of Mars Ultor dominated the Forum Augusti, the façade of the Pantheon was composed of eight monolithic shafts of grey Egyptian granite, forty feet high, set on a stepped base, and capped by Corinthian capitals in white marble; most of the rest of the building is also calculated in multiples of five Roman feet. These columns carried a marble entablature bearing an inscription in great bronze letters, stating that Agrippa built it in his third consulship (25 B.C.), and a large pediment embellished with a design in bronze, now lost but for the dowel holes used to affix it to the stone. Recent study of these suggests that the subject was a huge eagle settling within a wreath: a common symbol of imperial power.

Passing beneath the pediment, the visitor would find himself in a three-aisled porch formed by eight more of the huge Corinthian monoliths, arranged in pairs behind the first, third, sixth, and eighth columns of the façade. While the two outer aisles terminated in semi-domed niches displaying colossal statues of Agrippa and Augustus, the center one, framed by white marble Corinthian pilasters, developed into a barrel-vaulted entranceway that led to a pair of great bronze doors. This inner porch and the niches formed part of an intermediate block that also carried service staircases leading to the upper storys and the roof. Built, like the remainder of the building, of brick-faced concrete, on the outside it takes the form of a massive rectangle behind the pediment and roof of the outer porch; to ease the transition, it is given its own pediment and a crowning cornice. Ungainly and awkward, this intermediate block poses many problems that will occupy us further below.

None of this prepares the spectator for what confronts him as he finally passes through the great doors to reach the heart of the complex. A huge, domed rotunda 150 feet in diameter and 150 feet high, embellished with colored marbles, colonnaded apses, and soaring coffers, and capped by a circular opening or *oculus* that enables the direct rays of the sun to sweep slowly and majestically around the interior, it simply takes one's breath away. Above a floor paved with alternate squares and circles of colored granites, marbles, and porphyry, the rotunda rises 75 feet to the springing of the dome. Contrary to first impressions, it is not a continuous drum but composed of eight enormous concrete piers joined by Corinthian colonnades and backed by a screen wall. As in the octagon of Nero's Golden House **(G 6.49–6.50; H&F p. 162),** the apses created by this arrangement help to open up the interior, the more so as they are top-lit via a set of smaller, pedimented niches in the attic zone above. (This zone was drastically redesigned in the 1740s, but a small section was restored to its original state earlier in this century). Paneling and pilasters in yellow African marble, purple and white "peacock" marble from Asia, blue-white marble from Athens, and deep red Egyptian porphyry further enhance this symphony of light and color.

And finally, there is the dome, soaring above a relatively simple cornice of white marble. Its one hundred and forty coffers are arranged in five bands of twenty-eight, and are designed perspectively. Not only do they necessarily diminish in width as they rise, but the panels both have sloping sides and are displaced towards the top of each coffer, so that the rays from the *oculus* cast their upper sections into deep shadow even as they highlight the lower. The effect is to draw the eye both outward, into the coffers themselves, and upward, toward the blinding light of the *oculus*. By thus expanding the envelope of the dome, the coffers are to it what the apses are to the vertical walls of the rotunda. Each coffer was decorated with a gilded bronze rosette and edged with gilded bronze moldings.

Two questions naturally come to mind when one is confronted with an architectural phenomenon of this size, sophistication, and power: how was it built, and what does it all mean? To these, architectural historians of recent years have added a third, specific to the Pantheon itself: why, in a building of such obvious genius, is the transition from porch to rotunda so ungainly? Investigations during this century have done much to answer the first question; the second, despite some agreement over generalities, is still a problem; and a most ingenious solution has recently been offered to the third. To take each in turn.

The building rests upon a fourteen-foot-deep ring of concrete mixed with chunks of hard local travertine to minimize compression. Above this, the rotunda is of concrete faced outside with brick. Its piers, almost twenty feet thick, do much thereby to absorb the relatively limited outward thrust generated by the dome. For unlike cut stone vaults and domes, concrete ones are essentially homogeneous and rigid, and so have much less tendency to flatten out and to topple their supporting walls. As a result, Roman architects never needed to develop the complicated exterior buttressing systems that are so conspicuous a feature of, say, Gothic cathedrals. Any residual outward thrust was countered by loading the exterior of the dome with masonry, which redirects its weight downwards, but in doing so makes the extra-thick piers absolutely vital: the combined weight of dome and loading has been estimated at over 5,000 metric tons. On

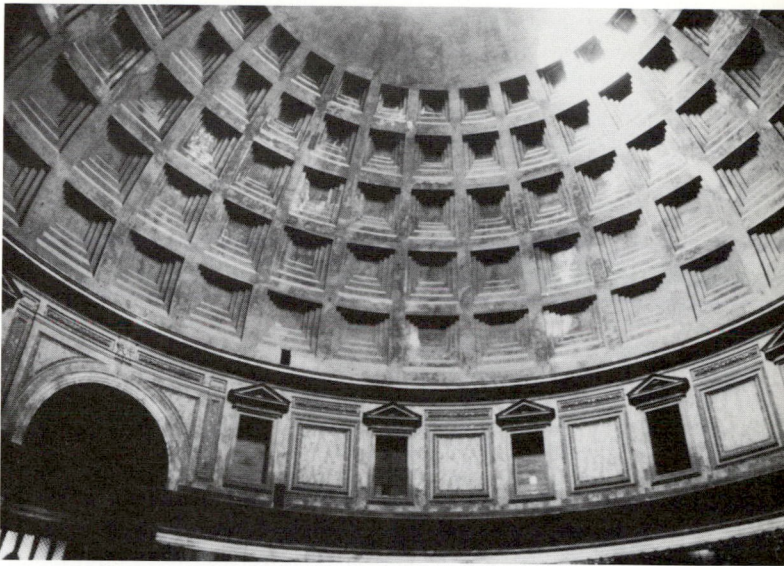

The Pantheon, Detail of Interior. (ALINARI/ART RESOURCE, NEW YORK)

the outer face of the dome, this masonry appears as the series of concentric steps that are so conspicuous a feature of the Pantheon's roof.

Most conspicuous from the exterior are, however, the superimposed series of brick arches set into the surface of the rotunda. Formerly it was believed that these were intended to deflect the immense weight of the dome away from the thin screen-walls of the rotunda and down into the eight enormous piers. Now it is recognized that they continue up into the dome itself, and must have served another function too: to stabilize the mass of concrete section by section as it was drying. As to the dome, gone are the days when it could be believed that when the rotunda's walls had been completed, Hadrian ordered it filled with earth liberally seeded with gold coins, so that the concrete fabric could be poured in safety and the building then opened up rapidly by the frantically digging slaves!

Instead, the whole interior must have been filled with scaffolding, for the concrete was actually poured over a vast wooden hemisphere, studded with wooden step-pyramids for the coffers. As it was poured, it first created the web of ribs between the coffers, then, as the layers of concrete dried, the panels themselves. Liberally mixed with pumice, the aggregate used was the lightest in the whole building. Finally, when all was set, the mass of timber was removed, and the vault revealed in all its glory: like the building itself, a triumph of that peculiarly Roman genius not only for organization, but for imaginative planning at all levels.

Nowhere are the Romans' unique talents more manifest than in the Pantheon's complex interrelation of design and meaning. In geometric terms, the interior of the Pantheon is a hemisphere set above a cylinder. If the hemisphere were projected into a sphere, this would just touch the center of the floor of the building. Not surprisingly, the few Roman historians to comment on it likened its rotunda to a great city and its dome to the vault of heaven, and more recent critics have detected a truly cosmic symbolism, an attempt to express the essential unity both of the divine (in an age that had grown increasingly skeptical of the old gods), and of the inhabited globe under Roman rule. In this view, it is "the temple of the whole world," to use a phrase borrowed from one of them. In fact, we know that it was indeed filled with the statues of many gods, including Mars and Venus, and that Hadrian often used it as an imperial audience hall, but little more.

The problem is not whether these interpretations are right: they are certainly *plausible,* and to some extent supported by evidence from other buildings and other texts, but architecture is an abstract medium and so necessarily somewhat open-ended in its symbolism. The matter is rather one of degree: was the Pantheon's worldly or its celestial "message" paramount, or was its meaning truly a seamless mixture of the two? Indeed, was it really a temple? Though its name suggests that it was, it is never explicitly called a temple, and its inscription contains no dedication, only the information that Agrippa "made" it. Furthermore, Roman emperors appear to have avoided giving audiences in temples.

Taking all this into account, and observing the definite imperial connotations of the pedimental eagle and the abundance of purple marble and porphyry in the building, a recent suggestion is that it was designed not as a temple but as an imperial audience hall, and that any religious connotations are entirely secondary. To develop the argument a little, one might propose that the statues of the gods which evidently gave the Pantheon its name were included as evidence of their favor to empire and emperor, and not necessarily as cult images in their own right. Two snippets of evidence, hitherto overlooked in the debate, might support this more worldly interpretation of its function: as we have seen, the caryatids included in Agrippa's original building were regarded as symbols of eternal subjection, and on April first, the feast-day of Augustus's divine progenitrix and the patroness of the empire, Venus, the sun rises exactly on the building's east-west axis. Of course, all this is not to decry the Pantheon's extraordinary power as a symbol of earthly unity under a unified cosmos, merely to re-orient its meaning towards the former. Its status as the supreme statement of the destiny and mission of Rome remains unchanged.

Finally, there is the puzzle of the awkward join between portico and rotunda. Were features such as the intrusion of the portico's pediment into the pediment of the transitional block, and the abrupt termination of the portico's entablature and the lowest cornice of the rotunda at the junction between the rotunda and the transitional block intended? Why are the portico columns more widely spaced than usual? Why is the pediment of the portico unusually tall in proportion to the height of these columns? Why do the two pediments have cornice modillions of different sizes, even though the pediments themselves are the same size? Why are the interior pilasters wider than the capitals they carry? Why is the brickwork of the transitional block only bonded with the rotunda in the lower levels of the building? And so on.

Taking these all together, it would indeed seem that the portico, as built, is a stop-gap solution to some problem that emerged in the course of construction. The key to the problem, as a recent article argues, lies in the two pediments: why are there two at all, when it would have been much simpler to roof the entire entrance complex at the same level? What if there had been a drastic change in plan during construction, compelling the architect to lower the portico's roof the 12 feet that now separates the apex of the first pediment from the second?

Roman Corinthian columns were usually designed so that their shafts occupied five-sixths of the total height, the capital the other sixth. These shafts were normally produced in multiples of 5 feet, the same basic module used by the Pantheon's architect throughout. The shortest ones were 20 feet high (complete column, 24 feet), then 25 (complete column, 30), 30 (36), 40 (48), and finally 50 (60). Now, it will be evident that the difference between the Pantheon's present 48-foot columns (including capitals) and the largest size in normal use, totalling 60 feet in height, exactly corresponds to the difference in the two roof levels. What if the Pantheon had originally been intended to have 60-foot columns, but the giant 50-foot shafts for them were suddenly for some reason no longer available?

An Egyptian papyrus of A.D. 118 mentions difficulties in supplying these 100-ton monoliths (almost double the weight of the 40-foot shafts), and numerous wrecks around the Mediterranean testify to the fate of many such cargoes. Furthermore, Hadrian was also engaged at that time in building a great temple to his predecessor and adoptive father, Trajan, which apparently used the 50-foot monster shafts too. Perhaps filial piety played a part in the hard choice between the two, but in any case the reduction in height would have had a much less drastic effect upon the Pantheon than upon the more traditional temple of Trajan, whose entire proportional scheme would have been predetermined by the selection of the 50-foot shafts, some of which may have already been in place. Rather than countenance the long delay that a new order would have caused, Hadrian may have authorized the substitution of the smaller shafts, many if not all of which might well have been immediately available from stock.

Of course, all this is only hypothesis, but it has the merit of explaining all the facts, and of making sense of a building which is both one of the most influential and most intriguing in the history of architecture. Certainly, these revisions affected its subsequent popularity not one whit. For whereas the Parthenon, for all its perfection, had sparked no imitations, and was hardly accessible to Westerners before the late eighteenth century, little Pantheons from Pergamon to Monticello testify to the truth of what Pope Urban VIII caused to be inscribed upon its porch: PANTHEON: AEDIFICIVM TOTO TER-RARVM ORBE CELEBERRIMVM. "The Pantheon: the most celebrated edifice in the whole world."

Hadrian's building program, too massive to discuss in detail here, was continued under his successors, enriching Rome and the provinces alike to a degree unimaginable only a century earlier. Yet by the end of the century Rome was in deep crisis again, to the effects of which we must now turn.

## The Third-Century Crisis, and Late Imperial Art

This is not the place to debate the reasons for the profound changes that transformed the Empire and eventually brought about its downfall. Renewed barbarian pressure, economic woes, the depraved or despotic personalities of not a few of the later emperors themselves—all had a part to play in the drama, as did the collapse of paganism and rise of Christianity. Suffice it to say that when Constantine built his triumphal arch in 315, celebrating his victory over his rival for the imperial purple, Maxentius, all had changed.

The Arch of Constantine (**J 273–274; G 6.89–6.91; H&F 5.66**) is a landmark in Roman art in more ways than one. First, it plunders reliefs from the reigns of the "five good emperors," presumably to assert that the good times had returned, but in effect betraying a distinct inferiority complex. For not only was the Empire now a semi-feudalized, absolutist despotism in a state of near-permanent mobilization, but the imperial classic style of these reliefs had been abandoned in the third century and could hardly be revived. The reliefs above the side-arches show what had taken its place: dumpy, dehumanized figures, often in frontal poses, their modeling reduced to the point where negative forms (drill channels, chisel cuts, and so on) define the figure more than positive ones. Confronting the observer, and so immediately establishing a kind of hieratic rapport with him, this sculpture is already medieval in that it explicitly rejects Greco-Roman humanism, as manifested in the organic, rational, naturalistic styles pioneered by the Greeks and dominant in Rome since the late republic. Instead, it substitutes a transcendent view of the universe that regards man as but a cipher and earthly things as mere delusion.

To the world of late antiquity, inner meaning and spiritual content are now all important, and the outer shell is just that—a carapace to be gouged, penetrated, and stripped away in search of a higher Truth. Though these attitudes are obviously well-entrenched in the philosophy of early Christianity, it must not be thought that they are unique to it, or stem principally from its teaching. In this respect, Christianity was but a part of a wider rejection of humanist paganism that, fueled by the appalling chaos of the third century (when no fewer than thirty emperors reigned in fifty years, usurpers ruled large sections of the Empire, and the Goths devastated whole provinces), manifested itself in a wide variety of transcendentalist philosophies, among the most influential of which was Neo-Platonism. Late antique portraits vividly chronicle this increasingly reductive and anti-classical trend, from the "Hard Style" of the third-century barrack-room emperors, through the frozen stereometry of the Tetrarchs and Constantine, to the emaciated, dematerialized features of early Byzantine notables (**J 270–272, 305; G 6.74, 6.87–6.88, 6.92; H&F 7.16**). Finally, after an unbroken history of over a thousand years, the art of portraiture itself simply died; when men's eyes were fixed on heaven, physical representation of the individual became irrelevant.

All this is not to say that the new trends were uniformly accepted, or proceeded at a uniform pace. Architecture had undergone its own revolution in the early Empire, and needed no second one. Though they use the Greek Orders in an even more blatantly cosmetic manner than before, and their capitals and moldings are modeled as "negatively" as the figural sculpture of the period, the Baths of Diocletian and Constantine's basilica are planned along lines that had been traditional ever since Augustus (**J 242–244; G 6.85–6.86; H&F 5.60, 5.62**). The sarcophagus of Junius Bassus, a Christian prefect of Rome who died in 359, even attempts a kind of neo-classicism to cloak its salvation cycle of Old and New Testament scenes (**J 301–302; H&F 7.12**). Yet the doll-like figures with their large heads and stilted actions owe much to the Constantinian reliefs, raising the possibility that what is intended here is a kind of creative synthesis of old and new. A generation later, the ivory diptych of the fiercely conservative aristocratic families of the Nicomachi and Symmachi attempts a full-blown classical revival, in the context of a pagan sacrifice to Jupiter (**J 303; G 7.19; H&F 7.19**).

When this ivory was produced, around 400, Rome's days as an imperial power were numbered. For strategic reasons, Constantine had already removed the imperial capital to the shores of the Bosphoros, enlarging the old Greek city of Byzantium there and renaming it Constantinople. When the Vandals crossed the Rhine into Gaul on the last day of 406, there were no troops left to oppose them. Chaos swiftly ensued as Spain and Africa fell to their advance; the East, guarded by the new capital, now stood alone, and Rome was defenseless. In the spring of 410, the Visigoths under Alaric stormed into Italy and advanced on Rome. The city fell by default on August 24th, and was plundered. True, an emperor was to reign in the West until 476, when the pitiful Romulus Augustulus (his name a caricature of those two giants of Roman history, the founder of the city and the founder of the

Empire) was deposed by Odovacar the Visigoth; yet it was in 410 that the power of Rome was finally broken. From the third century Rome had increasingly come to reject her classical heritage in the arts, and in the fourth the foundation of Constantinople had shifted the artistic center of gravity back to the East. Now, with Alaric's departure for juicier pickings in South Italy on August 28th, 410, Rome ceased to be the center of power as well.

## Summary

After the chaos of the Dark Age, the foundation of the polis and increasing contact with the Near East in the eighth century gave Greek art its first major impetus. Using a vocabulary adapted from Near Eastern and Egyptian models, artists competed to create rationally structured and visually credible images in free-standing and relief sculpture, and in narrative painting on vases. The Doric and Ionic Orders were invented, and together with the representational arts achieved their definitive, or "classic," form after the repulse of the Persians in 480–479. In their various ways, the Doryphoros of Polykleitos and the Parthenon represent both the climax of this development and a departure-point for further experiment. After Athens' defeat in 404, sculptors turned to exploiting the achievements of this high classic phase in a more personal manner, until (under the patronage of Alexander) Lysippos radically transformed the art, laying the foundations for the highly subjective creations of the Hellenistic period. In architecture, the Corinthian Order, invented in the fourth century, became ever more popular. Alexander spread Hellenism over the Near East, but as his empire broke up, Athens became the bastion of classicism, and Pergamon of the Asian baroque, while Alexandria produced a diverse and hybrid art that is often decorative and anecdotal in character. The effects of Roman intrusion were increasingly apparent after 200, as new tastes made themselves felt and massive quantities of treasure were transferred to the West.

While Roman art of the regal period and early republic is hardly distinguishable from Etruscan, this influx of plunder from Greece and the East after 200 both swamped the native traditions and created a superficially Hellenized material culture in Rome. In verist portraiture, architectural complexes, private homes, and numerous other contexts, late republican art sought to adapt Greek vocabulary to specifically Roman functions. Under Augustus, the need for a style to express the new ideology of peace through strength led to the development of imperial classicism, and much investment in such genres as ruler-portraiture and historical relief. During the first two centuries of the Empire, the Augustan achievement was further refined, and the republican invention of concrete architecture with its curvilinear forms was incorporated into the tradition. Monuments such as Trajan's column and the Pantheon represent the apex of this specifically imperial mode, completing the transformation of the legacy of Greece into an authentically Roman means of expression. The third-century crisis eroded these ideals, both in sculpture, where Greek organic naturalism was progressively abandoned for an ever more searching exploration of the soul, and in architecture, where the Greek Orders were reduced to mere window dressing. Often serving a new ideology, Christianity, late antique art represents the first stage in the rejection of Greek humanism, and the beginning of the medieval world.

## Textbook References

Whereas this Study Guide unit has aimed to balance art and its context, analyzing sculpture, painting, and architecture as products both of an inherited artistic tradition and of a wider social and political framework, in both Janson and Gardner the emphasis is on form. The authors coordinate numerous illustrations, important facts, thorough descriptions, and a close formal analysis in order to train their readers to discriminate between styles and to produce accurate and closely reasoned descriptions and evaluations of their own. By reading their work attentively, you will learn to sharpen your eye for art, and gain fluency in its language. Honour and Fleming, on the other hand, tend to emphasize context at the expense both of the individual work of art and of stylistic development; while one welcomes their discussions of the role and status of the artist, or of patronage, the result is a certain loss of continuity.

**J** Janson includes fewer monuments than Gardner but is careful to illustrate plans, elevations, and views of most of the architecture he talks about. His discussions are briefer (the Parthenon and Pantheon receive less than half of the space allotted to them by Gardner), and the treatment of the Hellenistic period is particularly cursory; the only minor arts included are Greek coins.

**G** Gardner's chapters are organized chronologically and by medium; they cover most of the major monuments in some detail, and occasionally include newly discovered or marginal work. This is the only one among the three textbooks to pay significant attention to town planning, but it neglects the so-called minor arts entirely.

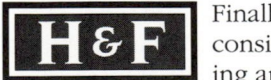 Finally, Honour and Fleming make a considerable effort to be both interesting and provocative, introducing concepts, themes, and issues overlooked in the other two textbooks, and challenging preconceived ideas. The

subject of the reactions to Greek art among neighboring peoples is extended from Etruria to the Balkans and Central Europe, and the normative value of the classical style is repeatedly called into question.

**Janson, Part I, Chapter 5: Greek Art, pp. 96–149.** Geometric, Orientalizing, black-figure, and red-figure vase-painting; kouroi and korai; architectural sculpture (temple of Artemis at Corfu, Siphnian treasury, temple of Aphaia at Aegina); Doric and Ionic Orders; Paestum; Perikles and the Athenian building program; the Parthenon, Propylaea, and Erechtheion; the Corinthian Order; town planning; the theater at Epidauros; classical sculpture (the Kritios Boy, Doryphoros, Delphi Charioteer, Olympia, and Parthenon sculptures); classical painting; Skopas, Praxiteles, Lysippos; Pergamene sculpture and the Great Altar; the Nike of Samothrace and Laokoon; portraits and coins.

**Chapter 6: Etruscan Art, pp. 150–157.** Tombs, temples, metalwork, and towns.

**Chapter 7: Roman Art, pp. 158–196.** Republican temples—Fortuna Virilis, Sibyl, Praeneste; forums; the Colosseum, Pantheon, Basilica of Constantine; houses; late Roman architecture; republican portraits; Primaporta Augustus and Ara Pacis; Arch of Titus; Trajan's Column; imperial portraits; Arch of Constantine; painting: Boscoreale, Villa of the Mysteries, portraits, Dura-Europos.

**Gardner, Chapter 5: The Art of Greece, pp. 124–181.** Geometric, black-figure, and red-figure vases; kouroi and korai; the Kritios Boy; the Doric and Ionic Orders; Paestan temples; architectural sculpture on the Siphnian Treasury, and at Corfu and Aegina; Severe style sculpture, including the Riace bronzes, Delphi Charioteer, and Olympia pediments; the Periklean building program and the Parthenon, Propylaia, Nike temple, and Erechtheion; the Doryphoros; classical vase- and wall-painting; Praxiteles, Skopas, and Lysippos; the Tholos at Epidauros; Pergamene sculpture and the Great Altar; Laokoon and Sperlonga; the Venus de Milo and other Hellenistic sculpture; the temple of Apollo at Didyma; the theater at Epidauros; Hippodamian and Hellenistic town planning; Hellenistic mosaics.

**Chapter 6: Etruscan and Roman Art, pp. 125–245.** Etruscan temples; tomb paintings; sculpture; Roman republican portraits; the temple of Fortuna at Praeneste; Pompeii; painting and mosaic; imperial architecture, including the Colosseum, Forum of Trajan, Golden House, Pantheon, and Baths of Caracalla; imperial sculpture, including the Augustus from Primaporta, Ara Pacis, Arch of Titus, Trajan's column, and sundry imperial portraits; late imperial art, including the Basilica and Arch of Constantine.

**Honour and Fleming, Chapter 4: The Greeks and Their Neighbors, pp. 94–135.** Geometric and Orientalizing vases; kouroi and korai; the Kritios Boy; black- and red-figure vases; the Periklean building program and the Parthenon; the Doric and Ionic orders; temple of Athena Nike and Erechtheion; architectural sculpture (Aegina, Olympia, the Parthenon); classical sculpture and the Doryphoros; Riace bronzes; Praxiteles; classical. vase-painting; funerary art; the tholos and theater at Epidauros; luxury arts and coinage; Scythian, Hallstatt, La Tene, Iberian, and Sardinian art; Etruscan art (jewelry, sculpture, temples).

**Chapter 5: Hellenistic and Roman Art, pp. 136–177.** The Alexander Sarcophagus; the Apollo Belvedere, Venus de Milo, Baker Dancer, Demosthenes, Euthydemos, Nike of Samothrace, Terme ruler; the Great Altar; Didyma; town planning; painting and mosiacs (the Alexander Mosaic, Villa of the Mysteries, and other Pompeian painting); art collecting and connoisseurship; Pompeian architecture; Praeneste; Roman temples and the Augustan building program; the Colosseum, Golden House, Trajan's Markets, Pantheon; Laokoon, Augustus from Primaporta, Ara Pacis, imperial portraiture; Arch of Titus, columns of Trajan and Marcus Aurelius; Sabratha, Baalbek and eastern architecture; baths of Caracalla and Diocletian; sarcophagi; Arch of Constantine.

## Study Questions

1. Explain the following terms: kouros, arete, basilica, auctoritas.
2. Describe the differences between the Doric and Ionic Orders, and discuss their development down to 450 B.C.
3. "Seek to know what pattern governs mankind!" (Archilochos, ca. 650 B.C.) How far can archaic Greek art be described as a quest for order?
4. In what ways did classical sculptors use drapery to articulate the forms of their figures? How does classical drapery differ from archaic?
5. The Greeks of the classical period often seem to be obsessed with moderation and the Mean. Examine the Parthenon and its sculptures from this point of view. How would a Spartan visitor to Athens in 432 or 404 have reacted to it?
6. The art historian W. B. Dinsmoor used the phrase "the beginning of the decadence" to characterize fourth-century art and architecture. Examine this statement in the light of what you know.
7. What effects did Alexander's conquests have upon the subsequent course of Greek art?
8. Hellenistic poets prided themselves on seeking the byways, rather than the highways, of their art. What new interests are displayed by Hellenistic artists, what new effects did they seek, and what new clients did they serve?
9. Why did the Romans want to acquire Greek art, how did they go about it, and to what uses did they put it?
10. "Generalization is the goal of Greek thought, but the Romans preferred the concrete and down-to-earth." How far does Roman portraiture reflect this difference? To what extent was Roman realism put at the service of expressing abstract principles and ideas?
11. "Greek architecture is the search for the perfect exterior; it was the Romans who discovered the interior." Discuss.
12. How far is it true to say that late Roman art is already proto-medieval?

## Glossary

**abacus**   the uppermost member of a column-capital.

**aegis**   a talismanic upper garment, scaly and fringed with snakes, worn by Athena and (sometimes) Zeus.

**agora**   the town center of a Greek polis.

**akropolis**   the citadel of a Greek polis.

**akroterion**   a figure placed at the lower angles or apex of a pediment.

**antefix**   the decorative termination of the cover-tiles at the edge of a roof.

**architrave**   the lowest member of an entablature; a lintel in stone or timber, carried from the top of one column or pier to another.

**arete**   personal excellence; (later) moral virtue.

**auctoritas**   personal authority.

**basilica**   a Roman exchange, assembly place, and court of law. Usually a rectangular building, divided into three aisles by interior colonnades, and furnished with a speaker's podium at the end opposite the door.

**cardo**   the main north-south street of a Roman legionary camp and (later) of Roman towns.

**caryatid**   female figure used in place of a column.

**cella**   the cult-room of a temple.

**centaur**   hybrid figure combining a horse's body with the torso and head of a man. Often a symbol of unbridled appetite and *hybris.*

**chiaroscuro**   Italian word for light and dark. In painting, a system of modeling form by the use of light and shade.

**classical**   work produced in the fifth or fourth centuries B.C. that subscribes to the "classical" principles of economy, clarity, consistency, and the supremacy of formal design.

**classicizing**   work produced after the fourth century B.C. that is intended to echo or re-create the classical.

**coffer**   a sunken panel in a vault, ceiling, or cornice.

**constantia**   endurance, "grit."

**consul**   the chief magistrate of the Roman republic. Consuls were always elected in pairs.

**continuous narrative**   a method of pictorial or sculptural narration in which the protagonists reappear at intervals along a frieze, so that the story unfolds as the spectator walks along or around it.

**contrapposto**   Italian word for "set against." A method of composition that balances engaged and relaxed parts of the body in a series of ordered cross-relationships, thereby achieving an overall harmony and balance of movement.

**cornice**   the uppermost member of an entablature, positioned just below the roof-gutter. In general, any molding provided to throw water away from a wall.

**decumanus**   the main east-west street of a Roman legionary camp and (later) of Roman towns.

**diptych**   originally, a hinged, two-leaved tablet used for writing; later a purely ornamental insignia of office for magistrates, usually of ivory.

**doryphoros**   spear-bearer.

**entablature**   the superstructure carried by columns, and sometimes used also to crown a wall.

**entasis**   the slight convex curve often given to the profile of a Doric column.

**epiphany**   an appearance in person of a god or goddess.

**forum**   the town-center of a Roman city (equivalent to a Greek agora).

**frieze**   the middle member of an entablature; any sculptured or painted band.

**gravitas**   seriousness, gravity.

**griffin**   a hybrid animal with the body of a lion and the wings and head of an eagle. Often a symbol of divine or royal power.

**hybris**   arrogance; any conduct which offends divine sensibilities and natural justice.

**iconic**   representational.

**iconography**   the "what" of an image; the study of representational schemata and their meanings in art.

**imperium**   executive power given to a Roman magistrate by the Senate and people; (later) dominion, empire.

**kore**   a girl or statue of one, always clothed.

**kouros**   a youth or statue of one, usually naked.

**krepis**   the stepped platform of a Greek temple.

**Lapith**   member of a Greek tribe chiefly remembered for its conflicts with the Centaurs.

**metope**   a panel, sometimes carved or painted, between the triglyphs of a Doric frieze.

**mos maiorum**   ancestral custom.

**necropolis**   the cemetery of a Greek polis.

**neo-classical**   work produced after the fourth century B.C. that is intended to echo or re-create the classical.

**nemesis**   retribution (usually for hybris).

**oculus**   an "eye." The hole left at the apex of a Roman vault or dome to admit light and air.

**patrician**   member of the hereditary aristocracy of Rome.

**pediment**   a gable.

**Pegasos**   a winged horse, offspring of Poseidon and the Gorgon Medusa, and tamed by Bellerophon.

**pilaster**   a pier engaged in a wall.

**plebeian**   any Roman who was not a patrician.

**polis**   a Greek city-state.

**princeps**   "first man"; the usual title of a Roman emperor.

**schema**   a pattern or formula.

**sophrosyne**   the self-knowledge that begets a measured self-restraint.

**stoa**   a covered colonnade used as a meeting place or promenade, and later, as a shopping mall.

**stylobate**   the upper step of a temple krepis.

**tholos**   a round temple.

**triglyph**   a projecting member separating the metopes of a Doric frieze, its face carved with three vertical bars.

**verism**   super-realism. Exaggeration of unflattering features to produce a map of experience, emphasizing the political credentials of the sitter.

**volute**   the spiral scroll of an Ionic capital.

## Artists, Patrons, and Important Personages

**Agrippa.**   Roman consul, general, and right-hand man of the emperor Augustus until his death in 12 B.C. Also a patron of the arts, whose buildings in Rome included her first set of public baths, the original Pantheon, and, more prosaically, a new sewer and water system.

**Alexander the Great.**   King of Macedon, 336–323 B.C. Conqueror of the Persian empire, Alexander was much concerned with his own portraiture, hiring the sculptor Lysippos, the painter Apelles, and the gem-cutter Pyrgoteles as court artists to this end. He also patronized the architect

Deinokrates, who is supposed to have advised him on the planning of the many Alexandrias that he founded during his campaign.

**Apollodoros.** Architect from Damascus. Minister of works to the emperor Trajan (A.D. 98–117), later adviser to his successor, Hadrian (117–138), who is supposed to have had him killed in a fit of anger at his criticisms of the Temple of Venus and Rome. His buildings in Rome included Trajan's Forum, Concert Hall, and Baths, and he also designed a great stone bridge across the Danube to facilitate supply of Trajan's Dacian campaigns. His dismissive attitude to Hadrian's architectural fancies ("go away and draw your pumpkins"), together with the evidence of the Forum itself, perhaps suggests an architectural conservative.

**Augustus.** First Roman emperor, 31 B.C.–A.D. 14. A vigorous patron of the arts, he boasted in his own testament that he found Rome a city of brick and left her a city of marble. He was responsible for restoring no fewer than eighty-two dilapidated temples in the city itself, left to decay during the civil wars, and in addition undertook numerous civic projects (fora, baths, gymnasia, theaters, and so on) in both Rome and the provinces. The most influential of Roman sculptural styles, imperial classicism, was created under his direct authority.

**Celer.** Chief engineer to the emperor Nero (A.D. 54–68). Associate of Severus in the building of Nero's Golden House, engineer of its colossal statues, hydraulic works, and mechanical devices such as the revolving ceiling of its main dining room; Celer also worked with Severus on Nero's pet public-works project, the Avernus-Tiber canal.

**Constantine.** Roman emperor, A.D. 311–337. Famed for making Christianity the official religion of the Empire (though he himself was only baptized on his deathbed), and founder of the new capital of Constantinople (modern Istanbul), he inaugurated the last great period of Roman imperial art. His Basilica Nova (actually begun by his predecessor, Maxentius) and triumphal arch are classic works of their genres, and the Constantinian portrait style represents the last major development in its genre before the Empire's fall. His Church of St. Peter was the prototype for all Christian basilicas until the Renaissance.

**Hadrian.** Roman emperor, A.D. 117–138. Polymath and Hellenophile, world traveler, architect, sculptor, painter, draughtsman, poet, and builder as no other Roman emperor. In addition to the Pantheon, the Temple of Venus and Rome, and his sprawling country villa near Tivoli, Hadrian patronized countless other projects in Rome and the provinces, sometimes (as at Athens) not merely donating libraries, temples, and fora, but rebuilding entire sections of the town. Irked at the architect Apollodoros's caustic criticisms of his designs, he is supposed to have had him killed.

**Hagesandros, Athanadoros, and Polydoros.** Sculptors from Rhodes, authors of the Laokoon group and of a large sculptural complex in a cave adjoining an imperial villa at Sperlonga. Masters of the "baroque" style, they seem to have worked either in the time of Augustus or of his successor, Tiberius (A.D. 14–37), who narrowly escaped death when the roof of the Sperlonga cave collapsed in A.D. 21.

**Hippodamos.** Architect and town planner from Miletos, active ca. 475–440. A theorist and author of a treatise on town planning and rational government, Hippodamos is credited with the first systematic exposition of the principles of the grid plan.

**Iktinos, Kallikrates, and Karpion.** Athenian architects of the Parthenon, 447–432 B.C. Iktinos was perhaps the theorist of the group, while other projects such as the rebuilding of the Akropolis walls suggest that Kallikrates was more of a master mason. Karpion is otherwise unknown.

**Lysippos.** Bronze-sculptor from Sikyon, active ca. 370–310 B.C. Extremely prolific, at home in many genres (gods, heroes, athletes, portraits, groups, and animal sculpture), and working in all scales from miniature to super-colossal, Lysippos was court sculptor to Alexander the Great (336–323). He was also a theorist, inventing a new canon of proportion which sought to increase the apparent height of his figures by slimming down the torso and reducing the size of the head. A master of illusion, he cultivated extreme delicacy of detail to enhance the credibility and impact of his work, and was a seminal figure in the transition from classical to Hellenistic.

**Mnesikles.** Athenian architect of the Propylaia (gateway) to the Akropolis, 438–432 B.C.

**Nero.** Roman emperor, A.D. 54–68. Best known for his megalomania and perverted sense of humor, Nero turned the great fire of Rome in 64 to his own advantage, appropriating the entire center of the city for his Golden House. Hiring Severus and Celer to carry out the work, Nero emerges as a catalyst of innovation in the arts, particularly architecture.

**Perikles.** Athenian statesman and leader from the 460s until his death in 429. Responsible for the Athenian building program, including the Parthenon, Propylaea, and theater of Dionysos, and alleged patron of the master sculptor Pheidias.

**Pheidias.** Athenian sculptor, active ca 470–425 B.C. Master of many media, including chryselephantine (gold and ivory), bronze, and marble, he specialized in images of the gods, particularly Athena. The supreme exponent of the high classic style in sculpture, he is recorded as having been chosen by Perikles to oversee the Athenian rebuilding program, and produced the colossal chryselephantine Athena for the Parthenon. Exiled for allegedly embezzling its ivory in 438, he fled to Olympia, where he spent the last years of his life making the even bigger chryselephantine Zeus for the god's temple there. In antiquity, he was regarded as the greatest of all Greek sculptors.

**Polykleitos.** Argive sculptor, active ca. 460–410 B.C. A specialist in bronze, he produced mostly statues of mortals (athletes and heroes), of which the most famous was the Doryphoros or "spearbearer." An exercise in perfect proportion and composition, and accompanied by a theoretical treatise entitled "The Canon," this immediately attracted a large following. Despite revisions by Lysippos a century later, the Doryphoros remained the paradigm of male perfection for the rest of antiquity.

**Polykleitos the Younger.** Argive sculptor and architect, active ca. 370–330 B.C. He is chiefly remembered for his tholos and theater at Epidauros: the former set a new standard of elegance in architecture, and created a model design for the Corinthian capital, while the latter represents a more-or-less definitive solution to the architectural and acoustical problems of the Greek theater.

**Praxiteles.** Athenian sculptor in bronze and marble, active ca. 375–325 B.C. Particularly renowned for his sensitive portrayals of Aphrodite and Eros, he revitalized the art of marble-carving with his exquisite handling of surface. His impressionistic *sfumato* (delicate gradation of light and shade) was much in favor with Hellenistic sculptors, among whom it swiftly became a cliché.

**Severus.** Architect, with Celer, of Nero's Golden House (A.D.

64–68). The domes and vaults of the remaining wing of the villa reveal him as a vigorously modern professional, the pioneer of Rome's "new architecture" of interior space, while the reports of his landscaping and other activities show him as an innovator in other ways too.

**Skopas.**  Parian sculptor and architect, active ca. 375–335 B.C. The great exponent of pathos in late classic sculpture, Skopas was also an entrepreneur, in demand for large architectural projects with extensive sculptural embellishment. His main work in this vein was on the Mausoleum at Halikarnassos and the temple of Athena Alea at Tegea, which he designed.

**Sulla.**  Roman consul, general, and eventual dictator (82–79 B.C.). Conqueror of the eastern monarch Mithridates and the first Roman to take Rome by assault, Sulla merits inclusion here because of the large-scale architectural projects initiated under his rule: the Tabularium (Public Record Office) at Rome and the Sanctuary of Fortuna at Praeneste. These mark the massive Hellenization of Roman architecture, the first large-scale use of arches and vaults, and the birth of a concept of the art as a political weapon.

**Trajan.**  Roman emperor, A.D. 98–117. In many ways as influential a figure in the development of Roman art as Augustus, Trajan both overhauled the imperial classic style in sculpture, and, through his court architect Apollodoros, created a new standard for imperial architecture. His column recording his successes in the Dacian Wars and the adjoining Forum and Basilica Ulpia together represent the definitive statement of Roman imperial art.

# Bibliography

## HISTORY AND CULTURE

Boardman, J. *The Greeks Overseas,* 2nd ed. London, 1980.
Brown, P.  *The World of Late Antiquity.* London, 1871.
Cornell, T., and Matthews, J.  *Atlas of the Roman World.* Oxford, 1982.
Crawford, M.  *The Roman Republic.* Glasgow, 1978.
Dudley, D. R.  *The Civilization of Rome.* New York, 1982.
Finley, M. I.  *The Ancient Greeks.* London, 1977.
Keuls, E.  *The Reign of the Phallus.* New York, 1985.
Levi, P.  *Atlas of the Greek World.* Oxford, 1980.
Millar, F.  *The Roman Empire and Its Neighbours.* London, 1981.
*The Oxford Classical Dictionary.*  Oxford, 1970.
Price, S. R. F.  *Rituals and Power: The Roman Imperial Cult in Asia Minor.* Oxford, 1982.
Schor, N.  *Reading in Detail: Aesthetics and the Feminine.* London, 1987.
Starr, C. G.  *The Ancient Greeks.* Oxford, 1971.
Walbank, F. W.  *The Hellenistic World.* Cambridge, 1972.

## GREEK AND ROMAN ART

Alsop, J.  *The Rare Art Traditions: The History of Art Collecting and Its Linked Phenomena.* New York, 1982.
Andreae, B.  *The Art of Rome.* New York, 1977.
Becatti, G.  *The Art of Ancient Greece and Rome.* New York, 1968.
Bianchi-Bandinelli, R.  *Rome: The Center of Power.* New York, 1970.
———.  *Rome: The Late Empire.* New York, 1971.
Brendel, O.  *Prolegomena to a Book on Roman Art.* New Haven, 1979.
Brilliant, R.  *Roman Art.* New York, 1974.

Charbonneaux, J., Martin, R., and Villard, F.  *Archaic Greek Art.* New York, 1968.
———.  *Classical Greek Art.* New York, 1972.
———.  *Hellenistic Art.* New York, 1973.
*The Encyclopedia of World Art.* New York, 1968. Articles on Greek Art, Roman Art, etc.
Henig, M., ed.  *A Handbook of Roman Art.* Ithaca, 1983.
Hurwit, J. M.  *The Art and Culture of Early Greece.* Ithaca, 1985.
L'Orange, H. P.  *Art Forms and Civic Life in the Late Roman Empire.* Princeton, 1975.
MacCormack, S.  *Art and Ceremony in Late Antiquity.* Berkeley, 1971.
Onians, J.  *Art and Thought in the Hellenistic Age.* London, 1979.
Pollitt, J. J.  *Art and Experience in Classical Greece.* Cambridge, 1972.
———.  *Art in the Hellenistic Age.* Cambridge, 1986.
———.  *The Art of Greece: Sources and Documents.* Englewood Cliffs, 1965.
———.  *The Art of Rome: Sources and Documents.* Englewood Cliffs, 1966.
Richter, G. M. A.  *A Handbook of Greek Art,* 2nd ed. London, 1969.
Robertson, C. M.  *A History of Greek Art.* Cambridge, 1975.
Schweitzer, B.  *Greek Geometric Art.* London, 1971.
Strong, D. E.  *Roman Art.* Harmondsworth, 1976.

## ARCHITECTURE AND CITY-PLANNING

Berve, H., Gruben, G., and Hirmer, M.  *Greek Temples, Theaters, and Shrines.* New York, 1963.
Coulton, J. J.  *Ancient Greek Architects at Work.* Ithaca, 1977.
Davies, P., Hemsoll, D., and Wilson Jones, M.  "The Pantheon: Triumph of Rome or Triumph of Compromise?"  *Art History* 10 (1987): 133–153.
Dinsmoor, W. B.  *The Architecture of Ancient Greece.* New York, 1975 (repr. of 1950 ed.).
Godfrey, P., and Hemsoll, D.  "The Pantheon: Temple or Rotunda." In  *Pagan Gods and Shrines of the Roman Empire,* ed. M. Henig and A. King, pp. 195–209. London, 1986.
Lawrence, A. W.  *Greek Architecture,* 2nd ed. New York, 1983.
Macdonald, W. L.  *The Architecture of the Roman Empire,* 2nd ed. New Haven, 1987.
———.  *The Pantheon: Design, Meaning, and Progeny.* Cambridge, 1976.
Nash, E.  *Pictorial Dictionary of Ancient Rome.* New York, 1968.
Percival, J.  *The Roman Villa.* Berkeley, 1976.
Sear, F.  *Roman Architecture.* Ithaca, 1982.
Travlos, J.  *Pictorial Dictionary of Ancient Athens.* London, 1971.
Ward-Perkins, J. B.  *Roman Imperial Architecture,* 2nd ed. New York, 1981.
———.  *The Cities of Ancient Greece and Italy: Planning in Classical Antiquity.* New York, 1974.

## SCULPTURE

Ashmole, B.  *Architect and Sculptor in Classical Greece.* New York, 1972.
Bieber, M.  *The Sculpture of the Hellenistic Age.* New York, 1960.
Boardman, J.  *Greek Sculpture: The Archaic Period.* London, 1978.
———.  *Greek Sculpture: The Classical Period.* London, 1985.
Brommer, F.  *The Parthenon.* London, 1979.
Hallett, C. H.  "The Origins of the Classical Style in Sculpture." *Journal of Hellenic Studies* 106 (1986): 72–84.
Haskell, F., and Penny, N.  *Taste and the Antique: The Lure of Classical Sculpture, 1500–1900.* New Haven, 1981.

Hinks, R. P.  *Greek and Roman Portrait Sculpture,* 2nd ed. London, 1976.

Lullies, R., and Hirmer, M. *Greek Sculpture.* New York, 1960.

Richter, G. M. A.  *Korai: Archaic Greek Maidens.* New York, 1968.

———. *Kouroi: Archaic Greek Youths,* 2nd ed. New York, 1970.

———. *The Portraits of the Greeks.* London, 1965; rev. by R. R. R. Smith, London, 1984.

Ridgway, B. S. *Fifth-Century Styles in Greek Sculpture.* Princeton, 1981.

———. *The Archaic Style in Greek Sculpture.* Princeton, 1977.

———. *The Severe Style in Greek Sculpture.* Princeton, 1970.

Stewart, A. F.  *Greek Sculpture: An Exploration.* New Haven, forthcoming.

Vermeule, C. C.  *Greek and Roman Sculpture in America.* Berkeley, 1981.

———. *Greek Sculpture and Roman Taste.* Ann Arbor, 1977.

## PAINTING

Arias, P. E., and Hirmer, M. *History of 1000 Years of Greek Vase-Painting.* New York, 1963.

Beazley, J. D. *The Developent of Attic Black-Figure,* 2nd ed. Berkeley, 1976.

Boardman, J. *Athenian Black-Figure Vases.* London, 1974.

———. *Athenian Red-Figure Vases: The Archaic Period.* London, 1975.

Bruno, V. J. *Form and Color in Greek Painting.* New York, 1977.

Cook, R. M. *Greek Painted Pottery,* 2nd ed. London, 1972.

Dorigo, W. *Late Roman Painting.* London, 1971.

Maiuri, A. *Roman Painting.* Geneva, 1953.

Picard, G. C. *Roman Painting.* London, 1963.

## THE "MINOR" ARTS

Boardman, J. *Greek Gems and Finger-Rings.* London, 1970.

Charleston, R. J. *Roman Pottery.* London, 1955.

Higgins, R.  *Greek and Roman Jewellery,* 2nd ed. London, 1980.

Jashemski, W. M. *The Gardens of Pompeii.* New York, 1979.

Kent, J. P. C., and Painter, K. *Wealth of the Roman World,* A.D. 300–700. London, 1977.

Kent, J. P. C. *Roman Coins.* London, 1978.

Kraay, C. M., and Hirmer, M.  *Greek Coins.* New York, 1966.

Richter, G. M. A. *Engraved Gems of the Greeks and Etruscans.* London, 1968.

———. *Engraved Gems of the Romans.* London, 1971.

———. *Furniture of the Greeks, Etruscans, and Romans.* London, 1966.

Rolley, C. *Greek Bronzes.* New York, 1983.

Strong, D. E., and Brown, D. *Roman Crafts.* London, 1972.

———. *Greek and Roman Gold and Silver Plate.* London, 1966.

# A White Garment of Churches
## Romanesque and Gothic

## Learning Objectives

The Middle Ages: the phrase only informs us that the period comes between two others, in this case the classicism and humanism of the ancient world and their rebirth in the Renaissance. In fact, many of the terms for this period—"the Middle Ages," "Romanesque," "Gothic"—were devised by those who saw this great age as but an interruption in the way they thought the world should be. But such prejudice is obsolete, and today we study the one thousand years or so that are called the Middle Ages more objectively, understanding and appreciating the achievements of this period more in terms of the aspirations of the age. And these achievements were many and considerable.

The title of this unit, "A White Garment of Churches," was the poetic way a medieval monk named Raoul Glaber described the visual effect of the great number of large churches built all across Europe starting about the year 1000. The most obvious feature of these buildings is also the most important: their religious purpose. For religion was all-important in the Middle Ages and, with few exceptions, medieval art, especially that which survives today, was created with but one aim, to please God. The excellence and permanence of the materials used in its creation reflect this goal.

In the Middle Ages the Church of Rome and its language, Latin, were unifying forces for all of western Europe. The church guided one's life from baptism at birth to last rites at death, and even beyond, to the Last Judgment and the Second Coming. In that age of political turmoil and economic uncertainty, the hierarchy of the Church filled the vacuum of secular power. Therefore the art of the Church assumed a significance beyond its religious context, reinforcing the political position of the institution. Naturally, much of the medieval art sponsored by the church was didactic, offering instruction in the faith which would lead to salvation. Most of it was produced by anonymous craftsmen, guided by a patron and sometimes an independent theological adviser. This art tends to be strongly conceptual in approach, with the clarity of its traditional message more highly valued than mere visual reality. Works of art that ignored tradition might even be considered heretical. There is little to distinguish religious from secular elements in the art or customs of the Middle Ages, for religion permeated all of life and, conversely, secular values influenced much within the church. Church and state were integrated, politically and artistically.

The Romanesque pilgrimage church, typified by the church of Paray-le-Monial, and the Gothic cathedral, exemplified by the cathedral at Chartres, are the products of nearly a thousand years of development of Christian art in the West. The styles, materials, and techniques of medieval art vary with time and location, as you will see as we examine the Early Christian church of St. Peter in Rome (ca. 333), the chapel of the Emperor Charlemagne at Aachen (792–805), a ninth-century plan for an ideal monastery (the St. Gall plan, ca. 820), and the contributions of imperial German art and architecture in the tenth and eleventh centuries. In this unit we will explore something of the historical and social contexts for a few of these great monuments of the Middle Ages.

Any discussion of medieval art involves a somewhat specialized vocabulary, and in the following pages you may encounter some unfamiliar terms. Of course, in the description of a church, you will recognize the round arch, the barrel vault, and the basilica plan from Roman architecture. However, many features discussed in this unit are medieval developments. The plan of a typical medieval church includes the nave, aisles, transept and apse, while in cross-section you should note the nave arcade, gallery or triforium, clerestory, vaulting (barrel or rib) and perhaps flying buttresses to support the highest rib vaults of the Gothic period. On the exterior, the church might receive sculptural embellishment in the tympanum over the doorway or have statues lining the jambs of the door. You will find these terms explained in a glossary at the end of the unit, where you will also find a list of names of important artists, patrons, and historical figures.

In this unit, you will learn to:

- Understand the impact of pilgrimage and monasticism on the development of Romanesque architecture and sculpture.

- Understand the structural and formal principles at the heart of the Romanesque and Gothic styles.
- Identify the debt to Roman forms in the Romanesque: how they were transformed to meet contemporary needs and to deal with the technical and structural limitations in architecture at the time.
- Recognize how Gothic was derived from Romanesque, through recombination and transformation of its basic structural decorative forms.
- Identify the attitudes in religious philosophy of the Romanesque and Gothic periods regarding the human body and how they affected its depiction in the visual arts.
- Understand the important technical innovations that made many of the important features of the Gothic style possible.

## Part 1
## THE EARLY MIDDLE AGES TO THE ROMANESQUE PERIOD

## The Age of Constantine

Christianity was but one of several new religions to be introduced in the eastern provinces of the Roman Empire. In part because of the inherited Judaic prohibition against graven images, the new religion was slow to develop its own artistic forms. At first Christians simply adapted the forms of pagan Roman art to suit their own purposes, and therefore their art is indistinguishable in any respect except subject matter. Even this is often not immediately evident, for the early representations of Christ show him as a philosopher or teacher **(J 301, 302; H&F 7.12, 7.14)** as the Good Shepherd **(G 7.18, 7.26; H&F 7.2),** or in the guise of the sun god Apollo **(G 7.10),** all familiar types in pagan art. More often Christ was represented symbolically by the fish, the lamb, or the Chi Rho monogram **(H&F 7.1).** The ambiguity of representations allowing a non-Christian as well as a Christian interpretation could be helpful in times of religious persecution when more overtly Christian imagery might prove compromising.

At this time Roman art itself was changing significantly. The illusionism of classical art was being replaced by other artistic goals, especially clarity of expression. This was most appropriate for Christian art, where illusionism was rejected in order to present ideas which were considered timeless in a style suitable for this didactic purpose. Generally, details were simplified, features were regularized, and movement became frozen. Eternal meaning became more important than tran-

sient beauty. The Roman legacy from this early Christian period can be traced throughout much of the Middle Ages.

In the fourth century came the decisive change in the fortunes of the Christian religion, one which was to have a profound effect on history. The man who became known as Constantine the Great (d. 337) was proclaimed the western Caesar in 305. Unfortunately, this title was also claimed by Maxentius, son of the eastern ruler. For their meeting at the Battle at Milvian Bridge in 312, Constantine, inspired by a dream, adopted the Christian Chi Rho monogram to lead his army into battle. The victorious Constantine interpreted his triumph over Maxentius as a sign from the Christian God. The next year, by the Edict of Milan, Constantine recognized Christianity as one of the tolerated religions of the Empire. Thus many historians consider the year 313 a convenient date to separate the ancient world from the start of the Middle Ages. In 325 Constantine, not only promoting but controlling Christianity, called a council at Nicaea to establish a uniform Christian doctrine. When the Nicene Creed held that Christ was both human and divine, making other beliefs heretical, it further opened the way for more direct portrayals of the human Christ.

With the official recognition of Christianity came the possibility of more prominent church buildings. Constantine's Church of St. Peter **(J 288, 289; G 7.4, 7.6; H&F 7.7)** built over the site of Peter's martyrdom and burial in the Circus of Nero, set the primary example for subsequent church architecture in the West. The plan, adapted from the secular Roman basilica **(J 242, 243, 244; G 6.48)** rather than the pagan temple, was a T-square design with a small apse projecting from the transept. The large church had a long colonnaded nave, flanked by double side aisles. The interior was lit by a row of windows beneath the timber roof, known as clerestory windows. The church of St. Peter was so influential that this type of basilican plan became known as a Petrine plan. In the fifteenth century, Constantine's by then dilapidated church, now known as Old St. Peter's, was destroyed to make way for the present church designed by Bramante and Michelangelo **(J 608, 626, 627, 700; G 17.32–17.34; H&F 11.29–11.31).** Therefore, architectural historians have had to glean details of the Constantinian structure from such diverse sources as old drawings and prints, literary accounts, and its influence on other buildings in order to reconstruct its appearance.

There are two major reasons for the prominence of Old St. Peter's. The first is political: this church gained in importance as its bishop, the Bishop of Rome (the Pope), with the considerable support of the emperor, asserted authority over other bishops. The second is spiritual: the church, with its shrine of St. Peter, was the most important pilgrimage site in the West, because Christ had entrusted Peter with a special mission saying, "You are Peter, the Rock; and on this rock I will build my church. . . . I will give you the keys of the Kingdom of Heaven" (Matt. 16:18–19).

Although he was only baptized on his deathbed, Constantine's conversion to Christianity was decisive for the survival and growth of the new religion. His example of imperial patronage and integration of church and state had tremendous influence on subsequent rulers throughout the Middle Ages. Various medieval rulers, including Charlemagne and Otto III, sought to emulate his example. Although Constantine had set these forces in motion, it was left to Emperor Theodosius I at the end of the fourth century to make Christianity the sole religion of the Empire.

## The Art of the North

The northern reaches of the Roman Empire were populated by various migrating tribes known collectively to the Romans as barbarians. They put increasing pressure on the Empire, and by the fifth century even Italy had suffered invasions by the Visigoths, the Ostrogoths, and the Huns. Eventually, the Franks occupied much of what is modern France; the Visigoths, Spain. The Ostrogoths and Lombards fought for control in Italy, while the Angles and Saxons inhabited most of England. Outwardly, many Roman customs were followed, just as Roman buildings were occupied and Roman roads were traveled. But without centralized and strong political authority in the West, there were no new building projects nor even repairs to existing structures. Both Roman civilization and its monuments succumbed to decay. Knowledge of Roman building techniques was lost as was the recipe for making concrete. Cities declined. Warfare was common.

The artistic heritage of the Northern tribes was radically different from that of Rome. The peripatetic nature of tribal life had, for the most part, precluded permanent architecture and monumental sculpture. Instead, their major art forms were portable, especially jewelry and metalwork. Often these were objects for personal adornment. They delighted in intricate patterns, whether based on abstract geometric designs or animal and human forms. However, depiction of the human figure is rare in this art, and when it appears, it is usually in an abstracted form where pattern governs **(J 361).** The naturalistic representation typical of classical art is never found. Although it is difficult to generalize about the type of designs, an aversion to empty spaces, known as *horror vacui,* is a guiding design principle for much Northern art.

For Anglo-Saxon England the excavation of the burial of a local ruler in a ship laden with goods has provided information on daily life and economic conditions in the seventh century. Examined first in 1939, this site at Sutton Hoo in Suffolk yielded coins and other objects which were evidence of extensive trade with places as far away as the Byzantine East and Coptic Egypt as well as Ireland, Merovingian France, and Scandinavia. The wood, leather, and soft materials had rotted away but the impression left

of the ship shows it was a type rowed by forty oarsmen. The king, possibly King Redwald of the East Angles (d. 625/6), was armed with helmet, shield, and sword. His garments were fastened with cloisonné enamel shoulder clasps and a belt with a large gold buckle **(H&F 7.47).** Artistically, one of the finest objects is a gold purse cover decorated with cloisonné enamel **(J 357; G 8.2).** The composition, which combines four groups of stylized animal and human figures with geometric interlaced forms, exemplifies the Northern interest in abstract decorative design. The enameling technique involved attaching thin metal strips to the metal surface to form partitions or *cloisons* into which various colors of enamel paste were placed before the work was heated to transform the paste into a hardened glass. This purse held thirty-seven gold coins and other pieces of gold, possibly a symbolic payment for the oarsmen.

The Romans had introduced Christianity into Britain by the fourth century, but the Anglo-Saxon invasions had disrupted its development. In 597 Pope Gregory the Great sent St. Augustine (d. 604/5) on a mission to convert the Anglo-Saxons. Augustine established a great church in southeastern England at Canterbury, which had been an important town in Roman Britain.

The formal structure of the Church had developed rapidly from the fourth through sixth centuries, during a period of great political, social, and religious turmoil. Some individuals renounced the world to live a contemplative life of solitude and prayer in the Egyptian desert, an ideal soon modified to allow communities of these monks to live together in monasteries. The monastic life was popular in part because it offered peace and stability in times of war and famine. Monasteries in fact flourished as centers of civilization as urban life declined. St. Benedict of Nursia (ca. 480–ca. 550) compiled a rule for a communal life for groups of monks living apart from the world which is still in use today. Drawing, in part, on earlier sources, the Benedictine Rule was intended to reform and purify the monastic movement. Monks were required to take vows of poverty, chastity, and obedience. Above all, St. Benedict prescribed common worship, the *opus Dei* or God's work, a practice which was to lead to an increasingly elaborate liturgy in the Western church. This need to codify practices reflects the rapidity with which the monastic tradition was growing in the early Middle Ages.

For missionaries such as St. Augustine, the most portable and powerful art form for the dissemination of Christianity was the manuscript. Although few could read, manuscripts were widely respected because they recorded the word of God; they were even considered sacred. Unlike ancient scrolls, these medieval books were written on leaves of parchment or vellum which were bound into a flat book or codex. The text would be written by a scribe. Sometimes the scribe would be responsible for any decoration as well, but more often pictures were done by a specialist, known as an illuminator. The small paintings are called miniatures, not for their size, as our use of the word today suggests, but for the red pigment, minium, used in the paintings. Manuscripts would often receive fine bindings of tooled leather, and a few of the most luxurious manuscripts had covers of gold embellished with pearls and precious gems (J 374, clpl 41; G 8.12). But even ordinary manuscripts were expensive to produce, in terms of both material and labor. In the early Middle Ages, most of those that were illuminated were for liturgical use rather than private ownership.

Some of the finest early medieval manuscripts to survive were produced in the monasteries of the British Isles. The style of the Lindisfarne Gospels (J 359, clpl 38; G 8.6) dating from about 698, owes a clear debt to the pagan metalwork tradition, such as that seen in the Sutton Hoo clasp and purse cover. This is most obvious in its decorative "carpet" pages, where line governs the design as surely as it does in cloisonné enamel. The meticulous planning behind the intricate design of one of these carpet pages becomes evident when you study the composition carefully and find that each of the non-geometric lines can be traced ultimately to an animal's body. On these pages the sense of rhythm and movement of the interlaced forms is held in balance by the even arrangement of color and form over the entire composition. The pages of the Lindisfarne Gospels and the even more elaborate Book of Kells (H&F 7.43), produced about 800, reward close, even microscopic, examination to appreciate fully the complexity of their design. An artist's love of variety and intricacy has never received a more perfect expression.

Much of the history of medieval art can be seen as the opposition and resolution of two distinct approaches to art: a northern desire for pattern versus a recurring interest in the classical art of the Mediterranean. The northern impulse toward abstract linear surface decoration, regardless of whether the human figure was included, is the opposite of the classical emphasis on the human figure, with its interest in mass and belief in ideal, mathematical proportions. Throughout the Middle Ages, the pendulum swings back and forth between these two poles: most medieval artists tried, however unconsciously, to satisfy both of these very basic desires, to use the human figure and to create a decorative pattern. Only with the Renaissance did the pendulum pause for long, and that was on the classical side.

## Charlemagne and the Carolingian Revival

By the eighth century, the civilization which had been Rome had nearly disappeared in the West. Politically disorganized, Europe was divided into small kingdoms and duchies that fought constantly with each other and with outside invaders, such as the Vikings from the North and the Moors in Spain. Famine and disease were perennial threats. But in Gaul, a strong and aggressive Christian dynasty, the Merovingians (486–751) ruled the land of the Franks. They were succeeded by a dynasty named for the greatest of all medieval kings, Charles the Great or Charlemagne (742–814). On Christmas day in the year 800, Charlemagne had himself crowned by the Pope as the first Holy Roman Emperor. In taking this title, Charlemagne made clear his intent to revive the glories of ancient Rome. By securing the blessing of the Pope, Charlemagne continued the tradition of Constantine in fostering an intimate, and mutually advantageous, association between church and state. Moreover, Charlemagne undertook an important program of imperial patronage of the arts. His biographer, Einhard, described Charlemagne's achievements for posterity, which is especially fortunate because little survives from this period.

Charlemagne's Palatine Chapel (J 363, 364, 365; G 8.16, 8.17; H&F 7.52–7.54) at his capital, Aachen (also known as Aix-la-Chapelle), is the only major Carolingian building to survive. The design by Odo of Metz provided a central octagon supporting a lobed dome, all enclosed in a sixteen-sided shell. The main altar was located in a small, square apse. Opposite this altar, two large stair towers emphasized the entranceway. This elaboration of the entrance is an early example of a westwork, a form associated with imperial power. From the throne room on the second story of the narthex, the emperor could address huge crowds gathered in the atrium below. With the permission of Pope Hadrian I, Charlemagne took marble fittings from ancient buildings in Rome and Ravenna to use in the chapel, almost as if he wished them to act like fertile seeds for his revival of the power and splendor of Rome. In emphasizing the imperial as well as the religious, Charlemagne was following the example of the Byzantine emperor Justinian. And both emperors, Charlemagne and Justinian, dedicated themselves to reviving the power and prestige of ancient Rome, politically and artistically.

Charlemagne valued the monasteries throughout his realm as stable outposts of civilization. Vikings destroyed the great church of St. Riquier (J 367; G 8.20, 8.21) at Centula, built by Angilbert, Charlemagne's son-in-law, in what was then the largest monastic complex in Christendom. Therefore the Carolingian ideal can best be studied in the St. Gall plan (J 368, 369; G 8.19; H&F 7.55), a plan devised about 820 for a Benedictine monastery. The plan survived only because it was used as scrap material in the binding of a later manuscript at St. Gall, in Switzerland. Throughout the Middle Ages, most monasteries were laid out according to the basic arrangement described in this plan. Detailed inscriptions describe the function of each building and area marked on the plan. The largest and most important building was the church, oriented with the main altar in the apse at the eastern end, toward Jerusalem, and the principal entrance at the opposite end, to the west. In the Middle Ages there was no accepted standard of measurement, so the church was designed by using the crossing square, formed by the intersection of the transept and nave, to provide the unit of measurement. This was believed to result in a building with geometrically harmonious proportions.

The St. Gall plan tells us much about monastic life as set down in the Rule of St. Benedict. Bells summoned monks to prayer, the *opus Dei,* at set intervals throughout the day, starting with Matins in the middle of the night and continuing to Vespers in early evening and later Compline. The cloister, a center of daily activity for the monks, was a grassy square enclosed by arcaded walkways located to the south of the larger church for protection from harsh north winds. In the refectory, monks ate together in silence while one read from a religious text. In addition to attending services, they spent part of their day in private prayer and reading, the rest at manual labor. Gardens and livestock areas ring the perimeter of the grounds to the south of the church. For sleeping, the monks retired to a sparsely furnished dormitory adjoining the south transept of the church. For monks too ill to work there was an infirmary. The cemetery was to be planted with apple, fig, laurel, and chestnut trees. The abbot was provided with a grand house, and a separate house was maintained for important guests. Such monasteries were intended to be entirely self-sufficient to allow the monks to live apart from the world.

Charlemagne's obsession with Roman civilization led to a number of important reforms, including a reform of the Latin language for greater clarity of expression and the reform of the script itself for an equal clarity of writing (somewhat surprising since Charlemagne himself never learned to write). The practical, clear new script, called the Carolingian minuscule, is the basis of our modern Roman alphabet. Used in conjunction with the ancient majuscule forms, the kind used on public monuments in ancient Rome, the Carolingian minuscule allowed scribes to organize their texts with greater visual emphasis. Education was a related concern and, although the great monasteries remained the major centers of learning, Charlemagne established guidelines for instruction to include Latin grammar, the psalms, musical notation, chant, and computation of the years and seasons. There were never many educated people, but scholars maintained contact with each other, exchanging letters and books and even traveling great distances to meet. The revival of scholarship was one of the most significant contributions of the Carolingian era.

Medieval manuscripts were produced in monastic scriptoria. From the work of scholars like Alcuin of York and the visual evidence of much of Carolingian art itself, it is clear that some ancient manuscripts survived the centuries and continued to be highly prized. Monks spent much of their time copying older manuscripts to preserve and disseminate their contents, both text and image. Of course, medieval copies are nothing like photocopied duplicates but rather are interpretive works of art in their own right.

The most classical of the major Carolingian manuscripts is a book known as the Coronation Gospels (**J 370;**

**G 8.9; H&F 7.57),** made about 800–810. The manuscript was said to have been found in Charlemagne's tomb when it was opened in the year 1000 by Otto III; thereafter the German emperors took their coronation oaths on this book. This luxurious manuscript has vellum pages dyed an imperial purple with letters written in gold and silver. The portraits of the evangelists revive the ancient subject of a poet or philosopher seated and writing. What is more astonishing is that they have been painted in an equally classicizing style which not only attempts three-dimensional modeling but even captures the illusionistic brushwork of antiquity (**J 371).** Such painterly considerations had not appeared for centuries. Suddenly the artist was concerned with showing a three-dimensional body in space, not an abstracted pattern against a background. There are no medieval evangelist symbols to intrude on the desired realism of these miniatures; only the flattened halo indicates the Christian context. Yet, on close inspection, it is clear that the artist has not worked out the problems of anatomy and perspective for himself, he has only superficially copied some of the effects he had seen in ancient art. This artist wanted to transmit a venerated tradition, not explore the natural world for himself.

In the Ebbo Gospels (**J 372, clpl 40; G 8.10; H&F 7.58)** ca. 816–835, a classical influence, similar to that in the Coronation Gospels, is nearly overwhelmed by northern medieval linear energy and expressionism. Even the lines of the drapery folds have an independent life, one which functions more as a surface pattern than as an attempt to define a three-dimensional form. Here the evangelists, accompanied by their symbols, work in an ecstatic frenzy to which even the landscape and furniture seem to respond. To express the fervor of the religious content, the artist has reverted to Northern traditions: the moment of Carolingian classicism was very brief. This style of the Ebbo Gospels appears on the sumptuous gold and jeweled cover for the Lindau Gospels (**J 374, clpl 41),** even more clearly combining the Northern metalwork tradition, exemplified by the Sutton Hoo ornaments, with Carolingian classicism.

Like the dreams of many empire builders before and since, Charlemagne's visions for a powerful Holy Roman Empire were short-lived. His son Louis the Pious (778–840) proved an ineffectual ruler, and when Louis died he split the territory into three sections for his sons. Their internal bickering, aggravated by renewed attacks from the Norsemen, soon led to the disintegration of the single political entity fashioned by Charlemagne. Charlemagne's contributions in the fields of language and the arts were, fortunately, more enduring.

## Ottonian Art

In the Germanic lands, the house of Saxony rose to power in the vacuum of the decaying Carolingian Empire. This period is known as Ottonian, after the three emperors named Otto who ruled in the tenth and early eleventh centuries. Like Charlemagne before him, the first Otto (r. 936–973) had himself crowned emperor by the Pope, an act which asserted a claim that the heritage of ancient Rome belonged to the West rather than to the Byzantine East. As he and his successors sought to rival the splendor of the eastern empire, artistic patronage was one area of competition. His son, Otto II (r. 973–983) married the Byzantine princess Theophano and under their son, Otto III (r. 983–1002), the Ottonian Empire reached its peak.

The art and architecture sponsored by the Ottonian emperors and their supporters shows the strong influence of the Roman past, both directly and filtered through its Carolingian and Byzantine interpretations. A prime example is the Church of St. Michael's at Hildesheim (**J 377–379; G 8.22–8.25; H&F 9.5),** started by Archbishop Bernward toward the end of the rule of Emperor Otto III. It is a monastic church resembling the Carolingian church of St. Riquier and the one on the St. Gall plan. In its bold massing of cubical forms it recalls ancient Roman buildings and anticipates features of the later Romanesque style. On the interior, an alternating system of columns and piers supported a flat timber ceiling, but much of the current appearance is the result of extensive restoration after the church was severely damaged in World War II.

Archbishop Bernward made the abbey at Hildesheim an important center of learning. He instilled in his pupil, Otto III, a love of ancient literature, and expressed his own admiration for the ancient past through his commissions. Bernward had visited Rome and was obviously influenced by what he had seen there. Rome was filled with examples of public monuments covered with narrative relief sculptures. The German archbishop was so taken with the column of Trajan (**J 265; G 6.65, 6.66; H&F 5.39)** that he commissioned a version of it for his church. Of course for this setting the exploits of the pagan emperor were replaced with scenes from the life of Christ. This column was cast in bronze, and Bernward also commissioned a pair of bronze doors for the church (**J 380; G 8.25; H&F 9.6).** These are the first known instances of monumental bronze casting in medieval art, amazing accomplishments technologically no less than aesthetically. Moreover, they mark the return to monumental relief sculpture which will become one of the dominant art forms of the later Middle Ages.

Each of the doors at Hildesheim has eight scenes, those on the left from Genesis and those on the right from the life of Christ. The medieval viewer would have understood immediately the contrasting references: on the left, to sin and redemption in the story of Adam and Even and the closing of the gates of Paradise after their expulsion; on the right, to the opening of the door to salvation through the sacrifice of Christ. For narrative clarity the figures act out the stories as if performing pantomime, their gestures clearly silhouetted against the plain ground. A similar technique is also seen in the narrative miniatures in a contemporary manuscript, the Gospels of Otto III (**J 381, 382, clpl 42; G 8.28; H&F 9.8).**

Vows of monastic silence must have resulted in a rich vocabulary of such hand signals upon which the artist could draw.

As the bronze works at Hildesheim reintroduced monumental narrative art, the late tenth-century Gero Crucifix in Cologne Cathedral (**J 375; H&F 9.2)** reintroduced large-scale sculpture of the human figure, unknown in Western art since the fourth century. The suffering image of Christ is life-sized, the oak polychromed in realistic colors to stimulate an empathetic response, encouraging the viewer to identify with the human nature of Christ and the torture he endured. This is a limited use of realism for a specific purpose. There is no interest in anatomy or musculature, for these are not relevant. If we compare this figure of Christ to an ancient work such as the Doryphoros (**J 179; G 5.61; H&F 4.31),** the contrast between classical and medieval approaches is immediately apparent. Far from being a naturalistic, let alone an idealized, representation, the Gero Christ with its expressive abstraction of form projects a strongly emotional appeal, a trait which is characteristic of much of later German medieval art.

The Ottonian contributions to medieval art were many. The splendor of Byzantium at the height of its second Golden Age engendered a spirit of rivalry in the German emperors which resulted in commissions for increasingly lavish works of art. In architecture, there was a continuation and expansion of the Carolingian ideal, with an even more emphatically Roman element. In fact scholars like Georges Duby even refer to a "cult of antiquity." The huge scale of many Ottonian churches anticipated the size of Romanesque buildings. At this time, too, there was a return to monumental sculpture in bronze and wood to decorate the large churches. Such monumental art forms, which would be fully resurrected in the Romanesque and Gothic periods, had been virtually unknown in the West since the fall of Rome. And finally, by their encyclopedic nature, Ottonian painting cycles, whether wall paintings in churches or miniatures in manuscripts, preserved and transmitted much of Early Christian and Byzantine iconography. These Ottonian contributions were crucial to the development of Romanesque art.

## Romanesque Art

Western Europe had experienced only two brief and limited periods of architectural achievement since the decline of the Roman Empire. Significantly, both periods are known by the names of the rulers who were the major patrons, the Carolingian and the Ottonian. But a new phase of building started in the eleventh century which truly rivaled that of ancient Rome. Coming at a time of relative peace and stability, it was spurred in part by a growth in the population which coincided with a period of increased prosperity. But the number of churches and abbeys built all over Europe at this time constitutes a phenomenon that cannot be explained by studies of economics and population alone. The Cluniac monk Raoul (or Rudolph) Glaber attributed it to "the friendly rivalry which led each community to seek to have a church more beautiful than those of its neighbors," causing Europe "to shake itself, cast off its ancient garment and clothe itself everywhere with a white robe of churches" (quoted in G. Duby, *History of Medieval Art,* Vol. I, p. 158).

Diverse in geography and patronage, this creative period is known by a general term which was derived from the style of the buildings themselves: Romanesque. Originally a term used pejoratively to indicate a debased Roman style using round arches and massive piers, the word Romanesque is used today to refer to much of the architecture, sculpture, and painting produced in the eleventh and twelfth centuries.

The Romanesque was the first medieval style to be truly European in scope. Increased mobility of the population encouraged this general uniformity in approach. Romanesque art is like the Roman in using permanent, monumental forms for architecture, sculpture, and painting. And, as in Roman art, the human figure is once again of primary importance. But the conceptual approach of the medieval style is different from either the idealistic or realistic approaches found in ancient art.

## Pilgrimage and the cult of saints

The increasing popularity of the so-called "cult of saints" motivated an increase in both travel and building activity at this time. This type of worship focused on the veneration of saints whose beneficial intercession was sought through prayer. Traditionally, the holiest Christian sites, such as the Church of the Holy Sepulchre in Jerusalem and St. Peter's in Rome, had been associated with the burial places of important religious figures. Not all churches were fortunate enough to have the tomb of a saint, but even the bones, garments, or other physical remains of a holy person were believed to possess miraculous powers, so people cherished whatever such relics they might be able to obtain. These might be an apostle's tooth, the skull of John the Baptist, a thorn from the crown of thorns, a container of the Virgin's milk, the arm of a local saint, or a drop of the blood of Christ. Originally relics were intended to aid devotion by making the presence of the holy person more tangible, but often the relics themselves came to be worshiped. These highly prized possessions would be acquired through whatever means possible—purchase, exchange, subterfuge, or even theft.

As befitting its importance, a relic would be enshrined in a reliquary made of precious materials. Typically, this might be a simple box-like container made of gold or enamel, or perhaps one with a gabled roof in the shape of a church. Some reliquaries took the form of the particular relic they held, for example, a foot shape for a bone from the foot of a saint, an arm shape for an arm. A special reliquary might be something more elaborate, perhaps a full statue of the saint. Such was the reliquary of Sainte Foi (St. Faith) made in the ninth century to house the relics of the young virgin martyr which the enterprising monks of Conques had stolen from another church. Its wooden core (incorporating a late Roman head or helmet) was covered with gold and jewels; the several additions and modifications over the centuries give evidence of the generosity and love of pilgrims to this shrine.

Liturgical objects, such as reliquaries, crosses, candlesticks, chalices, and croziers, form an important category of medieval metalwork, but examples are scarce because, especially in times of war or economic unrest, the material would be valued above its artistic merit and the works would be melted down. A twelfth-century treatise, *On Divers Arts,* describes many of the techniques used to create such works. The treatise was written by an anonymous German monastic metalworker who used the name Theophilus, but scholars believe he was the artist Roger of Helmarshausen, some of whose works survive. The author assumes his book will be of interest to other craftsmen accustomed to working, as he did, in a variety of media. This practice helps to explain the lively exchange of influences between various art forms in the Middle Ages. Covering a variety of topics from panel painting to stained glass to metalwork, his instructions are quite specific and straightforward: "When you are going to make ink, cut some pieces of [haw]thorn wood in April or in May, before they grow blossoms or leaves . . ." (Theophilus, *On Divers Arts,* p. 42).

A journey to visit a shrine containing relics was called a pilgrimage. It might be undertaken for many different reasons. Usually some sort of divine intervention was either desired or being acknowledged. In this age when medical knowledge was indeed primitive, people turned to religion for an answer to their physical suffering. Prayers were considered helpful, but relics, in particular, were valued for their miraculous healing powers. Therefore, many pilgrims were those afflicted with physical ailments seeking a cure, and they would attempt to get as near to the relics as they could, believing that proximity enhanced efficacy. In addition to their prayers, pilgrims would generally leave offerings at the shrine to ensure a miracle.

In the Middle Ages, most pilgrimages involved difficult journeys which might take several years of strenuous travel to complete. But in addition to any immediate assistance, a pilgrimage could be beneficial in terms of salvation when one's good deeds would be weighed on the Judgment Day. Works of art in the pilgrimage churches constantly reminded the pilgrims of these immediate and long-range benefits.

Of course, some went on a pilgrimage out of curiosity, just for the adventure and the chance to travel. Another reason for the increase in the number of pilgrims at this time was that such journeys had come to be used as punishment or penance for misdeeds; the worse the offense, the longer and more difficult the pilgrimage required. Whatever the motivation, the popularity of pilgrimages greatly increased travel and exchange of ideas in the Romanesque period. And the visits of pilgrims enriched church coffers, enabling the commission of more elaborate shrines and larger churches to attract even more pilgrims. Ironically, one result of the increased travel on pilgrimages was a growing skepticism about the authenticity of some relics, for observant and sophisticated travelers found many abuses, such as more than one church claiming to have the body of saint X, or too many bones for one body of saint Y, or, most notoriously, far too much wood for one True Cross. Nevertheless, the enthusiasm for relics is one of the main features of the Romanesque period, and it continued to be strong throughout the Gothic era.

Many of the pilgrimage churches of France not only attracted pilgrims to their own shrines but served as stops on the way to the great pilgrimage center in northwestern Spain, Santiago de Compostela (**H&F 9.20**). The pilgrimage to Santiago (St. James) was more popular than that to Rome itself, although the reasons for this are obscure. Pilgrims to a shrine usually purchased a badge to show that they had completed their pilgrimage, and for Santiago de Compostela the badge was in the form of a scallop or cockle-shell. In medieval art, St. James can usually be seen as a pilgrim, carrying a staff, wearing a cloak, and sporting the cockle-shell badge on his large hat. Guidebooks, such as the twelfth-century Codex Calixtinus, directed pilgrims to special points of interest along the main roads leading from various points in eastern and central France to Compostela. The great churches along these pilgrimage roads included the churches of La Madeleine at Vézelay (**J 408, 409; G 9.32, 9.33**), St. Lazare at Autun (**J 387**), Notre Dame of Le Puy, Sainte Foy at Conques, St. Front in Périgueux, St. Hilaire at Poitiers, St. Pierre at Moissac (**J 405, 406; G 9.27–9.29**), and St. Sernin in Toulouse (**J 383–386; G 9.4–9.6; H&F 9.18**). In Spain there were the churches of St. Isidore of León and the Cathedral of Santiago de Compostela itself. The styles of the architecture, sculpture, and painting of these churches show the spread of artistic influence along the pilgrimage roads. Together, these churches are evidence of the rich cross-fertilization in the arts which resulted from increased travel in the period.

## Monasticism and Cluny

The rapid growth in the number and size of monasteries during the Romanesque period was astonishing; the most representative type of Romanesque building is in fact the monastic church. Monastic communities were in the forefront of society, as centers of both intellectual activity and development in the arts. Their churches were built with the most permanent material available, stone. Two distinct criteria made stone the building material of choice: it was relatively fireproof and it provided fine acoustics for music. Moreover, the difficulty and expense of stone construction gave the material a certain prestige. But to construct heavy stone vaulting over a space as broad as a nave required significant structural developments.

In France, the development of the Romanesque style, as well as the flourishing of monastic power and influence, can be traced to some extent in the successive buildings at one site, the Benedictine monastery of Cluny in Burgundy. This monastery, which was to become the most powerful and wealthy establishment in western Europe, was founded in 910 on land provided by Duke William of Aquitaine. It was founded in an effort to reform the monastic movement which, over the years, had grown relaxed in its observance of the Rule of St. Benedict. Unlike most monasteries, which had to answer to local political leaders, Cluny was under the direct control of the Pope in Rome, a fact that gave this monastery added power and prestige.

Construction of the church at Cluny was an early priority. Unfortunately, little is known about this first building, a simple boxy structure, for it was quickly replaced with a larger, more elaborate building as the monastery grew larger and more powerful. This second church, known as Cluny II, had been started by 955 and was dedicated in 981. An early example of the Romanesque style, Cluny II was a cross-shaped basilican church, in plan and scale much like Early Christian churches such as Old St. Peter's (**J 288, 289; G 7.4, 7.6; H&F 7.7**). At the eastern end, however, it had three staggered apses or chapels to allow room for more altars and the display of relics. The nave wall was divided into three parts, a nave arcade, a gallery, and a clerestory level. A rounded tunnel or barrel vault of stone spanned the width of the nave. This type of vaulting had been known in ancient Rome, but the Early Christian churches, such as Old St. Peter's, had only timber roofs. Such heavy stone vaulting required thicker walls to support the weight and to buttress the thrust of the vault. At the western entrance to the church, the massing of forms included a monumental gateway, an atrium, and a two-story narthex. Thus the Early Romanesque style of Cluny II shows elements that can be traced ultimately back to imperial Rome through the contributions of the Early Christian, Carolingian, and Ottonian periods.

Of Cluny II only some foundations survive, for it in turn was replaced by the church known as Cluny III, begun about 1088 (**H&F 9.16, 9.17**). Cluny III was a truly monumental structure, as is evident even from the few fragments that survive today. Most of Cluny III was destroyed in the early nineteenth century when the site became a virtual quarry for local buildings after the repression of the monastery during the French Revolution. Originally the church measured over 600 feet in length. Its great size accommodated the many visitors and pilgrims who came to Cluny from all over Europe as well as the unusually large community of monks at Cluny,

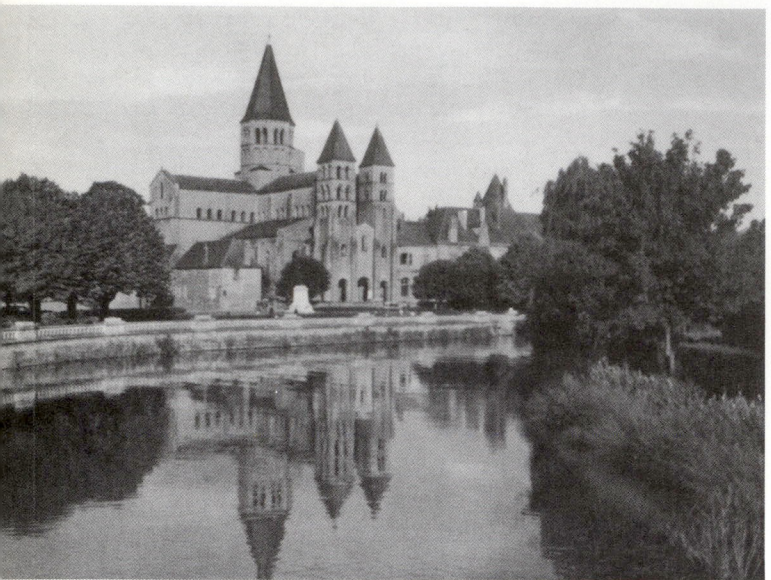

Paray-le-Monial, Exterior. ca. 1100. (EDITIONS ET IMPRESSIONS COMBIER, MACON)

such was the dignity, such the piety pervading them, one could well believe that the officiants were not men but angels." (Quoted in G. Duby, *History of Medieval Art,* Vol. I, p. 135.)

There were significant advances in the design of the new church. Rather than the rounded barrel vault of Cluny II, the vault of Cluny III had a more pointed profile. This made the vault both higher and structurally safer by directing the thrust so it could be buttressed more effectively. The pointed barrel vault became a characteristic of Burgundian Romanesque architecture, and the pointed arch would become ubiquitous in the Gothic period.

In a number of its architectural details Cluny III shows the direct influence of Roman and Early Christian monuments, many of which survived in the area. These features include engaged columns, pilasters, capitals, and moldings. This revival of Roman forms was obviously a conscious choice. Some scholars interpret it as a visual and symbolic link with the Early Christian period, associating it with the founders' intent to reform the monastic movement.

Despite the destruction of most of Cluny III, something of its original appearance is reflected at a reduced scale in other surviving churches. Perhaps the best example is the Cluniac priory church at Paray-le-Monial, a far more modest building about twenty-five miles from Cluny. The cross-shaped basilican plan of Paray-le-Monial is typical of many Romanesque churches in having a long nave with side aisles, transept, and choir with ambulatory and radiating chapels. Not only is each part of this plan clearly articulated, but the sense of the well-defined areas on the plan is not diminished on the interior, for one experiences each part as a separate segment of space when walking through the church. Even the length of the nave is divided into vertical units called bays, each comprised of one arch of the nave arcade with the three smaller arches directly above at both the gallery and clerestory levels. Strongly projecting pilasters and piers clearly define each bay. This sense of segmentation is an important feature of Romanesque architecture.

The exterior of the church of Paray-le-Monial clearly exemplifies this notion of segmentation. The various parts of the church—nave, towers, apse, and chapels—look as if they have been added together like so many building blocks. Even on this small church the vertical façade with its two massive towers is formidable, echoing the lost forms of Cluny III. At the eastern end, a huge polygonal tower at the crossing dominates the cluster of radiating chapels around the apse. The additive quality of the building parts makes one aware of the sculpturesque quality of the forms themselves. The austere stonework is ornamented only with simple arched corbel tables, a form which repeats and complements the round arches of the windows and serves to reinforce the basic geometric shapes of the parts of the building.

believed to number about 300 during the abbacy of St. Hugh (1049–1109). In fact, there was a waiting list to enter the monastery at Cluny, despite the long novitiate required to become a monk. Not only did the monastic life offer tranquillity in an age of turmoil; at this time the monastic schools were virtually the only place to receive a proper education, in part because they had the only extensive libraries. In an economic and social system which dictated that inheritance went to the eldest son (primogeniture), the monastery was a frequent choice for younger sons. While many joined because they wanted a religious life, it could also offer the ambitious an alternate route to a political career. Monastic ranks were further swelled by orphans and widows who had no one else to care for them. The popularity of this type of life is indicated by the fact that the tremendous rise in the number of monks and nuns in the Romanesque period far exceeded the general increase in population.

The plan of this mammoth church, Cluny III, is traditional, an elaboration of the basic Petrine plan with double side aisles, two transepts, and apse. The inclusion of an ambulatory and radiating chapels helped to solve the problem of traffic flow created by the large number of visitors and the need for each priest to celebrate mass daily. The Cluniac monk Raoul Glaber wrote proudly:

"Know that this House hath not its equal in the Roman world, above all in the task of rescuing souls that have come into Satan's clutches. . . . In this monastery, as I have seen with my own eyes, so great is the number of monks that it is customary for masses to be said without an instant's break from the peep of day until the hour of sleep, and

On entering the dark yet lofty interior of the church of Paray-le-Monial one is immediately aware that the mundane world has been left behind. In the Middle Ages, candles, some used in rituals, would have augmented the dim light admitted through the small windows. As at Cluny III, the thick walls supporting the stone barrel vault over the nave could safely be pierced only by small openings. But Romanesque builders willingly sacrificed light in order to lessen the danger of fire by using such a stone vault. Further, the acoustic superiority of stone enhanced the effects of the monastic chant. In the decoration of the church, classical details, such as fluted pilasters and a form of egg-and-dart molding, give evidence of the Romanesque builders' admiration of Roman monuments, evoking both the grandeur of the past and the aspirations of the day.

Like the small priory church of Paray-le-Monial, the great cathedral of St. Lazare at Autun **(J 387)** owes a debt to Cluny III. This influence can be seen in features such as the pointed barrel vault of the nave and the classicizing fluted pilasters with Corinthian capitals. In Romanesque France the most prevalent models for monumental architecture were still the vestiges of the Roman Empire. In this case, two surviving Roman gates to Autun, the Porte St. André and the Porte d'Arroux, provided specific models for the Romanesque builders. They are among several Roman remains still standing in Autun, which was an important town in Roman Gaul.

In a more experimental fashion the church of La Madeleine at Vézelay **(J 408, 409; G 9.32, 9.33)** combines Cluniac forms with local traditions. The survival of this church, as well as many others throughout France, was due in large part to the restoration work undertaken by E. E. Viollet-le-Duc in the nineteenth century. Built on a dramatic hilltop site, the Romanesque church of La Madeleine was consecrated in 1132. The church owned some important relics of St. Mary Magdalene. Conflating several stories in the Bible, she was believed to be the sister of Martha and Lazarus from whom Christ exorcised seven devils and who annointed the feet of Christ. Tradition said that she was present at the Crucifixion and that, as she stayed weeping by the tomb, Christ appeared to her with the message of his Resurrection. She was said to have become a penitent and a hermit and, especially in France, it was believed she came to Marseilles with her brother and sister to convert pagans to Christianity.

The church of La Madeleine at Vézelay is of great historical significance, not only as a pilgrimage site in its own right, but also as the starting point of one of the major pilgrimage roads to Santiago de Compostela. Recognizing this intimate association with holy pilgrimages, St. Bernard chose to issue his call for a Second Crusade to the Holy Land in 1146 from Vézelay. Despite the disastrous outcome of this crusade, King Philip Augustus of France and King Richard the Lion-Heart of England selected this same place to meet to set out on the Third Crusade.

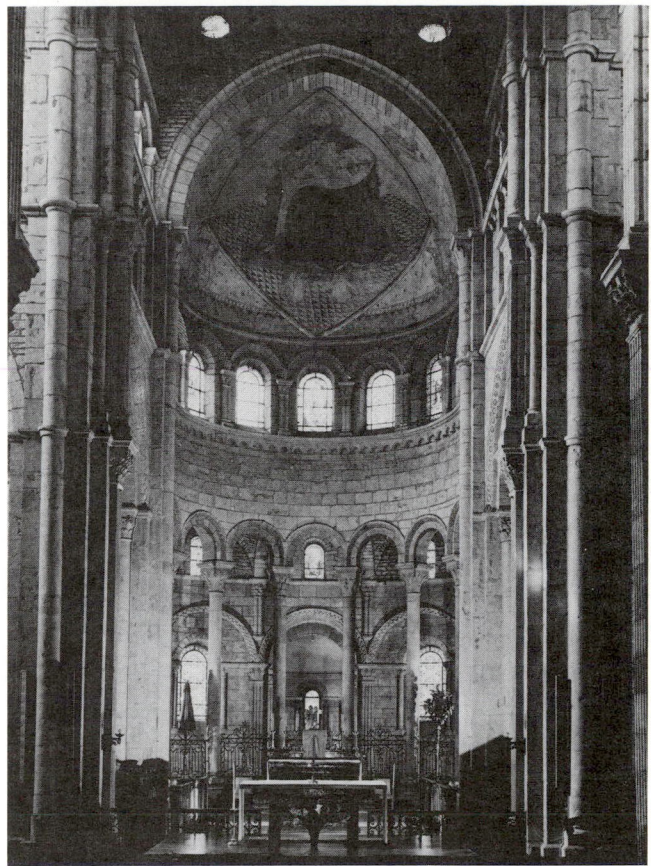

Paray-le-Monial, Interior. (GIRAUDON/ART RESOURCE, NEW YORK)

It is still easy to see how the medieval town at Vézelay developed in response to the needs of the pilgrims who climbed the steep hill to the church. Like tourists today, the medieval pilgrims wanted to buy guides and souvenirs, exchange currency, and find places to eat and sleep. Merchant stalls sprang up along these frequently traveled paths, to be replaced eventually by more permanent inns, shops, and dwellings. Thus, the plan of Vézelay, typical of those of many medieval towns, shows narrow, meandering streets which grew in a haphazard fashion, very different from the clarity of the imposed geometric grid plan of cities which started as Roman army camps. In towns constructed mainly of timber or wattle-and-daub, the large stone church dominated the town materially as well as spiritually. However, despite their mutual dependence on the popularity of the relics of St. Mary Magdalene, relations between the town and the abbey were often bitter. Such town and church disputes were as common in the Middle Ages as town and gown arguments in college towns today, but the level was often far more violent: one abbot of Vézelay was murdered in a local revolt in the early twelfth century.

## The revival of monumental sculpture

Although the arrangement of geometrically simple volumes of masonry itself, enhanced possibly by abstract ornamentation, is one of the chief features of the pilgrimage road churches, applied sculpture came to play an increasingly important role. Only a few isolated forerunners like the Ottonian Gero Crucifix anticipate this return to monumental sculpture. Some of the Romanesque architectural sculpture is purely decorative, but, beginning in the eleventh century, figural sculpture was increasingly used to teach and enlighten. A letter written by Pope Gregory the Great in the early seventh century had offered the rationale for such works of art in a church when he wrote that, "a picture is introduced into a church so that those who are ignorant of letters may at least read by looking at the walls what they cannot read in a book." The pilgrim crowds were there waiting to be so instructed. Didactic sculpture appeared not only on the façade but also on the interior, where historiated capitals on piers between nave and side aisle entertained and educated the pilgrim crowds as they made their way to the eastern end to view the relics.

The tympanum of the Last Judgment at the cathedral of St. Lazare at Autun **(J 407; G 9.30, 9.31; H&F 9.22)**, one of the few signed works in the Romanesque period, bears a remarkable inscription: GISLEBERTUS HOC FECIT, "Gislebertus made this." This inscription is all the more surprising because it appears directly beneath the feet of Christ. Generally in medieval art the subject was emphasized while the person who created it was but a servant to that goal. At Autun other inscriptions explain the scene of the Last Judgment to the viewers with the warning, "to let this horror appall those bound by earthly sin." The huge figure of Christ enthroned as Judge dominates the composition. Angels support his mandorla while to the side other angels sound the trumpets announcing the Day of Judgment. To Christ's left, souls are weighed to determine their fate, while on his right St. Peter with his keys stands ready to admit the saved to Paradise. On the lintel below, grouped to Christ's right among the saved, are apprehensive pilgrims, some wearing the cross badge to show they have been to Jerusalem or the cockle-shell badge of Santiago de Compostela. The nude souls on Christ's left, or sinister, side are doomed. Gislebertus has captured the state of sheer terror in one haunting, nightmarish image: giant, disembodied hands or claws ensnare the head of one sinner to pull him inexorably to his fate. In several cases, the artist has devised an eternal torture appropriate to the offense, such as the sin of lust resulting in a young woman's breasts being gnawed by serpents. Significantly, one of the damned is a miser, guilty of the sin of avarice, a timely reminder to the pilgrims to be generous when visiting the shrine inside.

The "realism" of such devils by Gislebertus is matched by various "eyewitness" accounts of the day. Our guide,

Raoul Glaber, described one devil he saw as "a sort of little man horrible to see, of low stature (it seemed), with a thin neck, haggard face, jet-black eyes, peaked, blubber lips, a mean, receding chin, a goatee beard, hirsute, pointed ears, a shock of touseled hair, dog's teeth, a tapered skull, a bulging chest, a hump on his back, flapping buttocks, filthy clothes" (quoted in G. Duby, *History of Medieval Art*, Vol. I, p. 74).

One of the finest sculptures at Autun is the seductive figure of Eve from the destroyed portal on the north transept. As Paul Crossley explained in the program, she is acclaimed as one of the first monumental nudes in medieval art. However, the artist was not so much interested in the human form itself as equating nudity, common in pagan Roman art, with sin. In the Middle Ages, Eve, who was considered responsible for original sin, was often contrasted with the Virgin Mary, called the new Eve, who provided the way to salvation through her son, Jesus Christ. Thus Eve was an appropriate choice to adorn the penitence portal at Autun.

On the interior of Autun Cathedral, Gislebertus and his assistants carved the massive capitals of the piers in the nave. For centuries visitors have marveled at the humor, charm, compassion, and vigor with which the scenes from the life of Christ and other stories are depicted. Some of the episodes, such as the Adoration of the Magi, are familiar. Others show more unusual moments before or after climactic events, such as the Dream of the Magi before the three kings reach Bethlehem, or the suicide of Judas following his betrayal of Christ.

## Cistercian reform

Throughout the twelfth century, as prosperity increased, so did the periodic reaction against wealth and worldly goods. One response to this malaise was the founding of the Cistercian Order as a reformed Benedictine order in 1098. The Cistercians believed in austerity. They sought purity in simplicity. Cistercian architecture, devoid of figural sculpture, stained glass, or other distractions, is the physical embodiment of this belief. The Cistercians, who wore habits made of undyed cloth, in contrast to the black habits of the art-loving Benedictines, became known as the "white monks." The great Cistercian St. Bernard of Clairvaux (1090–1153) railed against ostentatious display, that of Cluniac Benedictines in particular. He was especially caustic on the subject of the impropriety of decorating churches with carvings of beasts and grotesques, but his care in describing these sculptures shows how thoroughly he had studied their "comely deformity."

The Cistercians were the only monastic order to develop their own distinctive building style. In so doing, they contributed much to the development of medieval architecture in general, since this style remained consistent wherever the Cistercians went, disseminating the style throughout Europe. The well-preserved abbey at Fontenay **(H&F 9.34)** is typical of early Cistercian architecture. Its Burgundian forms, similar in basic outline to those at Cluny or Paray-le-Monial, have been stripped of their ornate sculptural overlay to be interpreted in the austere Cistercian style. The church, built from 1139 to 1147, has the rectangular eastern end typical of Cistercian design. Rather than embellishing the altar area with gilded paintings or sculpture, Cistercian builders preferred to let only the light of God, entering through clear glass windows in the flat eastern wall, enhance the high altar. As in many twelfth-century buildings, round and pointed arches co-exist; the barrel vault of the nave is pointed in profile, while round arches, traditionally associated with the Romanesque style, appear elsewhere. In the nave, each of the severely abstracted foliate capitals is slightly different in design, subtly combining the medieval love of variety with Cistercian austerity.

An early twelfth-century manuscript from Dijon, the *Moralia in Job* (**G 9.38; H&F 9.21**), shows the austere Cistercian approach to painting. There are no lavish full-page miniatures here; instead, the capital letters of major divisions in the text have been enlarged to allow room for pictures. These historiated initials tell much about daily monastic life, even humorous details like the fact that the tonsured monks wore old, ragged tunics for their hard manual labor in the fields and orchards. In style, the rhythmic movement of these elongated, energetic figures is reminiscent of Burgundian sculpture, such as that at Vézelay, but the colors are far more subdued than those in the Benedictine Bury Bible of Master Hugh.

## The contributions of Norman England

While the pilgrimage roads were important in the development and dissemination of Romanesque art, significant contributions came from other areas as well, such as Normandy in northwestern France. William the Conqueror (ca. 1027–1087) extended Norman rule to England following his victory at the Battle of Hastings in 1066. This story is recorded in one rare and most significant secular work, the Bayeux Tapestry (**J 416; G 9.35; H&F 9.19**), a picture chronicle of the Norman conquest of England embroidered in wool thread on linen, probably by women working in southern England. Both a historical document and a piece of political propaganda justifying the legitimacy of William's reign, it is done with the story-telling flair of the French *chansons de geste,* the tales of heroic deeds. For us it has the added fascination of providing a glimpse at everyday life in the late eleventh century, for it records the appearance of contemporary clothing, armor, weapons, and even the decoration of a Viking longship.

The Romanesque style in England has been popularly, if not completely accurately, associated with the Norman conquest. The introduction of a new style is seldom such a clear-cut matter. However, even a contemporary historian, the monk William of Malmesbury, wrote, "With their arrival the Normans breathed new life into religious standards, which everywhere in England had been declining, so that now you may see in every village, town and city churches and monasteries rising in a new style of architecture."

The finest of the English Romanesque churches is located in the far north of England. The cathedral of Durham (**J 391, 392, 393; G 9.17, 9.18; H&F 9.29**) looks more like a fortress than a church. Built on a defensive site on a cliff over the river Wear, the church is dominated by three massive towers, two on the façade and one at the crossing. It stands proud, confident, defiant; the embodiment of the military spirit of the age. Of course, Durham, too, was an important pilgrimage church; here the main attraction was the shrine of St. Cuthbert (d. 687), the bishop of Lindisfarne whose life story was recorded by a near contemporary, the Venerable Bede (ca. 673–735).

At Durham the most significant structural development in Romanesque architecture was made: the introduction of the ribbed vault. Durham Cathedral, started in 1093, was one of the first medieval buildings to incorporate ribbed vaulting (**G 6.54**). Roman builders had used groin vaulting to cover their vast public baths, but the technique had been lost. The groin vault can be imagined as the intersection of two barrel vaults at right angles. By transferring the thrust of the heavy vault to specific points at the corners of each bay, groin vaults allowed specific buttressing at these points rather than continuous buttressing along the entire wall. The massive piers of Durham carry most of this thrust but, hidden at the gallery level, what are, in effect, early versions of the "flying buttress" reinforce the piers where the pressure is greatest. This system of vaulting allowed the walls to be both higher and less massive. Most importantly, larger windows became possible. These advantages of the pointed arch, the ribbed vault, and the flying buttress were crucial to the development of the Gothic style, but Durham remains a Romanesque church. The height of the nave arcade serves to increase the feeling of spaciousness, as at Cluny III and Paray-le-Monial in France, but the effect is clearly segmented, with each unit of space, each bay, emphasized. Bold roll moldings and the incised chevrons, spiral flutings, and diaper patterns on the huge piers set Durham apart from the more classical decorative vocabulary of many French Romanesque buildings. The style of Durham was not an isolated achievement, but other English cathedrals, such as those at Ely and Gloucester, retain similarly massive Romanesque naves only amidst later Gothic additions, just as the Romanesque church at Vézelay itself received a new Gothic choir only seventy years after construction had been completed.

The Romanesque period was one of immense energy. Western Europe was regaining confidence and now took the offensive, sending Crusaders to the East and battling the Moors in Spain. International exchange, both commercial and intellectual, transformed Europe. For the first time since the fall of Rome there was a widespread interest in the West in creating monumental sculpture and painting to decorate large and permanent buildings. The church became the major patron of the age, building new churches and monasteries all over Europe. Structural developments, such as the stone barrel vault, the pointed arch, and the ribbed vault, ennabled architects to satisfy their patrons' desires for ever larger and safer churches. To decorate these buildings, now attracting a wider audience of pilgrim travelers, a more strongly moralizing and didactic approach to subject matter was combined with the traditional medieval conceptual approach to style. Then, in the early twelfth century, these Romanesque innovations in art and architecture were combined in an entirely new way to create the new, visionary Gothic style.

## Part 2
# THE HIGH MIDDLE AGES

## Gothic Art

Starting in France in the twelfth and thirteenth centuries, a new style developed which was called *opus francigenum* or French work. We know it as Gothic, a derisive name applied only in the sixteenth century to emphasize, indeed mock, the non-classical nature of the style by naming it after the earlier northern barbarian tribe, the Goths. The Gothic aesthetic differed dramatically from the Romanesque. In architecture, tall, light, open, unified spaces created through the use of the pointed arch and the ribbed vault replaced the dark, segmented spaces of the Romanesque church. In sculpture and painting, there was a new interest in the more realistic representation of the human body, both physically and psychologically. The new Gothic style developed first in French architecture and sculpture, but it soon spread to other art forms such as painting and metalwork. And radiating from France, the influence of this new style can be traced throughout Europe, for the Gothic, too, was an international style.

In these centuries the population of Europe had continued to expand, and there had been two hundred years of economic growth, especially in the cities. Politically, Europe, under the rule of the Capetians in France, the Plantagenets in England, and the Hohenstaufens in Germany, was more stable than before. These social, economic, and political factors were important in leading to the new period of architectural creativity.

The Gothic cathedral defines this age the way the monastic church had the Romanesque. The word cathedral comes from *cathedra,* the throne of a bishop. Usually located in a city, the cathedral was an administrative center for the Church, but more importantly, it was a spiritual center for an entire region. While religious services were performed there on a regular basis, the cathedral was certainly much more than just a house of God. The cathedral had an important civic function as well, often serving as town hall, court, market place, school, and meeting place. As Michael Wood mentions in the program, the entire population of Amiens, about 10,000 people, could fit inside the cathedral at one time. Religious plays enacted in front of the sculptured entrances attracted large crowds. The cathedral dominated daily life just as it physically dominated the town. In the competition for trade and commerce, a large and beautiful cathedral filled with relics was an important attraction for a city. Similar to the rivalry between Romanesque monasteries, a spirit of competition between towns, such as Chartres and Reims, to have the largest and most lavish cathedral encouraged new architectural and artistic feats as much as any religious motivation did. The height of the vaults, the amount of stained glass, the richness of the sculptural program all might be factors in vying to have the most stylish and up-to-date church in the area.

As urban cathedrals supplanted in importance the monastic churches, so large universities replaced monastic schools as the main centers of learning in the twelfth and thirteenth centuries. The universities of Paris, Bologna, Oxford, and Cambridge attracted scholars from all over Europe. At this time, Scholasticism was the leading method of theological and philosophical reasoning at the University of Paris. Perfected by such scholars as Peter Abelard and St. Thomas Aquinas, it was a technique of rational, systematic definition in which the works of the ancient Greek philosopher, Aristotle, were of primary importance. Preserved through the centuries in the Islamic East, these ancient writings came to be re-introduced into Western thinking as part of the blossoming cultural exchange between East and West, an exchange spurred by increasing travel and trade at the time of the Crusades. Aristotelian logic was used in an attempt to reconcile Christian faith and scientific reason. Moreover, the view that the specific elements in nature, including the human body itself, were more important than the Platonic universals parallels the new developments in the art of the Gothic period.

### *Abbot Suger and the abbey of St. Denis*

For the study of Gothic architecture, of primary importance is the royal abbey of St. Denis, located in what is now a suburb just north of Paris. Major aspects of the transition from Romanesque to Gothic can be traced in this one seminal work, in particular the sections of the church of St. Denis **(J 422, 423; G 10. 1–10.3; H&F 9.31, 9.32)** built by Abbot Suger (1081–1151). This sort of specificity is rare, but so was this patron. Suger, born of poor parents, had been raised in the Benedictine abbey of St. Denis from the age of ten. When he was named abbot in 1122, he took charge of a Carolingian church nearly 350 years old which was not only too small but in need of extensive repairs. This church, founded by the patron saint of France, St. Denis, was the traditional burial place for the kings of France. Suger, an able and ambitious administrator and businessman, shrewdly fostered ties with the ruling Capetian dynasty of France to enhance the power and prestige of his abbey. Indeed Suger became the trusted adviser to Louis VI and Louis VII and was selected to serve as chancellor of France when Louis VII left on crusade.

Suger started building campaigns at either end of the church of St. Denis. At the west he provided a narthex and an elaborate westwork crowned by two towers (the north tower no longer exists). At the eastern end he built a large choir with nine radiating chapels, which William Clark describes in the program. Suger had intended to replace the nave as well, but that was not accomplished until the thirteenth century.

Elements of the Gothic style—especially the pointed arch, the ribbed vault, and large clerestory windows—can be found in many Romanesque buildings. What was new at St. Denis was their masterful integration. Suger gathered the best workers from regions of France and from other parts of Europe as well. They were professional craftsmen, more likely to be secular than monastic. Working together on this major project, these craftsmen incorporated features from Burgundy and England, from Normandy and Western France, to create a building which satisfied Suger's theological and aesthetic demands. Suger wrote proudly about their accomplishments, but he does not refer to any of these craftsmen by name. Instead, it is the name and image of Suger which is found throughout the church.

The plan of the choir of St. Denis is derived from the pilgrimage road type, seen at Paray-le-Monial, with an ambulatory and radiating chapels now more shallow and more numerous, forming what is almost an undulating second ambulatory. The first impression is one of space and openness. Thin Gothic columns, rather than massive Romanesque piers, support the ribbed vaults. The moldings provide a linear, graphic articulation characteristic of Gothic art as opposed to the mural emphasis of Romanesque design. The structural advantages of the pointed arch and the ribbed vault were exploited to channel the weight of the stone vault, thus permitting more efficient, less massive buttressing.

One benefit of these structural developments was the possibility of having large windows filled with stained glass, the first time such coloring was used extensively. Suger defended this luxury by offering a theological basis for it, one which was directly associated with his church. A history of the abbey written in the ninth century glorified the third-century martyr St. Denis, the patron saint of France. However, the author inadvertently confused him with two others with similar names, Dionysius the Areopagite, the follower of St. Paul mentioned in the Bible, and an anonymous fifth-century writer known as the Pseudo-Dionysius, who wrote in Neo-Platonic terms about light as a primary source of faith and inspiration. When Suger read the writings of the Pseudo-Dionysius on light symbolism, he believed he was reading the thoughts of the founder of his abbey. Suger associated natural light with spiritual enlightenment. The jewel-like colors of the light coming through these windows also invited comparisons with the Heavenly Jerusalem described by St. John in the Book of Revelation. Suger called his new choir a "crown of light." In his treatise on St. Denis, Suger described three of these windows. Such documentation, especially something written by the patron himself, is exceedingly rare in medieval art.

Suger spared no expense in providing luxurious furnishings for his new choir. No doubt the words of condemnation of his great rival, St. Bernard of Clairvaux, "So riches attract riches, money attracts money," would have appealed to Suger as a practical policy. After all, Suger wrote that "the dull mind rises to truth through that which is material." Therefore, according to Suger, the richer the objects, the more effective they would be in encouraging contemplation of spiritual truth. Unfortunately, zealots and philistines have destroyed the majority of these treasures. The Huguenots of the sixteenth century and the madness of the French Revolution at the end of the eighteenth century are especially to blame. However, one of Suger's sumptuously jeweled chalices **(H&F 9.33)** escaped this fury and is now displayed in the National Gallery of Art in Washington, D.C. Except for a few such isolated objects and Suger's writings, only inventory listings and a few later paintings and drawings are left to record the splendor of the golden and jeweled furnishings on the high altar at St. Denis.

The Gothic choir of St. Denis was dedicated in 1144. The king of France, Louis VII, his queen, Eleanor of Aquitaine, and numerous bishops and other dignitaries participated in the ceremony. Suger, known for his showmanship, did not disappoint. The festivities demonstrated that Suger had successfully linked the royal abbey of St. Denis with the rising fortunes of the Capetian dynasty of France. He probably would have approved of the thirteenth-century project that filled his choir with a series of commemorative tombs honoring the ruling Capetians and the dynasty they emulated, the Carolingian.

Suger had endowed his church not only with material splendor but also with a new political prominence which helped disseminate the new style. The rise of the Gothic style took place in the lands under the strong, centralized control of the capable Capetian rulers.

### Chartres: the west façade

The impact of St. Denis was felt first in the rebuilding of the west façade of the cathedral of Notre Dame at Chartres **(J 428, 456, 457, clpl 48; G 10.13, 10.14; H&F 9.45)**, a

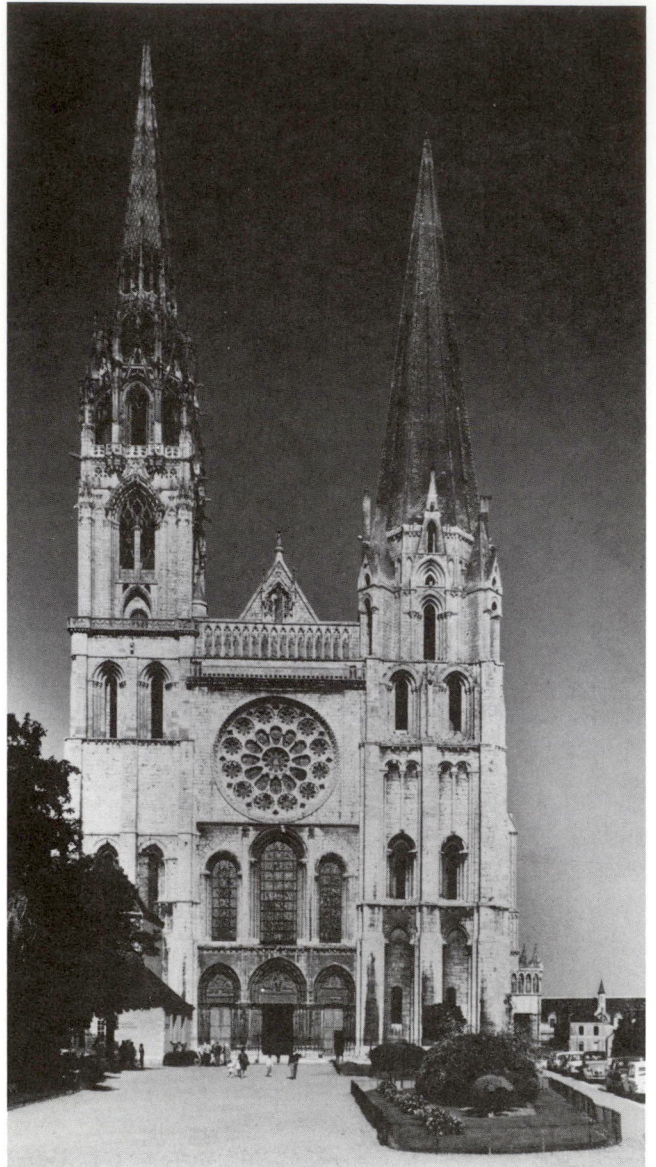

Chartres, West Façade, 1145. (SCALA/ART RESOURCE, NEW YORK)

The decoration of the western façade of Chartres is as important as its architectural design, for it contains the most complete and impressive Early Gothic sculptural program to survive. The three doorways are known as the royal portals, for their jambs are lined with statues of kings and queens of the Old Testament, the ancestors of Christ. Medieval viewers were encouraged to see an allusion to contemporary French royalty as well, as if the Capetian dynasty shared Christ's royal lineage.

The columnar appearance of the jamb statues at Chartres reinforces their architectonic role, continuing the Romanesque subordination of sculpture to architecture. But these early statues at Chartres are more fully three-dimensional than Romanesque works. For the first time since ancient Rome there is a hint of a living body beneath the folds of drapery. Despite the proximity in date between the sculpture at Chartres and Vézelay **(J 408, 409; G 9.32, 9.33; H&F 9.23),** the contrast between the calm, dignified Early Gothic figures and the agitated Romanesque relief sculpture is striking. Although several sculptors worked on the west façade, the work on the central portal by the anonymous sculptor, known as the Headmaster, stands out as being especially fine **(J 428, 456, 457, clpl 48; G 10.13, 10.14; H&F 9.45).** While the bodies of his figures remain static, symmetrical, and abstract, in these faces a new naturalism is evident, both physically and psychologically. They have a new self-awareness, and seem to the viewer to be cognizant, complex human beings, not mere actors in a religious drama. Thus they seem approachable, no longer remote and forbidding.

This awakening of interest in the earthly human being in monumental sculpture went far beyond the Ottonian and Romanesque examples, and it coincides with a renewed interest in the earthly life of Christ and his mother, the Virgin Mary, in the Gothic period. Chartres was but one of numerous Gothic churches dedicated to Notre Dame, Our Lady, who was especially beloved in the Gothic period. Little of Mary's story is related in the Bible, but she had been proclaimed Theotokos, Mother of God, in 431, laying the foundation for her increasing importance within the Church. A cult of the Virgin had been established by the Romanesque period, reaching its peak of popularity in the Gothic era. Worshipers directed prayers to this mother figure in hopes that she would act as an intercessor on their behalf, much as a feudal landowner would approach the king through a sympathetic intermediary at court. According to legend, Chartres had been built on a site where pagans worshiped a fertility goddess whose story paralleled aspects of the story of the Virgin birth. Moreover, Chartres possessed one of the most important relics of the Virgin, the tunic she was said to have worn when she gave birth to Christ.

Above the western portals of Chartres relief sculptures fill the tympana, the spaces above the doorways. The subjects of the tympana proclaim the message of hope and salvation offered through Christ. These tympana are

town southwest of Paris, where a fire in 1134 destroyed the façade and towers of the old church. The response to this disaster was immediate, and the fervor to rebuild quickly has been likened to the spirit of the Crusades themselves.

The geometric rationality of the new Gothic façade of Chartres reflects Suger's contemporary work at St. Denis. With logic and clarity the three enlarged portals suggest the three divisions of the interior, the nave and the side aisles. A round window filled with stained glass occupies the center of the rectangular grid of the façade. Two towers complete the façade, as had become traditional at such churches as St. Denis and numerous others. (Note, however, that the north tower was substantially rebuilt in the more ornate Late Gothic style.)

supported, literally and figuratively, by the Old Testament jamb statues below. On the right, the south tympanum presents scenes from the early life of Christ, culminating in the main image of the enthroned Virgin and Child. This south door, known as the Incarnation portal, celebrates the human Jesus. The north tympanum, showing the Ascension of Christ, celebrates his divine aspect. Thus the two side portals remind the viewer of the beginning and end of Christ's life on earth. Historiated capitals, arranged in a continuous band above the jamb statues, tell the story of the life of the Virgin and the life of Christ, serving to unite the design both formally and thematically. Finally, the larger central tympanum presents the image of Christ in Majesty surrounded by the symbols of the four Evangelists, the angel of Matthew, the lion of Mark, the ox of Luke, and the eagle of John. It is the Christ of the Second Coming, shown not as judge, but blessing and holding the book which offers the path to salvation.

The Gothic message carved on the façade of Chartres is clearly a positive one proclaiming man worthy of salvation. This stands in contrast to the tone of much of Romanesque art. On the tympanum of the Last Judgment at Autun **(J 407; G 9.30, 9.31; H&F 9.22),** for example, man was as likely to be considered a sinner threatened with damnation as a candidate for paradise. In the Middle Ages, when the concepts of heaven and hell were especially real, such a difference was significant. At Chartres, the new, more optimistic approach of the sculptural program parallels the new humanism in its style. Christ, who said, "I am the door" (John 10:9), now welcomed all to enter and be saved.

## The new cathedral of Chartres

In 1194 another fire struck Chartres, sparing the new façade but destroying the rest of the Romanesque church. Seeing the devastation, the townspeople at first despaired, believing that the tunic of the Virgin must have perished. But when the tunic was found amidst the rubble, miraculously safe and unscorched, it was taken as a sign that the Virgin wanted a new, more beautiful church built in her honor. Work began immediately.

Funding for such a major undertaking as a Gothic cathedral was never easy and naturally came from many sources. The church received revenues from the agricultural estates it owned and from levying taxes on trade fairs and the like. Donations were an important source. Members of the clergy who were independently wealthy would contribute, as would the local nobility and aristocracy. Additional revenues came from visiting pilgrims and from professional organizations such as guilds. But the cost was enormous, and financing the construction and decoration of a Gothic cathedral inevitably caused economic and social disruption throughout the region. Amazingly, the new cathedral of Chartres was completed within one generation, whereas most cathedrals took many decades, even centuries, to complete.

In designing the new cathedral of Chartres **(J 429, clpl 47; G 10.15–10.18; H&F 9.41),** the architect devised a plan with single side aisles in the nave which double in the choir to give it greater emphasis. The plan is shorter and the three radiating chapels more insular than they might otherwise have been because the practical and cost-conscious builders sought to re-use the crypt and the older foundations whenever possible. This sort of adaptation to existing conditions, rather than the imposition of preconceived ideals, is typical of medieval art. Therefore, the undulating, flowing space achieved by the numerous, shallow chapels in the choir at St. Denis was sacrificed at Chartres.

Nevertheless, the grandeur of the new cathedral at Chartres is evident throughout the building. On the interior, the nave vaults rise over one hundred feet. An interior space higher than a ten-story building remains awe-inspiring today in a world filled with skyscrapers, but to the medieval worshiper, accustomed to humble domestic structures of timber or wattle-and-daub, such an achievement in stone must have seemed miraculous. This, after all, was the intent. The cathedral towered over the other medieval buildings of Chartres and, as the program shows, its majestic silhouette continues to dominate the flat countryside for miles.

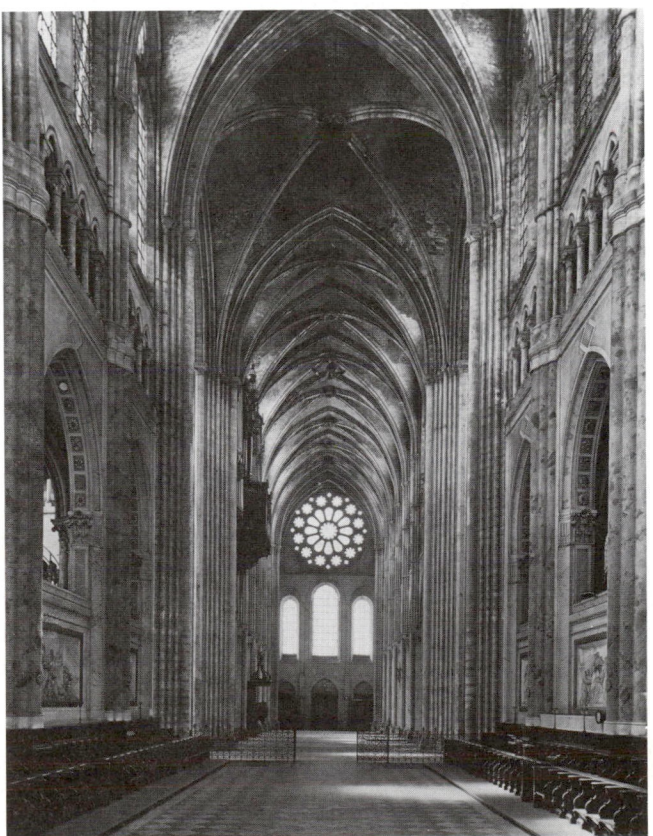

Chartres, Interior, looking east, 1194–1225. (MARBURG/ ART RESOURCE, NEW YORK)

Suger's innovations at St. Denis were exploited throughout the new cathedral of Chartres. Now the entire interior was perceived as a miraculous envelope for the flowing space, and Romanesque segmentation was subordinated to this new conception. Above all, the vertical is emphasized. The cathedral was designed to have lofty ribbed vaults reinforced on the exterior by flying buttresses, a method of buttressing that had been developed in the process of building the cathedral of Notre Dame in Paris **(J 427; G 10.10)** a few years earlier. Flying buttresses solved both structural and aesthetic problems. They provided maximum support for a vault where it was most critically needed, at the springing. Thus they relieved piers and walls of some of their buttressing function, allowing them to be less massive. And, because the flying buttresses were gracefully arched, open forms, and were exposed, rather than covered with a roof, they required less material to build, and allowed more light to enter the church. In addition to these familiar structural and aesthetic advantages, flying buttresses are also believed to have played an important role in controling a new problem: the effect of high winds on buildings of this unprecedented height. Today Robert Mark and others are using scale models and computers to test the effectiveness of such features in Gothic architecture in ways never imagined by the original architects.

From the interior of Chartres, the dramatic effect of the use of flying buttresses was most evident: the vaults now seemed to hover miraculously without adequate visible support. This was an amazing engineering feat. The upper walls, largely freed of any supporting function, were reduced to a minimum. Now the clerestory level looked like a wall of glass with windows as large as the arches of the nave arcade **(J 429, clpl 47; G 10.17).** The interior is suffused with the mysterious light from stained glass, a feature Suger emphasized at St. Denis. Chartres is unique in retaining more its original stained glass than any other major church of the period. The dominant colors of red and blue produce a mystical, glowing light, unlike anything in nature. Could heaven itself be any more beautiful?

The technique used to make stained glass was described by Theophilus in his treatise *On Divers Arts*. The artist would start by making a sketch of his design. This would be followed by a full-scale drawing known as a cartoon. Because the glass-making techniques of the day restricted the size of sheets of glass, pieces of glass had to be fitted together almost like a mosaic. After the various pieces of colored glass had been arranged on the cartoon, they would be joined together by H-shaped strips of lead. Details of the drawing, such as facial features and the lines of the drapery folds, were painted on the glass. Then a larger metal armature would join the smaller sections of the patterned glass together and secure them in the window.

Craftsmen, such as the glaziers who produced these large stained-glass windows, usually belonged to professional organizations known as guilds. Medieval guilds were something like the trade unions of today in that membership was required in order to practice the craft in a particular area. The guilds regulated training and apprenticeships; they also had rules to ensure the quality of the materials and the work produced by their members. But the guilds usually went beyond these professional duties to address the spiritual well-being of their members as well. They undertook charitable duties, participated in festivals for their craft's patron saint, and sometimes sponsored works of art, or even the decoration of whole chapels, in local churches. At Chartres, guilds and corporations donated over forty of the stained-glass windows. In theory such donations were given in pious thanks for past success in hopes that the prosperity would continue, but recent research suggests that less spiritual motives were sometimes involved

The subjects depicted in the windows in the west wall of Chartres amplify the sculptural program on the façade. The three subjects in the lancet windows are the Tree of Jesse, the early life of Christ, and the Passion of Christ. The Virgin Mary figures prominently in these episodes. The Tree of Jesse, a genealogical guide to the ancestors of Christ presented as a living family tree, had appeared in a window in Suger's choir at St. Denis and became very popular in manuscript illumination as well. At Chartres, the Tree of Jesse complements the statues of the Old Testament kings and queens on the Royal Portal, continuing the association between the Capetian kings of France and the royal lineage of the King of Kings. At the very center of the west wall the great rose window depicts the Last Judgment, the corollary to the Second Coming of Christ on the central tympanum. The planning of such intricate programs would not have been left to the artist but would have been worked out by learned theologians.

Around the nave and choir of Chartres, various windows **(J clpl 47; H&F 9.37, 9.38)** told stories from the Old and New Testaments and from the lives of saints and martyrs. For example, the shoemakers' guild donated a window telling the parable of the Good Samaritan **(G 10.35),** while the furriers displayed their own products, as Anne Prache explains in the program. Because stained glass was used to tell religious stories, it appealed to both the eye and the mind, for it illuminated the church literally and figuratively. As William Durandus, bishop of Mende, wrote in a thirteenth-century treatise on the symbolism of churches, "The glass windows in a church are Holy Scriptures, which expel the wind and the rain, that is all things hurtful, but transmit the light of the True Sun, that is God, into the hearts of the Faithful" (quoted in T. G. Frisch, *Gothic Art 1140–c.1450: Sources and Documents,* p. 36). Further, theologians compared the wonder of the transformation of clear light which became colored as it passed through stained glass without changing the glass, to the miracle of the transformation of God into Man through the birth of Christ to the Virgin Mary who remained a virgin: Mary remained as unchanged by the experience as was the glass.

## The transept façades of Chartres

In the new Gothic cathedral of Chartres, the transept façades received the sort of elaboration formerly reserved for the west façade alone. On each, the triple portals were recessed within deep porches which seem to embrace and protect those who approach while entertaining and enlightening them with religious stories through their detailed sculptural programs.

On the north transept, dating to the early thirteenth century, one notices immediately developments in the Gothic style since the west façade. As the style moves further away from the Romanesque, the jamb statues are less bound by the architecture. These Old Testament figures turn on their pedestals and look in different directions, their bodies no longer rigidly symmetrical. Furthermore, they are not quite so isolated but subtly interact with each other, with the sculpture above, or with the viewer. There is a new independence and a new humanity about them. Compared with the figures on the west façade, these statues are more three-dimensional, more naturalistic, as William Clark explains in the program. A range of expression and emotion animates their faces. Perhaps the most poignant figures are those of Abraham with his young son Isaac, whom he was willing to sacrifice to prove his faith. Their presence reminds the viewer of the path to salvation through sacrifice, while the reward in heaven is depicted on the tympanum.

This development in the representation of the human body at Chartres was not an isolated artistic phenomenon, but rather it parallels current intellectual developments, where there was an increasing interest in the factual. In the thirteenth century, philosophical and theological attitudes toward the human body were changing; the body was no longer seen as merely an unworthy prison for the soul. Theologians such as St. Thomas Aquinas reconciled the natural world of Greek philosophy with the teachings of the Christian faith. Aquinas wrote, "The soul has to get all its knowledge from the perceptible" (quoted in G. Duby, *History of Medieval Art,* Vol. II, p. 129). This attitude, in effect, sanctioned an increasing naturalism in art.

The regal scene of the Coronation of the Virgin appears on the tympanum of the central portal of the north façade of Chartres. This subject of Christ crowning his mother as Queen of Heaven was one of the most popular new themes introduced in Gothic art. As it often is in medieval art, the heavenly court is here modeled on the earthly court. Christ and the Virgin are shown as idealized royal figures of the day. But the importance of the Virgin Mary has been stressed here more than ever before. She is shown sitting next to her son, almost as an equal, with scenes from her life below. This new subject both reflects the importance of the cult of the Virgin and

is related to the theme of courtly love in contemporary secular art and literature. The Virgin is honored in other parts of the portal, too. Her mother, St. Anne, is represented on the trumeau, while above, the Tree of Jesse, the royal ancestry of Mary and Christ, is displayed in the archivolts.

On the south transept of Chartres, which followed soon after the north portals, the Gothic style has moved further in the direction of a naturalistic depiction of the human body. The jamb figures (**J 458; G 10.31, G 16.7**) on the south transept represent apostles and saints. One of the most popular is the military St. Theodore. The sculptor managed to make this historical figure so lifelike by using several new devices. We are seemingly confronted with a specific individual, not a generalized type. The contemporary thirteenth-century costume would have appeared especially convincing to the medieval viewer. St. Theodore, standing there wearing chain mail and carrying a sword, shield, and lance, looks like a knight ready to set out on a Crusade to the Holy Land. More subtly, the sculptor made the body appear so natural by showing the effect of standing, as we usually do, with one leg bearing more weight than the other. The use of contrapposto, well known in ancient art, has not yet been fully captured by the Gothic artist, but his incipient interest in the anatomical mechanics of the stance is clear.

## French High Gothic

Chartres is considered the earliest of the great High Gothic cathedrals, the classic age of French cathedral design. It became a popular model for the development of Gothic church design in the region around Paris, in part because its plan could be adapted for any scale.

One building to follow the plan of Chartres is Reims Cathedral (**J 461; G 10.32, 10.33),** the traditional coronation church of France which vied with St. Denis in national prestige. When fire destroyed the older structure in 1210, the new church was built in the High Gothic style by successive architects who worked on the building into the early fourteenth century. (Construction was delayed in part by conflicts over funding between the town, the archbishop, and the cathedral chapter, conflicts which resulted in serious riots in the 1230s.) Taller than Chartres, the cathedral at Reims is remarkable for a sense of verticality that is enhanced by its narrower nave. Details such as shafts rising from floor to vault emphasize the nave's great height, while the capitals balance this insistent verticality. The delicately carved foliate design of the capitals is both realistic and specific, the product of careful observation of the real world, as was the figure of St. Theodore at Chartres. The trend at Reims is toward a new elegance, refinement, and attenuation of form.

In contrast to the triumphs at Chartres and Reims, the cathedral at Beauvais (**G 10.29, 10.30)** is frequently cited as a morality lesson in the folly of excessive pride. In medieval art, pride was depicted as a rider falling from a high horse. The analogy is apt. Planned with the highest vaults in Europe (158 feet), the construction of Beauvais, begun about 1225, was never completed beyond the choir, for the buttresses and vaults collapsed in 1284. The vault was rebuilt with additional piers and ribs, in hopes that they would make it safer. The Beauvais failure and attempted remedy serve as reminders of the experimental nature of these engineering feats by medieval architects, who relied on such basic tools as a pair of calipers, a measuring stick, and a square to turn their theoretical knowledge of applied geometry and their practical knowledge of other buildings into a new cathedral. The specific reasons for the initial and subsequent collapses at Beauvais have been debated for centuries, with most theories concentrating on problems with the design of the choir, complicated by delays in construction due to problems in funding and the change of architects. In any event, the structural failure was followed by a financial one, and, in the early fourteenth century, the western end of the choir was simply walled up. The great age of cathedral construction had ended.

Many features introduced at Chartres were continued and expanded in other High Gothic churches such as Reims. One was the desire to use as much stained glass as possible, and at Reims even the tympana on the façade were glazed rather than sculpted. Also, new Gothic subjects received even greater prominence at Reims; for example, the Coronation of the Virgin was placed on the gable above the central portal of the western façade, the premier location on this coronation church.

The profusion of sculpture on the cathedral of Reims was unprecedented in quantity (over 2,000 figures) and unmatched in quality. The projecting portals of the west façade, in particular, display some of the most important examples of Gothic sculpture to survive. Although it would not be until Claus Sluter's sculpture for the Chartreuse de Champmol (J 469; H&F 9.76) that statues would appear totally independent from their architectural setting, at Reims the figures are now arranged in groups with a narrative context rather than as isolated individuals as at Chartres. These figures appear to be conversing with each other rather than lost in individual thought. In thirteenth-century art, the hieratic formalism of a purely conceptual approach increasingly gave way to the representation of more natural behavior.

Three distinct artistic styles are represented in the two scenes of the Annunciation and the Visitation (G 10.33; H&F 9.46, 9.49) on the façade of Reims. Most surprising are the figures of Mary and her aging cousin Elizabeth in the scene of the Visitation, which appear so classicizing that it was once thought they were ancient sculptures re-used on the Gothic façade. The Gothic artist, with his new interest in the natural world, apparently turned to classical models for guidance in achieving greater realism. But in medieval art there is no easy progression from abstraction to naturalism. This moment of thirteenth-century classicism was as short-lived as the Carolingian, but its brief

flourishing is far more difficult to explain, and not for lack of interest in the problem.

In terms of sculptural styles, Reims is best known for the courtly liveliness of the smiling Angel of the Annunciation. The mannered elegance of this figure follows the same conventions used in fashion illustration today: the small, well-coifed head with high cheekbones is set at an angle atop a long, thin neck, while the outward thrust of one hip makes the body seem to sway. The simple garment falls in deep, broad folds of drapery which accentuate the slenderness of the figure beneath. The lively play of light and shade makes the figure seem to move. Forsaking naturalism, the proportions are impossibly elongated.

This elegant, mannered style exemplified at Reims remained in vogue for over a hundred years, especially for statues of the Virgin shown as earthly mother and Queen of Heaven (H&F 9.47). The Virgin of Paris (J 462; G 10.38) is of this courtly type. Even the queen of France, Jeanne d'Evreux, wife of King Charles IV, owned a small gilded statuette of the Virgin and Child in this style, and the same style appears in miniatures in her tiny Book of Hours illuminated by Jean Pucelle (J 500).

This idealized Gothic approach is in direct contrast to the realism achieved in some Gothic sculpture, such as the figures of Ekkehard and Uta at Naumberg Cathedral (J 467; G 10.54; H&F 9.54). Although these German sculptures appear to be portrait likenesses, as does the St. Theodore at Chartres, the historical figures had been dead for centuries when the statues were made. The artists in both cases were concerned with the facts of nature, not the specifics of history.

One of the great patrons of the Gothic period was the pious King Louis IX (1214–1270), who ruled at a time when Paris was becoming the art capital of Europe. Louis's most important commission in Paris was the Sainte-Chapelle (G 10.27, 10.28; H&F 9.40) attached to his royal palace. Rather than trying to make it larger than any other building, he intended it to be more sumptuous. The Sainte-Chapelle was conceived as a giant reliquary to house the crown of thorns and the fragment of the True Cross which the king had bought from his cousin, the current Byzantine emperor. Golden reliquaries set with precious gems were the obvious inspiration for the design and decoration of the chapel. The walls of this Gothic building are almost entirely stained glass, the ultimate statement of the trend that had started with Suger's choir at St. Denis. What minimal stone surfaces remained on the interior disappeared beneath a dazzling display of sculpture, painting, and gilding. The antithesis of the Cistercian austerity at Fontenay, the Sainte-Chapelle offers the earthly miracle of extreme artistic refinement in continuing Abbot Suger's belief that the fine display of material splendor would naturally lead the mind to the contemplation of heavenly rewards to come.

A psalter belonging to the king reflects the style of his Sainte-Chapelle in its miniatures. Painted in the bright colors of stained glass, this Psalter of St. Louis (**J 484; G 10.37; H&F 9.48**) shows Old Testament scenes set in thirteenth-century guise. In the Gothic period more and more illuminated manuscripts came to be produced for individuals, first for royalty and high church officials and then, in later years, for any who could afford them. Most were religious books, but secular texts, such as the Romance of Alexander, became popular as well. A lively sense of humor animates many of these books, religious and secular alike, as is clear from the pages illustrated in the program. The increase in manuscript production was a sign of increasing literacy in society, plus evidence of a growing taste for luxury goods. This development parallels the shifts in patronage in other areas as well, from elaborate tombs and memorial chapels to small ivories and metalwork: what had once been the prerogative of royalty became the practice of the aristocracy and then spread to the wealthy and growing middle class.

## English Gothic

From France, the Gothic style spread throughout Europe. As with the Romanesque, each area adapted the style to local traditions, materials, and tastes. Always stronger in the North than in Italy, the Gothic style lasted well into the sixteenth century, and, in isolated cases, even later.

Despite the innovations in vaulting at Durham Cathedral, in England the Gothic style did not develop directly. Rather, it was imported from France. Once transplanted, however, the Gothic style grew in a distinctive way, sometimes borrowing again from the French and sometimes contributing ideas as well.

The first major building in England to employ the latest French Gothic style was Canterbury Cathedral (**G 10.40, 10.41; H&F 9.35**), where its archbishop, Thomas Becket, former friend of King Henry II and chancellor of England, had been murdered in 1170. A fire in 1174 destroyed most of the Norman Romanesque building and new construction started immediately, for the martyr's remains were already a major pilgrimage attraction. A magnificent shrine was prepared, and the story of the life and miracles of this controversial archbishop was told in the stained-glass windows of the new church. Over two hundred years later, Geoffrey Chaucer's ribald *Canterbury Tales* indicates the continuing popularity of this pilgrimage.

The architectural history of the new choir at Canterbury Cathedral is unusually well documented. One of the Benedictine monks of Canterbury, the chronicler Gervase, left a vivid eyewitness account of the fire and the circumstances of the subsequent rebuilding:

> And it was marvellous, though sad, to behold how that glorious choir itself fed and assisted the fire that was destroying it. For the flames multiplied by the mass of timber, and extending upwards full fifteen cubits [about 25 feet], scorched and burnt the walls, and more especially injured the columns of the church.

> And now the people ran to the ornaments of the church, and began to tear down the pallia and curtains, some that they might save, but some to steal them. The reliquary chests were thrown down from the high beam and thus broken, and their contents scattered; but the monks collected them and carefully preserved them from the fire. Some there were, who, inflamed with a wicked and diabolical cupidity, feared not to appropriate to themselves the things of the church, which they had saved from the fire. (Quoted in T. G. Frisch, *Gothic Art 1140–c.1450: Sources and Documents*, pp. 15–16.)

The new church at Canterbury was begun under the direction of William of Sens, a man described by Gervase as skillful in wood and stone. Presumably he came from Sens in France, as his name suggests. There are certain parallels between the early Gothic cathedral of Sens, as well as other early Gothic churches in France, and his work at Canterbury. Four years later, William of Sens, injured in a fall from some high scaffolding, was replaced by another William, known as William the Englishman. Thus, the French elements in the Canterbury design, such as the sexpartite ribbed vault, molded ribs, foliate capitals, and a three-part nave elevation, were combined with distinctly English elements in the execution. The most dramatic English feature is the use of two colors of stone, called bichromatic stonework. The selective use of dark Purbeck marble to accentuate the linear design results in a dimunition of the French Gothic verticality by emphasizing the horizontal lines. Both the linear interest and the horizontality would be characteristic features of English Gothic design.

Salisbury Cathedral (**J 438–440; G 10.42–10.45**) is considered the prime example of the Early English style of Gothic architecture. For English cathedrals it is somewhat atypical—first, because it was built on a fresh site unencumbered with earlier foundations and, second, because it was built in such a short time (between 1220 and 1258). Other than the addition of the pointed spire (and the punitive restoration of the cathedral by Wyatt in the eighteenth century), Salisbury never received the serious modifications most English churches underwent in later centuries. It is, like Chartres, that rare example of a Gothic cathedral conceived and executed within one generation. Salisbury is, therefore, especially useful in analyzing the English style and comparing it with the French. Where French Gothic churches stressed verticality, an insistent emphasis on the horizontal pervades English design: the long, low nave, only 85 feet high, about two-thirds the height of the slightly earlier nave at Chartres, is some 473 feet long. English, too, is the rectilinear plan with strongly projecting transepts and a flat eastern end borrowed from Cistercian architecture. Bichromatic stonework accentuates the horizontal sweep of the nave as it enhances the linear design, dematerializing further the wall surfaces already reduced by the larger openings for the nave arcade, triforium, and clerestory. Generally, the English were little interested in the structural innovations of the French Gothic; they exploited the new style for its decorative potential.

On the exterior, the towers and portals at Salisbury are understated compared with French design. Instead the entire façade is decorated with figural sculpture displayed in a series of niches which isolate the figures and, in terms of the overall design, serve to accentuate the horizontal lines.

The finest such screen façade in England is to be found at the cathedral at Wells, where it acts like a huge scaffold for the display of the largest collection of Early English Gothic sculpture to survive. Unfortunately, much of it is in extremely poor condition, but at least it survives: most English monumental sculpture has been destroyed, either by man or nature. In its day, with its original painting and gilding, this ensemble at Wells would have looked like a giant retable for an altar. It has been suggested that for special ceremonies, such as that on Palm Sunday, members of the choir would stand in hidden passages behind the statues to sing. These remarkable visual and auditory effects can only be imagined today.

Completed in 1239, the long, low nave of Wells is approximately the height of a side aisle in a French High Gothic cathedral. After a new tower and spire were built over the central crossing in the early fourteenth century, the additional weight caused the walls to buckle, so huge strainer arches were erected to counteract this force, a bold and imaginative solution to the problem. Paradoxically, Robert Mark's recent studies of the support for the Wells tower show that these dramatic strainer arches were far less efficient than the unobtrusive buttresses built against the walls. Again, as at Beauvais, modern scientific methods have shown us the limits of the medieval empirical approach.

A love of linear patterning can be found throughout the church at Gloucester despite the fact that the building spans the time frame from Early Romanesque to Late Gothic, embracing both the continuity and change evident in the nearly five hundred years which separate its Norman nave from its Perpendicular Lady Chapel. Gloucester received an incentive to rebuild the choir when the body of the murdered King Edward II (d. 1327) was deposited there. Unlikely as it sounds, this weak ruler, who had met such an ignominious end, became the object of cult veneration and soon pilgrims were flocking to Gloucester in great numbers, despite the fact that Edward II's saintly status was never officially recognized by Rome. The tomb for the king and the refurbishment of the choir around it were done in the latest style, the English Perpendicular (**J 441; G 10.46**). As the name suggests, the Perpendicular style emphasizes rectilinear elements as surfaces, whether stone or glass, are divided into repetitive traceried panels. The flat eastern wall of the Gloucester choir is filled with an enormous stained-glass window measuring approximately 72 feet by 38 feet. Dozens of figures are displayed in elaborate architectural niches which illusionistically continue in glass the actual stone tracery of the window. Abbots and bishops form the first rank; then, leading up through pairs of saints, male and female, come the twelve Apostles and, finally, the scene of the Coronation of the Virgin with angels above—a visual demonstration of the path from the earthly to the sublime, paralleling the social hierarchy of the feudal system with the king and queen at the apex. Above, the elaborate lierne vaulting studded with sculpted bosses of angels playing musical instruments must have made the choir of Gloucester seem like heaven itself.

The monastic cloister at Gloucester was built shortly after the choir and it introduces yet another new form of English vaulting: the fan vault. The small ribs seem more like moldings as they form conical starburst patterns at regular intervals along the sheltered walkways. This love of intricate linear surface pattern is the Gothic heir of the northern tradition in both pagan (the Sutton Hoo metalwork) and Christian art (the Lindisfarne Gospels and the Book of Kells). A similar type of fan vaulting was used for the magnificent Chapel of Henry VII at Westminster Abbey (**J 442; G 10.47**), built at the very end of the Middle Ages, when the Renaissance had already reached its peak in Italy: these English fan vaults date from the same time Michelangelo was decorating another vault in Rome, the ceiling of the Sistine Chapel (**J 615–617, clpl 77; G 17.24–17.26; H&F 11.21, 11.25**).

## Summary

Where the Romanesque was a style of walls and massive forms, the Gothic was a style of voids, of spaces enclosed within linear grids. Its chief characteristic was what Jean Bony calls the "skeletonization of the structure." The distinction is often summarized as Romanesque surface versus Gothic line. The Romanesque reminds one of fortifications while the Gothic seems a visionary style, one which anticipates the glories of heaven itself. The effects of each—the dark Romanesque church perceived as a series of segmented spaces and the bright, unified Gothic interior—were the result of changes in aesthetic goals as much as technological capabilities: the parallels with the changes in the representation of the human figure are striking. General trends in patronage varied as well in the two periods, for the major achievements of the Romanesque were monastic in origin, while in the Gothic they were secular and aristocratic. The quickening pace of structural innovation and stylistic change in the Gothic period may reflect the faster life outside the cloister.

Despite centuries of neglect and abuse, the ravages of war, puritans, decorators, and over-zealous restorers alike, great numbers of Romanesque and Gothic structures still survive over much of Europe, even if most of their original furnishings do not. After all, these buildings were constructed of strong materials and in a sound manner. And they were numerous. It has been estimated that in the Middle Ages there was one church or chapel for every two hundred people. Many still dominate their settings today just as they did in the Middle Ages. Tattered as it might be, Raoul Glaber would still find his "white garment of churches."

## Textbook References

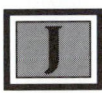 Janson's *History of Art* concentrates on formal analysis while offering an extended selection of works, especially for the Gothic period.

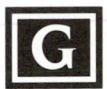 Gardner's *Art Through the Ages* provides a formal analysis of individual works along with important diagrams and maps. Both of these books tend to divide each period into sections according to the medium of the work of art and its nationality.

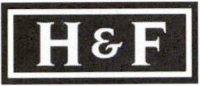 Hugh Honour and John Fleming's provocative *The Visual Arts: A History* places more emphasis on the context of artistic production than on analysis of individual works. However, these authors discuss and illustrate such crucial yet problematic works as Cluny, Santiago de Compostela, and Fontenay, which are not to be found in Gardner and Janson.

**Janson, Part I, Chapter 8: Early Christian and Byzantine Art, pp. 197–231.** Catacombs; Old St. Peter's; mosaics; San Vitale, Ravenna; Hagia Sophia; St. Mark's, Venice; Daphne.

**Part II, The Middle Ages: Introduction, pp. 238–241.**

**Chapter 2: Early Medieval Art, pp. 255–277.** Dark Ages; Sutton Hoo purse cover; Lindisfarne Gospels; Carolingian art; Palace Chapel, Aachen; St. Gall plan; Gospel Book of Charlemagne (Coronation Gospels); Gospel Book of Archbishop Ebbo of Reims; Ottonian art; Gero Crucifix; bronze doors of Hildesheim Cathedral.

**Chapter 3: Romanesque Art, pp. 278–299.** Autun Cathedral; Durham Cathedral; Moissac; Ste.-Madeleine, Vézelay; Bayeux Tapestry.

**Chapter 4: Gothic Art, pp. 300–359.** Abbey church of St. Denis, Notre Dame, Paris; Chartres Cathedral; Reims Cathedral; Salisbury Cathedral; Gloucester Cathedral; the Virgin of Paris; Ekkehard and Uta, Naumberg Cathedral; stained glass; Psalter of St. Louis; Jean Pucelle, Hours of Jeanne d'Evreux.

**Gardner, Chapter 7: Early Christian, Byzantine, and Islamic Art, pp. 246–293.** Catacombs; Old St. Peter's; mosaics; Good Shepherd sarcophagus; San Vitale, Ravenna; Justinian; Hagia Sophia; St. Mark's, Venice; Daphne.

**Chapter 8: Early Medieval Art, pp. 310–339.** Migration period; Sutton Hoo purse cover; Book of Lindisfarne; Carolingian period; Coronation Gospels; Ebbo Gospels; Palatine Chapel, Aachen; St. Gall plan; Ottonian period; St. Michael's, Hildesheim; bronze doors of Hildesheim; Gospel Book of Otto III.

**Chapter 9: Romanesque Art, pp. 340–369.** Durham Cathedral; St. Pierre, Moissac; Gislebertus; St. Lazare, Autun; La Madeleine, Vézelay; Bayeux Tapestry; *Moralia in Job;* Bury Bible.

**Chapter 10: Gothic Art, pp. 370–411.** Abbey church of St. Denis; Notre Dame, Paris; Chartres Cathedral; Sainte-Chapelle; Beauvais Cathedral; Reims Cathedral; stained glass; Psalter of St. Louis; the Virgin of Paris; Canterbury Cathedral; Salisbury Cathedral; Gloucester Cathedral; Chapel of Henry VII, Westminster Abbey; Ekkehard and Uta, Naumberg Cathedral.

**Honour and Fleming, Chapter 7: Early Christian and Byzantine Art, pp. 224–260.** Constantine; sarcophagi; The Good Shepherd; Old St. Peter's; basilica, mosaics; Justinian; San Vitale, Ravenna; Hagia Sophia; Lindisfarne Gospels; Book of Kells; clasp from Sutton Hoo; Charlemagne; Palatine Chapel, Aachen; St. Gall plan; Coronation Gospels; Ebbo Gospels.

**Chapter 9: The European Middle Ages, pp. 282–331.** Gero Crucifix; Ottonian art; bronze doors at Hildesheim; St. Mark's, Venice; Cluny III; Bayeux Tapestry; pilgrimage; Santiago de Compostela; *Moralia in Job;* Autun Cathedral; Gislebertus; La Madeleine, Vézelay; Durham Cathedral; ribbed vaulting; abbey church of St. Denis; chalice of Abbot Suger; Fontenay Abbey; Canterbury Cathedral; Chartres Cathedral; flying buttresses; stained glass; Sainte-Chapelle, Paris; Reims Cathedral; St. Louis Psalter; Ekkehart and Uta, Naumberg.

## Study Questions

1. Why was the Church of Old St. Peter's in Rome important?
2. What debt does Romanesque architecture owe to Roman architecture? to Carolingian? to Ottonian?
3. What was the importance of the pilgrimage roads?
4. Describe the influence of the cult of saints and the religious pilgrimage on the design and decoration of churches in the Middle Ages.
5. Why was stone vaulting preferred?
6. Why is Paray-le-Monial typical of Romanesque architecture in France?
7. What is unusual about the sculpture at Autun? Where does it appear? What are the subjects?
8. Who were the Cistercians? What were their contributions?
9. Outline aspects of continuity and change between Romanesque and Gothic architecture.
10. Is Durham a Gothic cathedral? Explain.
11. What structural developments made the High Gothic cathedral possible?
12. Discuss the significance of Abbot Suger.
13. What changes take place in the representation of the human form in medieval art?
14. Is stained glass crucial to Gothic architecture? Why or why not?
15. How does the English version of Gothic differ from French Gothic? How is it similar?

# Glossary

**abbey**   the buildings occupied by a group of monks or nuns, ruled by an abbot or abbess.

**aisle**   a passageway, especially one flanking the nave of a church and set off by a row of columns or piers.

**altar**   a table upon which the sacrament of the Eucharist is performed during the Mass.

**altar frontal**   a decorative panel covering the front of the altar table, either painted, carved, or embroidered.

**altarpiece**   the painted or sculpted panel placed on or above an altar.

**ambulatory**   the walkway around the apse of a church.

**angel**   a messenger of God, usually shown in human form with wings.

**Apocalypse**   The Book of Revelation by St. John the Evangelist, the last book of the New Testament, and, by extension, the events described in that book which will occur at the end of the world.

**apostles**   the twelve main disciples of Christ: Peter, Andrew, James, John, Philip, Bartholomew, Thomas, Matthew, James the Less, Jude (Thaddeus), Simon, and Judas Iscariot; Judas's place was taken by Matthias.

**apse**   a recess in a wall, especially the vaulted semicircular recess in the eastern wall of a Christian church.

**arcade**   a series of arches supported on piers or columns.

**arch**   a curved span made of wedge-shaped blocks (voussoirs); shapes include round, pointed, ogee, or horseshoe.

**archbishop**   the chief bishop of a church province.

**archivolt**   the molding around an arch.

**ashlar masonry**   stonework using squared blocks of stone in horizontal courses.

**atrium**   an open courtyard; the courtyard in front of a Christian church.

**baldachin**   a canopy, usually over an altar, throne, or tomb.

**baptistery**   the building or part of a church used for baptism.

**barrel vault**   a semicircular vault; also known as a tunnel vault.

**basilica**   the Roman colonnaded hall, a form adapted for Christian churches throughout western Europe. The longitudinal plan includes a nave with at lest two aisles and an apse at one end (usually the eastern end). The structure is lit by clerestory windows.

**bay**   a repeating vertical unit of space marked by architectural members.

**Benedictine Order**   an order of monks following the rule of St. Benedict of Nursia (ca. 480–ca. 550).

**bestiary**   a book with descriptions or depictions of various animals, both real and imaginary.

**bichromatic**   two-colored; see *polychrome*.

**bishop**   the church official in charge of a diocese.

**Book of Hours**   a private prayer book arranged according to the canonical hours of the Church: Matins, Lauds, Prime, Terce, Sext, Nones, Vespers, and Compline.

**boss**   the decorative carved projection at the intersection of ribs in vaulting.

**buttress**   a projecting support or reinforcement for a wall.

**canonization**   official declaration of sainthood.

**capital**   the upper part of a column, often decorated.

**cartoon**   a full-scale preparatory drawing for wall paintings, stained glass, or tapestries.

**catacombs**   subterranean burial places connected by passageways in ancient Rome.

**cathedral**   the principal church of a bishop containing his throne (*cathedra*).

**chalice**   a cup or goblet for wine, especially that used in the Eucharist.

**champlevé**   an enameling technique in which enamel fills hollows carved into a metal surface.

**chancel**   the part of the church from the high altar to the east reserved for the clergy and choir, often separated from the nave by a screen.

**Chansons de Geste**   stories of heroic deeds in medieval French verse. The most popular heroes were Charlemagne and Roland.

**chapel**   a small area within a church with its own altar.

**chapter house**   the building used for the business meetings of the monks or canons of a cathedral.

**chevet**   the eastern end of a church including the choir, ambulatory, apse, and radiating chapels.

**Chi Rho**   a monogram for Christ based on the first two letters of his name in Greek.

**chivalry**   a code of social behavior for medieval knights based on courtesy and consideration.

**choir**   the part of the church where the service is sung, usually in the chancel.

**Christ in Majesty**   the enthroned Christ, often surrounded by the symbols of the Evangelists.

**Cistercian Order**   a reformed Benedictine order founded in 1098.

**clerestory**   the fenestrated upper story of a basilican church.

**cloisonné**   an enameling technique employing thin metal strips attached to the surface forming partitions (*cloisons*) to hold the enamel.

**cloister**   an open courtyard surrounded by a covered walkway, usually next to the church in a monastic complex.

**Cluniac Order**   not a true monastic order, but a term used in recognition of the unusual power of the reformed Benedictine abbey of Cluny, which governed 1500 dependent houses.

**codex**   a manuscript in book form with pages bound together between stiffened covers, as distinct from a scroll.

**colonnade**   a row of columns supporting a beam.

**colonette**   a small column.

**column**   a circular pillar with a base and a capital.

**compound pier**   a pier with several shafts, common in Romanesque and Gothic architecture.

**contrapposto**   the Italian term used to describe the natural counter-positioning of the human body when one leg bears the weight and the other leg is relaxed, resulting in changes in the placement of the shoulders and hips.

**corbel**   a projection from a wall, often functioning as a supporting bracket.

**crenelated**   notched or indented, especially in reference to battlements.

**cross**   the instrument of Christ's crucifixion; the cross has been the main Christian symbol from the time of Constantine.

**crossing**   the area of a church where the transepts cross the nave and choir.

**crozier**   the staff carried by bishops and abbots.

**crucifix**   the figure of Christ on a cross.

**cruciform**   in the shape of a cross.

**Crusades**   eight Western military expeditions to the Holy Land in the eleventh through thirteenth centuries.

**crypt**   the vaulted area beneath the eastern end of a church.

**cult of saints**   the worship of venerated persons as intercessors, focusing on the miraculous powers of their physical remains.

**damp-fold** a method of depicting draperies as if the material were wet and clinging to the body.

**diaper** a repeated pattern of lozenges or squares.

**diptych** a painting or relief sculpture consisting of two panels which can be folded together.

**dome** a convex roof with a hemispherical or pointed vault.

**elevation** the vertical plane of a building.

**enamel** a vitreous substance which adheres to a surface when heated. The two main techniques in the Middle Ages were champlevé and cloisonné.

**Eucharist** one of the sacraments of the Christian church in which the bread and wine are consecrated and become the flesh and blood of Christ in commemoration of the Last Supper.

**Evangelists** the authors of the four Gospels, Matthew, Mark, Luke, and John. Often represented symbolically according to the vision of Ezekiel (Ezek. 1:5–14, Rev. 4:6–8): the angel or man of Matthew, the lion of Mark, the ox of Luke, and the eagle of John.

**façade** the front or face of a building which receives architectural emphasis.

**fan vault** lierne ribs arranged in a radiating, fan-like pattern; characteristic of the English Perpendicular style.

**fenestration** the arrangement of windows in a building.

**feudalism** the political, economic, and social structure of medieval Europe based on mutual duties and obligations, especially the promise of homage, military service, and labor in exchange for land.

**flying buttress** an external buttress carried on an arch or a series of arches to counteract the thrust of a vault.

**font** the receptacle used for baptismal water.

**fresco** painting on plaster, when the plaster is either wet (true fresco or *buon fresco*) or dry (*fresco secco*).

**frieze** a horizontal band of sculpture.

**gable** the triangular area of a wall under a ridged roof and, by extension, canopies of that shape.

**gallery** in ecclesiastical architecture, the story over the side aisle opening onto the nave.

**gilding** a surface covering of gold leaf, or of any shiny metallic substance resembling gold.

**glory** an aureole indicating sanctity, as a halo or nimbus around the head or a mandorla around the body.

**Gospels** the first four books of the New Testament, which record the life of Christ.

**groin vault** the intersection of two barrel vaults, sometimes accentuated with ribs.

**guild** a professional organization which often regulated training, materials, and standards for a particular craft.

**habit** monastic dress. The color and style indicated the order.

**halo** a disc or ring of light around the head of a sacred figure.

**heraldry** the distinctive armorial bearings of the nobility in the Middle Ages.

**hieratic** a formal, ritualized style fixed by religious tradition.

**historiated** decorated with narrative scenes, as historiated initials or historiated capitals.

**horror vacui** an avoidance of empty spaces in the composition of a work of art.

**icon** an image, especially that of a sacred person.

**iconoclasm** the destruction of images.

**iconography** the study of the symbolic meaning of a work of art.

**illuminated manuscript** a manuscript with colored or gilded decoration.

**jambs** the vertical sides of an opening such as a door or window.

**knight** a high military rank in the feudal system.

**labors of the months** occupations traditionally associated with a specific month, often depicted with the signs of the zodiac.

**lancet window** a tall, pointed Gothic window without tracery.

**lierne** a short, subordinate rib connecting two other ribs but not associated with the springing of the vault.

**lintel** the horizontal beam across the top of a door or window.

**liturgy** the form of public worship.

**lunette** a semicircular demarcation or opening.

**mandorla** an almond-shaped glory or nimbus, often shown surrounding the figure of Christ in medieval art.

**martyr** one who suffers or dies for belief in a cause.

**martyrium** a building commemorating the site where a martyr suffered, died, or was buried.

**Mass** the celebration of the Eucharist.

**mausoleum** an imposing tomb. The term refers to the tomb of King Mausolus at Halicarnassus, one of the Seven Wonders of the Ancient World.

**medium** (pl. **media**) the material or technique of a work of art.

**miniature** a painting or drawing in a manuscript.

**miracle** an event which cannot be explained by the laws of nature.

**monastery** the residence of a community of monks.

**mosaic** the decoration of a floor, wall, or vault with small pieces of stone or glass (*tesserae*) of different colors set in plaster or concrete. This form of decoration was popular in Roman, Early Christian, and Byzantine art.

**mural** a painting on a wall.

**narthex** a porch or vestibule of a church.

**nave** the central aisle of a church, extending from the entrance to the choir and usually flanked by side aisles.

**net vault** a vault with lierne and tiercerone ribs arranged in a net pattern.

**nimbus** a halo.

**ogee** an S-shaped curve; a form of arch popular in the English Decorated style.

**opus Dei** the work of God; the communal worship prescribed by St. Benedict for monks.

**orans** a gesture of prayer with the hands raised used in the early Christian church.

**Pantocrator** the Byzantine representation of Christ as Ruler of the Universe.

**parchment** an animal skin which has been scraped and bleached to be used for writing.

**parish** a district having its own church.

**pendentive** a method of supporting a dome over a square by using concave, triangular sections of masonry.

**pericope** a type of manuscript containing lessons from the Gospels arranged according to the liturgical calendar.

**pier** a solid masonry support.

**pilaster** a rectangular column attached to a wall or pier.

**pilgrim** one who journeys to a sacred place.

**pilgrimage** the journey of a pilgrim.

**pillar** a general term for a vertical architectural support, including piers, columns, and pilasters.

**plan** a horizontal section of a building mapping the arrangement of the parts.

**polychrome** decorated with many colors.

**priory** a monastic house dependent on an abbey.

**psalter** a book of the Psalms.

**pulpit** a raised platform for reading and speaking in a church.

**quadripartite vault** a four-part groin vault.

**relics**   the venerated remains of a saint, or objects closely associated with a saint.

**relief**   sculpture which, rather than being three-dimensional, stands in relief from a surface.

**reliquary**   a container for relics, usually decorated with precious materials.

**retable**   a carved or painted altarpiece placed on top of an altar.

**rib**   a molding accentuating the lines of a vault.

**ridge rib**   a longitudinal rib at the crown of a vault.

**rose window**   a round stained glass window with tracery resembling a rose. Usually placed at the center of one of the façades of a Gothic church.

**sacraments**   the seven rites of the church: baptism, confirmation, the Eucharist, penance, matrimony, holy orders, and extreme unction.

**sarcophagus**   a stone coffin.

**Scholasticism**   a theological and philosophical approach to faith based on reason, espoused by Peter Abelard and St. Thomas Aquinas among others. The writings of Aristotle were very important.

**screen façade**   a façade which masks rather than reveals the size or arrangement of the interior space.

**scriptorium**   the place where manuscripts were written in a monastery.

**serf**   the lowest rank of freeman in medieval society; a serf's movements were restricted by the lord whose land he worked.

**sexpartite vault**   a type of groin vault in which each bay is divided into six compartments.

**spire**   the tapering structure atop a tower.

**springing**   the point where the curve of an arch begins.

**squinch**   an arch or niche used to merge a rectangular space with a round or polygonal structure above.

**strainer arch**   an arch inserted to keep walls or piers from leaning together.

**string-course**   a horizontal molding on a building.

**tabernacle**   a canopied container for relics or for the Eucharistic wafer, and, by extension, a canopied space.

**tessera** (pl. **tesserae**)   a small piece of stone or glass used to compose a mosaic.

**tierceron**   a secondary rib running from the springing of a vault to the ridge rib.

**tracery**   decorative stonework on walls or windows.

**transept**   the transverse arms of a cruciform basilican church.

**tribune**   alternative term for the gallery of a church.

**triforium**   the arcaded wall passage of a church located between the nave arcade and the clerestory.

**triumphal arch**   a roman commemorative gateway; also the transverse arch at the eastern end of the nave of a church framing the altar area.

**trumeau**   the pillar in the center of a Romanesque or Gothic portal.

**tympanum** (pl. **tympana**)   the area between the lintel of a doorway and the arch above it, usually decorated.

**vault**   a masonry roof or ceiling constructed on the principle of the arch.

**vellum**   calfskin parchment, or, more generally, any especially fine parchment.

**vestibule**   an entrance hall or lobby.

**vestments**   the official garments worn by the clergy during a church service.

**voussoir**   the wedge-shaped stones forming an arch, the center one being the keystone.

**westwork**   the monumental towered western front of a Carolingian, Ottonian, or Romanesque church.

**zodiac**   the path of the sun, moon, and stars, divided into twelve compartments associated with the months: the twelve signs of the zodiac are named after constellations: Aries, (the ram), Taurus (the bull), Gemini (the twins), Cancer (the crab), Leo (the lion), Virgo (the Virgin), Libra (the scales), Scorpio (the scorpion), Sagittarius (the archer), Capricorn (the goat), Aquarius (the water carrier), and Pisces (the fish).

## Artists, Patrons, and Important Personages

**Abelard, Peter** (1079–1142). French theologian and Scholastic philosopher.

**Angles.** One of several German tribes to invade England in the fifth century after the withdrawal of Roman forces.

**Apollo.** In Greek mythology, the son of Zeus admired as the ideal in male physical beauty. Later associated with the sun god Helios (Sol).

**Bernward.** Archbishop of Hildesheim (993–1022).

**Capetian.** Ruling dynasty of France, 987–1328.

**Carolingian.** Ruling dynasty of France, 768–987.

**Charlemagne** (742–814). King of the Franks (r. 768–814) and first Holy Roman Emperor (r. 800–814); founder of the Carolingian dynasty of France. He extended the empire through military conquest and unified it through reforms in government, education, and language.

**Chaucer, Geoffrey** (ca. 1342–1400). First major English poet, best known for the humorous *Canterbury Tales,* about pilgrims traveling to the shrine of St. Thomas Becket at Canterbury Cathedral.

**Constantine** (d. 337). Roman emperor (r. 306–337) who nurtured the development of the Christian religion.

**Dionysius the Areopagite.** A follower of St. Paul mentioned in the Bible (Acts 17:34); in the Middle Ages confused with a later anonymous Neo-Platonic author (Pseudo-Dionysius) and with St. Denis, the patron saint of France.

**Edward II** (1284–1327). King of England (r. 1307–27) who, when deposed and murdered, became the unlikely object of cult veneration.

**Eve.** According to the Book of Genesis, the first woman, created from Adam's rib. When she succumbed to the temptations of the serpent to eat forbidden fruit from the tree of the knowledge of good and evil, God expelled Adam and Eve from Paradise.

**Franks.** Germanic people who conquered Gaul (France) in the sixth century.

**Gislebertus.** The main sculptor of the cathedral of Autun; his name is inscribed on the tympanum of the central portal.

**Goths.** Germanic tribe which started to invade the Roman Empire in the third century. Eventually split into two groups, the Ostrogoths and the Visigoths.

**Master Hugh.** English painter, sculptor, and metalworker active at the abbey of Bury St. Edmunds in the twelfth century.

**Huguenots.** French Calvinists (Protestants) at odds with the ruling Catholic majority in the sixteenth and seventeenth centuries.

**Huns.** Asiatic people who ravaged Europe in the fourth and fifth centuries.

**Jeanne d'Evreux** (d. 1371). Queen of France, wife of King Charles IV (1294–1328); important patron of the arts.

**Lombards.**   Germanic people who invaded Italy in the sixth century.

**Louis the Pious** (778–840).   Charlemagne's son who succeeded him as Holy Roman Emperor in 814.

**Louis IX** (1214–70).   King of France (r. 1226–70), later canonized as St. Louis. A strong and pious ruler, and major patron of the arts, he went on the Seventh Crusade in 1248 and died in 1270 on the Eighth and last Crusade.

**Merovingians.**   Ruling Christian dynasty of the Franks from the fifth century through the mid-eighth century.

**Moors.**   Muslim people of northwest Africa and Spain.

**Ostrogoths.**   The eastern Goths who conquered Italy in the fifth and sixth centuries.

**Otto I** (912–973).   King of the Germans (r. 936–973) and Holy Roman Emperor (r. 962–973) who came to control Italy and the papacy. Succeeded by his son, Otto II (r. 973–983), and his grandson, Otto III (r. 983–1002).

**Philip II Augustus** (1165–1223).   King of France (r. 1180–1223) who embarked on the Third Crusade after the capture of Jerusalem in 1187.

**Philip the Good, Duke of Burgundy** (1396–1467).   Credited by historians as the founder of the Burgundian state in the Low Countries, Philip the Good was also the longest reigning and one of the most important patrons of the arts. The son of John the Fearless, he became duke at twenty-three and during his reign, court life reached a new level of pomp and extravagance. Philip established the Order of the Golden Fleece in 1430. He had the finest collection of illuminated manuscripts then in existence and his patronage extended to the leading sculptors and painters of the period including Jan van Eyck.

**Pseudo-Dionysius.**   An anonymous fifth-century Neo-Platonic author who wrote of light as a primary source of faith and inspiration; known by this name because he was confused in the Middle Ages with Dionysius the Areopagite.

**Jean Pucelle** (d. 1334).   Manuscript illuminator active in Paris in the early fourteenth century.

**Richard I (the Lion-Heart)** (1157–99).   King of England (r. 1189–99) known for his military exploits including his participation in the Third Crusade.

**St. Augustine** (d. 604).   Sent to England by Pope Gregory to refound the Christian Church there. The first archbishop of Canterbury.

**St. Benedict** (ca. 480–ca. 550).   Compiler of the monastic rule which continues to be observed by Benedictine monks.

**St. Bernard of Clairvaux** (1090–1153).   Influential French Cistercian abbot and theologian.

**St. Denis.**   Third-century Christian martyr; patron saint of France.

**St. Hugh** (1049–1109).   Abbot of Cluny.

**St. James the Greater** (d. 44 A.D.).   One of the Apostles and the elder brother of St. John the Evangelist; his shrine at Santiago de Compostela became a major pilgrimage center in the Middle Ages.

**St. John the Evangelist.**   The youngest Apostle of Christ and one of the Four Evangelists; author of the fourth gospel and the Book of Revelation (the Apocalypse).

**St. Louis.**   *See* **Louis IX.**

**St. Peter** (d. 67 A.D.).   Apostle who became the first bishop of Rome. Traditionally shown as Keeper of the Gates of Heaven holding a large key or keys.

**St. Thomas Aquinas** (1225–74).   Italian Dominican theologian and philosopher noted for reviving and interpreting the works of Aristotle. His major work, the *Summa Theologica,* illustrates the Scholastic method.

**St. Thomas Becket** (ca. 1118–70).   Friend of King Henry II of England, who made Becket chancellor of England and then archbishop of Canterbury. Becket's murder in his own cathedral produced the greatest martyr saint in England, and pilgrims flocked to his shrine in great numbers.

**Saxons.**   Germanic tribe that invaded England in the fifth and sixth centuries.

**Sluter, Claus** (ca. 1360–1406).   Sculptor who worked for Philip the Bold, Duke of Burgundy.

**Suger** (d. 1151).   Abbot of St. Denis (1122–51); responsible for rebuilding the choir and the western end of the church in the Gothic style.

**Theodoric** (ca. 454–526).   King of the Ostrogoths; invaded Italy in 488 and established his capital at Ravenna.

**Theophilus.**   Pseudonymous author of the twelfth-century treatise *On Divers Arts;* possibly the German artist Roger of Helmarshausen.

**Visigoths.**   Western Goths who eventually established a kingdom in Spain.

**William the Conqueror** (ca. 1027–1087).   Duke of Normandy who became the first Norman king of England (r. 1066–1087) after defeating Harold at the Battle of Hastings in 1066.

## Bibliography

### MEDIEVAL ART

Alexander, J. J. G., and P. Binski, eds. *Age of Chivalry: Art in Plantagenet England 1200–1400.* Royal Academy exhibition catalog. London, 1987.

Arts Council of Great Britain. *English Romanesque Art 1066–1200.* Hayward Gallery exhibition catalog. London, 1984.

Beckwith, J. *Early Christian and Byzantine Art.* Harmondsworth, 1970.

———. *Early Medieval Art.* New York, 1964.

Brooke, C. *The Monastic World.* London, 1974.

Calkins, R. G. *Monuments of Medieval Art.* New York, 1979.

Demus, O. *Byzantine Art and the West.* New York, 1970.

Duby, G. *History of Medieval Art 980–1440.* New York, 1986. (Incorporates *The Making of the Christian West 980–1140; The Europe of the Cathedrals 1140–1280;* and *Foundations of a New Humanism 1280–1440.*)

Grand Palais. *Les Fastes du Gothique; Le siècle de Charles V.* (Exhibition catalog.) Paris, 1981.

Henderson, G. *Early Medieval.* Harmondsworth, 1972.

———. *Gothic.* Harmondsworth, 1967.

Hinks, R. *Carolingian Art.* Ann Arbor, 1962.

Kidson, P. *The Medieval World.* New York, 1967.

Kitzinger, E. *Early Medieval Art,* rev. ed. London, 1983.

Lasko, P. *Ars Sacra: 800–1200.* Harmondsworth, 1972.

Martindale, A. *Gothic Art.* New York, 1967.

Runciman, S. *Byzantine Style and Civilization.* Harmondsworth, 1975.

Shaver-Crandell, A. *The Middle Ages.* Cambridge, 1982.

Snyder, J. *Medieval Art: Painting—Sculpture—Architecture.* Englewood Cliffs, N.J. and New York, 1989.

Stoddard, W. *Art and Architecture in Medieval France.* New York, 1972.

Stokstad, M. *Medieval Art.* New York, 1986.

Swarzenski, H. *Monuments of Romanesque Art,* 2nd ed. Chicago, 1967.

Wilson, D. M. *Anglo-Saxon Art*. London, 1984.

Zarnecki, G. *Art of the Medieval World*. Englewood Cliffs, 1975.

———. *Romanesque Art*. New York, 1972.

## ARCHITECTURE

Bony, J. *The English Decorated Style*. Ithaca, 1979.

———. *French Gothic Architecture of the Twelfth and Thirteenth Centuries*. Berkeley, 1983.

Branner, R. *St. Louis and the Court Style in Gothic Architecture*. London, 1965.

Conant, K. J. *Carolingian and Romanesque Architecture*. Harmondsworth, 1959.

Fergusson, P. *Architecture of Solitude: Cistercian Abbeys in Twelfth-Century England*. Princeton, 1984.

Grodecki, L. *Gothic Architecture*. New York, 1977.

Krautheimer, R. *Early Christian and Byzantine Architecture*. Harmondsworth, 1975.

Kubach, H. E. *Romanesque Architecture*. New York, 1975.

Mark, R. *Experiments in Gothic Structure*. Princeton, 1982.

Panofsky, E. *Gothic Architecture and Scholasticism*. New York, 1957.

## SCULPTURE

Campbell, M. *Medieval Enamels*. London, 1983.

Forsyth, I. H. *The Throne of Wisdom: Wood Sculptures of the Madonna in Romanesque France*. Princeton, 1972.

Hearn, M. F. *Romanesque Sculpture*. Ithaca, 1981.

Sauerländer, W. *Gothic Sculpture in France 1140–1270*. London, 1972.

## PAINTING, MANUSCRIPTS, STAINED GLASS

Alexander, J. J. G. *The Decorated Letter*. New York, 1978.

Avril, F. *Manuscript Painting at the Court of France: The Fourteenth Century (1310–1380)*. New York, 1978.

Backhouse, J. *Books of Hours*. London, 1985.

———. *The Illuminated Manuscript*. Oxford, 1979.

Cahn, W. *Romanesque Bible Illumination*. Ithaca, 1982.

Calkins, R. G. *Illuminated Books of the Middle Ages*. Ithaca, 1983.

Cuttler, C. D. *Northern Painting from Pucelle to Bruegel*. New York, 1968.

Demus, O. *Romanesque Mural Painting*. New York, 1970.

Dupont, J., and C. Gnudi. *Gothic Painting*. Geneva, 1954; reprinted New York, 1979.

Grodecki, L., and C. Brisac. *Gothic Stained Glass: 1200–1300*. Ithaca, 1985.

Marks, R., and N. Morgan. *The Golden Age of English Manuscript Painting 1200–1500*. New York, 1981.

Mütherich, F., and J. E. Gaehde. *Carolingian Painting*. New York, 1976.

Nordenfalk, C. *Celtic and Anglo-Saxon Painting: Book Illumination in the British Isles 600–800*. New York, 1977.

Pächt, O. *Book Illumination in the Middle Ages*. London, 1986.

Robb, D. M. *The Art of the Illuminated Manuscript*. New York, 1973.

## REFERENCE WORKS AND PRIMARY SOURCES

Davis-Weyer, C. *Early Medieval Art, 300–1154*. Sources and Documents in the History of Art. Englewood Cliffs, 1971.

Frisch, T. G. *Gothic Art 1140–ca. 1450*. Sources and Documents in the History of Art. Englewood Cliffs, 1971; reprinted Toronto, 1987.

Hall, J. *Dictionary of Subjects and Symbols in Art*. New York, 1984.

Holt, E. G. *A Documentary History of Art*. Vol. 1, *The Middle Ages and the Renaissance*. Garden City, 1957.

Jacobus de Voragine. *The Golden Legend*. Translated by G. Ryan and H. Ripperger. New York, 1969.

Schiller, G. *Iconography of Christian Art*. 2 vols. London, 1971.

Theophilus. *On Divers Arts*. Translated by J. G. Hawthorne and C. S. Smith. Chicago, 1963; reprinted New York, 1979.

Thompson, D. V. *The Materials and Techniques of Medieval Painting*. London, 1936; reprinted New York, 1956.

# The Early Renaissance
## Florence and the North

## Learning Objectives

European art of the fifteenth century is as seminal to Western civilization as that of Greece and Rome. In fact, the term "Renaissance," by which this era is described, reflects a conscious return to many of the ideals which had thrived in antiquity. Renaissance, meaning "rebirth," was the name given to Italian culture by the very humanists who revived antiquity as a model for human behavior.

The impact of the Renaissance was enormous. It embedded the art of antiquity into Western culture. The Renaissance laid the foundation for subsequent developments in painting, sculpture, and architecture. Renaissance humanism established the study of liberal arts which we still pursue today.

Part 1 of this unit concentrates on Italy. A brief discussion of developments prior to the fifteenth century is followed by a more detailed analysis of the fifteenth century in Florence. Particular emphasis is placed on the geniuses of the first part of the century: Donatello, Masaccio, and Brunelleschi. Their rational, monumental, and humanly oriented art signaled the beginnings of new directions for sculpture, architecture, and painting. Humanity was both the subject and object of their work. Each of these artists worked with highly rigorous, rational, and measurable systems. Perspective, proportion, harmony, and idealism are some of the terms and concepts introduced in this section of the unit.

Venice is introduced at the end of the unit. An important link between the cultures of northern Europe and Italy, Venice was home to a remarkable school of painters who employed oil paint and studied nature and light to achieve visions at once naturalistic and also evocative. The discussion will concentrate on Giovanni Bellini, the greatest Venetian painter of his generation and founder of the Venetian school.

The second part of the unit will turn to northern Europe. There in the Burgundian courts and the thriving mercantile cities such as Bruges and Ghent, art was also revolutionized. While humanism and classicism did not structure perceptions, there was a forceful interest in the visible world which changed the direction of painting and sculpture. The results are a miraculous translation of visible reality into paint and a precocious injection of human character and personality into sculpture. The unit concentrates on Claus Sluter, the acknowledged master of Northern Renaissance sculpture, and Jan van Eyck, as well as Rogier van der Weyden for painting. These masters established a means to translate visible reality into paint which guided artists for the rest of the century. The unit closes with Albrecht Dürer and Matthias Grünewald, to trace the changes and developments in the North at the close of the fifteenth and beginning of the sixteenth centuries.

Throughout the unit an underlying issue is the functionalism of what was made. Each of the works discussed was not made as a work of art, but served a particular function. There is a fundamental relationship between that function and the material, subject, and size of the resulting work. The artists in question regarded themselves as artisans, supplying products to suit their patrons. Yet what they produced are regarded as unsurpassed works of art. The unit will try to convey how artists worked within the constraints of tradition and function to produce creative, innovative, interpretive, and highly aesthetic works of art. What they created was meant to be beautiful as well as functional, and it is hoped that the works under discussion can be appreciated on both levels.

You will encounter a whole host of terms; many may be unfamiliar. Others are familiar but now in a new context. "Humanism" and "Neo-Platonism" are key terms for understanding the culture of Florence; "perspective" and "proportion" are significant for understanding aesthetics; "school" is a term associated with related groups of artists. "Classical," "harmony," "balance" are all ideals adopted by artists of the time and re-used by historians to describe the aesthetic goals of the artists.

You will be encountering works of art of utmost beauty from two cultures, Italian and Northern, which are vastly different in appearance. Whereas in Italy natural observations were always moderated by generalization, by larger principles of order and composition, in the North nature was magnified, transfixed, and sometimes made more mysterious. In Italy the optimism about life and humanity—the love of beauty for its own sake—is palpable; in the North the fervent piety and respect for all creation is magical.

In this unit, you will learn to:

- Understand the reasons for the revival and adoption of classical forms in fourteenth- and fifteenth-century Italy.
- Recognize and identify a distinctly Northern European, non-classical tradition in the visual arts.
- Identify the goals of the Early Renaissance sculptors, painters, and architects and the works that represent their watershed achievements.
- Appreciate the new techniques in painting, sculpture, and architecture that made many of these achievements possible (and in some cases, failures).
- Recognize and identify the disguised symbols in Northern painting and understand the intellectual basis for such symbolism.
- Understand the various kinds of patronage—court, burgher, religious, communal—and how patronage both generated artistic activity and affected forms and themes.

## Part 1
## THE EARLY RENAISSANCE IN ITALY

## The Fourteenth Century

The late thirteenth and fourteenth centuries witnessed and grappled with extremes and paradoxes of all kinds. Immense wealth coexisted with dire poverty; great beauty thrived beside the most grotesque ugliness; ideals of love and compassion emerged in an age of the utmost cruelty and violence; life could be long and filled with suffering, or it could be pleasurable yet cut short at any moment; love of pageantry, rampant materialism, and wanton self-indulgence coexisted with ideals of austerity; debates raged over the relative merits of the active versus the contemplative life, the spiritual versus the temporal, and the universal versus the specific. Practical needs often modified ideals. The collective still found a need for individual leadership. Mercantile capitalism was curbed by the Church's prohibition of usury, yet the Church provided a solution by accepting donations of money or art as an expiation for the sin of moneylending. This promoted the flood of artworks for the Church from the thirteenth century on. A hierarchical mental framework underlay not only religious and philosophical principles but social reality as well. Yet such hierarchies were tempered by the egalitarian tenets of the universal Christian faith.

In this world where the most simple reality coexisted with an intellectual complexity we now find hard to fathom, the imperative for tradition was as strong as the irresistible impulse for change. Religious images in particular were governed by formulas for materials, composition, color, and content to make them efficacious and understandable. Yet they were also the products of creative minds who altered and reinterpreted in sometimes subtle and sometimes daring ways the traditional materials and subjects with which they were entrusted.

Artists then found themselves facing a difficult challenge. By introducing humanity and realism into traditional sacred subjects they could potentially profane them. Yet the impulse for change and the interest in making images accessible to the viewer was also strong, and the examples we shall see resolve the paradoxical needs of sacred and secular in remarkably inventive ways.

While collectivity was still an important force in social interaction, individual ingenuity and action also gained importance, finding their best expression in the resourceful mercantilism in Italy (the Italians led Europe in capitalist ventures), while knights and chivalrous deeds were glorified in the North. A competitive spirit which motivated countries, regions, and city-states also motivated families and individuals to proclaim their status through heraldry and personal insignia, family emblems and coats of arms, and eventually through portraiture of all kinds. There emerged a thirst for individual ideals in the form of sculpture (see Orsanmichele), paintings (of historic men and women), and literature, while war called for models such as Cicero, Caesar, and Hannibal. The role of the Virgin as intercessor on behalf of the faithful was endlessly celebrated. Entire cities such as Siena were dedicated to her; all regarded her as their protectress and guardian, and the events of her life were endlessly recounted in paintings and sculptures.

The universities, which had been founded in the thirteenth century and which fostered the scholastic system of learning best exemplified by St. Thomas Aquinas's *Summa Theologica*, were led into new avenues of inquiry and interest in the fourteenth century by the so-called humanists, of whom Petrarch is among the most celebrated. The humanists collected and translated Latin and Greek manuscripts, studied the ancient authors, and began to rethink humanity and religion in different terms.

Fourteenth-century Europe was marked by cataclysms of all kinds—floods, bank failures, wars, and famine—but no event was more destructive or more lasting in human memories than the Great Black Death of 1348. Gruesomely described in chronicles and literature from all over Europe, the plague claimed its victims swiftly and cruelly. Sufferers died within seventy-two hours, afflicted by bloody, foul-smelling boils, often alone and unattended. "Father abandoned child, wife husband, one brother another," wrote Agnolo di Tura, a chronicler of Siena, where more than half the citizens died. "Nobody wept no matter what his loss because almost everyone expected death." From one-third to one-half of Europe's population was swept away by this tidal wave of disease. People said and believed: "This is the end of the world." Demons and devils and the punishing hand of God extracting payment for human sin were seen as the source of this calamity.

Debate still goes on about the effect this event had on the arts. The Northern artworks under discussion (by the Limbourg brothers and Sluter) were created well after the plague, seemingly unaffected by what had gone before. Those promising geniuses in Tuscany—Giotto and the Lorenzetti brothers—died before the plague of 1348 or during it. Developments in Italy thereafter are more complex than this program has room to discuss. Suffice it to say that one style in fourteenth-century Italy did not simply supplant another, and there existed combinations of ideas and styles.

Merchants and the merchant class emerged as an important force in fourteenth-century Europe's economic, cultural, and political life. Italy's merchants and moneylenders dominated Europe, and Italian money exchange branches made the capitalist mercantile revolution possible. These merchants enjoyed great prosperity yet faced continual admonition against usury and moneylending from the church. By channeling some of their profits into church adornments, merchants could not only proclaim their wealth and family prestige; they could also expiate themselves from the sin of usury, thereby assuring the well-being of their souls.

The patrons were part of an era which thirsted for a more comprehensible and humanized expression of religious ideas. No doubt affected by St. Francis of Assisi (d. 1226), who preached a loving God and the beauty of creation, and whose Franciscan followers soon established monasteries all over Europe, the arts responded with an astounding new imagery. Foremost among those artists who changed the direction of painting was Giotto di Bondone. His monumental figures had mass, weight, expression, and action that were unprecedented in painting. His fame was instantaneous and his impact far-reaching. A truly transitional figure, still thinking in terms of the great unifying systems of thought to organize his chapel, Giotto created figures that are idealized, monumentalized, yet comprehensible mirrors of humanity, and in so doing, he transformed the direction of Western painting.

The program uses the Bardi chapel of Santa Croce in Florence **(G 15.15–15.16),** painted in the 1330s, to show how mercantile patronage affected art. The Bardi, one of Florence's great banking families, commissioned Giotto to illustrate the life of St. Francis on the walls of their family chapel, located just to the right of the main altar of the church of S. Croce. In three successive strips, Giotto recounted six important moments in the renowned saint's life, among them St. Francis's renunciation of wealth, the approval of his rule, his miraculous apparition at Arles, and his trial by fire. Each scene in the St. Francis cycle can

be taken as an individual composition. The characters within each scene are believable by virtue of their dimensionality, their individually characterized faces, and their convincingly portrayed emotions.

As John White explains in the program, perhaps the most moving of all the episodes, however, is the *Death of St. Francis.* In this remarkable fresco, we see Italian painting achieve new heights of mastery and attain new independence, as well as a new orientation towards realism, monumentality, and emotional pathos. Attending the body of St. Francis, who expired at forty-eight, worn and exhausted from lifelong privations, are his fellow Franciscans. While those flanking the saint maintain the dignity of a funeral ritual, those closest to the saint display deeply human emotions of grief and affection. Some kiss his hands and feet, others throw up their arms in sorrow, while in a startling display of anecdotal detail, one of the attendants slips his hand into the exposed wound on Francis's side, a wound which was part of the stigmata St. Francis received during his miraculous vision of Christ on the Cross. Here a follower doubts but has his faith reaffirmed. The great mystic who helped alter the direction of medieval thought is here depicted with the realism, compassion, and dignity which he himself helped foster. Giotto's figures gain mass, monumentality, and dignity from their almost schematic description, their clear, thick contours. Carefully balancing between the general and the specific, the sacred and the human, Giotto added features and gestures based on observation of nature to individualize each character, and to satisfy the decorative and narrative needs of his drama. Giotto achieved unparalleled greatness in his painting, and established a new syntax of painting because it was accessible to the onlooker not only in subject but psychologically, emotionally, and rationally. This was a great change from the schematic, symbolic, and psychologically remote pictorial language of the past.

The Bardi Chapel is an example of private patronage in fourteenth-century Italy. Our next example reflects communal patronage. In nearby Siena, a hill town that even today preserves much of its medieval flavor, another native style took hold which found one of its greatest exponents in that endearing genius Ambrogio Lorenzetti. One of two brothers who probably died in the plague of 1348, Ambrogio left behind a remarkable body of original paintings, each type a revolution of its kind. His Madonnas are among the most tender and affectionate ever painted, but the most often quoted of his contributions is the fresco cycle depicting the effects of Good and Bad Government, painted in the 1340s for the town hall of Siena **(J 495; G 15.22–15.24; H&F 9.55).** Painting in the visual equivalent of the vernacular syntax that so enlivens the charming narrative of Boccaccio, Ambrogio depicted the comforts of urban and country life under the protection of good leadership. In a bustling city, full of open shops where merchants trade or apprentices learn, we see the happy citizens, dancing ladies, richly attired riding parties. Just as revolutionary is the other half of this fresco, in which the benefits of rural life are described. The first Western "landscape," this mural takes us among the well-cultivated hills and valleys outside Siena's walls, where the peasants tend their crops or flocks, the gentry set out for a hunt astride noble steeds, and the poorer citizens go about on foot. Ambrogio's painting ranks among the first truly secular paintings to come down from fourteenth-century Italy.

Within this well-ordered hierarchy everyone seems contented and well cared for. Such an ideal, of course, could only be attained through the help of the Virgin Mary, to whom the city was dedicated and who protected Siena's wise rulers, but the ideal Ambrogio depicted concerned the pleasures of this world and not the concerns of the next. By infusing his image with endless details based on natural observations and thereby making it precociously real, Ambrogio invited a naturalism in painting that would fully develop only in the following century.

A more startling and dramatically different interpretation of life is found in the third example shown in the program: the Triumph of Death Fresco painted for the Camposanto at Pisa by a Sienese-trained artist **(G 15.25).** Whether or not this masterpiece was created after the Plague of 1348, this fresco (produced for a burial ground) sets forth the extremes of existence which so profoundly preoccupied fourteenth-century minds. A riding party sets out to find pleasure and stumbles across corpses in various states of decay. As we see, these elegant men and women recoil from the horror of what they see and smell. In another scene, a musical party composed of young men and women in the full bloom of their youth amuse themselves in a garden, completely unaware of the angel of death about to descend upon them. Here we know that they will soon face the certitude of death. Although they lack the awesome simplicity of Giotto's monumental Bardi chapel, these works of Ambrogio Lorenzetti and the Pisan painter speak to the onlooker on a similar level of accessibility, using greater amounts of detail, both anecdotal and realistic, to convey their message.

## The Fifteenth Century

Within this century many dramatic changes took place. Before 1400 few people could read, and only scholars were literate in Latin or Greek, but by 1500 the literacy rate among the entire populace was rising. Time was viewed by the medieval man as a continuum which originated with the Creation and headed ominously toward the Last Judgment. The Renaissance gave rise to a historical perspective of an epochal past, separate and distinct from the vastly different present. In particular, antiquity, which had been regarded as a pagan era—historically and religiously a misguided precursor to the onset of enlightened Christianity—was now seen as a golden age of great thinkers and heroes, writers and artists and builders who developed models for Renaissance artists and writers to emulate.

Man, in the medieval mind, was born tainted with original sin. Moreover he was dependent on the benevolence of Christ and on intercessors such as the Virgin to protect him from evil. By 1496 the philosopher Giovanni Pico della Mirandola (1463–1494) had written his famous *Oration on the Dignity of Man,* which reaffirmed man's special place in the center of the universe, midway between God and Matter. Man's role as an active participant in both worlds was upheld, and man's freedom of choice, his own character, and his strength of mind were viewed as important factors in man's own self-development. Life was still a matter of extremes, but in those extremes the individual was emerging as more significant, reliant as much on himself as on God in his path through this world. As his self-perception changed, so did the images man created change. Sculpted figures were freed from their surrounds; they became independent. Records of individuals abounded as painted or sculpted portraits. The depiction of religious subjects took on a much more secular tone. Where in the Middle Ages human beings were content to have their generically described proxies kneeling diminutively and circumspectly in the presence of a divine being who visually and symbolically overpowered them, Renaissance man stepped boldly and confidently—and sometimes arrogantly—into the world of divinity, and the distinction between the two realms became less clear. Thereby man became as much the focus of such images as the deity did, with profound consequences. Attention shifted more and more to humanity, and with this development we can find the birth of the modern concept of the individual whose duty it is to fulfill his or her potential.

It should come as no surprise, then, that we view the Renaissance itself largely through the accomplishments of its individuals: its leaders, humanists, patrons, and artists, all of whom shaped a culture that was unlike any other in reflecting their specific world, their temporal as well as their spiritual aspirations. Exceptionally gifted, these men had the courage to utilize their talents, the ambition to change their world, and the resources to commemorate themselves. Leonardo Bruni, the humanist scholar who wrote a history of Florence and helped guide his city through her troubles with the Milanese Visconti, was commemorated by his city with a new kind of tomb. Brunelleschi, who triumphed over the problem of the Cupola, was an instant hero. And the Medici family dominated fifteenth-century Florence with their wealth, their political aspirations, their humanistic orientation, and their patronage of the arts.

One of the conundrums of history is, "Do men shape events or do events shape men?" Modern scholars tend to view events as the more overpowering force; the nineteenth-century view of individuals shaping events in the Renaissance is now regarded by many as old-fashioned and is being replaced by new emphasis on historical context, on functions of works of art, on the role of tradition, and so forth. Regardless of our viewpoint, when we deal with the Italian Renaissance, we are forced to deal with individuals, and remain fascinated by their remarkable achievements.

Fifteenth-century Italian developments are complex: on the one hand, there is an urge for simplicity, order, cohesion and separation; on the other, a drive towards realism and intricacies of meaning. As the arts loosened themselves from their architectural contexts, independent forms of painting and sculpture emerged, and their formats became simpler. For example, the complex and additive nature of polyptychs which flourished in the fourteenth century were gradually replaced in the fifteenth by the single round, rectangular, or other single-paneled shape. While art still served various functions, the functions became more diverse and were often secular in nature. The development of mathematical perspective was an important organizing tool which not only endowed the image with a rationally conceived, spatially convincing atmosphere, but also gave it a cohesion and simplicity which was different from the more additive imagery of the previous era. The imagery that was developing was more accessible on human terms— intellectually, psychologically, in scale, and in subject matter. From Brunelleschi's dome on the cathedral at Florence to Donatello's *David,* we see an extension of these principles.

On the other hand, Renaissance artists and thinkers also saw the potential for increased sophistication in their subject matter inherent in the ever-increasing realism with which they portrayed their ideas. Perhaps inspired by Northern artists, whose realism contained equally complex iconographic programs, such paintings as Botticelli's *Birth of Venus* and his *Primavera* reflect a tendency wherein the content of an image is magnified and made more intricate by the very explicitness with which each component of the image is described. There is so much potential meaning in each element of Botticelli's paintings that a single, satisfying explication has yet to be found.

Finally, in all of our Italian examples we will discover a search taking place for ideas and for perfection—a quest for beauty which takes its models partly from nature, partly from antiquity, and partly from intellectual and spiritual needs.

## Florence

Already an important artistic city in the early years of the Trecento, Florence had eclipsed her Tuscan rivals by the end of the fourteenth century. Like most of Italy and much of Europe, Tuscany had been devastated by the Black Plague of 1348. But not all medieval Tuscan city-states recovered at the same pace. Lucca and Pisa ultimately became satellites of Florence. Siena, which did retain some territory and was a rival to Florence artistically as well as politically, began to languish economically.

Unlike the hill towns of Siena, Lucca, or Orvieto, Florence fills the bowl-like valley of the Arno River, embracing both sides of this watery access to the sea, enabling Florence to carry on a flourishing wool-finishing industry, a trade which extended throughout Europe as far as England in the fourteenth century. Wool, silk manufacture, but more importantly, banking and money-lending had earned Florence her wealth. Within her protective walls, over five miles in circumference, forty feet in height, and accented by fifteen massive gates and towers, lay a city boasting some 110 churches and monasteries, an impressive town hall with a nearby loggia, a venerable baptistry, a duomo, and hundreds of artisans' shops. Florence was thriving, although its population was still recovering from the setback of the plague. (From some 90,000 in the fourteenth century, it had probably declined by the early fifteenth century to about 45,000 to 50,000.) Even as it flourished, Florence faced continual threat from without. Her principal worry was Milan.

Milan's rulers, the Visconti, had extended their power over Piacenza, Bergamo, Cremona, and Pavia, and by the late fourteenth century were threatening Tuscany. In 1401 Florence was engaged in mortal combat, from which it was rescued only by Gian Galeazzo Visconti's sudden death from the Plague in 1402. The Florentine Republic survived, and the city saw herself delivered from extinction. If the Great Plague was seen as a punishment by God in 1348, it was seen as divine deliverance in 1402. But Florence's survival was also seen as a triumph of her leaders, of her fortitude, courage, and skill, and of her steadfast opposition to tyranny, which continued to be tested intermittently by the Milanese. Florence did not finally rid herself of the Visconti until the decisive battle of Anghliari of 1440, in which the Milanese were vanquished once and for all.

During these years of strife, Florence was guided by humanists. Her chancellors were scholar/teachers who found models for thought and guidance for behavior not only in the Bible but in classical sources. Coluccio Salutati (d. 1406) discovered lost texts by Cicero and used these and other texts from Republican Rome to defend freedom against tyrants. Leonardo Bruni (d. 1444) not only knew classical Latin but also Greek, and he revived the Greek concept of will and will power—the innate ability within human beings to discipline the self (called by Italians "virtu"). These brilliant scholars fostered the notion of self-determination as opposed to fate, turning Florentine minds to the thought of human, individual potential. In their work can be found that rebirth of a world seen in human terms which forms the basis of the Renaissance, even as it mingles with and takes expression in older and still venerable notions of spirituality and allegiance to family and tradition.

By the fifteenth century, the Florentine commune had gradually abdicated its rule to the "signori," leading families who gained their power from commerce, not from inherited nobility. The Albizzi, Capponi, Strozzi, Pazzi, and of course the Medici, took over the guidance of city affairs, reflecting the power of individuals to shape their own lives. By 1434 the Medici ruled in all but name; Cosimo de' Medici (who has been called a benevolent tyrant) chose to retain the appearances of being a mere citizen, abjuring all other titles, and using the existing political structure and the tools of artistic patronage to achieve his ends. With Cosimo began a Medici domination of Florence that lasted well into the next century.

Fifteenth-century Florence honored old ideas even while new ideals were emerging. Buildings such as the Baptistry and Orsanmichele, constructed a century or more earlier, supported decorations which reflected both old and new attitudes about humanity. Political and societal organizations such as guilds, confraternities, and families were the traditional context within which new attitudes and art forms were born.

## The Baptistry doors

Most surveys of art cite the Baptistry door competition of 1401 as a paradigm of the new developments in Florentine art in the early fifteenth century. The competition *is* useful, not only because the date (1401) conveniently falls at the century's beginning, but because of the inherent drama of the event. A competition is announced and many artists join the contest for the coveted prize: the commission to decorate one of the oldest and most revered monuments in Florence—the Baptistry. The winning artist (Ghiberti) does go on to glory and gains immortality as a sculptor, while the loser (Brunelleschi) becomes an architect, perhaps even more famous. Here facts rival fiction for power and suspense. In a larger sense, the Baptistry doors exemplify how changes emerge within a traditional context.

Since the patron saint of Florence was John the Baptist, her Baptistry, built in the eleventh century, was a particularly important site for decorations. Flush with wealth in 1330, Florence had commissioned the decoration of the first of three sets of bronze doors from Andrea Pisano, who cast scenes from the life of John the Baptist in relief, set within quatrefoil frames. Embellishment of the other doors was halted by the flood of 1333, a banking collapse, the plague of 1348, and subsequent economic decline.

But by 1401, the Arte di Calimala, the merchant's guild, decided that the financial reverses that had interrupted its support of the decorative program of the Baptistry had subsided sufficiently, and they mounted what was to become the most famous competition in the history of Italian art, the competition for the second pair of bronze doors for the Baptistry. Of the many artists who entered the contest, only six were selected: each was given a year to design and cast a bronze panel representing the same story, "the Sacrifice of Isaac." Bell-founders, goldsmiths and woodcarvers, all established men, competed. But

symptomatic of the spirit of the new age, they were outdone by two young upstarts (both barely twenty) whose competition models still survive. These reflect a new understanding of human form based in each case on the study of nature as well as of antiquity. The patrons narrowed their selection to two revolutionary works, preferring them over the more conventional solutions of others.

Brunelleschi's version **(G 16.1)** was the more dramatic of the two and utilized aggressively the quatrefoil design. In Brunelleschi's version, the obvious symmetry and aggressive shape of the quatrefoil itself gives form to the composition within. Abraham fills the right side, the angel the left, and Isaac the middle. Brunelleschi chose the most violent moment of the story, when Abraham's hand is stopped just short of Isaac's throat. The scene has the feel of battle between two protagonists rather than of divine intervention. Throughout, figures, drapery and forms take their cue from the quatrefoil. Look at Isaac's angular form and see how its bend reminds us of both the lobes and angles of the surrounding frame; the swirls of Abraham's drapery, the ancillary figures, all push into and bend in relation to the overall configuration of the quatrefoil.

In Ghiberti's version **(J 479; G 16.2),** the overall asymmetry of his composition (the essential characters are crowded into the right half of the picture) places Abraham in dead center. Both he and Isaac turn slowly and more gracefully in contrast to the rigorous geometry of the frame. Isaac is turned outward to us, so that the action projects in and out of rather than parallel to the frame, and gives Ghiberti the chance to show us a youthful nude form in great detail. Isaac's form almost gives the impression of an antique torso having been copied by Ghiberti to achieve such a well-muscled and beautifully proportioned form. One is so lost in admiring the figure that its purpose in the story is nearly forgotten, though we are quickly reminded when we consider the knife approaching Isaac's throat.

Action and counter action, push and pull, the formal and narrative are aggressively bound together in Brunelleschi's work, while a more subtle sense of gradual transition from one event to another in Ghiberti's narrative lessens the narrative and emotional tension, leaving us free to admire his artistic skill. Clearly the patrons made a decided choice in favor of perfected beauty, in favor of realism tempered by grace and artifice, while also showing a marked preference in both finalists for imagery that in part at least had an antique derivation. In its calm, engaging, and rationalized approach, Ghiberti's winning panel demonstrates one of fifteenth-century Florence's first steps in a new artistic direction.

## Orsanmichele and its niche sculptures

If the Baptistry competition reflects a new direction in the taste for relief sculpture, the embellishment of nearby

Orsanmichele demonstrates a remarkable change in the appearance of monumental sculpture.

Just a short walk from the Baptistry and Florentine Duomo sits a remarkable building called Orsanmichele, which now ranks as one of the world's greatest treasure houses of art. A former grain storehouse and grain exchange, Orsanmichele preserved a miraculous painting: *The Madonna of the Pilaster*. Popular worship of this image in the fourteenth century eventually rendered grain dealing within the same building impossible. Hence the painting was enclosed by a tabernacle completed in 1359, and as the grain dealers cleared out of the first floor, the arched openings were closed up and twelve tabernacles or niches were set up, each one given to one of the more important guilds which formed the company of Orsanmichele. Each guild was expected to supply a statue of its patron saint for its niche and would worship at this niche on that saint's day. Production of sculptures was again interrupted by economic reverses until the early fifteenth century, whereupon the new generation of extraordinarily gifted sculptors (including Ghiberti, Donatello, and Nanni di Banco) produced for the guilds statues of various patron saints. Nanni di Banco supplied for the masons and carpenters (Maestri di Pietre de Legname) their patron saints: the four crowned martyrs, or "Quattro Coronati"—four Christian sculptors who refused to make pagan images for the Roman emperor Diocletian **(J 536, 537; G 16.4).** Ironically, Nanni used Roman (pagan) portraits for his models to give physical form to his Christian saints. Taking on the dignity, the monumentality, and the reserve of Roman republican sculpture, Nanni's saints become at once historically immediate, identifiable with the past, and a model for the present. Antiquity is used in a double sense in Nanni's work then, both for narrative and aesthetic reasons.

Ghiberti worked at Orsanmichele a number of times (interrupting his activities on the bronze doors to do so). For the bankers (the Cambio), Ghiberti cast a bronze St. Matthew between 1419 and 1423, creating a noble and elegant bearded former moneylender who became one of the first of Christ's four original followers. Having designed the niche, Ghiberti ingeniously solved the problem of a halo for his saint by using the scalloped edges of the shell design behind the saint's head to serve this traditional function.

Comfortable with the Gothic conventions of elegance and linearity, Ghiberti used these devices to maintain the hierarchical superiority of his subject. Much closer to our world perhaps than the sculpture we saw at Chartres in the previous unit, Ghiberti's St. Matthew remains psychologically remote from us. Moreover, the conventions Ghiberti relied on maintain St. Matthew's decorative integrity with the architectural setting. Ghiberti's saint, with his tangle of hair regulated into lissome patterns and symmetrical ringlets, and with his gestures carefully balanced, adheres to aesthetic principles which had their origins in a previous century. Yet the unity of the whole figure, the integration of the pose and the graceful contraposto underneath the limpid drapery, shows Ghiberti's careful study of antiquity which endowed his sculpture with a totality and cohesion that look forward to future developments.

## Donatello's *St. George*

Between 1415 and 1417 a singular genius, Donatello, approached the armorer's commission for their patron, St. George, with unprecedented interpretive skills. Equally successful as the abstract symbol of the armorers, or as a model of courage for Florentine citizens, Donatello's *St. George* **(J 541; G 16.6; H&F 10.15)** is a revolutionary work because it is no longer simply a symbolic form but a potent psychological presence. Not content to describe his saint's appearance, Donatello grappled with the more difficult task of describing his subject's state of mind and succeeded in presenting him in such a way that St. George's courage seems to come from his character and not from divine intervention. How far this great work is from the nearly schematic and remote presences at Chartres cathedral! As you have seen in the program, the psychological description Donatello presented is complex and subtle. The courage in St. George's face is one born out of the recognition of danger joined with the resolve to marshal one's resources to resist one's fear and thereby overcome external threat.

Psychologically, philosophically, and formally, Donatello's St. George recalls the Greek ideal of "sophrosyne" in which self-knowledge begets self-restraint. It is coupled here with that other Greek concept, "arete," or personal prowess and personal excellence. If the metopes of the Parthenon (notably the victory of the Lapith over the Centaur) represented those ideals in ancient times, then they are recaptured in the fifteenth century in Donatello's St. George. He has nothing if not prowess; he demonstrates physical strength disciplined by a rigorous mind. Ancient values, born again in the Florentine idea of "virtu" (manly self-determination and active participation in public affairs), are silently yet grippingly expressed in Donatello's ever alert, ever vigilant character. Prowess, excellence, courage were all required during Florentine battles with Milan, and one should not be surprised to see a sculptor of the era express such ideals in a figure of the patron saint of those who manufactured weapons, shields, and other implements of war. With his feet firmly planted, his posture alert and guarded, his face a thoughtful essay on courage, this St. George displays the moral earnestness (the "gravitas") espoused by Florentine humanists. His thoughts turn inward while his attention is forever turned outward to the real world, where enemies abound and danger lurks.

Donatello's *St. George* retraces the original steps by which the real, historical, human George gained the courage to become a great warrior and thus to earn his place among the pantheon of venerated saints. His battered shield affirms battles fought and won. Donatello makes the human element as important in the sculpture as the symbolic one, if not more so. And thus a religious ideal is reconceived on a human scale, in human terms physically, and—more importantly—psychologically. Ultimately, Donatello's St. George becomes again an ideal, but he is a human model for us, a hero of this world.

Donatello took sculpture in a dramatic new direction with his *Saint George*. He integrated the mind and body of his character, giving him a compelling presence and identity. He also isolated and liberated his saint from his setting. The individual figure is no longer simply part of a larger architectural program, as was the case with the Gothic cathedral sculptures we saw. (Think back to Chartres, with its many figures still submerged—if somewhat independent—within the form and content of the cathedral itself.) Donatello's Saint George overpowers his niche; he is conceived in the round and can seemingly step out from his setting at will. The niche becomes a doorway permanently guarded by this ever vigilant knight.

The patronage and history of Orsanmichele demonstrates again the fifteenth-century Florentine mingling of sacred and secular, individual and communal, symbolic and real. Bred out of the competitive spirit of the age in which the guilds competed with one another in producing sculptures of their patron saints, the resulting complex had civic as well as religious implications. The various artists who produced sculptures for the niches of Orsanmichele interpreted their subjects in diverse ways; the most revolutionary was Donatello. His *St. George*, only the first of many memorable personifications he created, charted a new course in the history of Italian art. Man as hero has replaced saint as symbol as the heart of his new sculpture.

## Donatello's *David*

Discussions of Renaissance art all point to Donatello's *David* (J 548, clpl 65; G 16.12) as a groundbreaking accomplishment. Celebrated as the first freestanding statue to be seen in the round since antiquity, as you will remember from the program, *David* still elicits commentary on his unabashed and sensuous nudity, and on his perfection as an example of bronze casting. Sensitively fusing natural observation with idealization, motion with inaction, and engaging the viewer from every angle, Donatello's *David* does mark a turning point in Renaissance art, setting the taste for freestanding sculpture, for nudes, and for well-cast, sumptuous bronzes.

Despite its importance, there remains little firm information about the exact date of *David*'s production (dates range from 1430 to 1450), its original setting, and its exact patron. We do know it was done for the Medici for their private enjoyment, and it is first mentioned in 1469 as set atop a column in the center of the courtyard of the Palazzo Medici. Scholars now point to the interesting correlation between this colonnaded courtyard inspired by the antique (peristyle) court and the first classically inspired sculpture at its center. Fascinating connections have been established with various members of the Medici clan; some scholars see a connection with Cosimo, who may have adopted David as the emblem of his triumph over enemies during his exile in 1434, while the laurel leaves marking David's victory are connected with Lorenzo de' Medici.

Lack of precise dating prevents a definitive statement about just which Medici commissioned *David*, but that the family would adopt such a symbol with both biblical and classical connotations should not come as a surprise, since we know the Medici as humanists who looked to the Bible and to antiquity for their intellectual models. That *David* was intended for private enjoyment goes far to explain both his nudity and his reflective mood.

David's nudity and his quiet introspection are the most emphatic features of this subtle and complex image. His hat and boots and the feathered wing sliding up his thigh all underscore the soft, adolescent body exposed in its undress. Nudity of this type is traditionally a matter of private delectation and tells us more about the patrons' love of sensuality than it does about the artist's often mentioned homosexuality. We are placed in the position of voyeur by virtue of David's self-absorption. Having accomplished his heroic deed, David is posed not as victor, but as a vulnerable boy. His classically inspired hip-slung pose underscores David's pubescent delicacy and emphasizes his sensuality. While David languishes over this trophy (Goliath's head) he is lost in thought—perhaps considering the nature of his triumph—leaving us free not only to consider the biblical and moral implications of his story, but to meditate on youth and old age, on life and death, and on the transient nature of human perfection.

An engaging personality, David is also a complex symbol, derived from many sources; his story comes from the Bible, while Donatello's inspiration must have come both from antiquity and natural observation. When studied in books, *David* takes on the small scale and sensuous beauty of antique small bronzes. Individually owned, privately handled, often calm and introspective, these were nude figures (Hercules, for example) described in a state of inaction. Donatello might have had such a figure in mind, and transcending his source, made the figure nearly life-sized and gave it the credibility of a life study and the personality of a specific character. An antique cameo from the Medici collection reveals a possible model for the putti on David's helmet, while David's face has been related to the classical Antinous type (the youthful male beauty of antique legend whom the emperor Hadrian loved, mourned, and celebrated in so many images). David's pose displays Donatello's adaptation of the classical contrapposto, which here with its angled arms and bent knee gives a sprightly action and rhythms to the quietly passive figure. Yet the specific details of musculature and gesture are derived from long and thoughtful analysis of a model posed in Donatello's studio.

Despite *David*'s purpose as a personal belonging, its potency as a symbol was not lost on others. In an ironic historical twist, it became a Florentine trophy when the Medici were expelled from the city in 1495. While goods from the Palazzo Medici were sold at an auction at Orsanmichele lasting some days, Donatello's *David* was dislocated from his intimate courtyard setting and carted to the courtyard of the Palazzo della Signoria (also known as the Palazzo Vecchio) in full public view. *David*'s pedestal was emblazoned with four new civic coats of arms and *David* was transformed into a symbol of Florentine republicanism triumphing over Medici tyranny. Dwarfed by the enormous civic hall around him, *David* must have seemed a rather puny public symbol. The need for an emblem more suitable to the Palazzo Vecchio prompted the decision to place Michelangelo's purposeful and grandiose *David* in front of the Palazzo Vecchio in 1504.

## Brunelleschi's cupola

Perhaps no single monument symbolizes the triumph of the Renaissance more effectively than does Brunelleschi's cupola **(J 449, 450; G 16.15).** Capping Florence's great cathedral, Brunelleschi's dome presides majestically over the Florentine skyline and remains the one symbol by which Florence is best known. Appropriate for a cathedral which owed its existence to the competitive spirit of Brunelleschi's medieval ancestors, the cupola became the

largest dome Europe had seen since antiquity, marking Florence's triumph over her rivals with this impressive symbol of civic, sacred, and personal power, and creating a touchstone for future buildings to emulate or excel.

As we have learned in the study of Chartres, every medieval city had a cathedral (*duomo,* in Italian), which was the bishop's seat. The cathedral was maintained by the city and was at the heart of its identity. Thus when Pisa and Siena outdid Florence with their cathedrals in the late thirteenth century, the Florentines were not pleased. They set about correcting this imperfect reflection of their civic pride by having Arnolfo di Cambio design a large cathedral. Begun in 1297, and revised somewhat in 1367, the grand Duomo rose bit by bit, its long flanks composed of patterns made by alternate groupings of green, pink, and white marble, and the transepts and choir made up of five-sided arms embracing the octagonal shape from which the drum for the cupola would rise. In a fit of optimism characteristic of these early Florentine builders, they planned a dome larger than any they had ever seen and which they themselves had never experienced building. Perhaps they anticipated a roof for the dome analogous to that which covered the adjacent octagonal baptistry, but more likely they predicted that their descendants (for they knew they would likely not live to see the building completed) would have the solution. They predicted correctly. They left their descendants a problem which would become Florence's greatest architectural achievement when it was solved. And the solution sprang from the ingenious mind of Brunelleschi, whom we last met as a losing contestant in the Baptistry competition of 1401.

Filippo Brunelleschi, Cupola of Florence Cathedral, begun 1419. (MICK GOLD)

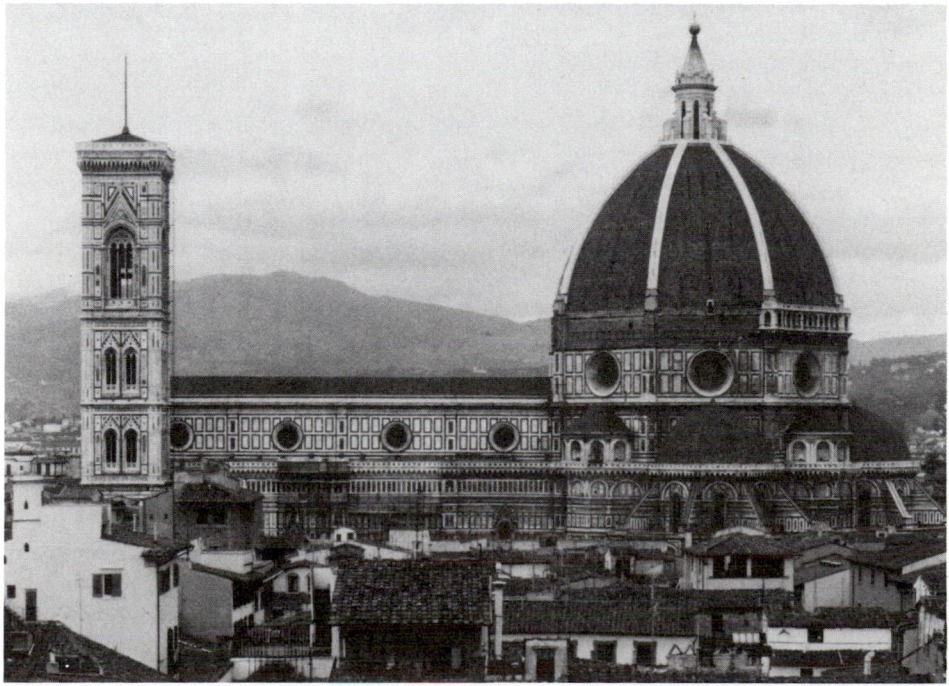

The firm assurance with which the cupola sits on its drum belies the struggle to achieve its creation. Work on the Duomo had come to a halt in 1410, when the building itself and the drum had been completed. How to build the dome remained a seemingly insurmountable technical and architectural problem. The Opera del Duomo (Cathedral Works), financed by the Arte de Lana (Wool Guild), consulted with various architects, including Ghiberti and Brunelleschi, about how to cap the drum. The great challenge was presented by the fact that the octagonal drum could not accommodate the buttress and scaffolding system traditionally used. No timbers were long enough to span the 140-foot diameter of the drum, nor were there any tall enough to rise to the top of the projected height of the dome. Another problem was that stones built over a scaffolding and held in place by a keystone would inevitably collapse of their own weight in a dome of this size built by conventional means. In 1417 Brunelleschi submitted a plan which ingeniously solved these and other problems. While proposing a revolutionary solution, Brunelleschi (perhaps fearing that others might steal his ideas) refused to submit the required models to the Opera del Duomo. For several years an impasse remained: a commission was not forthcoming without a model, a model was not forthcoming without a commission. Finally, the Opera relented and accepted Brunelleschi's proposal on condition that he submit a model.

Having studied Roman buildings such as the Pantheon, Brunelleschi had some good notions of ancient building techniques, which gave him clues as to how to support the weight of the dome without the aid of buttresses. But his solution was ingenious and unprecedented. Instead of one massive shell constructed as a single unit, Brunelleschi designed three shells, one inside the other: the inner one was to be about seven feet thick, supporting most of the weight, the middle one only three feet thick, and the outer shell thinner still. The two inner shells would be interconnected by a common ribbing, thereby making them structurally unified, but without being crushed from the weight of a single construction. Brunelleschi initiated the solution used for all great domes of the future (Michelangelo used it for his dome of St. Peter's, and Christopher Wren adapted the same principle for St. Paul's Cathedral in London). Brunelleschi's model convinced the Opera and he was allowed to proceed.

Adapting a complex network of herringbone brickwork to carry weight away from the ribbing, which he learned from the ancients, and overcoming innumerable problems (including the fear of his own workmen, who occasionally went on strike), Brunelleschi oversaw the construction of both inner shells, the stairways between them, gutters to throw off water, and openings to admit light and reduce wind force.

Built over medieval forms, Brunelleschi's dome is truly Renaissance in character. It both simplified and harmonized its setting, unifying the octagonal drum in a dynamic upward leap. The eight ribs of the external shell (sometimes compared to those of an umbrella) soar skyward and describe for all to see the simple, exact relationships which contribute to their whole. Brunelleschi's dome represents, it is often said, the triumph of individual will over collective doubts—the power of the *human* mind to solve problems. Its presence is a resounding individual accomplishment, crowning the collective effort that was the cathedral. Certainly that triumph of individual will remains today, one of the architectural miracles of the Renaissance.

## Brunelleschi and the Old Sacristy and Church of San Lorenzo

Brunelleschi's involvement with the Old Sacristy and Church of San Lorenzo (**J 551, 552**) is discussed not only because it resulted in two of the earliest Renaissance spaces in Florence but also because in the unfolding events the Medici, who became the leading family in fifteenth-century Florence, first appear as patrons within the traditions of communal religious life.

When the prior of the Church of San Lorenzo applied to the Signoria (city council) of Florence to tear down some houses in order to enlarge his church, he had a plan involving eight of the wealthiest members of the parish, each of whom would pay for building one of the chapels of the new church. Those chapels would become family chapels for burial sites and masses. Giovanni di Bicci de' Medici was the richest member of the parish and supported not only a chapel but also the sacristy. In 1419 Brunelleschi was commissioned to design and construct this vital space for San Lorenzo.

Completed fairly quickly because of Medici money, the "Old Sacristy," as it has come to be known to distinguish it from the New Sacristy created by Michelangelo a hundred years later, was constructed between 1421 and 1429, making it the first truly Renaissance interior space in all of Florence. Here Brunelleschi used mathematical and geometrical forms as visual and spatial analogues for the sacred purpose of the room. Gone are the lofty, superhuman spaces of Gothic cathedrals, where spirituality is given expression in the vast, diffuse, and overwhelming expanse. Instead, we find in this space a sanctity endowed by Brunelleschi's meditation on the purity of the circle, the perfection of the square. Inherently perfect, these simple geometric forms are also easily comprehensible, measurable and quantifiable, and lend to the space created from them an accesibility both intellectually and visually, which profoundly differentiates the sacristy from its medieval counterparts. Though wholly rational in its construction, this sacristy is no profanation of a traditional space, but it takes our rationality, not simply our faith, to engage in a dialogue with the most absolute perfection and the creator of it: God. No space in Florence is more reverent and conducive to contemplation. Its clean surfaces and sparing details (such as the fluted Corinthian pilasters and the continuous entablature) induce a sense of calm and reflection. It endows all who enter it with a dignity based on proportion and design. In that sense, Brunelleschi's sacristy does not diminish our sense of humanity, but underscores it, and thereby it establishes a different relationship with the divine within its walls. We are inclined to meditate on God, neither from fear, nor awe, nor out of a sense of our own inadequacy, but rather with a recognition of perfection which has its roots in our minds and its ultimate manifestation in God.

Meanwhile, Medici interest in the church of San Lorenzo itself continued; with their support, San Lorenzo became the first church in Florence to express early Renaissance ideas. Though initially supported by Giovanni di Bicci de' Medici, the construction was held up after his death owing to various financial difficulties which prevented progress on the transept and nave. Giovanni's son Cosimo de' Medici finally intervened in 1442 and lent the Commune 40,000 florins to complete the construction of the nave in exchange for the privilege of placing the Medici coat of arms in the nave and in the crossing, rendering the church in essence Medici property. Though the process of patronage was traditional, the scope was unprecedented and left the Medici family unchallenged in their proprietorship over San Lorenzo.

Though Brunelleschi retained the basilica shape of the church originally located on the site, he completely rethought the arrangement of San Lorenzo's interior and its spaces. Everything in the church is connected through simple mathematical relationships, not unlike the ones applied in the Old Sacristy. The module of the crossing square is repeated exactly once on each side to make the transept and four times to make the nave, while the aisle bays and side chapels are one-fourth and one-eighth of that square, respectively. Using "pietra serena," a gray-blue stone, to construct his Corinthian columns, Brunelleschi adapted a system of arches and entablatures with similar coloration to define and articulate the architectural system within the pure white walls. Such muted but distinct accents outline the shapes of the spaces and underscore the components out of which they are formed. Gone are the centuries of accretions and decorations found in medieval churches, and what remains is a simple, emphatic architecture that permits contemplation of its pure forms as a means of meditating on the divine.

Each of the components in his construction was measurable, quantifiable, and repeated in a regular predictable fashion. Columns (of an easily measurable height) were capped by a well-proportioned capital; how each component relates to another is clearly described by the pietra serena. Nothing impedes our study of the space and its components.

Standing at one end of the nave, Brunelleschi permitted the visitor to predict the length of the building and how it would look at the other end. Nowhere else in Italy could an artist of the time better learn the lessons of mathematical perspective as columns diminished in size at a rate equal to the regular intervals at which they were placed, and the crossing suggested a vanishing point somewhere behind the choir. Marching ahead of the viewer in a predictable, rational fashion, the sacred world also became in Brunelleschi's hands a perfected and well-modulated extension of our own, reaffirming man's importance in the scheme of things and making God comprehensible as the epitome of order and rationality.

## Brunelleschi and the discovery of perspective

Brunelleschi, as we have already seen, was one of the leading forces of the Renaissance. He completed medieval Florence's greatest architectural monument with a triumphantly Renaissance cupola; he transformed a medieval basilica into a purely Renaissance space. He made architecture obey new mathematical laws that were simpler, more comprehensible, and thereby more predictable than earlier methods. Brunelleschi's San Lorenzo, wherein one could comprehend the length and height and depth of the church simply by measuring the dimensions of a single module, also reflects Brunelleschi's remarkable contribution to painting: linear perspective.

Linear perspective made some fundamentally revolutionary assumptions about the nature of the surface upon which the painter was working. The medieval artist conceived his surface as a flat plane upon which images of symbolic significance would be placed; they might resemble but would remain distinct from our world. Gold was the preferred background, reflecting as it does a radiant and precious light and underscoring the elevated nature of religious subjects. Brunelleschi conceived of his picture plan as a window. Such an idea immediately transforms the relationship between the picture and the onlooker's world, making the picture an extension of, not a division from, the place in which the onlooker exists. Brunelleschi introduced the basic notion that parallel lines, placed at a right angle to the picture plane, would not actually meet, but appear to meet, converging at a single "vanishing point" at the center of a horizon line. Objects seen at various distances would be reduced in scale relative to their distance from the window, just as the columns within San Lorenzo marched ahead and got visibly smaller at a predictable rate. Such a system of perspective had far-reaching effects for painters, for it elevated the craft of painting to the level of a mathematical science; it rationalized and systematized the visible world, giving man yet another means of simplifying, understanding, and thereby controlling the world around him. Interestingly, few Renaissance artists adopted this system to methodically transform the visible world around them into an idealized order. Instead they employed it to give a more convincing presence to fantasies—to create idealized architectural spaces or to make the mysteries of faith more visually compelling. Such was the case with Masaccio.

## Masaccio's *Trinity*

Given the reverential and imposing qualities inherent in Brunelleschi's architecture, one should not be surprised to find a painter adopting its august language to give pictorial expression to religious ideas. Masaccio's depiction of the *Trinity* (God the Father, Son, and Holy Ghost) **(J 560, 561; G 16.28; H&F 10.2)** is given palpability as well as majesty by a Brunelleschian setting and a well-ordered one-point perspective. The coffered ceiling, the noble space, and mighty pilasters endow this image with certitude and power. The orthogonals that meet at the base of the cross give it an order and spatial extension that is wholly convincing.

While it is true that no other painting produced so early in the century more clearly expresses the principles of mathematical perspective, it is equally true that no painting shows more profoundly that this powerful illusionary tool was often used for paradoxical purposes. Here Masaccio uses the new-found tools for illusion to make visible that most irrational and mystical doctrine of the Christian faith: that Divine being has three manifestations, the Father, the Son, and the Holy Ghost; that three are one and one is three. Moreover, Masaccio's whole painting uses the modern tools of rational thought to provide what amounts to a pictorial essay on one of the oldest tenets of the Christian faith: human salvation through divine intervention.

That Masaccio's *Trinity* invokes and describes this process can be known when the whole image and the setting for the fresco is described. Set in the nave of the austere Dominican church of Santa Maria Novella, the fresco includes a skeleton above which appears the familiar reminder of mortality: "I was once that which you are and what I am you will also be." Kneeling above the skeleton are two donors (a man dressed in the costume of a Gonfaloniere and his wife). These donors are placed in a ritual pose and appear to supplicate the Virgin and John the Evangelist (the two traditional attendants to symbolic portrayals of Christ on Golgotha, or Christ Crucified). The image of Christ on the Cross occupies the center of the picture and is symbolically the center and the key to the solution of man's mortal dilemma. That God granted this solution is here portrayed by God the Father's stern and hieratically described presence holding the cross, thus literally and figuratively supporting the key to mankind's salvation, while the Holy Spirit flutters down, sending his blessing to the Son and forming a visual and symbolic link between Christ and God the Father. At once emblem and illusion, Masaccio's painting has all the force of a confounding apparition and all the conviction of a rationally described event. Relying on our rationality to understand what we see, it equally relies on our faith to believe it. By giving the appearance of material substance to a most sacred spiritual concept, Masaccio took a grave risk of demystifying and profaning it. That he succeeded in making his image as solemn and exalted as any examples by his forebears is testimony to Masaccio's genius, and proof that early Renaissance artists relied equally on tradition and innovation in shaping their images.

Though a fresco, Masaccio's painting resembles an altarpiece in its subject matter and size. But Masaccio avoided the multipaneled altar, adopting a single unit into which he placed his characters. All bound together by a perspectival system, they are linked to us by virtue of a space that is an extension of our own, but separated from us by their overpowering simplicity.

Endowed with a supramortal dignity, Masaccio's holy figures adopt the language of traditional religious icons in their postures and gestures. Frontal, hieratic, and resolutely uncommunicative—these lofty beings compel our obedience. Unlike Brunelleschi's humanely oriented chapel, which endowed man with a new-found dignity and importance, Masaccio's *Trinity* is a humbling reminder of man's mortality and a stirring exhortation to consider the spiritual instead of the physical meaning of life.

The identity of the patron for whom Masaccio produced this unusual monument is a matter of debate, though a Gonfaloniere of the Lenzi family still had a tomb in the floor below the fresco in the nineteenth century. The specific function of the fresco is also a mystery, for it has no exact surviving parallel. However, given its components—the skeleton, the donors, and the Trinity—its overall meaning as an essay on human mortality and salvation is compellingly clear.

## The Renaissance portrait

Personality has been both an implicit and explicit part of our discussion so far. Donatello and Masaccio both injected personality into their symbolic subjects, altering the direction of Renaissance sculpture and painting, while Brunelleschi's persona—his ingeniousness, courage, and determination—helped alter the direction of Renaissance architecture. Fra Angelico's private piety underlies the sensitive spiritualism in his paintings. When we turn to Botticelli, the cult of personality becomes not only a by-product but the focus of our discussion, involving, as it does, not only Botticelli himself, but his portraits of others, especially the Medici and the cult of personality which surrounded them in the second half of the fifteenth century.

Botticelli will also help us see again that, for the Renaissance, realism was never an end in itself. For those artists like Botticelli, who were closely associated with the Medici and their intellectual preoccupations with the Neo-Platonic academy, realism permitted the introduction of very complex iconographic programs which rivaled medieval examples for intricacy and sophistication.

In an age when the individual had increasingly become the focus of philosophical interest, portraiture logically emerged as an important art form. Having both public and private uses, portraits celebrated the living, commemorated the dead, and proclaimed associations between families and friends. Portraits in many media flourished in Florence, including sculpted busts, drawings, and wax likenesses (most of which are now lost). Botticelli's *Young Man Holding a Medal* (ca. 1470), now in the Uffizi, allows us to consider two of the most popular forms of portraits in fifteenth-century Florence, the medal and the painted portrait. The painting also allows us to consider how sophisticated and complex portraiture had become by the third quarter of the century, since one image contains two likenesses in a single fascinating context.

The object which the young man presents so prominently is a portrait medal. Medals were among the most highly prized, artistically refined, and personal forms of portraiture which Florence helped popularize. Medals were an ideal format in which to express the Renaissance notion of persona. A profile likeness was accompanied by a personal device and a motto. Generally no larger than the palm of the hand, medals were a perfect union of the private and the public. Made in multiples, medals were exchanged, worn on chains, sewn onto hats or even harnesses, and became an effective means to proclaim one's personal association with another. That seems to be the case here; Botticelli used a gesso cast of an actual medal made for Cosimo de' Medici. The medal was cast on the occasion of Cosimo's achieving the title "Pater Patriae" from the Florentine Signoria shortly before his death in 1464. Just why the young man holds Cosimo's medal and who he is remains unclear. Early scholars proposed that we were presented with a portrait of a medalist proudly displaying one of his most famous commissions. Scholars today feel that we may be looking at a member of the Medici family affirming his family lineage by showing a medal of one of his most illustrious ancestors. Some have gone so far as to identify the sitter as Lorenzo di Pierfrancesco de' Medici, a second cousin of Lorenzo the Magnificent and frequent patron of Botticelli, as we shall see later on. Regardless of the young man's identity, his presence is compelling and animated and exists halfway between the world of the ideal and the real.

Here is a young man whose beauty verges on perfection and falls short only by virtue of the deliberate asymmetry of Botticelli's faithful transcription. Youthful, sensuous, handsome, the young man holds us in his thrall not merely by his beauty nor by his forthright look in our direction, but by the character which animates his entire face. Holding our gaze steadily, the young man seems so lively we almost expect him to speak and tell us about the medal which he holds for us to see. Held up to engage us, the medal also becomes a barrier between us and the sitter. This balance between guardedness and approachability parallels the portrait's balance between real and ideal. The gaze is both steady and shy, the expression

both wary and vulnerable. The sitter is remote not from lack of interpretive skills on the artist's part, but by deliberate choice; both artist and sitter are obeying the conventions of formality imposed on portraiture of the period, which was intended to convey the sitter's identity, his social standing, his affiliations, and, at times, some philosophical or intellectual ideas, instead of divulging the intimate secrets of personality. Thus the medal, the sitter's costume, and the setting (a bird's-eye view of an idealized Tuscan landscape) are "devices," visual symbols to give us clues about how the sitter intended us to understand him. Specific to the time and place in which they were created, most of these meanings are now lost to us, but we can still understand how far both patron and artist have come in transforming likeness into a cohesive personality—an intellectual, physical, and psychological whole.

## Botticelli's *Adoration of the Magi*

One of Botticelli's most celebrated pictures is his splendid portrayal of the visit to Christ by the three foreign kings who followed the star and worshiped him in the stable of his birth. Regarded as the first Gentiles to recognize Christ, these kings were taken as the founders of the Christian faith and viewed as personifications of devotion. As the interest in the Magi grew during the fifteenth century, so did the levels of meanings associated with them. And Botticelli's *Adoration* is (if current interpretations are correct) among the most complex and daringly original of them. Much discussion centers around the figures of the Magi and their retinue, many of whom have such distinctively specific features that they must be viewed as portraits. Their presence in the foreground, dominating the true subject (pushed up and back) is taken as an indication of how daringly contemporary Renaissance Florentines had intruded into holy pictures and, more specifically, how arrogant the Medici had become in their self-glorification. Just who all the people are and why they are in this picture is still a matter of conjecture. If the Medici are present, they may have been included not because of their own ambitions but because of someone else's. The painting may not show us how the Medici saw themselves, but how other Florentines saw them. If current scholarship is correct, the donor in this grandiose assembly of the Magi and their retinue is not the red-clad figure in the center of the picture, or either of the two figures standing confidently to the far right or the left (traditional spots for donors), or any of the more prominently portrayed individuals. Our donor (one Guasparre dal Lama, ca. 1411–1481) soberly looks out at us nearly hidden within the crowd assembled to the right, and points to himself lest we forget who he is. A minor "exchange broker" of questionable ethics with variable fortunes, Guasparre, flush with money around 1472–1475, commissioned the *Adoration* for his small family chapel in Santa Maria Novella. Just who else besides Guasparre is represented in this picture is unclear, though most scholars accept this as a depiction of the Medici family, among them Cosimo de' Medici (d. 1464, known by then as Pater Patriae) as the old Magus. His son, Piero de' Medici (d. 1469), may be shown in the center discussing some point of presentation etiquette with Giovanni de' Medici, while Giuliano de' Medici (d. 1478) looks disdainfully on from the left. Above them, looking out, is Lorenzo de Giovanni de' Medici, while to the right we see an idealized profile portrait of Lorenzo the Magnificent. At the right, coolly regarding the onlooker with a steady gaze as if momentarily distracted from the proceedings by our presence, is Botticelli.

Botticelli's presence should not surprise us, since the tradition for artists' portraits was already established. What fascinates us is the reason for Guasparre dal Lama's nearly disappearing into a virtual re-assembly of the Medici family tree. There seems to have been no official connection between Guasparre and the Medici despite Guasparre's activities as an exchange broker. Perhaps the answer lies in the Medici association with the "Compagnia de' Magi," the lay confraternity dedicated to the Three Kings which operated out of San Marco and whose chief function was the production of the "Fiesta de' Magi," a pageant in which worshipers made offerings to the church in the spirit of the Magi. The *Adoration* has also been associated with the Feast of Corpus Christi, a ritual procession which began in Santa Maria Novella and traveled to the Duomo, to which the Medici have also been connected. Were the Medici merely seen as archetypes of the Magi and their likenesses taken from the medals and used here to lend specificity to an otherwise sacred event? Was Guasparre hoping to elevate himself in the eyes of his fellow Florentines by publicly associating himself with the Medici, or perhaps flatter them into patronizing him? Or did Botticelli simply use Medici as models with the hope of attracting Medici patronage?

Regardless of the answers to these questions, which may never be known, it is evident that the sacred and symbolic function in this altar picture has been joined with temporal political, social, and financial motives. All are deftly woven into an image overflowing with lifelike human beings, who despite their believability have taken on the dignity, the grace, the refinement, and perhaps the meaning of symbols. Each part of the picture and the placement of each character must have had symbolic significance. The obvious references include the stable and collapsed temple (the fall of paganism and rise of Christianity) and the star (the Magi's guide); more subtle is the significance of the placing of laurel plants directly above Guasparre's head and Lorenzo de Medici's. Botticelli's *Adoration* has all the artifice of theater, all the specificity of history, and all the abstract symbolism of a grand and sacred ritual. It demonstrates perfectly how realism was adopted by Botticelli to add increased complexity and sophistication to the symbolism of his pictures.

## Botticelli's *Primavera* and *Birth of Venus*

Probably the best-loved pictures of the Renaissance, Botticelli's *Primavera* (**H&F 10.39**) and *Birth of Venus* (**J 594, clpl 73; G 16.60**) stand as enduring expressions of feminine beauty. The two pictures are also outstanding examples of domestic pictorial decoration that has transcended its function and risen to the level of timeless art.

The *Primavera* has been closely connected to Marsilio Ficino's letter of 1478 to the young Lorenzo di Pierfrancesco de' Medici:

> Venus, that is to say, Humanitas, . . . is a nymph of excellent comeliness, born of heaven and more than others beloved by God all highest. Her soul and mind are Love and Charity, her eyes Dignity and Magnanimity, the hands Liberality and Magnificence, the feet Comeliness and Modesty. The whole, then, is Temperance and Honesty, Charm and Splendor. Oh, what exquisite beauty! My dear Lorenzo, a nymph of such nobility has been wholly given into your hands! If you were to unite with her in wedlock and claim her as yours she would make all your years sweet.

Standing in the center of her own garden and walled off (like the Florentine courtyard) from the outside world, the "Christianized" Venus (note her halo of leaves) or secularized Virgin invites us into her paradise with a gesture equally associated with blessing and welcome. Treading weightlessly on a carpet of flowers, she points toward the three graces, while above her Cupid blindly shoots his arrows of love. To the right, we see the West Wind (Zephyr) chasing his beloved Chloris, who is transformed into the beautiful Flora, while to the left Mercury, dressed in a flaming cloak, plucks golden apples (or oranges). Why Zephyr and Flora are shown is unclear, though they were sometimes compared with Adam and Eve, while Mercury, completely ignoring the female pulchritude so near, is absorbed with the fruits of this magical garden. Just what message was intended remains a puzzle to scholars, but no one disputes that feminine ideals of grace, of love, and of fertility are at the center of the image. A feminine ideal other than Eve or the Virgin Mary has emerged. Allusions to three elements (air, earth, and fire) abound. The painting sometimes described as the pendant to the *Primavera*, Botticelli's *Birth of Venus*, certainly makes a strong allusion to the regenerative power of water, the fourth element.

Hailed as the first Renaissance depiction of a classical female nude, Botticelli's Venus is carried across the waters on a sea shell by sea winds. She modestly covers her perfect body with arms and hair (emulating the traditional Venus Pudica type which Masaccio earlier used so ironically in his description of the Fallen Eve's nakedness). Born from the seafoam produced by the mingling of Uranus' testicles with the ocean—Venus is the mythological Eve, born from Adam's rib.

Though as convincingly massive as the fabled lost Venus by Apelles, that ancient model which some scholars suggest Botticelli was trying to re-create, our Venus is nevertheless so light and graceful as to defy gravity. In an image replete with movement and transition, the *Birth of Venus* (like the *Primavera*) remains static and stable—balancing motion with stability, line with volume, decoration with description. Graced with the most delicate of color schemes, Botticelli's two paintings are equally composed of a sophisticated non-classical linearity. Edges which simultaneously define dimensional forms and create graceful linear arabesques across the image testify to Botticelli's sensitivity and gift for line. Elastic, taut, springy, and attenuated, Botticelli's line has a life of its own which describes complex rhythms and patterns throughout his pictures, and lifts his forms, giving them lightness, fluency, suppleness, and exquisite grace.

Most sources now suggest that the two paintings (though one is panel and the other canvas) were commissioned for the wedding of Lorenzo di Pierfrancesco de' Medici to Semiramide Appiani in May 1482. All agree that the complex mingling of antique themes with Christian morality had as its source the work of Marsilio Ficino, who believed that the revelations of the Bible, the ideas of Plato, and the figures of Classical mythology were all related. Equally important were Ficino's theories of three types of love (carnal, human, and divine) and their relationship, and his use of the three graces to express elements of these ideas. Using St. Augustine as his starting point, Ficino argued for the compatibility of Platonic ideas and Christianity. In Botticelli's *Primavera* and *Birth of Venus,* we see an artist working closely with an intellectual patron, giving pictorial form to his specialized, personal, and humanistic ideas—ideas central to the very particular kind of humanism that flourished at the so-called Neo-Platonic Academy of the Medici. But Botticelli's genius gave these ideas such transcendent pictorial beauty that his paintings have risen above their special, Neo-Platonic, meanings and retain an enduring significance.

## Donatello's pulpits, San Lorenzo

If the creative impulse of individuals can be seen as the overriding force of the Italian Renaissance, and their personalities have become an important part of our discussion, then Donatello's pulpits **(H&F 10.17)** become especially significant, because they show us how far a great creative spirit can go in its own independent development. As Donatello's last works, his pulpits reveal a mind digging deeper and deeper into a private reality to create imagery so highly personal and so far removed from the conventions of the time that it becomes inimitable. The phenomenon of "late style" which we shall see again in the works of Titian, Michelangelo, and Rembrandt here emerges with remarkable originality.

The pulpits were once thought to have been commissioned by Donatello's old friend Cosimo, who revived the early Christian custom of paired pulpits from which the Gospel and Epistles were read, but scholars now suggest that Donatello may have intended one to be used as a pulpit and one to be used as a tomb for Cosimo which was to have been incorporated into a high altar for the church of San Lorenzo. (Cosimo is presently buried directly under the site of the high altar in the crypt.)

What is unquestionable is Donatello's wholly personal and original interpretation of traditional subject matter and his daring use of materials—in this case, cast bronze. In scene after scene depicting episodes of Christ's Passion, Donatello pushes far beyond the limits of narration and technique. His depiction of frenzied grief deals not with appearances but with essentials, from flailing screaming to numbed immobility. In the center of those nightmarish scenes is the *Lamentation,* with its cut-off figures and its empty spaces mingled with overcrowded tangles of humanity. Beneath cascading waves of weightless figures lies the dead Christ, his crushing heaviness borne by a row of mourners. Equally remarkable are the "Three Marys at the Tomb"; here, instead of projecting the episode deep into fictive space as he did with the death scene, Donatello reverses himself and projects a radically unprecedented stage set out into our own space. This not only stresses the physical presence of the tomb but underscores the miracle of the Resurrection—the tomb is, of course, already empty. The Marys are startlingly human in their reaction to this miracle: one clutches the pillar to support herself, while another stares wildly into the casket.

Perhaps most compelling of all is Donatello's interpretation of the Resurrection. Here the dead Christ, having descended into Hell, rises again. Most artists well into the Renaissance treated the subject in its most traditional fashion: Christ is shown defying gravity and lifting delicately into heaven. Donatello, true to his far more personal understanding of this most sacred of miracles, describes the terrible struggle of tortured and decayed flesh trying to come out of that most terrible of sleep—death. Christ is no hero here in the ordinary sense, but a most memorable description of the miraculous power of the spirit over matter; the battle is being won in a slow but inexorable struggle, as Christ's soul reconquers his worn and tired body and forces that body once more to animation.

Using every tool at his disposal, Donatello makes his images at once real and compelling, yet summary. Christ emerges from a jumble of sleeping soldiers, their sleep prefiguring their much more lasting death to come. They are wildly active in their sleep, haunted by nightmares; one soldier with his drawn sword looks as though he is about to ward off an unseen enemy, another reaches into Christ's tomb as if to hold him back, while Christ himself seems far more tired and weary in his state of awakeness.

In this, his last work, Donatello's use of materials is even more daring than earlier. Disregarding the requirements of refinement and polish, he used not only wax alone, but wax dipped in cloth or seared with hot irons to obtain diverse textures. The wax from which the mold for the bronze is made is cut and scoured and gouged to produce unprecedented effects, not seen in conventional bronzes or even in Donatello's own work. A raw and crude power results.

Donatello filtered his imagery through the prism of his own experience, giving heightened believability, accessibility, and emotional expression to his works. Like Rembrandt, Donatello can be viewed as a genius who so transcended the limits of his time that he touched a universal human chord in all of us. In his old age, Donatello seems to have felt free to explore his inner vision and to have felt less harnessed by his patrons. His inner vision was absorbed, as it often is in the works of older artists, with thoughts of death and mortality. His need to give shape to that vision required him to move away from direct and literal description. Yet his cumulative skill and the wisdom of his experience allowed him to take advantage of his material more directly, to let it speak seemingly more crudely but far more powerfully. Michelangelo's *Pietàs*, Titian's *Pietàs* and Rembrandt's late self-portraits all seem to descend from Donatello's late, immensely personal essay on mortality. If his *David* proclaimed his technical and anatomical skills to all the world, Donatello's pulpits established him in his old age as a visionary.

Donatello interpreted his subject matter so personally that the results are no longer explicable within established traditions. No one could have predicted Donatello's version of the crucifixion based on what had come before. Donatello tested the limits of convention to a powerful and raw expression. His saintly characters had become impossibly vulnerable and his human characters daringly unreal. In a wild phantasm that has all the irrationality of a nightmare, all systems, all reality, all rationality is gone—leaving only the subjective ephemera of experience, emotion, and intuition. Donatello's hallucinatory visions on the pulpits looked far ahead to the future, when artists and whole cultures explored the deeper recesses of the psyche. In these last works, the Renaissance as we have come to understand it was left behind, but the very fact that the pulpits were created by one of the exemplary geniuses of the Renaissance demonstrates just how much we owe this seminal period of art. For to the Renaissance we owe not just the first rudimentary notions of self since antiquity, nor the first inklings of the interior workings of the mind, its intellect, its rationality, and its self-discipline. From Donatello's last effort we learn that the stage has been set for understanding the much more complex world of dream and fantasy, which is among the most modern and current preoccupations of our time.

## Venice

Before turning to the North, we should remember that developments in Renaissance Florence were paralleled elsewhere with many divergent styles and techniques. Among the most celebrated achievements in fifteenth-century art are those in Venice, that fabled city of canals and colored bricks which first sprang up as a refuge against barbarian hordes at the fall of the Roman Empire. Safe and secure in its marshy retreat, Venice thrived and developed a vast trading empire in Turkey and Greece. The wealth and splendor that resulted made Venice one of the legendary cities of Europe.

Chief of its fifteenth-century painters was Giovanni Bellini, who is justifiably called the father of Venetian painting. Bellini set the stage for all the great artists to come, and they came in extraordinary numbers: Giorgione, Titian, Veronese, and Tintoretto are just the most famous of the scores of genial painters who thrived in the Venetian climate. For this reason and because Bellini came to know Dürer, the subject of part of a later section, we should consider Bellini, if only briefly.

Born into a family of painters that included Jacopo (his father) and Gentile (his brother), Giovanni (ca. 1400–1470) was well aware of artistic developments in Florence and elsewhere. Drawings from the family studio show us that Jacopo already understood perspective and had an interest in the sculptural remnants of classical antiquity. His knowledge was combined with a particular sensitivity to nature and light, which some scholars claim were in part inspired by Northern realists. Giovanni certainly adopted the technique of oil painting which had gained use in the North and exploited its potential to create subtle areas of color, light, and atmosphere, and to introduce areas of the most detailed realism into what might otherwise have been abstracted forms. Called a "poet of natural appearances" (Pope-Hennessy, p. 51), Giovanni Bellini is regarded as the most accomplished portrait painter of his generation. One of his greatest efforts in portraiture was that of Leonardo Loredan, who was Doge of Venice from 1501 to 1521. A remarkable examination of the Doge's face, Bellini's painting conveys it with the most lifelike detail, and we can see right away how much more attention there is to light playing over the surface of the form, when compared to Botticelli's portrait with its more emphatic use of contour. As light plays over the surface, we are aware not only of the sitter's face but of the texture of his skin, the moistness of his eyes, the sumptuousness of the brocade, and the beauty of the embroidery which surmounts the Doge's hat. Silent, still, nearly stonelike in its remoteness, the portrait is nonetheless remarkably lifelike, animate, and real.

Bellini's portrait maintains aloof distance from the viewer, which is in keeping with the dignity of his sitter's rank. Chief officer of his city, the Doge was the duke of the Venetian Republic, elected for life by its nobles. Doge in one of Venice's darkest hours, Doge Loredan (like Leonardo Bruni in Florence) guided Venice through her perils with the League of Cambrai, an alliance of Venetian enemies who defeated Venice time after time in battle. Leonardo Loredan skillfully employed the tool of diplomacy to save his city from ruin. Exploiting inherent suspicions among the members of the League, Leonardo

Loredan turned them against one another and regained for Venice many of the territories lost in the wars. His gaunt, thin, unsmiling face, which Bellini so compellingly portrayed, reveals some of the steely determination, the cunning mind, and the deft diplomatic skills so carefully concealed behind this imposing face.

Perhaps a year after painting his still-famous portrait of Doge Loredan, Giovanni Bellini turned to a traditional religious subject, the *Pietà* (now in the Accademia, Venice), and interpreted it anew. Traditionally shown weeping over her deceased son, touching his wounds or embracing his neck, the youthful Virgin was often accompanied by Angels or John the Evangelist. In this late example of his work, Giovanni Bellini changed the young Virgin into an old woman, aged by grief; she huddles over the body of her dead son, which seems about to slip and fall to the ground. The ineffable tragedy takes place in the still and silent world of nature, where—isolated and alone—the aged Mary weeps over her loss. The distant hill town and penumbral sky set a reverential and poetic mood for the entire scene.

Using nature and reality to underscore the sentiment of a story exemplifies the lyrical orientation of Giovanni Bellini and his school. Renaissance Florence appealed most strongly to the rational and intellectual aspirations of her citizens; Venice and her painters appealed to the heart. We do not linger long on the systems (if there were any) by which Giovanni laid out his landscape, or his rules of proportion or his canons for Beauty. Instead we find ourselves caught up in the emotion of the image, in which the old woman's personal loss transcends any specific origin and becomes a timeless essay on grief and endurance. Lulled into silence by her private mourning, nature has stood still, time has stopped, and the momentary translates seamlessly into the eternal. Here feelings are not limited to individual characters but are steeped into the whole aesthetic message of the picture. Such an appeal to our subjectivity, then, has its roots as much in the Renaissance as did the rational objectivity of Renaissance Florence.

Just a few years earlier (c. 1485) Giovanni Bellini painted what must be considered one of his greatest masterpieces: the so-called *Stigmatization of St. Francis* **(J 592, clpl 72),** now in the Frick Collection in New York. St. Francis (d. 1226), one of Europe's most influential religious figures, abandoned his wealth and embarked on a life of austerity and piety. His affectionate relationship with the creator and creation helped revolutionize humanity's thinking on the fundamental issues of the nature of God and the nature of man. Key to St. Francis's development was his vision of the crucified Christ. This mystical occurrence resulted in Francis's receiving the stigmata (the wounds of Christ) which, according to legend, he retained until his death. Untold numbers of pictures recount the life and death of this important saint, of which Giotto's Bardi Chapel (ca. 1330) in Santa Croce should be especially familiar.

Most earlier representations of this subject concentrate equally on Francis and the vision of the crucified Christ. Instead, Bellini chose no specific subject and focused instead on the mystical union the saint and the natural world resolved. St. Francis stands outside the door of his rocky retreat, transfixed by the holy emanation of light. Diminished, not overwhelmed by his surroundings, St. Francis here seems part of nature; his meditation on Christ and on nature is celebrated in a communion with them both. If man was the measure of all things in Florence, he is part of a continuum here, and is integrated into nature in a manner which gives importance to them both. Nature, not just man, is a means to know God, and therefore nature, not just man, becomes worthy of depiction.

And how beautifully nature is described here! The liquid, viscous, and translucent properties of oil paint were never more effectively utilized to transcribe the light, the air, and the wonderful texture of the visible world. With all the skill of a keen observer and a lover of natural things, Giovanni Bellini rivals his northern counterparts (from whom such an orientation surely comes) in his ability to describe the phenomena of creation. But unlike the artists we shall discuss later, Bellini introduces a more selective note: his light, though clear, and his hand, though meticulous, do emphasize some details and de-emphasize others. Very likely those that are emphasized (such as the grapevines) had important symbolic significance (a symbol of the Eucharist), but Bellini's more integrated vision also endows his painting with an emotional intensity shared by the figure of St. Francis. Ironically, for a city so devoid of nature (except water), Venice produced a school of painters who developed the theme of landscape more fully than any other of the time.

Letting us enjoy the natural and irregular forms with which the visible world abounds, Bellini did order it according to laws of perspective, though in the St. Francis picture, a vanishing point can be found to the far left of the scene (instead of the mid-center vanishing point commonly found in Florence), drawing our eye along and through the vast natural panorama. Clear, precise, and methodical, Bellini was ultimately not rational in his aims, but evocative, subjective, and meditative. Bellini is celebrating Francis, whose writings contained such charming praise of "Brother Sun" and "Sister Moon" and who regularly addressed nature's creatures as "Brother Donkey, Brother Fly and Brother Bird." As we observe St. Francis's own ecstasy set within the very subject of his reverence, we too become meditative and spiritual—our thoughts and emotions drawn into the mystical reverie before us. Here nature and saint become equal models for our consideration, refreshing our minds as well as our hearts by their beauty and goodness.

If fifteenth-century Florence gave us artworks that provide us with a psychological and rational framework for reality, fifteenth-century Venice introduced artworks that provide us with an experiential framework for reality. Life in Florence, as seen through the art of its day, was one of paradigms, ideals, and perfection. Through self-mastery and proper application of his talents, the individual could strive to emulate the ideals promoted in the images all around him. The art of Venice charted a more emotional and ultimately more far-reaching path for humanity by exploring the subtle and evocative world of mood, feeling, and experience. Florentine art promoted the figure as the subject for art, and so it became in the grand figurative language of the sixteenth century. Venetian art promoted the notion of humanity as the subject for art and thereby paved the way for many of the developments we shall see in the seventeenth century.

---

## Part 2
# THE EARLY RENAISSANCE IN THE NORTH

---

## The Art of Northern Europe

The realism achieved by the early generation of Flemings has often been called mystical because of the reverence and care with which they treated their subjects. Such systems and rational methods of transforming reality into paintings as we saw evolved in Florence were not regularly applied; instead the artist viewed himself not as an intellect as much as a magician, whose observational abilities were harnessed by technical facility to produce minutely accurate replications of nature, which even today we regard as nothing short of miraculous. One feels in Northern painting that there was not the overriding search to unlock intellectual keys to the universe, but the irresistible impulse to describe it. One could also argue that the culture had two conflicting goals—to make the mysteries of faith more visible and at the same time to make them more mystical. Scholars have suggested that the thirst to make the abstractions of religion more concrete came at a time when the efficacy of religion was waning—when many of the older rituals were more strongly codified and emulated, but were empty of meaning.

Another thread that enters the discussion at this point is the role of humanism in the North. Learned scholars had much in common with each other in the North and in Italy, searching through similar ancient texts. But it is fair to say that in the North the critical readings of texts led not only to the adaptation of ancient models by scholars, but more importantly, it led to a critical reading of biblical texts and therefore a fundamental questioning of the tenets of faith as set down by the Church. Certainly by the early

sixteenth century, the North and Italy had parted company, for they were no longer unified under a single universal faith once the Reformation was underway.

The view that emerges about man is more pessimistic, critical, and censorious than one finds in the South. Man in Dürer's world was still tainted with sin, but sin could now be understood in more complex manifestations than mere mortality.

One could argue that Italy, safe and undisturbed by the intellectual revolution of the Reformation and related cultural upheavals, could less interruptedly pursue the aesthetic and philosophical aims which her humanistic and idealistic culture had embarked on. Art uplifted, it pleased, it moved hearts and stirred souls. In the North it served a more critical, didactic, and self-governing purpose, reminding people of their weaknesses more often than providing them with encouraging ideals of their strength. Though Northern art, too, began to interest itself in purely aesthetic issues late in the fifteenth century, medieval preoccupations with mortality and divine deliverance lived on well into the first decades of the sixteenth century. Just as Dürer's mind remained steeped in religious mysticism, so too did that of his contemporary, Mathias Grünewald, painter of the mighty Isenheim altar. In this epic-sized masterpiece, the mortality, the frailty, the suffering of humanity (mirrored in a suffering Christ described as no one had shown him before) is once more hideously confirmed. Painted for those who suffered disorders of the skin, the painting became an unforgettable reminder of human limitations which cannot be overcome without divine intervention. Anyone who looks at this great work is instantly confronted with the very darkest hour of the human condition, and for the moment, at least, the bright, optimistic, sunlit world of the Renaissance seems to have gone out forever, leaving behind a harsher, grimmer reality. That we are heir to both views of humanity exemplified in the North and South is proven by the diverse paths mankind has taken since it moved beyond the Renaissance. Our world has produced great heroes; it retains a faith in individuality, and the sanctity of each life is an avowed idea. And yet our reality still falls short of these ideals; our history of violence and cruelty remains unabated, and fewer people have, as Grünewald's audience did, the hope which the Isenheim altar embodied.

### The arts of Burgundy

Burgundy emerged as a distinctive region in the early Middle Ages, administered by its own rulers. Called dukes, they rapidly gained power rivaling that of kings, and their story is one of successive generations seeking to affirm their prestige, power, and dynasty. Like the Medici in Florence, the Burgundian dukes used art to elevate family prestige, but their needs were overtly dynastic instead of covertly employed to enhance power within a republican context.

Philip the Bold (1342–1404) figures prominently in our story for he ranks as one of the most lavish patrons in a family of renowned art lovers which included Jean of Berry. Like the Italians we have come to know, he inherited a competitive spirit that impelled him to strive to outdo his rivals. Chief among Philip's enterprises was the Chartreuse of Champmol. Unequalled in France, even in the king's court, for the lavishness of its decoration, the Chartreuse was a Carthusian monastery near Dijon whose cornerstone was officially laid in 1385. Thereafter Philip spent enormous amounts on a complex intended to include a monastery, a main cloister, and a smaller cloister designed to contain the tombs of the dukes.

When Philip died suddenly in 1404, his treasuries had been depleted by the expense of the monastery, but his funeral was nonetheless elaborate and lavish. A convent lent the Carthusian monk's habit in which Philip had wished to be robed on his death bed. His sons pawned the family silver to pay the initial funeral costs. The monks of Chartreuse formed a procession to take Philip's body from the Castle of Hal, where he had died, to the Chartreuse in Dijon. There, with great pomp, he was placed in one of the most magnificent tombs ever created.

Claus Sluter, a sculptor from the Netherlands, received the commission to create Philip's tomb. Sluter's genius transformed the traditional function of tomb sculpture into one of the greatest landmarks of fifteenth-century sculpture. Adapting the requirements of the tomb to underscore the rank, dignity, and prestige of the Burgundian dukes, Sluter also commemorated the deceased individual: Philip. Furthermore, Sluter changed the static, frozen, and passive nature of the tomb into an animate, active, and perpetual reenactment of the very funeral procession which carried Philip to his final resting place.

The recumbent duke, resplendent in his white Carthusian gown, is set apart by the dark, somber alabaster slab that supports his body. The inert, motionless quality of his effigy is counteracted by the angels who are engaged in the act of placing a cushion under his head.

Beneath them is a system of arches in which a procession of Carthusian mourners express their sorrow at the loss of one of their chief patrons. Generally treated as supporting figures whose role is analogous to the pillar figures on cathedrals, Sluter's "pleurants" are wholly independent of their niches, using that setting as a space within which to define the active and highly individualized movements. Unified by their nearly identical Carthusian robes, and rendered faceless and anonymous by their drawn-up hoods, the monks nevertheless reveal themselves as individuals by their distinctive actions, no two of which are alike. As one wrings his hands, another wipes tears from his face and yet another twists his body in agony. Each one of the mourners reacts in a wholly personal way to the grief which Philip's death inspired, while maintaining the dignity required of a funereal ritual. By so effectively individualizing the mourners, Sluter not only conveyed Philip's importance to them as Carthu-

sians, but to them as people, and so this monument to Philip celebrates not only his role as a ruler but his human ties to the members of the monastery he loved.

Often called the culmination of the Gothic, with its fulfillment of individualized, more natural, and more animated figures, Sluter's great sculpture can equally well be described as Renaissance for the complete integration of each figure with its well-proportioned forms and the deeply felt fusion of mind and body. Sluter's mourners behave the way they do because they feel, they have hearts and minds, and their bodies convey most effectively what their deliberately obscured spirits experience. Such a wholly integrated human interpretation of sculpture is surely a conception that fulfills much of our understanding of the Renaissance, with its increased emphasis on humanity, individuality, and emotion.

Sluter's tomb sculpture is a further development of yet another great monument he supplied to the Chartreuse, the so-called Moses Well **(J 470; G 18.1; H&F 9.59)**, which anticipates by over a decade Donatello's deeply felt and highly characterized saints in Florence. A fragment of

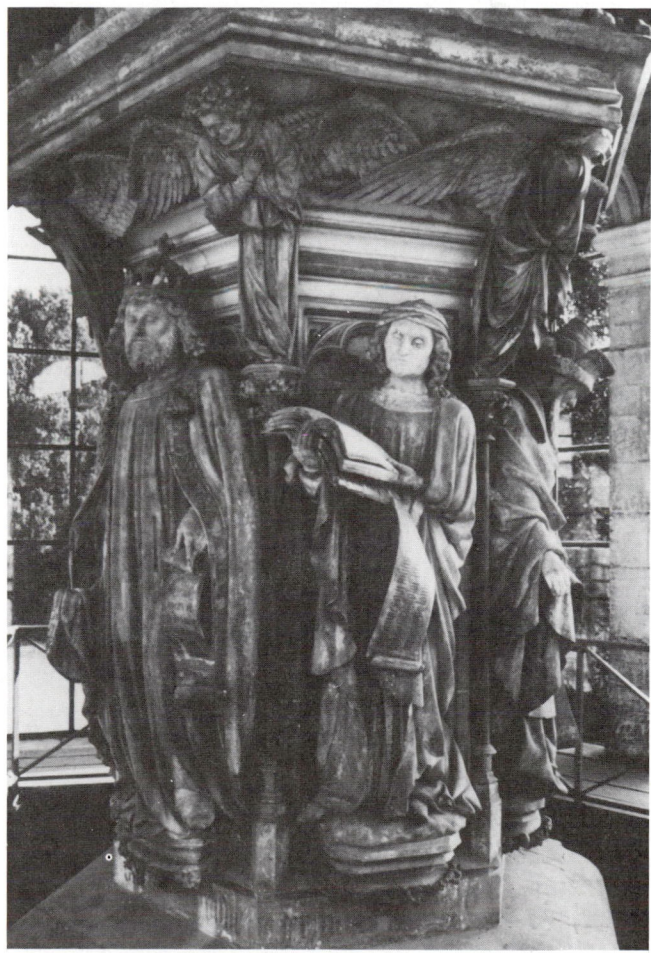

Claus Sluter, Well of Moses, Detail of David and Jeremiah, 1395–1406. Dijon, Chartreuse de Champmol. (KAVALER/ART RESOURCE, NEW YORK)

a large complex devoted to the Crucifixion, Sluter's Well of Moses (ca. 1395–1403) was partially destroyed during the French Revolution. The Crucified Christ, attended by Mary and John, is gone, leaving us with the base consisting of Old Testament figures whose role was to predict the Messiah of the New Testament placed over them. Effectively independent of their setting, these awesome old sages proffer scrolls upon which are inscribed their prophetic messages. Each of these men is animate—alive in terms of gesture, in the realism of his costume and the volume of his figure, but also as a personality. These are men of character, of mood, of conviction, and of temperament. They invite us to consider their message not simply by virtue of their role as abstract symbols, but by their compelling personalities and presence. Short of grabbing us by the collar and forcing us to read their texts, these men could not be more potent in their role as introducers to the event taking place (which once took place above them).

## The Très riches heures du Duc de Berry

Jean de Berry, Philip the Bold's brother, rivaled Philip in the extravagance of his expenditures on art. Instead of a monastery, Jean built castles; his palaces in Bourges, Poitiers, and Paris—just to name a few of the most famous—were legendary. Adorned with equally legendary sumptuous objects, none has become as celebrated as Jean de Berry's Book of Hours (J 504–506; G 18.4, 18.5; H&F 9.56), which today has become a kind of paradigm of princely luxury placed in the service of a religious exercise. The Book of Hours, a type of book containing the Hours of the Virgin and a Psalter, assisted individuals in the practice of private devotion and had become highly popular. Of all the Books of Hours to come down to us, none is as splendidly decorated as the Très riches heures du Duc de Berry (now in the Musée Condé) which was started in 1413 and not finished at the time of Jean's death in 1416. It was produced by the so-called Limbourg brothers, Paul, Herman, and John, who were the most celebrated illuminators of their day. Active in France and Flanders between 1399 and around 1439, the Limbourg brothers may have come from the Lowlands, where they, like many of the artists we have studied, learned the meticulous craft of goldsmithing before turning to the art of manuscript illumination.

The Très riches heures reached a pinnacle of manuscript illumination and led the way for the development of later panel painting, which is why most discussions of early Northern painting center on them. Their refined, elaborate, and delicate style must have appealed to the elevated and courtly tastes of Jean, and so did their subject matter. Each of these marvelous pages outlines with precise accuracy a religious event associated with the Hours of the Virgin, and an event in the life around the duke which could typically be associated with a month of the year.

In these richly illustrated images the medieval system of thought which associated the act of prayer with various stages in biblical history is evident. "Matins," for example, depicts as one might expect "The Fall of Man and the Expulsion," which here is viewed through a lens of fantasy. Refinements of grace and artificiality make the story comprehensible merely as symbol, providing none of the grandiose pathos which so revolutionized Masaccio's "Fall," with which the Limbourg brothers' illustrations have so often been compared. Dainty, graceful, and ritualized, the Limbourgs' Adam and Eve do not permit any lack of manners or grace to intrude on the fairy-like atmosphere of the scene. And such an atmosphere is a matter of choice, since there is ample evidence the Limbourg brothers must have known Italian art. The crouching Adam in the Fall has been compared to Brunelleschi's more potent figure of the Baptistry Commission Panel. Page after page lavishes attention on the rich attire, the pageantry and ceremony of such scenes as "The Meeting of the Magi at the Crossroads" and the Adoration of the Magi. Such luxuriousness clearly served the tastes of the patron well.

But even more famous than the section illustrating the Offices of the Virgin are those which accompany the calendars. Each month is illustrated by an example of secular life which is characteristic of the time of year. Blending topographical accuracy with sensitivity to landscape and details of courtly and peasant life, the calendar illustrations are among the most detailed visual accounts of life in the early fifteenth century that we possess. Here again, painstaking realism is linked with other systems of knowledge—above each scene is a zodiac characteristic of that month. In January, we see Jean himself seated at a court banquet, with a fireplace screen deliberately arranged behind him to set off his head and underscore his place in the scene. Adapted from a traditional theme of an old man by a fire associated with January, the Limbourg brothers made it a specific celebration of their patron in one of his glorious residences. In several instances, October for example, we see a vast castle filling the expanse of the background. Many scholars suggest that these realistic depictions of castles are indeed portraits of those owned by Jean himself. October is equally famous for the informality and harsh realism of the scene portrayed—the peasants farming and sowing the soil. Scowling and thin, the sower has a deathlike pall, which alludes to notions of mortality within a scene of fertility and hopeful regeneration.

Of the many contributions the illustrations by the Limbourg brothers make, the ability to miniaturize and make convincing scenes of an epic scale, to incorporate intimacy into panoramic visions, and to unify the whole of a scene by wonderfully captured light and convincingly cast shadows, had a lasting impact. In these miraculous pages, the Limbourg brothers set the stage for much of what was to follow in Northern art. Called the final masterpiece of the International Gothic style, the Limbourg brothers' *Très Riches Heures* can, like Sluter's work at Champmol, be viewed as the first steps towards Renaissance painting in the North. Ironically, Jean de Berry and the Limbourg brothers all died in 1416, before the great Book of Hours was finished, but what had been accomplished is still a high point in the history of art.

# Northern Painting

In turning to the developments of painting in the North, the program takes us to the mercantile centers such as Bruges where trading, banking, and manufacture had developed a comfortable bourgeois life. Banking and moneylending were a nearly exclusive province of the Italians, and there were Italian patrons among the supporters of the Northern painters we discuss. The sacred and the secular commingle in a new and startling way in Northern painting, as the examples we discuss will reveal. Dedicated to an exploration of all that is visible, these paintings have a religious purpose behind their precocious realism. Far ahead of Italy in the degree of natural observation that was incorporated into religious paintings, the realism found in Northern art further mystifies and complicates the religious symbolism contained within the images, leaving us to marvel and wonder about the exact meaning of each magically described detail.

## Jan van Eyck's *Man in a Red Turban*

Portraiture—the art of creative likenesses of individuals—is a familiar theme. We have found portraits in sacred contexts—the donors kneeling circumspectly and unobtrusively in Campin's *Annunciation* (**J 509, clpl 60; G 18.6**), for example—and the tradition goes back more than a century in both Italy and the North. Think back on Botticelli and Bellini as well. Early likenesses favored profile renderings that concentrated on recording the personal qualities to identify an individual, stressing social standing or piety over any other potential of likenesses.

When the program introduces Jan van Eyck's *Man in a Red Turban* of 1433 (**J 515; G 18.11**), it presents a remarkably precocious example of portraiture. Here no religious pretext is needed for the artist to take a likeness of an individual; simply recording him is justification alone. What a remarkable step this was. It is no accident that it should be the product of Jan van Eyck. A Flemish master of uncertain origins, Jan ranks as one of the most innovative artists of his day, who turned not only portraiture but religious painting in new directions. Probably trained as a miniaturist, Jan's early works were illuminations not dissimilar to the examples we saw by the Limbourg brothers earlier. Jan also adapted the medium of oil paint (which appears to have been known) but applied it in a new and experimental way, fulfilling its potential as never before. His skill at transcribing detail is nothing short of extraordinary and, coupled with his mastery of oil, set the stage for new developments. Of all of Jan's works, none is more startling or more remarkable than his portrait *Man in the Red Turban*. For perhaps the first time in a thousand years, the subject stares out at us and makes contact. Though we now take such contact for granted, it had not been part of the artistic vocabulary for many centuries, and yet it emerges here with such confidence and matter-of-factness that it seems to have always been conventional. Such lack of tentativeness often marks original contributions by great artists, for they had the courage and conviction to see their new ideas take form.

Carrying Jan's signature: "Als Ich Kan [As I can] Joh. de Eyck fecit [made it]"—and dated October 21, 1433, the painting seems to be proclaiming Jan's ability, in fact his *right,* to make portraits, simply because he has the skills and techniques to do them! With the refined skill of a miniaturist, the intensive observational skills of a master, and the flexibility of oil paint, Jan captured every detail of his subject's face. The brow is built up of each minute hair, and the lined skin is faithfully mapped. Details of this portrait will show that Jan even reproduced the fine hairy stubble of an unshaven face. But most remarkable are the eyes, which confront us frankly, confidently, and soberly. Tiny dots of light (reflections from a studio window?) glisten on the moist eyes and these clues, together with the intensity of the expression, which seems to concentrate on itself (as though the subject were looking in a mirror), the relative informality (note the unshaven face), and the red turban (which we associate with workers' wear) have led to the suggestion that this was a self-portrait. Jan's revolutionary work may have been the result of the artist's working to satisfy his own interests and curiosity within the privacy of his studio. Still, the signature and date also indicate that Jan valued his portrait, affixed it in time and place, and identified it for others, which may suggest that the subject was someone else, or that the self-portrait was painted for a purpose other than simple self-interest.

Regardless of the sitter's identity or the circumstances which brought the portrait about, when we look at Jan's *Man in a Red Turban we* find an early, precocious, and well-developed example of a type of portrait which soon flourished, both North and South. Northern portraits seem to have concentrated more on details, while Italian examples built upon a general, more idealized form. Jan's portrait is a sophisticated essay on the balance between general forms and specificity as well as an exercise in form that has meaning, and form described for its own sake. Though charted in minute detail, the geography of the face is contained within the totality of a carefully premeditated overall design. The thin pale features compete with, but are not overpowered by, the large, swirling turban resting on the head. The turban's twists and folds are a virtuoso display of drapery design that is nearly as artificial as the likeness is real—and the juxtaposition of such opposites finds a perfect equilibrium in the hands of a master like Jan, for whom the turban, the face, and the cloak become a beautiful exercise in light, form, texture, and color.

We begin to look for thought and character and though we cannot penetrate the sitter's reserve, we recognize that we have made contact, for the first time, with a person alive in time and space, and whose distance from us is a matter of choice. This man would, it seems, rather look at us and pass his own judgment about what he sees than reveal more of himself than he desires to the strangers staring at him. Here, as in Italian portraiture, we encounter the manifestation of individuality within a civilization that was accelerating the pace at which its art forms and their subjects were liberating themselves from collective anonymity. Though symbols and ideals may have first taken on forceful personalities in Italy during the fourteenth and early fifteenth centuries, as the works by Giotto and Donatello show, the portrait had its greatest early development in the North with Jan van Eyck. When we consider the later developments in the North, with Albrecht Dürer among others, such a circumstance should come as no surprise, for in the North, the complex nature of man and his condition was early on an important subject for artists, writers, and thinkers. Portraits with the psychological intensity revealed in Jan's can be seen as an early nascent manifestation of this interest. The unchallenged master of observation, Jan, to paraphrase the great scholar Max Friedlaender's words, knew fabrics like a weaver, buildings like an architect, the earth like a geographer, plants like a botanist and one could add (at least on this occasion) man, like a budding psychologist.

## Symbolic reality: the Arnolfini wedding portrait

A year after Jan described our turbaned man with such insightful skill, he produced yet another revolutionary portrait, which remains (on the basis of what survives today) unique in Netherlandish painting. In this famous work now regarded as a paradigm of portraiture and early Flemish painting style, we obtain a rare glimpse into the private life of individuals. Portraiture often required a momentous occasion, and so here we are witness to the betrothal or wedding of the Lucchese merchant Giovanni Arnolfini and Giovanna Cenami **(J 516, clpl 62; G 18.12, 18.13),** who were married in a civil ceremony in Bruges in 1434, the year inscribed prominently in the painting.

Appointed special knight by Philip the Good, Giovanni Arnolfini may have come to know Jan—who also inscribed the picture (a brilliant fusion of symbol buried within tangible forms) with the statement "Jan was here." "Here" is the bridal chamber, and Jan describes it down to the last detail while infusing it with the sacredness appropriate to this fundamental step in human life: matrimony. Each object within the room is endowed with special significance and at the same time with the tenderness and special stillness which haunt Jan's pictures. Employing the simple vertical division we know

from Jan's *Rolin Madonna* **(H&F 10.25),** Jan seamlessly joins two worlds, that of the merchant Giovanni—a world of commerce, action, and leadership—and that of Giovanna, the wife—domestic, chaste, pure, submissive, and fecund. Giovanna places her long tapering fingers into Giovanni's outstretched hand, while his other hand makes the same mute gesture of welcome we saw in Botticelli's *Primavera.* Both have covered their heads while taking this sacred vow, though they have apparently removed their shoes, in keeping with their place at home. The dog, sometimes a symbol for fidelity, is also used to designate erotic desire. The candle, associated with images of the Annunciation, also alludes to the "marriage candle" which was carried in the bridal procession and burned until the couple consummated their vows. Clean and orderly, the room symbolizes the purity of the bride, which is also expressed in the color of her dress, combining allusions to love, faithfulness, and purity. St. Margaret, the patron saint of mothers, is represented in a small sculpture near the bed, and Giovanna's domestic role is reflected by her placement deep inside the room, near the bed. Giovanni seems to have just come in through the unseen door, his wider world reflected by his placement nearer the window. As if regarding the painting as a pictorial certificate of marriage, Jan placed his inscription (testifying to his presence within the room as legal witness) just above the convex mirror, which shows in its reflection the artist at his easel, accompanied by a second witness required for a civil ceremony.

Just how unique the painting really is is difficult to determine. Was this portrait, like many others, now lost? Is it the sole surviving example of a popular type? Was it preserved for the present out of mere historic accident, or does its survival reflect the value placed on the artist's skill or the solemn, almost spiritual connotations of the image? Was Giovanni importing to Flanders a marriage portrait custom more common in Italy? No Italian examples exactly like this type survive from this period to clarify the question, nor do we have answers to these and many other intriguing puzzles presented by this remarkable painting. Witness to the wedding of his friends, Jan van Eyck expressed the solemnity of the ritual. Used to giving material presence to holy things, he gave a holy feeling to his description of even mundane reality. He also alluded to the wealth and social status of his friends, and described their home with such fidelity that one still feels his presence. "Jan van Eyck was here." "Only a moment ago . . . his voice still seems to linger in the silence of this room," as Huizinga so eloquently states (*The Waning of the Middle Ages,* p. 259).

Interestingly, Giovanni is described with great specificity, the portrait leaving no doubt that this is the same person Jan had portrayed in Berlin. But what of Giovanna? Her porcelain perfection, delicate features, and blank expression find their closest parallels in portrayals of the Madonna, and not in nature. This is puzzling, because Jan was a skilled portrayer of women, as his portrait of his own wife, Margaretha, painted in 1439, will testify. Was Jan an actual witness to the ceremony? If not, would he not have had access to portraits of both husband and wife? Did he feel it more important to show Giovanna's conformity to the ideals of femininity on the eve of her wedding than to portray evidences of character that might indicate some deviation from that norm of perfection?

## Rogier van der Weyden's *Last Judgment* Altarpiece

In the mid-fifteenth century, Rolin, chancellor to Burgundian dukes, extravagantly underwrote charities and commissioned great masterpieces. In 1434–1435 Rolin had Jan van Eyck paint a Madonna. In 1443 he commissioned the Hotel-Dieu, a hospital for the poor, and inspired King Louis XI to state that he, Rolin, had impoverished enough people to make a hospital necessary. A few years later, Chancellor Rolin engaged van Eyck's great follower, Rogier van der Weyden, to paint a large and impressive polyptych of the Last Judgment (it is nearly eighteen feet wide when open). Finished and installed when the hospital was dedicated in 1451 but probably painted around 1448, the *Last Judgment* is presented as a well-orchestrated rite when the altarpiece is open, and when closed, it celebrates its donors (Chancellor Rolin and his second wife with their coats of arms) by portraying them in fictive niches, kneeling and adoring fictive statues of saints: Sebastian and Anthony. Unlike van Eyck's *Rolin Madonna,* which was privately used for personal devotions and later donated to Notre Dame of Autun (where it was used as a memorial), here ritual, rank, and hierarchy are punctiliously observed—perhaps because of the more sacred nature of the subject matter, or because the function of the painting was always as the altarpiece for a church.

Rogier has also shown a change in style—his naturalism (though still highly detailed) is more selective than van Eyck's, giving a greater overriding sense of order to his image and underscoring the sober message of the painting, which is taken in part from the book of Revelation (20: 11–15): "Then I saw a great white throne and him who sat upon it. From his presence earth and sky fled away. . . . I saw the dead, great and small, standing before the throne . . . and the dead were judged by what . . . they had done."

Christ in glory, joined by a tribunal of apostles and saints, blots out the worldly sky with his celestial fire. Cloaked in a furling scarlet robe, he transcends time and space, hovering on his arc of light, his feet resting on a symbol of his sovereignty over the entire earth. All eyes are turned to the Supreme Judge who, staring out beyond our world, seems aloof to the proceedings he has initiated. His angels call forth long-dead souls who break the earth's crust and beg for his redemption. One by one their souls are weighed. Rogier's gift for precise descrip-

tion makes the end of the millennium believable and comprehensible, yet the ceremony of judgment retains its awesome solemnity through the mighty pageantry. Stained with original sin, humanity faces its reckoning in the same state as the original sinners, Adam and Eve. Indeed Adam and Eve come to mind in more than one depiction of mankind coming to be judged—reduced to puny insignificance against the transcendent splendor of the Almighty Creator and Ultimate Judge.

Long the subject in relief sculpture over cathedral doors, the Last Judgment had found its way into painted imagery already in the previous century. Rogier's version utilizes the rainbow (symbol of God's covenant with man and symbol of the Trinity); a lily and sword represent the innocent and the damned; Christ shows the wounds of his passion; and instruments of his martyrdom are held by angels to either side, signifying the necessity of faith as well as charity to gain entry into heaven.

Flanked by the Virgin interceding for the righteous, St. John, and the trumpeting angels, the Archangel Michael holds the scale that weighs the souls. As the blessed make their way into paradise to Christ's right (our left), the damned reluctantly proceed to Hell and fling themselves voluntarily into the fires, reflecting the words of a local theologian, Honorius of Autun, who affirmed: "The weight of sin upon the conscience is enough to make the damned fall into Hell, as heavy as lead."

No subject could have been more appropriate to the ill and dying, and no artist more successfully unified the symbolic with the real, or to greater effect.

## Albrecht Dürer

While late fifteenth-century painters like Hans Memling were essentially looking back to their great forebears for inspiration, there emerged in Germany a singular artist, Albrecht Dürer, who is universally accepted as looking forward to the Renaissance. Although he was born of medieval parents and raised in a medieval climate, Dürer's massive intellect, diverse interests, and technical mastery carried him forward in new directions. However, he never quite abandoned his heritage, and his career can be described as a strange comingling of the old with the new.

Despite his role as a benchmark for the dawning Northern Renaissance, Albrecht Dürer occupies a unique place in the history of Northern European art and in our discussion. He is the first figure we have seen whose personality emerges as an element in his artistic expression. Every discussion of Dürer, consciously or unconsciously, includes aspects of his personality or character in describing his work. Events from his personal life, quotes from his journals, opinions culled from letters are systematically applied to explanations about the form and content of his complex imagery. Dürer also fostered the apprehension of himself as a sensitive and inspired personality whose special talent set him apart from other men. We see him as an artist in the modern sense of the term, and we tend to evaluate his work as we would a modern artist's. This is not completely wrong, for Dürer in some ways worked like a modern artist—often creating prints without a contract from a patron, relying on his imagination and his skills to make a work that would appeal to his audience. Dürer's massive legacy of letters, diaries, and journals, together with his exceptionally large body of self-portraits (which form a visual autobiography), give us a fuller account of his life than is normally the case for artists of this time. Dürer has left us with a clearer insight into himself as a man as well as an artist. Thus, we are compelled for the first time in this discussion to stop and consider an artist's life before we consider his work.

Born in Nuremberg in 1471, Dürer spent his youth in that city which was fast becoming a center for humanistic studies. A precocious youth, he studied goldsmithing with his father, but his skill at drawing (a self-portrait done at thirteen now hangs in the Vienna Albertina) brought him an apprenticeship with the painter Michael Wolgemut, then the leading Nuremberg painter and also a woodcut artist. Dürer remained with Wolgemut from 1486 until 1489, learning the craft of painting but also the techniques of drawing and woodcut making. This experience instilled in the young man a deep affinity for linearity which formed the basis for his art for the rest of his life.

From the start of his career to the end of his life, Dürer had a special curiosity about the world around him which he translated into drawings and watercolors of exceptional brilliance. His rendering of the *Wire-Drawing Mill* (ca. 1489) (West Berlin, Staatliche Museen, Kupferstichkabinett) was followed by hundreds of nature sketches recording the beautiful, the fascinating, and the bizarre. In 1489 began the first of Dürer's journeys that took him to Colmar where he sought out the renowned engraver Martin Schongauer (who died just before Dürer arrived in 1491). Dürer returned to Nuremberg to marry Agnes Frey, a wealthy burgher's daughter, in 1494, and then almost immediately set out for Italy alone, inspired by his friend, the Nuremberg humanist, Willibald Pirckheimer. Venice made a deep impression on Dürer, as did the great Venetian painter Giovanni Bellini, who received him warmly and loaned him drawings. While in Venice, Dürer concentrated on studying "the naked pictures of the Italians" and took pains to learn anatomy; here began his lifelong interest in the human figure. Dürer's fascination with nature extended to landscape, and among his most celebrated watercolors were the vistas he encountered during his trip through the Alps (*Welsch Pirg*-Oxford). Having returned from Venice in 1495, Dürer was busily producing woodcuts, engravings, and paintings.

In 1500 Dürer painted the third of his memorable self-portraits, which you encountered in the program. Having first portrayed himself as the faithful and youthful lover in 1494, and then the sophisticated "Venetian Gentleman" in 1498, Dürer in 1500 painted himself in the frontal and imposing convention traditionally reserved for the image of Christ (**J 670; H&F 10.41**). Idealized, yet carefully and accurately transcribed, Dürer's last known oil self-portrait seems to reflect his self-perception as an artist whose creative power derived from God, and who, by creating images, was (even more than the average Christian) an imitator of Christ. Now popularly misconceived as self-indulgently flattering, this portrait is also often seen as an exemplar of Dürer's nearly neurotic self-obsession and his deeply felt religiosity.

In the year 1520, Dürer (this time accompanied by his wife) set out on a trip to the Netherlands, via Cologne. Dürer kept meticulous journals and filled his sketchbooks with numerous studies of people and animals. He sketched dogs of all sizes, monkeys, and a walrus, and tipped zoo keepers to let him spend time studying a live lion. In Antwerp, Dürer encountered the dazzling Aztec treasures newly arrived from America: "All the days of my life, I have seen nothing that rejoiced my heart so much as these things, for I saw amongst them wonderful works of art, and I marveled at the subtle ingenia of men in foreign lands. Indeed I cannot express all that I thought there."

At Ghent, he went to see Jan van Eyck's nearly one hundred-year-old painting of the *Adoration of the Lamb,* while at Bruges he spent time admiring Michelangelo's *Madonna and Child,* carved in 1503 for a Bruges merchant.

Having heard that a whale "much more than a hundred fathoms long" had been beached by a storm at Zierikzee in Zeeland, Dürer embarked on a bitterly cold day to see it. Nearly shipwrecked on the way, Dürer came down with a cold from which he never fully recovered. He returned to his beloved Nuremberg at 50, in failing health and with flagging energy. Sensing his own mortality, Dürer painted his last painting in 1526—the *Four Apostles* (**J 673, clpl 90; G 18.41; H&F 11.5),** as it is now known—for the town hall of Nuremberg, and gave it to the city fathers as a lasting memorial. Grand, austere, and monumental, the *Four Apostles* did not remain in Nuremberg; relinquished to the Elector Maximilian I, it was moved to Munich the year after Dürer died.

Fervent, petulant, doomed to fits of melancholy, troubled by frightening nightmares, and nearly obsessive in the application of his meticulous craft, Dürer put every facet of his experience and much of his personality down on paper. Often generous, he was thrifty and cost conscious, as his journal entries tell us. A lifelong Catholic, he greatly admired Erasmus and Luther, the fathers of the Reformation. Restless, he traveled a great deal, but remained a loyal citizen of Nuremberg and gave his final effort to his native town. Endlessly searching for keys to perfection, Dürer also recognized the futility of his quest. Subject to moments of self-pity, he was also capable of humor and possessed an insatiable curiosity. His understanding, however, and his expression of it, was largely visual. "Sight is the noblest sense of man," he once wrote.

"To paint is to be able to portray on a flat surface any visible thing whatsoever."

Dürer spent a lifetime pursuing experience, knowledge, fortune, and fame. It is hard to say what exhausted him more in the end: his pursuit of thrift, his quest for natural curiosities, or his endless search for an intellectual key to the massive details of nature he had assembled. Ultimately Dürer was a great describer, and a visionary, but not a synthetic interpreter. He looked intensely, passionately, and indiscriminately at the visible world or the imaginary one, and left behind an unprecedented legacy of drawings, watercolors, engravings, and paintings. These show us that Dürer did not discover many new truths, but made visible those old truths that his heritage had taught him to see.

## Dürer's *Apocalypse*

The frightening predictions of St. John's Book of Revelations lurked in medieval minds near the century's end. The program used Dürer's *Apocalypse* (**J 669; G 18.36**) to introduce his work, for it appropriately reflects the millennial fears that obsessed Northern minds in the late 1490s, just as Dürer was coming of age. Anticipating or exploiting such fears, Dürer established instant fame for himself by his first published book: an illustrated Apocalypse, printed in 1498, which uses fifteen elaborately carved woodblocks to make St. John's arcane visions materialize. One of Dürer's most famous scenes was that of the *Four Horsemen* as described in *Revelations:*

> And I saw, and behold a white horse: and he that sat on him had a bow; and a crown was given unto him: and he went forth conquering, . . . (Rev. 6,2)

> And there went out another horse that was red: and power was given to him that sat thereon to take peace from the earth, . . . (Rev. 6, 4)

> And I beheld, and lo a black horse; and he that sat on him had a pair of balances in his hand. . . . (Rev. 6, 5)

> And I looked, and behold a pale horse: and his name that sat on him was Death, and Hell followed with him. . . . (Rev. 6, 8)

Using his keen observation of nature, his fertile imagination, and his awesome linear skills, Dürer described the imminent cosmic holocaust that would consume evil and establish a New Jerusalem where the righteous could gather to live at the end of time. Done in the years when people enthusiastically purchased indulgences to assure a place in heaven, Dürer's illustrations of the seven candlesticks, the Four Horsemen of the Apocalypse, the Babylon Whore, and the Destruction of the Earth by Fire must have struck a deep nerve. His artistry has made these images transcend his time, and they remain an indelible part of the popular consciousness.

Using that most abstract of all pictorial means—pure line—Dürer manipulated it with such skill (making it long here, short there, bending it, twisting it, contorting it in impossible convolutions to describe turning drapery or curling hair) that he managed not only to outline St. John's seven candlesticks surrounding God's fiery face, but to model them in space and surround them with atmosphere and shadow. The four horsemen ride on hairy nags, their steeds trampling a multitude of effectively described men and women, while locusts swarm, cataclysmic fires burn, and a mountain plunges into the sea. An eagle shrieks overhead: "Woe, Woe, Woe." Multitudes of details, pictorial effects of every kind; textures, colors, and emotions splash before us in a dazzling and frightening profusion. And all are derived from the simplest of means—black line—here used with such mastery that its equal has never been found. Heir to the attenuated, contorted, and stylized vision of Rogier van der Weyden, Dürer concentrated on its linear aspects, creating a new style, even more excessive in its convoluted linearity and its explosive visual power.

Dürer's *Apocalypse* marks his first great success as a printmaker. Not commissioned, it was produced for a mass audience. Texts printed in Latin and German were supplied but the images were most important and were released without text as well, letting the pictures speak for themselves. Barely twenty-nine when the apocalyptic year, 1500, finally arrived, Dürer lived another twenty-eight years in the new era. Though he contributed to new developments in those years, he also pandered to older traditions. Religious prints, particularly woodcuts, remained an important aspect of his output for the rest of his career. Dürer produced serial narratives more often than any other printmaker. (These were sold at fairs by his wife Agnes, who often nagged Albrecht about the family income.) "The Large Passion," "The Life of the Virgin," and "The Small Passion," as well as other individual prints, were made for a largely devout, still generally illiterate and God-fearing public, which, despite the changes wrought by the Reformation, thirsted for pictures to tell them the biblical stories they all knew by heart.

Woodcuts were a fairly ancient and somewhat crude technique, which involved chipping bits of wood to leave raised edges that would be inked and then printed to make the inked impression on a paper with the image carved out of the block. Engraving was a far more refined, taxing, and meticulous process which Dürer brought to unsurpassed perfection. Using a metal engraving tool called a burin and a copper plate, Dürer gouged out the lines from his plate which would catch ink and register dark when printed. His ability to render texture, light, volume, shadow, and infinite detail on relatively small surfaces makes Dürer's engravings among his most celebrated achievements.

Among Dürer's best-known early engravings is his *Adam and Eve* of 1504 (**J 671; G 18.37**). Showing Eve coolly removing the apple from the snake's mouth as she prepares to offer it to Adam, Dürer has surrounded his figures with the forest of Eden and the creatures in keeping with traditional interest in high symbolic content. Simultaneously, and more importantly, this is Dürer's crowning effort in his exploration of ideal figure types—ideals which he sought not so much in direct observation of live models, but in the surviving examples of antiquity. Not surprisingly, Dürer's Adam finds his ancestry with the Apollo Belvedere in Rome, while Eve has sometimes been compared to the Medici Venus. Aware of the Vetruvian canon, Dürer was forced to abandon it to satisfy the visual needs of the image, extending Adam's left leg beyond the required proportion (in which the body equals eight head lengths).

Much as the cat ensnares the mouse, Dürer's Eve has caught her husband and caused mankind's downfall—leading to the ensuing development of four different temperaments: the elk symbolizes melancholy, the hare the hot-blooded sanguine temperament, the cat the choleric, and the bull, the phlegmatic.

Dürer's Adam and Eve are not the tragically flawed creatures who fled howling from Paradise, as Masaccio portrayed them. Instead they are the embodiment of perfection—ideal human beings from a golden age and from whose downfall can be traced the development of the human temperament, which is the key to human suffering. Here is symbolic language speaking of new concepts—the human condition is explored not so much in terms of sin and salvation, but a biblical theme is used to trace more modern concerns with the human psyche and temperament. Adam and Eve do not remind a medieval worshiper of religious matters, but speak here in a more secular sense—these are paradigms of an intellectual exercise which struggles with artistic, aesthetic, and human issues of a more general nature. This refined presentation must have appealed to the earliest connoisseurs of prints, lovers of learned discourse and beauty. The subject matter might have been medieval, but the presentation is remarkably modern.

Nine years after his *Adam and Eve,* Dürer executed yet another of his masterworks, his *Knight Death and the Devil* of 1513 **(J 672)**. This amazing image harks back to the Dürer of the *Apocalypse,* showing us a frightening world beset by demons and death. Despite the occasional burst of optimistic sun which shone in from the South, in the North there more often rose up the compelling obsession with darkness and death that is visible here. Dürer's Knight, however, seems resolute against his tormentors, moving steadfastly forward, the epitome of courage. He reminds us of several Italian works of an earlier age. Donatello's *St. George* and his great monument to the condottiere Gattamelata in Padua may have helped inspire Dürer, who we know went as far south as Venice at least twice in his life. He might even have seen Verocchio's Colleoni monument unveiled in Venice in 1495. Dürer's great stallion finds its counterpart in the four golden horses—Greek masterpieces—that graced the top of San Marco, while the knight and his armor were drawn much earlier from life in 1498 by Dürer with a note saying, "This was the armor of the time in Germany." Dürer's demons have their ancestry in the imaginative creatures of his predecessor Martin Schoengauer, though Dürer's imagination endowed them with equal measures of horror and comedy. What strikes us finally about this image is the purposeful and courageous progress of the horse and rider, the commanding authority expressed by the knight, whose lance cuts across the whole picture in a powerful stroke, and whose sword punctuates the forward thrust of the horse and its determined rider. As his dog slinks noiselessly along, we nearly hear the jingle of the knight's trappings and the steady clip clop of ironshod hooves. The figure of Death seems powerless to do more than warn our rider, while the devil acts more like an entourage than a threat.

## *St. Jerome in His Study,* 1514

A year after describing his resolute knight, Dürer portrayed his vision of contemplative life. Seated deep within the comfortably but sparingly appointed room is St. Jerome, the renowned fourth-century scholar, who is best known for translating the Bible into "Vulgate," or Latin. A favorite theme of Dürer's, Jerome is deeply absorbed in his task and sanctified by it, as the light from his halo is brighter and purer than any other visible in the room.

Using the limited medium of engraving, in which fine black lines register on white paper, Dürer has miraculously described a complex vision. Light streams convincingly through leaded windows, which cast their shadows on the plastered walls of the niches into which they are set. We recognize the wood grain of the beams overhead, and from there our eyes linger over meticulously detailed accoutrements of the study and can nearly count the hairs on the lion and dog.

Inspired by Jan van Eyck's mystical interiors, the room has some of van Eyck's dramatic perspective as well; the vivid orthogonals give the room a convincing illusion of depth and endow St. Jerome's environment with as much importance as the saint himself. Replete with meaning about St. Jerome as a historical figure and as an exemplar of the contemplative life, Dürer's engraving also reflects an important turning point in cultural thought. Giving us not just a symbol, but a real setting, the engraving sets out for us one ideal environment for human activity—the study. In this image, man is sanctified not only by the life of the soul, but by the activity of the mind. Human intellectual thirst, philosophical discourse, and rational thought were extolled in the medieval concept of the "vita contemplative." But here this concept is given expression not as a symbolic ideal but as a specific reality: were it not for the obvious symbols of St. Jerome—the lion and the cardinal's hat—we would regard this image as a scene of any scholar-monk at work in his comfortable study. Though originating in the retreat from worldly life in the

Middle Ages, the contemplative life shown here by Dürer is not simply an image of a life given over to spiritual contemplation, but a celebration of perfect civilization: the life of the mind which in solitary activity endows man with dignity, with purpose, and with the best this world has to offer.

## Melancholia I

Called the third in the great triad of master engravings that includes *Knight Death and the Devil* and *St. Jerome in His Study, Melancholia* **(G 18.40)** has also been linked with Dürer's earlier *Adam and Eve* of 1504. There Dürer first explored the theme of the origins of man's temperament—while in the *Melancholia* of 1514 he fused medieval concepts about the humor of melancholy with contemporary ones. Most often discussed of all the humors, Melancholy was seen in medieval times to be symptomatic of sloth and weariness brought on by despair. Later it became associated with the introspective intellectual qualities of the contemplative man. By Dürer's time, Melancholy was also identified with creative genius. Marsilio Ficino of Florence linked melancholy with the frenzy of genius in poetry, philosophy, or art (*De vita triplici*, 1482–1489) while Agrippa of Nettesheim (Dürer's contemporary) reiterated these ideas in his *De occulta philosophia* of 1509–1510. Scholars speculate that Dürer must have known this text. In his *De anima* of 1548, Dürer's friend Philipp Melancthon described Dürer after his death as possessed of this most noble state of melancholy ("Melancholia generosissimi Dureri"). Besides Dürer's identification with the subject of Melancholy as a creative artist, sources point to the production of the work in the months following the death of Dürer's mother in May of 1514. A latent obsession, this compelling essay on artistic frustration might have been triggered by a specifically tragic moment in Dürer's own life. It calls up Dürer's warning to his pupils not to think too intensively about art, for "it can lead to the mind becoming overcast and the melancholy spirit taking the upper hand."

Regardless of its origins, Dürer's *Melancholia* ranks as his most renowned though puzzling image. (Seemingly explicit, the image is ultimately elusive—inducing in the onlooker the very state of mind the engraving portrays.) Within an undefined space of vaguely classical derivation, the winged daughter of Saturn stares broodingly into nothingness. Surrounded by discarded tools used for mathematics, measurement, and crafts, Melancholy has slumped into idleness; the limits of her knowledge have rendered action useless, and yet the depth of her understanding gives her no rest or peace. A blazing meteor streaks across the evening sky, the night further illuminated by the puzzling nocturnal rainbow (perhaps alluding to judgment or the brief but imperfect illumination possible through human thought), while that sinister night creature, the bat, spreads his wings to announce the presence of Melancholy. Instead of earth, the element associated with Melancholy, we find a dusky sea, which may refer to the black bile or humor which predominates in melancholic spirits.

The many tools for measuring may refer to that most encompassing of the arts, architecture. This may be a commentary on the imperfection of human activity in contrast to God, the architect of the universe, though scholars continue to debate the meaning of many objects contained within this complex image. The dog, long associated with Melancholy, lies curled up at her feet, while tools of the artisan are strewn about.

Melancholia's surroundings are as disturbingly disordered as Jerome's are reassuringly neat, and her passivity is as restlessly futile as Jerome's is fruitfully active. Of the three ideas described in the master engravings, Melancholia is the one which relies on the mental state of its symbol to carry forth the tale. Her dark frown and glowing eyes, her bent pose, all convey effectively her state of frustrated meditation.

If the *Knight* and *St. Jerome* can be viewed as expositions of the active and the contemplative life, then *Melancholia* can rightly be called an intellectual portrait of Dürer himself. Based on ideas then current, the *Melancholia* is and remains a puzzling assembly of symbols whose significance is still debatable. Why is that ladder leaning up against the wall? Why is the putto astride a grinding wheel and what is he scribbling? To what do all the symbols allude? Of all Dürer's master engravings the *Melancholia* is the only one which bears a title, and perhaps it was the only one to need it. As we study the title another puzzle emerges. Is it a Roman numeral I or is it instead the symbol for self—the *I* of *Ich?* Both interpretations are possible. Absorbed by ideals and deep in the quest for artistic perfection and absolute beauty, Dürer recognized the limits imposed by such a struggle. More than one scholar has pointed out the "Faustian shadow" cast by this image, which falls not only on creativity, but on any quest for perfection. No doubt Dürer experienced these moments himself. Ironically Dürer died just ten years before the historical Dr. Faustus went to his own reward. Dr. Faustus, you will recall, sold his soul to the Devil to learn the very secrets of perfect beauty which Dürer himself had so actively pursued.

## Grünewald's Isenheim altarpiece

The program ended with a startling and horrifying altarpiece which is by an artist as mysterious as Dürer is knowable **(J 667; G 18.34, 18.35; H&F 11.4).** Although we know that this Gothart Neithart (Mathias Grünewald) and Dürer died within months of each other, Grünewald's death is called the end of the last chapter of Gothic art, while Dürer's is considered the close of the first chapter of Northern Renaissance art. Both artists had courtly connections and both were called on to produce a variety

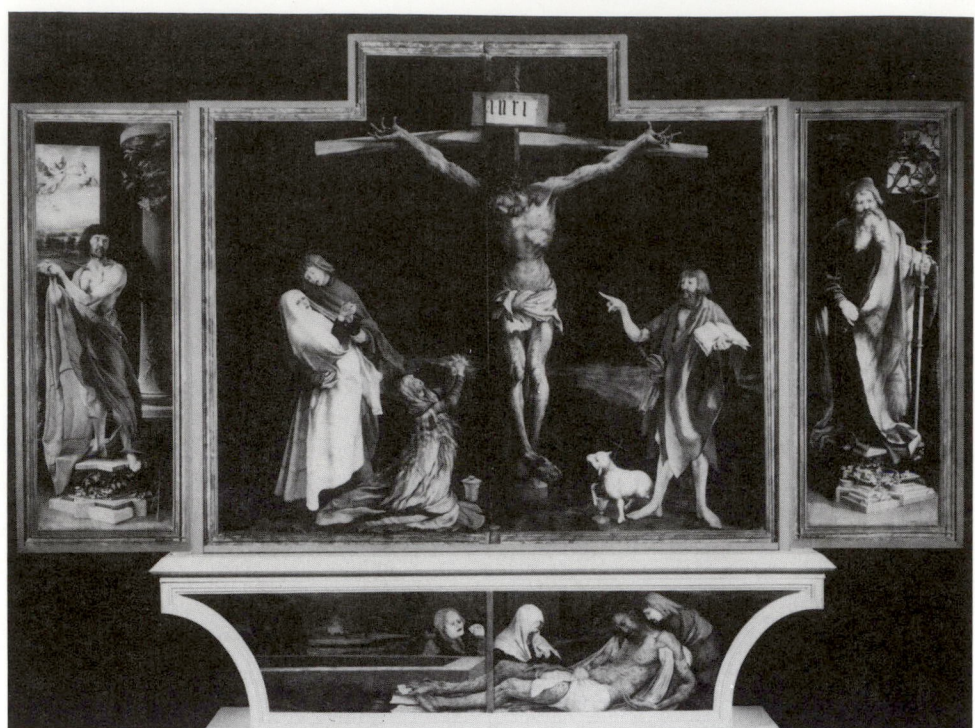

Matthias Grünewald, The Isenheim Altarpiece, Crucifixion, 1510–1515. Colmar, Musée Unterlinden. (Giraudon/Art Resource, New York)

of diverse works (Grünewald, for example, was a designer of waterworks for the Archbishop of Mainz). But Dürer, though a painter, was most effective as a printmaker, while Grünewald concentrated primarily on being a painter. The two artists once shared a patron, the merchant Heller, whose altar by Dürer got wings by Grünewald in around 1508–1510. But Dürer can be seen as looking southward to Italy for inspiration, and to the writers of humanist circles for at least some of his pictorial sources, while Grünewald remained untouched by Italian culture.

Dürer, as we know, on at least one occasion turned to visionary writings (those of St. John and his Revelations) to produce his *Apocalypse* of 1498. Grünewald's work can be linked with another mystic, St. Brigdet of Sweden, whose fourteenth-century *Revelations* were published in Nuremberg in 1501–1502. Her words come to mind when considering Grünewald's most famous masterpiece, done for the Antonine monastery of Isenheim. The Antonines were renowned for their "vita contemplativa"; and they also ran a hospital devoted to diseases of the skin, including the nearly gangrenous infection brought on by the plague and St. Anthony's fire, or ergotism, an often fatal skin disease produced by eating grain infected with the ergot fungus. The hospital became a pilgrimage site for sufferers.

The first stage of treatment for those who came took place in front of the great and complex altarpiece by Grünewald executed between 1505 and 1516. Nine panels composing triple wings folded over carved and painted sculpted shrines of St. Anthony flanked by St. Augustine and St. Jerome. The outer wings of the altar presented the onlooker with the Crucified Christ, suffering not only from scourges and the Cross but also from every imaginable torment of the skin. Here Brigdet's words (produced in the fourteenth and popular well into the sixteenth century) come to mind:

> The crown of thorns was impressed on his head; it was pushed down firmly covering half his forehead, and the blood, gushing forth from the prickling of thorns, ran down in many rills over his face, hair and beard so that it seemed like a river of blood. . . . After he breathed his last human breath, his mouth gaped open so one could see his tongue, his teeth, and the blood in his mouth. . . . His feet were cramped and twisted about the nails as if they were on hinges.

In Grünewald's monumental painting, Christ has taken on the suffering of the world in a very real and gruesome sense, and those looking on who suffered would know that in him lay their redemption and hopefully their cure. In an era when the efficacy of religious totems was waning, Grünewald seems to have turned up the volume, so to speak, to give his image more power. Christ's torture is not simply described, but embellished and made epochally cruel. The drama is portrayed not merely in realistic dimensions, but in superhuman ones. Though working in a medieval context here, Grünewald takes a great leap to the psychologically gripping and mystically transporting images of the seventeenth century, when Catholic cultures reaffirmed the importance of images to convey the irrational and magical powers of faith. Both ages saw efficacy waning, and both combatted it with intensified emotion and theatrical display. The medieval view had begun to regard the human body as more than an unworthy prison of the soul, and thereby introduced naturalism into art. In an ironic twist, that naturalistic vision is here used to show a body that is not only a prison but a torturer. And yet, that image of a prison is designed to provide release. It is painted on an icon dedicated to relieving pain.

Both symbolic and emotionally gripping, Grünewald's dark and gloomy crucifixion shows on the left those mourners traditionally associated with the event: Christ's mother, here seen as a nun, expresses dignified compassion and grief, while Mary Magdalen abandons herself to sorrow, wringing her hands in a manner that echoes Christ's twisted fingers nailed to the cross. To the right, John the Baptist says; "He must increase but I must decrease," to explain his role in man's redemption. With nearly hallucinatory power, Christ looms over the entire scene; the more we look, the more he dwarfs his mourners and establishes his importance in the whole event. Grünewald portrays an equally harrowing entombment in which the Magdalen, John, and the Virgin take on masklike faces of sorrow; Christ's death has clearly diminished them and transformed them into emblems of grief.

On Sundays and special feasts, the outer wings were opened to reveal an array of scenes as dazzling as the outer scenes were gruesome. The *Annunciation,* the *Incarnation* (also called the *Nativity*), and the *Resurrection* are all symptomatic of Grünewald's original treatment of traditional subjects.

To the left, Mary, made visible by the pulled-aside red curtain, receives and is visually overpowered by the angel who delivers the divine decree—the light within the room becoming increasingly penumbral and mystical as it nears the area of the holy protagonists. A master of perspective, Grünewald has treated the subject we saw by Campin quite differently. Besides reversing the order of the characters (having the angel on the right is most unusual), Grünewald also changed the location of the mystery, using the Gothic vaulted church (as van Eyck often did) and exploiting changes in scale to keep the scene active and moving—as though it were continually taking place just now before our eyes. Grünewald reversed his proportional relationships in his middle scene, where the monumental Madonna visually overpowers the rest of the scene. Happily cuddling her child in a cloth reminiscent of the tattered loincloth of the Crucifixion, the Madonna sits in a mystical setting; behind her are mountains whose peaks are enveloped by clouds and celestial fire. God and his Heavenly Host stream down in beams of light. As Mary sits humbly on the ground, surrounded by a few rude belongings, she is venerated by a small crowned figure, enshrined by a glowing aura, a figure many scholars have identified as Mary again in another state of being. This small and unusual figure is joined by a host of glorious angels within a gorgeous and ornate tabernacle. Here in these panels Grünewald shows himself to be a master of forceful description as well as a brilliant interpreter of light. Light of all kinds abounds in his center panel—from the cloudy natural light from the landscape to the right, to the blinding effects of celestial glory, to the shining auras and penumbral emanations for the heavenly hosts, Grünewald was able to visualize them all with brush and oil paint.

Balancing interior spaces to the left with exterior spaces to the right, Grünewald controls this phantasm with careful, simple organizing principles. His Resurrection, set on the darkest of starry nights, is shown at the moment when Christ, now as immaculate as he was once blemished, lightly ascends from his tomb—his fair countenance surrounded by a radiant aura that casts its light over the sleeping soldiers. As the human flesh is transformed into divine, once more Grünewald describes this transformation by dissolving Christ's form into pure light—a process given even greater effectiveness by the sharply defined edges of every material substance that lies beneath him.

## Summary

Grünewald's Isenheim altar closes our discussion of Renaissance art. It shows us how diversely humanity was interpreted during the fifteenth and early sixteenth centuries. Clearly humanity and nature were the focus of interest in both Northern Europe and Italy. But in Italy, reality was perfected and translated into art. Only the daringly expressive images of the late Donatello show us the quest for ideal beauty abandoned in favor of a more subjective and tragic vision. For many Florentines, life, as seen in the art of its day, offered paradigms and ideals. Through self-mastery, the individual could strive to emulate the ideals promoted in the images around him. Calm, temperate, clear, and beautiful, the art of Florence offered an optimistic and structured view of the world.

In Venice, the arts charted a more emotional and ultimately more far-reaching path for humanity by exploring the subtle and evocative world of mood, feeling, and experience. Florentine art promoted the figure as the subject of art and fostered the great figurative language of the sixteenth century, while Venetian art helped pave the way for developments of the seventeenth century.

In the North, humanity was subjected to a more far-ranging and critical analysis. Viewed within the context of creation, humanity never consistently rid itself of the taint of sin, corruption, and mortality. As Grünewald's masterpiece shows us, God's grip on man's mind was as strong, if not stronger, in the closing years of the fifteenth and early decades of the sixteenth century than it had been earlier. This urge to come close to God fostered the

Reformation that ultimately rent the fabric of a unified church. It also reaffirmed a more democratic and egalitarian view of life that found its most glorious artistic expression in the art of Holland in the seventeenth century.

In sum, the artists of early Renaissance Italy established the aesthetic criteria by which we still judge art today. Problems of ideal proportion, of harmonious integration of parts to the whole, of the properties of line and color, the problem of masses in space, and the figure in landscape all trace their origins to Italian art between 1300 and 1500. By contrast, the artists of Northern Europe first met the challenge of realism head on and established the first of many periods in the history of Western art when faithful transcription of visible reality was the ultimate challenge. We see echoes of van Ecyk's influence in the detailed visions of such artists as Gerrit Dou or William Harnett. No longer mystical, such realism still fascinates, but has never surpassed the accomplishments of the first great visionaries of the fifteenth-century Netherlands.

## Textbook References

**J** Janson's chapter on the Late Gothic covers both Northern and Italian masters and applies the concept of Gothic to all Northern artists to the end of the fifteenth century, as well as to Giotto. While this opinion is not compatible with that of the program, which considers the art from this period to be Renaissance, the chapter includes a valuable discussion of oil paint as adopted by Northern artists. Materials and styles are emphasized and explained. Janson traces developments in Florence and then takes the reader to other developments in Bologna, Padua, and Orvieto. Later fifteenth-century Italian artists like Luca Signorelli, Andrea del Verrocchio, and Domencio Ghirlandaio are included. These are worth reading about if you are interested in knowing about how Donatello, Brunelleschi, and Masaccio affected later fifteenth-century Italian art.

**G** Gardner covers the Early Renaissance with a particularly valuable discussion of early Italian painting and gives you the background for Giotto. The other outstanding sculptors and painters of the period are also discussed, as is the impact of the Black Death on the visual arts. Following her useful discussion of the bronze door competition, she fleshes out the developments of Donatello and includes the important and exquisite paintings by generations of painters after Masaccio. There is an insightful discussion of Renaissance portraiture and the chapter provides information on Bellini's brother-in-law, Mantegna, who adopted Florentine illusionism in a sophisticated and independent

manner in northern Italy. Besides Sluter and Burgundian court art, Gardner's chapter on the Renaissance outside of Italy follows Northern art all the way through the sixteenth century. It includes other Northern painters, among whom Hugo van der Goes is particularly important for later Italian developments. Discussions on German painting and woodcarving are worth reading to understand this important medium.

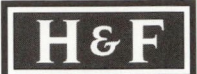 In the space of a single chapter, Honour and Fleming take us from the Gero crucifix of the tenth century to Claus Sluter. They divide the theme between sacred and secular, a division that becomes increasing important for the next chapter. Giotto, Sluter, and the Limbourg brothers are all seen as closing the Gothic. Conceptually, Honour and Fleming's approach is valuable and distinctive for emphasizing the function of artworks and relating the function to the form. In their next chapter, the authors make thought-provoking and valuable comparisons between Florence and the North throughout their discussion, so that you get an immediate sense of the differences and similarities between the two cultures. There is an extensive exploration of the diverse types of art that emerged: the portrait bust, the terracotta relief, the statuette, the humanist tomb, domestic easel painting, cassone, as well as the new use of old mediums (wall frescoes and the like).

**Janson, Part III, Chapter 1: "Late Gothic" Painting, Sculpture, and Graphic Arts, pp. 370–380.** Painting—Flemish: altarpieces, portraits; Campin, van Eyck, van der Weyden, van der Goes, Bosch. French, Swiss, and German: portraits; religious themes; Witz, Fouguet, Stosz. Sculpture: altar shrines. Graphic arts: woodcuts, engraving; Schongauer, the Master of the Hausbuch.

**Part III, Chapter 2:  The Early Renaissance in Italy, pp. 391–435.** Florentine painting: religious frescoes and altarpieces; Masaccio, Veneziano, della Francesco, Uccello, Castagno, Lippi, Fra Angelico. Sculpture: biblical reliefs and figures; Donatello, di Banco, Ghiberti, Quercia. Architecture: cathedrals, chapels, plans; Brunelleschi, Michelozzo. Central and Northern Italian painting: religious themes, portraits, mythology; Mantegna, Bellini, Botticelli, Cosimo, Ghirlandaio, Perugino, Signorelli. Sculpture: Tombs, religious reliefs and figures, portraits; della Robbia, Rossellino, Pollaiuolo, Dell'Arca, Verrocchio. Architecture: palazzos, cathedrals; Alberti, Sangallo.

**Gardner, Chapter 15: The "Proto-Renaissance" in Italy, pp. 528–547.** Early Italian painting: religious themes and altarpieces, Berlinghieri, Duccio, Cavallini, Giotto, Cimabue, Gaddi, Martini, Lorenzetti. Sculpture: pulpits, reliefs, doors; Pisano.

**Chapter 16:  Fifteenth-Century Italian Art, pp.**

**548–597.** First half fifteenth century—Italian painting: religious and battle themes; da Fabriano, Masaccio, Uccello, Castagno, Veneziano, della Francesca, Fra Angelico, Lippi. Sculpture: reliefs, portraits, religious themes; Brunelleschi, Ghiberti, Quercia, di Banco, Donatello. Architecture: cathedrals, chapels, palazzos; Brunelleschi, Michelozzo. Second half fifteenth century—Italian painting: mythological and religious themes; portraits; Pollaiuolo, Ghirlandaio, Botticelli, Signorelli, Perugino, Mantegna, Messina. Sculpture: tombs, portraits, reliefs; Rossellino, Settingnano, della Robbia, Verrocchio, Pollaiuolo. Architecture: cathedrals, palazzos; Alberti, Sangallo.

### Chapter 18: The Renaissance Outside of Italy, pp. 654–707. Flemish painting: religious themes; Broederam, Campin, van Eyck, van der Weyden, Christus, Bouts, van der Goes, Bosch. French and German painting: Fouquet, Dürer, Grünewald, Quatron, Lochner, Witz, Stoss, Pacher, Schongauer. Sculpture: religious figures; Sluter. Illumination: Pucelle, the Limbourg brothers.

### Honour and Fleming, Chapter 9: The European Middle Ages, pp. 282–331. Ottonian art: illumination, crosses, cathedrals. Italian Romanesque architecture: cathedrals (Pisa, Florence, Venice); baptisteries (Pisa, Florence). Northern Romanesque architecture: Cluny, St. Etienne, St. Sernin; Santiago de Compostela; Speyer, Maria Laach; Durham. Sculpture: Autun, Vézelay, Perigord. Illumination: Stavelot Bible. High Gothic architecture: St. Denis, Fontenay Abbey, Amiens, Chartres; Canterbury, Lincoln. Painting: Martini, Lorenzetti. Sculpture: Southwell Minster and Percy Tomb; Reims; Sluter. Stained glass: Chartres, Amiens, Sainte-Chapelle. Illumination: Limbourg brothers, the St. Louis Psalter. Secular Gothic architecture: Naumberg, Cologne; Fossanova; San Francesco, Assisi. Painting: religious panels and frescoes; Berlinghieri, Cimabue, Duccio, Giotto. Sculpture: Antelami, Pisano, Maitani.

### Chapter 10: The Fifteenth Century in Europe, pp. 332–365. Italian painting: religious themes, altarpieces, and mythologies; Masaccio, Robbia, Mazzoni, Fra Angelico, Uccello, Lippi, Della Francesca, Ghirlandaio, Botticelli, del Cossa, Mantegna, Bellini, and Dürer. Sculpture: bronze doors, biblical figures, portraits, and reliefs; Ghiberti, Donatello, Pollaiuolo, Settignano, and Verrocchio. Architecture: palazzos, chapels; Brunelleschi, Michelozzo, Alberti. Flemish painting: portraits, altarpieces; van Eyck, van der Weyden, Chritus, Bouts, van der Goes.

## Study Questions

1. The Renaissance has been characterized as the emergence of the individual over the collective spirit. Is this a correct assertion? How would you refute or substantiate it?
2. What kind of balance is struck between sacred and secular interests in the Renaissance?

3. Much has been made of the Neo-Platonic Academy in Florence. Did this Academy have an effect on the arts? To what extent?
4. Would Brunelleschi's solutions to the cupola of the cathedral at Florence and his designs for San Lorenzo have been possible without a trip to Rome? If yes, why? If not, why not?
5. Why would an artist like Masaccio be attracted to a rational system like perspective to depict his *Trinity?* What effect does perspective have on the image?
6. Donatello has been called a master of his material. Can you think of ways in which the material he used was exploited to strengthen the message of his image?
7. How does the use of visible reality differ in the work of Jan van Eyck and Masaccio? How does this signify a difference in the cultural outlook of the two regions in which these artists worked?
8. Where does portraiture emerge as an important subject first, in the North or in Italy? Why?
9. Oil paint has been discussed as an important medium for Renaissance painters. What are its properties and how does it affect the appearance of paintings?
10. Landscape emerges as an important element in two regions we have discussed. Where and how?
11. Grünewald's use of visible reality is different from Dürer's. How and why?
12. Some works under discussion were not made for any particular patron. Which were they, and how does lack of specific patronage affect their appearance?

## Glossary

**altarpiece** a decorative screen, a painting, or a set of painted or carved panels set upon or behind and above an altar.

**Apocalypse** the last book of the New Testament, also known as the Revelation of St. John the Divine. The book contains numerous eschatological visions which were often represented in early Christian art.

**book of hours** a type of book containing the offices of the Virgin and a psalter, used in private devotions.

**camposanto** burial ground.

**Carthusian Order** monastic order founded by St. Bruno (ca. 1030–1101) at Chartreuse of Champmol in 1084. An eremitic order, its life was, and still is, one of prayer, silence, and extreme austerity.

**Chartreuse of Champmol** Carthusian monastery built by Philip the Bold (1342–1104) between 1385 and 1393 and dedicated to the Trinity.

**commune** medieval form of government collectively organized of representatives of the commercial and professional guides.

**confraternity** a society devoted to a religious or charitable cause.

**cupola** a semicircular or polygonal domed vault.

**device** a symbolic image often derived from classical antiquity and frequently used on medals.

**doge** chief officer of the city of Venice; elected for life by the nobles who alone had the right to vote.

**duomo** cathedral.

**engraving** the process of incising a design onto a plate of metal or wood with a sharp tool for the purpose of printing. The plate when inked will impress a relief picture onto the paper.

**Gonfaloniere di Giustizia** the communal minister of justice, the most important civil authority in medieval Florence.

**hieratic** an elevation above the ordinary human level usually established by formal devices such as large scale, frontality, rigidity of pose, and lack of human expression.

**humanism** a doctrine or way of life centered on human interests or values. A philosophy that asserts the dignity and worth of man and his capacity for self-realization through reason and that often rejects supernaturalism.

**illuminated manuscripts** manuscripts found from the third to the fifteenth century, which were decorated with colored designs and pictures and written in elaborate calligraphy. Early ornamentation consisted of intricate initial letters and calligraphy which reflected the scribe's training. Later the picture itself dominated the text.

**intercessor** one who prays, petitions, or entreats in favor of another.

**keystone** the central stone at the top of an arch which braces the two sides.

**Matins** morning prayers.

**monumentality** a term applied to a work of art that is often, but not always, of a large scale; of an elevated idea; and of an impression of formal grandeur, nobility or simplicity of conception, enduring significance or architectonic quality.

**Neo-Platonism** the ideas of Plato modified in later antiquity by Aristotelianism and the work of Plotinus. It expresses the concept of the world as an emanation of the One with whom the soul is capable of being united in trance or ecstasy.

**perspective** a system of representing three-dimensional objects on a two-dimensional surface which creates an illusion of depth and space. There are several types of perspective, including linear, parallel, angular, and oblique.

**pietra serena** a clear gray Tuscan limestone used in Florence.

**pleurants** mourners.

**prie-dieu** a French phrase literally meaning "pray God." A prayer desk which has a bar for kneeling and a support to hold a book.

**primavera** Italian for spring.

**Psalter** a devotional book containing the Psalms. In the Latin West there was both a biblical and a liturgical Psalter. The biblical contained the Psalms with no additions. The more common liturgical Psalter was divided into eight sections in accordance with the Benedictine rule that monks were to recite the Psalms in full every week.

**pulpit** architectural term for the platform from which a Christian priest delivers his sermon. It is surrounded by a parapet and is reached by stairs. The pulpit is often placed on the north side of the nave and is sometimes covered.

**quatrefoil** four arcs joined together to make a clover form and used as a decorative motif popular in Gothic architecture and design.

**Quattrocento** term commonly used to designate fifteenth-century Italian art.

**Renaissance** a period in Western history and culture (15th and 16th centuries) which renewed the ancient's concern with man and meant an increasing preoccupation with the importance of the individual and with secular life. These ideas were embodied in a philosophy called humanism.

**sacristy** a room in a church where sacred vessels and vestments are kept and where the clergy vests.

**Signoria** the governing council of Florence.

**stigmata** marks corresponding to the wounds in the hands, feet, and side of the crucified Christ, sometimes appearing on the corresponding portions of religious persons after prolonged meditation, and believed to be a token of divine favor.

**tabernacle** a receptacle for the consecrated elements of the Eucharist: an ornamental locked box fixed to the middle of the altar and used for reserving the host.

**Trecento** term commonly used to designate fourteenth-century Italian.

**Trinity** the central doctrine of Christianity; the belief that God is comprised of three parts: God the Father, Christ the Son, and the Holy Spirit.

**virtu** the ideal of manly self-discipline in a public sphere.

**woodcut** a relief printing technique which uses a wood block for printing. The cutter carves a design onto the surface of the block, parallel to the wood's grain, with special tools. In printing the ink catches on the uncarved areas and creates a picture when impressed on paper.

## Artists, Patrons, and Important Personages

**Arnolfini, Giovanni.** Lucchese merchant who settled in Bruges. Important patron to Jan van Eyck.

**Arte de Lana.** The wool guild of Florence; it supported the efforts to build the cupola of the Florentine Duomo.

**Arte di Calimala.** The merchants' guild of Florence; it underwrote the decorations of the Florentine baptistery and in 1401 sponsored the competition for the baptistery doors, won by Ghiberti.

**Bardi Family.** A leading banking family of Florence, who served the kings of France and England during the fourteenth century. Though flush with wealth in the 1330s which enabled them to afford Giotto's services for the family chapel in S. Croce, they had catastrophic losses when they overextended credit to the Duke of Burgundy and King Edward the III of England between 1339 and 1341.

**Bellini, Giovanni** (1430–1516). Founder of a Venetian school of painters that included Giorgione and Titian, Bellini was the great early Renaissance interpreter of landscape, mythology, and sacred subjects, endowing them with great poetic spirit and human feeling.

**Botticelli, Sandro** (1445–1510). Florentine painter. A pupil of Fra Filippo Lippi, Botticelli was patronized by the leading Florentine families, including the Medici. He worked chiefly in Florence, leaving only to participate in the decoration of the Sistine Chapel in 1481–82. The linearity, grace, and poetic sense of his work have strong parallels with contemporary Sienese painting.

**Brancacci, Felipe.** Patron of the Brancacci family chapel, which contains Masaccio's fresco cycle.

**Brunelleschi, Filippo** (1377–1446). Florentine architect. Trained as a goldsmith, he was also a talented sculptor and entered the competition for the Florentine baptistery doors. After losing to Ghiberti, he turned to architecture and created, among other masterpieces, the dome of Florence Cathedral, an engineering feat unrivaled in his own time and still celebrated to this day.

**Bruni, Leonardo** (1370–1444). Florentine chancellor (1427–44) who guided Florence through her troubles with the Visconti of Milan. A humanist, Bruni took courage, and inspiration, from ancient Greek and Roman writers, whose examples he used as models for contemporary Florentine patriotism. His *History of the Florentine People* took nearly thirty years to complete, and this achievement was celebrated in Bruni's tomb, done ca. 1445–50 by Antonio Rosselino in S. Croce.

**Cambio.** The bankers' guild of Florence; it commissioned Ghiberti to cast a bronze St. Matthew between 1419 and 1423 for their niche at Orsanmichele.

**Corazzi.** The armorers' guild of Florence, for whom Donatello executed his marble St. George between 1415 and 1417 at Orsanmichele.

**Donatello** (1386–1466). Renaissance Italy's greatest sculptor. From his St. George to his Mary Magdalen, Donatello injected personality, character, and mood into his figures. He had an unerring sense for materials as well as form and is one of the earliest artists whose career shows distinguished and original developments at every phase of his life.

**Dürer, Albrecht** (1471–1528). Painter and engraver. Dürer is regarded as the greatest of all German artists. His graphic works outnumber his paintings, and he raised engraving to the level of great art. Dürer's two trips to Italy helped bring Italian art to the North, but his greatest contributions to Northern European art were his keen observation, his thirst for knowledge, and his unsurpassed skill as a draftsman.

**Ficino, Marsilio** (1433–1499). Florentine philosopher, who under the patronage of Cosimo de' Medici gained access to the ancient manuscripts in the Medici library and established the Platonic Academy at the Medici villa at Careggi. His great contribution to the thought of the period was his revival of Plato, whom he studied through the works of St. Augustine, and whose ideas he reconciled with Christianity. Ficino placed man at the center of the universe and also espoused the notion of Platonic love—a non-carnal affection through which God could be contemplated and celebrated.

**Ghiberti, Lorenzo** (1378–1455). Goldsmith and sculptor who won the 1402 competition for the bronze doors of the baptistery in Florence. He worked on these doors from 1403 until 1424 and then was commissioned to produce the third doors, on which he worked from 1425 until 1452. Ghiberti's work retains a decorative and refined delicacy, testimony to his training as a goldsmith. His *Commentaries* are the first autobiographical material from a Renaissance artist.

**Giotto di Bondone** (1266–1337). One of Renaissance Italy's greatest painters. Giotto was a pupil of Cimabue and recognized as revolutionary by both Dante and Boccaccio. His development of massive, monumental, and grandiose figures which relate to and yet are elevated above the human realm forever altered the direction of Florentine painting. Giotto's altarpieces (Ognissanti Madonna), his fresco cycles (Arena Chapel, Padua; Bardi and Peruzzi chapels, S. Croce), and his crucifixes (S. Maria Novella Cross) are all significant departures from past traditions and have never lost their place as some of the greatest accomplishments of Western art.

**Grünewald, Mathias** (ca. 1460–1528). Mathias Gothart Niethart, called Grünewald; one of the most original painters of Northern Europe. His work departed from tradition in both its imaginative use of light and its exaggerated, evocative realism. His Isenheim Altar is considered his greatest work.

**Guasparre dal Lama** (ca. 1411–1481). A Florentine money-changer now known as the patron for Botticelli's *Adoration of the Magi*, which features portraits of the Medici family.

**Jean of Berry** (1340–1416). Jean, Duc de Berry; brother of Philip the Bold. A lavish patron of the arts, he built palaces in Bourges, Poitiers, Paris, and elsewhere. He is best known for the manuscripts he commissioned, especially the Limbourgs' *Très riches heures du Duc de Berry,* which is the epitome of late medieval illumination.

**Limbourg brothers.** Paul, Hermann, and John Malouel; the most noted Franco-Flemish illuminators of their time (fl. before 1399–ca. 1439). They trained with a goldsmith in Paris and then worked primarily for the Duc de Berry. The *Très riches heures du Duc de Berry* (1413–ca. 1416) and the *Heures d'Ailly* (ca. 1402) are two of their most important works.

**Loredan, Leonardo.** Doge of Venice, 1501–1521.

**Lorenzetti, Ambrogio.** Painter active in Siena between 1320–1347. Brother to Pietro. A great painter in a school of remarkably original painters, Ambrogio was probably a pupil of Duccio. Ambrogio's great contributions include the first known landscape in medieval art and a highly original group of altarpieces.

**Maestri di Pietre de Legname.** The masons and carpenters guild that commissioned Nani di Banco's production of the "Quattro Coronati" for their niche at Orsanmichele.

**Masaccio, Tommaso Giovanni di Mone** (1401–1428). The first great painter of the Italian Renaissance. His training is unknown, but he was influenced by the great generation of older Florentine sculptors, Nanni d'Antonio, Donatello, and Brunelleschi. His frescoes are known for their balanced and harmonized compositions, figural modeling, and use of space. They were profoundly influential among younger artists including Fra Filippo Lippi, Fra Angelico, and Michaelangelo.

**Medici, Cosimo de'** (1389–1464). Statesman and banker, called "Pater Patriae" for his role in Florentine political affairs. Virtually Florence's ruler, Cosimo understood the necessity of appearing to adhere to republican virtues. His patronage was legendary; he helped Ficino establish the Platonic Academy and commissioned works of Brunelleschi, Donatello, and Ghiberti, among others. A humanist himself, Cosimo collected an enviable library, now part of the Laurentian library.

**Medici, Lorenzo de'** (1449–1492). Lorenzo the Magnificent, grandson of Cosimo, son of Piero the Gouty. Educated like a prince, Lorenzo gained the leadership of Florence upon the death of his father in 1469. In 1478 the Pazzi Conspiracy resulted in an attempt on his life (his brother Giuliano was killed), and in the aftermath Lorenzo retained his hold through skilled diplomacy. Lorenzo's patronage equaled that of Cosimo. He commissioned works from Botticelli, Donatello, Pollaiuolo, Filippino Lippi, and Ghirlandaio, among others. Lorenzo himself was a poet and friend of artists and philosophers.

**Medici, Lorenzo di Pierfrancesco de'** (1463–1503). Cousin of Lorenzo the Magnificent; frequent patron of Botticelli and probable patron of his *Primavera* and *Birth of Venus*.

**Medici, Piero de'** (1416–1469). Son of Cosimo, father of Lorenzo, Piero was known as "the Gouty" because of his ill health. Equally munificent as a patron, Piero was responsible for Benozzo Gozzoli's fresco cycle in the family chapel; he was also the patron of Pollaiuolo, Alberti, and Fra Filippo Lippi.

**Memling, Hans** (ca. 1430–1494). Painter of the Flemish school. Born in Mainz. Probably pupil of Rogier van der Weyden. Settled in Bruges ca. 1465 and was extensively patronized by the guilds there, as well as by the Burgundian court. His style is based on Rogier van der Weyden and Jan van Eyck.

**Philip the Bold of Burgundy** (1342–1404). Youngest son of King John II of France and brother of Jean, Duc de Berry, Philip became the Duke of Burgundy in 1363. By marriage to Margaret, heiress of Flanders, Philip created a significant state which lay between France and Germany. As a patron of the arts he built the monastery of Chartreuse of Champmol.

**Pico della Mirandola, Giovanni** (1463–1494). A leading humanist philosopher who joined Ficino's Platonic Academy in Florence in 1479 (he was 16). His most important work is the Oration on the Dignity of Man of 1486 in which he affirmed man as an independent entity, capable of achieving perfection through his own efforts, rather than having to depend on God's grace. This was a revolutionary idea which reflects the new humanely oriented culture that existed in the fifteenth century, particularly in Florence.

**Rolin, Nicolas** (1380–1462). A well-known patron of arts; chancellor to Philip the Good of Burgundy.

**St. Francis of Assisi** (ca. 1182–1226). Founder of the Franciscans. Son of a wealthy cloth dealer in Assisi, he took a vow of poverty and devoted himself to Christ. His personal, affectionate, and happy affirmation of the creation and the Creator helped change the direction of Western civilization, which began to view God as more accessible and tolerant than had been the case earlier. Canonized in 1228, Francis was one of the most important subjects for artists from the fourteenth through seventeenth century.

**Salutati, Coluccio** (1331–1406). Chancellor of Florence from 1375 to 1406 and the first of its humanist chancellors; his success enabled other humanists (notably Leonardo Bruni) to follow. Like Bruni, he found in antiquity models for contemporary behavior, and among his notable efforts was his "On the Labors of Hercules," in which he used the myth as an exposition on the values of active civic life.

**Sluter, Claus** (ca. 1350–1406). Leading Northern sculptor of the late fifteenth century and court sculptor for Philip the Bold. Sluter's raw and expressive realism signaled a departure from the elegant and courtly refinement of Northern sculpture of the time.

**Van der Weyden, Rogier** (1399–1464). Pupil of Robert Campin and follower of Jan van Eyck, sharing with him the rank of the greatest painter of fifteenth-century Flanders. He was favored at the court of Philip the Good and also patronized by his chancellor, Nicolas Rolin. His subdued emotional tenor adds dignity and powerful tension to his works.

**Van Eyck, Jan** (ca. 1390–1441). Considered the greatest painter of Northern Europe in the early part of the fifteenth century. Sometimes credited with inventing oil paint, van Eyck certainly exploited its potential with precocious skill. In 1425 he became court painter to Philip the Good, who not only commissioned work but sent van Eyck on diplomatic missions.

## Bibliography

### PART 1

### General: Italy

Baron, H. *The Crisis of the Early Italian Renaissance.* Princeton, 1966.

Baxandall, M. *Painting and Experience in Fifteenth-Century Italy.* New York, 1974.

Berensen, B. *Italian Painters of the Renaissance,* rev. ed. London, 1967.

Berensen, B. *Italian Pictures of the Renaissance.* 7 vols. London, 1957–68.

Borsook, E. *The Mural Painters of Tuscany from Cimabue to Andrea del Sarto,* rev. 2nd ed. Oxford, 1980.

Burckhardt, J. C. *The Civilization of the Renaissance in Italy.* Trans. S. G. Middlemore. Phaidon, 1965.

Cennini, Cennino. *The Craftsman's Handbook.* Trans. D. V. Thompson. Dover, 1954.

Cole, B. *Giotto and Florentine Painting 1280–1375.* New York, 1976.

———. *Italian Art 1250–1550: The Relation of Renaissance Art to Life and Society.* New York, 1987.

———. *The Renaissance Artist at Work.* New York, 1983.

———. *Sienese Painting from Its Origins to the Fifteenth Century.* New York, 1980.

Crowe, J. A. *A History of Painting in Italy,* 2nd ed. 6 vols. London, 1903–14.

Freedberg, S. *Painting in Italy, 1500–1600,* Pelican History. Baltimore, 1971.

Freemantle, R. *Florentine Gothic Painters from Giotto to Masaccio.* London, 1975.

Gilbert, C. E. *Italian Art, 1400–1500: Sources and Documents in the History of Art.* Englewood Cliffs, N.J., 1980.

Hartt, F. *A History of Italian Renaissance Art.* New York, 1979; 3rd ed., 1987.

Larner, J. *Culture and Society in Italy 1290–1420.* New York, 1971.

Meiss, M. *Painting in Florence and Siena after the Black Death.* Princeton, 1951.

Panofsky, E. *Renaissance and Renascences in Western Art.* 2 vols. Stockholm, 1960 (1-vol. ed., 1965).

Pope-Hennessy, J. *The Portrait in the Renaissance.* New York, 1966.

White, J. *Art and Architecture in Italy, 1250–1400.* Pelican History of Art. Baltimore, 1966.

Wind, E. *Pagan Mysteries in the Renaissance.* New Haven, 1958.

### Architecture

Heydenreich, L. H., and Lotz, W. *Architecture in Italy, 1400–1600.* Harmondsworth and Baltimore, 1974.

Murray, P. *Renaissance Architecture.* New York, 1971.

Murray, P. *The Architecture of the Italian Renaissance.* New York, 1963.

Pevsner, N. *An Outline of European Architecture.* Harmondsworth and Baltimore, 1960.

Wittkower, R. *Architectural Principles in the Age of Humanism,* rev. 3rd ed. London, 1962.

### Sculpture

Pope-Hennessy, J. *Italian Gothic Sculpture.* London, 1955.

———. *Italian Renaissance Sculpture.* London, 1958 and 1971.

Seymour, C. *The Fountains of Florentine Sculptors and Their Followers from Donatello to Bernini.* Cambridge, Mass., 1933.

### Drawings

Ames-Lewis, F. *Drawing in the Italian Renaissance Workshop.* London, 1983.

Berensen, B. *The Drawing of the Florentine Painters.* 3 vols. Chicago, 1938.

### Individual Artists
#### Giovanni Bellini

Dussler, L. *Giovanni Bellini.* Vienna, 1949.

#### Botticelli

Ettlinger, L. D., and Ettlinger, H. S. *Botticelli.* London, 1976.

## Brunelleschi

Prager, F. D. and Scaglia, G.   *Brunelleschi: Studies of His Technology and Inventions.* Cambridge, Mass., 1970.

## Donatello

Bennett, B. A., and Wilkins, D. G.   *Donatello.* Oxford, 1984.

Hartt, F.   *Donatello, Prophet of Modern Vision.* New York, 1973.

Janson, H. W.   *The Sculpture of Donatello.* 2 vols. Princeton, 1957 (1-vol. ed., 1963).

## Ghiberti

Goldscheider, L.   *Ghiberti.* London, 1949.

Krautheimer, R., and Krautheimer-Hess, T.   *Lorenzo Ghiberti.* Princeton, 1956; 2nd ed., 1970.

## Giotto

Cole, B.   *Giotto and Florentine Painting, 1280–1375.* New York, 1976.

## Masaccio

Cole, B.   *Masaccio and the Art of Early Renaissance Florence.* Bloomington, Ind., 1980.

# PART 2

## General: Northern Europe

Benesch, O.   *The Art of the Renaissance in Northern Europe.* Cambridge, Mass. 1945.

Cuttler, C. D.   *Northern Painting from Pucelle to Bruegel.* New York, 1968.

Huizinga, J.   *The Waning of the Middle Ages.* London, 1924.

Meiss, M.   *French Painting in the Time of Jean de Berry: The Late Fourteenth Century and Patronage of the Dukes.* London, 1967.

Meiss, M.   *French Painting in the Time of Jean de Berry: The Limbourgs and Their Contemporaries.* New York, 1974.

Snyder, J.   *Northern Renaissance Art: Painting, Sculpture, the Graphic Arts from 1350 to 1575.* New York, 1985.

Stechow, W.   *Northern Renaissance Art 1400–1600: Sources and Documents.* Englewood Cliffs, N.J., 1966.

## The Netherlands

Crowe, J. A., and Cavalcaselle, G. B.   *The Early Flemish Painters.* London, 1857.

Davis, M.   *National Gallery Catalogues: Early Netherlandish School,* 2nd ed. London, 1955.

Detroit Institute of Arts.   *Flanders in the Fifteenth Century: Art and Civilization.* Detroit, 1960.

Elst, J. van der.   *The Last Flowering of the Middle Ages.* Garden City, N.Y., 1944.

———.   *Early Netherlandish Painting from Van Eyck to Bruegel.* London, 1956.

Panofsky, E.   *Early Netherlandish Painting: Its Origins and Character.* 2 vols. Cambridge, Mass., 1953.

Valentiner, W. R.   *The Art of the Low Countries.* Garden City, N.Y., 1914.

Weale, W. H. J.   *Hubert and John van Eyck: Their Life and Work.* London, 1908.

## Prints and Drawings

Hind, A. M.   *An Introduction to a History of Woodcut.* 2 vols. Boston, 1935.

Schretlen, M. J.   *Dutch and Flemish Woodcuts of the Fifteenth Century.* London, 1925.

Whinney, M.   *Early Flemish Painting.* New York and Washington, 1968.

# The High Renaissance

## Learning Objectives

The previous units traced how medieval man emerged from the philosophical and cultural context which had subordinated him intellectually, ethically, spiritually, physically, and hierarchically beneath the supremacy of God. In the Renaissance, man gained new assurance, climbed some of the hierarchical rungs, and a new balance was struck—a balance and harmony that found an expression in the arts. Perspective, canons of beauty, and nature were used to order and mirror reality back to humanity. Man's self-importance was indicated by the revival of the portrait with increasingly life-like representations of saints as human beings—stressing their historical not their symbolic reality—and with images that reflected man's secular preoccupations as well as his religious ones. In the sixteenth century the old balance changed. Extremes between realism and idealism pushed farther and harder in both directions. The direction that art would take depended increasingly on the artist himself, who was now emerging as a truly creative artist instead of a trained artisan who realized the ideas of others.

This unit will deal with those artists whose contributions rose above all others. We will be considering, for the first time, artistic development and the issues of style pursued more self-consciously than before. We will trace the careers of the three most prominent artists of the first half of the sixteenth century: Leonardo, Michelangelo, and Raphael. We will follow Leonardo from Florence to Milan where his *Last Supper* was created, and we will watch Raphael and Michelangelo in Rome, working for the Popes, who during the first three decades of the sixteenth century made Rome the artistic center of Italy.

We will then consider Venice, a city rich with native talent, a city remote from the struggles that beset most of the rest of Italy and a haven for artists from all over Italy. There we will see the feminine aspect take on a role equal to or greater than that of the male ideal that had so dominated Florence and Rome. The reasons are complex. Much of what we see created by Giorgione, Titian, and Veronese was created for private patrons, who enjoyed sensual subject matter. But the issue goes deeper than that. Venice herself was portrayed as a woman and the complex mythology which Venice created helped foster the development of a powerful femininity that had as many far-reaching consequences as the more virile expression of humanity found in Florence and Rome would have.

We will encounter important terms and concepts such as those at the center of the artistic debate that raged between Venice and Florence over the relative merits of "disegno," or drawing, favored in Florence, and "colore," or color, favored in Venice. "Chiaroscuro," the means of modeling figures through light and shade, joined even more sophisticated uses of perspective to give pictures greater overall cohesion. Sculpture, like painting, became more integrated, and often more deliberately imitated the antique. Antiquity became the standard against which many artists and patrons measured themselves. The scale of art becomes important as gigantic sculptures and grandiose painting cycles reflect the increased ambitions of patrons, and the desire of artists to excel even the ancients. Finally, the figure became the principal subject for artists. Painted, sculpted, or drawn, portraying real, biblical, or mythological characters, the figure was, to artists and patrons alike, the most important theme of art.

In this unit, you will:

- Comprehend the ideals of High Renaissance culture elevating human thought and creative expression to a new summit;
- Recognize the shared characteristics of geometric simplicity, harmony, and balance for compositional designs in painting, sculpture, and architecture;
- Appreciate the true nature of artistic genius as the combination of mind, spirit, and technique as witnessed by the masterpieces of Leonardo, Michelangelo, and Raphael;
- Know how the artists serving the city-states, republics, and papacy came into a new level of patronage which elevated the social rank of artists to privileged positions;
- Understand how the theological conflicts of the sixteenth century bringing Rome under doctrinal (Martin Luther, Henry VIII), and physical attack (Charles V's

Hapsburg mercenaries) were mirrored by the anti-classical distortions of the Mannerist style;

- Perceive the stylistic differences between the Florentine school's continuing use of the basic elements of clearly defined masses, geometric forms, and line versus the Venetian style's shift towards sweeping angles, enhanced color, and more intense interest in a painting's emotional mood;

- See that the human figure reaches its ultimate apogee as a sacred and profane subject through its appearances in Michelangelo's divinely modeled projections, Raphael's debating ancient philosophers, or Giorgione's carousing bacchants, and Titian's fleshy love goddesses.

## Part 1
# THE HIGH RENAISSANCE IN ROME

## Historical Background

In the sixteenth century, humanity ascends to greater levels of importance intellectually and takes on a larger-than-life dimension. Rome, Milan, and Venice join Florence as important artistic centers. The men who rule—the Popes, the princes, the statesmen, as well as the artists—all seem to take on a greater presence. The artists in particular are celebrated as giants elevated by the virtue of their creative genius. Many of them—Raphael, Michelangelo, Leonardo, and Titian—are still famous. These titans of creativity gained sufficient stature so that their lives were not simply chronicled but surrounded by myth by their less than reliable biographer, Giorgio Vasari, in his *Lives of the Most Excellent Italian Painters, Sculptors and Architects* (Florence, 1550). In more than one instance a prince or Pope stooped down to pick up an artist's brush, and the patrons (who once ruled supreme) were more often than not reduced to the role of awe-inspired spectator of the miracle of creativity, which they were privileged to have paid to come about.

Larger than life impressions are made by the rulers as well: Charles V, Pope Julius II, and Henry VIII, for example. Together with artists and thinkers they gave full vent to their aspirations, their appetites, and their ambitions. Struggles resulting from conflict among them seemed more cataclysmic, while their accomplishments appeared more astonishing and their failures more spectacular. Everything seemed to have taken on a larger scale. Sixteenth-century buildings became more monumental, as if to compete with ancient Rome itself. Likewise, sculptural and painted programs were not simply large but gigantic; over life-sized bulky, muscular heroes abounded, as a taste for colossi swept through parts of Italy.

This, then, was an era of grand schemes—and an age which sometimes saw grand schemes fail. The era began with calls for reform in the North and unity in the South. Neither was successfully accomplished. Machiavelli's *The Prince*, a seminal treatise on political science, was written in 1513, a time of great potential. A Medici had become Pope Leo X and his brother was Duke of Nemours. Machiavelli composed his work as a guide for a prince to gain power and free Italy from foreign powers. But the deaths of the Duke and the Pope destroyed Machiavelli's plans and he was forced into exile. In the North Erasmus's *Praise of Folly* in 1509 urged the translation of the Bible into the vernacular and asked for clerical reform. Martin Luther produced a vernacular Bible and, fueled by righteous indignation over what he deemed Catholic deviation from the true faith, urged not only reform but Reformation. A new Protestant church emerged, after 1517, but it soon became fractious, and Luther died disappointed in the disunity of the new church, the moral laxity of his contemporaries, and the apparent survival of the diabolic Catholic church. Unremitting in his attempt at producing a male heir, Henry VIII married six wives, but he was ultimately thwarted. His kingdom was handed on to his daughter, one of Europe's greatest monarchs, Elizabeth I. Even the so-called "Holy Roman Emperor," Charles V, who successfully sacked Rome in 1527, was overwhelmed by the turmoil of Europe; in 1556 he abdicated, retreating to a monastery and leaving the empire to his son, Philip II. If expectations seemed higher, more centered on success in this world, then disappointments often seemed greater and the sufferers seemed to recover less easily.

The social status of some artists escalated and, as has been stated, so did the scale of their output. Issues that artists confronted became, to some extent, purely formal—that is, art became a specialized intellectual discipline and its properties were discussed. Debates emerged as to the relative merits of "schools" of artists—and their approaches to art. In Florence drawing was the highly valued key to all art and "disegno"—drawing—held connotations of intellectual control, of manual preparation guided by intellect, of line and contour as the supreme components of art. In Venice, by contrast, "colore," or the properties of color, reflected a more spontaneous working method in which artists worked less premeditatively and allowed the act of painting itself to guide the artist as he worked.

In either case, new value was placed on the artist's inspiration. His creativity was something apart and distinct from the mere manual training of the artisan. But the inspiring muse did not cooperate with Renaissance artists any more fully than it had with their creative forebears in antiquity. While we have many universally celebrated masterpieces, we also have from the sixteenth century a high incidence of failures. From this period we have records of artists deliberately smashing their efforts, as Michelangelo did with a late Pietà; or art works being unfinished or failing technically, as with Leonardo's *Madonna and St. Anne* (H&F 11.14) or his famous *Last Supper* (J 601; G 17.3; H&F 11.13). Artistically, accomplishments were astonishing. In Italy, where we shall turn first, the succession of geniuses which had brought the early Renaissance into such spectacular flower continued unabated. Raphael, Michelangelo, Leonardo, and Titian are names you may already know and whose works will be discussed here.

While it was common for artists in the fifteenth century to practice more than one medium—to be architect, painter, and sculptor as Giotto had been, or as Verrocchio was—in the sixteenth century we see artists emerging who are true polymaths. Leonardo was, in fact, a scientist, who explored anatomy and engineering as seriously as he did painting. Michelangelo was a poet as well as a painter and sculptor, while Raphael was both architect, painter, and designer of prints.

Moreover, all of these artists relied on drawings to formulate their ideas. While this is not new, since drawing was a fundamental tool for artists from time immemorial, more drawings survive from the sixteenth century, and they help us trace the creative evolution of an idea more effectively than before. Spontaneous, immediate, and direct, drawings were valued as a closer and more personal expression of the artist. Drawings, like the artists who made them, survived in the sixteenth century because they had gained a new value among discerning patrons. Vasari, who wrote our invaluable biographical history of Italian artists, also collected their drawings enthusiastically and was himself a painter. Finally, even in Venice, where landscape was born, the figure reigned supreme. It was the first and only challenge for the serious artist, and it was used to explore not only reality, but ideas in the complex world of art and patronage that was sixteenth-century Italy.

## The Renaissance Man: Leonardo da Vinci

A logical place to begin our new unit is with Leonardo da Vinci, the oldest and in many ways the most influential of the artists under discussion. Famous not only as a painter and sculptor and superlative draftsman, Leonardo was a far-ranging intellect who pursued science, mathematics, anatomy, and engineering with equal energy. Leonardo produced only about fifteen known works but most of them remain part of our common cultural language. His *Mona Lisa* (J 603; G 17.4; H&F 11.15) is so familiar as to have endured countless parodies. His *Last Supper* so

transcends its time and function that it comes as a surprise for most students to learn that in this effort Leonardo was working in a tradition more than two centuries old. Leonardo's *Vitruvian Man* emblazons the cover of countless texts on the Renaissance and stands as an emblem of the Renaissance fusion of mathematical and physical ideals.

Leonardo, the man himself, embodies our commonplace notions of the Renaissance man, gifted as he was in so many disciplines. Leonardo is a useful place to begin our discussion because he has much in common with his Northern near-contemporary Dürer, whom we met in our previous unit. Both men left behind a vast body of writings which tell us a great deal about their lives. Both lived via their sight, calling it the most noble of senses, and both had an insatiable visual curiosity. But while Dürer was passionate and precise, Leonardo was searching for systems and principles even in the clumps of grass which he, like Dürer, liked to draw and thus record. Record keeping of all kinds dominated their lives: drawings, visual notes, diaries, and other writings were a passion equal to that of eyesight and with marvelous results in both cases.

Leonardo was also very different from his Northern counterpart. Leonardo lived far longer and demonstrated far wider ranging interest than Dürer. Where Dürer had an insatiable visual appetite, Leonardo had a life-long scientific curiosity.

It is, in a way, strange that Leonardo should crop up in discussions of the sixteenth century, born as he was when the fifteenth had just reached its halfway mark (1452). But such was his impact on later developments that he belongs to the next century. Born in Vinci, a town near Florence, Leonardo was the illegitimate son of a lawyer and a servant. Early on he demonstrated a sensitivity and compassion to living things which he would carry all his life. Quick, alert, but guarded, Leonardo seems to have set himself apart (and in that trait we witness a mentality not unlike that which ruled Dürer). Apprenticed at fourteen to one of fifteenth-century Florence's greatest masters, Andrea del Verrocchio (who was equally gifted as a painter and as a sculptor), Leonardo's genius first emerged as he assisted Verrocchio on a painted altarpiece depicting the *Baptism*.

Interestingly and appropriately, for an artist as influential as Leonardo, we first encounter his impact on others in a masterpiece left unfinished—abandoned when Leonardo found greener pastures in Milan. Even unfinished, *The Adoration of the Magi* (J 599) had an impact on other artists. Leonardo's efforts began traditionally enough—with a contract dated 1481 that still survives, drawn up between himself and the monks of San Donato a Scopeto. Leonardo was to produce the *Adoration* in twenty-four or, at most, thirty months, a rather typical space of time. In undertaking the commission for this altarpiece, Leonardo was fired with youthful ambition and has, to the eyes of many art historians, overreached himself. First he attempted to crowd an overwhelming number of figures into his compositions (the count has run as high as sixty-six by some historians), a taxing job for any painter, but even more challenging for a painter devoted to achieving a sense of harmony and balance in his picture. Next Leonardo attempted to incorporate many details he observed from life—the active, energetic horses, for example; the full-leaved tree; and the diverse and elaborate gestures and expressions on each of his Magi's faces. These he bound into a totality that had as many elements of artifice, of dreamlikeness, of near irrationality as it had system and logic and cohesion. The steps which run to the broken top of a ruin, the horse which bolts through the arch, the tension in the participants all make the picture seem like an apparition.

The elderly brooding figure to the left and the one looking out at the right are just two of the many puzzles which have intrigued scholars and fed the imaginations of painters. Variously identified as philosophers or personifications of ages, they have also been ascribed to Leonardo's own personality. Here we find yet another parallel with Dürer and another manifestation of how closely these works stay to the spirit and personality of the creator. Visions, dreams, or nightmares come from the artist's experience. So, the artist's psyche now becomes one of the underlying and perhaps the deciding factor in the creation of an art work. Regardless of their origins, these old men established a type for the "elder," a new bearded sage that cropped up regularly in the images of later artists.

Leonardo's unfinished masterpiece lays bare the very genesis of its creation. The many drawings which underlay the work still survive, showing us an artist not simply preparing, transferring, and executing his design, but continually searching, changing, rejecting, and re-adapting his final image. He also fundamentally reversed the relationship between darkness and light. While all previous artists had applied small areas of shadow to model figures drawn on a light ground, Leonardo made his figures emerge out of darkness. Dusky and smoky, hinting at atmosphere as well as drama, Leonardo's imaginative rethinking of light and shade revolutionized the way artists understood light, shadow, and form. Leonardo's working method and his vision were a radical departure. Oil paint helped make this possible, liberating the artist from the more mechanical and unforgiving medium of tempera. Made of pigment suspended in egg white, tempera dried quickly and was not conducive to broad and energetic brushmarks or over-painting. Oil paint suspended pigment in the more viscous, slower-drying medium of oil and permitted greater variety in rendering texture, color, transparencies, and opacities. But the use of oil is only part of the story.

Having lifted himself above the level of the artisan or craftsman, the sixteenth-century artist took on the burden of creativity. Leonardo could not resist the impulse to pursue the quest even at the expense of the finished work.

Like his later artistic descendants, such as the famed Don Quixote, Leonardo sometimes tilted at windmills. But even the act of tilting provided a fertile legacy. Unfinished, the work has impact, for each barely described character has power and conviction; nuance has never spoken more effectively, and the picture became a sort of lesson piece for young painters. The innovative compositional language, the new syntax of drama, and the artist's ability to wring out gestural diversity and expressive subtlety from each of his figures challenged every artist who saw the picture to match or excel him. Vasari was probably truthful when he says that the young Raphael was speechless before it. How could he fail to recognize the brilliance of a composition that is at once cohesive and simple, yet complex, and consisting of so many different figures and objects? The impressive array of figures (in part derived from earlier masters like Masaccio) were beguiling, and we shall meet some of them again in Raphael's Stanze.

The patrons in this effort seem nearly incidental—just a vehicle for Leonardo's creativity—and it is his impact on other artists which has become the focus of our story. Though their picture remained unfinished, the monks of San Donato waited patiently for fifteen years before giving up and calling in a much less genial painter, Filippino Lippi, to paint another *Adoration* for their altar.

Leonardo departed meanwhile for Milan, where he inspired a whole school of followers. Leonardo spent two decades in Milan working for the Sforzas. When Leonardo applied to Ludovico Sforza, he was dealing with a city that was entirely different from the one with which Florence had battled until 1440. Long the stronghold of the Visconti dukes, Milan (which boasted the largest duomo in Europe) has the distinction of being the first duchy to be inherited and ruled by a hired condottiere or soldier of fortune. Ludovico Sforza, a parvenu, bent on proving himself a worthy successor to the Visconti dukes into whose family his father had married, supported a lavish court, interested in mathematics, printing, science, and technology. Unlike Lorenzo de' Medici, whose banking ancestry had supported an aristocratic life, Ludovico was much less gracious and refined. Yet he has been called a more lavish and discerning patron than Lorenzo, who, unlike his grandfather, Cosimo, did not commission the greatest works of his generation. In keeping with his militaristic heritage, Ludovico hired Leonardo, not so much because he was a painter but because he was a master engineer, gifted at war machines and defensive systems of all kinds. Leonardo must have sensed this would appeal to his potential patron, for in a surviving letter addressed to Duke Ludovico Sforza, he lists his accomplishments as engineer and mechanic first, and mentions painting as a mere afterthought. Instability dogged Ludovico, who ended his days a captive of France alone in a dungeon, while Milan was finally annexed to the Holy Roman Empire in 1525 by Charles V.

Fascinatingly, Leonardo, this most intellectual of artists, was attracted to a court which was far less literate than Medicean Florence, but it was more scientifically inclined. Ludovico Sforza has been described as a brutal, direct, and somewhat sinister man, who, though a good patron for Leonardo, lacked the intellectual refinements one associates with the Medici. Leonardo, on the other hand, disdained the literary interests of the Medici, preferring Ludovico's interests in machinery and mathematics. Some scholars also suggest Leonardo preferred a despot to an aristocrat. In Milan, Leonardo, besides designing fortifications and military machinery, applied his engineering skills to courtly entertainments and central heating. He painted portraits of Sforza's mistresses and designed costumes, theatrical productions, and music among other fairly trivial pursuits. He also pursued an equestrian monument which would go Verrocchio's Venice one better—showing Ludovico's father Francesco on a rearing charger. Ludovico seems not to have been sufficiently impressed by this work to pay for its casting and from this disinterest a masterpiece was lost. Most importantly, Leonardo had time to pursue his own inclinations. During this period the bulk of the famous Notebooks, of some five thousand pages came into being. Notes, drawings, diagrams, and sketches crowd on each page, tracing the quicksilver observation, the rapid changes of attention, the thirst to know and to understand by one of the greatest minds of all time.

## Art above reality: Leonardo's *Last Supper*

In 1497 Leonardo received a commission from more traditional quarters, the friars of S. Maria delle Grazie. For their refectory, Leonardo was asked to paint a standard subject: the Last Supper—a scene which adorned countless similar refectories elsewhere in Italy, particularly in Florence. Appropriate for a subject in a room where monks gathered to take their meals, the Last Supper by Leonardo's time had taken on a fairly standard appearance: Christ was to be in the middle, and his twelve apostles arranged on either side of him—except Judas, who traditionally was isolated on the other side of the table.

Leonardo's *Last Supper* (**J 601; G 17.3; H&F 11.13**) looks traditional at first. But on second glance we see that he has created an entirely new vision. He shows us apostles reeling from the news that one of them is a betrayer. Psychological shock waves of response wash over the figures, dividing them, organizing them, giving meaning to the moment. Compared to the decorative, additive, and linear style of Botticelli's *Adoration* discussed in the last unit, Leonardo's *Last Supper* displays a totality that is breathtaking. Seemingly sculpted out of the very atmosphere that surrounds them are figures of the highest possible refinement who interact in a way that is at once dramatic and highly cultivated. They exist in a space that is perfectly mathematical and seems thoroughly compatible with them, so that the entire realm is

of a higher order than is possible in nature. On closer examination, the carefully contrived scale of the figures, which makes them appear so balanced in relation to the space, is illogical. They are much too big for the room's scale. Seeking the illusion of perfection, Leonardo, like all great artists, understood the necessity of a lie in order to tell a more effective truth.

Having dipped his vision into darkness, Leonardo let light fall on his characters selectively, smoothing their features with a vaporous haze which has been given such names as "sfumato," (smoky), or chiaroscuro (meaning light and dark). Adding drama and lending another element of cohesion to the work, this smoky atmosphere has its origins in Leonardo's intensive study of light. But it is employed as an artistic device and is recognizable as part of the picture's artifice. Each of the faces of the apostles in the *Last Supper* has an expression which also has its roots in Leonardo's intensive study of nature. But this is not nature simply retranslated into pigments on a wall surface. This is nature selectively adopted, to give the right expression of concern here, the proper sense of shock there, and which choreographs a drama in a sensitively arranged pantomime. Intense, distilled, and artfully woven into the schema, the psychological intensity of Leonardo's *Last Supper* reverberates through the image like a well-pitched tuning fork striking just the right note.

The dramatic action and compositional cohesion (achieved by grouping his figures into threes), the sublime perspective, and the atmospheric, suffused, yet contrasting lighting of Leonardo's *Last Supper* render tradition for this subject obsolete. And in keeping with the new spirit of the times, the fame of the *Last Supper* was nearly instantaneous and has remained unabated until today. Apparently thirsting for the new pictorial language it expressed, artists flocked to the *Last Supper* with enthusiasm, copying it in drawings and engravings and through them spreading its influence throughout Italy and Europe. Its impact could be found in such diverse artists as Raphael (whose drawing of the composition is thought to form the basis of an engraving by Marcantonio Raimondi). Just how Raphael came to know the *Last Supper* is one of the much debated questions among art historians. Dürer adapted the *Last Supper* in his own woodcuts. Besides affecting many other less notable contemporaries, Leonardo's masterpiece also influenced numerous illustrious artistic descendants, among them Rubens and Rembrandt in the seventeenth century, who copied or adapted figures from this nurturing wellspring of art.

What Leonardo produced was revolutionary and demonstrates how far, intellectually and formally, the artists of the sixteenth century had gone past their forebears. In his cohesive, perfected vision, consisting of a perfectly realized one-point perspective occupied by graceful, grand, and perfect beings, more perfect than anything in our own world, Leonardo lifted art *above*

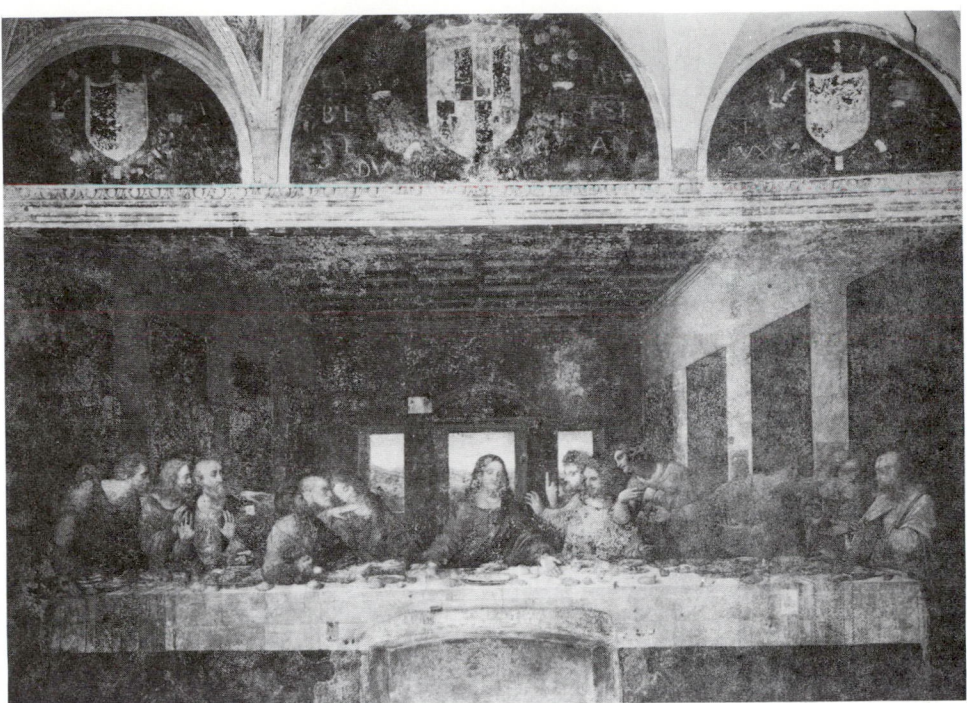

Leonardo da Vinci, *The Last Supper*, 1495–1498. Milan, Sta. Maria della Grazia, Refectory. (SCALA/ART RESOURCE, NEW YORK)

existence; it is no longer simply a window which extends our own world into the fictive one displayed on the picture surface.

Here, instead, we find that art has, through its aesthetic properties, created a world which in its perfect idealization exists as art. No symbols, no archaic or iconic formulas such as we saw in the past lift this picture beyond our realm; here artistry and artifice achieve that end. The artist's hand is everywhere and the work proclaims Leonardo's genius—it takes its identity from him; and so we see our first exemplar of how grandiose schemes, and the ambition of men to give vent to their visions, leads to a different kind of masterpiece. The power of human inventiveness has never been more evident and the shortcomings of human technical skill never more tragic.

Parallel to the ink that has been spilled discussing the *Last Supper* as artistry is the discussion that traces its destruction. Even in Leonardo's lifetime, the *Last Supper* began to suffer from the Milanese cold and damp. Working not simply in *buon fresco* (wet plaster with pigment mixed into it to make a permanent bond with the wall), Leonardo added *fresco secco*—pigment applied on the dry or drying surface to obtain the nuances of light and shadow not possible in the fast-drying buon fresco method. Technically, the work is a spectacular failure and little of what was Leonardo's vision remains. Even in Vasari's day, it languished in gloomy darkness and little could be seen. The painting was repainted at least twice in the eighteenth century alone. Though continual restoration preserves some shadow of the masterpiece, it is essentially lost. Because of Leonardo's impatience to achieve through any means, fair or foul, the essence of his

vision, its longevity was sacrificed. How like some artists today, who struggle, who study, who test and experiment for the moment, and how unlike the craftsmen of Leonardo's time, whose tried and true methods yielded images that lasted indefinitely, even if they lacked the explosion of genius which produced Leonardo's *Last Supper*.

Leonardo's life after the fall of Ludovico in 1499 to France was peripatetic. He returned to work in Florence periodically, but also worked in Mantua, Venice, and Rome, and he ended his days working for Francis I of France. Francis set Leonardo up in a fine house and seems to have required little of him except conversation, and we still have a record of Francis saying: " 'that he did believe that no other man had been born who knew as much as Leonardo, both in sculpture, painting and architecture, so that he was a very great philosopher' " (Kenneth Clark, *Leonardo* [London, 1939], 1967, p. 156).

Leonardo's legacy is complex, as the noted art historian Kenneth Clark has eloquently pointed out. On the one hand, Leonardo's refinement of form, his deliberation over gesture, composition, and expression has been so carefully calculated so as to outdo any Greek masterpiece in the restraint and artifice of its appearance. These methods fundamentally attracted many artists and affected their way of working. Leonardo can be called the father of academic painting, which emerged in the seventeenth century and adopted systems of learning and working much like those used by Leonardo. It is no accident that he would be hailed among the heroes of the Academicians in the seventeenth, eighteenth, and nineteenth centuries. On the other hand, Leonardo injected deeply romantic feelings into his work, and those strong emotions are heightened by the strongly contrasting lighting he used, the mysterious and evocative settings he created, and his supreme mastery of human expression. Romanticism and Academicism were often rivals, but on more than one occasion overlapped, and in Leonardo's art they coexisted in one remarkably gifted mind.

## Tortured Genius: Michelangelo

If Leonardo is viewed as the paradigm of the Renaissance man, then Michelangelo surely has come down as the acknowledged paradigm of the Renaissance artist. Possessed of prodigious talent, unsurpassed technique, and bold aspirations, Michelangelo was, nevertheless, tortured by his muse—a captive of that melancholy temperament which Dürer, as we have seen, so eloquently pictured as the by-product of thought and creativity in his great engraving. The son of minor nobility, Michelangelo Buonarroti was born in 1475 in the outskirts of Florence, lost his mother at age six, and was early on (in 1488) apprenticed to Domenico Ghirlandaio, the leading fresco painter in Florence—whose training later stood Michelangelo in good stead. Michelangelo soon joined the sculptor Bertoldo di Giovanni, who was teaching in a school set up by Lorenzo de' Medici in the garden of San Marco, and there Michelangelo was absorbed by the collection of antique works Lorenzo had assembled. Early biographers recount Michelangelo's precocious re-creation of an antique faun's head that so captured Lorenzo's attention that Michelangelo's genius was instantly recognized. Whether fact or fiction, such legends are typical of the mythic stature artists like Michelangelo achieved, even in their own day.

In 1494 the Medici had fallen from power and, nineteen years old, Michelangelo set out first for Venice (where it is possible that he met Dürer), then for Bologna, and finally for Rome. There, Michelangelo's dual nature—a mind steeped in antiquity, which he both emulated and rivaled, and a heart grasped by faith—found expression in his early Roman years. And both facets informed his art throughout his life. For Jacopo Galli, Michelangelo produced a marble Bacchus so near in type to ancient models that surviving drawings of it by Maerten van Heemskerk make it seem like any other antiquity in a collection of ancient marvels. For a French cardinal, Jean Bilhères de Lagraulas, Michelangelo undertook in 1498 the carving of a marble *Pietà* which Jacopo Galli firmly stated would be "the most beautiful work of marble in Rome, one that no living artist could better."

Using marble quarried from Carrara in 1497, the year in which Leonardo had contracted to undertake the *Last Supper* for the refectory in Milan, Michelangelo lived up to Galli's claims and even surpassed them. Completed after the Cardinal's death in 1499 and meant for his tomb in St. Peter's, Michelangelo's *Pietà* elicited the same instant acclaim in Rome that Leonardo's *Last Supper* had

won in Milan. both were marvels of artistic perfection, but Michelangelo surpassed Leonardo in technical mastery—his *Pietà* remains to this day a virtuoso display of marble carving, while Leonardo's mural is now a ruin. As we look at the figure of Mary with the dead body of Christ slumped across her lap, we may remember Bellini's evocative painting of the same subject, discussed in Unit III. Based on a Northern prototype, the Italians endowed their interpretations of the Pietà with beauty, beatific sorrow, and the exquisite pain that comes from witnessing not merely a tragic subject, but artistic perfection. Michelangelo's sculpture, when compared to Bellini's painting, is, however, more concerned with artistic perfection than emotion, and reveals Michelangelo's training in Florence, where emotion was subordinated to idealized beauty and refinement. Besides its obvious virtuoso carving, the St. Peter *Pietà* demonstrates Michelangelo's searing analysis of nature. He, too, like Leonardo, dissected bodies to learn more about anatomy, and he, like Leonardo, used what he learned not merely to imitate nature, but to perfect his art.

An assembly of details is compiled within Michelangelo's composition that looks forward to the sixteenth century, much as the *Adoration of the Magi* by Leonardo looked to the future. Despite the detail, neither of these works is additive in the fifteenth-century sense of the term; rather, each expresses a *unity* born of a bold design and a daring use of composition to dominate and encompass details. Achieving the perfection of the small personal table-top bronzes which became so popular in the sixteenth century, Michelangelo's oversized *Pietà* sits on a rounded base that designates it a work apart. It is the only work Michelangelo signed—perhaps his fame became so great he had no need to sign his works later on.

### Antiquity challenged: Michelangelo's *David*

As you will remember from the program, Michelangelo returned to Florence in triumph early in 1501, and a new ruler for life, a Gonfaloniere (Pietro Soderini), was soon to be elected. He encouraged Michelangelo to remain in Florence. Michelangelo's first effort there was to mark him again as an artist of superhuman ability who triumphed where others had failed. Michelangelo decided to take on the challenge of a flawed marble block over fourteen feet high. It was quarried in 1464, and harked back to a commission involving Donatello. Nothing had come of it since Donatello's death in 1466. Michelangelo's return to Florence renewed the hopes of the Cathedral Opera (directors of the Cathedral works) that this block could be salvaged and a David could be carved.

Michelangelo began work in August, 1501, apparently aware that he was competing not only with antiquity but with his great Florentine predecessor, Donatello, whose bronze *David* then graced the courtyard of the Palazzo Pubblico. Three years later, in 1504, Michelangelo's colossus was finished. A look at it reminds us that

Michelangelo had seen the Apollo Belevedere in Rome, and had its heroic view of humanity in mind. Like the ancients, Michelangelo saw the nude male as an emblem of beauty, virtue, and strength. Like them, he adopted the same ideals of virility coupled with a self-mastery: Here, too, is the same pose of one leg resting, one leg supporting, which causes the hips to swing and the body to twist in subtle, taut rhythms. But this is no mere emulation of an ancient type—here, Michelangelo has surpassed antiquity and found a hero for Florentine Renaissance. Despite his seeming perfection, David does not possess the harmonious proportions of his ancient counterparts. Just as his head and face are larger and more expressive, Michelangelo has chosen to emphasize David's hands and feet, which adds to the awesomely gigantic appearance of the whole. David's animated expression registers thought, and a defined personality replaces the calm, psychologically neutral heroes of classical antiquity. Because of the limitations of the shallow block in which he worked, Michelangelo's *David* **(J 611; G 17.20; H&F 11.22)** has one principal view—the front—though the sides and back are important as well. But that disadvantage was turned into an advantage, making David's glance, his thought, his far-off look, in sum, the space around the work, as important as *David*. This idea transcends the more self-contained figures of antiquity.

Vasari, Michelangelo's admirer and biographer, acclaimed *David* as a triumph over antiquity: "Without any doubt this figure has put in the shade every other statue, ancient or modern, Greek or Roman." After some debate, Michelangelo's sculpture was placed before the Palazzo Vecchio (where it remained until 1878, when it was moved inside the Accademia). With *David*, Florence added another hero to the pantheon created by Donatello and his contemporaries. *David* expresses familiar ideals of fortitude, valor, and physical and intellectual perfection. Yet in *David* they have a grander scale than we have seen since antiquity, and his frankly pagan derivation and nudity are for the first time deliberately associated with a public, civic emblem of Florence. With *David*'s deliberated placement in front of the Palazzo Vecchio, historical conditions in Florence must be remembered. Having recently expelled the Medici, the Florentines made *David* a symbol of independence from Medici tyrants, as they had Donatello's *Judith and Holofernes* and his *David*, which had been captured from the Medici after their expulsion and had been turned into emblems of civic triumph.

If Michelangelo took on mythic proportions in the minds of his admirers, his output also took on grandiose dimensions. The demure adolescent of biblical times had been transformed by Michelangelo into a superhuman, giant entity—his immense physicality seen as the visual expression of divine intervention which gained him victory over Goliath. but this, like Donatello's *St. George*, is a moment of challenge, as well as of victory—though

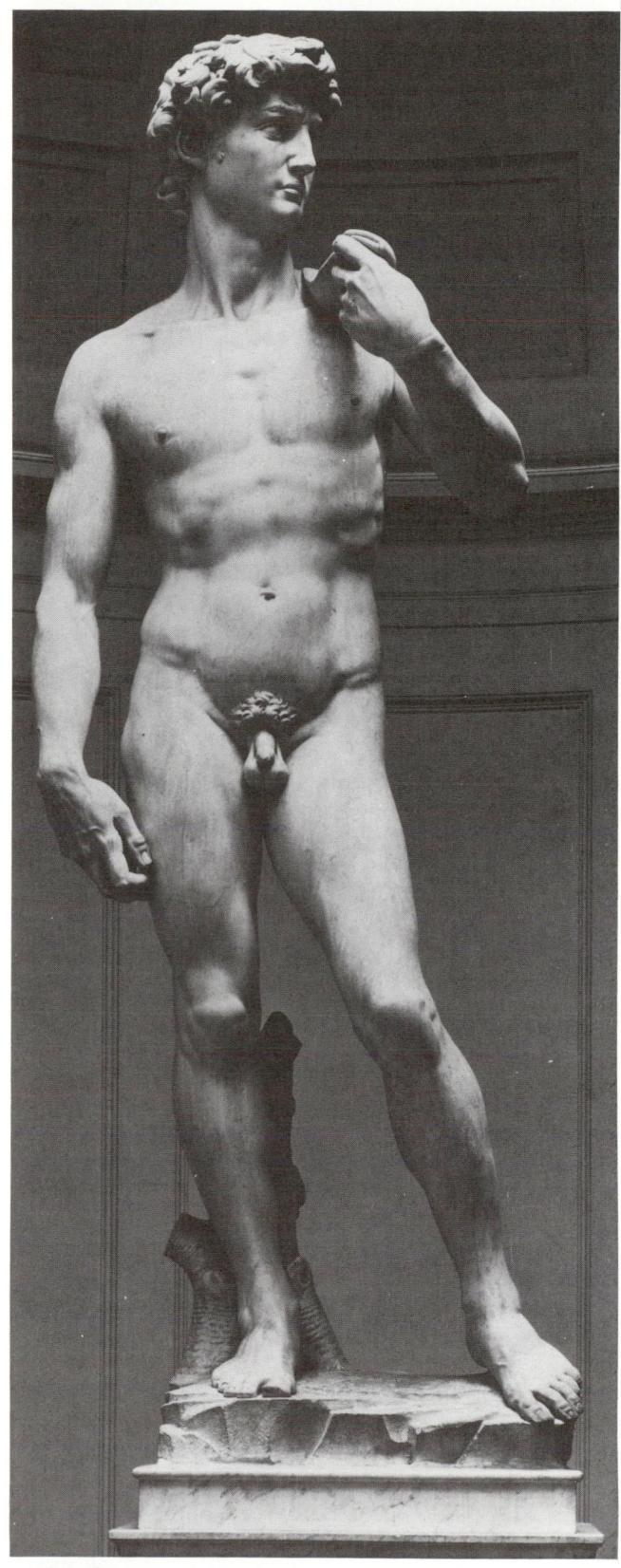

Michelangelo, *David*, 1501–1504. Florence, Accademia. (ART RESOURCE, NEW YORK)

David's triumph cannot be in doubt. Standing before the Florentine city hall, *David* watched over his city, protecting her against any Goliaths, and to the minds of some historians, *David* was particularly aimed at the gathering Medici forces to the south, in Rome.

## Thwarted ambition: the tomb of Julius II

In 1503, the year before Michelangelo completed his *David*, Giuliano delle Rovere was elected Pope Julius II and in Julius, Michelangelo met his match in ambition, and his nemesis in a patron. Julius must have known about Michelangelo from contact with him in Florence and nearby Bologna, and upon his election, he turned his thought almost immediately upon his own tomb. The monument to Julius's earthly glory and guardian of his mortal remains, as well as a magical assistant of the spirit into the celestial realm, Julius's tomb was also an especially significant testament to his role as supreme pontiff. Seething with ambition for glorification of himself and the papacy, Julius saw in Michelangelo an artist who could materialize his own ambitions. Julius contracted him in 1505 to plan and construct the biggest and most ambitious tomb ever created for a pope. Thus began what for Michelangelo was to be the bane of his existence for forty-two years and resulted in, for lack of better terms, nearly complete failure. The tomb was not built according to plan, nor placed in its originally planned site. Drawings, letters, and contemporary accounts from Ascanio Condivi and Vasari assist in the reconstruction of the tomb in its various phases, which was originally supposed to consist of over forty figures united within an architectural frame, and was to be erected in the biggest and most important church in Christendom: St. Peter's. It became, forty-two years later, a mediocre wall tomb in one of Rome's least significant churches: S. Pietro in Vincoli. It ended up incorporating only one of the many figures Michelangelo had created for the work, his *Moses* **(J 612; G 17.21; H&F 11.24),** which was transformed from an ancillary role to primary focus. The rest of the figures Michelangelo struggled over are scattered—some are in Florence and others in Paris. The tomb crops up in scholarly studies, not as a chapter in Michelangelo's life, but as a continual interruption in the flow of his other work. Changes in circumstance, in funding, and in Michelangelo's own ideas helped transform the original conception into the final product and scholars continue to debate not only the original design, but its various transmutations.

It is a fascinating if difficult story, involving a remarkable artist and patron. Sixty years old when he ascended to the papal throne, Julius II was driven by his ambition to strengthen the secular power of the papacy. A brilliant strategist, he enlarged the papal territories to include Bologna and Perugia, changing sides and alliances whenever necessary to achieve his ends. Paying lip service to demands for reform, Julius resorted to the wholesale promotion of indulgences to enrich his treasury, needed not only for his military exploits but his lavish patronage of the arts.

Like the Medici before him, Julius II recognized that art could enhance his own prestige and that of the church, and he transformed Rome. Under his instigation, St. Peter's was enlarged and expanded by Bramante and Michelangelo **(J 625–627; G 17.32–17.34; H&F 11.29, 11.31)**, a project that far outlived its patron and artists, lasting one hundred and twenty years. St. Peter's was not re-dedicated until 1626, but on completion, was a fitting monument to the foremost church in Christendom. Employing Michelangelo and Raphael, Julius supported the creation of the greatest pictorial monuments of the Renaissance: the Sistine Chapel **(J 615–617, clpl 77; G 17.24–17.26; H&F 11.21, 11.25)** and the Vatican Stanze (or apartments). Thus, while Julius's own personal monument (among the first projects he undertook as Pope) did not live up to his expectations, his other projects have earned him a permanent place in the pantheon of Renaissance patrons.

When Michelangelo and the Pope negotiated over the tomb, Michelangelo supplied him with drawings of various designs, one of which suited Julius. A contract was drawn up for a tomb to be about twenty-six by thirty-two feet, three tiers high, and incorporating forty figures. Michelangelo set out almost at once for Carrara in Northwestern Italy, noted since Roman times for its excellent white and colored marble. Letters record his impatience for the materials to arrive and while he fretted, Michelangelo witnessed one of the most momentous rediscoveries of antiquity. It had a profound impact on his own artistic development. Early in January, 1506, a man was digging in a vineyard on the old Esquiline Hill of Rome and hit a niche that held a legendary masterpiece of ancient Greece: the Laocoon group. Renaissance humanists knew of it from the admiring account of Pliny in his *Natural History* (ca. A.D. 47–70); Pliny described it as "a work superior to all paintings and sculptures."

It is not difficult to imagine the excitement of Julius, Michelangelo, and Giuliano da Sangallo (his architect) when the work was rediscovered. Julius already owned the famous Apollo Belvedere, from which Dürer took much inspiration for his *Adam and Eve*, and which Michelangelo studied for his *David*, as we saw earlier. Julius added the Laocoon group to his statue court in the Vatican Belvedere. There Michelangelo was able to study it thoroughly and learned from its twisting, struggling figures, as well as its well-muscled forms. More than one scholar has also pointed out that the Laocoon was a particularly fitting subject for Michelangelo to study, since it displays humanity as tragic victims of divine wrath, a theme that finds a parallel in Michelangelo's own work.

Surely Michelangelo suffered from the wrath of his patrons, from his own temperament, and his spirituality. The first blow came with the ill-fated tomb for Julius. Once Julius had decided on a great tomb, his choice of location, St. Peter's, led inexorably to an even more ambitious project: to tear down the old church and build a new one. Donato Bramante was handed the most important building project Renaissance Italy had ever seen. Absorbed in his new project, Julius either lost interest in or lacked money for the tomb, and Michelangelo left Rome, angry and bitter, arriving back in Florence April 17, 1506, the day before the foundation was laid for the grand new church in Rome.

Six years later, in 1512, the Pope sensed his own imminent death; he pressed Michelangelo once more to work on the tomb. New plans were made and new contracts drawn up, and the following year, on February 20, 1513, Julius II died, leaving money in his will to continue the project. From 1513 to 1516, Michelangelo worked almost without interruption, struggling to meet the deadline (seven years) to complete the monument. He created the slaves (now in the Louvre) **(J 613–614; G 17.22–17.23; H&F 11.26)**, which are as famous as they are difficult to interpret. Celebrated for showing even greater progress with the human form than was seen in his *David*, the slaves merely hint at meaning, while *David*'s purpose was abundantly clear. Michelangelo's symbolic language had by then become increasingly personal and generalized. These two male figures can be seen first and foremost as Michelangelo's celebration of the male body which he admired above all else. Drawings tell us that these figures were intended to be set inside niches, a tradition we recognize as going all the way back to Orsanmichele. But here the niches were simply frameworks for independent figure studies. What these figures were intended to convey is nearly as debatable as the details and progress of the whole tomb project.

Clearly inspired by the Laocoon group, the two slaves are a study of restless sleep and impotent, wakeful struggle. The sleeping or dying slave is propped by a simian creature behind, perhaps intended to visualize the notion of art aping nature. Is our figure intended to represent art as soon to be awakened by the arrival of Pope Julius the patron, or sleeping after his death? Regardless of its exact meaning, if a single one was intended, the meaning is conveyed through a figure that is both muscular and voluptuous. Its arm extending behind the head, the sleeping slave adopts a pose most often associated with a woman, as she was interpreted, recumbent within nature, by Giorgione in his famous *Dresden Venus* of 1509, discussed later in this unit. Such sensual and vulnerable physicality is paradoxically expressed by Michelangelo in a body of gigantic proportions and prodigious muscularity, a muscularity that is much more fluid and integrated within the totality of the body than was the case with *David*. Sweeping, generous, and supple rhythms unify and articulate the figure. Michelangelo has also brilliantly contrasted narrative *passivity* within a visually active form—the upstretched arm, the bent knee, and the turning torso all lend vitality and energy to this mysterious somnambulant hero. Intimations of the tortures of dreams, the struggle between

the mind and the body, which absorbed Michelangelo's thought, are poignantly expressed.

His awake counterpart is coiled and twisted, conveying a violent struggle and establishing him as an opposite principle. Both figures have come to be seen as ideations of the old Neoplatonic ideas of man struggling to escape the prison of the body and to liberate the spirit. These ideas were nascent in Donatello's time and were still current in Michelangelo's day. But interpretations of Michelangelo's slaves in these terms have to do with art historians turning to known aspects of Renaissance culture to understand unknown ones. The truth is, Michelangelo's slaves are not in their intended context, they are highly personal, and so idiosyncratic, yet so elemental, that they have become receptacles for the most complex iconographic interpretations as well as the most simple ones.

The slaves do show us that with Michelangelo, the patrons seem to have been relying on the artist not only to supply creativity by means of design and technical ability, but to supply meaning—to provide ideas. Certainly for Michelangelo, the idea itself was increasingly important in his work, and the struggle to formulate an idea, as well as to liberate it then from the material, are both reflected in the way in which he worked.

Two years after creating the slaves, Michelangelo completed the *Moses* **(J 612; G 17.21; H&F 11.24)** which now is the central component in the much reduced and much maligned tomb that finally got installed in S. Pietro in Vincoli. In this mighty Old Testament figure, the direct descendant of Sluter's and Donatello's formidable prophets, we see the high degree of finish and resolution to which Michelangelo's figures could come when he had the time. Clearly related to the Sistine ceiling figures, which themselves had grown out of Michelangelo's earlier experiments with the Julius tomb, the *Moses* has the troubled and earnest gaze we first found in *David*, and, in fact, is in many ways David's seated and aged counterpart. Still physically potent, Moses is even more invincible than David, having added spiritual authority to his physical energy.

A penultimate chapter in the story of Julius's tomb came in 1518 when members of the della Rovere family once again pressed Michelangelo for the tomb. In 1519 Michelangelo sent a promise for four figures and these have been identified with the four so-called "Prigioni," or Prisoners, now in the Accademia in Florence. Apparently the tomb had been redesigned at this point as a wall monument, and the four prisoners were intended to be architectural supports in the forms of human figures. Taller than the slaves, more massive, and largely unfinished, the four prisoners had a far-reaching influence not only on our conception of Michelangelo, but also on our understanding of finish. Until Michelangelo produced these works, artists were expected to work in detail and then grind, sand, and polish marble until it was smooth and provided a sense of completion. Though Michelangelo himself doubtless aimed at a greater level of completion for these works, the germ of his idea is so clear and the idea itself becomes sufficiently important that they are valued in their present state. In fact, they inaugurate an appreciation for a rougher, more crudely chiseled marble which reflects a belief in truth to materials as elements of beauty. The name "prisoners" is appropriate on a variety of levels. Interpreted in Michelangelo's time to mean caryatid or Atlas, the Italian name "Prigione" expresses the load-bearing function which these figures were intended to serve. Their poses and gestures have meaning when considered in this context.

However, these figures take on other meanings because they are still imbedded in their marble. We seem to witness their perpetual struggle to liberate themselves, and Michelangelo's struggle to free them. Romantic interpretations view the marble as an active force enveloping the figures and resisting their attempts to free themselves. To more modern eyes, the block is part of Michelangelo's formal device—it set the limits to which his figure's arms or knees or heads could reach. The block represented a shape and scale which gives form and proportion to Michelangelo's figures not merely out of necessity, but out of his desire to remain true to the materials. The block, the living stone, is magically transformed in the artist's hands. Whether Michelangelo intended his figures to remain as they are or not, the process of becoming is what remains, and, while such raw and roughly chiseled forms had little impact on Michelangelo's immediate descendants, they had a profound influence in the nineteenth and twentieth centuries. Artists as diverse as Rodin, Picasso, and Henry Moore would be impossible to understand without them. By failing to complete the tomb for Julius, Michelangelo succeeded in affecting art more profoundly than if the tomb had been a success.

## The triumph of genius: Michelangelo's Sistine Chapel

Michelangelo had left behind the cantankerous Julius II and shaken the dust of Rome off his feet in 1506. He probably expected to stay in Florence permanently, but Julius was not about to let him get away so easily. In 1508, over his objections, Michelangelo was pressed back into papal service, not to complete the tomb, but to undertake a vast painted ceiling, the vaulted roof of the Sistine Chapel (named after Pope Sixtus V) (**J 615–617; G 17.24, H&F 11.21, 11.25**), which, among other functions, served as a setting for the conclave of Cardinals when electing a new Pope, as it still does today. Its walls had been decorated during the late fifteenth century with murals by a largely Florentine team of painters, including Botticelli and Ghirlandaio. Though Michelangelo was as hesitant about this project as he had been delighted about the tomb, he was destined to complete the Sistine Chapel in four years, and thereby produced an unprecedented

decorative scheme for a ceiling which (to contemporary minds as well as our own) literally and figuratively overpowered the wall decorations below. Most important to consider was that Michelangelo here worked almost entirely alone. He decided on the overall design, having rejected his patron's choice of the lives of saints. Michelangelo's independent action was a significant enough novelty that his biographer Condivi mentioned it, though scholars think that a theologian helped Michelangelo plan subjects for each area: the Old Testament Prophets, the Sibyls, and the nine scenes displayed across the center of the ceiling. But Michelangelo conceived how the figures and the architecture would appear and interact, and remarkably, he also painted much of it singlehandedly.

What strikes us immediately is the size and grandiose conception of the mural. Narrative, symbolic, and decorative conventions have all been re-thought, and they all spin on one central all-encompassing idea—the figure. Equally striking is the fact that figures perform any number of functions, from sculptural embellishment to embellishment in place of architectural form. Figures play both the major and minor roles as characters of the Old Testament and antiquity. They are brought together to give meaning and historical perspective to man's origins in Genesis and his salvation through the church. Capping the events from the New Testament described on the wall, Michelangelo used the ceiling to link the Old Testament with the New, and with the church, by illustrating the episodes from Genesis which describe the early phases of Creation. He also depicted the Prophets and Sibyls who predicted the coming of Christ and Christianity.

What he produced has rightly been described by Howard Hibbard as "the most grandiose pictorial ensemble in all of Western art" (*Michelangelo*, p. 108). Painting quickly and evolving his thinking at a much faster pace than was possible in the slow, laborious process of carving stone, Michelangelo seemed to give full vent to his frustrated ambitions for Julius's tomb. Considering painting an inferior art to sculpture, Michelangelo emulated the sculptural qualities of his forms through paint, giving his forms a three-dimensional appearance that is unique to his work. The male figure dominates the scheme here, too, and is celebrated in its many poses and gestures. Close parallels can be found between the slaves of the Julius tomb and the so-called nudes flanking the narrative panels, given the job of holding the fictive medallions between them. By using the human figure to express such diverse functions, Michelangelo was consciously or unconsciously emulating the ancient Greeks, who saw in the human body the prism through which most ideas could be expressed. In the Sistine ceiling, as well as in his sculpture, Michelangelo affirmed the human figure as the challenge and true subject for great art.

More than one scholar has commented on the fact that the loss of the Julius tomb was perhaps the greater gain of the Sistine Chapel. In this supreme dynamic expanse, Michelangelo presented a textbook of figures for generations of later artists. The works of Raphael, the Carracci, Caravaggio, Rubens, and Rodin, just to name some of the first that come to mind, would be impossible without it. With the surge of creative effort, Michelangelo succeeded in dwarfing and outmoding all of the chapel's previous decorations, and rendering them charming but obsolete. The transition here was not subtle or gradual, but dramatic, and its effects were immediate. Scholars now accept the story that Raphael, whom we shall discuss shortly, crept into the Sistine Chapel while it was in progress, and soon altered his own work in the Vatican to reflect what he had seen, learned, and greatly admired.

With the centuries of grime now being lifted from the surface of these murals, we know Michelangelo to have been a superb colorist as well as draftsman. His subtle range of exotic pinks, green blues, lavenders, and reds make a stunning contrast to the bold modeled volume of each of his figures. These colors share and often exceed the intensity of color found in his only known panel painting, the *Doni Holy Family* in the Uffizi. Since the colors have been revealed, controversy has raged about how much of the surface might have been removed, though consensus seems to fall on the side of the conservators for now.

Working rapidly, often close to exhaustion and, as he himself jokingly remarked, perhaps permanently bent from lying supine on his scaffolding, Michelangelo pursued his vision with single-minded determination. His initial explorations of the ceiling narratives of the Flood and the Drunkenness of Noah soon gave way to a fuller, freer, and more ambitious treatment of his narrative. While his earlier scenes owed clear debts to Masaccio, Jacopo della Quercia, and others, Michelangelo's *Creation of Adam* and the scenes leading up to the *Creation* all show him reaching the full height of his powers as a draftsman, narrator, and interpreter of the human form. His *Creation of Adam* (**J 616; G 17.26; H&F 11.25**), though rooted in medieval thought, was revolutionary in creating obvious physical and compositional parallels between creator and created. Here Michelangelo also, as in his other works, was celebrating the spiritual message through heroic, masculine corporeality. Sight and touch seem here to express a paean to the sculptor as well as a paean to creativity—to the ultimate creativity of God and its lesser but still awesome emulations in the hands of man. God is, in fact, a Daedalus—the first sculptor.

More than one artist had such notions as Albrecht Dürer has shown us. But Michelangelo left no doubt that man himself was to be celebrated, his physicality a perfect vehicle to express the nobility of his soul. Even in a story usually tainted with man's downfall, Michelangelo has produced an unsurpassed celebration of man's rise from God himself. The moment Michelangelo picked is unusual. God and man come together yet they actually part. God here has already touched Adam and given him life—

the supreme sculptor has provided the spark of life, and departs.

In an ironic twist, Michelangelo stopped painting after his singlehanded triumph with the Sistine Chapel. He did not paint during the lifetime of his arch rival in Rome: Raphael. Perhaps taking a clue from the successful workshop Raphael directed, Michelangelo once more took an assistant, who was, in fact, a collaborator: Sebastiano del Piombo. A Venetian who traveled to Rome, Sebastiano executed a number of works after Michelangelo's drawings, and Michelangelo busied himself with renewed work on the Julius tomb, among other sculptural and architectural projects.

As you will remember from the program, the Northern antipathy for Rome was given full vent in the sack of 1527. A fuller account is provided later in this chapter. Michelangelo did not leave as so many artists did. He stayed on to produce a new kind of image that reflects renewed piety, of himself and his patron. In 1533 Pope Clement VII decided that the Sistine Chapel, so brilliantly embellished under the patronage of Julius II, needed a new decoration on the altar wall, and began toying with the idea of a new mural. Though he died before it could be undertaken, leaving Michelangelo with the delusion that he could return to the Julius tomb, his successor, Paul III (Alessandro Farnese), stated that he had waited thirty years to have a work by Michelangelo and pressed for the decoration to proceed. The result was the *Last Judgment* (**J 618; G 17.35–17.36**), perhaps the most famous version of that subject ever painted before or since. When we compare it to Rogier van der Weyden's version done nearly one hundred years before, we see instantly how far Michelangelo had traveled in his creative journey. The work has been described as using the human figure to express all that is possible in the art of painting. And yet the heroic vision of humanity seen above has been abandoned, together with the iconographic conventions of subject. Here humanity seems flawed, gestures express inner anguish, and human shortcomings are everywhere apparent. Christ the judge has sent down the seven angels to awaken the dead from the four corners of the earth. Figures bend, turn, twist, and move in every conceivable action. Yet human limitation and divine perfection are the themes of these figures and the message is compelling. It might come as a surprise to know that Christ, here cast in the same heroic mold as Michelangelo's *David,* his prisoners, and his prophets, adopts a gesture that traces its origins back at least two centuries (to the Camposanto in Pisa). In this vast tapestry of interwoven figures, suspended in an eerie sky, Michelangelo seems to have abandoned nearly every convention attached to this subject. But not all.

Christ's raised right arm calls the souls on the left to rise into paradise, while his lowered left hand condemns the figures on his left (our right) to hell. Struggle, torment, and inexorable power—the awesome act of judgment itself is the subject here, not its symbolic significance but its manifestation of cosmic inevitability. Though the interpretation was wholly modern, the function of the chapel was still traditional. The Sistine Chapel was used, among other things, to celebrate the festival of All Saints and to reflect this function, Michelangelo included a group of saints gathered below Christ. The feast days of Lawrence and Bartholomew were particularly associated with the building of the Sistine Chapel, and Michelangelo enlarged these two saints and added a particularly poignant and autobiographical note to the Bartholomew.

Martyred by being skinned alive, Bartholomew is here shown holding his flayed skin, which bears not the saint's likeness but the hapless portrait of Michelangelo himself. Not a simple artistic vanity, this detail embodies Michelangelo's sharing of the age-old belief in saints as intercessors and his fervid aspirations to his own ultimate salvation. Even Pope Paul himself, who had indulged his carnal appetites before becoming Pope, fell down before the finished work at its unveiling, responding to its combined power as artistic image and compelling icon.

In this last of his great frescoes, Michelangelo, who helped invent the paradigm of high Renaissance optimism in his youth, turned in his old age to a subject that was centuries old and that lowered humanity to the humble and flawed state to which it had fallen since the demise of antiquity. Embodying the paradoxical and often mutually contradictory impulses of an era in which the material and the sensual were viewed in direct opposition to the spiritual and the ascetic, Michelangelo's heart and mind had been transformed not only by this ancient conflict but by the more directly consequential condition of his own aging. Just as Dürer had expressed his artistic and spiritual frustration through his *Melancholia*, done in the closing years of his life, so Michelangelo's outlook became more pessimistic, antimaterialistic, and spiritual as he grew older.

Living in Rome, he would have been witness to the devastation of the Sack, and its profound effect on the self-confidence of the church. Chaos and destruction inevitably remind humanity of the vanity of earthly things, and turn thoughts toward the more enduring values of the spirit. The Reformation did not make Michelangelo doubt the validity of his faith; it increased and intensified his orientation to spiritual matters.

When Michelangelo's *Last Judgment* was completed in 1541, he had lived sixty-six years and was old by contemporary standards. Yet he would work on for twenty-three years more, turning more often to architecture and drawing, and becoming increasingly spiritual and deeply pious. In 1536 he had befriended Vittoria Colonna (1490–1547), a great and creative woman whose wisdom and spirit had attracted attention. His poems to Vittoria speak of a feverish piety, and pessimism, and seek the direct communion with God which the Protestants espoused. Faith alone was important and guilt seemed to weigh heavy on his shoulders. Many critics believe Michelangelo's *Last Judgment* reflects his and the era's

new religious orientation—a Counter Reformation spirit filling the air, strengthening the church and her supporters against the religious ferment in the North.

While Michelangelo's poetry, drawing, and sculpted work reflected a greater piety, his architectural projects were designed to enhance the public prestige of the city which adopted him formally as a citizen in 1537. The Capitoline Hill **(G 17.29–17.31)** was redesigned (but not completed in his lifetime) to house the grand imperial Roman bronze of Marcus Aurelius—and thereby mingled the messages of power of ancient Rome with those of his own day. He added designs for the Palazzo dei Conservatori and the Palazzo Farnese, but his most important Roman architectural project was his work on St. Peter's **(J 625–627; G 17.32–17.34; H&F 11.29, 11.31)**. Michelangelo undertook the project of completing designs for the façade of the church whose enlargement and rebuilding under Julius II had originally interrupted work on Julius's tomb and which now languished half built.

Michelangelo's designs for the building were altered after his death, but elements of the façade decoration reflect his intent. Like much of his architectural work, the articulating elements—the pilasters, the windows, the entablature, and the ribs and double columns around the drum of the dome—all express a dynamic presence that activates the building and overpowers the structural elements. The bold vertical thrust of the daringly emphatic pilasters, with their alternatingly large and small windows set between them, disguises the wall and overtakes the visual language of structure. Each of the elements forces the eye to rise and gives the whole façade a decorative, energetic unity. Michelangelo's architectural forms were adapted from classical sources, much as Brunelleschi's had been, but his use of these forms was as personal and creative as his interpretation and utilization of the human figure.

### The art of the intangible: the *Rondanini Pietà*

In the last years of his life, increasingly isolated and solitary (his friend Vittoria Colonna had died in 1547), perhaps as an exercise in piety, perhaps sensing his own mortality, Michelangelo set out to make a sculpture for his tomb, or simply tested himself with a work of a challenging composition. The result was a series of Pietà studies. The final one, known as the *Rondanini Pietà* **(J 568)** is a memorable effort. Michelangelo struggled with the simple, elemental conception of a single figure holding a dead weight. Here free to indulge his own creative urge to the fullest at a time when his internal vision seems to have far surpassed his ability to express it in stone, Michelangelo chipped away at the marble, feverishly destroying the original idea (note the broken off arm at the left) and pursuing it once more with a tighter grouping. Six days before he died Michelangelo was still working. What remains is a glorious ruin.

Michelangelo's vision was now so ephemeral and internal that it was no longer satisfied by the new style he himself had helped to foster, and his final effort remained almost totally unfinished. Its unformed, wraithlike creatures are worlds away from the heroic beings who populated his earlier work. Reduced to the most elemental forms, his sculpture anticipates the foundation of modern abstraction, allowing twentieth-century eyes to admire it more for its lack of finish than had it been completed. Subdued, meditative, and resigned, his figures no longer express the energy, buoyancy, and self-confidence of his earlier works. Even the *Last Judgment* does not prepare us for the gaunt and insubstantial forms the *Pietà* had become. Testament to Michelangelo's genius, this germ of an idea can be read by our modern eyes. We need no further explication to understand its message of grief and death—yet we have no way of ever fully knowing what Michelangelo himself intended. Perhaps he, too, had been lost in a search. But his partial discovery supplies us with more nourishment to our spirits than do many fuller explanations by lesser talents.

## The Art of Perfection: Raphael

If Michelangelo suffered torments of doubt and his long career traces both his triumphs and failures, Raphael, his younger rival, was his opposite both in temperament and in style. While Michelangelo struggled, Raphael produced with ease. Michelangelo clung stubbornly to his own inner vision, while Raphael managed to please his patrons without sacrificing any integrity. Raphael's reputation as the creator of the most perfect and sublime paintings ever known persisted down through the centuries, and was challenged seriously only in the twentieth century, when scholars turned away from the whole notion of "great" and placed more emphasis on the origins, development, and *oeuvre* of a given figure.

Raphael's rise to prominence was meteoric, and his life the most romantic of all the biographies Vasari compiled. An orphan, Raphael (Raffaello Santi or Sanzio) was precociously talented; his superiority shone out even in his earliest works. His gifts soon came to the attention of the foremost patron in Rome: the Pope. Raphael charmed all who knew him with his beautiful appearance, his grace, and excellent manners. His premature death in 1520 was greatly mourned, and his funeral contrasts with those of Leonardo and Michelangelo. Leonardo had died in exile in the arms, they say, of a French king. Michelangelo died alone, his ebbing strength pouring out in one last struggle, with a vision so intangible as to be ultimately elusive. Raphael died at the full height of his powers, and you will recall no doubt the poignant epitaph by Pietro Bembo quoted in the program: "This is that Raphael, by whom in life our mighty mother Nature feared defeat; And in whose death did fear herself to die." Raphael's body was placed at his request in the pagan/Christian monument, the Pantheon, an appropriate burial site for an artist steeped in ancient as well as Christian traditions.

Since Dante celebrated Giotto for having outshone Cimabue, a notion had been born that some artists were differentiated by their talents and genius. By Raphael's time, such genius was increasingly valued. Leonardo, Michelangelo, and Raphael were considered great in their own time, and their extraordinary talents were celebrated. Having a great artist in residence was a matter of pride to a patron and a city. It was the standard by which the culture of a city was, to some extent, measured. Patrons went to considerable pains to obtain works by a celebrated master, as contemporary documents indicate. And in the sixteenth century, the numbers of art collectors increased well beyond the limits of the papacy and the nobility. Vasari, a Florentine biographer, had a particular bias for Florentine masters and his paeans to them were sometimes excessive, but his work reflects a real value that was placed on creative genius in the sixteenth century. To Vasari, Raphael represented an artist of "supreme judgment," whose work was flawless and justly deserving of his great reputation.

In 1500 Raphael was seventeen, Leonardo was forty-eight, and Michelangelo twenty-five. Though the youngest of the titans of the early sixteenth century, Raphael was in many ways the most traditional. Born in 1483 to a painter father, Giovanni Santi, in Urbino, Raphael was orphaned in 1494. And by 1500 we know he was working in the workshop of the leading Umbrian painter, Perugino, from whom he learned to perfect the sweet-tempered, transcendently beatific faces that adorn his many charming Madonnas. Perugino also bequeathed Raphael a deep respect for studying nature and the habit of looking at other artists for models. Leonardo, Michelangelo, and Raphael were trained in the traditional workshop system, but only Raphael seems to have continued workshop practice in his own career. Content to explore and study the visible world in his own inimitable way, Leonardo, for example, conformed to no known workshop system, and Michelangelo, though he used assistants on occasion, more often than not eschewed them, as the many unfinished sculptures he bequeathed us testify. Only Raphael seems to have been secure in his ability to convey directions to his assistants with his designs and drawings so that his vision could be transcribed into finished works prepared by them. His reliance on assistants increased with the size and number of his commissions. Raphael's fame was such that the demand was great, coming not only from Rome, but from discerning collectors eager to obtain examples of his work.

Archives still preserve a whole series of letters exchanged between Alfonso, Duke of Ferrara, and his agent in Rome that recount the Duke's frustrated attempt to cajole or to threaten Raphael into living up to his promise to provide the Duke with a *Triumph of Bacchus* for his *studiolo* (or private study). Raphael died without fulfilling his promise to the Duke and the letters show the Duke alternately impatient, irritated, but ultimately reluctant to annoy the great Raphael, lest his chances of getting the work become nil.

Raphael's origins within the cooperative enterprise that was the Quattrocento studio, and his utilization of this organization to fulfill commissions towards the end of his life, have inaugurated various searches for the authentic Raphael among his many assistants. Tools of connoisseurship and refined technical analysis are applied to cull Raphael's hand from the many others with whom he collaborated. But our understanding of Raphael is complete only when we understand him as developing a new pictorial language (a new style), but employing it within a traditional workshop context. Even Raphael's style has many discernible sources besides Perugino, as one should expect from an artist trained to look, copy, and emulate. We know that Raphael looked at Leonardo's work, standing transfixed before his unfinished *Adoration* in Florence. Somehow, though exactly in what manner is uncertain, Raphael even managed to learn of Leonardo's *Last Supper* in Milan. And Raphael was, as biographers tell us, anxious to see what Michelangelo was doing in the Sistine Chapel and must have seen it when it was half-finished, adding a portrait of Michelangelo to his own work in the Vatican as a tribute. Other Florentine and Umbrian artists affected him, too—and one proof of his genius was his assimilation of all these sources into his own pictorial vocabulary.

When Raphael left Florence for Rome in 1508, he was merely twenty-five but had a strong reputation. Upon his arrival, he was soon summoned by Julius II to decorate the Pope's private apartments in the Vatican. The fresco decoration for the three rooms (stanze) absorbed much of Raphael's time from 1509 until his death eleven years later. Of the three rooms, it is the first, the Stanza della Segnatura, which is most celebrated. Here, in the Pope's private library, where sessions of the Papal Court of Justice (Segnatura Gratiae) were held, Raphael gave visual forms to ideals which probably owe their subject matter to the humanistic orientation of Julius II. The two walls, as the program will have shown you, compare, contrast, and express the unity between the antique world of philosophy and its Christian manifestation in theology. Contained within the hemispherical contours of the wall are images of such cohesion, balance, and perfection that they have become canons for generations of subsequent artists. By using the simple language of contrast, Raphael eloquently visualizes the differences and the similarities between the classical and Christian worlds.

In the *Disputa* the Christian realm is described as the union between the celestial and the material. The celestial rises above the human world, where a majestic array of saints float weightlessly beside the Holy Trinity (in which the three figures are placed against a traditional gold ground—harking back to the venerable treatment of holy subjects by fourteenth- and early fifteenth-century paint-

ers), while the message from these holy beings to the humans below is transmitted across the deliberately empty and translucent void by divine inspiration. The message is received, transcribed, and spread by God's earthly authorities, the saints, bishops, and popes of the church. Here the truth, the authority, and the revelatory nature of Catholic doctrine is celebrated. The shape and structure of the space and forms take the overall shape of the wall as its guide, giving the entire image a logic and cohesion to its context.

By contrast, the *School of Athens* (**J 630; G 17.17; H&F 11.19**) celebrates the search for answers in antiquity, which finds its ultimate answer in the Christian world. Here we see a horizontal frieze of men in the exact spot where a celestial void occupied the *Disputa*. Men, not God, are the focus of this picture. And their accomplishments are expressed by a man-made edifice: the lofty architecture (borrowed from Bramante's designs for St. Peter's) that surrounds them and sets them off. The two cornerstones of ancient philosophy, Aristotle and Plato, are shown in the exact center of the picture and are crowned by a series of arches that rise above them. As Plato (a Leonardo-esque old man) points skyward to the absolute world of "ideas" which he espoused, Aristotle points downward in his affirmation of the unceasing study of all material existence to understand the truth. To the right in the foreground, mathematicians and astronomers gather around the great Euclid, while to the left we see Pythagoras (who discovered the harmonies between numbers and music), and Heraclitus (the famed misanthropic philosopher whose theory of flux and change was all important to Plato), brooding alone in a pose clearly derived from the Sistine Chapel. Heraclitus may have been based on Michelangelo himself. Certainly no one who knew the solitary genius could have failed to recognize Raphael's brilliance in appropriating Michelangelo's face and adopting a Michelangelo-esque pose for the ancient philosopher.

Though most scholars point to the harmony and balance, as well as the use of perspective and symmetry, to underscore the central importance of Plato and Aristotle, it is less often noted that within this vaulted space, at once continuous and yet more perfect than any likely to be seen in our own world, the figures tend to be isolated, and the *division* of human schools of thought is also emphasized. Figures in the foreground are bunched in groups; Aristotle and Plato point in opposite directions, and here and there isolated figures crop up. In a language that is both subtle and sophisticated, Raphael has envisioned not only the dignity and achievement of human thought, but also its limitations—its lack of cohesion, its fractious independence, its divisiveness.

Without divine guidance, man discovers partial truths—important and consequential, but without the cohesive totality that is Christian enlightenment. How is that totality expressed in the *Disputa*? Look back at it and see how the figures flow in huge sweeps both above and

Raphael, *The School of Athens*, 1510–1511. Rome, Vatican, Stanza della Segnatura. (SCALA/ART RESOURCE, NEW YORK)

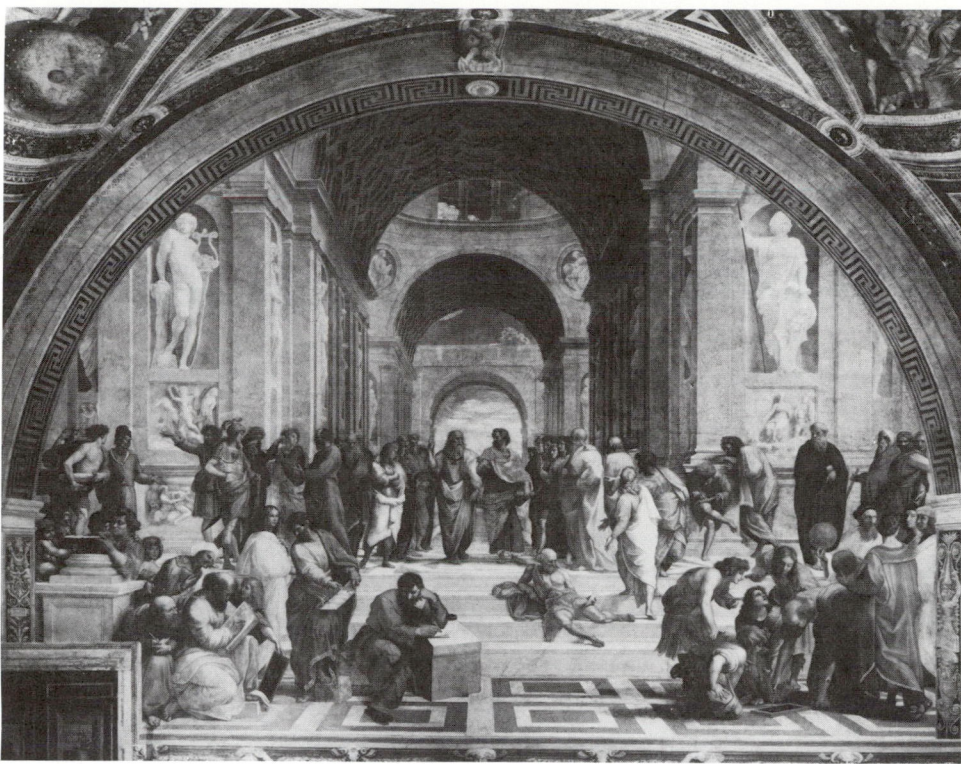

below—and how the miracle of the Mass, represented by the altar placed in the center of the composition, provides the link to the enlightenment and grace only faith can bring. Where in the *School of Athens* architecture enveloped the figures, here the figures *are* the architecture, sweeping through the vast open space of the sky, suspended by the mystical powers of faith and defining by their very being the space in which they exist.

Here in the lofty confines of the Stanza della Segnatura, on the two arched walls two exalted realms are shown, one mortal and the other divine. Both address the momentous issue of a search for truth. Raphael's lucid, majestic, and sweeping compositions lay out the meaning of his message and convey the erudite wisdom of his protagonists. Guided by the blueprint of measured squares, and the canons of perspective, we are presented with a knowable space, but one that we perceive to be more lofty, more majestic, and more spiritual than those we can encounter in the less elevated world of our own lives. These murals use fictive space as an analogue to the exalted sagacity of the venerable philosophers and saints described within. And, while the one is rational, the other is sublimely irrational. Yet both reflect contemporary thought, which sought unity and resolution. Assembling all the ancient philosophers known to the Renaissance, they come alive and coexist in the single cohesive frame of space and time. Reconciling Christian and pagan

thought had long been a goal of Renaissance thinkers, but no artist before or after Raphael expressed that goal more comprehensively or more beautifully. Raphael's *School of Athens* has become the paradigm of Renaissance classicism. Its fusion of dignified, comprehensible space, ennobled humanity, and a harmonious as well as grand sweeping vision, became a virtual academy for later painters, and it will come as no surprise to learn that Raphael was regarded as the supreme model for those eras when academic painting was at its peak, the seventeenth through the nineteenth centuries.

Raphael worked for Julius until the Pope's death, and after his death had one more opportunity to immortalize him. Raphael's *Sistine Madonna* of 1513 uses the unkempt, sunken features of the dying Pope to depict St. Sixtus, and it has been generally agreed that this most glorious of all Raphael's Madonnas (the only one to be painted on canvas), was hung by Julius's funeral bier—indicating that Julius's funeral, if not his final resting place, was as art-filled as his life had been.

If Raphael's work in the Vatican was a remarkable essay on ancient and Christian philosophical ideas, then his work in the Villa Farnesina can be described as a celebration of a wholly pagan world. Built around 1508–1509 for the Sienese banker Agostino Chigi, the Villa Farnesina (so named for the Farnese family that later owned it) was designed by Baldassare Peruzzi and was

**105**

meant to be a place for Agostino to enjoy his mistress Imperia, the most famous courtesan in all of Rome. The design of the palace was a Roman villa and its interior decoration was consistently and charmingly pagan. It contains Raphael's first important secular work, the *Triumph of Galatea* **(J 631; G 17.18),** painted around 1511–12 in the wall of a great hall on the ground floor called the Sala di Galatea.

The ceiling, with its mythological/astrological symbols celebrating the date of Agostino's birth, and was painted by Baldassare Peruzzi, while the lunettes were painted by Sebastiano del Piombo, whom we remember as having been Michelangelo's assistant. But the most successful work in the entire room is Raphael's *Triumph of Galatea*. The subject was known through the *Metamorphosis* of Ovid, and the poetry of the contemporary Poliziano, and is based on the story of Galatea, a goddess who loved Acis and was loved by the grotesque Polyphemus. Having lost Acis to Polyphemus (who killed him with a rock) she turned her dead lover into a river, and descended into the sea to escape the undesired carnality of Polyphemus. To tell his story, Raphael probably consciously chose Botticelli's *Birth of Venus*, that charming early Renaissance emblem of classicism, and reversed many of its ideas.

Where Venus emerges from the sea, Galatea returns to it; where Venus is calm and the embodiment of stability, Galatea is a virtuoso description of a form in movement; where Botticelli's image is the embodiment of grace and restrained action, Raphael's is filled with ebullient action. Perched in the center, Galatea turns her head one way, her torso another, and her knee in the opposite direction, building up a sense of torque and movement which could propel her out of her seaborne chariot. Echoing her twisting motion is the pair of Tritons to the right who move in exactly opposite directions, making a dizzying criss-cross of movement, while in the foreground, a Triton is described energetically grasping his Nereid with bold sweeping gestures. Even the sky is alive with the amorini who all take aim at Galatea. Oblivious to them, Galatea looks upward, expressing the superiority of platonic over carnal love.

Raphael's sources must have been many, and include antique monuments. The nymph with her curving, windswept veil has antecedents in ancient art, as does Galatea herself, who reminds us of the antique fleshy Venuses, perfect in proportion, abundant in form, and neutral in character. The brick-red cloak which surrounds her is reminiscent of the predominant color in ancient Roman paintings, and one wonders if Raphael could have seen one.

Space in this work is as secondary in consideration as it was important in the Stanza paintings, indicating that Raphael chose form, composition, color, and his spatial conception to suit the purposes of his painting. Here, in a work intended to be decorative and sensuously amusing, the figures all occupy a shallow, tapestry-like space which makes their actions seem part of a fantasy, which is what was intended. Amusing, imaginative, delightful, and charming, this work is as light and frothy as the *School of Athens* was serious.

Like Botticelli's *Birth of Venus* and the Titians discussed later in this unit, Raphael's *Galatea* represents the sensual, and sometimes overtly sexual subject matter that Renaissance patrons commissioned for their private enjoyment. Couched in antique references, these pictures gave patrons the opportunity to consider the nude female, to enjoy sensuous reveries while looking at them. Far more bawdy and earthy than any fifteenth-century examples, Raphael's Galatea is, nevertheless, the chaste counterpart to Titian's more lustful Venuses.

Raphael continued in much the same vein in his contribution to the Loggia di Psyche painted some five years later (between 1518 and 1519) in the same villa. As the program points out, Raphael had to rely on his assistants, particularly Giulio Romano, to complete the work, but extant drawings indicate how carefully and beautifully Raphael worked out the figures, and how ingeniously he treated the problem of the ceiling and its division into fields of narrative.

His solutions fulfill the purely decorative, secular function of the images and add playful references to sophisticated illusion. As if the ceiling were some enchanted garden, green bowers bursting with flowers and fruits rise up and divide the space into sections. The blue airy space behind the bower seems like open sky, and the stories of Cupid and Psyche are shown as though painted on an awning stretched between the bowers and tugged by the air and wind moving over it. An added conceit limits the stories to only those which took place in heaven, and the figures sitting among the bowers seem to be looking up at some episodes or simply existing in their airborne garden. Though much was produced by assistants, the best of the figures were designed and perhaps executed by Raphael, and the enchanted world owes it overall conception to his imagination.

You will likely recall the program recounting Raphael's legendary involvements with women, and certainly from the loving way he drew them, one could readily imagine Raphael succumbing to their charms. On the other hand, apocryphal stories about artists in love with their models originated in antiquity and were known in the sixteenth century through Pliny. It might well be that Vasari was embellishing his life of Raphael, and making him rival the ancients even in his love life, by adding an allusion to an ancient legend in his biography of that most perfect of artists.

The Villa Farnesina has been called the end of a chapter. The inspired humanistic, ambitious, and enthusiastic paganism which had influenced the tastes of Leo X and Agostino Chigi, as well as Raphael, came to an abrupt end, not only with their respective deaths within eight years of the completion of the Farnesina, but with the sack of Rome by the armies of Charles V, in 1527.

Reformers in the North, who shored up their arguments against the pagan, materialistic, and decadent world of Rome, turned, interestingly enough, to the ancients to supply models to shore up their beliefs. Tacitus, the Roman historian, was published in Germany in 1515, and his stories of Arminius, who rose up against the Romans in A.D. 9, captured the imaginations of contemporary Germans, who found in him the ideal exemplar: honest, courageous, and uncorrupted by Roman sensuality. Arminius was one model; the Revelations of the Bible provided yet another: Rome and the Pope were described as the anti-Christ, and apocalyptic imagery in the North often showed the papal tiara as associated with the Whore of Babylon. Resentful of the demands on their pockets to indulge papal projects and no longer convinced of Catholic doctrines regarding indulgences, confession, as well as saints as intercessors, Protestants not only formed their own religion but developed a deep enmity for Catholicism and the papacy in Rome. Political, religious, and cultural motives culminated in the fall of Rome on May 6, 1527, when ten thousand vehemently anti-Catholic soldiers, in an army of mixed recruits numbering over thirty thousand, fell on the city and occupied it until February, 1528.

To Rome it was as though history had repeated itself; just as the barbarians had destroyed the ancient Roman empire, so now barbarians were destroying the Renaissance one. As the troops descended on Rome they were swept up in an orgy of murder, rape, and pillage. Someone carved Martin Luther's name with a pike on one of Raphael's frescos in the Stanza. Churches were sacked, their contents thrown into the streets, where chalices, altarpieces, and holy vestments were hacked to bits. Paralyzed with fright, Pope Clement VII had to be told to take refuge in the fortress of the Castel Sant' Angelo (Hadrian's Tomb), and the Bishop of Nocera held up the Pope's skirts so he could run there faster. The rich were held for ransom, others were mutilated for their belongings: fingers chopped off for rings and arms for bracelets. Historians have estimated the dead on the first day to have numbered eight thousand.

Broken and defeated, the Pope surrendered to Charles V, but remained prisoner in the Castel until he escaped in early December. Having no other recourse, Pope Clement was forced to come to terms with the Emperor. What were his conditions? Not the reform of the church, not the important issues of the country; they were political and familial. A cousin to Pope Leo X, Clement VII wanted the Medici restored in Florence (which had ousted them as soon as Rome fell). With Charles's support the Medici were once more returned to power in Florence, and the papacy, much diminished in power, prestige, and influence, survived in Rome, a city now burned-out and half its population dead or in exile.

Clement survived for only seven more years. He was succeeded by Paul the III, whose alteration of Clement's plans for the wall of the Sistine Chapel from a Resurrection to a Last Judgment is seen as a change in Rome's spiritual climate. It is true that the vital artistic energy that had thrived in Rome changed, and artistic developments elsewhere now take our attention.

## Part 2
# THE HIGH RENAISSANCE IN VENICE

In the sixteenth century, as the program noted, Venice entered what is known as its Golden Age. Venice, like Rome, had built a myth about herself that traced her origins to the time of the dissolution of the Roman Empire. Created as a watery refuge from the Huns who invaded Italy in 421 B.C., Venice thrived and grew, building her city on hundreds of wooden pylons sunk deep in the marshy soil and using the surrounding waterways for a traffic of gondolas, barges, and other kinds of boats. Rising dreamlike from the sea, her splendid palaces, treasure-laden churches, and quiet canals extended in a meandering pattern. Venice had briefly lost some of her edge as a trading center in the late fifteenth century, when new trade routes to the East were found by Spanish, English, and Portuguese explorers, but Venice continued on a reduced scale in the sixteenth century to trade in spices, glass, and other goods. Venice often aroused the enmity and jealousy of other Italian city-states, particularly Rome. Julius II in 1508 instigated the League of Cambrai, consisting of Louis XII of France, Maximilian I, Henry VIII of England, Ferdinand of Aragon, and the Medici of Florence, which attacked the Venetians in the battle of Agnadello in 1509, and Venice lost many of her territories.

But her defeat was temporary. Using her skill at diplomacy, Venice, led by Doge (from the Venetian dialect for "leader" derived from the Latin *dux*) Loredan, whom Bellini so beautifully immortalized, set one member of the League against the other. By 1510 Julius II was quarreling with the French, changed sides, and revoked his excommunication of the Venetian State. The Venetian State had prevailed and the Venetian myth had been strengthened. Guided by a stable government consisting of a Doge who served for life, and served by a body of loyal patricians, Venice saw herself guided by her patron, Saint Mark, toward the ideals of justice and peace, and remained a stable government in a time when other Italian cities witnessed violent upheavals. The Medici, exiled in 1494, returned to Florence in 1512 assisted by a Spanish army, and were thrown out once more in 1527, only to have Charles V assist in re-establishing them as hereditary dukes in 1530. Rome had just been invaded and brought to her knees in 1527. But Venice remained serene, and "Serenissima"—the most serene republic—was the name by which she was known through the long centuries of her existence.

Most serene, a city of mystery and strange opposites, where carnival lasted for much of the year and whose courtesans were legendary all over Europe, Venice was and is unique. Jewel of the Adriatic, white swan of cities, phantom, mirage, abhorrent, green, slippery, and decadent, Venice was and is everyone's dream or nightmare. Venice has inspired more poets and writers and has hosted more visitors bent on amusement or reverie than any other city. Her buildings formed a network of confusing streets and alleys that confound all but those born there. Her painters, true to their heritage, created the first pictures in which the viewer lost himself, drawing him in just as the streets and byways lured the visitor into the heart of this magical city.

Venice quite naturally gathered about her a myth, a myth that was consciously fostered and encouraged.

## The Venetian myth

A particularly Venetian expression of her myth can be seen, as the program showed you, in the staircase leading up to the Doge's palace. Designed in 1500, the solemn and imposing staircase was embellished in 1566 by Jacopo Sansovino with sculptures—colossal descendants of Michelangelo's *David* who served much the same function. Mars, the God of War, and Neptune, God of the Sea, were ancient gods, adapted as part of the symbolic language which, in the sixteenth century, grew increasingly classicizing in its subject matter. Skilled at war and ruler of the Adriatic, Venice and her leaders gave visual form to this proclamation by the two figures whose idealized and superhuman musculature establish their purpose first and foremost as symbols. In a subtle way, these sculptures, whose massive presences and ancient attributes make them a far cry from any medieval sculpture, show us that a notion not dissimilar to medieval thinking has once more emerged. These are personifications, rather than persons, and though freestanding, they make sense only in the larger context in which they exist: on the staircase, with the Ducal palace behind the Lion of St. Mark presiding above them. In adopting such a symbolic system of communication, Sansovino, like other sixteenth-century sculptors, was retracing the steps in a complex train of thought that had its origins in the myth-building practices of the ancient Romans and which had been adapted to an anti-materialistic, anti-physical, and anti-human but still symbolic system of the Early Christians. Though symbolic expression became increasingly human throughout the Middle Ages, as we have seen, the human form gained the greatest credence in sculpture in the fifteenth century, when it became a natural form as much as a symbolic one.

Now, in the sixteenth century, the emphasis has shifted back again to the highly stylized and consciously classicizing forms such as Sansovino's figures, and to a more symbolic language and symbols that must of necessity express something larger than themselves—and bespeak a higher order. Here that higher message is the myth of Venice, and it is a myth that has been fostered and interpreted in various ways until the present day.

The creator of these sculptures was Jacopo Sansovino, who fled Rome in 1527 to escape the sack and took refuge in Venice. Jacopo had been born in Florence in 1486 as Jacopo Tatti and there was apprenticed to the sculptor Andrea Sansovino, from whom Jacopo adopted his surname. In 1505, not yet twenty, Jacopo set out for Rome, lured there by the marvels of antiquity which had attracted so many other artists, including some of the ones we have studied, such as Donatello and Brunelleschi. Though trained as a sculptor, Sansovino was also an architect, and in that discipline he made his greatest contributions.

The most celebrated of all Sansovino's commissions was the Library of St. Mark, designed to define one side of the small piazza leading from the Quay to Venice's most venerable church, San Marco. The Library was begun in 1537, and was completed after Sansovino's death, following his design. Sansovino proved himself equally adept at adjusting the design of the building to serve both its interior and exterior functions. The Piano Nobile, or first floor, of this magnificent two-storied structure was intended to house a collection of manuscripts the Venetian Republic had inherited; it also provided reading rooms, a vestibule to be used as a classroom for nobles, and offices for the procurators, while the ground floor, the Primo Piano, was, as was customary, used for shops. The reading room required good lighting, well supplied by the large east-oriented windows. Just as important, if not more so, was the Library's function to define the side of the piazzetta which looked across to the Palazzo Ducale.

Sansovino succeeded brilliantly. Adapting a system of columns and arches that he knew well from such famous Roman monuments as the Colosseum and the Theater of Marcellus, Sansovino created an imposing façade that would upon completion be twenty-one bays long. Double-tiered, and Doric Order sits above the Ionic in perfect and correct form. The façade marches forward in dignified, measured pace—the discreteness of each bay made more emphatic by Sansovino's daring use of light and shadow. The windows are set deep within each bay and are cast in shadow, while the half-columns project outward in a sculptural fashion and are bathed in light. Alternating patterns of dark and light result, which are at once distinct and knit together into a single entity by the emphatic entablature. Sansovino's Library added a certain majesty to Venice's most important square and in so doing, also contributed substantially to her image as the queen of cities.

Echoes of Sansovino's mythic and classicizing vision are evident in yet another contribution to the area around St. Mark's—the so-called Loggetta, built at the base of the Campanile beginning in 1538. Derived from the ancient

Roman form of the triumphal arch, the Loggetta was intended to serve as a gathering place for the nobility, and provided a suitably theatrical and magisterial background to the public processions which originated within its precincts. Four niches flank the larger arches and these, as you will remember, have figures within. Above is a series of reliefs illustrating Venice as Justice in the center panel, while the bronze figures below represent Minerva, Apollo, Mercury, and Peace: Minerva, the civilizing goddess who fights for just causes; Apollo, who represented the rational and cultured side of life; Mercury, who personified eloquence and reason; and the embodiment of Peace, which results from the combined efforts of these benevolent forces. When the noble rulers of Venice gathered beneath these deliberate references to ancient ideals, their meaning would have been obvious and the august images of antiquity would lend their authority to the rank and power of Venice's ruling class.

The program quotes Sansovino's own description of his meaning in the construction of his Logetta and its many images, and these words deserve repetition here:

> The city of Venice has by far surpassed all other republics in time, by means of its admirable government and by being still in its first condition. This continuity can only be said to come from one cause, namely its senators' unsurpassed wisdom; because they have given it a good foundation in religion and justice, it has lasted and will last a long time. Since the ancients represented Pallas as wisdom I decided that this figure should be Pallas, armed and in an alert and lively attitude, because the wisdom of these elders of ours in public affairs is unique and without rival.

Venice herself was personified as a beautiful woman, and nowhere is she more gloriously depicted than in Paolo Veronese's *Ceres Renders Homage to Venice* (**G 17.69**), painted for the Doge's Palace in 1575. Decorating the ceiling, this huge and monumental oil painting is testimony to Veronese's brilliance. A consummate, urbane, and sophisticated painter, Veronese transformed what might have been a dry allegory into a celebration of feminine beauty and bounty in a virtuoso display of illusionism, grace, and some humor. Seated on a richly appointed throne, in a sumptuous array of silks and brocades for which Venice became famous, Venice takes the form of a beautiful, sensuous woman. Her earnest expression does not hide her allure and appeal. As an elderly Lion of St. Mark sits at her feet, rather like a large overgrown tabby, Ceres, the goddess of agriculture, and Hercules, the personification of physical prowess and courage, pay homage.

Hercules seems to contemplate the lion, which bears a humorous resemblance to the trophy skin he holds modestly over himself; Ceres and her two putti attendants offer the fruits of their bounty to the city. Bathed in a warm light, the scene is one of enchantment and serenity. Guided by peace and justice (who may be the figures flanking her), Venice herself embodies a Golden Age. No artist surpassed Veronese in the lightness and sophistica-

tion of his vision, effortlessly mingling the official with the human so that each is enriched. Unabashedly physical, material, and sensual, Veronese's image of Venice is also tranquil, serious, and touched with equally light measures of humor and pathos—its evanescent mood capturing the essence of the real Venice as well as perpetuating her myth.

The program's last example of mythic Venice is the image of *Paradise* on the end wall of the Sala del Maggiore Consiglio in the Palazzo Ducale, painted in his shop between 1588 and 1593 by Jacopo Robusti Tintoretto, one of the great Venetian triumvirate of Golden Age painters. In a chamber that contained the largest beamed ceiling known in Europe until the nineteenth century, up to one thousand nobles or more gathered to elect their Doge. This Sala has some obvious parallels to the Sistine Chapel in Rome, and it is significant that in this secular counterpart to the more sacred function of the Sistine Chapel (where the Pope was elected), a sacred subject would be chosen. More important, the subject was Paradise, surely intended to allude to the earthly paradise that was Venice, thanks to the just and wise rule of the Doge and the nobles. A pictorial colossus and painted analogue to the larger-than-life images of Venice's attributes done by Sansovino much earlier, Tintoretto's *Paradise* is occupied by literally hundreds of figures—the elect of humanity—many of whom were portraits of the donors who paid for this enormous painting.

Measuring twenty-three by seventy-two feet, the picture was the largest painting on canvas in the world, and its message—the mass of blessed humanity illuminated by the celestial light of heaven—overrode its aesthetic merits. Technically a marvel, the work is not a masterpiece, but an example of the pictorial myth building that began long before the dawn of the Venetian Golden Age and lasted well into its declining years. Venice was, in fact, already in a decline economically when Tintoretto produced this work. But the Serenissima would survive, secure in her marshy retreat for two centuries more. Her government would serve as a model for cities looking at alternatives to monarchies in the seventeenth century. Her ultimate decline would not occur until 1797, when Napoleon became her first invader and planted the "tree of liberty" on Venetian soil. From this blow, the Serenissima would never recover.

## Painters of Poetry and Sensuality

The painters who contributed pictorial celebrations of the Venetian myth were a remarkable body of native talent. Spawned by the great Bellini, an unprecedented school of painters was active in sixteenth-century Venice. Giorgione, Titian, Veronese, Tintoretto are all giants. Possessed of great originality, a feeling for the medium of oil paint, and a love of the human figure as well as nature, the Venetian painters often concentrated on narratives centered on the female form. They, too, adopted classical subjects, but theirs were the stuff of reverie and fantasy. Sensuous, poetic, and dreamy, Venetian painting eschewed the rational, masculine, heroic visions of Florentine artists and poured out paintings filled with tantalizing goddesses, nude and voluptuous, or stories of love (Venus and Adonis), of death, and of bacchic rites.

A taste had emerged for pictures called "poesie," fantasies that today have defied exact interpretation and which most likely were painted as subjects for secular meditation, much as religious pictures had been painted for sacred meditation. Such poesie depended on the viewer to help create the story; like Raphael's Chigi (Farnese) Palace commissions, they were for private enjoyment and contemplation. Bellini had painted such a picture: his *Feast of the Gods* **(G 17.50)**, done in 1514 for Alfonso d'Este. His pupil Giorgione developed the "poesie" further; in fact, many scholars credit Giorgione with the invention of the subjective, elusive imagery of the true poesie.

Giorgione (Giorgio Barbarelli) was born in Castelfranco, near Venice, in 1477, and he died very young (age thirty-three) in 1510. Like Raphael, Giorgione was celebrated for his beauty, for his grace, and for his romantic early demise, and like him also, Giorgione had a special affinity for the female form. Besides being inspired by Bellini to look and learn from landscape, Giorgione was influenced by Leonardo, whose stay in Venice probably helped popularize the "sfumato" approach to painting, where gradations from light to dark are so soft and subtle that the painted forms seem to be enveloped in a gentle smoke.

Giorgione's most famous poesie is his picture now called *The Tempest* **(J clpl 79)**, which has defied all attempts to interpret it. And we know from X rays that Giorgione himself changed his mind about what to paint midway through, changing the figure at the left from a nude woman dangling her feet in the water to a dressed man, perhaps a soldier, who is fully clothed and is standing upright. Set at opposite sides of the landscape, with a town in the background and classical ruins in the middle ground, the scene is charged with feeling, not only because of the enigmatic nature of the two opposing figures, but because of the approaching storm. Why is the woman sitting there nursing her child? Is she a gypsy? Is she a forest nymph unaware of the soldier seeing her? Is she the embodiment of the fecundity of nature, the regenerative powers of rain and earth? Why is the man standing there? Is he the male analogue, whose gender is reaffirmed by the phallic-shaped broken column just behind him? No known literary subject shaped Giorgione's thinking that we know of. Instead, his innate picture-making sense, his interest in the female form and the male form, and the countryside around Venice seem to have coalesced into one of the most memorable and elusive pictures of the Renaissance, and his feeling for not only the beauty, but the power of nature, is here given its

earliest expression. This may well be the first storm captured on canvas.

Like Dürer's *Melancholia*, which was mentioned in the previous unit, Giorgione's *Tempest* is a milestone because it was painted (so far as we know) purely from Giorgione's imagination and probably to suit himself. No known commission brought this work into being. Though we know it was in the collection of Gabriel Vendramin in 1530, it is not certain that Vendramin commissioned it, or even that he bought it directly from Giorgione, since the artist had died twenty years earlier. Giorgione shows us an *artist* who is emerging and supplanting the artisan and who shares much in common with artists working today—who take it for granted that their own imaginations and their own creative spark inspire the production of an image. How unlike the bulk of what was painted well through the eighteenth century. Giorgione put his creative force first in his *Tempest*. It became the impulse for the *Tempest* and to his artistic independence is added work of unspecified meaning, purely subjective in purpose, requiring imagination on the viewer's part as well.

Giorgione developed another milestone in his theme of nature and humanity in his depiction of a reclining Venus, asleep in the landscape. Reclining nudes had been the subject of marriage chests (*cassone*), where they were sometimes painted inside the lids. Giorgione revolutionized the subject by placing his lushly sensuous, appealingly vulnerable, yet wholly natural reclining nudes into a landscape, and weaving the forms of the landscape so that they are an extension of the figure, or the figure is simply another aspect of the landscape. The illusionistic properties of oil paint are used to describe soft, pliable skin, cool, shiny satin, as well as earth and sky—all set in a waning golden light. This multitude of textures and colors exploits oil paint to its fullest. With this calm, rather simple correlation between the resting Venus and the placid natural setting, a new type of subject gained popularity: the reclining nude.

Deliberately creating works of this kind to appeal to the frankly sensual appetites of private collectors, Giorgione's slightly younger contemporary, Titian, could hardly supply them fast enough. Over a period of twenty years, we know that Titian produced at least six paintings of a nude woman lying on a bed. The *Venus of Urbino* **(G 17.63; H&F 11.37)**, done for the Duke of Urbino, is a probable copy of a lost example Titian had painted for Charles V. The setting is a bedroom, and the woman is now more like a courtesan, aware of the onlooker, coolly gazing with frank interest out at us. Her body is described with an even more sensuous feeling for skin and flesh than Giorgione shows, but this example is chaste in comparison to the *Danae* Titian painted between 1544 and 1545 for Cardinal Alessandro Farnese. This work, with its overtly sexual scene, in which Danae is preparing for the loving embrace of Jupiter, who arrives as a shower of gold, provoked this comment: "The nude which Your Reverence saw in Pesaro in the apartment of the Duke of

Urbino looks like a nun beside this one" (Hope, p. 89). Titian took this work to Rome personally in 1545, where Michelangelo saw it and commented that it was too bad the Venetians could not draw better. The two great artists met, an encounter described by Vasari, and though pleasantries were exchanged, it seems these two titans of art were so disparate in their views of what true art was that they found no real common ground. Michelangelo's firm belief in drawing and Titian's equally firm love of paint and color forever divided these artists. To Michelangelo, drawing was the ultimate rational tool which guided the artist's hand and gave rise to a heroic conception. Even in 1545, when Michelangelo's ideas about art had become more ephemeral and elusive, he would not yield on the value of drawing over the more intuitive and subjective approach to art espoused by Titian. Nevertheless, Michelangelo's very last works share in their form the emotional and irrational spirit, a kinship with Venetian art which he refused to acknowledge in words.

## Masters of the Sacred Subject: Titian, Veronese, Tintoretto, and Palladio

Churches and confraternities were important patrons during Venice's history, and besides Bellini, whose sacred subject matter was discussed in the previous unit, Titian, Veronese, and Tintoretto all made remarkable contributions to the history of religious painting. Their religious paintings, like their secular works, exhibit a particularly Venetian feeling for light as it plays over forms, dissolving edges, melting one form into another, emphasizing both a psychological and physical atmosphere. Their counterpart in architecture was Palladio, whose classically inspired churches still reflect the Venetian sunlight, just as Titian's pictures seem to capture it.

### A *new grandeur of size and form:* Titian's early altarpieces

One of Titian's earliest efforts was a triumphant work, *The Assumption of the Virgin* (**H&F 11.35**), executed for the Church of the Frari. Painted as the high altar for the Friar's Minor between 1516 and 1518, the *Assumption* is over twenty feet high and the largest and most important painting done in Venice at the time. Set between and beneath several tiers of lancet windows in the Gothic church, and seen through an arched choir screen, the painting had to have bold forms and colors to successfully compete with and complement the bright light and emphatic forms of its surroundings. These considerations of function and setting were important to Titian in his formulation of the painting. He also looked at the artistic developments outside Venice. More than one scholar has pointed to the monumental forms of Raphael's *Sistine Madonna* of 1513, which may have inspired Titian, while

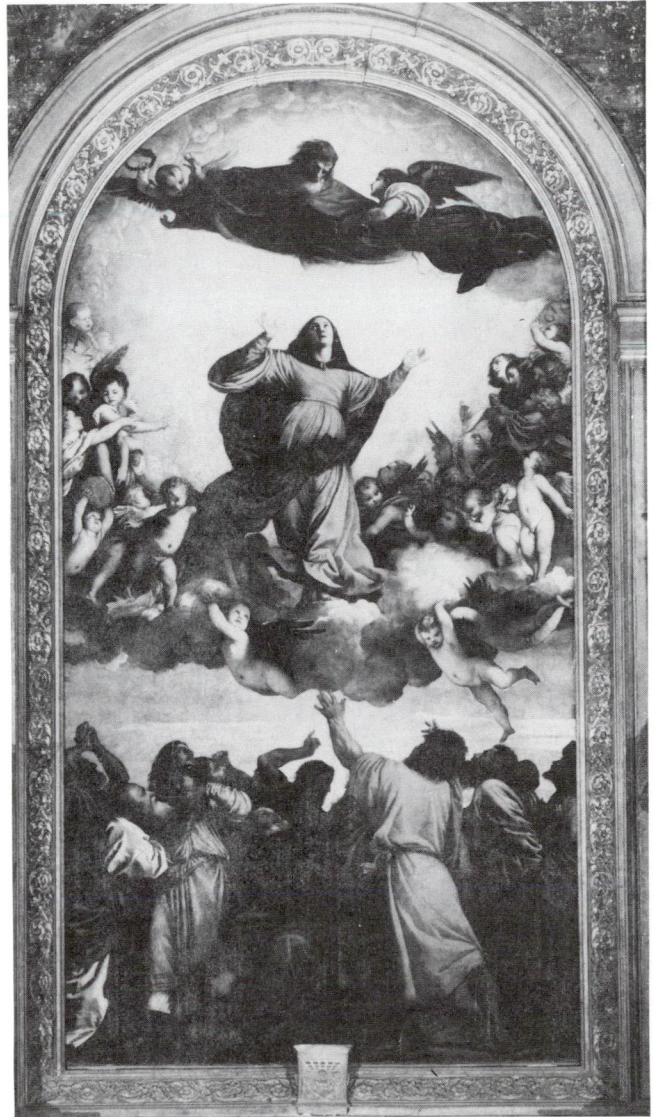

Titian, *The Assumption of the Virgin*, 1520.  Venice, San Francesco dei Frari. (Scala/Art Resource, New York)

the double-tiered composition of Raphael's *Transfiguration* (**H&F 11.27**) is also sometimes discussed in relation to Titian's work.

Regardless of Raphael's possible influence, Titian was his own man, working within the tradition of this subject to develop a revolutionary interpretation. Unlike earlier interpretations of the Assumption (the ascent of the Virgin Mary into heaven) in which the Virgin is symbolically suspended in mid-air, frozen and unmoving, Titian has shown the scene in dazzling movement. His majestic, fully sculptural figure of the Virgin is rising heavenward, her robes aswirl with wind and light passing over her moving form. A cascade of angels assists her ascent. Received into a nearly blinding celestial light, she reaches up to God the Father, who, bearded and ascetic, is nearly as ephemeral in this work as he was material and substantial in Michelangelo's Sistine ceiling. An angel messenger listens to God's instructions and prepares to offer the Virgin the crown of heaven. A series of sliding, tilting forms lends visual energy to the action Titian portrayed. Below, the gathered apostles register their astonishment and awe at this miracle, alternately praying, gasping, and reaching up for her. Feeling, motion, and light all come together in a glorious, characteristically Venetian vision. In its transitoriness, the *Assumption* anticipates the baroque, and in its poetic mood, it remembers Bellini.

Titian's conception was so original that the Friars had doubts about accepting it at first, but when the painting was set in place, Titian's exploitation of the surrounding architecture, as well as of the choir screen which frames and sets off the painting, convinced them that it not only belonged, but was a masterpiece. The pure colors, bold design, and brilliant lighting all effectively overcame the limits of setting. In its exploitation of setting, in its emphasis on subjective experience over rational portrayal, and in the sophistication of its illusion, Titian's painting, like much of Venetian art, set the stage for the development of baroque art in the seventeenth century.

Titian's reputation was established with this work, and within three years he received another commission in the same church. The Pesaro family commissioned an altarpiece in 1519 (**J 635; G 17.62;**), which Titian completed after seven years' work in 1526. Jacopo Pesaro was Bishop of Paphos in Cyprus and as commander of the papal fleet in 1502 had won a battle against the Turks. Titian had painted a votive picture of Jacopo Pesaro around 1506, and in the Frari painting he enlarged on his theme of Jacopo Pesaro paying homage to the Madonna for his grand victory against the Turks. We see Jacopo kneeling to the left, praying to the Virgin in much the same position as the donors in Masaccio's *Trinity*, while to the right, other members of the Pesaro family also kneel in veneration. Jacopo is presented to the Madonna by St. Maurice, the warrior saint, who holds the Pesaro coat of arms aloft on a flag, while St. Peter represents Pesaro's role as papal commander. High above them all is the enthroned Virgin, who no longer occupies the center frontal position of traditional altar pictures, but has been moved to one side; moreover, her throne has been turned sideways. X rays show us that Titian experimented with the architectural setting until he fixed on the large imposing columns behind the figures. These lend a magisterial dignity and solemnity to the event. They also balance and lend weight to the otherwise rather small figures within the large canvas.

Titian's injection of asymmetry and deep airy space into this religious subject was inspired. It adds an element of narrative, and binds the actual and sacred characters together in a convincing, slightly informal fashion. Regal and elevated, the Madonna tilts her head down to acknowledge Jacopo, while the Christ Child playfully offers his toe to St. Francis, who acts as intercessor to the sober assembly of Pesaro family members to the lower right. Perhaps impatient with such ceremonies, not unlike the infant Christ above him, the youngest member of the Pesaro group looks out at us, a winsome and captivating child whose striking presence underscores Titian's brilliance not only as a painter of grand altarpieces, but of portraits. So beautifully conceived as to seem devoid of all contrivance, the Pesaro altar anticipates the developments of the seventeenth century. Venice, home of theater and carnival, of fantasy and reverie, was the natural home to theatrical and staged works like Titian's Pesaro altar. It was also the wellspring for that most theatrical of all ages, the baroque.

This painting is so balanced and harmonious within its overall asymmetricality that we never bother to question its logic, but if we did, we would find that it has none. Where is this assembly? What are those columns? Here, as in the seventeenth century, effect is everything. Staging the event is more important than mere logic, just as the effect on one's senses and emotions is more important than rationality. If Michelangelo and Raphael induced a sense of awe with their intellectual triumphs, Titian earned his viewer's empathy and admiration for his engaging and charming illusions.

Titian, like Michelangelo, lived to a venerable old age. And in his old age, Titian developed a wholly different, highly personal, and deeply felt interpretation of religious subjects. He seemed haunted by the events of Christ's passion, and painted images of Christ's flagellation, the lamentation over Christ's body, and his burial. Titian's *Entombment*, painted in 1559 for Philip II of Spain and now in the Prado, is one of the finest of these late works. Transcending all previous treatments of this familiar subject, it is an elemental portrayal of grief and pathos. Unlike his earlier narratives, Titian has given this *Entombment* almost no setting. Looming out of a darkened background, the Virgin, John, and Nicodemus lean over Christ's lifeless form—his limp weight given wordless emphasis by the arm which dangles uselessly over the edge of the sarcophagus.

Pushed forward, up against the picture surface, the *Entombment* is nearly oppressive in its concentration of figures. We are at once impelled to come closer and impelled to back away. Christ's body is shown frontally, but at an eerily tilted angle—echoes of the asymmetry which added narrative spontaneity to the Pesaro altar. Here the ancient, venerable, symmetrical, vertical icons of Lamentation have been set askew, leaving us to ponder not only the mystery of Christ's death, but the reality of his dead weight, a reality further underscored by the awkwardly bent figure seen from behind, who helps lower Christ's feet into the tomb. Behind this red-cloaked figure (who adds nearly the only color note in the whole picture) a ghost-like Magdalen races up, set off by a cloud-streaked sky (becoming the first in a triad of leftward-leaning figures ending in the dead Christ himself). Her haunting gesture has a ghost-like after image in the looming darkness behind the Virgin. Is this a mirror (an odd device for an entombment), or is this hand simply a residue from an earlier hand placement that Titian left behind, pleased with the effect?

Here Titian has used his medium in a daring way. Instead of describing material and texture, instead of celebrating the sensual physicality of his subjects, paint here dematerializes his forms, reaching beyond their external appearances to their essences. Broadly applied, scraped, and scumbled, paint seems to tremble on the very surface of the canvas—alternately describing eccentric dabs on its grainy texture and coalescing into these tragic characters emerging out of a nightmarish dream.

Like Michelangelo's Rondanini *Pietà* and Donatello's pulpits, Titian's *Entombment* has stripped away earlier conventions to find this vision. This vision is made possible only by the cumulative experience of thought and imagination ripened by age and wisdom. Like Michelangelo and Donatello, Titian had explored the meaning of death with a new understanding, perched—as he was—on the edge of the same chasm. Understanding death's finality, accepting its inevitability, and expressing its tragedy, Titian reached into the core of his humanity for this universally affecting image.

## Poetic license: Veronese's *Feast in the House of Levi*

In 1571 a fire broke out in the Dominican church of S. Giovanni de Paolo and destroyed the *Last Supper* in the church's refectory—a masterpiece by Titian. The priors turned not to the aged Titian but to his younger contemporary, Veronese, for a replacement, and they got more than they bargained for. His *Last Supper* **(J clpl 86; G 17.68; H&F 11.35)** transforms the traditional sacred meal into an elaborate banquet, set beneath an arcade reminiscent of Sangallo's architecture and attended by dwarfs, dogs, nobles, German soldiers, Moorish slaves, and presided over by an imposing-looking gentleman in a striped gown who acts as a sort of maitre d'. So many incidental details are added, including the man on the stairs at the left who has suffered a bloody nose, that the true nature of the scene—Christ gathered with his apostles—is nearly obscured, and one has the impression that the holy men are gathered for this solemn occasion at one of the most popular eating places of sixteenth-century Venice.

Grandiose in scale, the *Last Supper* is a magnificent portrayal of diverse figures and architecture, and became the touchstone for many later works by such important painters as Tiepolo. However, its accomplishments were obscured by its digression from tradition, and Veronese was hauled before the Inquisition in 1573 to answer some serious questions. Medieval in origin, the Inquisition, that holy office designed to prevent heretical actions or expressions, was revived during the Counter Reformation. When asked by the papal inquisitors to justify his inclusion of so many incidental figures, Veronese explained: "We painters take the same license the poets and jesters take. . . . If in a picture there is some space to spare, I enrich it with figures according to the stories . . . and I paint pictures as I see fit, as well as my talent permits." He then went on to say that he took liberties just as Michelangelo took liberties when painting the *Last Judgment* with figures all in the nude. Forcing the tribunal to defend Michelangelo, Veronese was instructed by the Inquisition to change his painting, but chose instead to preserve the integrity of his creation and altered the title instead to a more acceptable subject: *Feast in the House of Levi*. A landmark case that has interest for twentieth-century American legal history with its adamant defense of first amendment rights, Veronese's trial was also important in its own day.

In this exchange we witness not only an artist taking creative license and defending it—but also not altering his work to suit authority. We also see the church particularly sensitive to the charges of impropriety. Chastened, or at least reaffirming its legitimacy in the wake of the Reformation, the church embarked on a crusade to reaffirm the value of pictorial representation of sacred mysteries against the charges of idolatry and secularism aimed against it by the heretical reformers of the North. However, for pictures to retain their sacred impact, they needed to conform to certain proprieties, and works like Veronese's *Last Supper* were far too vulgar and commonplace to be acceptable. We will witness this same sensitivity again a few decades later in the early seventeenth century, when the revolutionary genius of Caravaggio had the audacity to use the body of a drowned whore as his model for the dead Virgin.

## The church reborn as a temple: Palladio's *S. Giorgio Maggiore*

As you will recall from the program, Andrea Palladio, the most gifted architect of sixteenth-century Venice, considerably changed the Venetian façade with his church designs. Most important of them was his church on the island of S. Giorgio Maggiore, across the lagoon from San Marco. Like Sansovino, Palladio went to Rome in 1542, where he adopted the name Palladio from the antique name Pallas, and where he enthusiastically studied ancient buildings and Vetruvius's treatise on architecture. The fruits of his studies were born in Venice, in such masterpieces as the Church of S. Giorgio Maggiore **(J 662–663; G 17.54–17.55; H&F 11.42)**. Built on the island of the same name, which had once been the refuge of Cosimo de'Medici during his brief exile from Florence in 1433, the island was home to a Benedictine monastery. Between 1559 and 1580 Palladio contributed designs for enlarging the monastery and the creation of a new Church of S. Giorgio. Considered one of his greatest sacred works, Palladio's church has literally become a Christianized temple.

Two temple porches, one superimposed on the other, compose its simple, dignified façade and resolve the problem of accommodating nave and aisle within the church to the exterior form of temple design. The nave is reflected by the triangular pediment clearly supported on two pairs of columns set on high bases, while the side aisles are reflected in the lower, wider pediment supported by paired flat pilasters on the side. Smaller triangular pediments, of the same proportions as the central one, flank it on either side and enclose the sarcophagi and portrait busts of two doges who had been patrons of the monastery, while statues of St. George and St. Stephen are set in the niches between the paired columns. Compact and harmonious, the façade gains dignity, clarity, and a special prominence by being built of white Istrian marble. This uniform color not only lends integrity to the whole façade design, but reflects the light from the water and sky, making S. Giorgio shine like a transported temple under the bright, clear Venetian sky. Like all Venetian artists, Palladio developed a particular sensitivity to and love of light, both outside and inside his buildings.

In its august simplicity, S. Giorgio added a new, more aggressive classicism to Venice and seems an expression of Venetian civic pride as well as Venetian piety. Its austere façade must have made a considerable impression on Venetians used to the complex, busy, and fussy exteriors of many Venetian churches. Most important, however, is Palladio's purposeful re-adaptation of pagan temples into a Christian church—not a mere borrowing of a column, or of a modular design. Palladio found in his day that the most eloquent expressions for the church were the new benign forms taken from its former enemy. Here they do not express paganism, but rationality, harmony, and serenity. Though he preferred the uniform, cohesive expression of the circle, he limited that desire to the shape of his dome, acceding to the requirements of worship and using a Latin cross plan for the church itself. Not unlike Brunelleschi before him, Palladio thought like a Roman about space. He wanted to shape it, define it, and give it a rational, dignified expression that would underscore the worshipper's harmony within the environment.

Within the building, all is whiteness and light. Adapting the semi-circular "thermal windows" (from *thermae* meaning baths) he saw in Roman baths, Palladio placed them strategically to give better light and softer shadows to the whole. His belief in white was emphatic: "Of all the colours, none is more proper for churches than white, since the purity of the colour, as of life itself, is particularly satisfying to God." The overall space is easily read from any point in the room; the observer's eye is guided by the large central dome and the half-columns and piers, as well as by Corinthian pilasters that are ranged in a regular pattern throughout the space. The space is tangible, moving softly, serenely, and gracefully—defining the building as well as being defined by it. Light, pure, and nearly unembellished, its precise cross arms and vaults curve, mold, and embrace the space around us.

Palladio's genius lies not only in his original adaptation of ancient sources, but in his utilization of them to create buildings that seem to exist in a self-contained, ideal world of their own creation. This self-possession, this cohesion, is an intuitive and idiosyncratic refinement of ideas developed by Brunelleschi and learned from the ancients. Though its origins are visible, Palladio's use of them is his own. Brunelleschi had inaugurated the simple, unadorned interior; Palladio adapted it, making light play a more prominent role. By making his walls white and reflective, he made his interiors seem to glow from within and exhibit the sensual love of light that is so particularly Venetian. Like other Renaissance architects, Palladio borrowed from antiquity, but his adaptation was in many ways subjective. Palladio was reaching for effect sometimes at the expense of logic. In that respect, Palladio was the quintessential Venetian artist, shaping and affecting his onlooker's experience just as Titian, Veronese, and Tintoretto did in their paintings. There is no real logic in superimposing one tall colonnaded porch over another to make a façade, yet the effect is so aesthetically satisfying and convincing that we are no more inclined to question it than we are to question the logic of Titian's *Pesaro Altar*. S. Giorgio became one of Palladio's most enduring legacies. Its flexible, graceful, and pleasing adaptations of ancient forms nurtured generations of architects. Palladio's work was the classical style of the future. English eighteenth-century architecture is unthinkable without it, and so is the architecture of that epitome of Rational thought, Thomas Jefferson. If Palladio's architecture supplied a seminal and quintessentially Venetian treatment of light and texture, the paintings within the church reveal the talents of the third of that triumvirate of Venetian painters, Tintoretto.

### The artist as dramatist: Tintoretto and S. Giorgio Maggiore

Jacopo Tintoretto, like Titian and Veronese, was a master of oil painting with a particularly sensuous and exuberant feel for his medium. Like them, he used paint to portray not only form, but light. In his hands both light and form were dramatic in their intensity. The son of a dyer (hence his nickname, "little dyer"), Tintoretto's training is unknown, though some sources say he studied briefly with Titian, only to be cast out by a master jealous over his precocious student's talents. Probably an apocryphal story, Tintoretto's talent was not. He had a flair for dramatic, personal, and unconventional narrative which found great favor in Venice. He spent years working for one confraternity, the Scuolo di San Rocco, for whom he painted a stupendous array of Old Testament and New Testament scenes, including an over forty-foot-wide depiction of the Crucifixion **(H&F 11.39)**, which became a wellspring for later artists, including Rubens.

Tintoretto's decorations in the Church of S. Giorgio Maggiore were done shortly before his death in 1594, and reveal an artist at the height of his creative powers. Here we see two scenes, one familiar, the *Last Supper* (**J 645; G 17.67**), paired with one less familiar, the *Fall of Manna* (an Old Testament subject taken from Exodus, which shows God's chosen people saved by God by this gift of food from heaven). The subjects were chosen by the Prior of San Marco to focus on the theme of the Eucharist, the central mystery of the Mass celebrated on the altar situated between the two pictures. Tintoretto's *Last Supper* is as startlingly spiritual as Veronese's (done some twenty years earlier) was remarkably profane. Here, in a daring departure from convention, Tintoretto has placed the apostles' table at a dramatic angle to the picture plane, where it recedes far into the tenebrous shadows of the room's deep interior. Christ's halo illuminates the scene, together with the flame from a lamp in the foreground, which gives the whole image an eerie glow. Christ does not sit as tradition would have him (think of Leonardo's example and even Veronese's), but is standing, offering the food to his apostles, saying "Take, eat, for this is my flesh." If the mystical light, in a nocturnal scene that anticipates the dramatic lighting of Caravaggio, were not enough to underscore the miraculous nature of the story, then the spectral angels, formed merely by touches of light, help confirm it. Having learned from Titian that to depart from reality helps make a more convincing theater, Tintoretto pulled out all stops. Every action is not merely drama but melodrama; the staging is not merely unusual, but eccentric; the lighting has gone beyond the merely vivid to the hallucinatory.

The mysterious darkness of the *Last Supper* is contrasted by the morning light and external setting of the *Fall of Manna*, where Moses' followers busy themselves picking up God's blessing, as it falls like golden rocks from the sky. Absorbed in their desire for food, the true nature of the miracle has still escaped them; only Moses and the excited man seem aware of what has transpired. In both works, Tintoretto has fused fact with fantasy, theatricality with mundane reality into a blend that is uniquely his own. His massive, bending, and heroically conceived figures owe some of their conception to Michelangelo and the copies of his sculptures that Tintoretto used to draw incessantly. Incidental details like the man driving the donkey, or the cat raiding the food basket, are clearly taken from life, and it is Tintoretto's oddly effective conflation of two such diametrically opposed ways of working that give his images their dramatic power and their appealing humanity.

Painted at the end of the sixteenth century, Tintoretto's two paintings show us an artist building on and transcending the clear, harmonious, and lofty world of the early sixteenth century, to a pictorial vision which eschews clarity for drama, and harmony for effective pictorial discord, to add additional piquancy and narrative flavor to his image. The Council of Trent, which had met from 1545 to 1563, had declared that images were particularly important to portray the mysteries of religion. The Council, a product of the attempt to counter the rise of the Reformation (hence Counter Reformation), clearly saw that art continued to have a purpose for the church. Mysteries and faith had been bound to images whose purpose was to move the viewer through drama and pathos. What better tradition to mine than the Venetian one, with its poetic, subjective, and emotional pictures that date back to the foundation of its school? Tintoretto, whether conscious of the Counter Reformation or not, clearly shared many of the same goals.

In searching for new ways to tell familiar stories, Tintoretto led the way to a whole new range of images in the following century. Through his own style and subject matter Tintoretto affected the future of painting. From the full-scale scenes of daily life which we call "genre" that became so popular in the seventeenth century, to the dramatic, darkly shadowed works of such Counter Reformation artists as his pupil El Greco as well as Caravaggio, Tintoretto shaped the art of the future with his unabashedly personal style. Testimony to the universality of his vision, even Rembrandt, that least Catholic of all painters, owed a debt to Tintoretto as well as to Titian. Tintoretto's direct and spontaneous way of manipulating paint, pointed, like Titian's, to the art of the future.

## Life in the Country Villas of the Veneto

### *Palladio and Veronese at the Villa Maser*

You will likely recall the pleasant excursion to country life outside Venice with the discussion of Palladio's Villa Maser and the decorations by Veronese which embellish it. Built between approximately 1560 and 1568, the Villa Barbaro at Maser, an area north of Venice, was designed for the Barbaro brothers, who were fast friends of Palladio's. The villa was not simply a gorgeous retreat, but a working farm, and its owners were educated aristocrats. One was a mathematician, an editor of Vitruvius, and an ambassador, the other a prosperous man of the world.

It is likely that the unusual design of this villa—in which a portico extends along the full length of the building, and the family quarters occupy the rooms of the piano nobile upstairs—was a collaboration between Palladio, the painter Veronese, and the Barbaro brothers. Joining the functional farm buildings with the more refined living spaces within the illusion of a continuous façade, the Villa Maser appears to be one building on the outside and another in its interior. Here, through the imaginative treatment of Veronese, illusionism is given full reign, and the classicizing tastes of patrons not unlike Agostino Chigi in Rome, whose Villa Farnesina Raphael

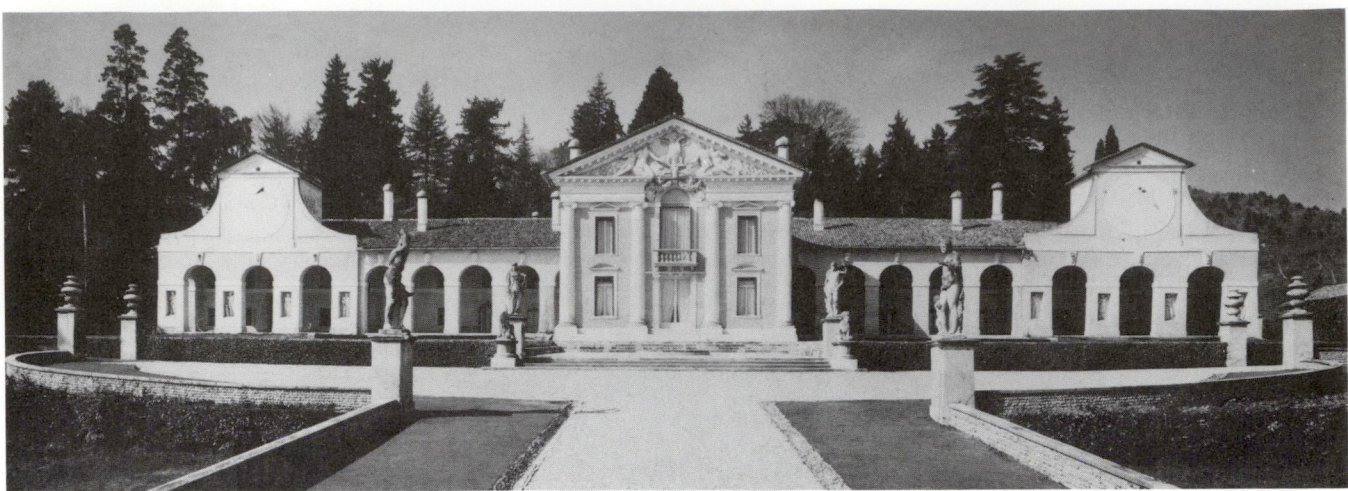

Palladio, *Villa Barbaro,* façade. 1565. (SCALA/ART RESOURCE, NEW YORK)

had so charmingly decorated, are seen again. These tastes, however, are purely Venetian.

Probably inspired in part by ancient Roman wall painting **(J clpl 24; G 6.28; H&F 5.17)**, Veronese has seamlessly created a fantasy in which the members of the Barbaro family become part of the illusion. In the central hall the fictive dome displays an Olympian splendor—we see a pantheon of deities and allegorical figures taking their ease. Diana is being affectionately sniffed by one of her hounds, Zeus abstractedly dangles his arm over his eagle, and the whole assembly is presided over by the illuminating powers of Aurora, sitting comfortably astride her lizard-like chariot. Other mythological characters and events decorate the lunettes and pendentives, while a series of fictive columns and arches are the stages upon which family members gaze down on themselves in yet another and inspired level of illusionism. A young man holding a book gazes distractedly down from one side, while a gloriously attired Venetian lady and her aged maid, together with the family parrot and spaniel, look down from the other. The lady may be Antonia Giustiniani, the wife of Marc' Antonio Barbaro. From the balcony she is surveying the garden room, in which Veronese painted fictive columns flanking painted vistas of mountains and seas, some with ancient ruins, and all lush and serene in their Arcadian splendor. To complete the fantasy, Veronese created a trompe l'oeil door which has been suddenly opened, and a Barbaro child stares curiously in, perhaps attracted by the music she hears coming from the room.

For Venice, as this Veronese masterpiece has shown us, the Renaissance was a time to enjoy the sweetness of life—to indulge in the luxury of painting, music, architecture, and letters, all of which enrich and ennoble the lives of those educated and fortunate enough to enjoy them. In a synthesis and leap of imagination that was unprecedented, Veronese created a fictive world in which the wellspring of the Renaissance (antiquity), its fruits (the arts of music, letters, and architecture), and their beneficiaries (the Barbaro family), all coexist in a single, unified fantasy world that is actually built around, and lived in by, the very people pictured in the fantasy! Such a daydream was possible only in a city like Venice, which seemed to live out a dream of its own creation.

A culmination of the particularly sensuous, playful, and illusionistic tendencies in Venice which irreverently mixed reality and fiction as nowhere else, Veronese's Maser frescoes became a textbook for later artists, as did many other sixteenth-century works we have seen. Veronese initiated the tradition for illusionistic wall paintings in Venetian villas. His influence reached well into the eighteenth century, when Gianbattista Tiepolo, the last great master of the fresco medium, looked over his shoulder many times at the grand and glorious examples set by his forebear.

## Summary

During the sixteenth century, we have seen artisans blossom into artists—creative geniuses, who shared equally in the benefits and the drawbacks of that elevated station. Set apart and above ordinary people by virtue of their talents, artists were often doomed to a futile quest to make their inner visions materialize. Though benefiting from fame and on occasion wealth, a good many artists we encountered in this unit were subject to a melancholy temperament, and struggled with their creativity.

All the artists shared a common interest in the challenge presented by the human figure. Michelangelo's heroic nudes, Leonardo's perfect beings, Raphael's essays on numerous figures in diverse and exquisitely drawn poses, Titian's sensual beings, all are responses to that challenge.

In Florence and Rome, the figure was an intellectual subject, symbolizing the ideas and ideals greater than any human could attain in reality. In Venice the figure became a vehicle to express or elicit emotion. Human experience was woven into Venetian imagery in many subtle and evocative ways. It made myths and allegories more appealing, religious images more accessible, and made them the carriers of great human themes which transcend their subject. Love and death, the destructive and regenerative forces of nature, themes that would absorb human thought for centuries more, found some of their finest and most profound expressions in Venice. And, while the humanistic secular vision was eclipsed in Rome with the sack of 1527, Venice and her culture endured secure in her watery refuge throughout the century.

The Venetian school and the artists of Rome and Florence forged a lasting legacy for later generations. Michelangelo's Sistine ceiling and Raphael's Stanze were virtual textbooks of figures for artists well into the nineteenth century. Their intellectual and rigorous approach to art as a concept, and to the figure as the vessel for ideas, fed the academic orientation of art in the next century, and forms the basis for the work of the Carracci, Poussin, and the French Royal Academy that was founded in 1647–1648.

At the same time, the theatrical, evocative, and emotionally stirring imagery of Titian and Tintoretto made the revolutionary work of Caravaggio possible. The Venetian school inspired and sustained artistic creativity in the North as well as in Italy. No great Northern painter of the next century—Rubens, van Dyck, Rembrandt, Velázquez—can be understood without studying the work of Titian.

Thus, the great masters of the sixteenth century were truly titans. Their bold vision forever altered the course of Western art. None of the artists who succeeded the giants like Michelangelo and Titian surpassed them in the scope and grandeur of their visions. And none achieved the mythic status these sixteenth-century titans enjoyed. Though famous and honored, Rubens, van Dyck, Velázquez, and the other great names of the next century fit more comfortably within the context of their times. Refined, educated, and aspiring to the status of gentlemen, they no longer towered over others in the manner of Michelangelo or Raphael. That we tend to see all artists through romantic glasses is testimony to the lasting impact the genius of such artists as Michelangelo had. Heir to the belief in the individual, they realized the ultimate potential of that idea. Later artists may have gone as far, but none have been able to exceed them.

## Textbook References

**J** The textbooks essentially cover the same material regarding sixteenth-century art, but with slightly different emphases. In two chapters, Janson covers what he terms the High Renaissance in Italy, followed by Mannerism. His discussion in the first

of these chapters introduces the important notion of genius and its impact on the art of the High Renaissance. Beginning with Leonardo, he then traces the careers of the most influential artists, without making a strong division between Venice, Florence, and Rome. Later ("Mannerist") developments are treated in the second of the two chapters, where Tintoretto, El Greco, Parmigianino, Bronzino, and Correggio are discussed. Emphasis is placed on the impact of certain artists like Tintoretto and Correggio on the seventeenth century. The last phase of the sixteenth century, in which the works of Cellini, Primaticcio, Giovanni Bologna, Vasari, and Palladio are cited, gives Janson's discussion particular balance and breadth.

**G** Gardner covers all of sixteenth-century Italian art in a single chapter. Beginning with the High Renaissance in Florence, she provides an extensive discussion of Leonardo, and includes a valuable analysis of the meaning of classical art as it applies to him. After a brief discussion of Giulio Romano and Mannerist architecture, Gardner turns to Venice, where she deals first with the architects Sansovino and Palladio. Then she traces the Venetian school from its beginnings with Giovanni Bellini and Giorgione. The Venetian themes of sensuality, arcadian fantasy, and voluptuous femininity are the subject of a particularly good discussion, and Titian's development from his pastoral images to his Pesaro Altar and beyond is covered. Tintoretto and Veronese are placed in the context of Venetian Mannerism, with the latter artist's anticipation of the Baroque ending the chapter.

**H & F** In a single chapter, Honour and Fleming cover artistic and cultural developments in Europe between 1500 and 1600. Citing the Reformation as the single most important event of the period—one that affected art and culture as well as politics and history—Honour and Fleming build a useful and subtle discussion of the Reformation and its origins in Northern humanism. From there, they turn to the High Renaissance in Italy with discussions of works by Roman, Florentine, and Venetian masters. After a brief explanation of the development of Mannerism, its influence on France is demonstrated through the work of Jean Goujon and the emergence of women artists, especially Sofonisba Anguissola, the most famous woman artist of her time. El Greco, a student of Tintoretto, is used to illustrate the mystical direction of Catholic art at the end of the sixteenth and the beginning of the seventeenth century.

**Janson, Part III, Chapters 3 and 4: The High Renaissance in Italy** and **Mannerism and Other Trends, pp. 436–476. Chapter 3: The High Renaissance in Italy, pp. 436–463.** Painting—religious and mythological themes and portraits; Leonardo, Michelangelo, Raphael, Giorgione, Titian. Sculpture—religious and mythological figures; Michelangelo. Architecture—churches, public buildings; Bramante, Michelangelo.

**Chapter 4: Mannerism and Other Trends, pp. 464–476.** Painting—religious and mythological themes and portraits; Fiorentino, Parmigianino, Bronzino, Tintoretto, El Greco, Correggio, Savoldo, Veronese. Sculpture—religious, mythological, and portrait figures; Cellini, Berruguete, Primaticcio, Bologna. Architecture—churches, public buildings, palaces and villas; Vasari, Ammanati, Palladio, della Porta, and Sacchi.

**Gardner, Chapter 17: Sixteenth-Century Italian Art, pp. 598–653.** Paintings—religious themes, portraits, mythology; Leonardo da Vinci, Raphael, Michelangelo, del Sarto, Correggio, da Pontormo, Fiorentino, Parmiginanino, Bronzino, Romano, Bellini, Giorgione, Titian, Tintoretto, and Veronese. Sculpture—mythological and religious figures, tombs; Michelangelo, da Bologna, and Cellini. Architecture—churches, palaces and public buildings; Bramante, Sangallo, Michelangelo, Romano, Sansovino, and Palladio.

**Honour and Fleming, Part 3, Chapter 11: Harmony and Reform, pp. 366–405.** Northern: Painting—allegories, religious themes, portraits and landscape; Bosch, Grünewald, Holbein, Cranach, Dürer, Altdorfer. Sculpture—altarpieces and tombs; Torrigiano and Reimenschneider. Italy, High Renaissance: Painting—religious and mythological themes; Leonardo da Vinci, Raphael, Fra Bartolommeo, Michelangelo, Giorgione, Lotto, Titian, Tintoretto, Veronese, Correggio, Parmigianino, Spranger, Bruegel, and El Greco. Sculpture—religious and mythological figures; Michelangelo, Goujon, Bologna, Cellini. Architecture—churches, public buildings, palaces and villas; Bramante, Michelangelo, Sansovino, Palladio, Romano.

## Study Questions

1. How does the use of the human figure in the sixteenth century compare with its use in the fifteenth century?
2. Nature is an important subject in the sixteenth century. Where, and how, does it compare to its use in the fifteenth?
3. How do patrons and society view some artists in the sixteenth century? Is this different from the previous era?
4. What role does Rome play in sixteenth-century artistic patronage?
5. The question of finish and completion arises in the sixteenth century. Whose work can you think of that centers on this issue and what circumstances affect it?
6. Several artists in our discussion develop a "late style." Who were they and what is its nature?
7. Does sixteenth-century religious art function the same way or differently from the way it had in the fifteenth century? Explain.
8. Much of the art work we discussed was made for private patrons. What is the nature of this kind of art work and how is it different from sacred art?

9. Art in Venice is different from that of Rome or Florence. How and why? The nude figure emerges as a dominant form in sixteenth-century painting and sculpture. Whose work shows a deep interest in this subject and why?

## Glossary

**academic**  term applied to art being taught in an academy with a regular system of learning. This is in contrast to the apprenticeship system regularly practiced from medieval times through the seventeenth century. The first stirrings toward academic thinking are found among Florentine theoreticians of the sixteenth century, who championed "disegno" over "colore" and stressed the importance of studying the human figure. Numerous quasi-academies sprouted up during the late sixteenth and early seventeenth centuries, the most famous of them the Carracci academy in Bologna. The French king established the earliest formal academy to teach art in Paris around 1647.

**buon fresco**  the true fresco method, in which pigment is applied to a surface of wet plaster, which upon drying, bonds permanently with the plaster. Most surviving frescoes in Italy done between the fourteenth and eighteenth centuries adopted this technique. Its opposite, "fresco secco," was not as long lasting.

**chiaroscuro**  derived from Italian, *chiaro* (light) and *oscuro* (dark), the term alludes to the creation of an illusion of space, through contrasting areas of light and shadow, on a two-dimensional surface.

**colore**  Italian word for color, reflecting the Venetian practice of emphasizing color and light in the creation of pictorial forms; the theoretical counterpart to "disegno." Venetian painting, with its blurring of edges, its building of volume through changes in color and the presence of light, as well as its practice of painting directly on the canvas, often without preparatory drawings, was a distinctively intuitive and less rational approach to art than Florentine "disegno."

**disegno**  Italian word for design, or drawing. Though drawings were the basis for all Italian art, they gained a new intellectual framework in sixteenth-century Florence. There drawing came to be viewed as a demonstration of the eye guided by the mind, and the best means by which well-ordered, balanced compositions could be achieved. Linear qualities—edges and contours—were stressed in Florentine art, which, even when color was absent, could be clearly understood. Theoretically, Florentine "disegno" opposed the Venetian notion of "colore."

**fresco secco**  the opposite of true or buon fresco. In fresco secco, pigment suspended in glue is applied to a dried plaster surface. Certain colors, particularly blue, were often applied in this manner, and have flaked off in the intervening years. Leonardo's experiments with pigments and glues in his *Last Supper* have shortened its lifespan considerably.

**icon**  an image or likeness, usually of a religious figure, such as a painted panel representing Christ or the Virgin Mary.

**putto (pl. putti)**  a representation of a naked cherubic infant, often with wings. Used sometimes as decorative devices, putti were also used to represent love or angels.

**romanticism**  like academic art, romantic art really flowered in the late eighteenth century with artists like Goya and Fuseli who stressed feelings and emotions over rationality and intellect. But like academic art, romanticism had antecedents earlier, particularly in the art of sixteenth-century Venice, where the concept of "colore" together with highly expressive subject matter that appealed to emotions was prevalent.

**Serenissima**   Italian word meaning most serene; traditional epithet of the city of Venice.

**sfumato**   Italian word meaning smoky. Developed by Leonardo da Vinci, sfumato is a means of modeling figures through the subtle use of light and dark in a hazy atmosphere.

**Sibyls**   Greek and Roman prophetesses, who were believed to have foretold the coming of Christ.

**stanza**   Italian for "room."

## Artists, Patrons, and Important Historical Personages

**Bramante, Donato (Donato di Pascuccio d'Antonio)** (1444–1514).   Italian architect. His early training is undocumented, but it is believed that he began his career as a painter. As of 1482 he was working as an architect, completing commissions for Duke Ludovico Sforza, Pope Julius II, and various churches. His reputation rests on his later Roman works, where subtle adjustments were made to heighten the play of light and shade across a surface and to enhance the strong sculptural effects.

**Charles V** (1500–1558).   The single most important European ruler of the first half of the sixteenth century, Charles spent his life trying to unify Europe, a goal that was ultimately elusive. He was crowned Holy Roman Emperor in 1530. Though a Catholic, Charles sacked Rome in 1527 to punish Clement VII for having sided with the French against him. A discerning patron of the arts, he made Titian his court painter, knighted him, and paid him many honors. In 1556 Charles retired to a monastery, taking with him some of Titian's pictures, which provided solace and inspiration in the last years of his life.

**Chigi, Agostino.**   A Sienese banker who commissioned Baldassare Peruzzi to build the villa which is today known as the Villa Farnese (1508–09).

**Condivi, Ascanio** (d. 1574).   An insignificant Italian painter, Condivi's claim to fame is as Michelangelo's biographer. In 1553 he published the *Life of Michelangelo*, a biography based on his intimate friendship with the artist; it contains what amount to verbatim quotations from the master. The book is the most accurate record of Michelangelo's life that we have. Michelangelo seems to have taken some exception to Vasari's account, printed in 1550, and Condivi's biography is the result.

**Francis I of France** (1494–1547).   King of France 1515–1547. During his reign Milan was under the domination of France, and he contributed to the unstable political clime of the period by fighting Charles V continuously from 1521 until past 1536. Francis greatly admired Leonardo, who lived under the protection of the King at the end of his life.

**Giorgione** (Giorgio Barbarelli) (ca. 1477–1510).   Together with Bellini, Giorgione is one of the important early members of the Venetian school, whose influence on Titian is particularly significant. In Giorgione's inventive hands the nude, "poesie," and landscape all became part of the Venetian painter's vocabulary. His early death parallels the tragic loss to art of Raphael.

**Julius II** (1443–1513).   Possessed of enormous ambition, Giuliano della Rovere became Pope Julius II in 1503. Julius was a great patron of the arts. He is remembered for his commissions for the Sistine Chapel ceiling paintings by Michelangelo, the Stanze frescoes by Raphael, and the plans for St. Peter's by both Bramante and Michelangelo.

**Leonardo da Vinci** (1452–1519).   Considered the towering intellect of the Renaissance, Leonardo was a scientist, philosopher, mathematician, engineer, sculptor, and painter. Devoted to understanding physical reality, he spent years dissecting bodies and studying plants, animals, and natural phenomena: light, storms; water and air. His observations filled thousands of notebook pages which are a valuable document of a brilliant intellect tackling the problems of visible reality. Leonardo worked in Florence, Milan, Rome, and France for patrons that included Ludovico Sforza, Cesare Borgia, and Francis I of France. As an artist, Leonardo contributed a new understanding of light, atmosphere, and exquisite beauty.

**Luther, Martin** (1483–1546).   Luther began as a priest. A great biblical scholar, he produced the German vernacular Bible in 1522. His opposition to the sale of indulgences and to papal secularism helped spawn the Protestant Reformation. In 1517 he posted his Ninety-five Theses, an attack on ecclesiastical abuses which caused the populace to take a closer look at the role of the church. In 1521 he successfully defended himself against papal attack in the Diet of Worms. Supported by German princes, Luther ultimately succeeded in establishing the Protestant Church.

**Michelangelo Buonarroti** (1475–1564).   Florentine painter, sculptor, and architect, Michelangelo is universally celebrated as one of the supreme artists of all time. His idealizing conception of the human form established the figure as the ultimate challenge to the artist and made the heroic nude male embody superhuman ideals. Apprenticed to Ghirlandaio, Michelangelo took his inspiration from Donatello, Masaccio, Giotto, and the ancients. A highly spiritual man, Michelangelo's later life reflects a deepened religiosity, which is evidenced in his *Last Judgment* and his late Pietàs.

**Palladio, Andrea** (1508–1580).   Indoctrinated into ancient literature and architecture by Giangiorgio Trissino, Palladio succeeded in translating antique forms into the schemes developed by the architecture of the Renaissance. Throughout his career he built numerous villas, palazzos, and churches, developing a form of architecture which combined the ideas of Bramante and Roman antiquity. In 1570 he published the treatise *I quattro libri dell' architettura*, which was a comprehensive account of the theory and practice of architecture, rooted in Vitruvius and the result of Palladio's prolonged study of Roman buildings.

**Paul III** (1468–1549).   Interested in the arts, Alessandro Farnese began the Palazzo Farnese in 1517. Upon his installation as Pope Paul III in 1534, he commissioned Michelangelo to paint the *Last Judgment* in the Sistine Chapel and began to enlarge his palazzo, commissioning Antonio da Sangallo to take charge of the expansion. Sangallo was followed by Michelangelo and Vignola, and the palazzo was finished by Giacomo della Porta in 1589. Farnese's son Alessandro, known as the "Cardinal Farnese," is acknowledged as a great patron of his time.

**Peruzzi, Baldassare** (1481–1536).   An Italian painter and architect, Peruzzi began his career in Siena as a painter, under the direction of Pinturicchio. He built the Villa Farnese for Agostino Chigi, and helped with its decorative frescoes. Popes Leo X and Clement VII were among his other patrons. He was one of the first architects of St. Peter's, although his most important building was the Massimo alle Colonne Palace, which was completed after his death.

**Philip II** (1527–1598). King of Spain, 1556–1598; son of Charles V. His spare yet elegant appearance was depicted in famous portraits by Titian and Sir Antony More. Lover of books and pictures, Philip was also a strong champion of the Roman Catholic Counter Reformation, and the Inquisition grew strong in his reign. During his stewardship the Spanish Empire attainted its greatest power and widest geographical domination.

**Raimondi, Marcantonio** (ca. 1480–1534). An Italian print-maker best known for his association with Raphael. His engravings spread the designs of Raphael and were largely responsible for introducing Raphael in the North. Apprenticed to the painter-goldsmith Francia (Francesco Raibolini), Raimondi developed an instinct for describing the ideal beauty of the human form in the formal vocabulary of classical sculpture.

**Raphael (Raffaello Santi** or **Sanzio)** (1483–1520). Born in Urbino, Raphael's earliest training was with his father, Giovanni Santi. He was most influenced by the Umbrian painter Perugino, whom he assisted for several years. In 1504, Raphael arrived in Florence where the works of Leonardo, Michelangelo, Fra Bartolommeo, and Verrocchio deeply affected him. By 1509 he was in Rome, where Julius II immediately hired him to paint the Vatican stanze. Most famous of these were the frescoes for the Stanza della Segnatura, but his efforts included the Stanza dell' Incendio and the Stanza d'Eliodoro. Raphael also painted a long series of Old Testament scenes for the Vatican, produced mainly by his assistants. Among his last paintings were the frescoes he added to the decorative scheme of the Palazzo Farnese. There his *Triumph of Galatea* and the Cupid and Psyche cycle are ranked as the finest secular decorations done in early sixteenth-century Rome.

**Sebastiano del Piombo** (1485–1547). Sebastiano's early training is uncertain; he first appears as a young artist in Giorgione's circle. He adopted Giorgione's use of atmospheric form and the poetic meditative mood. Additional influences were found in Raphael's compositional solutions, the rounded figural arrangements, and the monumentality and anatomical force found in the works of Michelangelo. In his day Sebastiano was a notable portraitist, completing portraits of such dignitaries as Pope Clement VII, Cardinal Salviati, and Cardinal Ciocchi.

**Sansovino, Il (Jacopo Tatti)** (1486–1570). Pupil of Andrea Sansovino, whose name he adopted, and Bramante, Sansovino was both sculptor and architect. His career encompasses commissions for sculptures in Florence and Rome and for architectural monuments, including the Library of S. Marco, in Venice. Throughout his life Sansovino adhered to the harmonious principles of the classic High Renaissance style.

**Sforza family.** The Sforza's descended from a family of condottiere. When Francesco Sforza married a Visconti daughter, he inherited the principality of Milan and became the first condottiere to gain a duchy. His son Ludovico (Il Moro) ruled Milan for eighteen years, from 1481 to 1499, and attracted a number of important artists there; most famous of them was Leonardo.

**Tintoretto, Jacopo Robusti** (1518–1594). One of the triumvirate of great Venetian painters, along with Titian and Veronese, Tintoretto was a leading painter for Venetian churches and patricians. Bonifazio de' Pitati is thought to be Tintoretto's primary teacher and in 1545 Pietro Aretino became his first important patron. Tintoretto's most important efforts were the fifty-odd paintings produced over a period of twenty-three years for the Scuola di San Rocco of Venice. Including Old and New Testament scenes, these paintings are the most comprehensive decoration made by a single artist. They show Tintoretto to be an original interpreter of traditional subjects, capable of injecting drama and great realism into his works. Though his figures are stylized, they are joined by direct observation from nature in the form of anecdotal details that enrich his imagery and keep it engaging.

**Titian (Tiziano Vecellio)** (ca. 1487–1577). The greatest Venetian painter of his time, Titian was patronized by some of the great heads of state, including Pope Paul III, Francis I of France, the emperor Charles V, and Philip II of Spain. His early training was possibly derived from working with the mosaicist Sebastiano Zuccato and with both Bellinis. However, Giorgione, with whom he collaborated in 1508, was to have a great impact on his style. Titian adopted Giorgione's technical innovation of atmospheric unity of space through color but altered it to create extroverted figures who are not absorbed into the space. The physically vigorous figures who move freely in an airy, fresh world become the hallmark of his style. Later European painting is impossible to understand without him.

**Vasari, Giorgio** (1511–1574). Painter and architect, Giorgio Vasari painted in the Palazzo Vecchio and designed the Uffizi Palace, both in Florence. Today, however, he is best known for his history of Italian art, *Le vite de' piu eccellenti pittori, scultori e architettori* (1550). A valuable source on sixteenth-century artistic theory, the book is also the most important source for the art and lives of Italian artists from Cimabue to Vasari's time.

**Veronese (Caliari), Paolo** (1528–1588). One of a triad of great Venetian painters, including Titian and Tintoretto, Veronese was chiefly interested in the depiction of sensuous, richly textured scenes which were more concerned with decoration than movement or emotion. He was apprenticed to Antonio Badile of Verona, and his style is indebted to the painters of Verona for their technique of intense luminous color areas, to the local architect Michelle Sanmichelli, and to the Brescian masters Moretto and Savoldo and their interest in the figure. Veronese was highly regarded in his own time. His urbane sophistication, wit, and wonderful poetic sense make his paintings appealing, charming, and grand. Veronese was especially important to later Venetian painters such as G. B. and G. D. Tiepolo.

**Vitruvius Pollo.** As a Roman architect, Vitruvius held an official position from Augustus for the rebuilding of Rome. Today he is best known for the treatise *De Architectura*, probably written before 27 B.C., and the only technical work of its kind to have survived from antiquity. The treatise was not a theoretical explanation of architectural aesthetics but a practical handbook. *De Architectura* was rediscovered during the Renaissance and Vasari produced one edition.

# Bibliography

## GENERAL

Cellini, B. *Autobiography.* Ed. J. Pope-Hennessy. London, 1960.

Klein, R., and Zerner, H. *Italian Art, 1500–1600: Sources and Documents in the History of Art.* Englewood Cliffs, N.J., 1966.

Leonardo da Vinci. *Leonardo da Vinci on Painting: A Lost Book (Libro A)*. Berkeley, 1964.

Michelangelo, *Complete Poems and Selected Letters of Michelangelo,* 2nd ed. Ed. R. N. Linscott. Trans. C. Gilbert. New York, 1965.

Palladio, Andrea. *I quattro libri dell 'architettura*. Venice, 1570; reprinted in facsimile, Milan, 1951.

Rosand, D. *Painting in Cinquecento Venice*. New Haven, 1982.

Shearman, J. *Mannerism*. Harmondsworth and Baltimore, 1967.

Smyth, C. H. *Mannerism and Maniera*. Locust Valley, N.Y., 1961.

Vasari, Giorgio. *Lives of the Most Eminent Painters, Sculptors and Architects*. Trans. G. du C. De Vere. 10 vols. London, 1912–15.

## THEORY

Blunt, A. *Artistic Theory in Italy, 1450–1600*. Oxford, 1966.

Summers, D. *Michelangelo and the Language of Art*. Princeton, N.J., 1981.

## PAINTING, SCULPTURE, AND DRAWING

D'Ancona, P. *The Farnesina Frescoes at Rome*. Milan, 1955.

Delogu, G. *Veronese: The Supper in the House of Levi*. Milan, 1948.

Freedberg, S. J. *Painting in Italy, 1500–1600,* rev. ed. Pelican History of Art. Harmondsworth and Baltimore, 1975.

*Italian Drawings in the Department of Prints and Drawings in the British Museum,* 4 vols. Vol. II: Wilde, J. *Michelangelo and His Studio,* London, 1953. Vol. III: Pouncey, P., and Gere, J. A. *Raphaela and His Circle,* 2 vols. London, 1962.

Pietrangeli, C. et al. *The Sistine Chapel, a New Light on Michelangelo: The Art, the History, and the Restoration*. New York, 1986.

Pope-Hennessy, J. *Italian High Renaissance and Baroque Sculpture*. 3 vols. London, 1963.

Pope-Hennessy, J. *Italian Renaissance Sculpture*. London, 1963.

Popham, A. E. *The Italian Drawings of the Fifteenth and Sixteenth Centuries in the Collection of His Majesty the King at Windsor Castle*. London, 1949.

Seymour, C., Jr. *Michelangelo: The Sistine Chapel Ceiling*. New York, 1972.

Shearman, J. *Raphael's Cartoons in the Collection of Her Majesty the Queen and the Tapestries for the Sistine Chapel*. London, 1972.

Walker, J. *Bellini and Titian at Ferrara: A Study of Styles and Taste*. London, 1957.

## ARTISTS

### Giorgione

Baldass, L. von. *Giorgione*. Trans. J. M. Brownjohn. New York, 1965.

Conway, W. M. *Giorgione: A New Study of His Art as a Landscape Painter*. London, 1929.

Phillips, D. *The Leadership of Giorgione*. Washington, D.C., 1937.

Pignatti, T. *Giorgione*. Trans. Clovis Whitfield. London, 1971.

### Leonardo da Vinci

Clark, K. *Leonardo da Vinci: An Account of His Development as an Artist,* rev. ed. Harmondsworth and Baltimore, 1967.

Goldscheider, L. *Leonardo da Vinci*, 6th ed. London, 1959.

Heydenreich, L. H. *Leonardo da Vinci*. 2 vols. New York, 1954.

Kemp, M. *Leonardo da Vinci: The Marvellous Works of Nature and Man*. Cambridge, Mass., 1981.

Popham, A. E. *The Drawings of Leonardo da Vinci*. New York, 1945.

Wasserman, J. *Leonardo da Vinci*. New York, 1975.

Zubov, V. P. *Leonardo da Vinci*. Trans. D. H. Kraus. Cambridge, Mass., 1968.

### Michelangelo

Ackerman, J. S. *The Architecture of Michelangelo,* 2nd ed. Harmondsworth and Baltimore, 1971.

Camesasca, E. *The Complete Paintings of Michelangelo*. Intro. L. D. Ettlinger. New York, 1969.

De Tolnay, C., ed. *The Art and Thought of Michelangelo*. Trans. N. Buranelli. New York, 1964.

Goldscheider, L. *Michelangelo: Paintings, Sculpture, and Architecture,* 5th ed. New York, 1962.

Hartt, F. *Michelangelo*. New York, 1965.

———. *Michelangelo Drawings*. New York, 1971.

Hibbard, H. *Michelangelo,* 2nd ed. New York, 1985.

Morgan, C. H. *The Life of Michelangelo*. New York, 1960.

Salmi, M., ed. *The Complete Work of Michelangelo*. 2 vols. London, 1966.

Symonds, J. A. *The Life of Michelangelo Buonarroti,* 3rd ed. 2 vols. New York, 1899.

### Palladio

Ackerman, J. S. *Palladio,* rev. ed. New York, 1978.

### Raphael

Beck, J. *Raphael*. New York, 1976.

Fischel, O. *Raphael*. Trans. B. Rackham. 2 vols. New York, 1948.

Johannides, P. *The Drawings of Raphael with a Complete Catalog*. Berkeley, 1983.

Jones, R., and Penny, N. *Raphael*. New Haven, 1983.

Salmi, M. *The Complete Works of Raphael*. New York, 1969.

### Jacopo Sansovino

Howard, D. *Jacopo Sansovino: Architecture and Patronage in Renaissance Venice*. New Haven, 1975.

Lorenzetti, G. *Jacopo Sansovino, scultore*. Venice, 1910.

### Tintoretto

Newton, E. *Tintoretto*. London, 1952.

Pallucchini, R., and Rossi, P. *Tintoretto: Le Opere sacre e profane*. 2 vols. Milan, 1982.

Tietze, H. *Tintoretto: The Paintings and Drawings*. New York, 1948.

### Titian

Hope, C. *Titian*. New York, 1980.

Rosand, D. *Painting in Cinquecento Venice: Titian, Veronese, Tintoretto,* New Haven, 1982.

Tietze, H. *Titian: Paintings and Drawings,* 2nd ed., rev. London and New York, 1950.

Wethey, H. E. *The Paintings of Titian*. 3 vols. London, 1969–75.

### Veronese

Pignatti, T. *Veronese*. 2 vols. Milan, 1976.

Piovene, G., and Marini, R. *L'opera completa del Veronese*. Milan, 1968.

# Realms of Light
## The Baroque

## Learning Objectives

The seventeenth century was one of the most complex eras in the entire history of art and also one of the most important. Most of the subjects we now take for granted as the established themes for artists: still life, landscape, people in rooms or engaged in normal activities became popular in this century. It was an era that made the onlooker as important as the artist had been in the sixteenth century. Effect was everything. When we look at a seventeenth-century work, we react to what we see, we experience what the artist has meant for us to experience. The artist has become a producer, a stage designer, a manipulator of reality. The relationship between viewer and object is the fundamental issue for the period.

The unit first takes you to Rome where the church, triumphant and extravagant, has transformed the city architecturally, as well as through paintings and sculpture. We will concentrate on the presiding geniuses active in Rome: Borromini the architect; Caravaggio the painter; Bernini the sculptor. Pietro da Cortona and Poussin are introduced to demonstrate the diverse tastes, styles, and pictorial effects that were achieved in seventeenth-century Rome. You will encounter new concepts: subjectivity, theatricality, illusionism, and see old concepts such as classicism revived.

After Rome, we shift to Vienna, where baroque architecture profoundly affected the shape of the city and then Madrid, the other leading cultural and political center of the early seventeenth century. There we will see native Spanish art in the hands of Velázquez become among the greatest of the period. Working for Philip IV, great-grandson of Charles V, Velázquez produced memorable portraits of the royal family. He stressed the paradox of their existence, human and vulnerable, yet set above and apart ordinary humanity by their position. In Madrid we also consider the courtly art of van Dyck and Rubens, who, together with Velázquez and other artists working for the court, faced the problems of expressing the authority and power of their subjects, while making them seem real. Here we are introduced to the concept of the court portrait and have a chance to compare the accomplishments of three of its greatest practitioners.

Finally, we consider Holland, where an entirely different art was produced for different patrons. In Holland, we find artists facing the challenge of looking at ordinary reality and transforming it into art. Largely Protestant, mercantile, and republican, the Dutch culture admired honesty and disavowed pretention. We will see their great accomplishments in the group portrait, a particularly Dutch subject, made by Frans Hals and Rembrandt. Rembrandt's contributions to "history" painting, as well as portraiture, are considered. Though of its place and time, Dutch art is universal in its appeal because of its straightforward realism and its compassionate interpretation of humanity. While many images are impregnated with allusions and meanings scholars are still trying to interpret, Dutch still lifes, landscapes, portraits, genre, interiors, and city views have at their core a belief in the beauty, the rightness, and the value of ordinary things. It is a view we have inherited and which still shapes our lives.

Besides "baroque," the term most often used to define this century, you will encounter such diverse terms as "illusionistic," "realistic," "subjective," "theatrical," and "decorous" during your readings.

In this unit, you will:

- Recognize the characteristic traits of the baroque style through identification of its pliant treatment of light, mass, space, and texture.
- Realize that the vigorous manipulations of art and architecture in this era are directly addressing the theological crises of the Counter Reformation;
- Appreciate how the discoveries of a microcosmic reality in the laboratory, a rational system of natural physics, a new geo-political world of previously unknown continents and oceans, and a helio-centric solar system were stimulants to broader artistic horizons;
- Understand the extraordinary leaps from the idealization of the High Renaissance to the striking realism of the baroque.
- Comprehend how baroque painting, sculpture, and architecture were built upon the structure of the Classical and High Renaissance periods; yet a clearly

distinguishable enhancement of these earlier styles identifies the baroque age;

- Recognize the special architectural features of baroque architecture including: complex spatial patternings, heavily articulated niches and recesses, convex and concave surfaces, integration of applied ornamentation, and an overall effect of dynamic movement throughout the exterior and interior surfaces and voids;

- Learn about the two visible strains of the visual arts demonstrated by the energetic and romantic style of Cortona, Rubens, and van Dyck versus the cool and academic approach of the Carracci, Poussin, or Vermeer; this emotional versus rationalist dualism harkens back to the Venetian/Florentine dichotomy of the Renaissance and previews the Romantic/Realist debates of the nineteenth century;

- Come to an enhanced enjoyment of baroque art as the visible mirror of a dramatically evolved realm of human knowledge and expression.

## Part 1
## THE BAROQUE IN ITALY AND AUSTRIA

## Historical Background

The sixteenth century saw the triumph of the human figure in art. For artists working in Rome and Florence it was the ultimate artistic challenge, embodying ideas and ideals greater than any single individual. The figure was the acknowledged means for an artist to demonstrate his abilities as a draftsman, painter, or sculptor. For Venetian artists, the human figure was part of a more comprehensive look at the human condition. Venetian painting, in particular, occupied itself with human dreams, fantasies, tragedies, loves, and sensual interests. Venetian "poesie" and mythological and religious subjects contained within them a deep core of human emotion. The techniques of Venetian painters reflected this concern. The tactility of the paint, the interest in light, atmosphere, and nature all make Venetian imagery more accessible, intellectually and emotionally.

Seventeenth-century art seems to have been especially nourished by Venetian developments. All of the overriding geniuses of seventeenth-century painting—Rubens, Rembrandt, Velázquez, and Caravaggio—looked to Venice for inspiration. The Counter Reformation, which asserted Catholic faith in the wake of Protestant challenges, particularly emphasized the value of art to inspire the faithful, and so a whole raft of images emerged that stressed the emotional and rapturous side of religion. Scenes of martyrdoms, conversions, visions, and

mystical experiences became increasingly important in Catholic countries, and artists sought ways to make their images comprehensible and affecting in human terms. A definite realism was necessary to convey the human side of religion, and that was combined with the need to convey emotional states—penitence, ecstasy, pain, and euphoria. Human models were studied intensely and utilized in varying degrees to express meaning. Caravaggio, seventeenth-century Italy's most revolutionary artist, took naturalism to its greatest extreme. He combined his realism with a well-developed understanding of artifice. Composition, dramatic lighting, and carefully calculated actions were effectively melded into his lifelike characters. The inspiration for such a revolutionary departure came from the work of Titian and Tintoretto, among others.

The intellectual and classicizing tradition represented by Michelangelo and Raphael also passed on to the seventeenth century. A whole "academic" movement developed, which placed antiquity and the art of their greatest Renaissance exponents on a pedestal, and which emphasized a rigorous education for students that was seen as an alternative to the old workshop system that had gone before. Both formal and informal "academies" existed. "Academy" was a term adopted to indicate the intellectual orientation of teachers as well as students. From the quasi-academy of the Carracci in Bologna to the official academy established by the French artists in 1648, the seventeenth century saw the birth of true academic art. With academic art came all the intellectual baggage such institutions embody: theories of art, theories of style, hierarchies of value, and systems of teaching. Often viewed as stultifying today, academies then gave a new credibility and stature to the artist, making him a full-fledged member of the intellectual community. At the same time, academies offered a standard for art, which successive generations of artists could either accept or reject, and thereby formed a point of departure for many artistic movements in the future.

Finally, this was a period that emphasized narrative. Storytelling rose to a new level in the seventeenth century. For academicians and many discerning collectors, histories (biblical or mythological) were the ultimate challenge of the artist and ranked highest in the hierarchical ladder of art. But even the so called genre painters told all kinds of stories, and such non-narrative images as still lifes often had a strong overtone of message, if not story, embedded in them. When looking at seventeenth-century art, it is especially important to consider in how many ways the artist controlled what is seen and what meaning is conveyed through setting, lighting, gesture, pose, and expression; through color, figure type, and so on. Naturally, for an age steeped in tradition and interested in narration, there was an official position—taken by the church, for example—of the right and wrong way to tell a story, something we have already seen with Veronese in the previous unit. In this unit Caravaggio and Rembrandt sometimes run afoul of their patrons. How artists tell stories (and the stories they tell) becomes more diverse, more sophisticated, and more independent.

Again, you will see the region, the city, the function, the artist, and the patron of a work of art strongly shaping the outcome. At the same time, more and more independent artists worked without patrons for a market, particularly in the North, but also in Italy. These artists tried to anticipate what would sell; they were no less "commercial" or "professional" than those who worked under contract for a specific patron, and most artists did both. They produced work on demand for a particular patron, and had a stock of images available for sale through dealers or to visitors to their shops and studios.

We return to Italy, and more specifically to Rome, to begin our story. But before we do, we should set the stage by considering the changing philosophical, scientific, and literary changes that parallel those of the arts in this vital period. During the seventeenth century, thought and experience were fixed on reality, and fundamental philosophical steps had been taken in the direction of human experience by such great minds as René Descartes (1596–1650). "I think, therefore I am," he said, affirming not only his wish to understand the basis of reality, but also the centrality of each individual in forming an understanding of it. Man is the filter and prism through which experience and reality flow. To affirm the certitude of existence, man mirrored back to himself the complexity of the physical, psychological, and experiential aspects that made up reality. All these complexities are reflected in the visual arts. Art became alternately more real and more theatrical, more emotionally gripping, and more interpretive of humanity. Just think of Velázquez's candid portraits of the Spanish Royal family or Rembrandt's profound sympathy with his burgher patrons. The seventeenth century began with the work of Shakespeare (1564–1616), and ended with that of Leibnitz (1646–1716). The former was, like Descartes, deeply interested in humanity, the latter, in logic. Shakespeare's Hamlet said: "To be or not to be: that is the question," in a soliloquy within a play (1603) that reflects Shakespeare's own interest in the world of the senses and the world of the mind. Knowledge of oneself was the only true certainty, and a strong autobiographical strain ran through the works of artists like Rembrandt (who painted himself more than forty times, over the years of his triumphs and tragedies) and Bernini. Autobiographical elements are also evident among writers; it shapes all of Shakespeare's work, and that of Cervantes (1547–1616).

This interest in humanity affected visual art in many other ways as well. In this era when royalty and the papacy asserted their rights and privileges, a whole spate of themes that fused the person with his position emerged. The royal portrait flourished in all its manifestations (astride a horse, standing, in formal attire, or in graceful informality); the allegorical picture cycle that celebrated royal or papal accomplishments was widespread; royal entertainments were recorded and the results of conflicts between empires were documented. Callot's *Miseries of War* describe in minute and excruciating detail the effects of war on the lives of people.

Besides Popes and rulers, a whole range of subjects emerged that reflected the lives of ordinary people. In Holland especially, where Protestantism eschewed traditional religious subject matter, a whole new panoply of subjects was built on the lives of the sturdy, practical burghers who inhabited the cities and towns of the seven United Provinces. Portraits recorded their likenesses; genre scenes described their lives and fantasies; landscapes, seascapes, and townscapes described the environment in which they lived and worked; still lifes showed us the precious objects they owned, what they ate, made, and traded.

Not only human likenesses, but human emotions were examined and depicted by artists throughout seventeenth-century Europe. From rapture to tears, languor to reflection, deep meditation to sudden laughter, we see every nuance of human expression interpreted by the sensitive minds and hands of such artists as Rembrandt, Frans Hals, Caravaggio, and Bernini. States of mind, states of time (from the momentary to the timeless), social conditions (wealth, poverty, and everything in between) were depicted; in sum, every facet of human existence found its reflection in the imagery produced during this era.

Artists shared with scientists a fascination with and exploration of the optical and mechanical basis of reality, so the program introduces the new developments in science as well as in art. It should come as no surprise that the nascent scientific interests we saw emerging in the works of Leonardo da Vinci, and to a lesser extent in Dürer in the previous century, also had a corollary in science. Anatomy, geography, and planetary studies made great strides in the sixteenth century. But Copernicus remained unread; his *Book of the Revolutions of the Heavenly Spheres,* published in Nuremberg in 1543, has been described as the all-time worst seller.

In the seventeenth century, science rose to new levels of importance and interest. Times seemed conducive to re-evaluating accepted notions of reality. Just as Descartes could reconsider the fundamental issue of knowledge, science could begin to question fundamental issues of reality. Between 1606 and 1619, Johannes Kepler published his three laws of planetary motion, disproving by direct observation the long-held belief that planets moved in circles. Galileo Galilei (1564–1642) published his seminal work, *Dialogue on the Two Great World Systems,* in 1632; in it he reaffirmed Copernicus's theory that the earth was not the center of the universe. Galileo also refined and improved the telescope, thereby increasing his ability to study the actual paths of stars and planets. Galileo was a hero to the Italians—feted by Venice, the

Medici, and the Jesuits, whose own telescopes affirmed many of his discoveries. But Galileo eventually ran afoul of the church, which found that his theories challenged church doctrine, and the famous trial of 1632 ensued. The judges (among them was Cardinal Francesco Barberini, brother of Urban VIII) assured that science became divorced from faith. In the long run, knowledge gained from rigorous proof and experiment changed our understanding of the world. In the short run, faith remained the reality of the mind and became increasingly divorced from material reality. Issues of faith took precedence over the discoveries of science, and also provided comfort in an era of human misery brought on in large measure by issues of religion as well as political struggles. Wars of religion and territory were endlessly waged by rulers anxious to expand their empires and to subdue their rivals. Rulers shaped not only the lives of their subjects but the arts as well.

This was an age when monarchs claimed absolute authority through divine right, and an age that saw this claim challenged. Though the kings of France and Spain endured, Charles I of England was beheaded, in part because of his unrelenting claim of absolute authority. If thrones could not always be held, the images of authority artists created for these rulers have survived, reflections of an age whose promotion of authority, power, and religious beliefs yielded a terrible harvest of conflict.

Most of these conflicts trace their origins back to the sixteenth century. The Spanish Armada was defeated by the British in 1588. The Dutch revolted against Philip II in 1566 and again in 1572, and embarked on a struggle for independence from Catholic and Spanish domination. In 1579 seven provinces (Holland, Utrecht, Gelderland, Overijssel, Drenthe, Friesland, and Groningen) united against the Spanish. They became known as the United Provinces and officially gained their independence in 1648. France, ruled alternatively by Protestant and Catholic rulers, endured civil wars for thirty-six years beginning in 1562—wars which finally achieved the toleration of the French Huguenots in 1598. Germany endured the Thirty Years War, lasting from 1618 to 1648, once more centered on battles between Protestants and Catholics.

Questions of faith, then, started wars, and influenced philosophy. Thomas Hobbes, offended and horrified by the continual warfare of his day, published the *Leviathan* in 1651, in which he concluded that only absolute and sovereign power could maintain the peace in which humanity and an orderly society could thrive. Hobbes derived his authority from his scientific reasoning and mechanistic view of life—a view countered by Blaise Pascal (d. 1662), who, though a scientist, became deeply religious and stated: "The heart has its reasons that the mind cannot know." Separation of the material from the spiritual could be fatal to man, and his words echo down to us in our age of science triumphant.

The sixteenth century had already expressed disillusionment with man and material existence. Mich-

elangelo's late poems and his late works are a far cry from the triumphant vision of his earlier work, becoming instead deeply mystical. Shakespeare, too, delivered sobering observations on humanity: "What a piece of work is man! how noble in reason! how infinite in faculties! . . . And yet to me what is this quintessence of dust? Man delights not me" (Hamlet, Act 2, Scene 2). The seventeenth century came to terms with itself in diverse ways. In Holland, there emerged an unsentimental, pragmatic, tolerant, and compassionate view of humanity, while in France and Flanders the view was more veiled in idealized rhetoric. In Italy, where we shall turn first, Rome struggled to retain its spiritual, political, and artistic primacy. In contrast to the merchant class of Holland, it was the ruling class of France, Spain, and Italy that set the styles and shaped subject matter. Bent on promoting authority, power, and stability, the royal and clerical patrons of Paris, Antwerp, Madrid, and Rome ignored all uncertainty. They created their own reality in an opulent, theatrical display of architecture, sculpture, and painting. The greatest artists of the era emerged in both bourgeois and noble settings, as exemplified by Rembrandt in Holland and Velázquez in Spain. Rembrandt achieved greatness for his compassionate view of ordinary people and Velázquez for his unsparingly honest view of everyone from king to jester. In this era when subjectivity and objectivity were strongly opposing tendencies, Italy exploited subjectivity (playing to the mentality and emotions of its citizens) to affirm that most subjective of truths, faith, while Holland valued a more objective view of all humanity. Spain's greatest artist mixed objectivity and subjectivity in his own unique way, showing us the tragic and fragile humanity of both the rulers and the ruled.

## Counter Reformation Rome

As the strength of the Reformation grew in the North, the Catholic church developed strategies to oppose it. In 1540 St. Ignatius Loyola founded the Jesuit Order, a militant branch of the Catholic order whose spirituality and religious zeal marshalled the resources of Catholicism and formed an antidote to the flagrant and decadent humanism of Rome before the sack of 1527. St. Charles Borromeo (d. 1584) and St. Philip Neri (d. 1595) were characterized by a deep piety, charity, and charismatic leadership. Both revived the faith and contributed to the vitality of Catholicism in the late sixteenth century. They were guided by Popes of similar mentalities. Pope Gregory XIII (1572–1585) and Pope Sixtus V (1585–1590) came from mendicant orders and lived lives of relative austerity, piety, and rigor.

A whole spate of images was born that reflected and affirmed spirituality and mysticism. Agostino Carracci's *Last Communion of St. Jerome* (ca. 1592), is characteristic of the somber piety these late sixteenth- and early seventeenth-century images possessed. Visions, martyrdoms, repentance, and spiritual ecstasy (such as the one experienced by Philip Neri) increasingly became the subjects for artists. Some were moving and had a far-reaching impact on art, such as Federigo Barocci's *Noli Me Tangere*. Others were less inspired, like Federigo Zuccaro's *Conversion of St. Paul* **(J 818).** But all reflected Rome's stature as it became the leading city in Italy politically, economically, and artistically.

Home of the papacy, center of religious as well as cultural activities, seventeenth-century Rome enjoyed a great renewal of prestige and artistic glory. Gianlorenzo Bernini, the native Italian artist, dominated her artistically for most of the century, while foreign artists flocked there by droves. They were attracted not only by the artistic heritage and artistic ferment to be witnessed in Rome, but by the possibilities of patrons, both domestic and foreign, to be had there.

The lure of Rome must have been irresistible to an artist active in the early decades of the seventeenth century. Michelangelo and Raphael had worked there, and by the seventeenth century their names were legendary. Collections of antiquities abounded. Rome's churches and palaces were being restored, enlarged, and refurbished, or new ones built, making opportunities of all kinds available to artists with ambition and talent.

Rome, as the program pointed out, was a cosmopolitan center, conscious of its role as the leading city of Christendom, and possessed of the wealth and the patrons who wished to see Rome regain the splendor she enjoyed before the Reformation. New impulses for patronage joined old ones. The circles around the Pope were still noted for their erudition, their refinement, and their interest in art. Privately, these patrons collected works of the utmost sophistication. Publicly, they commissioned buildings and decorations that would promote the glory of Rome and Catholicism.

The Popes of the early seventeenth century came, like the Renaissance Popes, from important families: Aldobrandini (Clement VIII, 1592–1605); Borghese (Paul V, 1605–1621); Ludovisi (Gregory XV, 1621–1623); Barberini (Urban VIII, 1623–1644); Pamphili (Innocent X, 1644–1655); and Chigi (Alexander VII, 1655–1667). These Popes were cultured, educated, and sophisticated. Their interests in art extended beyond the public commissions to private collections which were amassed with fair means and foul. They traveled in circles that included other sophisticated erudite collectors, such as the Marchese Giustiniani and Cassiano dal Pozzo. They, like their late sixteenth-century predecessors, however, wished to make Rome reflect the grandeur of the church and the supremacy of the faith. A remarkable pool of talent was at their disposal. Some, like Francesco Borromini (1599–1667), were primarily architects; others, like Gianlorenzo Bernini (1598–1680) and Pietro da Cortona (1596–1669) were polymaths, equally gifted in architecture, sculpture, or painting. Still others, like Caravaggio (1573–1610), concentrated exclusively on painting. All put their stamp on the city.

## The reshaping of Rome

Changes in Rome's façade were already apparent in the late sixteenth century. The mendicant popes, Gregory XIII (1572–1585) and Sixtus V (1585–1590), had sponsored great building programs and enlarged its streets before 1600 had dawned. The purpose of enlarging those streets was to link the main religious buildings together along some clear and straight access. And in fact, the most famous sites for devotions, S. Croce in Gerusalemme, S. Florenzo, S. Maria del Popolo, and St. Peter's, were, by the early seventeenth century, all accessible by large and accommodating straight thoroughfares. The chief attraction of these streets were the churches, however, and thus Rome was transforming its physical and material form to help shape the experience of the visitor. Besides the churches themselves and the streets leading up to them, the architects who were actively redesigning Rome's appearance also considered the spaces around the churches: the squares, the fountains, and the size of the space which the building would occupy. As a result, seventeenth-century Rome became the tourist's adventure it still is today. From the long, imposing, and impressive setting for S. Agnese in the Piazza Navona, the visitor might stumble into the smaller, more intimate, and yet spatially aggressive façade of S. Maria della Pace, where, as was seen in the program, architects tried to use setting, interior, and exterior space to shape experiences of the visitors to their buildings.

The program also took us to the Piazza Navona, and in so doing, transported us back to the middle of the seventeenth century when that most munificent papal patron Urban VIII had died (1644) and his successor Innocent X (Pamphili) chose the Piazza Navona as the centerpiece for his own patronage, and a celebration of the Pamphili family. The buildings that line and define this long and majestic piazza include the papal palace (a commission given to Borromini but later completed by others) and the church of S. Agnese, a project taken over by Borromini in 1653 and completed after his designs **(J 712; H&F 13.17).** Marking the center is a huge Egyptian obelisk, a forgotten trophy of ancient Roman conquest which Innocent had found broken and neglected on the Via Appia. It crowns a fountain created by Bernini between 1648 and 1651 as the centerpiece of the piazza: the Fountain of the Four Rivers **(H&F 13.6).**

Set inside a shallow basin of water, four over-life-sized personifications of rivers (the Nile, the Danube, the Ganges, and River Plate) sit atop rock formations that are are irregular as the obelisk is geometric. These are strewn with trees, a lion, and horse, and from each side water from the Aqua Vergine (Rome's most celebrated water source) pours out; moving and energetic, the figures are a perfect foil for the rushing water.

The fountain, church, and piazza are not just parts of a whole; they interact and are interdependent in a manner that is unique to the seventeenth century and is part of the aesthetic of the baroque. The piazza itself takes its shape from antiquity, having been the site of a hippodrome inaugurated by Domition in A.D. 86. The buildings that line the piazza also define it, marking it as a space and not simply a long street. Three fountains articulate the square itself, with the *Fountain of the Four Rivers* marking the center point and thereby pointing to and interacting with the key building of the square's façade: S. Agnese.

With S. Agnese, Borromini revolutionized how façade and surrounding spaces interrelate, making the church active in its engagement with the piazza by virtue of its concave façade. The two side entrances to the church recede in, as though the space of the piazza itself was an active force. Thereby a reciprocity between space and architecture is established which is fundamental to the understanding of architecture in the seventeenth century and is a principle which underlies the relationship between viewer and image as well. As the façade responds to the "pressure" of the square, S. Agnese's dome pushes out and up aggressively against it. Here an active, plastic arrangement of architectural forms develops which is sculptural in its dynamism.

Equally important to Borromini's contribution to S. Agnese is his use of proportional relationships which allow the dome of S. Agnese to take on a principal role in the perception of the façade. Based on the dome of St. Peter's (which has it origins with Brunelleschi's cupola on the cathedral in Florence), Borromini's dome has been heightened and enlarged. It rises nobly and aggressively from a tall drum, articulated by paired pilasters which form compatible rhythms with the paired pillars composing the two flanking towers.

The program showed you two more examples of Borromini's work to demonstrate his development. In 1634 Borromini received the commission to design the church of S. Carlo alle Quattro Fontane **(J 707; G 19.13–19.14),** near the Palazzo Barberini which earned the sobriquet "S. Carlino" by virtue of its small size. Begun in 1638, it was finished three years later. Here Borromini eliminated the concept of anthropomorphic architecture. His little church discards any logical multiplication or division of modules to create a rationally comprehensible whole. Though geometry informs this building, it is deliberately ambiguous and such fundamental conventions such as corners, which help us define where we are, have been eliminated. What results is a dynamic, flowing, and aggressive space that surrounds and tantalizes those who enter the building. Recognizable structural elements like pillars and entablatures still articulate the interior, but the oval dome supported by half arches, the pendentives, and the overall space are composed of geometric shapes so complex and so elusive that scholars disagree as to the shapes from which they are derived. Called an oval intersected by four circles, the space has also been called the juncture of two equilateral triangles joined at their bases.

This dazzling complexity of intersecting geometric forms to create a dynamic interior space found further expression in Borromini's S. Ivo della Sapienza **(J 710–711; G 19.15–19.17),** done between 1642 and 1650. As the program pointed out, this was a revolutionary work. Composed of two interpenetrating equilateral triangles, the ground plan produced a star-hexagon. Here corners are not eschewed, they become so dominant and numerous so that they confuse rather than orient the visitor. The entablature no longer marks the separation of the main space from the dome, but defines the very complexity of the star-hexagon floor plan. Space and architecture interact with dynamic intensity, with space seeming to carve out the walls and the walls seeming to carve out the space. Lit from a series of windows in the dome, the whole space is alive with light and energy, its mystery derived from the complexity of the space which the light makes so visible. Ill defined, ambiguous, the boundaries between wall and support completely dissolved, this room is no longer rational and comprehensible, but confusing and disorienting. S. Ivo's star-shaped plan (based on a symbol of wisdom) celebrates a knowledge higher than human capacity. Here the unreason of the space is the physical analogue to the unreason of faith. S. Ivo, like Caravaggio's paintings and Bernini's sculptures, shapes human experience in a conscious and calculated manner, reaching into the viewer's emotions, rattling the viewer out of his rationality and lifting him towards the subjective level of faith. The ultimate expression of this tendency in architecture is Bernini's colonnade for Saint Peter's.

## Painting in Rome

Rome's private patrons, those like Cassiano dal Pozzo who collected antiquities with enthusiasm and who already judged art by aesthetic standards alone, together with the artistic riches which Rome already boasted, drew countless artists to Rome from other regions. French, Flemish, Dutch, and an occasional German artist were drawn there by the score. Some like Nicolas Poussin and Claude Lorraine would make it their home permanently, while others, including many Dutch artists, flocked to Rome for only a short time. No matter who came to Rome in the first decades of the seventeenth century, he was overshadowed there by a single artist, Caravaggio.

### A *meteoric presence*: Caravaggio

Michelangelo Merisi was born in Caravaggio near Bergamo in 1573. He came of age after Titian, Veronese, and Tintoretto had died, but he seems to have taken some inspiration from these great Venetians. Like them, he learned to paint directly on the canvas and, like the Venetians, he looked to nature for his models and used human experience as his themes. But even when we recognize his sources, the work Caravaggio produced in

Rome was stunning. He burst on the Roman scene sometime around 1592 or 1593 and painting was never quite the same again.

Caravaggio's earliest efforts helped popularize images of ordinary life for the collections of private patrons. In 1596 Caravaggio joined the household of Cardinal del Monte and for him he painted such works as *Self-Portrait as Bacchus* and *Concert of Youths* which you saw in the program. Each of these pictures had far-reaching influence. The *Bacchus* is so strongly based on visible reality, on a model (himself) posed in the studio, that its actuality overrides its purported mythological theme. Its verisimilitude (notably the flaws on the apples, on the carefully described leaves and grapes) is balanced by its artificiality, both in its staging and in its careful composition. If we look at the devices Caravaggio uses, we recognize them as old friends.

The table ledge which divides our world from that of Bacchus appears in countless Venetian pictures; the pose Bacchus assumes has its derivation (as do many of his figures) in the work of Michelangelo; the still life traces it origins back to Pompeian painting. Artists have looked out at the viewer from countless religious pictures. What is startling here is that Bacchus not only looks out at us, he reaches toward us, engaging us as never before. He offers the onlooker a glass of wine, invoking our sense of taste, touch, as well as sight and invites us into a sensuous reverie. Time is invoked, as it had been by other artists depicting moments of conversion or instances of martyrdom. But here time is the present; our engagement with this picture is immediate and direct. We are not witness to a historic event, but are engaged by the picture as its equal counterpart. Here, then, is the mark of a truly great artist; he has taken elements from the past and reused them as never before; he has charted new directions for painting and introduced a level of realism which rivals and transcends that of the Flemings a century earlier.

A similar tone is set with the youths gathered for a concert. Though partially damaged, the picture still gives us much of Caravaggio's original intention. Staring out at us, much like Bacchus did, the lute player engages us, invoking once more not only our sense of sight, but hearing, touch, and taste. For all their straightforward realism, these two pictures and others like them were not simple pictures, and they were made for a sophisticated patron: Cardinal Del Monte.

Cardinal Del Monte represented the Grand Dukes of Tuscany (the Medici Dukes who now had unquestioned leadership of Florence, which had become an artistic backwater compared to its age of splendor in the fifteenth and sixteenth centuries). Del Monte followed the traditions of the Medici Popes, living splendidly and enjoying theaters, banquets, and parties that were often decadent and licentious. Boys dressed up as girls and danced, it was said, and this life of the senses was reflected and celebrated by Caravaggio's candidly realistic images. When the Cardinal was older, he became more pious but he remained a lifelong supporter of artists, including Andrea Sacchi, a much more conservative and conventional figure than Caravaggio.

Caravaggio soon gained contracts for altarpieces as well. His most important early Roman commission was to paint scenes from the Life of Saint Matthew for the Contarelli Chapel of S. Luigi dei Francesi which he produced between 1599 and 1602. Cardinal del Monte likely intervened on Caravaggio's behalf to obtain this commission and by 1600 the first two pictures, the *Calling of Saint Matthew* **(J 693, clpl 94)** and *The Martyrdom of Saint Matthew* had been completed. These were, first and foremost, narrative pictures and how they tell their stories is the key to Caravaggio's genius. The first image is understated in its drama and nearly genrelike in its narrative; while the second is as horrifyingly dramatic as the first was calm. According to Matthew's own gospel, Jesus saw a man named Matthew seated in the custom house where he was tax collector and Jesus said to him: "Follow me."

Caravaggio shows us the custom house, with Matthew seated at the table, surrounded by assistants helping to count out money. Jesus has stepped into the room and points across it to Matthew, and has issued his command; both words and gesture are echoed by a sharp beam of light which illuminates the tax collector, apparently startled and amazed by this sudden interruption. While those to his left have looked in the direction of the disturbance, those to Matthew's right are still busily counting coins, an indication that we are viewing the very instant of Christ's entry into the room.

Despite its straightforward approach, the scene is carefully planned and staged. Plain, dark, and spare, the room lets us concentrate on its occupants; their clothes, faces, and gestures picked out with great detail and accuracy. Spot-lighted faces strangely devoid of expression register a deep intensity. Chiaroscuro, so effectively employed by Leonardo and Titian, has become even more dramatic. Dark and light are now two extremes. Meaning is here dramatically conveyed almost abstractly; the beam of light, Christ's gesture and the rightward posing of each figure lend significance to the story. These allow the whole composition to move in the direction of Christ and his command. In a gesture we recognize from Michelangelo's *Creation of Adam,* Christ is transforming Matthew from a tax collector to an apostle and martyr.

In the *Martyrdom* Caravaggio has reversed a number of formal devices he used in the previous scene to underscore the difference between Matthew's calling and his death. Here light floods in from the left, instead of the right. It illuminates an otherwise dark and nightmarish scene where violent action and thunderous noise replace the calm and quiet of the "Calling." Executioner and victim are brought together in the center of the scene, in marked contrast to the distance between Christ and Matthew in the "Calling." Matthew lies helplessly beneath the feet of the swordsman (a device borrowed from

Titian) who prepares to behead the saint. He grasps Matthew forcefully to obtain his submission, while Christ only had to point across the room to make Matthew obey him. Raising Matthew's arm, the executioner points it to the angel handing down the martyr's palm, while surrounding figures flee in terror. Conversion and martyrdom were the expected subjects for a painter of the time, but how brilliantly, originally, and daringly these traditional themes are handled! Meaning and nuance are enriched and brought out not only by how each image is handled, but by how one scene contrasts with another.

The moment of conversion is balanced by the moment just before martyrdom. The one is filled with promise and mystery, the other is excruciatingly dreadful in its inevitability. While the Conversion shows us mundane reality transformed by a miracle, the other scene reveals the horrifying reality of a saintly martyrdom. Both are compact, close-up, intimate glimpses into saintly life. These scenes crowd up toward the viewer, draw the onlooker in and cause him to pull back. The dialogue between image and viewer has become intense, interactive, and dynamic. It is a painterly parallel to the relationship between architecture and space in Borromini's churches. Caravaggio must be appreciated for more than his ability to selectively use a prosaic reality, a dramatic light, and effective staging. He also knew how to use them to convey different experiences to his viewers.

Caravaggio's lateral paintings for the chapel eventually won him the contract for the altarpiece, but here the artist, just like the sculptor who preceded him in trying to make a satisfactory altarpiece, ran afoul of the clergy. The sculptor Cobaert's work was rejected for its poor quality; when Caravaggio first attempted to show *St. Matthew and the Angel,* it was rejected for its originality. Here Caravaggio went too far with his naturalism. He portrayed Matthew as a short, stocky, thick-necked peasant who is getting a reading lesson from a beautiful angel. Matthew's rough, dirty feet stick out at the viewer and this among other parts of the picture offended the clergy's sense of decorum. It had to go and it was quickly snapped up by Caravaggio's discerning friend and patron, Vincenzo Giustiniani: an altarpiece entered a private collection as a work of art.

A few months later Caravaggio supplied the Clergy of San Luigi with a more conventional and therefore acceptable picture. A dignified, venerable, and clearly literate Matthew bends over his gospels, the text placed on a desk. An angel hovers overhead giving Matthew spiritual dictation. Never mind that this angel is one of those churlish looking models who leered provocatively out from Caravaggio's genre pictures; his street urchin face is offset by a sufficient amount of swirling angelic drapery. Furthermore, St. Matthew himself looks intelligent, refined, and appropriately ascetic as well as spiritual; his features have an uncanny resemblance to the many portraits done after St. Philip Neri's death mask. Caravaggio carefully revised the onlooker's experience in the two

works. In the first, there is an intimate, even affectionate relationship between the spiritual messenger and the earthly recipient. Their two realms are differentiated by the vastly different characterization of the rude, yet endearing, peasant saint who looks earnestly and intensely at the message the beautiful angel is guiding him through; we seem to witness the moment of some special revelation as the saint registers awe and amazement at what he is writing. In the accepted work, that easy intimacy and close rapport is broken; the revelation is supplied in a sufficiently airborne fashion but wary concern has replaced awe and inspiration on Matthew's face. In the first example we experience humble but sincere faith; in the second, refined but less convincing spiritual illumination.

Caravaggio's success with the Contarelli chapel soon earned him a new commission for the decoration of the Cerasi chapel in Santa Maria del Popolo. For the Cerasi chapel Caravaggio once more supplied the twin themes of conversion and martyrdom between 1600 and 1601.

In this chapel he contrasted the *Conversion of St. Paul* **(G 19.26; H&F 13.1)** with the *Martyrdom of St. Peter.* Placed on the walls flanking the main altar, these two scenes (like those in the Contarelli chapel of S. Luigi Francesi) exploited and utilized the light source from the window and the scale of the setting. Here the episodes are both dramatic, but the conversion, with Paul thrown back, stunned and blinded, is the more sudden and explosive of the two; while the martyrdom of Peter is a moment of transition. Condemned to death by crucifixion, Peter requested that he be crucified upside down in deference to Christ whom he feels unworthy to follow in a similar martyrdom. Caravaggio presents us with the executioners engaged in the slow, laborious task of raising the cross with its burden on the bottom.

As the program pointed out, were we not to know the subject of Caravaggio's *Conversion of Paul,* we might think it was a depiction of a riding accident. The great spotted horse looms over the fallen saint and is more prominent and central in the image than is Paul, the actual subject of the story. On his way to Damascus to obtain arrest warrants for Christians, Paul was thus converted to the faith and became one of Christ's most eloquent and influential followers. As in Caravaggio's earlier scenes of miracles, mysteries of faith are conveyed by means of light and intense mood but restrained expression, rather than by the more conventional and literal tools at artists' disposal. Aware only that a man has fallen, the horse steps over him and in so doing, his lifted hoof hovers precariously over Paul's vulnerable form. This momentary danger underscores Paul's insensate condition; seeing nothing, oblivious to the horse, Paul hears only God's words: "Saul, Saul, why do you persecute me?" Caravaggio saves his picture from simple prosaic realism by his careful staging and understated facial expression. Crowded, claustrophobic, and dramatic, the picture concentrates on horse and groom, and the saint. All else is darkness. The horse and Paul are picked out in high relief against the dark by the blinding light through which God's message is carried. Paul falls out of the picture almost into our space in a manner not unlike the Bacchus reaching out to us with his wine.

Caravaggio's importance for European painting was profound. He spawned innumerable followers in Rome and Naples, as well as in Holland and France. These artists adopted Caravaggio's use of realism, his sense of lighting, his subject matter. Themes of musicians, card sharks, and the like flourished in Holland and Flanders thanks to Caravaggio's work, while in Italy, painters particularly responded to his use of highly realistic and unrefined models, embellished by such artificial devices as lighting and staging. Caravaggio's scenes of violent action like his *Boy Bitten by a Lizard* or his *Judith Killing Holofernes* spawned a hole host of imitations, the most striking being those by Artemesia Gentileschi (1593–1652) the most successful woman artist of her day and whose own experience with rape has often been ascribed to her obsession with this theme **(H&F 13.9)**.

Contemporary critics did not universally approve of Caravaggio's approach to art. Bellori criticized his followers for imitating forms that were "vulgar" and that suppressed the "majesty of art." "Some artists began to look enthusiastically for filth and deformity" (Engass, Brown, p. 76). He praised Caravaggio for adopting realism, however, for he "came upon the scene at a time when realism was not much in fashion and when figures were made according to convention and manner and satisfied more the taste for gracefulness than for truth" (Engass, Brown, p. 77).

Caravaggio's death was sudden and violent. He had traveled to Naples from Sicily, where he was attacked by armed men who gashed his face. Wrongly imprisoned, he was released but was disoriented, and caught a fever after searching for his lost belongings along a beach in the full heat of the sun. He died several days later, aged forty, according to Bellori; according to another document, he was only thirty-six.

## The art of tradition: Pietro da Cortona

Caravaggio was a revolutionary artist. He eschewed classical antiquity and refused to "invent" his figures, substituting keen observation of people from all walks of life for the study of ancient marbles and the art of Raphael. Caravaggio's independence from tradition earned him the admiration of collectors and at times caused him trouble with conservative patrons. Caravaggio, like Michelangelo, relied on his own artistic inventiveness and his own inclinations about how a particular subject should be treated, or invented his own. Other artists followed more conventional patterns, letting patrons pick the subjects and using traditional formulae to visualize them. While Caravaggism became an influential style for painters, especially during the first three decades of the seven-

teenth century, there were other schools of thought in Rome. Many artists still took their inspiration from antiquity from Raphael, and spoke in the exalted and majestic visual language that Bellori had preferred. One of the most gifted of these artists was Pietro da Cortona (Pietro Berrettini) who was born in Cortona in 1596 and died in Rome in 1669.

The contemporary biographer, Passerei, tells us that Pietro first studied with some minor Florentine painters, but that his real inspiration came from his travels to Rome. There he studied antiquity, Raphael, and Michelangelo. From ancient artifacts he copied scenes of ancient rites, pagan ceremonies and bacchanals. He also made a copy of Raphael's *Galatea,* the most "baroque" and also the most pagan of Raphael's images.

Just as Caravaggio had come under the protection of Cardinal del Monte, Pietro gained the patronage of Cardinal Giulio Sacchetti. Sacchetti was, in turn, very close to Cardinal Francesco Barberini, nephew of Pope Urban VIII. Pietro soon enjoyed a distinguished career and gained important commissions. Sacchetti was, like many other Roman patrons, passionately interested in antiquity and he chose for Pietro some antiquarian themes to paint. The most famous of these is the *Rape of the Sabines,* which Pietro painted for him in 1629. Pietro depicted a well-known episode of Roman history that comes down to us from Livy and Plutarch. Short of women, the ancient Romans invited neighboring groups including the Sabines to a festival. At a prearranged signal, the young Roman men seized the Sabine women and carried them off. Plutarch says they did this to assure bonds with their neighbors and to insure children. From this incident comes the custom of lifting the bride over the threshold of her husband's house.

Like Caravaggio's *Bacchus,* this picture reflects the personal interests of a private patron and is intended to decorate his palazzo. But unlike Caravaggio, Pietro tried to re-create antiquity aesthetically in depicting his subject, and he completely ignored the more prosaic reality with which Caravaggio enlivened his interpretation of mythology.

Pietro strove to tell his story with decorum and dignity. His compositions, forms, and figures all trace their origins to the very epoch he was trying to revive. A series of abductions takes place in a shallow frieze across the picture surface, a device borrowed from ancient reliefs. To the left, the unfortunate married woman has been seized, her reaction one of annoyance rather than fear, while the sturdy Roman soldier seems literally to have his hands full. Next to him another soldier prepares to lift his prize and the question is not so much her reluctance as his ability to get her airborne. Beside him another soldier has succeeded and carries off his trophy while shouting encouragement to his fellow Roman. His bride throws up her arms in a gesture we should recognize from Caravaggio's *Burial of Christ*. Here the gesture lacks the serious pathos of Caravaggio and becomes in part a formal device to give this figure more lift, to move the composition across the surface of the picture to the right, and to counteract the leftward direction of the soldier holding her.

Filled with solid, weighty figures that look like ancient statues come to life, this scene has some of the wistful nostalgia we found in Venetian painting of the previous century. The dappled light and ample bodies remind us of Veronese, and the mythic feeling owes its charm to Venetian traditions as well. Though momentous, this scene is neither ponderous nor frivolous or tragic. Pietro managed to maintain the dignity of his subject, despite its potential for licentiousness. The women are properly dignified, but not terrified (as Caravaggio might have painted them) and the men are sufficiently strong to carry them off, but do so with a certain decorum (and not with the violence we would expect from Caravaggio or his followers). Though Pietro was the most talented exponent of the "baroque" style, meaning that he believed in an art of dynamic movement and energetic compositions, he, like his counterparts who advocated "classicism," also believed in decorum, especially in the treatment of mythological subjects. In re-creating a classical theme, Pietro, who loved motion, energy, and a sense of dynamism in his pictures, restrained himself to keep within the spirit of his story. After all, this is a scene about antiquity, an epoch Pietro regarded with reverence and respect.

This scene about motion is as controlled and calculated as the historical "rape." Everything is prearranged and plotted within a balanced composition. At least one device, a single movement repeated in different stages, should be familiar from Caravaggio's *Entombment of Christ*. Notice how the figure lifting the Sabine woman is essentially repeated three times to describe the action across the picture. This device traces its origins all the way back to Giotto, and from there to classical antiquity. The Parthenon reliefs include for example, a reclining, semi-reclining and seated figure, and these three figures are essays on the human body in different states of repose. This particular visual device was sufficiently important to find exponents from various theoretical camps, and in Pietro's time, those camps were sharply divided.

In the Rome of Pietro's time, art was sufficiently independent to warrant debates about issues of style and their relative merits. As is true of any theoretical issue, what is one thing in theory becomes something else in practice. Though Pietro belonged to the camp of baroque artists (in that he favored energetic diagonals and vividly moving forms and twisting bodies) he presented, in his *Rape of the Sabines,* all these diagonals in a series of carefully plotted figures, whose mass, dignity, and proportions have many of the characteristics of the so-called classicists, as exemplified by Poussin, who is mentioned later on. For our purposes it is best to consider Pietro's work in contrast to Caravaggio, for it is a vastly different world from his. Here imagination, antiquity, idealism, intellectual rigor, carefully modulated actions and emo-

tions give this image a feeling of control, balance, charm, and restraint despite the somewhat dramatic subject matter. It appeals above all to the mind. Pietro tried to re-create a golden age, to satisfy the personal erudition of a patron who likely showed the work only to a small circle of like-minded friends. That circle greatly admired the art of antiquity. To them, the kind of ideals expressed by such classical works as the metopes of the Parthenon, with their measured actions, controlled forms, and triumphant vision, were to be valued, emulated, and if possible, re-created. That Pietro fulfilled his mission is evident from his career. Pietro produced grand decorative schemes for erudite patrons in Rome as well as in Florence.

Pietro's grandest masterpiece was his ceiling fresco done for the "gran salone" of the Palazzo Barberini between 1633 and 1639 **(J 698).** With this commission we encounter a seventeenth-century pope, Urban VIII (Maffeo Barberini), who equals Julius II for his taste and impact on Roman art. His tomb in Saint Peter's has been compared to Julius' ill-fated project; in fact, Urban VIII made more changes in Saint Peter's than any Pope since Julius. A lover of art, Maffeo Barberini was an early patron of Caravaggio, and by the time he became Pope in 1623 he was well prepared to use art to advance his own and his family's prestige. Urban VIII is generally recognized as the most self-aggrandizing Pope in an age of self-aggrandizement. By 1633, with the help of Maderno and Bernini, the Barberini family had built the largest family palace in Rome and shortly thereafter they selected a small army of painters to decorate it.

The over-riding theme of these decorations was the glorification of the Barberini family. One ceiling was devoted to the theme of their wisdom. Pietro da Cortona was chosen to decorate the largest ceiling in the reception room, following a scheme to apotheosize the Barberini family developed by the sycophantic family poet: Francesco Bracciolini. Trying desperately to restore himself to favor in the Barberini household, Bracciolini developed a grandiose scheme of visual allegory greater and more complex than any since Raphael's Stanza. In an era already used to myth building (consider Tintoretto's vast assembly in the Palazzo Ducale of Venice) Pietro's ceiling reached new heights of exuberant veneration.

What strikes us about the ceiling at first glance is its overwhelming energy. Never before have so many figures crowded into such a lofty fictive space and moved with such unbounded energy towards the center of the ceiling. Here Pietro was able to give full vent to his love of movement, and lives up to his reputation as the greatest exponent of the baroque style. As if drawn by some unseen force all the figures stream to the climax of the allegory: Divine Providence signaling Immortality to crown with stars the three bees who represent the Barberini family. Surrounded by laurel, signifying Urban's gifts as a poet, the bees are also accompanied by personifications of the theological virtues holding emblems of the Papacy: the tiara and the keys of Saint Peter.

Urban's erudition, his wisdom, and his many virtues are woven together in a complex tapestry of mythology, symbol, and narrative.

Such abstruse imagery could easily have been deadly in the hands of a lesser talent, but Pietro used it as an opportunity to create a playful and energetic illusion. The actual limits of the ceiling have been replaced by a soaring, infinite space that transports us into the magical world of ideas and myth. Fictive architecture defines the borders for the narrative episodes and the apotheosis above, but the borders themselves are freely transgressed by characters that seem impelled upward by the force of the receding space. There, in the glorious light and clouds, Divine Providence issues her decree and the entire action concentrates humorously enough on three rather oversized and chubby bees who act as emissaries of the only actual humans in this whole complex of ideas: the Barberini. They are surrounded by wholly imaginary beings. Charming, smiling, enchanted, and playful, these personifications of ideas happily perform their roles as a supporting cast to the main actors, the bees. And, as if to humorously underscore the point that only the spectator's vantage point matters, he paints the bees though they had just swooped out of our space and were just approaching this celestrial world. This, of course, means that all the divine personifications are seeing three bees feet first. Logic has no place in the realm of illusionism, and by asking such questions we see how irrelevant they must be to a fantasy such as this.

Every swirling, moving figure plays its appointed role well and remains part of an overall design that unifies the entire scheme despite its many distinct parts. Like Caravaggio, Pietro recognized the potential of illusionism, but he playfully created and destroyed illusion at will. And by artfully confusing the onlooker about what is "real" and what is not, he ultimately reminds the viewer that the entire image is in fact a fantasy, and that in fantasy, rules of logic and reality can and should be abandoned. Thus, the spectator is engaged in this image as never before in a ceiling painting. The very fact of its illusionism is ultimately a reminder of our separation from what seems to be so accessible and tangible. In an era when illusion became an important issue for artists, they approached that issue with remarkable sophistication. Pietro's ceiling was the stepping-stone for a whole series of other experiments with deep space, numerous figures, and complex subjects. Pietro's suave and light-hearted approach was not superseded however until the eighteenth century, when the Venetian Giambattista Tiepolo added the final chapter to the now lost art of allegorical ceiling frescoes.

## Master of the classical style: Poussin

Pietro, as we have seen, was equally adept at decorative allegories and classical mythologies. Learned, imaginative, and humorous, Pietro was the talented counter-part to a painter of a much more serious temperament, his opponent in form, style, and often in content. If Pietro was the exponent of the baroque, then Poussin was the great exponent of seventeenth-century classicism.

A native French artist, Nicolas Poussin (1594–1665) settled in Rome permanently and made his living supplying easel pictures to private clients. Poussin has been called the most intellectual and learned painter who ever lived. His pictures often amounted to visual philosophical treatises, and satisfied the intellectual orientation of a particular sphere of clients that included briefly Cardinal Francesco Barberini (nephew of Urban VIII), who, however, generally preferred less rigorous logic in his pictures. One of Poussin's lifelong patrons was Cassiano dal Pozzo, friend of Galileo, scholar and ardent archeologist, whose palace had become a kind of miniature university, replete with books and artifacts, particularly ancient ones. Cassiano tried to record all surviving traces of Roman antiquity by collecting prints and drawings, and by commissioning artists to fill over 23 volumes with copies of antiquities. Cassiano, like Pietro da Cortona's patron, Sacchetti, was a member of an erudite circle of collectors whose tastes ran to classical themes, subjects as well as styles. Pietro's *Rape of the Sabines* was one of his most "classicizing" works, meaning that it conformed to ideals of balance, stability, seriousness of form and content. Poussin's entire oeuvre represents his quest to find the forms and subjects that adequately expressed his own interpretation of the antique.

Poussin thrived in the rarified intellectual environment of Cassiano dal Pozzo and his group. During his lifetime, Poussin built up a repertoire of ancient figure types, compositions, and architectural motifs which were used to re-create antiquity in scenes that are both sober and filled with a deep nostalgia. One of Poussin's most celebrated works is his *Shepherds of Arcadia* **(G 19.61),** an austere assembly of four figures gathered round a lone tomb set deep in the natural paradise that was Arcadia. The message they read is sobering, "I too am in Arcadia" (Et in Arcadia Ego)—signifying that even in Arcadia, death can be found. Taking the form of an epitaph on the tomb, the meaning is subtle. Evoking nostalgia for a shepherdess now lost (has she reappeared to the shepherds who reflect on her life?), the image touches on the grander theme of death itself. It is treated with dignity and deep emotion. A golden Venetian light (inspired by Titian) adds warmth and nostalgia to these sad yet noble figures. Poussin has filtered both his subjects and his forms through the rigorous filter of his intellect, culling out all imperfections and removing any false notes that would detract from the serious and meditative mood of his scene. Carefully arranged around the tomb, which blocks out our view of the landscape, the shepherds bring our thoughts back to the subject that dominates the image. In an image where time has been suspended, Poussin has provided a thoughtful discourse on time. He brings to mind not only that the Golden Age of classicism was destroyed by time, but uses the metaphor of the tomb to consider the more universal notion of mortality. Poussin represents the most classically conscious artist in a classically conscious age and his *Arcadian Shepherds* demonstrates the most intellectual orientation of seventeenth-century art. His art, however, deals ultimately with human themes. In this rigorous composition and its starkly arranged forms, the theme is death and mortality. Art, as we have seen, alternately affirmed, ignored, or denied humanity, substituting or supplanting humanity with issues of faith. In an era seeking to confront reality, age-old human concerns lie at the core. No matter how one views life, death is inevitable and unescapable. The seventeenth century, caught up with the notion of transience, found its thoughts turning on more than one occasion to that fundamental issue.

## Master of Motion and Illusion: Bernini

What Pietro da Cortona was to pictorial illusionism, Gianlorenzo Bernini was to sculptural illusion. Born in Naples, the son of a Florentine sculptor, Bernini came to Rome with his father in 1604–05. A prodigy, Bernini studied the work of Michelangelo and Raphael, as well as ancient sculpture. But he did more than imitate those whom he admired. Like all great artists, Bernini strove to make his sources part of his own unique vision. He was fascinated by movement, and his ability to describe an action in process, and to capture a moment of it, marks him as a seventeenth-century artist. Movement was an important aspect of Caravaggio's art and that of Pietro da Cortona. But describing action in paint is a less difficult task than trying to capture it in sculpture.

The program concentrated on Bernini's *David* (**J 702; G 19.16**) to show how far Bernini could take a single figure in action. David, as you will recall, had been established as a challenge to figure sculptors by Donatello. Subsequent sculptors provided their essays on David, the most famous of which was Michelangelo's colossal marble of 1504. Alert and ready for action, Michelangelo's *David* was nonetheless static. Bernini, instead, shows us David in the moment just before his stone is discharged from its sling. His jaw set, his lips pressed, and his face tense with concentration, David's body is coiled like a spring just before release. David's action implies the presence of Goliath somewhere in the immediate vicinity.

The spectator, in certain positions, could feel like the target, adding another level of illusion (besides that of action) to this masterpiece of frozen movement. Bernini, like Michelangelo and Donatello, looked at nature as well as antiquity as sources. David's well-muscled body and torso are an artful mixture of antique sources and studies from life. Bernini's biographers tell us that Maffeo Barberini helped hold up a mirror so that Bernini could use his own face as a model for David's. Bernini also had a particular sensitivity to texture and the ability to describe it in marble. Look at David's arm and shoulder and see how effectively he describes the hard, thin muscles stretched along the bone of the forearm, the thicker, denser muscles of the shoulder and the soft, delicate tissue of the under arm.

Bernini left his sculpture uncolored, as had Michelangelo, so that the miracle of transforming the marble into a human form is fully revealed. Bernini worked much faster than his Renaissance predecessor. He finished his David in a mere seven months, proof of his virtuoso talent as a carver. But what he turned out so quickly is a masterpiece of description instead of interpretation. Life-sized and beautifully conceived as a figure in motion, it describes that figure turning and twisting in preparation to throw. In concentrating on the momentary, Bernini's *David* lost some of the grander associations attached to the heroic figure sculptures of the Davids of the past. In witnessing the moment of transition, one is not impelled to consider the more encompassing idea of transience. In admiring the specificity of this action and the lifelikeness of the body engaged in an act, however heroic, the concept of hero is somehow diminished. Anecdotal ripples emanate from this figure instead of the epic rhythms that accompany Michelangelo's *David*. Art has truly returned to the human scale, to human dimension, and a human level.

To achieve something more awesome and grandiose, it must return to myth and compound the number of figures and actors in its theatrical assembly. And even then, it must retain a level of humor and lightness in order to sustain the credibility of its message. Bernini also relied on theater to elevate and increase the power of his message. That is nowhere better expressed than in the Cornaro chapel of S. Maria della Vittoria, which he produced twenty years after completing his remarkable *David*.

Urban VIII died in 1644 and for a brief time Bernini did not enjoy papal favor. Innocent X, who had a horror of nudity in art, preferred blander fare than Bernini's extravaganzas, but a private commission came Bernini's way which has won him immortality. Cardinal Federigo Cornaro asked Bernini to convert the left transept of S. Maria della Vittoria into a family burial chapel, a project Bernini completed in 1652. Bernini adopted the subject matter common in Carmelite churches: the ecstasy of St. Teresa (**J 703; H&F 13.5**). Founder of the Discalced (or Barefoot) Carmelites, St. Teresa was canonized in 1622, and her "transverberation," the piercing of her heart by divine love, was mentioned in the proclamation of her sainthood. What Bernini did with this fairly standard commission was to transform the chapel into a theater, the main altar into a stage, and the walls into box seats occupied by members of the Cornaro family.

We know Bernini was a lover of theater and well versed in its discipline. John Evelyn, the famous English diarist, reported that during his visit to Rome in very eyes. Bernini has managed to transform marble into vapor, into churning drapery and gleaming unearthly flesh. The entire ensemble—figures, light, action, and stage—transports us into Teresa's emotional state, helping us to see what she is experiencing and to feel it as well.

Here Bernini manipulated and mixed his media with unprecedented freedom and originality. Using the natural light from a window above the stage, he simultaneously emphasized and dramatized the light illuminating Teresa's vision, and made it thoroughly artificial by carving and gilding out literal rays of light behind the two figures. This is the ultimate illusion. The most immaterial substance, light, has been given material definition and shape. Yet within the context of the image, it is, like everything else in the image, completely natural and convincing. Though carved in the round, Teresa and the angel are set apart from us behind a stage and we see them as though they were a picture or a theater event, one that is discussed by the carved portraits of the Cornaro family to the right and left. Like a hallucination, this ecstasy is remarkably real, but ultimately elusive. Traditional boundaries of painting, sculpture, and architecture no longer exist in Bernini's world. They are crossed at will to achieve the total effect he desired. That effect was deliberately illogical and subjective, and designed to appeal to the emotions rather than reason. In this goal, Bernini, like seventeenth-century Rome's interpretation of Saint Teresa, was a product of his times.

The historical Saint Teresa was, in fact, a fairly pragmatic and practical person. A Spaniard, she became a nun who after periods of ill health began to have a number of visions. She wrote about them matter of factly, not giving them too much importance, devoting her energies instead to the reaffirmation of the strict Carmelite rule. She established the discalced Carmelites, the barefoot order, devoted to poverty, charity, prayer, and hardship. During her life she toiled ceaselessly, founding seventeen convents in Spain and writing about her accomplishments in various tracts. But when the church canonized her forty years after her death in 1582, it was more interested in emphasizing her fervid spirituality, and immortalized her as the saint whose ecstatic vision affected her physically as well as emotionally.

A true son of his time, Bernini accepted and reinforced this subjective and one-sided interpretation of Saint Teresa. His depiction of her vision is now the image by which she is best known. We know he followed her own account of her vision accurately in describing his scene, but left us with a rather skewed understanding of her life and character. But ultimately, Bernini left us with an indelible affirmation of faith, in an era when the efficacy of faith was waning. Though we no longer respond simply to the affecting message Bernini's St. Teresa conveys, we can still admire the means by which Bernini brought it about. Heirs to the science which supplanted religion, we are keen to know how tricks of illusion are achieved. And yet, Teresa's message still haunts. Science

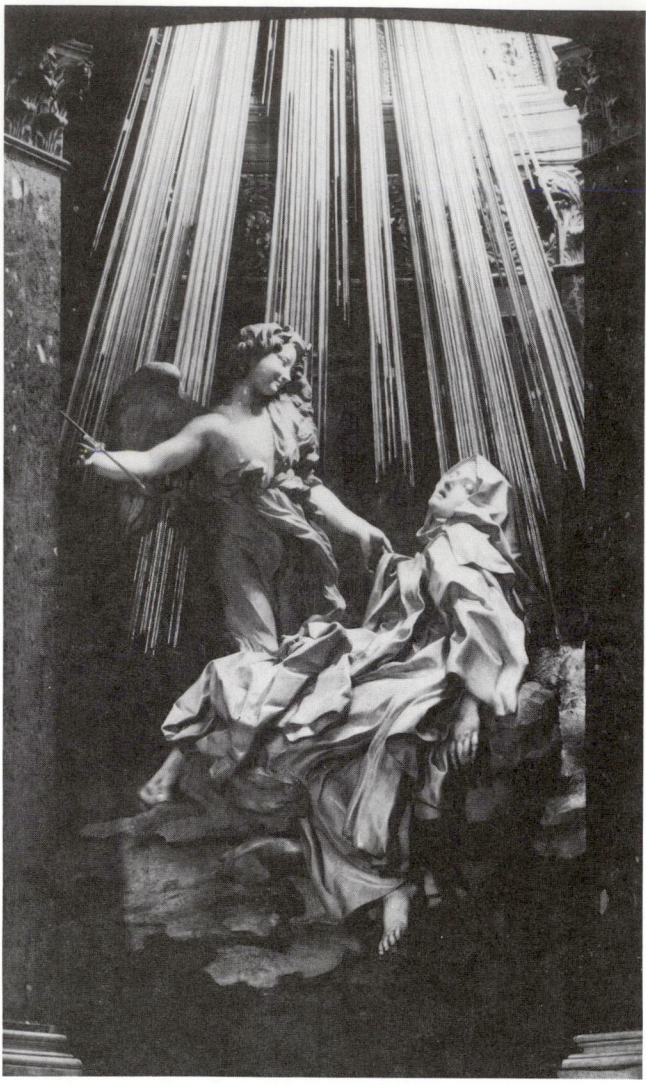

Gianlorenzo Bernini, *The Ecstasy of Sta. Theresa*, 1645–1652. Rome, Cornaro Chapel, Sta. Maria della Vittoria. (SCALA/ART RESOURCE, NEW YORK)

1644, "Cavaliero Bernini, Sculptor, Architect, Painter & Poet . . . gave a Publique Opera (for so they call those Shews of that kind) where in he painted the Seanes, cut the Statues, invented the Engines, composed the Musique, writ the Comedy and built the Theater all himself" (Hibbard, p. 179). That experience clearly stood him in good stead with the Cornaro chapel.

The altar has been transformed into a miniature stage, defined by dark green, mottled marble pillars and pilasters. The curtain has been drawn to reveal a startling scene. Illuminated by a blaze of divine light, St. Teresa lies in a swoon, suspended on a cloud. Her head thrown back, her lips parted, she is about to be pierced by an arrow of divine love. Teresa is transported in a vision of divine ecstasy and Bernini has presented that moment to us, as though it were a vision. The whole image hovers in another dimension and threatens to vanish before our has led us to expect greater and greater clarity and now shows us infinitely greater mysteries. Perhaps the great mystics were right. Certainly Teresa has continued to fascinate and was the subject of several important biographies down to the twentieth century. One wonders if her fame would have been as great if Bernini had not left us with this memorable illusion in which she was the star.

## Austrian Baroque

The arts of Rome, as the program stated, had an international impact. Foreign artists flocked there and returned to their native countries bringing with them the knowledge of Caravaggio, Bernini, and Borromini. One particularly important architect who learned from Bernini and Borromini was Johann Bernard Fischer von Erlach (1656–1723), who was the first important architect to emerge North of the Alps since the age of the cathedrals. Trained as a sculptor, Fischer von Erlach probably worked with Bernini and his assistants. Inspired equally by the art of antiquity and the forms of the baroque, Fischer von Erlach also forms a significant transition from the age of Baroque to the age of Reason, since he had contact with the inaugurator of rationalist philosophy: Baron Gottfried Wilhelm Leibnitz.

After spending twelve years in Italy, Fischer returned to Austria where he introduced baroque architecture to the imperial court. The small principalities and the churches in Austria were anxious to rebuild after the ravages of the Thirty Years War. Fischer found employment at a number of important sites. In 1705 he had become chief Imperial Inspector of all Buildings for Court and Festivities and he produced the great palace at Schönbrunn in around 1690. But his masterpiece was the great Karlskirche begun in the eighteenth century. It, like the philosopher who helped design its program, is the epitome of logic. Born two years after the end of the Thirty Years War, which had torn apart Germany, and which was so effectively portrayed in the prints of Callot that the program showed you (**G 19.63**), Leibnitz set about proving God's existence through sheer logic. Summing up the Platonic, scholastic, and Cartesian arguments, Leibnitz argued that this is the best of all possible worlds, filled with more good than evil, and within which man has free will, and is created by the best of all possible beings: God.

The Age of Reason had dawned and its confident rationality informs every part of the Karlskirche (**J 718–719**). The church fulfills a vow made by Charles VI to build a church dedicated to St. Charles, should Vienna be delivered from the plague of 1713. When it was, Charles was true to his promise. Though dedicated to the great Counter Reformation saint, Carlo Borromeo, the church also makes reference to Vienna's self-proclaimed position as heir to Rome by virtue of being capital of the new Holy Roman Empire. The symbolic references are arranged in a rational, comprehensible order. Two triumphal columns adapted from ancient Rome flank a gabled portico, all of which are embellished with scenes from St. Charles's life. Each element of the façade can be read separately and fuse not only the ancient with the recent past, but secular and sacred themes. The symbolism inherent in the elements of the façade stress the power of the Austrian emperor while proclaiming the dignity of the church. In this era, when the right of kings was viewed as divinely given, more than one monarch seized on the importance of faith to lend credence and the strength of tradition to his reign. But Fischer von Erlach is credited with developing the most successful language of imperial architecture, suitable not only for churches but for palaces and other imperial buildings.

Fischer von Erlach's sources are as clear as they are diverse. The dome and flanking towers are based in principle on the façade of Borromini's S. Agnese, while the interior space is a more rationalized rearrangement of Borromini's designs. The authority of ancient and baroque forms was recognized and successfully adopted by Fischer, but arranged to suit the intellect, not the heart. Paying civilized homage to the saint who delivered Vienna from the plague, the Karlskirche introduced an era that believed that existence could be defined, and ordered. The parts of this church, though originating from diverse sources, have been made compatible with one another. Each speaks to the reason first and stands as a reassuring monument to the human intellect. Unlike Borromini, who intended to confuse, disorient, and ultimately suspend the viewer's sense of logic, Fischer von Erlach wanted to affirm it. Balance, symmetry, and carefully plotted proportions give each element of the Karlskirche façade a comprehensible role to play. Each of the parts is clearly and deliberately defined. Sufficient space is left between elements so that they neither crowd nor blend together, but retain a dignified sense of isolation. The two antique columns are flanked by shorter but wider towers, that, with the columns, compose a pairing of elements flanking the portico and the dome. The arrangement is eminently logical and predictable, even as it is made up of eclectic and disparate sources. The whole façade is a carefully considered arrangement of horizontal and vertical elements, played off against accents of curves. Decorations are sparing and restrained, adding only enough embellishment to reduce the severity of the arrangement.

Fischer von Erlach's legacy can be found in a number of important monasteries that were built along the banks of the Danube during the late seventeenth and early eighteenth century. Inspired by the triumphal spirit that swept through Europe after the defeat of the Turks in 1687, these new monasteries were viewed as a triumph of civilization over barbarism. They were as luxurious and splendid as any royal residence and many of them contained imperial residences. Most famous of these is the monastery and church of Melk, begun in 1702 on the design of Jakob Prandtauer, a follower of Fischer von

Erlach. Presiding majestically on a knoll overlooking the Danube, Melk's graceful yet imposing design, with its twin towers and curved entryway, retains the rhythmical curves and undulating forms that originated in seventeenth-century Italian architecture. Here those forms are repeated, giving a sense of layering and rhythm that endows the whole structure with a massiveness, yet lightness, that demonstrates the smooth but decisive transition of architecture from the seventeenth to the eighteenth century.

Melk, like its contemporary monasteries, contained luxurious apartments, banqueting halls, a library (regarded now as a temple of knowledge), and richly decorated churches. The theme that runs through Melk, as well as the Karlskirche, is the glory of civilization built on the combined forces of faith, education, monarchy, and priesthood. The abbot of Melk was a great landowner. He served as imperial counselor and when he commissioned Jakob Prandtauer to design his monastery in 1700, his tastes were appropriately aristocratic and prideful.

The façade, as seen from the banks of the river, is both closed and open, giving a sense of the interior from what is visible through the gate and the towers. That interior is no longer walled off and remote from civilization, but a superior, more refined, and more luxurious extension of it. Triumphal monasteries like Melk were built nearly everywhere in Europe during the eighteenth century and signal the final outburst of ecclesiastical energy generated by the Counter Reformation over a hundred years before. Traces of the monastic building were lost when Napoleon, with his anticlerical sentiments, swept through Europe at the end of the eighteenth century, closing many of them, destroying their treasures, and obliterating their presence in history.

## Part 2
# THE BAROQUE IN SPAIN AND THE LOW COUNTRIES

The churches and monasteries of Austria, which flourished at the end of the seventeenth century, point to the importance the courts of Northern Europe had for artistic development. Sponsored for the most part by monarchs, these buildings were the last great expression of a courtly art that, during the seventeenth century, was one of the prevailing forms of patronage. Madrid was the leading center of Northern Europe, ruling a vast empire that extended to Naples in Italy, and presiding over the truculent and ultimately independent Protestant United Provinces, as Holland came to be known. The arts that sprang from both environments—the aristocratic and largely Catholic environment of the courts and the more ordinary and humble environment of bourgeois Holland—is the subject of Part 2 of this program.

During the first part of the seventeenth century, Spain was the leading power of Europe and then entered a period of decline. Philip IV (reigned 1621–1665), grandson of Charles V, produced a son (Charles VI, r. 1666–1700), who was the result of so much inbreeding that he was essentially incompetent as ruler and as a human being. Charles's rule was the last of the Habsburg Spanish line; lacking an heir, the kingdom reverted to the French Bourbons. The Spanish empire at the time had an entrenched bureaucracy, a powerful church, and a court that lived conspicuously well in contrast to the poor. Largely peasants and laborers, this poor class had little chance to improve its lot, as no strong merchant class existed in the Spain of that era. France, ruled briefly by the regent, Marie de' Medici, until her son, Louis XIII, came to his majority, rose to greater and greater prominence. With the advent in 1643 of Louis XIV, who married Philip's daughter and thereby eventually gained the Spanish crown, France was in the ascent and was destined to become the leading cultural and political force of Europe in the late seventeenth and early eighteenth centuries.

Flanders, still under Catholic Spanish rule (as a result of calculated dynastic unions), also had a powerful church and noble class, but since the fifteenth century Flanders had been a city of merchants and burghers. While the artists of Spain served mainly the church and the nobles, in Flanders patronage extended to the bourgeoisie.

Holland, which had established itself as the United Provinces to gain independence from Philip II's rule, was, by contrast, a land of primarily Protestant merchants, traders, and patricians. Enjoying a prosperity brought on by trade, the Dutch enjoyed a fairly high standard of living. Citizens of Dutch towns like Amsterdam, Haarlem, Rotterdam, Utrecht, and Delft tended to live modestly, placing great value on thrift, on honest labor, on dignity and tolerance. The teachings of John Calvin emphasizing austerity were particularly influential.

Pragmatic and practical, the Dutch were unashamedly materialistic, having a deep respect for well-made objects of all kinds and an intense curiosity about the natural world. Cartography, horticulture, navigation, and optics were all pursued with passion and interest. Natural and man-made objects were traded and collected. Paintings, the ideal medium to reflect Dutch interests, were particularly favored. They could and did describe the people who collected them, their homes, their towns, and the landscapes around them. Paintings also depicted the objects they collected, the plants they so loved, and the historical and biblical ideals to which they clung.

The art of Spain, Flanders, and Holland, then, was deeply affected by the patrons who supported it. Artists in each country were keenly aware of visible reality and recognized the potential of art to replicate or interpret that reality. How reality was treated depended not only on the patron but on the mind and orientation of the artist.

# Spain, Flanders, and France

The program pointed out how similar court life in Europe was, regardless of the region. Kings ruled England, Spain, Flanders, France, Germany, and Austria. All used artists to proclaim their authority and their dignity through images that often traced their origins back to antiquity. The program introduced you to those great Northern artists who were patronized by nobility: Rubens, van Dyck, and Velázquez. All three artists were members of guilds, operated large workshops, and were deeply influenced by the art of Italy, which they visited in the early years of the seventeenth century. All entered noble service. Rubens worked for the Gonzaga of Mantua and then became painter to the Habsburg regents. Van Dyck began his career as chief assistant to Rubens and ultimately became court painter to Charles I of England, who knighted him. Velázquez held various posts in the court of Philip IV, and aspired to a knighthood which he attained after much effort in 1659. All of these artists used their polished manners, their sophistication, and their skill at flattery to rise within the court, and all worked within well-established conventions when producing courtly art. The commonality of their patrons' interests and the originality with which each artist fulfilled his requirements were exemplified in the program by the theme of the royal portrait.

Royal portraits of all kinds were much in demand during the seventeenth century. But of all royal portraits, those that showed the king astride a magnificent charger had the longest history and were perhaps the most difficult to interpret anew. The equestrian monuments of the Romans lived on in the Renaissance and found special favor in the seventeenth century. The program showed you equestrian portraits of Philip IV of Spain by Velázquez and of Charles I by van Dyck. These trace their origins back to the Marcus Aurelius statue that the program has mentioned and more recently to Titian's great portrait of Charles V on horseback, which is still in the Prado (Spain's national museum, in Madrid). Like their ancient ancestors, these images were used to promote a myth about rulership rather than reality about an individual. Each of these artists made what could be a tiresome and dry allegory into a masterpiece.

Van Dyck showed an armor-clad Charles (H&F 13.8), who was known as a superb horseman, confidently astride the royal mount, so relaxed and self-possessed that there could be no doubt about his authority over horse or subject. Attended by the riding master, who regards him with the proper respect, Charles rides through an archway embellished with swirling drapery that alludes pictorially to Roman imperial imagery. A more overt reference to royalty is the coat of arms leaning against the base of the pillar. Casual, graceful, yet convincingly lifelike, Charles has been subtly but effectively flattered by van Dyck, who has rightly been called the inventor of the English royal portrait.

Velázquez's equestrian portraits are truthful and forceful. His Philip IV on horseback is a brilliant essay on symbol fused with reality. Kingship and power were durable concepts which individuals momentarily fleshed out and realized. Velázquez shows us Philip earnestly and seriously fulfilling his regal role. Both horse and rider are superbly trained. Philip holds the reins of power correctly and with dignity, but his face and body are not infused with the graceful majesty and ease with which van Dyck endowed Charles. Velázquez's insightful vision caught a person at once more vulnerable (by virtue of his straightforward humanity) and more authoritative, by the seriousness with which he assumes royal responsibilities. It is perhaps an historical irony that van Dyck, whose interpretation of his subject fused the notion of kingship with the person of the king, and showed his subject so at ease in his role, was artist to a king who was eventually beheaded by his subjects. Velázquez, whose interpretation maintained a clear distinction between the person and the persona, did not live to see his patron's kingdom succumb to a less violent but equally destructive force, the weakness of offspring that were the results of dynastically arranged intermarriages.

Besides the emblems of mastery and authority that equestrian portraits represented, royal portraits took many other directions as well. In order to introduce the unsurpassed grace and grandiloquence of Rubens, the most sophisticated and successful of all painters working for kings, the program compared Rubens' portrait of Philip IV with that of Velázquez. Velázquez was honest and sober enough not to flatter his subject by glossing over his physical shortcomings or by injecting a different character into that which the real Philip showed in life. Instead, in Velázquez's hands, Philip becomes, despite, or perhaps because of, his evident humanity, a commanding and palpable presence. Differentiated from others by his evident self-command, his seriousness, and his devotion to duty, as well as the external manifestations of his royal position, Philip seems not to have felt it necessary that his painter flatter him. His position was evidently so secure that Velázquez's faithful yet grand interpretation of his subject was sufficient, and clearly desirable. Velázquez, after all, became Philip's court painter. Rubens, though an admired visitor, was retained by less prominent courts for the most part.

Rubens' portrait of Philip IV, which the program also showed, interprets the king very differently from Velázquez. Here opulence of dress and setting, vivacity of paint, and attention to details of grooming distract the onlooker from the inherently sober and melancholy Philip.

Rubens was twenty-two years older than Velázquez and unlike him was an international figure. Serving as a diplomat as well as court painter (it was a diplomatic mission that brought him to Spain), Rubens was knighted by Charles I. A great collector, connoisseur, and courtier, he was the ideal painter for royal patrons. In his hands even the most abstruse allegories came to life through the sensuality of his paint and the brilliance of his inventiveness.

The program showed you what amounts to Rubens' most famous royal allegory: the series of pictures which reflect the Regency (1610–1614) of Marie de' Medici, wife of the assassinated King Henry IV and mother of Louis XIII of France (**J 726**). Rubens happened to be in Florence in 1600, the year of the proxy marriage between Marie (the youngest daughter of Francesco I de' Medici) to Henry of Navarre and witnessed the ceremony held in the Florentine cathedral. When Marie sought Rubens out in 1622 to paint a series of pictures for her palace in Luxembourg, she was a widow in conflict with her son and his adviser Cardinal Richelieu; eventually, she was exiled to the Spanish Netherlands. As a diplomat, Rubens advised Philip IV to use his influence to restore Marie (a fellow Catholic) to the French court, but was unsuccessful. She died in 1642, secluded in a convent in Cologne, living a much more austere life than that to which she had been born.

Rubens' cycle of pictures uses every means at his disposal to flatter Marie and to support the fiction that her marriage and regency were an enormous success. Rubens seems to have sufficiently liked Marie personally so that his flattery was sincere, and, as the program pointed out, Rubens the artist was much more at home with grand conceptions than small ones. Many parallels have been drawn between Rubens and Michelangelo, both of whom grappled with vast projects, projects that symbolized a whole world view and embraced elevated notions about humanity, or at least the ruling class. But the Marie de' Medici cycle is not simply grand, it is grandiose, and its inflated pretensions vastly exceeded the capacity of Marie to live up to its meaning.

Nevertheless, the cycle is a wonderful example of brilliant decoration, opulent splendor, sensuous and vivid figuration, as well as a lightness of touch that is not unlike Pietro da Cortona. The program showed you all the images of this splendid series, which is now in the Louvre. We saw Henry, resplendent in armor (as Philip and Charles have been shown) tamed like Mars before the portrait of his "Venus" (a scene that deviates profoundly from the truth, since Henry was an inveterate womanizer who generally neglected his wife after the birth of their son). Next came the proxy wedding which Rubens had been fortunate enough to witness in Florence. Most famous of all the episodes is Marie de' Medici arriving at Marseilles (sketch, **G 19.43**) where gods and mortals pay homage to the great Medici princess, now French queen, as she sets foot on French soil. Never has royalty made a grander entrance either in painting or in reality, as Marie, resplendent in her gold embroidered white satin gown, disembarks from the Medici vessel that has brought her to shore. An assembly of mythical and actual figures register their reverence and joy in their arrival. Rubens touted Marie's enlightened patronage of science as well as art (an

indication that the rebirth of science was considered an important accomplishment). Marie, after all, did come from Galileo's native city, and in 1622 Galileo was still celebrated (his trial had not yet taken place). Her willing and peaceful transfer of power to Louis XIII at his majority in 1614, with its requisite imperial symbols (soldiers, triumphal arch), once more belies reality. Rival to her own son, Marie had to carefully disguise her true intent, even in the meaning of the pictures she had commissioned from Rubens. Yet no one who saw them could fail to comprehend their self-aggrandizing message.

Every inch a queen in the myth Rubens created for her, Marie in real life lacked the intelligence and diplomatic skills of her own painter. Outwitted and outmaneuvered by Richelieu and her son, she was eclipsed as a power and even as a patron. Her second cycle, *The Triumphs of Henry IV,* was, at Richelieu's instigation, taken away from the artist of her choice, Rubens, and given to an old and old-fashioned Italian, Cavaliere d'Arpino—no doubt to prevent Marie from promoting her cause with any more effective propaganda from the brilliant hands of Rubens.

Rubens, as the program pointed out, continued to serve royal patrons. He painted the portrait of Philip IV while in Madrid on a diplomatic mission; he frequented the English court, concluding a peace treaty between England and Spain in 1629–30. (This accomplishment became part of his epitaph.) During each mission he found time to discuss art with, and to paint flattering portraits of, nobles. His self-portraits reveal his ease in royal circles.

Rubens' portrait of himself with his first wife, Isabella Brant, painted in 1609–10, shows us a painter who lived the life of a courtier. Beautifully and richly dressed, he surrounds himself not with the accoutrements of his trade, but with the appurtenances of the gentleman. Refined, well-mannered, and cultivated, Rubens was the intellectual and social equal of the nobles for whom he painted pictures. Though we have records of Philip IV having initial doubts about diplomatic missions being performed by a painter who lived by his hands, he soon had sufficient confidence in Rubens to instruct him to negotiate the peace between Spain and England.

Rubens gained his diplomatic skills through a classical education and through his experience with court life. He gained his knowledge as an artist from the art of Italy. The program illustrated a number of copies, particularly by Titian, that Rubens made. Titian and Veronese sustained Rubens' interest in his tactile, vigorous approach to painting and his sensuous interpretation of the human form. But Michelangelo and Caravaggio handed him a vocabulary of gestures, movement, and the vigorously sculptural forms he so loved. Rubens, like all great artists, looked widely and absorbed his sources deeply. Raphael, Leonardo, and the Carracci were all quoted and absorbed into his own lavish portrayal of form. Lusty, elegant, and charming, Rubens' personages, like Michelangelo's, are inherently larger than life. His energetic compositions, filled with diagonal movements, spiraling figures, and expansive gestures, fulfill the highest ambition of painting done in a grand manner.

Such an approach intensified Rubens' many religious works which followed the traditional subjects associated with Catholic patrons. His *Raising of the Cross* **(J 725; G 19.38),** done for Antwerp Cathedral, is, like much of his early work, particularly inspired by Venetian painting. In this case, it quotes from Tintoretto's grand *Crucifixion* scheme done for the Scuola di san Rocco. Here is a particularly good example of how Michelangelo (who inspired Tintoretto) made the figure the true subject for artists and how, in the seventeenth century, the figure was set into motion thanks to the inspiration of Venice. As a series of generously muscled figures elevated Christ, they gave Rubens the chance to describe the active figure from every conceivable angle, and by placing the scene at a diagonal to the picture plane, he endowed the whole image with added energy. Christ himself becomes an essay on the ideal nude male body, and his physical perfection becomes an analogue for his spiritual triumph. Looking heavenward, Christ here ignores pain, does not give in to suffering, but considers only his forthcoming ascent into heaven. In this respect Rubens responds to Caravaggio's work as well. Confident in the faith this painting embodies, Rubens' *Raising of the Cross* was painted for Flanders, which had remained steadfastly Catholic. Making visual analogies to the host, which was also raised up during the Mass performed at the altar where this picture hung, it reflects the same religious fervor found in contemporary Italian subjects.

The program also showed you Rubens' *Last Judgment* painted around 1615–1617 for a convert to Catholicism, Wolfgang Wilhelm, Duke of Neuburg. Having built a Jesuit church there, he wanted the *Last Judgment* for the high altar. Twenty feet high, this great altarpiece remains a diminutive variation on the great *Last Judgment* fresco by Michelangelo which inspired it. Like Michelangelo, Rubens used the image as an essay on the nude human figure shown in diverse poses. But Rubens reversed many of Michelangelo's ideas. Christ is no longer the mighty hero dominant visually and physically over the scene, as Michelangelo had portrayed him. Here he is aloof, idealized, and remote in his celestial realm. Rubens chose to emphasize the blessed, shown at Christ's right, all massed together in a great river of human flesh. Female bodies are a greater and more sensuous aspect of the whole, probably satisfying Rubens' own fascination with the female form, while the abundance of blessed souls no doubt satisfied a newly converted patron about the correctness of his choice of religions and the potential benefits of his philanthropies involving the church and the altarpiece.

Despite the fact that Rubens helped to negotiate a peace treaty between England and Spain in 1629–1630, war was a matter of fact in seventeenth-century Europe until 1660. And Rubens, as the program pointed out,

produced his own commentary on its horrors in *Allegory of Peace and of War* (National Gallery, London). Using the allegorical method by which most of his ideas were conveyed, he did not choose to portray the actual effect of destruction and violence in a specific battle as Caravaggio might have done. Instead human vulnerability is more generally portrayed in the guise of myth; the goddess Venus, whose nude sensuality makes her even more vulnerable, cannot subdue the armed Mars. He and his warriors subdue the fallen figures who crouch in terror. Rubens himself added the meaning of the woman at the left, which the program quoted: "That grief-stricken woman clothed in black with torn veil, robbed of all her jewels and other ornaments, is the unfortunate woman, Europe, who for so many years now, has suffered plunder, outrage, and misery."

Rubens, by then a widower retired to private status, married a woman, Helena Fourment, many years his junior, and devoted himself to painting what pleased him. The result was a series of unsurpassed paintings which capture the glowing texture of Helena's skin, hair, and fur-skin robe. Heir to Titian's glorious nudes, Rubens' paintings of Helena are more specific. As she covers herself with a cloak in a pose called *Helena as Venus,* her body seems more exposed, more tactile, and specifically flesh than any of Titian's more explicit reclining nudes. Standing, her condition seems more momentary and therefore more distinct. *Helena as Venus* is really a portrait of Helena standing naked, appealing, and trustingly vulnerable before the eyes of her husband who, in the privacy of his studio, captures her appearance in paint. Though the picture surely took days or perhaps weeks to execute, it seems rapidly done, taking in every drawn breath, every movement, every nuance of a brief moment.

Though it can be discussed within the realm of figure painting, which Titian and Michelangelo had done so much to make the artist's only subject, this charming picture is equally a portrait, and it gains strength from Rubens' brilliant fusion of the two. Heir to a grand tradition, Rubens was also a product of his time, looking directly at nature when he wished and describing in his own inimitable way what he saw.

The paintings Rubens produced for himself are, like his portraits of Helena, among his most enduring works. Our discussion of Rubens ends with his landscapes, painted when Rubens had acquired a country house in Steen. Perhaps the most famous of these is his *Landscape with the Castle Steen,* a work that would inspire English landscape painters of the following century. Gainsborough, in particular, was affected by this great paean to nature. Here the landscape is not merely recorded, but made alive. Lines of trees, roads, and rivers coil around the hills and valleys, alternately compressed together or swinging away from one another in an epic panorama. Growth and decay are both embodied in a work that describes the essence as well as the details of nature. An artist fascinated with movement and transition, Rubens could make the most static of all subjects, the peaceful and motionless countryside, become an essay of energetic and restless activity. The sun seems to actually rise in the sky as we behold its rays dissolving the darkness. Trees seem to rustle and move from an occasional breeze. They also become our guides, moving us into the vast expanse this landscape encompasses. Though based on an actual place, Rubens has endowed it with the power of fantasy. That was part of Rubens' greatness—that he wished to, and did, lift ordinary reality to a higher level, just as his great sixteenth-century ancestors had done.

His fellow courtier and painter, Velázquez, turned in a different direction. He seems to have been inspired to probe and examine reality more deeply, distilling from it an essence that is as powerful in its own way as Rubens' extraordinary vision was. Velázquez's portraits of Philip have already been mentioned. Velázquez spent his career portraying members of the royal family. Perhaps one of his most poignant images is the *Portrait of Baltasar Carlos on Horseback,* which shows the tiny prince already trained to become a king. His pallid features and guarded face make the trappings of power which he holds so effortlessly seem oppressive and tragic; we know that the young prince died in 1646. Though he himself was consumed with aspirations to nobility, Velázquez the artist sensed the sacrifice of freedom, spontaneity, and self-indulgence which positions of royalty demanded from those who fulfilled them; this role affected their lives from birth. Velázquez, who had the insight to consider the person as well as the persona, was criticized by some contemporaries for his portraiture. Cassiano dal Pozzo, Poussin's patron in Rome and secretary to Cardinal Francesco Barberini, was in Madrid with the Cardinal in 1626. He found Velázquez's work to be "melancholy and severe" (Brown, p. 64).

Velázquez could be severe, in large part because he was truthful. His early works are masterpieces of straightforward realism inspired perhaps by Caravaggio, but with none of Caravaggio's added conceits. The greatest of Velázquez's early depictions of daily life is his portrayal of the *Waterseller of Seville* **(J 752).**

Painted some time between 1618 and 1623, the picture adopts an austere palette, a restrained composition, and a subdued emotional tone which transforms a scene of quotidian reality into an essay on human dignity. As simple and monumental in form as the water jug which he holds, the water carrier has a presence ennobled by age and privation. His sunbaked face is deeply lined. His expression is thoughtful and reflective. It betrays none of the cynicism or bitterness one might expect from a life in the streets. Instead, we read a deep seriousness not unlike that of the meditative saints who were the subjects of so many paintings in the seventeenth century.

If one theme of Velázquez's painting is the dignity of poverty, another, as in similar works by Caravaggio, is that of the senses. Guided by our sense of sight, Velázquez makes us consider our sense of touch. This painting is a thoughtful and virtuoso examination of surfaces and textures. From hair and skin and cloth, to the water-beaded surfaces of the pottery (one rough, one smooth), to the thin and light glass, to the coin held lightly between the fingers, this is an essay on touch. On some fundamental level, this picture equates sight, the most basic of senses, with that most elemental necessity, water. In a series of logical progressions we move from the noble vessel that contains it to the figure who drinks it.

Like Caravaggio, Velázquez understood the purpose of such paintings—to both visualize and help the viewer experience the portrayed theme. Painted for a private patron, *The Waterseller* was clearly an exercise designed to impress patrons and to gain entry into higher circles. We already know Velázquez accomplished this.

An equestrian portrait (the ancestor to the one we saw earlier) won Velázquez King Philip's attention. The painting was so highly regarded that it was publicly displayed. Velázquez thenceforth became court painter and moved to the palace. There he was absorbed in painting the portraits and histories required by the king. Encouraged by Rubens, whom he met in 1628, he also went to Italy in 1630, arriving in Rome when it was alive with diverse talents. Caravaggio had long since died, but his influence had spread and his works were still visible in churches and private collections. Hundreds of other artists worked in Rome when Velázquez was there, including Pietro da Cortona and Nicolas Poussin.

Upon his return to Spain, Velázquez painted history subjects like those admired and supported in Italy, but treated in his own independent fashion. *The Forge of Vulcan* reflects Velázquez's Italian experience. Here we see Apollo entering Vulcan's forge and telling him of his wife Venus's infidelity with Mars. The shop is no Olympian refuge, but a contemporary blacksmith's work place, and the ancient god is here described as a scrappy, sinewy blacksmith, sweaty with exertion, and stripped down to a leather apron due to the heat of the forge. His assistants are similar types, but distinctive individuals, all of whom listen and respond like ordinary mortals to this shocking news. Caravaggio introduced this kind of fidelity to contemporary reality into his work, but Velázquez made the scene much more mundane and real by including a faithfully described setting in a way that Caravaggio generally eschewed. This device takes an extraordinary legend and gives it new meaning by making it ordinary. Only Apollo stands apart by virtue of his halo and his olive branch, striking a rather odd note in the whole scene, making all of the rest of it even more strikingly prosaic.

Velázquez continued to explore and solve anew the problems of representation in the portraits that remained the backbone of his career. The program showed you three remarkable examples: *Philip IV in Brown and Silver* and the portraits of two court jesters, Pablo de Valladolid and the dwarf Calabazas. Each is revolutionary in its own way. In Philip's portrait, the brown, white, and black of his costume become a tapestry of brush marks that chart what Velázquez's eye caught when looking at Philip. Intuitive, responsive to what is seen, not what is known, Velázquez was working directly on the canvas, as the Venetians had done, without any drawings to guide his mind, simply letting his eye do the work. The result anticipates the manner in which the impressionsists worked—using dabs of paint and short direct marks from the brush, which coalesce into the form without benefit of drawn contour. These brush marks are as distinctive as handwriting and as immediate as a paint sketch. Their spontaneous language endows a dry formal portrait with a vivacity that transcends its type.

*Pablo de Valladolid* is an equally striking work. Here Velázquez eliminates nearly any reference to background, leaving it merely the roughly worked-in neutral color that etches out Pablo's form as emphatically through a contour as Philip's form had been created without contour. Here as in his waterseller, Velázquez dignified the ordinary. His forthright portrayal of a man whose job it was to invite ridicule and laughter evokes the pathos of his condition, without condescension. Equally important, by presenting a figure devoid of any reference to space around it, Velázquez has transcended the Renaissance notion of figure and space, transcended the conventions of the full figure portrait introduced by the Venetians of the previous century, and helped guide the way to the monumental figure paintings of Manet in the nineteenth.

Most shocking, and without successors, was Velázquez's last portrait of the jester Calabazas. Probably painted in the last few years of his life (Calabazas died in 1639), the tragic figure confronts us in almost claustrophobic intensity. Crouched in a chair, his twisted face and form are heart-wrenching. Velázquez takes an unsparing look down at this pathetic form, which seems more vulnerable and yet more dignified by being viewed from above. We seem to witness the very painful act it must have been for Calabazas to sit and pose for the artist. His eyes incapable of meeting ours, his lips parted in a forceful smile that conveys endurance as well as tolerance for those who laugh at him, Calabazas' most moving feature is his hands. Holding one clenched hand in his other, Calabazas seems to steady it, but in attempting to hide an infirmity our attention is drawn to yet another of his frailties. That clenched hand is a symbol for the secret inner life that Calabazas did not share. With a sensitivity that was at once compassionate and yet direct, Velázquez instinctively probed his subject's heart, and described for us an elemental human tragedy. Aware of his imperfections, Calabazas endures and perseveres. Real human courage endows him with dignity and real human defects endow him with tragedy. In portraits such as this, Velázquez emphasized the essential humanity of his art and thus, with Rembrandt, joins the ranks of the very greatest artists of the period and perhaps of all time.

Velázquez's most celebrated accomplishment is *Las Meninas,* or Maids of Honor **(J 754, clpl 104; G 19.37; H&F 13.26),** painted in 1656. In this remarkable work,

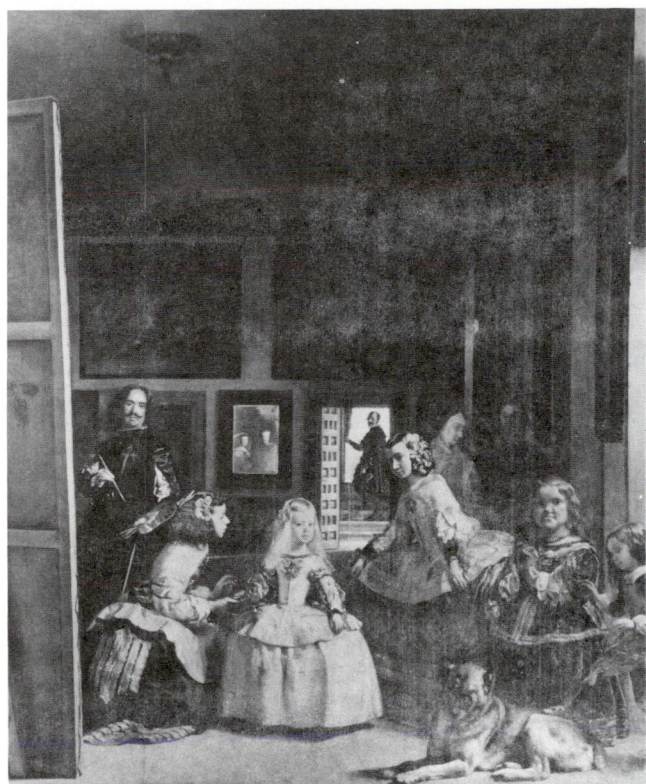

Diego Velázquez, *Las Meninas,* 1656. Madrid: The Prado. (SCALA/ART RESOURCE, NEW YORK)

Velázquez again played with reality. Like Bernini, Caravaggio, and Rubens, Velázquez freely crossed the boundaries between one type of work and another. In *Las Meninas,* the self-portrait, the group portrait, the theme of the artist in his studio (which had gained coinage in this century), "genre" (scenes of daily life), and interior scenes are fused and mingled as liberally as are the levels of reality. The role of the spectator has been re-interpreted as well.

Velázquez shows us a studio that looks like a room. It was actually the prince Baltasar Carlos's bedroom until his death in 1646. Velázquez described the room, emphasizing light from the windows and pictures on the wall. His description resembles Dutch interiors that became popular subjects in Holland (as we shall soon see) going so far as to add the door with the figure in it as the Dutch often liked to do. But unlike Dutch interiors, Velázquez filled his foreground with figures. These are not ordinary figures; they are the Infanta Margareta, born in 1651, two years after the marriage of Philip and his fourteen-year-old-niece, Mariana of Austria. Flanked by two attendants, a small child, and a dwarf, Margareta became part of a group portrait. She looks smilingly out at the onlookers—very possibly her parents—whose faces are reflected in the mirror behind her head. Next to them stands the newly knighted Velázquez, at work on a large canvas so the theme of the artist in his studio and the self-portrait is seamlessly added into the mix. Is he at work on a large double portrait of Mariana and Philip as has sometimes been suggested? Or is he at work on the very painting we see, which now becomes the subject within the subject? Or is this a very personal, sensitive, and poetic portrait of a room, painted for an individual to whom that room had special significance by the artist for whom the room became equally important? The room of a dead prince has become the creative work space for an artist. That artist, who lived in the palace and had daily contact with the king, doubtless knew what would please and touch his patron. By showing him that room filled with people whom he loved, portrayed by the artist grateful for its use, Velázquez may have been subtly honoring the dead as well as the living. That this picture hung in the king's private offices indicates that whatever the true meaning of this amazingly direct yet endlessly complex image, it had special appeal to Philip. For the twentieth century, *Las Meninas* is the ultimate demonstration of Velázquez's position as a child of his era. Like Bernini, Caravaggio, and Pietro da Cortona, Velázquez produced sophisticated essays on reality. But never had someone taken what appears to be a straightforward description of it to make something so mysterious.

Velázquez, though he worked for a king, had an artistic temperament that had as much affinity with non-aristocratic circles as it did with royalty. It is not surprising that in *Las Meninas* Velázquez was dealing with themes that are essentially Dutch in their treatment. Velázquez was clearly inspired by, and he inspired in turn, the exceptional flowering of realism found in Dutch painting of the seventeenth century.

# Holland

The culture and civilization of seventeenth-century Holland was built around the experiences and interests of the ordinary person. The merchants, traders, and bankers who supported art in other cities of Europe were joined by even more diverse ranks of society in Holland. According to one English diarist of the time, even shoemakers collected paintings. The people who supported this luxury were, in fact, a very practical kind. They respected trade, economy, and work. Keenly aware of their national history, which involved a protracted effort for independence from Spain, they valued independence, religious tolerance, and collective effort.

The Catholic nobles whose faith, taste, and status so affected the art discussed in the first part of this unit had only a limited impact on Dutch art. The landed nobles in Holland were not wealthy, and the Protestant faith had largely supplanted the Catholic. John Calvin's religion gained a good many followers. In this Protestant faith, God was the absolute authority; man's duty was to glorify Him, not through the renunciation of the world, but by hard work and material gain, and by the eschewing of all frivolities. Calvinism also firmly supported republican rule. Hence the United Provinces saw the growth of an urban, middle-class culture. Towns like Haarlem, Utrecht, Amsterdam, Delft, and The Hague thrived on cloth finishing, brewing, manufacture, and trade.

The countryside around these cities was low and flat. It was gained by building a system of canals, windmills, and dikes to drain off the sea. Low hills, dunes, and forests dotted the vast plains dissected by rivers and canals that led to the coast. Of the seven united provinces, Holland, fed by several branches of the Rhine and set along the long and protected part of the North Sea coastline, had the greatest number of cities: The Hague, Gouda, Delft, Rotterdam, Leiden, Amsterdam, and Haarlem.

Each of these towns had, as elsewhere, guilds of all kinds that regulated trades and manufacture. Professions from doctors to rhetoricians had organizations. For a region concerned with defense, there were numerous militias and civic organizations. Artists belonged to a guild and they were generally regarded among the lower ranks of society. Outside Holland few gained much fame. Only Rembrandt's reputation reached beyond the limits of his native country. Yet Rembrandt, like many of the other artists of seventeenth-century Holland, worked within a market system, driven by demand. Collectors tended to buy works by type rather than by artist (a still life, a landscape, and so on) and as tastes changed, artists' fortunes rose and fell with the market unless their style or subject changed. Hence a good many artists, including Rembrandt, faced financial difficulties. More than one endured chronic indebtedness and bankruptcy. Others became innkeepers or traders to supplement income. Records of suicides and madness are tragically plentiful.

Yet the lure of income was so powerful that hundreds of artists practiced their trade in Holland, producing a flowering of art so rich and so diverse that it has been called Holland's Golden Age. For roughly one hundred years the combined impulse to describe what is seen and to state what is known inspired men and women of talent and vision. "A perfect painting is like a mirror of nature," Samuel van Hoogstraeten, the Dutch painter and theorist, stated in 1678. And so Dutch paintings seem to be. Nature, in the form of people, places, and things, stands before us as unvarnished truth. Yet embedded within these seemingly straightforward images is the sometimes still obvious, at other times elusive, intellectual baggage of the time. Intimations of mortality, of social commentary, of religious symbolism flash out or are elucidated by the efforts of cultural historians. Many of these ideas are now alien or misunderstood. Yet what makes Dutch painting still speak to us is its orientation in human life. Our basic human condition remains unchanged and no culture ever spoke more directly to us about ourselves than the artists of seventeenth-century Holland.

## *Dutch landscape*

The program introduced Dutch art by first showing you examples of Dutch landscape, and certainly the Dutch established landscape painting as an important theme for artists. The largely urban and middle-class collectors of landscape no doubt enjoyed seeing images of the world which they inhabited, for that was the kind of landscape that most artists portrayed. Though a few like Rembrandt made imaginary views, the majority of artists painted factual descriptions. These included views of the seas, the coasts, the flat stretches of landscape, the towns, and the streets of the time. Some painters introduced the warm and sunny light of Italy into their portrayals of the raw and damp Dutch climate. Of all Dutch landscape painters Jacob van Ruisdael has been acknowledged as the greatest master. His *View of Haarlem* **(G 19.57;** comparable painting, **H&F 13.35),** for example, is a brilliant formal exercise and a sensitive portrayal of atmosphere, sky, earth, and water. Elemental in its structure, with its emphatic horizontal division that separates air from earth, it is a sophisticated and subtle transcription of natural effects. As damp, moisture-laden clouds soar overhead, we see a distant panorama of Haarlem with its cathedral, its windmills, and its bleaching fields. Here Ruisdael celebrates the glory of creation, not on an epic but on a human scale. Human industry, human labor, and human construction find their place within the greater industry, labor, and construction of God. Man and nature achieve a harmony here which anticipates the logical and pragmatic deductions of Leibnitz, that this is, indeed, the best of all possible worlds.

Embedded in pictures like Ruisdael's landscape, or the many seascapes and townscapes that artists produced between 1600 and 1700, were a good many other meanings, some overt, some so subtle as to escape detection. For a society reared in the longstanding tradition of symbolism, the portrayal of certain kinds of vegetation, or certain seasons, or certain times of day, brought to mind allusions to seasons of the year, hints at mortality, the vanity of human pursuits, and others kinds of allegories. Like other subjects favored by the Dutch, the landscape transcribed reality but also gave it meaning. Landscape paintings helped signify man's place in the scheme of the natural world. For the Dutch, as viewed through their great landscapes, man lived in a nourishing and accommodating environment in which the great forces of nature worked in predictable cycles and sustained life.

## Scenes of daily life

Life as it was carried on under ordinary circumstances became the vast and encompassing topic for scores of Dutch artists. Some concentrated on the minor dramas, the romantic encounters or the labors conducted within the privacy of the Dutch home. Other artists, like Pieter de Hooch, created a balance between the people who lived in the homes and the homes themselves. De Hooch became the most famous portrayer of the complex spaces that make up the Dutch interior. He specialized in painting courtyards, houses, and interiors such as the *Courtyard of the House in Delft* that the program illustrated. Here the Dutch values of cleanliness, orderliness, frugality, and domestic harmony are charmingly portrayed. Giving us a view into the neatly brick-lined courtyard, with its cultivated arbor, de Hooch shows us a woman and child quietly and contentedly going about their tasks. An open door permits a view through the hallway of the house, where we see another woman standing at the open doorway looking out into the street. Humble, patient, and protected, this is ordinary life raised to the level of great art by a master composer. Using a sophisticated sense of scale and lighting he described any number of spaces, from deep and narrow to shallow and large ones. Exploiting our own experience, he allows us to infer even more spaces from the doorways he merely described. Overt symbolism has never existed more comfortably with a seeming slice of life. As the broom and bucket lie in the foreground, they are the natural appliances of domestic life. But in this scene of neatly arranged bricks, trimly dressed people, and austere rooms, the broom and bucket are simply the most overt symbols of order in an image devoted to this theme.

How people lived was just as fascinating to artists as where they lived. A wide range of images traced people in love, at play, drinking and carousing, playing at cards, making music, or simply eating. Human appetites were acknowledged; human weaknesses mocked; human values praised. The program showed you examples of the great "genre" (that is, daily life scene) painters such as Jan Steen, who specialized in tavern scenes and people boistrously enjoying themselves, and pointed out the themes which Steen and others treated. Steen's *Drunken Couple* satirizes intemperance, showing the disorder, the moral laxity it brings about. Painted with insight into human actions, and a gift for visual narrative that was unsurpassed, Steen's paintings make humor and laughter a part of painting.

Perhaps the greatest painter of domestic life took an entirely different approach. Jan Vermeer, whose scenes of quiet domestic life are among the most celebrated masterpieces in the history of art, chose to suspend time rather than evoke it as Steen did. In Vermeer's hands the humble, uneventful act of reading a letter, pouring milk, or opening a window becomes an event of the noblest simplicity. Here ordinary humanity and the fruits of ordinary human labor transcend time and place. They become emblems of human endurance and celebrations of the greatness of ordinary things.

Illuminated by light from a window, Vermeer's characters exist in a sheltered, closed off, internalized world. Though forthrightly portrayed, the actions they engage in are full of gentle mystery. *The Woman Reading a Letter* **(J 749, clpl 102)** stands before a map. Does this refer to the distance that separates her from the letter's sender? Cast in light, her simple form has the simple monumentality of Velázquez's *Waterseller*. Though she, like the waterseller, is engaged in an action, that moment is forever suspended in time.

Vermeer's faultless intuition about composition has enabled him to create a stable, balanced arrangement out of seemingly randomly placed, asymmetrical forms. Although pulled aside at random so she could gain clearer light to read, the chairs also act to enclose the woman and to weave her into the elemental geometry of the painting. The wall, the map, the woman, the chairs, and the table are all discrete and defined shapes, and link together like pieces of a puzzle. If any part were missing, the puzzle would be incomplete. At the same time, although this is a complete and specific image, its visual cropping and its narrative allusion to a world beyond that of the room help to place it in a larger context, making its intimacy and its solitude all the more effective.

## Portraits

Vermeer, de Hooch, Jan Steen, and other artists who dealt with genre, made convincing references to humanity without referring to known individuals. The woman in Vermeer's *Woman Reading a Letter* does not need to be identified in order for us to understand the picture. Yet the specificity of her features has such verisimilitude that it verges on portraiture. Perhaps this is because portraits and other likenesses of individuals abounded as never before in Holland. Besides individuals, couples, and families, the Dutch confraternities, militia companies, and professional organizations routinely ordered their likenesses taken by portrait artists. Challenging the artist's ability to record, interpret, and compose, the portrait became the theme through which some of the greatest works of all time were produced.

Two artists, Frans Hals and Rembrandt, emerge as giants in the field of portraiture. Active in Haarlem, Frans Hals contributed some of the earliest new directions in group portraiture. His early triumph was his *Banquet of the Officers of the St. George Militia of Haarlem,* one of three portrayals of the St. George militia he painted. (He himself belonged to this group from 1612 to 1616.) Hals made his reputation painting civic guard pictures such as this one. He faced the difficult challenge of effectively portraying each of the officers and subalterns who had paid to be painted, and arranging them in some interesting and dynamic fashion. His effective use of sashes and banners to weave together and energize the group, together with his individual characterization of each member, makes his civic guard pictures among the most lively and spontaneous ever painted. Unlike Vermeer, who suspended time, Hals emphatically and vigorously evoked it. Seemingly caught in a split second of movement, the *St. George Militia* shows how effectively paint could capture an instant. With Hals, the temporal aspirations of his patrons became his aspirations as an artist during his early career. These are men who seem happy with themselves, comfortable with their positions, and

completely at home in their environment. But as Hals matured, he gained a deeper insight and followed his own inclinations.

Frans Hals worked well into his late seventies or early eighties. When he grew old, his vivacious, painterly way of painting had become old-fashioned, and Hals was reduced to penury. People preferred the polished, courtly, and flattering portraiture of artists like Bartholomeus van der Helst, who today have none of the stature Hals is accorded. Hals's reputation was sufficient for the city of Haarlem to award him a small pension late in life, but his commissions for group portraits were few and far between. His last great efforts were for the group portraits of the regents and regentesses of the Old People's Home in Haarlem **(J 733),** painted in 1664. Here we can see how Hals's understanding had deepened, and his sense of the momentary has ripened into a more durable and timeless portrayal.

Frank and dispassionate, Hals set down the faces of five old women. One senses that they operated the Old People's Home efficiently and responsibly, and that their charity was leavened by a healthy belief in the dangers of overindulgence. As the women sit quietly, practiced in the art of patience and self-restraint, one reads such virtues as austerity, chastity, abstemiousness, strictness, and forbearance in their faces. While Dutch society was already leaning toward more sumptuous dress, more ornate belongings, and more refined manners when this work was done, Hals shows these regentesses displaying the old-fashioned strengths that once made their country great. The ravages of age are in no way glossed over, but are meditated upon and deepen the sense of humanity. How different these women are from the self-congratulatory Marie de' Medici whom Rubens flattered. They have character, and that is what captures our attention. One appears dignified, another a bit pompous, and yet another quietly confident. They all seem to judge Hals and perhaps find him wanting. Did they blame his penury on lack of responsibility? Or did they, old and hopefully wise themselves, recognize the skill and value of this talented old man's now outmoded style? Regardless of the answer, the painting itself is a remarkable document. Faces and hands loom out and are spotlighted in an otherwise dark and sober image. They are a compelling essay on the ravages of time in a scene where time itself has been suspended.

As Frans Hals was working in Haarlem, another great master of the portrait emerged in nearby Amsterdam: Rembrandt van Rijn. He had arrived in Amsterdam from Leiden in 1631 and soon earned a living painting group portraits. One of his most celebrated early works is the *Anatomy Lecture of Dr. Tulp.* Anatomical studies, as you will recall, were an important development for artists and doctors in the sixteenth century. Vesalius, the founder of modern anatomy, was physician to Charles V and Philip II. By Rembrandt's time, interest in how the body really worked was sufficiently great that public anatomical lessons were annually given by the head of the surgeons' guild during the winter, so the corpse (generally an executed criminal) would not decay.

Rembrandt's anatomy lesson, produced when he was twenty-six, is celebrated as a masterpiece of originality. It deviated from all the established conventions of the type by placing the corpse at a diagonal to the picture, thereby allowing Rembrandt to group the students asymmetrically to one side and Dr. Tulp to another. Seated in his chair, Dr. Tulp is holding, with his forceps, the tendons and muscles that control the hands and lecturing on how they work, as the other members of the surgeons' guild look on. Most of them are listening to Tulp's voice and reading from the open anatomy text by Vesalius placed at the corpse's feet. Rembrandt reveals not only their faces but their intense interest, showing us the complex workings of the human mind even as he portrays a lesson in the workings of the human body. He also evokes the sense of touch and hearing as well as sight. The corpse itself is an equally important part of the image, lending a message of tragedy, and adding the theme of sacrifice and death to an image about life. Most traditional anatomy lessons obscured the head, or diminished the amount of the corpse that could be seen, but Rembrandt made the corpse the focus around which the rest of the image spins.

Rembrandt's brilliant fusion of portraiture and narrative resulted in what is certainly the greatest group portrait of all time, and one of the most celebrated masterpieces by an artist many considered the greatest artist of all time:

*The Nightwatch* (**J 737; H&F 13.28**). Commissioned in 1639 as part of the decoration for the new great hall in the headquarters of the Kloveniersdoelen (Company of Musketeers), Rembrandt's huge canvas originally portrayed two officers and sixteen men life-sized. Cut down when it was moved, several of the figures from the original canvas have been lost. The subject was the militia company of Captain Frans Banning Cocq, who stands in his black suit, white ruff, and red sash, attended by his lieutenant bearing a halberd and wearing yellow. As they stride out towards the onlooker, the rest of the militia prepares to line up for the march. Men check their muskets, others arrange their banners, still others prepare their pikes. A drummer at the right awaits the signal to begin tapping out the beat of the march. This most casual moment is chosen to portray that most official of images: a group portrait. And to confuse matters, Rembrandt has added about ten figures whose purpose in the picture has never been explained.

Who is the small girl, running through the group with a dead bird hanging from her belt? Several other smaller figures rush about, seemingly unnoticed. Are these just passers-by in the street in front of the building where Captain Cocq's group has gathered? These unexplained yet dramatic figures, together with the rather random assembly of the militiamen and the selective lighting (not unlike that we saw in Caravaggio), have endowed this group portrait with such a strong narrative sense that it has often been called a history painting—that is, a painting

Rembrandt van Rijn, *The Night Watch* (The Company of Captain Frans Banning Cocq), 1642. Amsterdam, Rijksmuseum. (SCALA/ART RESOURCE, NEW YORK)

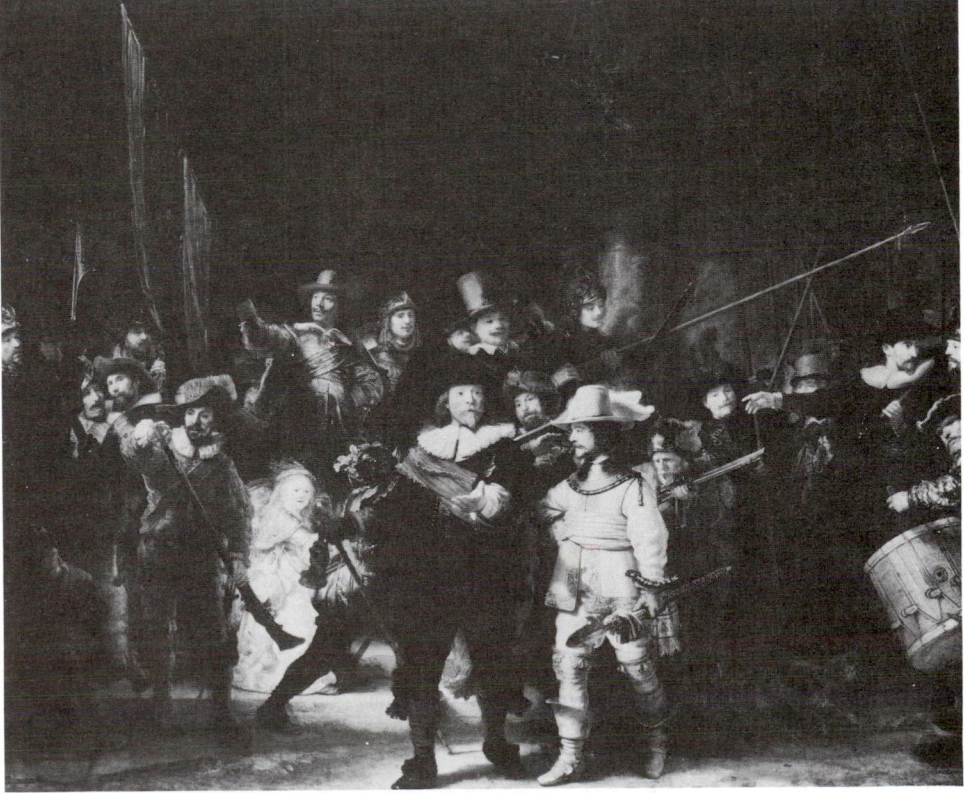

where figures are gathered to "tell" a story, usually a story taken from the Bible or from classical antiquity. Certainly the composition comes from that watershed history painting, Raphael's *School of Athens;* here Captain Cocq and his Lieutenant take the place of Plato and Aristotle. Whether or not Rembrandt's group tells any specific story or event has not been discovered. It has been suggested that *The Nightwatch* commemorated Captain Cocq's militia's participation in the festivities of Marie de' Medici's visit to Amsterdam in 1638. Certainly they seem to be preparing for something. Equally certain is that the abundance of activity and paraphernalia lends interest to a painting of an otherwise unprepossessing man. Capable of fiction, Rembrandt was too good a portraitist to fail to record the rather dull features of Captain Cocq, known as the dumbest man in Amsterdam.

Rembrandt's seamless fusion of history and portraiture is nowhere more evident than in *The Jewish Bride*. Painted some twenty years after the *Night Watch,* it has been variously described as a portrayal of biblical characters (perhaps Isaac and Rebecca), historical figures, or actual contemporaries of the artist. The program used it as an example of how Rembrandt developed the medium of paint. Here palette knives, sponges, fingers, and brush handles, as well as brushes, have worked the surface of the paint so that the viewer always remains conscious of paint as material. But at the same time, this stuff—this paint—coalesces into such a convincing portrayal of two people, their clothes, their ornaments, and their hair, that it reverberates more strongly and more convincingly with the truth than any illusion does. But outward appearances here allude to a deeper internal meaning.

As the man presses his hand to the woman's breast, she tenderly and solemnly holds it there, and both seem lost in the deeply felt emotion of the moment. In this specific moment a universal meaning has been elucidated. Late in life, when Rembrandt's personal losses had been great (his wife Saskia had died, all their children but one had died in infancy), Rembrandt produced this poignant expression of human love. The emotional bond between these two people is profound, its consequences tragic. For the inevitable result of love, as Rembrandt well knew, was loss. Death brings parting, and it is this dual message which echoes through Rembrandt's great work. In this pinnacle of Western art, Rembrandt has shown us ennobled humanity. This is not the idealized physical perfection of the ancients or of Michelangelo. This is not humanity ennobled by divine intervention or by some grandiose deed. These are two ordinary people ennobled by their own humanity, by the one emotion—love—which makes a human being think beyond self-interest and concern himself about another. Rembrandt's late pictures are enduring lessons about the human condition. They show us humanity and reconcile us to our fate. Filled with understanding, compassion, tolerance, and forgiveness, they help us to understand and accept ourselves for what we really are.

Rembrandt was a great portrayer of humanity. He was also a remarkable autobiographer: his self-portraits trace his life. Rembrandt enjoyed wealth and endured bankruptcy. His last years were spent in greatly reduced circumstances, and increasing isolation. Yet his self-portraits retain a detachment that disavows self-pity and affirms a self-sustaining spirit within. Of all the self-portraits the program illustrated, the one at Kenwood House **(J 740; H&F 13.29),** painted around 1661, is among the most famous. Here we see Rembrandt the artist. He confidently holds the tools of his trade, wears a painter's cap, and stands before a blank wall inscribed only with the perfect Euclidian circles. His position between these two circles not only emphasizes the imperfection and irregularity of the human form, but demarks him as specific, present, and real (as opposed to ideal). Using elemental paintmarks that defy description, Rembrandt has set down his massive form, his fur-lined coat, his palette and brushes, and has described his graying, curled hair (badly in need of a trim, it seems). He seems to be sizing himself up, looking into his own soul as he describes his own face. He draws us in and engages us, yet ultimately remains unyielding to any maudlin or pitying interpretation. His work remains his salvation and his identity. Though self-critical, Rembrandt knew himself well enough to understand his own talent. And so he painted himself as a commanding and towering presence. His head is the apex of an enormous pyramid that fills the painting nearly to each edge. Though far more irregular than the circles behind him, Rembrandt's humanity seems nearly as elemental and far more important.

When Rembrandt died in 1669, he was sixty-three years old and alone. Almost his entire family had died before him. There was insufficient money or interest for a large funeral, nor did anyone erect a monument. His only epitaph is his work. Now regarded as the greatest interpreter of humanity in paint, Rembrandt in his own lifetime was world-famous, but not the social equal of his patrons as Rubens and van Dyck or Titian had been. It is true that Leopoldo de' Medici, one of the last of the Medici grand dukes, visited Rembrandt in Amsterdam in 1667 and asked for a self-portrait to add to the collection of self-portraits he had been assembling in the Uffizi. Rembrandt had other foreign clients, including the Sicilian noble who purchased his *Aristotle with the Bust of Homer* (mentioned in the program). But in Rembrandt's last years, the richest painter in Holland was a master whose name is now all but forgotten. Adriaen van der Werff, who lived until 1722, was knighted and lionized by kings and princes. He was widely regarded as the greatest Dutch painter. But his work was not really Dutch at all. It was French. Its mannerisms, its refinement, its psychological distance, its technical polish, its love of grace all wove a spell of unreality and myth over art, which had in the hands of Rembrandt looked so penetratingly and honestly at humanity. Adriaen van der Werff clearly fulfilled the aspirations of his own day better than Rembrandt did, but

Rembrandt has fulfilled the aspirations of our own. Like Velázquez, Rembrandt was re-appreciated and re-valued in the nineteenth century when Impressionism broke the grasp of French academic painting on tastes and aesthetics.

## Conclusion

When the seventeenth century drew to a close, the direction of art and the center for artistic greatness had changed once more. Rome, which had been a leading center for much of the age, now languished. Papal funds dried up, and though artists and visitors still flocked to Rome to see the sights, it was no longer the thriving center for artistic developments it had been earlier. As science steadily supplanted faith, religious art was decisively eclipsed and the role of the church became secondary in art. The secular spirit, which made such substantial headway in the seventeenth century, became the primary influence in the following century.

Europe's nobility, led by the French, remained important patrons in the eighteenth century, but their tastes had changed. Rejecting the serious, elevated subject matter supported by the classicists and building on the exuberant imagery of the promulgators of the baroque style, the rulers of the early eighteenth century preferred lighter and more sensuous stuff. The energetic, vigorous imagery of Bernini, Pietro da Cortona, or Rubens was supplanted by the frothy delicacies whipped up by artists like Boucher and Fragonard. Increasingly refined to the point of effeminacy, the art of the early eighteenth century was that of the boudoir, full of sensuality and frivolity.

Having examined nearly every conceivable aspect of visual reality during the seventeenth century, artists of the eighteenth decided to suspend it, making art that appealed more to the imagination or the intellect. As people accepted this world as the best of all possible existences, they seemed to abandon their inhibitions and gave themselves over to great intellectual or sensual pursuits. If the seventeenth century was the great age of physics and drama, the eighteenth became the era of the encyclopedists, the comedians, and the fabled seducers.

In a century that began with Caravaggio, and that included artists as diverse as Rubens, Rembrandt, and Velázquez, humanity came to terms with itself and its environment. No other earlier period had looked more deeply or penetratingly into the human heart, and no other period had ever attempted to catch in images the wide spectrum of human existence. It was left to the following era to escape once more into pure fantasy, into play, into dreams, and sometimes into nightmares. If humanity is portrayed as more intellectual in the eighteenth century than it had been in the past, its art no longer consistently mirrored its greatest aspirations, but often served much smaller, more constrained, and narrower concerns. Following the path that would inexorably lead to the notion of art for its own sake, art in the eighteenth century could be both smaller and larger than life. But rarely did it serve as the mirror of life that was the art of the seventeenth. In that great century, when pictures seemed to step into the realm of the viewer, when sculptures seemed an extension of the physical world of the spectator, when art conspired to confuse, transport, teach, admonish, and mimic, art seems to have gained the stature, the energy, and the very pulse of life within its painted and sculpted confines. When the century ended, art had stepped back and regained a separation from life which the nineteenth century has once more tried to cross.

The seventeenth century bequeathed later generations an enormous legacy. A host of artistic subjects was introduced that remained a staple in artistic repertoires well into the twentieth century. Landscape, still life, scenes of daily life, as well as portraits, have outlasted the myths, religious paintings, and other histories which all European artists of the period tackled. And while histories by such academic and intellectual artists as Poussin remain abstruse and inaccessible to all but the initiated, Dutch histories reach out to us by virtue of their humanity. Perhaps no other culture or period looked more honestly or more compassionately at humanity, giving us the means not only to understand the past but to tolerate and accept the present as well.

## Textbook References

After a brief introduction, Janson launches into a discussion of baroque developments in Italy and Germany. He begins his discussion with Caravaggio and his important follower, Artemisia Gentileschi, and follows with the contributions to Roman art of Annibale Carracci and his followers, Guido Reni and Guercino. Architecture and sculpture are treated next, beginning with Bernini, and followed by Borromini and Guarini. Italy's influence on Germany then follows, using Fischer von Erlach, Melk monastery, and works by Balthasar Neumann and Dominikus Zimmerman's designs as examples. Flanders, Holland, and Spain are treated in the next chapter, beginning with Rubens and van Dyck, followed by Dutch painting organized by school: the Utrecht Caravaggisti, the Haarlem School (Hals and Judith Leyster), and Amsterdam (primarily Rembrandt). Spanish painting focuses on the still life painter Sanches Cotan, the religious works of Zurbarán, and the developments of realism in the art of Velázquez. France and England are the focus in the final chapter, beginning with Georges de la Tour, Le Nain, and the classical work of Poussin. Architecture concentrates on Mansart, Perrault, and the work at Versailles. Janson leads from there right into the development of the French Rococo. English developments begin with architecture, using the works of Inigo Jones and Christopher Wren as the major examples, and ending with the paintings of Hogarth, Gainsborough, and Reynolds.

**G** After a useful general introduction, Gardner begins her discussion of the baroque with Italy, where she concentrates first on developments in architecture and sculpture, reviewing the contributions of Giacomo Vignola, Maderno, and Bernini before moving on to Bernini's sculpture. Her discussion of painting begins with the important contributions of the Carracci family of Bologna and the major works by the leading Bolognese artists active in Rome: Guido Reni and Guercino. Caravaggio is the principal figure in the next part of the chapter, but he is placed in the context of his influence on Domenichino and Artemisia Gentileschi. Spanish developments are revealed through those artists closest to Caravaggio: José de Ribera, Zurbarán, and Velázquez. Flanders is characterized with the art of Rubens, whose English connections lead on to a brief discussion of van Dyck, followed by a treatment of Dutch artists, including Honthorst, Frans Hals, Rembrandt, Vermeer, Kalf, and ending with Ruisdael. French painting begins with a discussion of Georges de la Tour, influenced by Caravaggio, and includes the work of the genre painter Le Nain, the etchings of Callot, and the classical vision of Poussin. Architectural development includes the works of Mansart, Perrault, Charles Le Brun, focusing on Versailles, and the Church of the Invalides. French sculpture, with the works of Puget and Girardon, is followed by a treatment of English architecture, with emphasis on the works of Inigo Jones and Christopher Wren.

**H&F** In a single chapter, Honour and Fleming trace the developments of the seventeenth century, starting first with Rome and offering a valuable list of important artistic and historical landmarks. They begin with Caravaggio and Giordano Bruno's burning for heresy in Rome in 1600, the year before Caravaggio's *Conversion of St. Paul*. Caravaggio and the Carracci are followed by a brief discussion of baroque art and architecture. Rubens and van Dyck lead into a discussion of easel painting in Italy, where Artemisia Gentileschi, Guido Reni, and Guercino are given important mention. Bernini, as a portrait artist and sculptor, as well as architect, is given extensive treatment, followed by a discussion of Borromini. Contemporary developments in painting, with special focus on the works of Poussin and Claude Lorraine, are then mentioned. Velázquez and Zurbarán are used to trace developments in Spain. Dutch art is introduced with the work of its greatest master, Rembrandt. There follows a discussion of other types of painting: still life, landscape, and genre painting. England and France are covered mainly by architectural monuments, with Wren's St. Paul's Cathedral, Coysevox, and the decorations for the Palace at Versailles used as exemplars of important royal patronage.

**Janson, III, Chapters 6–8: The Baroque in Italy and Germany, pp. 499–568.** Painting—Rome: religious works, ceiling frescoes; Caravaggio, Gentileschi, Carracci, Reni, Guercino, da Cortona. Architecture and sculpture: St. Peter's, Bernini, Borromini, Guarini. Architecture in Germany and Austria: cathedrals by von Erlach, Prandtauer, Munggenast, Zimmerman.

**Part Three, Chapter 7: The Baroque in Flanders, Holland, and Spain, pp. 522–537.** Flanders and Holland: Painting—religious and historical themes, landscapes and portraits; Rubens, van Dyck, Terbrugghen, Hals, Leyster, Rembrandt, van Goyen, van Ruisdael, Saenredam, Heda, de Heem, Steen, Vermeer. Spain: Painting—Cotan, Zurbarán, Velázquez.

**Part Three, Chapter 8: The Baroque in France and England, pp. 538–569.** France: Painting—mythical subjects and genre scenes; de la Tour, le Nain, Poussin, Lorraine. Architecture—Palaces and churches; Perrault, Hardouin-Mansart, Le Brun, Coysevox, Le Vau. Sculpture—Girardon, Coysevox, Puget, Clodion, Falconet. French Rococo: Painting—Fragonard, Chardin, Vigée-Lebrun. England: Architecture—Jones, Wren, Vanbrugh. Painting—Hogarth, Gainsborough, Reynolds.

**Gardner, Chapter 19: Baroque Art, pp. 708–767.** Italy: Architecture and sculpture—churches and sculptures with religious or mythological themes; della Porta, da Vignola, Maderno and St. Peter's, Bernini, Borromini, Guarini, Longhena. Paintings—ceiling frescoes and chapel adornments; religious and mythological subjects; Carracci, Reni, Guercino, Caravaggio, Domenichino, Gentileschi, Rosa, Pozzo. Spain: Altarpieces and portraits—de Ribera, Zurbarán, Velázquez. Painting in Flanders and Holland: Religious themes, genre scenes, portraits, landscapes, and still life studies; Rubens, van Dyck, van Honthorst, Hals, Rembrandt, Vermeer, Kalf, van Ruisdael. France: Painting—de La Tour, Le Nain, Callot, Poussin, Lorraine. Architecture and sculpture—chateaux, palaces, and churches; Mansart, Perrault, Le Vau, Le Brun, Hardouin-Mansart, Le Vau. Mythological subjects by Puget, Girardon. English architecture: public and religious buildings; Jones and Wren.

**Honour and Fleming, Chapter 13: The Seventeenth Century in Europe, pp. 446–477.** Roman baroque: Painting—ceiling frescoes, altarpieces, Caravaggio, Carracci. Northern: portraits, mythological scenes, genre paintings by Rubens and van Dyck. The easel painting in Italy: Gentileschi, Reni, Guercino. Sculpture and architecture in Italy: Bernini in St. Peter's and S. Maria della Vittoria; Borromini. French and Spanish baroque: religious subjects, portraiture, and landscapes; Poussin, Lorraine, Zurbarán, Velázquez. Dutch painting: portraits, genre scenes, religious themes, still life subjects; Hals, Rembrandt, Kalf, Ruysch, Cuyp, van Ruisdael, Hobbema, de Hooch, ter Borch, Leyster, Vermeer. England and France: architecture and architectural interiors—Wren, Coysevox, Perrault, Le Vau, Lebrun, Hardouin-Mansart.

## Study Questions

1. Compare how artists of the sixteenth and seventeenth centuries interpreted the human figure. Are they similar or different? How? Give examples.
2. How did the seventeenth century view humanity?
3. The portrait emerges as an important theme in the seventeenth century. Can you name at least four different types of portraits? Who were the patrons, what were the motives behind the portraits, and how does that affect the end result?
4. Compare how van Dyck and how Rembrandt treated portraiture. Who were their subjects? How did each artist interpret his sitter?
5. Compare Rubens' and Velázquez's portraits.
6. Compare Bernini's *Ecstasy of St. Teresa* with Velázquez's *Las Meninas*. How is reality manipulated in each image?
7. Compare how reality is manipulated in Rubens' Marie de' Medici cycle and Velázquez's *Surrender at Breda*. Who were these works painted for? Whom was the artist trying to please? How does their use of realism compare to Rembrandt's in his *Anatomy Lesson of Dr. Tulp* or to Vermeer's in his *Woman Reading a Letter*?
8. Time, change, and movement were often evoked by baroque artists. Can you cite three works from the program that evoked a sense of the momentary and of movement?
9. Suspending time, making the momentary seem timeless, was another means open to artists. Can you give at least three examples of such works and describe how the artist achieved that effect?
10. Storytelling was an important challenge for artists. Compare how Rembrandt used narrative in his *Oath of the Batavians* with Caravaggio's *Calling of Matthew*. Are they similar at all? Are they different? What devices do they use to tell their story?
11. Seventeenth-century artists often manipulated their viewers. Compare how Borromini, Bernini, and Caravaggio manipulated the viewer's experience.
12. Compare how the onlooker relates to the image in Caravaggio's *Bacchus*, Pietro da Cortona's Barberini ceiling, and Velázquez's *Las Meninas*.
13. Seventeenth-century artists evoked emotions of all kinds. What emotions do you experience when looking at the following: Caravaggio's *Conversion of Paul*; Bernini's *Ecstasy of St. Teresa*; Velázquez's *Portrait of Calabazas*; Rembrandt's *The Jewish Bride*.
14. More than one artist in this chapter ran afoul of his patron. Who and why?
15. Subjectivity and objectivity were the two great extremes in the art of the seventeenth century. What works can be cited as examples of each extreme and how were those extremes achieved?

## Glossary

**Apotheosis**  elevation to mythic or divine status. This was a popular device in seventeenth-century art, used to extol the virtues of various noble families.

**baroque**  name given to the art of the seventeenth century; derived from the word "barroco" or irregularly shaped pearl. It implies the dynamic use of opposing ideas (concavity and convexity; dark and light; straightforward realism and artificiality) within one image or construction.

**Caravaggism**  term used to describe the dramatic effects of contrasting light and shadow made popular by Caravaggio and continued by the Caravaggisti.

**Counter Reformation**  the Roman Catholic movement which strove to meet the Protestant challenge head-on through a new militancy, affirmation of faith, use of saints, and active promotion of Catholic doctrine.

**decorum**  propriety and good taste required in conduct and appearance. Decorum was an especially sensitive issue among the official Counter Reformation patrons.

**discalced**  unshod or barefoot.

**easel pictures**  term applied to relatively small paintings painted for private collections.

**equestrian portrait**  a portrait in which the subject is seated on horseback. In the seventeenth century it was a popular form for the painted portrait; previously it occurred more often in sculpture.

**genre**  a category of painting which realistically depicts scenes from everyday life.

**Gesamtkunstwerk**  German for a complete work of art, mingling architecture, painting, sculpture, and music. The term was first coined in connection with Gothic cathedrals but is equally appropriate for baroque extravaganzas, such as Bernini's Cornaro Chapel.

**illusionism**  the tendency in art to distort appearance and deny the integrity of the material from which the painting is created or the surface on which an image is painted. Painting and sculpture become increasingly illusionistic beginning with the Renaissance, conjuring up fictive representations of dimensionally convincing figures and deep space. In the Baroque period, artists cross the boundaries between architecture, painting, and sculpture. Bernini in particular made sculpture seem like painting and architecture behave like painting, as did the architects Borromini and Maderno.

**penitence**  the quality or state in which an individual repents his sins or faults. A popular Counter Reformation theme ("The Penitent Madalen," "The Penitent St. Jerome," etc.).

**realism**  the degree to which an artist emulates nature. The term has been very loosely applied in the history of art. During the seventeenth century "realism" was nearly always balanced by abstraction.

**subjectivity**  the opposite of objectivity, based more directly on the intuitive feelings of the individual. Subjectivity in art affects both artist and viewer. The artist becomes the prism through which a theme is interpreted and creates an image intended to affect the feelings and emotions rather than the intellect of the onlooker.

**theatricality**  heightened drama in a work of art, achieved through composition and the use of contrasting colors and light.

**transverberation**  the rapturous transformation caused by an ecstatic vision.

## Artist, Patrons, and Important Personages

**Bernini, Gianlorenzo**  (1598–1680). Sculptor, architect, painter, playwright, theatrical designer, caricaturist, Bernini is universally acknowledged as the leading European sculptor of the seventeenth century. Born in Naples, Bernini was a prodigy, trained first by his father Pietro. Much of his inspiration also came from antiquity. Bernini arrived in Rome as a youth and it remained his home. He worked for the leading Roman families, including the Borghese, for whom he created his early masterpieces of life-sized figures, in motion: *David, Pluto and Proserpina,* and *Apollo and Daphne* of 1619 and 1625. When Maffeo Barberini became Pope Urban VIII (1623–1644), Bernini became the architect for Saint Peter's, designing its great colonnade and the Baldacchino of 1624–33, set over the main altar. Less favored under Innocent X (1644–55), Bernini produced perhaps his most famous "Gesamtkunstwerk," the Cornaro Chapel, featuring the *Ecstasy of St. Teresa,* between 1645 and 1652. The virtual czar of art in Rome throughout most of his life, Bernini worked in a style that rivaled nature in its verisimilitude, yet refused to be limited to one level of reality. Using his knowledge of theater, antiquity, and materials, Bernini produced a highly illusionistic, theatrical, and energetic imagery. His portraits exude vitality and spontaneity; his figures are essays on motion and energy; his architecture is classical yet animated.

**Borromeo, Charles** (1539–1584). Canonized 1610. A noted Counter-Reformation saint and a nephew of Pope Pius IV, Borromeo was ordained as the archbishop of Milan. He was deeply pious, ascetic, and an active reformer and a teacher (he established a number of seminaries). He aided the plague victims of 1576, and as penance for the plague, his symbols are a cracked skull or a rope around his neck.

**Borromini, Francesco** (1599–1667). Generally considered the most original architect of the Roman baroque, Borromini began his career around 1620 working with Carlo Maderno and then joined Bernini as his chief assistant working on the designs for St. Peter's and the Palazzo Barberini. Differences between the two resulted in Borromini working on his own from 1633 on. Problems with sites and existing buildings always hamper architects, but when Borromini was able to give full vent to his vision, he produced extraordinarily revolutionary buildings. Abandoning the long-held principles of symmetry, axis, and simple geometry, Borromini mingled geometric shapes to derive eccentric and exciting shapes for his interiors; his exploitation of concavity and convexity made his building façades come to life with a dynamism that was unprecedented. His most famous works—Sant' Ivo della Sapienza (1642–1660), San Carlo alle Quattro Fontane (1638–1646), Sant' Agnese (1656–1660)—remain touchstones of the Italian high baroque.

**Callot, Jacques** (1592/93–after 1635). A printmaker, Callot was apprenticed to the goldsmith Demange Crocq and worked in Rome with the engraver Philippe Thomassin. Callot moved to Florence in 1611, and found favor in the Medici court, where he created spirited and witty descriptions of the elegant daily life and festivities. The themes of his prints ranged from light-hearted to an almost didactic seriousness. His compositional skill and appealing subjects ensured his success as one of the most popular graphic artists. Today, Callot's importance relies on his dissemination of themes which would become popular in the eighteenth century among artists such as Watteau and Goya.

**Caravaggio, Michelangelo Merisi da** (1573–1610). A revolutionary painter, Caravaggio's meteoric career altered the direction of seventeenth-century painting and influenced so many artists that Caravaggism is a style ascribed to the Northern and Italian artists who followed him. Born in Caravaggio in northern Italy, Caravaggio studied with a minor master. His style was shaped by Venetian painting, particularly Titian, whose use of dramatic lighting and habit of working directly on the canvas without many preparatory drawings, Caravaggio emulated. Caravaggio arrived in Rome around 1593, working at first for private patrons like the Florentine Cardinal del Monte. For him Caravaggio prepared secular mythologies expressed with such straightforward realism that the effect was startling. His reputation was made and Caravaggio enjoyed a number of important commissions for churches, including the St. Matthew pictures for S. Luigi dei Francesi, the *Madonna di Loreto* (Rome, S. Agostino), the *Conversion of Paul* and *Martyrdom of St. Peter* for the Cerasi chapel of Santa Maria del Popolo, and the *Entombment of Christ* for Santa Maria in Vallicella.

Possessed of a violent temper, Caravaggio fled Rome after killing a man. His life thereafter was itinerant; he worked in Malta in 1608, earning a knighthood, but a quarrel caused him to flee for Syracuse, where he arrived in October of 1608. He moved on to Messina, Palermo, and Naples, where he was attacked by hoodlums and wounded. Shortly thereafter he embarked for Rome but was arrested by mistake in Port' Ercole. He died of fever without ever reaching Rome again. Caravaggio successfully fused extreme realism and artifice. His dramatic lighting, broad and deliberate compositions, and thoughtful use of expression and color all contrast with the frank, unvarnished realism with which his characters are portrayed.

**Cortona, Pietro da (Pietro Berrettini)** (1596–1669). Considered the leading Roman baroque painter of his day, Pietro was born in the Tuscan town of Cortona. He studied in Florence with minor figures, and then moved to Rome. There the works of Raphael, the Carracci, and Michelangelo, as well as surviving monuments of antiquity, deeply affected him. He drew antique artifacts incessantly and soon came to the attention of the leading antiquarian Marcello Sacchetti through whom he met Cassiano dal Pozzo. For these patrons, Pietro provided sumptuous and decorative revivals of "classical" art, such as his famous *Rape of the Sabines* of 1629. For other patrons, like the Barberini, Pietro was the ideal artist to provide the allegories and decorative schemes that were so much in favor at the time. His greatest palace decorations are his ceiling for the Palazzo Barberini and his walls and ceilings for the Palazzo Medici. Flattering his patrons, Pietro's decorative schemes are filled with fantasy, ebullience, and charm. They anticipate the more delicate, frothy interiors of the rococo.

**Fischer von Erlach, Johann Bernhard** (1656–1723). An Austrian architect, Fischer von Erlach was the greatest of those who replaced the traveling Italian virtuosi who dominated seventeenth-century Austrian architecture. His early buildings, the church of the Trinity, Salzburg, and the Karlskirche in Vienna, reflect the baroque plastic traditions of Borromini. Later in life he turned to the cooler, more classical style of French design. His most celebrated effort is the Karlskirche of 1715.

**Galileo Galilei** (1564–1642). Italian astronomer, mathematician, and physicist, Galileo laid the foundation of modern experimental science. A student at the University of Pisa, Galileo went to Florence in 1610 and worked for the Grand Duke of Tuscany. The darling of Europe for his experiments with the telescope, Galileo ran afoul of the Catholic Church with his publication of *Dialogue on the Two Chief Systems of the World* in 1632. He was called before the Inquisition, forced to recant his assertion that the earth revolved around the sun, and placed under mild house arrest. Galileo continued to work in seclusion and his impact on science was enormous. His trial marked a clear division between the world of science and that of faith.

**Hals, Frans** (1581–1666). One of seventeenth-century Holland's most original artists, Hals is the master of the group portrait. To this type, Hals added spontaneity, vivacity, and a freshness that had never been seen before. He had an unparalleled gift for capturing the momentary and fleeting aspects of life. Direct and informal, his portrayals of children, laughing revelers, musicians, and women has indelibly tinged our perception of Dutch seventeenth-century life. Chronically plagued by debt and out of fashion in his maturity (despite the fact that he had more group portrait commissions than any other painter in the Haarlem of his day), Hals developed a deeper and more penetrating style later in life. His most famous early group portrait is his *Banquet of the St. George Civic Guard Company* of 1616, while his fusion of genre and portraiture finds perhaps its greatest expression in his *Laughing Cavalier*, dated 1624 (London, Wallace Collection). His late great works are the portraits of the *Regents of the Old Men's Alms House* and the *Regentesses of the Old Men's Alms House* done around 1664, two years before he died. Here the momentary has been replaced by a wise, stoic, and memorable analysis of the effects of time on the human face and character.

**Hooch, Pieter de** (1629-after 1684). The exact contemporary of Jan Vermeer of Delft, de Hooch was also from Delft. De Hooch can rightly be called the greatest master of domestic interiors. His portrayals of courtyards and rooms, with people unself-consciously going about daily chores, are masterpieces of perspective and order. Their neat arrangement of forms echoes the Dutch love of cleanliness and tidiness and lifts such ordinary subject matter to the level of art.

**Leibnitz, Gottfried Wilhelm** (1646–1716). Foremost philosopher of the early eighteenth century; often depicted in the arts. A rationalist metaphysician, and writer on logic, mathematics, science, law, history, linguistics, and theology, Leibnitz coined the notion that this was the best of all possible worlds, created by the best of all possible Gods. He laid the cornerstone for the rational view of life that emerged in the eighteenth century. While a jack-of-all-trades for the German nobility, he continued his own research and corresponded with other scholars. He also helped found the German Academy of Sciences in Berlin.

**Loyola, Saint Ignatius** (1491–1556). Canonized 1622. Founder of the Jesuits and a leader of the Counter Reformation, Ignatius sought reform by encouraging education and frequent partaking of the sacraments. He is often portrayed alongside Christ, who had appeared to him, often wearing the initials IHS on his breast. Ignatius was declared the patron saint of spiritual exercises.

**Marie de' Medici** (1573–1642). Wife of Henry IV of France, daughter of Francesco de' Medici, Grand Duke of Tuscany. She married Henry in 1620 and gave birth to Louis XIII. After Henry's assassination in 1610 she became regent until 1617. Her policies reversed many of her husband's and were unpopular. Marie lacked the intelligence and diplomatic subtlety to understand the peril in which she was placing herself. After the rise of Cardinal Richelieu in 1630, Marie was exiled to the Netherlands and never returned to France. Her greatest accomplishment is the series of paintings she commissioned from Rubens to celebrate her regency.

**Neri, Saint Philip** (1515–1595). Canonized 1622. Son of a Florentine notary, Philip Neri founded the Oratorians, a lay society devoted to religious discussions and charitable acts. Philip was unconventional, charismatic, and devoted to the laity. He practiced harsh austerities himself but did not demand them of others. Instead he preached about love and spiritual integrity. Neri experienced divine ecstasy in 1544 and it is in this state of spiritual passion that he is most often depicted. None of these images is based on actual knowledge of his face. They, like the portrayals of the ecstatic St. Teresa, are based on Counter Reformation conventions for saints.

**Philip IV of Spain** (1605–1665). King of Spain, Naples, and Sicily. Son of Philip III, Philip IV reigned during a period of Spanish decline. At war on and off with the Netherlands until 1648, he was forced to accept the independence of the United Provinces at the Treaty of Münster in 1648. Wars with France depleted Spanish resources and resulted in a humiliating treaty with France in 1659. His successor, Charles II, was unfit to rule; Spain thereupon became a Bourbon possession. Philip's greatest accomplishment was that of patron. Velázquez was his court painter, with the result that there are more portraits of Philip and his family than of many other royal subjects. These are masterpieces of penetrating observation of Philip's essential humanity.

**Poussin, Nicholas** (1594–1665). One of the greatest French painters, Poussin has been described as the most intellectual artist who ever worked. After working in Paris, Poussin settled in Rome in 1624, living there permanently except for a brief stay in Paris between 1640–1642. Poussin worked almost exclusively for erudite private patrons who greatly admired his visualizations of ancient subjects most of which had serious philosophical overtones. Poussin's balanced, harmonious, and carefully planned compositions, his monumental figures, and his classical subject matter rank him as the leading exponent of classicism in the seventeenth century.

**Rembrandt van Rijn** (1606–1669). The greatest painter of Holland, Rembrandt is perhaps the most profound interpreter of humanity that ever lived. Having trained with some minor masters, he set up a studio in his native Leiden, where he painted portraits, histories, and some genre figures. These are remarkable for their sensitivity to light, expression, and material, as well as for their ability to convey drama. Around 1631 Rembrandt settled in Amsterdam and established himself as a leading portrait painter with such works as *The Anatomy Lesson of Dr. Tulp*. He married Saskia van Uylenborch, the daughter of a wealthy burgher, and bought a fine house. In 1642, the year he completed his revolutionary portrait *The Nightwatch,* Saskia died. Rembrandt's fortunes declined. A more elegant type of portraiture became fashionable, and he refused to change his style to suit the tastes of the time. His work became increasingly more personal and more profound. Rembrandt explored great human themes with compassion and understanding. Among his late great works are his *Jewish Bride*, perhaps the greatest essay on human love, and *The Return of the Prodigal Son,* which is a monumental discourse on reconciliation.

**Rubens, Peter Paul** (1577–1640). The leading Flemish artist of his age, Rubens was a diplomat and courtier as well as painter. He served the nobility of Spain, France, Italy, and Flanders, as well as England. Charles I knighted him in 1630. Born at Siegen in Westphalia, Rubens trained in Antwerp with minor Flemish painters. His travels to Italy in 1600 in the service of Vincenzo Gonzaga of Mantua exposed him to the great traditions of Italian, particularly Venetian, painting. Titian especially inspired Rubens, who developed an opulent, vibrant, and energetic style ideally suited to the histories, allegories, and royal portraits that were required of him. His commissions were so extensive that Rubens operated a vast studio, assisted by specialists in animals and still lifes, for example.

**Ruisdael, Jacob van** (1628/29–1682). Called the greatest Dutch painter of landscape, Jacob van Ruisdael was born in Haarlem. The nephew of a landscape painter, Solomon van Ruisdael, Jacob learned from him and from studying the natural effects around him. He traveled to Scandinavia around 1644 and in the 1650s to western Germany. He settled in Amsterdam in 1656. Ruisdael developed a heroic, panoramic vision of landscape. Sensitive to the most subtle effects of light and atmosphere, he fused these to a sense of monumentality. Grand themes, such as mortality, or the landscape as an expression of the whole creation, enter his work. His views of towns, such as *The Bleaching Fields of Haarlem* or his *Jewish Cemetery,* give an epic vision of humanity's place in the scheme of nature.

**Steen, Jan Havicksz** (1625/26–1679). A native of Leiden, Steen is considered the leading seventeenth-century painter of lively bourgeois life. He is best remembered for his genre-like treatments of old Dutch proverbs and his humorous portrayals of Dutch foibles. During his long life Steen painted numerous scenes with such subjects as "The Music Lesson," "The Effects of Intemperance," "The School," "The Oyster Eater," and so on. Mingling satire, humor, caricature, and the study of nature, these images show Steen to have been a student of human nature and a great storyteller through pictures.

**Teresa of Avila, Saint** (1515–1582). Canonized in 1622. A Spaniard, Teresa was born to a good family and joined the Carmelites. In middle age she founded a new order under the strict forms of the original Carmelite rule—the Discalced or Barefoot Carmelites. She wrote extensively, recounting her early ecstatic revelations in an autobiography, but also wrote books of devotional instruction and an account of the seventeen convents she founded in a period of twenty years. Frank, practical, gay, and witty, she is best known through Bernini's *Ecstasy of St. Teresa,* which uses her account of being pierced by the arrow of divine love—an account which was particularly valued during the Counter Reformation.

**Urban VIII** (1568–1644). Born to a Florentine family, Maffeo Barberini became Pope Urban VIII in 1623. While still a cardinal he had befriended Bernini and as Pope he made ample use of Bernini's talents, commissioning him to remodel the Church of S. Bibiana and to build his tomb. Urban also made Bernini architect of St. Peter's in 1629. Urban's influence on Rome artistically was second only to that of Julius II in the sixteenth century.

**van Dyck, Anthony** (1599–1641). Second only to Rubens among Flemish painters, van Dyck was a master portrait painter. An associate of Rubens between 1618 and 1620, van Dyck traveled extensively to Italy and England, where he was knighted and acted as principal painter to the English court. He is credited with inventing the English royal portrait, infusing his sitter with an effortless sense of grace, majesty, refinement, and ease. Though inspired by Venetian painting and the work of Rubens, van Dyck evolved his own personal manner of painting. More precise, more dispassionate, and more distant from his subjects, van Dyck's coolness, his suave sophistication, and his ability to endow his sitters with effortless nobility laid the foundation for English portraiture for centuries to come.

**Velázquez, Diego** (1599–1660). The greatest Spanish painter of the seventeenth century and one of the most important artists of the Western tradition. Born in Seville, he studied with Francisco Pacheco. In 1623 he entered the service of King Philip IV and spent the rest of his life rising through the ranks of royal employees, finally earning a knighthood in 1658. His oeuvre consists mainly of portraits of the royal family, but also includes religious subjects, nudes, and histories. Fusing a straightforward realism with a subtle understanding of the requirements of rank and power, Velázquez produced images of startling originality. He, like Rembrandt, appreciated the fundamental humanity of all of his subjects, and also daringly broke with convention when his own inclinations went beyond the constraints of a particular subject. *Las Meninas* is the most famous example of his fusion of various subject types.

**Vermeer, Johannes** (1632–1675). Vermeer was born and lived in Delft. There he transformed the ordinary domestic environment into images of timeless beauty. His genre subjects dwell on one or two figures, quietly absorbed in some mundane task. Sensitive to color, shape, form, and light, Vermeer's paintings are visual poetry—graceful, quiet, and lyric. Regarded as the finest master of genre, Vermeer suffered financially his whole life. He died bankrupt and Anthony van Leeuwenhoek, the "father of microbiology," was appointed his executor.

## Bibliography

### GENERAL

Bazin, Germain. *Baroque and Rococo Art.* New York, 1974.

Blunt, Anthony, ed. *Baroque and Rococo: Architecture and Decoration.* Cambridge, Mass., 1982.

Fokker, Timon H. *Roman Baroque Art: The History of a Style.* London, 1938.

Freedberg, Sydney J. *Circa 1600: A Revolution of Style in Italian Painting.* Cambridge, Mass., 1983.

Gerson, Horst, and ter Kuile, E. H. *Art and Architecture in Belgium, 1600–1800.* Baltimore, 1960.

Kitson, Michael. *The Age of Baroque.* London, 1976.

Martin, John R. *Baroque.* New York, 1977.

Norberg-Schulz, Christian. *Baroque Architecture.* New York, 1985.

### GENERAL: ITALY

Engass, R., and Brown, J. *Italy and Spain, 1600–1750: Sources and Documents.* Englewood Cliffs, N.J., 1970.

Haskell, F. *Patrons and Painters: A Study in the Relations Between Italian Art and Society in the Age of the Baroque,* rev. ed. New Haven, 1980.

Howard, Deborah. *The Architectural History of Venice.* London, 1981.

Lees-Milne, James. *Baroque in Italy.* New York, 1960.

Waterhouse, Ellis Kirkham. *Baroque Painting in Rome.* London, 1976.

### GENERAL: DUTCH

Alpers, S. *The Art of Describing: Dutch Art in the Seventeenth Century.* Chicago and London, 1983.

Haak, Bob. *The Golden Age: Dutch Painters of the Seventeenth Century.* London, 1984.

Kahr, Madlyn Milner. *Dutch Painting in the Seventeenth Century.* New York, 1978.

Nash, J. M. *The Age of Rembrandt and Vermeer: Dutch Painting in the Seventeenth Century.* New York, 1972.

## ARTISTS

### Bernini

Hibbard, Howard. *Bernini*. Harmondsworth, England, 1976.
Rosenberg, Jakob; Slive, Seymour; and ter Kuile, E. H. *Dutch Art and Architecture, 1600–1800*. Baltimore, 1979.
Stechow, Wolfgang. *Dutch Landscape Painting of the Seventeenth Century*. Oxford, 1981.
Wittkower, Rudolf. *Gianlorenzo Bernini: The Sculptor of the Roman Baroque,* 3rd ed. rev. Oxford, 1981.

### Borromini

Connors, J. *Borromini and the Roman Oratory: Style and Society*. Cambridge, Mass., and New York, 1980.

### Caravaggio

Friedlaender, W. F. *Caravaggio Studies*. Princeton, 1955.
Hibbard, Howard. *Caravaggio*. New York, 1983.
Hinks, Roger P. *Michelangelo Merisi da Caravaggio*. London, 1953.
Spear, Richard E. *Caravaggio and His Followers*. New York, 1975.

### Hals

Baard, H. P. *Frans Hals*. New York, 1981.
Slive, S. *Frans Hals*. 3 vols. New York, 1970–74.

### Rembrandt

Bredius, A. *Rembrandt: The Complete Edition of the Paintings*. New York, 1969.

Haak, B. *Rembrandt: His Life, His Work, His Time*. New York, 1969.
Slive, S. *Rembrandt and His Critics, 1630–1730*. The Hague, 1953.
Rosenberg, J. *Rembrandt: Life and Work,* rev. ed. Ithaca, 1980.

### Rubens

Baudouin, F. *Pietro Paolo Rubens*. New York, 1977.

### Ruysdael

Slive, S. and Hoetink, H. R. *Jacob van Ruysdael*. New York and Amsterdam, 1981.

### Velázquez

Brown, J. *Velázquez, Courtier and Painter*. New Haven, 1986.
Kahr, M. M. *Velázquez: The Art of Painting*. New York, 1976.
Lopez-Rey, J. *Velázquez' Work and World*. Greenwich, Conn., 1968.

### Vermeer

Slatkes, L. J. *Vermeer and His Contemporaries*. New York, 1981.
Wheelock, A. K. *Jan Vermeer*. New York, 1981.

### Zurbarán

Brown, J. *Francisco de Zurbarán*. New York, 1974.

# An Age of Reason, An Age of Passion

## Learning Objectives

Unit VI begins with reminders that scientific discoveries revolutionized human perception. Compared with the Renaissance or with the decades following the fall of Rome, the most radical shift of human attention in the period from roughly 1700 to 1850 concerns the new awareness of *nature*. With "man as the measure of all things," nature had been seen as a backdrop to human activities. When the earth itself was removed from the center of the universe as a result of Copernicus' discovery of the heliocentric system, earth's inhabitants also gradually lost their commanding position in creation. They were *in* nature, a part of it, like the trees that begin to become so prominent in Western art in the seventeenth century. The prominence given to the natural environment, and the demand for increasingly naturalistic representations, are features of the styles that you should associate with eighteenth- and nineteenth-century art. You should ask yourself as you consider each work of art, "How does it reflect nature? Which aspect of nature does it reflect?"

The introduction of subjectivity in mainstream art is another theme in the treatment of this period, related to the interest in nature, but sufficiently important to be considered as a separate issue. You should recognize how subjectivity is reflected in various ways, and how it increases over the decades.

One of the issues confronted has to do with the nature of Romanticism and of Classicism. You should understand the meaning of "Romantic" as an aesthetic term of description, and grasp its implications in terms of expression and form: it should be clear that Classicism *retains* the human figure as the center of interest, and classical subjects are about human actions; Classical form presents a finite world controlled by the artist who closes off both sides, and furthermore offers only a shallow stage for action, thereby channeling the viewer's attention, while Romantic art offers greater freedom to the viewer in terms of greater space and consequently less control by the artist.

One constant aim in studying art history is always recognition of an individual artist's style. This problem demands great subtlety of analysis in making problematic attributions, but even at an introductory level it requires close attention to every aspect of a work, *including subject matter*. You should know the characteristic subjects of each of the artists taken up in this chapter, as well as the characteristic formal features of their work.

Finally, you should grasp the role of the academic system in European art and consider how it developed a very high standard of skill but also tended to inhibit thinking about the possibilities of art that enable it to remain alive, which means relevant to its time.

In this unit, you will:

- Understand how the nature of one's relationship to society was conveyed in the visual arts through transformed images of the state, monarchy, church, and the commonplace;
- Recognize how the philosophical polemics of the eighteenth-century Enlightenment instigated the sweeping social and political revolutions of the nineteenth century with the visual arts often out on the barricades at the "cutting edge";
- Understand how the scientific Rationalism which inspired a monument such as Diderot's thirty-five volume *Encyclopédie*, and the treatises of Descartes, Newton, and Locke, inspired artists towards a sensibility for an empirical observation and visual investigation of life;
- Perceive how the capricious, trifling, frivolous themes favored by courtly painters of the rococo period represented the last gasp of an unchallenged monarchy endowed with the divine rights of kings,
- Appreciate how classical antiquity provided the models for the American and French revolutions as Athenian plutocracy and Roman republicanism influenced the "Declaration of Independence" and the "Declaration of the Rights of Man" as well as the pictorial calls to arms painted by West, Trumbull, and David, the architectural designs of Jefferson, or the sculptures of Houdon;
- Comprehend how artists such as Goya, Blake, Constable, Turner, Friedrich, Gericault, and Delacroix

explored new limits for the art of painting and gave birth to a Romantic attitude about art's potential for individual or societal salvation;

■ Enjoy viewing the continuing aesthetic conflict between the disciples of Raphael's/Poussin's classicism (such as Mengs, David, Gros, Ingres) versus the more subjectively and emotionally directed painters who imitated Titian or Rubens (including Fuseli, Turner, and Delacroix). A fascinating challenge is to trace how the Academic classical style is used to legitimize and defend the established regime in power while the Romantic style tends to question authority and raise human consciousness about the need for change.

## Part 1
## ROCOCO AND
## NEO-CLASSICISM

## Historical Overview

The most characteristic and monumental creation of the eighteenth century in Europe was not a building, not a sculpture, not a painting. It was the thirty-five volume *Encyclopédie ou Dictionnaire des Sciences, des Arts et des Métiers.* In the form it took, and in its intellectual orientation, it is the work of its editor, Denis Diderot, although the mathematical section was under the care of his co-editor, Jean d'Alembert. Published over a period of twenty-nine years, 1751–1780, the *Encyclopédie* contained articles written by one hundred and eighty of the greatest intellectual figures of the time, and the work thus covers the entire field of knowledge as known at the time.

As if the century knew that, with it, an epoch was dying, it totaled up its assets in this intellectual last will and testament, detailing the legacy that it would pass on to the modern world.

It is amazing to realize the depth and range of knowledge that was developed in the period termed the Enlightenment, or the Age of Reason. Generated by Isaac Newton's discovery of universal order, by René Descartes's rationalist philosophy, by John Locke's philosophy of empiricism and freedom, by Francis Bacon's method of inductive reasoning, which effectively destroyed the authority of medieval scholasticism, the *Encyclopédie* reflected the rationalistic and scientific mentality of advanced eighteenth-century thought and found support among the newly rising class of wealthy merchants and financiers.

In this scientific paradise, new kinds of saints labored for the betterment of humankind. They produced powerful instruments with which to explore space: the planet Uranus was found by William Herschel (with his sister-assistant Caroline) in 1781, thereby doubling the known

extent of the solar system. Mathematics made possible the development of astronomical research which revolutionized the earth sciences. Mapping expeditions demonstrated the shape of the earth and new instruments made possible previously undreamed of accuracy in cartography. Exploration was undertaken in the eighteenth century, as in the Renaissance, for commercial purposes, but with the further motivation of scientific research: when James Cook made his voyages of discovery in the South Seas, he was accompanied by Joseph Banks, who made a large collection of biological specimens previously unclassified by Linnaeus, who had published his *Philosophia Botanica* in 1751. This work established the system of botanical classification and, incidentally, had a direct impact on art, with wild flowers appearing on porcelain and in still life painting where earlier only the cultivated varieties had been favored.

It should be noted, however, that the entire phenomenon of eighteenth-century naturalist aesthetics that we see in both Rococo art and that of the subsequent classical revival is the artistic expression of the same impulse that was investigating the natural world in so many ways. That investigation was proving that nature in its regularity and order was essentially rational—controlled by reason, and for many this was evidence of God's intelligent rule of the universe.

Freedom, reason, and humanitarianism were the overriding concerns of the Enlightenment. Investigations carried on by the physical sciences characterized one side of the period's ambition. The other side turned its attention to social examination and analysis. The theory of the divinity of kings was destroyed along with the undermining of ideas of divinity itself by the widespread Deism of the period. Frederick the Great, in 1740, the year that he came to the Prussian throne, wrote a devastating attack on Machiavelli's *The Prince*, the work that had provided the basis and justification of absolute monarchy from the sixteenth century on. Influenced by Voltaire, with whom he had a long and stormy friendship, he had the revolutionary concept that the ruler was the servant of the people. At that time, Voltaire's influence was far-reaching, since he was in touch with the leading intellectuals in Europe and by precept and example taught the lessons of social justice. The conclusion of *Candide*, "Let us cultivate our garden," expresses Voltaire's practical philosophy of common sense, and also makes use of a metaphor—the garden, which to those living in the eighteenth century was a central focus of aesthetic interest.

Rousseau's influence was, however, even greater in the long run. His advocacy of the natural man, the "noble savage," made an incalculable impact on the sensibility of Western civilization. He declared the central idea of his political thought in the opening sentence of his great work, *The Social Contract*: "Man is born free, and is everywhere in chains." This was the century of the American *Declaration of Independence* and Bill of Rights, the supreme achievements of the Enlightenment, and the French Revolution, its deformed and tragic child.

From the point of view of sensibility, the eighteenth century in France breaks in half, the earlier years given to the expression of youthful enjoyment and high spirits, the latter period to high seriousness and moral earnestness. The extreme formality of life at Versailles under Louis XIV ended with his death in 1715, and the reaction was not unlike children being let out of school. A taste for naturalism in the sense of the unexpected, the *uncontrolled* emerged as if released from the constraints of absolutism in form. In this characteristic of the period, called the Rococo, one can see the link with the second half of the century, which was equally responsive to naturalism, although a naturalism interpreted in *rationalist* terms. Making one's way through the intellectual history of the seventeenth and eighteenth centuries, one must be aware of the shifting meaning of such words as rationalism, naturalism, classicism, romanticism. Like dancers in a reel, they combine and recombine, changing meaning as they change partners.

## The Rococo

The term Rococo was derived possibly as a complex pun on "barocco," with "rocaille," and "coquille," referring to the rocks and shells that appear frequently as motifs in the decorative arts that flourished so notably in the period. The gentle curving of Rococo forms is highly suggestive of the new, graceful, and relatively more relaxed style of living, which contrasted sharply with the straight lines and absolute right-angles of Louis XIV forms that matched the austere grandeur and strict ceremony of his Versailles Court, as well as with the classicizing interpretation given to Baroque style by French artists.

One has only to compare the façade of St. Peter's designed by Carlo Maderno (ca. 1607) with its dynamic colonnades designed by Bernini (1656) to the east façade of the Louvre (1667–1670) **(J 763; G 19.65; H&F 13.37)**, and to Versailles (1669–1685) **(J 765, 766; G 19.66, 19.67, 19.68; H&F 13.36)**, to see the difference in French and Italian Baroque style. The St. Peter's façade builds towards a climax from its outer limits toward its central portal, and from ground to dome. Its great colonnaded arms reach out into space, setting up a dramatic relationship with the embraced visitor that is analogous to the theatricality of Bernini's sculpture as seen, for example in *The Ecstasy of St. Theresa* **(J 703; G 19.11 and p. 520; H&F 13.14, 13.15)**. Bernini had in fact been invited to design the east façade of the Louvre, but the several Italian Baroque compositions he submitted were all rejected.

As designed by Louis Le Vau, Charles Le Brun, and Claude Perrault, working together, the composition of the Louvre's east façade distributes interest more evenly than that for St. Peter's, with shallow projecting pavilions at each end of the long colonnade of coupled columns and

a central pavilion that is distinguished by a pediment. There is no climactic build-up toward the center. The entire façade of three stories is made to appear like a Roman temple by treating the ground floor as a platform, and screening the upper two stories behind the colonnade to achieve a stately grandeur.

Comparing Versailles with contemporary Italian style, one sees again the preference for classical distance rather than Baroque interrelationship. Like the Louvre façade, the façades of Versailles are flat and shallow; the expression is as impervious as a geometric theorem. The famous gardens are indeed a statement of the triumph of the rationalism of geometry over nature, with rationalism interpreted as an instrument of control: they are laid out in geometric shapes, and the plants and shrubs have been clipped to fit the cerebral realm of French classicism. By contrast, consider the English country villa in classical Palladian style, surrounded not by the cones, cylinders, and cubes of French rationalism, but by the "natural" garden **(J 792; G 20.5; H&F 14.10)**. Nature somewhat helped with a pond here, a cluster of trees there, and views more various than nature had arranged.

In France, then, the reins of Louis XIV formalism were thrown off with something like giddy relief. Instead of the regal receptions of Versailles, social life began to center more on private salon entertainment in the elegant new *hôtels*—town houses—that were becoming fashionable. Nevertheless, however less formal, life for the aristocracy remained lavish, and days and nights were lived for entertainment. In such a society, taste becomes a value above morality. Poor taste in clothes, speech, or manners was an intolerable social offense. Good taste was evidenced in the preference for the delicate, the dainty, the graceful, the subtle, the nuanced, the witty. Colors to match this sensibility had to be pastel, and soft pinks and blues and lavenders took the place of the rich royal red and purple and gold of Baroque splendor. Rococo themes centered on leisure, love, and fashion, and the dramatic verve of Rubens gave way to the lyrical tone of Rubens' great followers, Jean-Antoine Watteau (1684–1721), François Boucher (1703–1770), and Jean Honoré Fragonard (1732–1806), the outstanding masters of three generations of Rococo painting in France.

French painting in the seventeenth century had been dominated by the Royal Academy of Painting and Sculpture, established in 1648. Under the directorship of Charles Le Brun (1619–1690) in 1663, the Academy took on the form that set its practice for more than two centuries, based on rules of art. It was within the walls of the Academy that the quarrel between the "Poussinistes" and "Rubenistes" developed, a theoretical quarrel that centered on the question of the superiority of drawing or color. Drawing was held to appeal to reason because it dealt with the apprehension of form which was understood as a mental activity: a form is *conceived* and thus exists in the mind, the realm of ideas which by definition are *abstractions*. Color was held to appeal to the senses because it dealt with visual phenomena: color is *perceived* and thus exists in nature, the realm of perceptions, which by definition are sensually *real*.

This duality has had a sturdy life in Western thought that goes back to ancient Greece, with form associated with classical order, balance, and restraint—the control of the mind in confrontation with the apparent chaos of nature; color associated with anti-classical irregularity, asymmetry, and emotionalism—the mind overwhelmed by the senses, by the demands, that is, of nature.

In the seventeenth century, classicists upheld Poussin as the model for the orderly, intellectual tradition. Although an artist of the Baroque, Poussin's style in painting, like that of French architects, imposed a classicizing mentality on his compositions, as can be seen in *The Burial of Phocion* (1648) **(G 19.62)**, which is spatially Baroque, but expressively and formally classical in its somber, stately rhythm and its emphasis on clearly rendered forms. But supporters of the color school, the "painterly" style, as we shall refer to it from here on in this book, began to counter-attack the negative connotations of color/emotionalism. Directly or indirectly responsive to Locke's conception of the priority of the senses as a means of knowing, they made a radical shift in aesthetic values that raised the perception of both human nature and the physical phenomena of the earth to a superior rank over the conception of ideas. In the new view, there was no issue of the mind being overwhelmed by nature. Instead, a new ideal relationship of harmony between all features of nature arose. The result in art is the further development of situating human beings harmoniously *in* nature, which had been a feature of Northern painting since the fifteenth century.

With Le Brun as director, the classicizing Poussinistes dominated the Academy, founded in 1648, for the first few decades of its existence. After his death, the urge toward naturalism burgeoning in Western culture in Italian and Northern Baroque could begin, by the end of the century, to assert itself even within the French Academy, and by 1715, with the death of Louis XIV, the Rubenistes were triumphant. Signaling the shift in taste was Watteau's admission to the Academy with his painterly *A Pilgrimage to Cythera* **(J 106; G 20.14)**, and the creation of a new category called "fêtes champêtres," outdoor parties, which was added to the traditional biblical, mythological, portrait, landscape, and still life subjects.

## Jean-Antoine Watteau

Watteau was French only by the accident of war. The area of Flanders where he was born became French by military treaty six years before his birth. He was therefore ethnically Flemish and heir to the great Flemish tradition of sensitivity to atmosphere, fastidious concern with how things looked, and a taste for color harmony. When he left his native town of Valenciennes, however, he did not travel to Brussels to learn his métier, but to Paris.

He was fortunate to win the interest of the artist who was in charge of the works of art in the Luxembourg Palace and as his assistant there was able to study its great cycle of paintings by Rubens on the life of Marie de' Medici, as well as works by Titian and Veronese. He was therefore steeped in the Venetian, painterly tradition. Admitted to the Academy as a student in 1709, however, he also had training in the classical-based academic style. As a result, his mature work shows complete mastery of

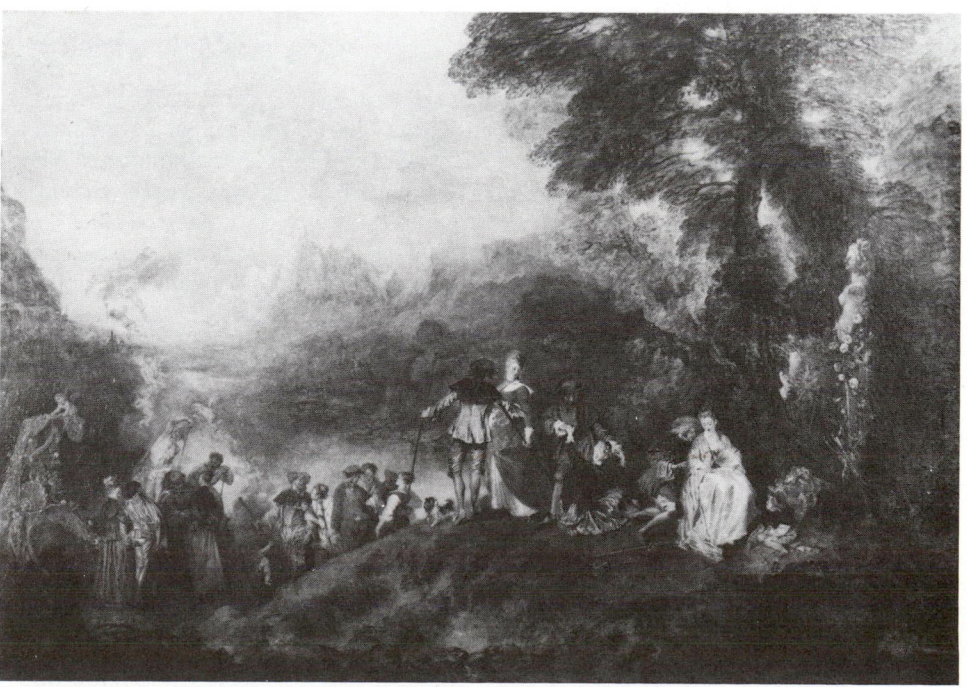

Antoine Watteau, *A Pilgrimage to Cythera*, 1717. Paris, The Louvre. (Josse/Art Resource, New York)

form and color. To this he added the temperament of a poet, and in his *Cythera*, as well as other "fêtes champêtres," he created the most lyrical pictures in French art.

The title of the painting is sometimes taken to mean a pilgrimage "to" Cythera and sometimes "from" Cythera—the island where Venus, born of the sea foam, was wafted ashore, the island of love and beauty. To this viewer, it seems that the pilgrims of love are going *to* the island, since the three couples at the right give the impression of three stages of readiness to embark. The three young women are dressed in high-style imitation peasant garb, with shepherdesses' crooks as part of their costume. The first at the far right appears to need some persuading, the one on the ground allows herself to be helped to her feet, while the third looks back to be sure she is not going to be deserted by her friends as the young man beside her holds her waist as if to steady her already-given consent. At the bottom of the hill all hesitancy has been overcome as the lovers prepare to embark on the fantastic golden, flowered-bedecked, shell-decorated gondola for their trip into the misty, dream-like distance. As is characteristic of Watteau, his figures are small, and are integrated in the flickeringly lighted landscape. They are arranged in small, irregular clusters linked by a continuous line that, starting at the left, rises and falls with the shapes of the landscape. The composition is further unified by a general golden-green tonality. Trees, shore lines, and distant mountains all add to the impression of naturalistic irregularity that suggests the freedom of the outdoors and the loosening of emotional constraints, while the artist retains a kind of behind-the-scenes control through color and line.

There is an entirely new expressive quality in Watteau's masterpiece. It is both stately and lively, like a minuet, a popular couple-dance in Watteau's time, and indeed has much of the graceful, ongoing regularity of the minuet rhythm. The period was one in which decoration of all kinds played an important role in aristocratic life, and the arts were preeminent as decorative accessories to living, not only as applied to domestic furnishings and clothes, but also to performance. Ballet, music, and plays with music were immensely popular. Since Watteau was close to theatrical circles, it has been suggested that his painting was inspired by one or another, perhaps several, comedy-ballets. In one, *La Vénitienne* (The Venetian Woman), a character sings to the gathering around him,

> Let everyone embark for Cythera!
> To be happy one must take risks
> But the wind is never contrary
> When one knows how to please:
> Young hearts, come all of you,
> There are no reefs to fear.

*Cythera* reminds us that Watteau was a Northern artist close to the Dutch and Flemish genre tradition, that is, painting of everyday life, usually of leisure moments and most often of rural subjects. This "fête galante" is a variation of genre that shows aristocrats at leisure, playing at the game of love. But it raises genre above its usual level by transforming it into a mythology and giving it an expressive resonance that communicates its universal meaning—the transience of youth and love. Watteau was ill with tuberculosis and knew his own life—and loves—would be brief. Perhaps the mood of reverie and what has often been described as melancholy in his work is due to this sad self-awareness. Or perhaps the artist's sensitive nerves were attuned to catch a subliminal melancholy in the period, like a leit-motif bass almost unnoticeable under the far more perceptible treble of playful gaiety.

It was Watteau's genius that he was able to invest genre with an expressive content that time and again deepened the meaning of his paintings. *Gersaint's Signboard* (1720) (W. Fleming, clpl 402) seems at first to be a charming genre piece showing fashionably dressed art connoisseurs looking at paintings in the shop of M. Gersaint, Watteau's personal friend. But the paintings hanging on the walls tell us that the painting is a kind of declaration of the artist's aesthetic allegiance—they are all either in the painterly style of the Venetians, or of Rubens and Van Dyke, or suggest Northern still life or genre. In the foreground, however, most prominent, is a portrait of Louis XIV, in the style of Le Brun, about to be dumped in a box. The painting thus turns out to be a statement of allegiance to nature and modernity versus the outworn formalism of the dead monarch.

*Gersaint's Signboard* displays Watteau's mastery of scenography through manipulation of light and color, as well as through the pose and gestures of his figures: pink and lavender are shot through with lustrous accents of silvery light, while the subtly striped costume of the seated woman at the counter also gleams like polished silver and echoes the pinks and lavenders, complemented with pale green. As in *Cythera*, the figures are disposed in irregular groups but describe a gently undulating, continuous line that starts at the left, here rising and falling in three waves across the picture plane. Oblivious of viewers, the human "actors" are intent on their interacting with each other or with paintings, and the sense of movement as well as speech is vivid. Every figure is given an active pose, including the dog biting fleas, expressing, perhaps, Watteau's sense that there were indeed "fleas" in the ribbon-and-bow culture.

Playfulness and role-playing are central to Rococo aesthetics, and one may still be transported to this make-believe world by visiting the eighteenth-century galleries in the Frick collection in New York City. On these walls Boucher's cherubic children play at philosophy and science, and Fragonard's eternal adolescents play at love.

## François Boucher

Boucher executed decorations for the most lavish *hôtels* in Paris. His most illustrious patron was Mme de Pompadour, the favorite of Louis XV, for whom he painted countless panels and designed motifs for porcelain made at the famous Sèvres factory. He also executed cartoons for tapestries woven at Beauvais, among which is *The Chinese Wedding*, a reminder that a widespread taste for Chinese-style decorations, chinoiseries, was an important feature of the period. This taste was partly mediated by Jesuit artists who worked in the court of the Chinese emperors, and by the fast-growing trade with the Orient. It should be noted that Boucher and others applied Chinese *motifs* in their designs for furnishings, but were unaffected by Chinese compositional methods; it would take another hundred years or so for European artists to look seriously at non-Western objects as works of art.

Boucher's favorite motif was the nude female figure (**G 20.15; H&F 14.3**), which he displayed as mythological figures in settings of Arcadian nature or in intimate interiors. Exuberant and erotic, but classically three-dimensional, his work synthesizes the Italian and Northern Baroque. His sumptuous color, warm, vibrant tonality, and large, swelling forms placed close up to the picture plane clearly reveal his primary debt to Rubens. He chose his subjects for the opportunity they gave him of displaying his mastery of color: the pink-pearl skin tones of the Venuses he painted in one guise or another are set off against great swags of rich drapery and the darker skin tones of the male consort. The artificiality of the setting is typical of Boucher's Rococo style, less naturalistic than Watteau's, but naturalism is in fact peculiarly interlarded with artifice in Rococo and to understand the style one must place the idea of artificiality in the context of Rococo culture and see its positive aspects. In our own time we prefer freshness, honesty, reality as we know it in our everyday lives. But artifice is the work of imagination, and although imagination in the Rococo period was put to services that were not noble, high-minded, or inspiring, what was created was nevertheless work of the human spirit—on its day off from serving nobility.

Surely Boucher's *Odalisque*, shown in the program, is not high-minded. There is not even the pretense of a divine immortal in this fleshy, very much alive Venus of the couch. Here is Boucher at his naturalistic best, with rumpled bedclothes, smooth pink skin, luxurious velvet, pearls and porcelain, feathers and ribbons, a chamber-music piece for the delectation of the senses.

## Jean-Honoré Fragonard

Fragonard's life spanned the last decades of Rococo and the whole period of Neo-Classicism, sadly becoming old-fashioned when he was at the height of his powers. Winner of the Prix de Rome at the age of twenty, accepted to membership in the Academy at thirty-two, he was successful from the start and had no difficulty finding wealthy patrons for his paintings of flirtatious love-making in well-cosmeticized gardens. Shortly after becoming Louis XV's new favorite (Mme de Pompadour having died) even Mme Du Barry gave him a grand commission for large mural-size works to decorate her boudoir in the late 1760s, but by the time he could finish them, Madame had embraced the new Classical style and refused what now was no longer fashionable.

Fragonard seems to paint with air, so light and light-hearted are his visions of love, and youth, and beauty. Using pastels, a medium that came into use prominently in the Rococo period, and a technique of rapid execution, he created works of artfully sophisticated social comedy that are unmatched in Western art. The story behind *The Swing* (**G 20.16**) is typical and reveals a great deal about the period and its art patrons: The Baron of Saint-Julien outlined his idea for the painting, explaining that he wanted it to represent his mistress seated on a swing pushed by a bishop; he wished to have himself placed in a position where he could observe the legs of the woman in the swing, and, he added, "better still, if you really want to make your picture lively . . . " All Paris heard this story and the painting became famous together with the painter.

The feathery lightness of Fragonard's forms is nowhere better seen than in his *Bathers* (ca. 1765) (**J clpl 107**). Air, water, earth, and the firey-red drape constitute the elements in which these nature nymphs exist in perfect harmony as if they have materialized out of the environment. The swaying foliage caresses them as it forms an enchanted bower in which they desport themselves, floating in the air or on the water, and their entire pastel world seems to be in never-ending motion. Typical of Rococo but carried to its extreme are the composition's infinitely irregular forms that freely interpenetrate with each other and with the space that surrounds them. But Fragonard controls this apparent irregularity with a Classical triangle design that rises from the lower left to its apex in the red-draped figure and descends to the lower right corner. It is strange, in this picture of nymphs at play, to notice the weird grotesques that lie jumbled along the lower margin of the scene. They do indeed almost escape notice, and one can only wonder at their possible meaning.

## Jean-Baptiste Chardin

Although the dazzling ebullience of Rococo tends to distort our perception of the period, a mere glance at the painting of Jean-Baptiste Chardin (1699–1779) acts as an instant corrective to such an unbalanced view. His mature life coincided with Rococo, he, like Watteau, Boucher, and Fragonard, was even attracted to Dutch and Flemish painting, and yet, Chardin was not a Rococo artist. It is instructive to observe that the masters he turned to, and the lessons he derived from the Northern masters were not the same as those of the Rococo painters. Intent on atmospheric effects and on bravura color, Rococo artists took their cues primarily from Rubens and Van Dyke, while Chardin was attracted to the masters of still life and genre, Northern painting's generally more sober aspects.

Chardin studied with several academicians and attracted the attention of Antoine Coypel, who hired him to do some decorative details for door panels. In his first assignment, Chardin was to paint a gun in the hands of a sportsman. Coypel, a highly trained, painstaking technician, drilled into him the importance of every stroke in getting the right value, in bringing out the form and the texture of the gun so as to give it its full pictorial meaning without allowing it to be obtrusive in the overall composition. This was the foundation of Chardin's art, based on minute observation and exquisite care for every stroke of the brush.

In 1728 he applied for membership in the Academy and submitted as his credentials two still life paintings. Nicolas de Largillière, a distinguished member of the Academy, thought at first that they were the work of a Flemish master. When he discovered they were by Chardin, he called them to the attention of the Director, who accepted him to full membership, an extraordinary move, both because a probationary period was usually required before full membership was bestowed, and because the paintings were still lifes, which no one in the Academy took seriously. The hierarchy of subject matter as structured by the Academy placed history, biblical, and mythological subjects at the top, portraits next, landscapes next, and still life at the bottom. But Chardin is that exception in the history of art, an artist who was appreciated by his fellow artists from the first, who won early admiration from connoisseurs, and who never lost his status as a master throughout all the changes in fashion that have occurred in the two centuries since his death. His place has remained secure as one of the greatest colorists French art has ever known.

Chardin's trips to the Paris suburb of Fontainebleau, where he carried out some decorations, were the only occasions on which he ever left Paris. His world was small, his experience completely inward, and his painting is a distillation of the inward experience of color and form. He never tackled big subjects, he stalked only one game—art.

While his contemporaries painted their high-style works of the "upstairs" aristocratic life, Chardin painted the "downstairs." His settings were often the kitchen or pantry, and for still lifes he chose lowly copper pots, earthenware jugs, and raw food, as in his *Kitchen Still Life* (ca. 1730–1735) **(J 779)**. Here is the characteristic compositional strategy of the artist, with shapes balanced against other shapes to create wonderful contrasts and rhymes. Although the black and white illustration deprives us of Chardin's color, it teaches us an important lesson about his painting, since it reveals the subtle gradations in values, that feature of a color that refers to

its lightness or darkness. In this still life, the range is from almost pure white (the eggs) to very dark (the jug, and the deep shadow under the ledge of the counter), with infinitely small changes in-between. Also to be observed here is the way the counter comes forward, as if it protrudes beyond the picture plane into "real" space. Used often by Chardin, the device is termed *trompe l'oeil*, which literally means "fool the eye." It appeals dramatically to the tactile sense of the viewer. Chardin's genius lies partly in his ability to appeal to the rational faculty (the cerebral mind) through his formal abstract relationships while also appealing to the senses through texture, color, and those objects in the furniture of the world which he chooses to paint.

In *Back from the Market* (1739) **(J clpl 108)** we see how the darks and lights translate into color. From white blouse through closely modulated beiges, tans, copper brown, purple brown, down to the blackish-brown bottles and deep shadow, accented by the washed-out blue of the pinafore, the colors shift through their restrained range, creating an atmosphere of high seriousness that underlines the profound importance of bread, and wine, and the people who provided the "upstairs" eating comforts.

There is a hint of narrative clinging to *Back from the Market*—the young girl at the back door with a dimly seen man standing outside, and the expression on the principal figure's face, with her sidelong glance—that emerges more strongly in *Grace at Table* (1740) **(G 20.19)**. A woman and two small children are about to dine. The two girls hold their hands clasped in prayer, while the woman, their mother one believes, looks somewhat vacantly but sadly at nothing, her face thoughtful as she sets the platters on the table. There is no man, no father, present— his absence seems to be the subject of the story. All the possibilities of treacly sentiment are there, and yet, by virtue of the formal and coloristic restraints imposed on the scene by the artist, it escapes sentimentality: circles and ovals and cylindrical forms are set in a rectangular corner, and soft transitions from light to dark, close harmonies within the family of somber tans and browns, give the picture its classical dignity.

## Art for a New Clientele

Insofar as modern life is dominated by middle-class culture, the modern period can be said to begin in England in the eighteenth century. Among the most striking features of the emerging middle-class society were the spread of literacy and the enormously broadened variety of reading that began to proliferate. In addition to the Bible and the classics, the newly enlarged reading public began to enjoy reading about itself—its problems, its aims, its needs, its values. This is the period in which the English novel took form in the hands of Henry Fielding, who satirized human faults and presented virtuous living as the greatest aim of civilized men and women, and of Samuel Richardson, whose sentimental moralizing made those faults easier to avoid and those virtues easier to live by.

## William Hogarth

It is not surprising to find, in this reading public, a taste for art that was equally didactic and moralizing. The outstanding artist of the Rococo period in England, William Hogarth (1697–1764), is the Fielding of painting. The three series of engravings which brought him enduring fame, *The Harlot's Progress* (1732), *The Rake's Progress* (1735) **(J 786, 787; H&F 14.6)**, and *Marriage à la Mode* (1745) **(G clpl 20.20)**, are like visual novels, with plots rising to a climax and ending with an always sad denouement, of course, because the main characters were object lessons in the disgrace and death that inevitably befalls unvirtuous living.

Although at first glance Hogarth's art seems to have no relationship to Rococo as represented by Watteau, Boucher, and Fragonard, on further consideration it becomes evident that he is dealing with much the same subject matter—love, flirtation, and extravagant living—but shows their seamy side, which is only hinted at in paintings of the French school. In formal style, too, his lively curvilinear figures and interior decorations show that the English Channel not only separated England from the continent, it also linked it.

## Jean-Baptiste Greuze

For Richardson's analogue, however, one must recross the channel to consider the painting of Jean-Baptiste Greuze (1725–1805), who knew Hogarth's engravings and planned to execute a large series in the same vein, using French people and scenes. The project was not completed, but his paintings *The Village Bride* (1791) **(J 825)** and *The Punished Son* (1777–1778) **(G 20.36)** show us his French "translation" of Hogarth. In the former, inspired probably by *Marriage à la Mode*, the irate father and conciliating mother flank the young people who, we know from the chicks on the floor, are expecting a chick of their own, without, it seems, benefit of clergy. We can expect a happy ending, here, however, since the couple's arms are already linked. *The Punished Son*, however, will have to live with his guilt, since he has arrived back home after his prodigal wanderings too late to see his father alive.

Greuze was accepted into the Academy only as a genre painter. He was for many years, however, the favorite artist of Diderot, who admired what he saw as naturalism in Greuze's painting, and who thoroughly approved of his didactic representations of Virtue Triumphant and Vice Punished; and his work was eagerly acquired by aristocratic collectors who enjoyed his sentimental moralizing in depictions of quaint country people and the lower classes. After the Revolution, however, he sank into oblivion and was poverty-stricken when he died.

## Historicity and Neo-Classicism: The Second Half of the Eighteenth Century

Historicity refers to a method of studying history based on research. It assumes that scientific methods of classifying evidence and organizing information produce an objectively truthful account of the material under investigation. It is thus linked to the rise of science with its reliance on experimentation and demonstration that we have already considered. In art, historicity arises during the Renaissance with such an artist as Andrea Mantegna, who studied antiquity; thus, when he painted his *St. James Led to Martyrdom* **(J 589; G 16.63)** he dressed the centurions in the authentic costume of Rome.

The concept of historical authenticity was innovative. For the most part, the Renaissance dressed its historical and biblical figures in fifteenth-century garments, so that the Madonna and the saints looked like contemporary Florentines or Venetians. Authenticity of facts was equally dispensable. The Early Renaissance had hardly gone beyond the concept of history expressed by the scholarly ninth-century bishop of Ravenna, Agnellus, who, as Herbert J. Muller recounts in *The Uses of the Past* (1952, p. 237, n. 1), wrote in his biographies of his predecessors, "Where I have not found any history of any of these bishops, and have not been able . . . to obtain [authentic] information concerning them, in such a case, in order that there might not be a break in the series, I have composed the life myself, with the help of God and the prayers of the brethren."

Gradually, contemporary dress, objects, and architecture began to seem inappropriate for subjects dealing with the past, and a rudimentary sense of history began to appear. The development was slow. The concept of scientific history hardly existed. Empirical science itself was in its infancy in the seventeenth century; we find anachronisms and representations that give only an impression of, say, Egyptian architecture, or the Near East, even in the work of Poussin, who was very much aware of history.

But, as noted above, the scientific spirit of the eighteenth century applied its attention not only to the physical universe but also to civilization. A passionate interest in history, in the modern scientific sense emerged along with scholarly research into the past. At the beginning of the eighteenth century when Herculaneum, near Naples, was rediscovered after having been buried under the volcanic matter that erupted from Mt. Vesuvius in 79 A.D., it drew little attention. But forty years later, at mid-century, when Pompeii was rediscovered, the consequences were dramatic. Times and events must be ready for each other;

we can only see what we are prepared to see. The latter discovery was meaningful because by that time the social forces including the scientific spirit that had been germinating for three hundred years had matured. The revelations of Pompeii—the life-style of an aristocratic civilization painted on its walls and discernible in its surviving architectural ruins—had an enormous effect on the European mind **(J 247, 277, 278, 282; clpls 21, 23, 24; G 6.21–6.27, 6.31, 6.32, 6.34–6.36, 6.38, 6.40; H&F 14.5, 14.16–14.19, 14.21, 14.22)**.

Interest in classical learning, alive since the Renaissance, had been satisfied by a knowledge of Latin and Greek philosophic, poetic, and dramatic literature. With the rediscovery of Pompeii, this interest now extended to the visual arts and decorations, and in the fourth quarter of the century the gracefully fanciful forms of Rococo begin to disappear from furniture and interior architecture in favor of classical linearity as well as classical motifs. The French lagged somewhat behind the English in responding to classicism, as evidenced by women's fashions: In England one sees the new sheer white muslin dress and flowing drapery in portraits by Reynolds and Romney **(H&F 14.16)**, while in contemporary France, the taste for extravagance in costume and life-style was led by Marie Antoinette, wife of Louis XVI, who ascended the throne in 1774.

In England, where the absolutism of a Louis XIV and his minister Colbert were unknown, the whimsicality and frivolity of Rococo did not develop, as we saw with Hogarth. Here the century was split lengthwise in its sensibility, rather than at its chronological center. One sees two tastes, for reasoned orderliness and for emotional naturalism (or Hogarthian realism) thriving side by side. Often intertwined, but often in tension, the two responses are exemplified by the expression—often encountered in eighteenth-century writing—of a favorite duality, the head and the heart. One of the most famous letters of the period is Thomas Jefferson's to Maria Cosway at the height of his infatuation with her, which he wrote in the form of a dialogue between his head and his heart; his head won out, eventually.

## Architecture in England and France: Palladian, Gothic, and Neo-Classical Taste

The new taste in architecture that appeared in England about 1720 was a direct rejection of the flamboyant Baroque as seen in John Vanbrugh's *Blenheim Palace* (1705–1722) **(J 785; G 20.4)**. Huge, irregular in its profiles, full of variety and dramatic contrasts, Blenheim represented the essence of Baroque style, and focused criticism against such extravagant, artificial expression, in favor of a more natural, thus more reasonable, style. As Alexander Pope remarked of Blenheim, " 'tis very fine, But where d'ye sleep, or where d'ye dine?"

Something there is more needful than expense
And something previous ev'n to taste—'tis sense.

What seemed sensible to the English mind was the serene orderliness of Palladio, whose influence was already present in seventeenth-century England through Inigo Jones. Lord Burlington and William Kent together designed Burlington's *Chiswick House* (begun 1725) **(J 702; G 20.5)**, where the pedimented temple front mounted on a platform is flanked symmetrically by recessed, austerely plain rectangular wings, and an octagonal dome rises at the center of the structure's body. Compositionally, the villa is an organization of geometric parts assembled in such a way as to give a rational, orderly effect. The triumph of Palladianism lasted for more than fifty years, and certain features of the style persisted for more than a century.

Side by side with Palladianism, however, one must consider the Gothicizing villa *Strawberry Hill*, renovated by Horace Walpole at mid-century (1749–77) **(J 802; G 20.21)**. Here, such features as the medieval crenelated roof edges, pointed-arch windows, and the donjon evoke the impression of Gothic architecture, stirring the Romantic imagination that dreams of far away and long ago. It should be noted, however, that Walpole's villa betrays certain features of symmetry that remind us of the period's underlying demands of reason, while Burlington's *Chiswick House* and other examples of sophisticated Palladianism carry a charge of yearning after the classical past that is in itself a Romantic longing. Both Classicizing and Gothicizing continued to flourish throughout most of the nineteenth century.

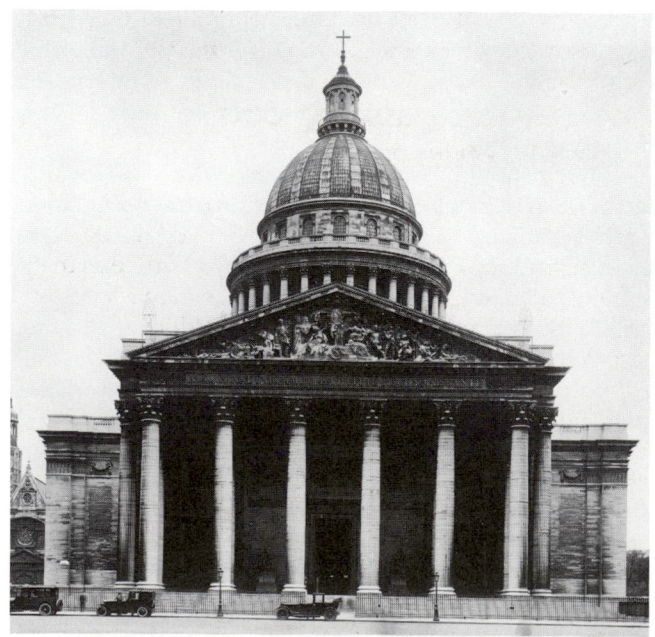

Jacques-Germain Soufflot. *The Panthéon* (Ste. Geneviève), Paris, 1755–1792. (ART RESOURCE, NEW YORK)

In Paris, Jacques-Germain Soufflot's *Church of Ste.-Geneviève* (1755–92) **(J 795; G 20.25)**, secularized during the Revolution and renamed the Panthéon, also reflects this aspect of the period's double-sided awareness, but expresses it altogether differently. Here again, as in Burlington's secular villa, there is the Roman temple front on a podium. The outer skin of the building is stark, bare-looking. The dome, however, with its open screen of columns and its slender rise to the lantern gives a very different impression. Inspired by St. Paul's in London, it is not Gothic but somehow it shares in a Gothic feeling. This impression is supported by the fact that Soufflot actually applied a theory of minimum support for maximum weight, for which the paradigm was taken to be the Gothic church. The slim columns that support the dome combine lightness with strength, thereby satisfying this theory, which was seen as an aspect of naturalism, since the origin of the column was the tree trunk. Whereas Gothicizing in England was expressed through superficial motifs, in France it had a structural basis. The Panthéon synthesizes the period's rationalist (classicist) and naturalist (romantic) tendencies in French terms.

As the century moved toward its final decades, classical tendencies became increasingly and more severely geometric. Claude-Nicolas Ledoux's drawing for his design for the Barrière de Clichy of the 1780s shows an austere rectangle crowned by a triangle (the pediment) with the flat, unadorned wall of the façade articulated by five columns along the lower story, and three arch segments surmounting the center three bays between the columns. But the most radical architectural thinker of the period was Etienne-Louis Boulée (1728–1799). His gigantic conceptions were composed of solid geometrical forms that expressed the essence of mathematical beauty, as indeed was his intention, made clear in his *Design for a Memorial to Isaac Newton* (1784) **(J 796; H&F 14.22)**.

## Neo-Classical Painting and Academic Theory

In painting, the competition between the two sensibilities, naturalism and Classicisim, was resolved during the second half of the eighteenth century by a synthesis that we might call naturalistic Classicism, but which is usually termed Neo-Classicism. The crux of the difference between Neo-Classicism and ancient Classicism lies along the cut that divides idealism from naturalism: the high-classicism of fifth-century Greece retained the control of the ideal over naturalistic features, as exemplified by the canon of Polyclitus, which applied a strict proportional system of units in designing the human figure, part-to-part. In Neo-Classical figures, by contrast, individualizing features impart a realistic expression to ideal types that tips the scale in favor of naturalism.

Neo-Classical style in painting has two principal sources. It is the invention of a brilliant German classicist, Johann Winckelmann, and of academic theory as it had developed by the eighteenth century. Winckelmann settled in Italy in 1755, where he devoted himself to the study of art. His masterpiece, *The History of Ancient Art*, was published in 1764 and marks the beginning of modern art history, since it is the first *stylistic* study of art; before Winckelmann, the history of art had been told in terms of artists' biographies, that is, who did what and when. Strangely, Winckelmann's aesthetic theory is based on ancient *Greek* art, of which he never saw an original example and which he only knew through Roman copies. Nevertheless he perceptively discerned such stylistic changes as the shift from the "severe" style of the fifth century B.C. to the "graceful" style of the fourth, and his work is a major monument in the history of aesthetics. He conceived of classical art as the embodiment of "noble simplicity and quiet grandeur" and proceeded to interpret what he saw in accordance with his concept; as Jonathan Swift had observed earlier in the century,

> Philosophers who find
> Some favorite system in their mind
> In every way to make it fit
> Will force all nature to submit.

Since Winckelmann's judgments about art were formed in accordance with how well the work exemplified his theory, it is not so surprising that he found in the studied classicizing artificiality of Anton Raphael Mengs the finest modern painter, on a par with Raphael himself.

The aesthetic credo of academic theory was "to delight" and "to instruct." "Delight" meant the appeal to the sensual pleasure of the eye by means of harmonious color and attractive proportions, shapes, and formal relationships that are comprised in the word *design* or *composition*. But delight was understood as more than satisfying retinal sensation: the delight of the eye was communicated to the mind, and pleasure therefore was created in the imagination. To "instruct" meant to teach a moral lesson, to edify, to inspire. Delight and instruction could not be separated, however, because what was morally uplifting (instructive) was also seen as setting up pleasurable ideas in the mind, and what was delightful to the imagination was also uplifting, because harmony, proportion, grace, and all the other qualities of beauty created a state of mind in which good feelings existed.

Academic theory rests heavily on Aristotle's theory that humans have "instincts" for harmony and imitation. This notion was extended to include the imitation of noble deeds and ideal beauty: To make nobility understandable would be to make it loved, since we love what we understand; to make it loveable would then make it desirable, since we desire what we love; to make it desirable would make it worth pursuing, since we pursue those things we deem desirable. Academically trained artists learned that it was their duty to depict nobility, by making it understandable, loveable, desirable, and worth pursuing. They emphasized the good as being the beautiful; clarity and precise drawing were visual equivalents for Reason.

To achieve nobility of imagery, one had to follow academic guidelines, beginning with subject matter. The subject itself should offer opportunity to portray a noble idea. Academic painting thus became the depiction of virtue, the supreme buzz-word of the eighteenth century. Heroism, self-sacrifice, ideal love, the triumph of good over evil, and the representation of eternal, universal truths were the predominent themes, and the subjects to illustrate them were found in the legendary deeds of ancient heroes, of gods and goddesses, and of biblical narratives, both Old and New Testament.

The second concept in academic theory pertained to ideal beauty. The problem was to understand the nature of beauty, and to express it through art. Since nature presented to our eyes only individuals, and since individuals were only imperfect reflections of the Absolutely Perfect, it followed that it was useless to copy nature exactly: one had to select. One of the oldest legends of art concerns exactly this problem. It tells how the great Greek painter Zeuxis created his painting of the most beautiful woman in the world, Helen, the prize over which the Trojan War was fought. He assembled a group of beautiful women and chose from each her most beautiful feature. His Helen was thus the composite of beauties, selected from nature, but made into an ideal, a type, rather than a rendition of any one individual. Academic artists in the eighteenth century used classical sculpture as the bases of their figure compositions in order to achieve ideal proportions; the *Apollo Belvedere* and the *Venus de' Medici* were particularly recommended for careful study.

Third, academic theory was concerned with character. Ideal physical types had to express ideal character types, and the image had to meet a reasonable person's reasonable expectations. For example, an artist wishing to depict ideal strength would use for his model a classical sculpture of Hercules.

A fourth concept had to do with expression. Descartes had systematically described the human passions in a treatise published in 1649, and as Director of the French Academy, Charles Le Brun used that text as a basis for illustrating the physical manifestations of emotion. These illustrations codified facial expressions so that one could find a formula for every emotion. Around 1760 the faces in Raphael's tapestry cartoons were engraved with captions labeling each emotion portrayed, so that artists could use the engravings like a dictionary.

The final criterion for academic painting is decorum. Decorum required that all elements in a painting had to be proper in accordance with the circumstances depicted: for example, costume and architecture had to be historically accurate; characters and actions shown had to be socially and morally acceptable: what was trivial, unjust, cruel, poor, wretched was to be avoided except as such

qualities contributed to the overall uplifting message of the composition, and then only depicted with utmost restraint. It would be poor taste—indecorous—to show the poor and the sick too emaciated or diseased. It is in the theory of decorum that one sees most clearly the social bias of academic art, since acting with reserve and aloofness was the mark of high class and education.

## Jacques-Louis David and History Painting

Academic theory achieved its fullest realization in Neo-Classicism during the last quarter of the eighteenth century, and Neo-Classicism itself found its greatest exponent in Jacques-Louis David (1748–1825). David's reputation has had as rocky a career as David himself had during his lifetime. Adored by his student-disciples, severely criticized by his academic peers, head of the most famous *atelier* in Europe, thrown into prison as an enemy of the Revolution to which he had been utterly dedicated, his reputation once more regained, he died neglected, in exile. In the century and a half since his death his work has continued to be admired by some and deprecated by others.

David was born in Paris in 1748 and died in Brussels in 1825. His life spans the event-packed period that included the violent transitions from monarchy to republic, from republic to empire, from empire to monarchy restored. Modern France did not have an easy birth. Crisis after crisis swept through the nation during those volcanic years, and David lived at the center of the greatest storms.

His artistic talent was recognized early and he was taken to Boucher, a family friend, who introduced him to *his* former pupil, Joseph-Marie Vien, who had also studied with Fragonard. Vien had moved from Rococo to a hesitant Classicism still flavored with Rococo elements, and David's early painting reflects this influence. He competed for the Academy's coveted Prix de Rome for three years, driven to attempted suicide by his annual failures, until he succeeded to gaining the award in 1774.

The routine followed by students at the French Academy school in Rome was rigorous. Up at five, drawing from the model from six to eight, studies in various churches and palaces during the day, and at the newly established Vatican Museum. Students were also required to make sketches of street life, and to continue their studies of classical literature, the well from which they would draw their inspiration and subject matter. Plutarch's *Lives* was probably the most intensely and widely read ancient work among the artists, and David's copy is heavily annotated in the margins.

For David, his first months in Rome were a period of intense searching. He had a fiendish capacity for work and was able and willing to learn from everyone. From a fellow student, a sculptor, he learned to develop his contours so that the points of articulation were clearly felt as rests, or accents, as in music, between the forms representing arms, legs, torsos, and so on; the contour lines were like the melody, carrying the energy along from rest to rest. The joints, wrists, elbows, knees are turning points, like rocks in a flowing river, changing the direction of flow, gathering the energy around them so that there are splashes, little or big explosions of force striking this point or another, as the river flows on. In the great paintings of the 1780s, *The Oath of the Horatii, The Death of Socrates, The Lictors Returning to Brutus the Bodies of His Sons*, one seems to see this lesson applied. But there were so many discussions, conflicting points of view, arguments that went on constantly among the students, and, finally, David reached a saturation point. He felt utterly confused, and unable to work. Vien, now director of the Rome school, sent him south to Naples, and this proved to be the turning point of his life. His experience at the archaeological sites at Pompeii amounted to a conversion. "I realized," he wrote later, "that to proceed like the ancients, and like Raphael—that was truly to be an artist. Then all my thoughts turned to this aim which the Greeks had attained, and which Raphael approached so near. I no longer despaired of arriving. . . . I still had many bad days, great dejections, cruel miscalculations, frightful agonies, but I had confidence that I would save myself, and the ardor of my will did not rest."

In 1780 David returned to France, and the following year he exhibited his *Belisarius Begging Alms*, which brought him immediate success. Some academicians criticized the color, which they found harsh, but the younger artists flocked to him as their new master. He opened a school in his studio, and his pupils included many of the painters who would become prominent in the following artistic generation. Soon he was granted a studio in the Louvre, a privilege for artists that had begun during the reign of Henry IV. He became a member of the Academy in 1783.

That year, many soldiers and officers were returning from America where some no doubt had been republicanized. The French government was all but bankrupt, and the years immediately preceding 1789 were increasingly tense. Like many others, David became more politically aware, and he found himself more and more drawn to the intellectuals, the poets, and the artists whose republican sentiments were the most radical.

In 1782 the government commissioned David to execute a painting on the ancient Roman subject of the Horatii, whose basic theme is loyalty. Convinced that he could paint such a work only in Rome, he returned there. The news that David was working on a painting of great importance went through the salons of the city, and by the time the painting was finished and ready to be viewed, interest was passionate. All Rome was talking about the picture and everybody who was anybody came to see it. An eyewitness wrote, "Every day it was like a procession; princes and princesses, cardinals and prelates, monsignori and priests, bourgeoisie and workers—all came [hoping to be allowed in] to view the painting." Even the Pope asked to see it, and David allowed the painting to be taken to the Vatican but refused to go himself. He had become, like many French intellectuals, a firm anti-papist.

In Paris his success with *The Oath of the Horatii* (1784) **(G 20.38; H&F clpl 14.20)** was equally smashing, but,

Jacques-Louis David. *The Oath of the Horatii*, 1781. Paris, The Louvre. (ART RESOURCE, NEW YORK)

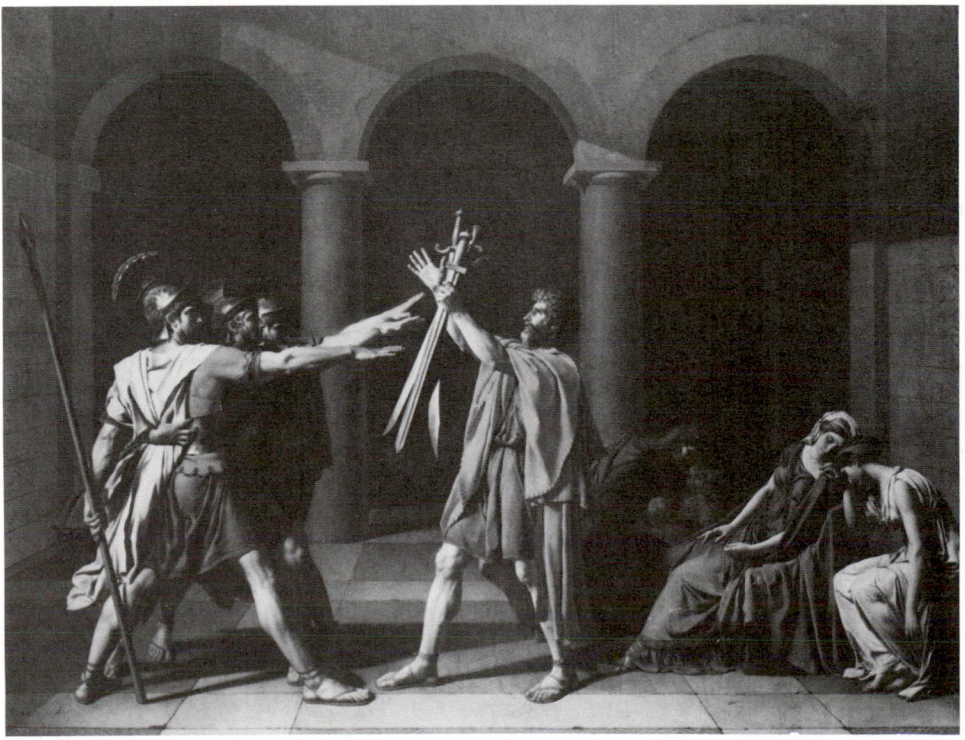

just as with *Belisarius*, there was negative criticism and even increased hostility on the part of the Academy leadership. David's painting was hung in the Salon exhibition of 1785 in an unfavorable position, but popular pressure forced its rehanging. Hailed as the Corneille of painting, since one of Corneille's great classics was his *Les Horaces*, David was recognized as the chief of the French school as well as the leader of the Neo-Classical movement.

The painting depicts the elder Horace with his three sons as they are about to leave to fight the sons of the enemy family, the Curatii. At the center, the father holds up three swords towards which his sons, at the left, stretch their unbending arms as they swear a do-or-die oath to defend the honor of the family, while the women of the family, at the right, are slumped in grief, and the children are encircled protectively in their nurse's arms. Severe Greek Doric columns support three arches against which this dramatic scene is played, masculine courage and duty on one side underlined by the contrasting feminine acquiescence and helplessness on the other.

In most ways the painting is a model of Classical composition. The action takes place as if on a stage, within a space box that is shallow and totally closed at the back. It is structured by stable horizontal and vertical elements, in which a triangle rises from each of the lower corners to its apex on the fist of the father. The forms are arranged symmetrically, with a central axis, and both sides of the pictorial field are closed off by figures which face toward the center. The figures are in stable, fixed poses, and their rhythms are slow and stately, like the rhythm of the architecture.

Departures from orthodox Classicism, however, can be discerned, most strikingly in the focus of the scene: instead of being located in a vanishing point at the rear, it is in the foreground. The perspective lines converge on the fist of the father, whose fingers are clasped around the swords. Furthermore, the sons are arranged isocephalically, in a space so compressed that the overlap between them is almost in one plane, as in Greek vase painting **(J 141, 142, 143; G 5.9, 5.10, 5.11)**, a feature that raised the ire of the Academicians. It should be noticed, however, that by placing his figures in this unconventional, flat-plane relationship, David emphasized the climactic point at which the eyes of the three sons were directed in unison, the same point at which the father looks—again, the wrist holding the swords, the emblems of the family's honor.

Stern morality and austere form are united in the *Horatii*, as they are in David's *Socrates Drinking the Hemlock* (1787) **(J 826)**. As in the earlier painting, loyalty is again the theme, but here it is loyalty on the even higher plane of Truth. The political martyr points upward, as in Raphael's *School of Athens* **(J 630; G clpl 17.17; H&F clpl 11.24)**, signifying the realm of perfect Ideas (including Truth) to which he is committed. The starkly bare walls speak, like Socrates, of the plainness and simplicity of

Truth. Here, however, a very slight compromise with strict classical form has been made by opening up the left side into deeper space than the shallow stage on which the action takes place. The philosopher-hero bids farewell to his followers who, including the man under the arch and the three departing on the stairs, number twelve, evoking sentient associations between this self-sacrificing martyr and Jesus Christ.

This evocation is far more pointed in *The Death of Marat* (1793) **(J 827; G clpl 20.39; H&F clpl 14.19)**, and to understand it requires a glimpse into the aesthetic context in which such a painting was created.

As we have noted, the transformation of Western European thought beginning with the Renaissance reached flood-tide momentum during the Enlightenment. Two conflicting views of reality, two ways of knowing, competed for authority, and in the end science and history won out. But the painting of historical events belonged to a well-established tradition of iconographical forms, postures, gestures, and groupings rooted in religious imagery. The death of Christ—depicted in Lamentations, Pietàs, Depositions, Entombments—provided the archetypal compositions for all death scenes.

As humans, and human deeds, replaced Christ and sacred acts in the historical and scientific imagination of the eighteenth century, the mortal hero surrounded by his aides emerged and took the center stage, dying in the same poses, and accompanied by the same gestures of grief formerly given to Christ and the saints. But whereas the death of Christ called forth religious emotion, the death of the hero summoned up its secular counterpart, moralizing fervor, the sentiment that we have seen pervading eighteenth-century sensibility. The French Academy exhibitions of the last quarter of the century were filled with scenes from history illustrating loyalty, courage, generosity, honor, and self-sacrifice in the service of one's country. While some depicted medieval and Renaissance subjects, most were drawn from legends of ancient heroes which provided ideal examples of virtue for the heroic aspirations of the present. Symbolic of national glory with countless stories of virtuous deeds admirably suited for illustration, classical history perfectly accorded with the moralizing and historicizing appetite of the day, satisfied its emergent self-conscious nationalism, and met the needs of artists for appropriate subject matter. Archaeologically sophisticated artists began to rove through the centuries with brush and palette in search of virtue, but the *modern* hero represented in his climactic moment of heroism was slow to appear. Heroines remained nearly invisible.

Classicism deals with Socratic, eternal truths. Only time could provide proof of the authenticity of the universal, eternal quality of an act or event, and the heroism of a deed had thus to be tested by that controlling measure. It followed, therefore, that no modern event merited depiction since there was no way to test its true quality, nor could a modern leader surely deserve the immortality conferred by art: How was one to know whether future events would justify his admittedly heroic-seeming act as truly heroic? Furthermore, how could one even *look* heroic in modern dress?

It was Benjamin West, the backwoods-born American, who became painter to the king of England, whose practical mind and lack of classical education in his youth led him to depict a modern hero in modern dress. His *Death of General Wolfe* (1770) **(J 812; G clpl 20.35; H&F 14.17)** shows the British general who died on the battlefield after securing the capture of Quebec and with it, the whole of Canada for England, in 1759. By eighteenth-century standards, this was still recent news, and although Wolfe was called "the hero of Quebec," West was the only major artist to see him as a hero worthy of eternal life through art. He placed Wolfe on the ground, slumped in the arms of his aides, reminiscent of Christ in many paintings. Where in a painting of the Crucifixion there would be a cross, he has placed a flag, its secular, nationalist analogue.

Other Americans working in England, notably John Singleton Copley and John Trumbull, and eventually some English artists followed West in taking up modern history painting, always with symbolic, evocatively religious poses and groupings, but the French had remained aesthetically loyal to the Caesars and their like.

In 1789 the French Revolution broke out with the fall of the Bastille. David associated himself with the most radical of the revolutionary groups, the Jacobins, led in 1792–93 by Jean Paul Marat, a man totally uncompromising in his revolutionary republican zeal. In the view of Charlotte Corday, associated with the Girondists—more moderate republicans—he was the personification of evil, and she resolved, like Brutus, to slay the tyrant who had inflamed the passions that unleashed the Terror. She managed to gain access to his bath—where he worked because only water soothed the terrible effects of the skin disease from which he suffered—and stabbed him. One might wonder who the hero of this drama was; some might say Corday. But David and his fellow Jacobins saw the assassination as the death of a great hero, and it is as a hero that David has represented him.

Marat has fallen over against the side of the bathtub, holding in his left hand the accusatory note that Corday placed between his fingers. Still holding a pen, symbol of his lifework for which he was martyred, his right arm hangs limply down to the floor in the position associated with Christ in many Crucifixion scenes (see, for example, **J 468, 527, clpl 63; G 18.25, 18.55, clpls 17.41, 18.14;** and an interesting variation, where Christ's death is foreshadowed by the limply hanging arm of the Christ child, **J clpl 82; G 17.43; H&F clpl 11.39**). The few accessories—wooden table, a few writing articles, the head wrapping, all of humble materials—highlight the exceptional drama of the event, and everyday objects are thus turned into powerful symbols, analogous to the wood, nails, and humble crown of thorns of the Passion.

Marat's wound is depicted with classical restraint, with only a few dabs of red paint to remind the viewer that the martyr's blood has been spilled. The background is blank, not a defined place in this world but like the gold heavens of medieval art, symbolic of eternity. The stark horizontal-vertical organization also conveys the permanence of timelessness.

Despite David's cool Classicism in such paintings as the *Horatii, Socrates,* and *Marat,* there is a warm naturalism that gives life to his figures, and one is reminded even of Chardin in the peculiar animation in the still life objects. His clarity of vision enhances the illusion of reality in the timeless, abstract world of ideas that he embodies with heroes, giving us the kind of experience we have in dreams, so very real and so ambiguous at the same time.

## *Part 2* ROMANTICISM AND REVIVALS: THE FIRST HALF OF THE NINETEENTH CENTURY

The period following the French Revolution is stylistically somewhat reminiscent of that following the High Renaissance. Perhaps in reaction against the Revolution's debauched decline into the Terror, Classical composition and images of civic virtue associated with the Revolution no longer satisfied the mood of the end of the century. Possibly, after several decades, high-mindedness had simply lost its fascination. Beginning in the early 1790s, in illustrations by John Flaxman **(G 20.40)**, one sees a kind of manneristic elongation of form together with peculiar juxtapositions of scale characteristic of Parmigianini and other sixteenth-century masters. This taste even enters David's painting in his post-revolutionary period, and becomes a hallmark of the style of Jean-August-Dominique Ingres (1780–1867), David's most brilliant pupil. Emerging a little later but contemporary with this manneristic mode, a painterly style revived features of Baroque art through the influence of Rubens on several prominent artists, but most particularly on Eugène Delacroix (1798–1863). His birth a generation after Ingres's removed him from the classicizing atmosphere that prevailed in Ingres's student years, and gave him the sensibility that made him the standard bearer for the opposing camp, thus extending the old Poussiniste/Rubeniste quarrel into the nineteenth century, when it was seen as the opposition of Classicism and Romanticism.

## Romanticism

Classical art can be described in terms of its network of ideas that taken together add up to a theory which serves as an objective guide for artistic practice. No one theory comprised of a bundle of rules lies behind Romantic art. Classical art, as we have seen, is concerned with generalities and universals. Romantic art, on the contrary, is individualist, depending on the artist's subjective response to experience. It places its confidence not in rules but in feeling, which is not accessible to rules. For Classical art there are well-established standards which constitute a body of ideals; for Romantic art there can be no such system of standards since general controls are contrary to the needs of individual expression. Rather than a set of regulations, Romantic art comprises an assortment of loosely held notions that take their authority from the artist's private, subjective response to experience. Subjectivity harbors an emotional response to experience that by-passes reason and reaches directly into the realm of feeling and intuition. As such it can be lyrical, coolly elegiac, passionate, violent, and anything else that lies in the gamut of human emotions.

Lines between rational and irrational, classical and romantic, and all such dualities, blur in the reality of life. But dualities are a convenience and can be useful if one remembers that, like all models, they are abstractions. One can recount the entire narrative of art history in terms of naturalism and abstraction, or painterly and linear forms, or rationalism and irrationalism, or Classicism and Romanticism, or a number of other dualities. No element in the pairs is ever pure. We have only to remember that David's Classicism was a Romantic reconstruction and nostalgic evocation of the ancient past to see how impure such dualities are. But insofar as dualities are useful abstractions, the opposition between objectivity and subjectivity perhaps affords particularly apt, particularly modern insights into the conflicting modes of thought and feeling that divide a David from a Blake or a Goya, or, in the next period, a Delacroix from an Ingres.

The new period's emotional and intellectual difference from the Enlightenment era can be recognized by its taste for emotion-arousing contemporary literature. While David and his generation read such ancient classics as Plutarch and Homer, Géricault and his contemporaries were reading books written in their own time by authors such as Byron and Sir Walter Scott (ironically, about time long past). Byron and Scott between them sum up much of the period's romantic feelings, Byron with his aristocratic radicalism, Scott with his dreams of Gothic adventure, knights in clashing armor, and maidens in distress saved by chivalric courage.

One particularly striking aspect of Romanticism deserves special attention. Possibly because of the continuing broadening of horizons that had brought to Europe a new awareness of the world beyond its borders, a strong taste for the exotic appears in European art, and often enough this taste has aspects of a peculiar, perverse liking for the weird, the erratic, and eccentric, and even the hair-raising and the horrible. One should be alert to the many guises in which this feature of nineteenth-century art appears.

# Napoleon

The towering figure of the first fifteen years of the nineteenth century was Napoleon, whose ideals of government were as distant from those that fueled the Revolution as those that separate an empire from a republic. This was not so apparent at first, and many idealists, including Beethoven, saw in Napoleon a liberating force. How David saw him is recorded in his *Napoleon Crossing the St. Bernard Pass* (1800) (Rosenblum/Janson clpl 4), one of the two greatest portraits painted of him—the other is by Ingres. "It is not with swords that one wins battles," Napoleon told the artist whom he had commissioned to do the work, "I wish to be painted serene on a wild horse." Storming up the mountain in the footsteps of the great commanders of the past—one sees the names of Charlemagne and Hannibal carved in the stones under his own name—Napoleon is indeed calm as the winds of war blow him upwards, cape flying, towards victory. David has returned to his pre-Revolutionary style, inspired by the verve and color of Rubens.

These qualities in Rubens seduced one of David's favorite pupils, Antoine Jean Gros (1771–1835), away from the master with whom he studied and whom he never ceased to venerate. Gros's Davidian classicizing works have been forgotten, while his artistic fame rests on paintings characterized by Baroque drama, violent movement, and spirited color. Gros met Napoleon in Italy in 1796 and was commissioned by the then General to select the works of art that Napoleon intended to carry back to Paris as war booty. He became part of Napoleon's intimate circle, and was able to observe the hero in action. As a result, he created some of the most effective battle paintings in French art. His battle horses owe a direct debt to Rubens and are a legacy that he will pass on to Géricault.

Gros's most famous painting is *Napoleon in the Pest House at Jaffa* (1804) **(G clpl 21.14; H&F 15.2)**, recording the real event when plague swept through the French army at Syria in 1799. Gros portrays Napoleon as a secular saviour, touching one of the horrible sores of an infected man, thereby demonstrating not only his fearlessness but linking him with the iconographic tradition of Christ healing the sick, and the various saints healing plague victims. The artist situates him in an exotic setting of Moorish architecture (introducing Near-Eastern exoticism into European mainstream painting), and composes his groupings so as to leave a space around the principal figure, arranging his lighting to focus on the central scene and to function symbolically as healing power.

Not only Rubens, but behind Rubens, Michelangelo, in whom Baroque art has its ultimate source, makes his presence felt in this huge work. In the nude plague victim on his knees, the legs seemingly powerless, we recognize the broken body style of Michelangelo's late Pietàs, while in the figure seated in shadows with his head supported in his hands we find a quotation from the *Last Judg-*

*ment*—the depiction of the eternally damned man. Gros's scene is, in fact, a kind of Last Judgment, with the light and shadow dividing those who will be saved by grace of the "saviour" from those who will die.

Napoleon is seen again as the benign Christ in Gros's *Napoleon at Eylau* (1808), where he is depicted riding through a battlefield strewn with the dead and dying, his arm raised in the gesture of blessing.

## David's Studio

Other students in David's studio were also transforming or deserting the lessons of the master. François Gérard (1770–1837) developed a cool, elegant classicism with a certain Rococo eroticism. Anne-Louis de Girodet-Trioson (1757–1824) reflects the period's Mannerist moodiness and formal elongations. He was one of a number of artists who responded to the new period under the Empire, followed by the Restoration of the Bourbon monarchy, with a revival of interest in religious sentiments. They searched for new meaning in religion, finding their imagery not in the grand themes of the past, centered on Christ, the Madonna, and the saints, but in quieter subjects, and humble people.

Surveying the situation around 1800, one may also pause for a moment to consider a strange group of painters (and writers) whose works have found the obscurity they deserve, but who, as a group, represent a part of an archaizing taste for linearity that will find its ultimate fulfillment in the genius of Ingres. This group was called "Les Barbus" (the Bearded ones) because they wore beards, which at the time was not the fashion, but which symbolized their identification with ancient times. They also garbed themselves in Greek mantles. They require our attention because the phenomenon they represent—the search for purity, inner peace, and quietude, for a return to a primitive, golden age before civilization, and particularly before the Renaissance had (in their view) corrupted humankind—has surfaced again and again in the past two centuries. We will recognize this impulse in the Pre-Raphaelite movement, in Van Gogh and Gauguin, and in the counter-culture movement of the 1960s which, however, found its expression in music more than in the visual arts.

Out of David's studio, then, we see the emergence of a number of different styles inspired by elements from the recent to the most remote past, and from exotic distance. It is exactly this variety of styles that typifies nineteenth-century art and architecture. As if a great menu of historical dishes were offered, artists picked and combined them so as to create their own individualistic gourmet feasts.

## Jean-Auguste Dominique Ingres

With the distance of more than a century separating us from the emotions and time-bound taste of the period in which Delacroix and Ingres (1780–1867) were the acknowledged leaders of their respective movements, Romantic and Neo-Classical, progressive and conservative, respectively, we are today able to see the contributions of each, and to evaluate them in terms of what we know has been the subsequent history of art. The result of such reevaluation has been to render greater respect to Ingres as a *progressive* force in painting than he was given in his lifetime, when he was admired only by the conservatives—the academicians of the École des Beaux Arts and the wealthy bourgeois whose portraits he painted.

Indeed, Ingres saw himself as a conservative, and had nothing but disdain for innovations. "There are not two kinds of art, there is only one," he wrote. "It is the one based on timeless, natural Beauty. Those who seek elsewhere deceive themselves, and in the most fatal manner. What do these so-called artists mean when they preach the discovery of the "new?" Is there anything new? . . . Our task is not to invent, but to continue." And again, "Pure and natural beauty need not surprise us through novelty: it is enough to be beautiful. But men are in love with change, and in art change is often the cause of decadence."

Among those who did "preach the discovery of the new," Ingres was seen of course as hopelessly old-fashioned and his self-important manner did not help. He provoked ridicule with his self-image as a public figure of profound respectability and the seriousness with which he treated himself and his honors—member of the Institute, Professor of the École des Beaux Arts, awarded the Grand Cross of the Légion d'Honneur. It was this pompousness that provoked Delacroix into making some of his epigrammatic remarks about Ingres, one of the most famous of which was that "Ingres achieved the complete expression of an incomplete intelligence."

Conservatives were associated with the discredited Classicism of David, and with the failed rationalism of the Enlightenment. And yet, when we look at the works of Ingres—this self-styled arch-Classicist—apart from his portraits, we have to account for visions that are not at all rational, whose reality lies in the realm of the imagination and can be approached only through symbol. How does he do this? How does he reconcile the demands of realistic appearance with the demands of those aspects of nature that are invisible? It appears that he achieves this by submitting his acute powers of observation to his miraculous sense of rhythm. Ingres was a gifted musician and a well-trained violinist; he played second violin in the municipal orchestra of Toulouse, where he went when he left his native town of Montauban to study art before going to Paris in 1797. Not infrequently his drawn line evokes in one the sense of music made visible.

Ingres won the Prix de Rome in 1801 but was unable to leave for Italy until 1806. In the meantime he began to get portrait commissions and one sees even at this early date, in his portraits of Mme Rivière and that of her daughter, those elements of his style for the female figure that would remain constant—the classical fullness of form that seems all flesh, without bone or muscle within firm yet soft contours, and the command of decorative patterns and textures that rivals Jan van Eyck.

In 1806 Ingres was commissioned to paint the Emperor in full glory, and produced his *Napoleon I on His Imperial Throne* (1806) (Rosenblum/Janson clpl 11), a staggering synthesis of free-standing sculpture as seen in the Zeus at Olympia by Phidias with the painted image of God the Father by Jan van Eyck, the center panel of the Ghent altarpiece which had been brought to Paris and was on exhibition in the Louvre between 1799 and 1816. Although the great chryselephantine statue of Zeus had not survived the destruction of the ancient world, it was among the wonders of classical antiquity and minute descriptions did survive so that, in addition to a Greek coin bearing the image, Ingres had available a vivid word picture of the forty-two-foot gold and ivory masterpiece.

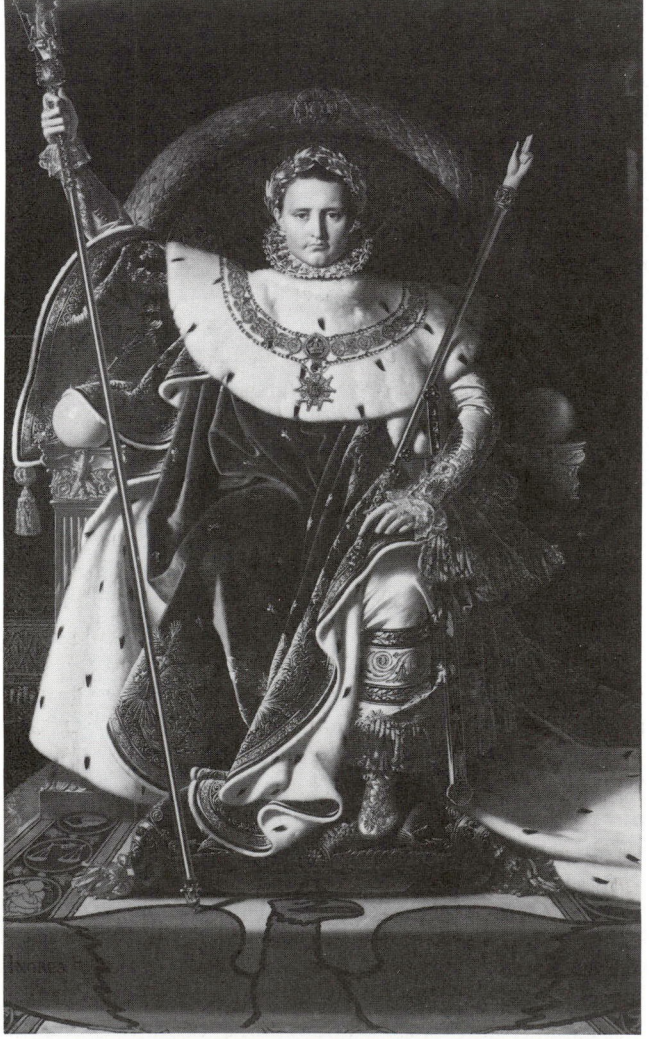

Jean-Auguste Dominique Ingres. *Portrait of Napoleon Enthroned*, 1806. Paris, Musée de l'Armée. (GIRAUDON/ ART RESOURCE, NEW YORK)

From the description he learned that Zeus was seated on a throne, holding in his left hand his sceptre surmounted by an eagle and in his right hand the goddess of victory, Nike. The left arm and shoulder and the lower part of the god's body were covered with golden drapery decorated with brilliant enamels; an olive wreath of gold with green enamel crowned his head. The splendor of the huge image of gold and ivory and brilliant colored enamels was totally in harmony with Ingres's temperament. But as a man of the nineteenth century he was also impelled by the spirit of naturalism, and he seems to have read the description as if it were overlaid with the breathtaking realism of Van Eyck's God the Father (**J 512; G 18.8, 18.9**).

Napoleon is portrayed iconically (frontally), in a rigidly symmetrical composition. Despite the huge bulk of the heavily draped figure, he and his throne seem to be levitated, like Zeus carried on the wings of his eagle. The imperial eagle is indeed at Napoleon's feet. But the Emperor holds the sceptre of Charlemagne, and the Hand of Justice unites him with the authoritative past. They symbolize his descent from the first emperor of the Holy Roman Empire, while the arch of the throne surrounds his head like a halo, fusing the image of the king of the gods with the Christian image.

Ingres's close study of the Eyckian style is evident in the way he painted with infinite detail the designs of the jewels, the ornate gold embroidery, the decorations on the sword sheath, and in the attention he paid to effects of light: typical of Van Eyck, one sees a window reflected in the ivory globe on the left arm of the throne. Iconic realism should be a contradiction in terms, but the Flemish masters had brought it off, and so does this French master, four centuries later. Such is the majesty of tradition.

The erotic tendency that we have seen formed an important element in the new sensibility of the period was not missing from Ingres's imagination. In him it seems intimately linked with a mysterious sense of energy. In the nineteenth century new insights were arising with regard to the nature of energy, and artists, with their own superior antennae, often arrive at insights that are analogous to those of science, even without scientific knowledge, simply on the basis of their response to intellectual currents that are present in their environment. Is it possible that Ingres could have had such unformulated insights into the interchangeability of mass and energy? In many works he seems to have been preoccupied with the question of power, and how power is exerted. His Napoleon is an example, and his nudes, too, exude a fascinating and compelling energy. His *Jupiter and Thetis* brings together his *Napoleon* with a female half-draped figure in one of the summit masterpieces of the century.

In this painting we are made acutely aware of the power of physical mass in contact with the energy of emotion. Lithe, svelte, almost slithering, Thetis tweaks the nose of this Ruler of the Gods, trying to persuade him to help her son, Achilles. She leans provocatively against him, her arm and breast pressing his thighs. Jupiter, massive, cloud-born, a frontal figure of authority similar to *Napoleon*, derives his power from his male virility, symbolized by his thick dark hair and beard, but also by his position as Ruler, while Thetis must solve her problem of power through the energy of sexuality.

Painting as sensual delight, as a delectation offered for the enjoyment of all the senses, but particularly the visual and tactile, reached its height and virtual end in the work of Ingres. No artist since has appealed so powerfully to the sensation of touch, and indeed, the history of modern art traces the effort to expunge from painting all evocations of physical sensations that spring from the experience of phenomena other than the painting itself. Modern art—what we shall be calling *modernist* art—has sought to achieve pure visibility analogous to the way music is pure sound, without reference to subject matter outside of itself. We shall return to this important matter in subsequent units, but for the moment, we may take Ingres's *Grande Odalisque* (1814) as a superb example of the artist's ability (and desire) to appeal to the viewer's memory of sensations of touch **(J clpl 113; G clpl 21.22)**.

An odalisque is a female slave in a sultan's harem, an object of sexual desire, kept always polished, perfumed, cosmeticized. She is a work of art in a collection of similar *objets d'art*, an object of luxurious pleasure, pampered and cared for to give her the perfect health and beauty required by the royal voluptuary to whom she belongs. Ingres's odalisque is apparently never allowed to have her feet touch the ground, to judge by the way he has painted the pink, smooth, soft, wrinkle-free soles of her feet. The artist shows her titillatingly half-exposed, half-hidden, surrounded by padded luxury, in an atmosphere of Oriental languor as imagined by a European voluptuary, which Ingres must certainly have been. The lavish display of silks, satins, furs, jeweled ornaments, and peacock feathers evokes the exotic ambiance of the seraglio, and is arranged so as to maximize its sensual effect on the viewer—firm flesh touched lightly by soft feathers, smooth body lying on wrinkled bedclothes, soft cool skin pressing into soft warm velvet. Even in a pre-Freudian world, the slave's grasp of the handle of her peacock fan must have been capable of arousing explicit sexual associations.

The elongated mannerist figure style that is characteristic of Ingres from the very beginning of his career is in no other work so spectacularly justified. Attacked by critics for its "arbitrary anatomy," its "three extra vertebrae," *Grande Odalisque* is a superb example of Ingres' "visible music," as well as his affinity with the Northern tradition, in its complex interconnected linear flow, its rhythmic contrasts—note the fifteenth-century Flemish angular, staccato bunching of drapery, as seen also in *Jupiter and Thetis*, contrasted with the long uninterrupted contours of the odalisque's figure—and in its harmony of two main colors, blue and flesh-pink, deco-

rated with notes of gold and green, with recurring accents of bright orange.

*Grande Odalisque* is one of several versions of this subject that Ingres painted during different periods of his career; see, for example, *Odalisque with a Slave* (1842) **(H&F clpl 15.18)**. It might also be observed that his portraits of French women are European counterparts to the Oriental odalisque. They, too, are lavishly cared for, clothed, of course, but bejeweled and enframed in settings that express their privileged position, their role as precious objects that have been bought and paid for, and cared for with the respect that expensive objects always command, as seen in *Madame Moitessier* (1851) **(H&F 15.6)** and in the glorious *Comtesse d'Haussonville* in the Frick Museum in New York, among many others.

## Henry Fuseli, William Blake: The Subjective Mode

In England, Mannerist tendencies appear earlier than in France. Henry Fuseli (1741–1825) created weird images that gained much of their effect from the artifice of elongation, as in *The Nightmare* (ca. 1781) **(J 816; G 20.41)**. In Fuseli we also see possibly the earliest appearance of the anti-rationalist current which flows through much of the art of the first half of the nineteenth century. He was a major influence on William Blake (1757–1827), whose linear art seems almost magically to extend visually the pure spiritual ecstasy of his poetry. "Imagination," Blake wrote, "is the divine vision, not of the world, nor of man, nor from man as he is a natural man, but only as he is a spiritual man." Strangely, both David, the arch-rationalist, and Blake, the visionary, were driven by the same fanatical determination to regenerate humankind.

A Gothicizing taste is strong in Blake, who, like Fuseli, invented a style that features elongation which may be sixteenth-century Mannerist in inspiration but also seems to be derived from the long, elegant lines of Late Gothic International style, as seen in *Pity* (ca. 1795) **(G 20.42)**. His forms are distinguished by a wiry line that has the growth energy of Gothic art, the nervous tension of Dürer, and the muscularity of Michelangelo, while the passion of his vision gives expression to the growing self-awareness, the subjectivity, that has characterized the modern age. The taste for linear art went hand-in-hand with the taste for archaizing or primitivizing, notable revivals whose appearance we have noted in France in the years around the turn of the century. The alternate Baroque tradition of Rubens that surfaced in Gros found an even more spectacular heir in Théodore Géricault (1791–1824).

## Théodore Géricault

Géricault's first success came with his dashing portrayal of an *Officer of the Imperial Guard* (1812) **(J clpl 115; G clpl 21.16)**. The verve, the twisting, turning movement, and the color constitute a kind of visual manifesto of his debt to Rubens, but it is above all his love for horses that is projected into his representation of the majestic, fiery charger, one of countless examples in nineteenth-century art in which an animal is the vehicle for the artist's emotional expression. It is indeed interesting to observe how often in this period artists used *unthinking creatures* to express that direct, unreasoning contact with reality that is at the heart of the subjective, romantic mode. Géricault's passion for horses led to his adulation of one of the famous circus riders of the day, Franconi, whom he tried to imitate physically. It also led to his early death: at the age of thirty-two, he fell from a horse and died of complications from the injuries he sustained. Géricault thus belongs to that extraordinary group of artists who leave a permanent mark in the history of art despite their tragically brief life span.

Although he won critical approval and a gold medal for his *Officer of the Imperial Guard* at the Salon of 1812, Géricault's second submission to the Salon, in 1814, met with disappointing reviews. *The Wounded Cavalier* (Friedlaender fig. 51) was found to be faulty in drawing, in proportions, and in color, and the artist did not send to the Salon again until 1819, when he submitted the painting for which he is most famous, *The Raft of the Medusa* (1819) **(J 837; G 21.15; H&F clpl 15.5)**.

Géricault spent two years in Rome (1816–18), where, to judge from his great work, he seems to have studied Michelangelo through the eyes of Caravaggio's dramatic realism. Returning to Paris, he searched for a subject that was big enough to contain the new ideas he found in himself as a result of his Italian experience. His need to make a large statement, however, should also be understood in the context of the period, which perhaps was reacting against the neatly finite rational expression of the late eighteenth century—Beethoven's Ninth Symphony, for example, was composed between 1817 and 1823. It was while Géricault was in this waiting, searching mood that there occurred one of those scandals that erupt from time to time, catching the imagination of an entire nation.

A French ship *The Medusa*, bound for Africa, foundered in the Mediterranean. There were not enough lifeboats aboard for all of the passengers, and a raft was quickly made, onto which some of them were loaded, with the intention that the raft would be towed by the lifeboats. According to various versions of what happened, the ropes were either rotten, or were deliberately cut. In any case, the raft was swept away, left to float with about a hundred and fifty people on it. The ordeal lasted for twelve days, during which every kind of horror was reported to have taken place, including cannibalism. People fought each other, were thrown overboard, or simply died of hunger and thirst. About fifteen survivors were finally picked up and brought to Paris. Two of them published a pamphlet attacking the naval ministry and the government for incompetence and malfeasance, and the terrible incident became a national, political *cause célèbre*. The radicals and other anti-Bourbon political

dissidents, by now including Géricault, sympathized with the survivors, and the artist found in the event everything for which he had been looking: a contemporary event with political content of national significance, satisfying the dramatic longing for adventure, offering to the imagination the most frightful, gruesome scenes, and calling forth the most profound feelings of anger against injustice.

Géricault set to work with his customary passionate energy and thoroughness. In accordance with the scientific attitude by then recognized as a requirement for modern history painting, he gathered every scrap of available information. He interviewed the survivors, and made portraits of them which he eventually inserted in the painting. He read all published material. He studied the sick and dying in hospitals and sketched cadavers in all kinds of twisted, contorted positions. He had a raft built, and went to the seaside where he floated it, in order to sketch its movement; he made sketches of the sky and clouds.

The finished painting is a dramatic distillation of the event. The huge composition (16 feet by 23 feet) is structured by a triangle that takes its rise at the bottom left-hand corner, rises along a daring diagonal to its apex, and drops abruptly only part way down where it is cut by the picture margin. The irregular triangle receding into pictorial depth is thus not Classical, but Baroque. The desperate reaching, turning figures of the anonymous crowd thrust upward to the figure of the black man who signals a ship on the distant horizon, reminding one that this is, in the Western tradition, a *salvation* picture. Furthermore, for this monumental statement, Géricault has gone to the greatest of monumental artists, Michelangelo, in whose *Last Judgment* **(J 615; G clpl 17.35)** one sees the reaching scramble of the saved as well as the inspiration for some of the other figures derived from the damned.

Along with the scientific developments of the century, an interest in the insane began to claim serious attention. A doctor friend of Géricault's, professionally concerned with dementia, asked the artist to make a series of studies of the insane. The portraits that resulted from this commission are masterpieces of sympathetic observation. *The Insane Woman* (1822–23) **(G 21.17)** is not represented as wildly mad but as somehow grimly knowing, her helpless incompetence sadly but unsentimentally revealed by the untied strings of her bonnet. The face of *The Madman* (1821–24) **(J 838)** is simply infinitely sad, as if deprived of purpose. They are like people seen on any present-day city street, and the realism of the handling is an example of that realistic current that persists in French art and emerges with such virility later in the century in Daumier and Courbet.

## Francisco de Goya y Lucientes

Interest in abnormality was not always scientific or sympathetic. Sometimes it took the form of thrill-seeking entertainment, as when people visited insane asylums to watch the deluded behavior of the inmates. In the painting of the most powerful artist of the period, Francisco de Goya y Lucientes (1746–1828), madness is a metaphor for the dark, demon-ridden side of human nature, which in his view was more normal, in the sense of more prevalent, than the bright side. It is also a symbol of the crumbling world, the death of order, the triumph of chaos which he perceived as the meaning of the world-shaking events of his time.

No clearer demonstration of the difference between the Classical mind and the Romantic mood can be adduced than through a comparison of Jacques-Louis David, in his purest classicizing period, the 1780s, and his exact contemporary, Goya, in a work of the same years, *St. Francis Borgia Exorcizing a Dying Impenitent* (1788) (Rosenblum/Janson fig. 23). In the former, death is heroic and public; in the latter it is grotesque and private. David's paintings of the Horatii, of Socrates, of Brutus, of Marat are evenly lighted, suggesting the clear-mindedness of those protagonists. *Exorcizing* is handled with strong contrasts of dark and light, underlining the conflict that is described specifically in terms of the priest's small figure and pale halo and the dying man's highlighted deathly pallor contrasted with the dark menace of the monsters that loom over him. The murky, nocturnal atmosphere is illuminated by a glowing red, suggesting the fires of hell. The moon-like window lets in some daylight, but it is partly covered by the dark drapery, like the veil of madness that has closed over the demonized man. Notice that the equal lengths of the window's crossbars, silhouetted by the light of day, are in contrast to the religious cross held by the ineffectual-looking priest: the measure of reason is beyond the space of this sick room, the world, which religion can no longer save.

Unlike the healthy, reddish-toned ideal beauty and nobility of the Enlightenment's classical immortal figures, whose names we know, this anonymous dying man is a twisted, tormented, greenish near-cadaver, gasping for breath, stiffened with hysteria, the dreadful image of the new modern-age Everyman, frail in his pitiful mortality.

Goya's first important work, begun in 1777 and continued for almost ten years, was a series of tapestry cartoons—compositions painted to serve as designs for tapestry. On the surface they seem typical of Rococo lightness, delightfully colored and full of charm and spontaneity. But Goya's scenes of picnicking and playfulness have a note of the sinister—a man is vomiting, in the picnic scene; a young woman caged in a golden-gleaming carriage is contrasted with a street vendor, poor, but out in the open, free, in *The Crockery Vendor* (ca. 1778).

In the early 1780s Goya attracted the attention of Don Gaspar Melchor de Jovellanos, the future minister of Charles IV. Jovellanos was one of the most enlightened aristocrats of the Spanish court, and through him Goya became a part of the circle of leading intellectuals and artists of Spain whose interests ranged over the entire spectrum of the period's social and moral problems. With the support of Jovellanos, Goya secured important portrait commissions and his brilliant style produced some of the most remarkable portraits in European art of the 1780s and 90s. One of the most original is his portrait of a child, *Don Manuel Osorio Manrique de Zuniga* (1788), in the Metropolitan Museum. The boy, in a brilliant red suit, holds a tether which is tied around a leg of a small dun-colored bird. Three cats stare greedily at the bird, which holds in its beak a card with Goya's name on it together with the symbols of a painter: palette, brushes, and a maulstick. A birdcage with smaller birds rests on the floor opposite the cats. It seems that Goya, self-identified as the tethered bird, already feels himself demeaned and menaced by those around him, for whom he is a plaything. He had his revenge, a dozen years later, when he painted his group portrait of the *Family of Charles IV* (1800–1801) **(J 833; G clpl 21.9)**.

In 1799 the artist became First Painter to the king and was commissioned to do this group portrait. One can only wonder at the supreme arrogance of people who could afford to see themselves so utterly without physical charm. A French novelist remarked that Charles and Maria Luisa looked like the corner baker and his wife after they won the lottery. They glitter with jewels and decorations as if to dazzle the viewer into not noticing how homely they are.

It is clear that Goya is recalling the great portrait of the royal family, *The Maids of Honor* by Velázquez **(J clpl 104; G clpl 19.37; H&F 13.16)**, including as his predecessor had done a self-portrait at his easel. But instead of placing his figures in Baroque depth, he disposes them frieze-like, in a shallow space box, with a strongly directed light coming from the left side so that the figures are almost like cutouts against the background. Sixty years later Manet, influenced by Goya, will be severely criticized for the "playing card" flatness of his painting, a technique that he seized on, as we will see, for the power of its expressive impact. Goya's prophetic modernity can also be seen in the way he drags the paint over the surface, suppressing individual textures in favor of the texture of paint itself.

During the 1790s, with his morbid view of humanity reinforced by the Terror in France, Goya painted a number of scenes of mass madness, including *The Burial of the Sardine* and *The Procession of the Flagellants on Good Friday*. In such works Goya captures completely the savagery, the abandonment, the emotional drunkenness and hysteria that possess people in a crowd, especially when seized with religious fervor. As a man of the Enlightenment, Goya was hostile to what he saw as the superstitions of religion, and in *Sardine*, a Spanish ritual parade in which a sardine is buried as a substitute for a roasted pig, signifying the end of Carnival and the beginning of Lent, he depicts the puppet-like movements of people in a state of catatonic nightmare. The image suggests the horror of watching zombies dance. A grinning mask on a huge banner hovers like evil itself over this people's bacchanal. On the sidelines, the watchers loll against each other, as drunk as those in the parade. It is indeed a world gone insane.

It is in such works as these that we find that Goya has made the most overt and acute break with the past. We have noted anti-classicizing tendencies in French and English painting but Goya goes even further. Instead of the graceful, flowing line of the Mannerist revival, Goya gives us an abrupt, jagged line; instead of interconnecting arabesques, as in the Baroque and Gothic revivals, one has interslicing angularities; instead of pleasing harmonies one has sour dissonances, and with these characteristics formally underlining the separateness of people locked into their own delusions, one enters the modern world of the lonely crowd, the isolated individual in a spiritual wasteland that is alien, frightening, full of despair and undefined menace. It was in the 1790s that Goya wrote, "The world is a masquerade. Face, clothing, voice—all is a lie. Everyone seeks to appear what he is not; all deceive each other, and no one knows himself." The age of anxiety, as Auden will call it, opened out of the Enlightenment, and Goya is the greatest of the artists who confronted the monstrous irrationality that lurks constantly at the corners of the rational world, ready—like a cat watching a bird—to spring the moment that Reason sleeps, as he shows us in *The Dream of Reason Produces Monsters* (1794–1799) **(G 20.44)**.

### The Third of May, 1808

In 1808, Napoleon invaded Spain. French troops occupied Madrid. When rumors spread that the youngest son of the deposed King Charles IV had been carried off to France, protesters attacked the French troops in the streets of the city on May 2. The French fired on the crowd, and by evening the Spanish fighters had been subdued and were carried off to the firing squad to be shot at dawn on May 3. The action started the first guerilla war, one of the most savage wars in history.

Goya recorded the events of May 2 and May 3, and the hideous atrocities committed in the following years, in two paintings executed in 1814, and in a set of etchings under the title of *The Disasters of War* on which he worked over a period of years beginning about 1810, but which were not published until thirty-five years after his death. The etchings are unparalleled in the entire history of art for their savagery, for the vile barbarity of the acts they depict, unmatched even by Jacques Callot: castration, live dismemberment, impalement **(G 21.11; H&F 15.3)** are graphically described as if, like the demonized man, Goya himself were trying to exorcize the horrors not of imaginary demons but of acts committed by humans that he had seen or heard reported during the French occupation.

After the defeat of Napoleon in 1814, the Spanish Parliament established a regency council in Madrid. Goya wrote to the council expressing his wish "to perpetuate with the brush the most notable and heroic deeds of our glorious insurrection against the tyrant of Europe." It is the scene of the aftermath of the insurrection, however, that has become Goya's most famous painting, *The Third of May 1808* (1814) **(J clpl 114; G clpl 21.10; H&F clpl 15.17)**.

On a hill at the outskirts of Madrid, with a church and government building in the background, the anonymous protesters are being executed officially by a French firing squad. At the moment caught in the painting, a shirt-sleeved man, on his knees, eyes staring but head erect, has defiantly thrown up his arms as he faces the rifles point blank. His white shirt is brilliantly lit, gleaming against the contrasting red blood, black sky, and murkily shadowed, uniformed soldiers of the squad. Compared to the few dabs of red paint in previous death scenes, Goya's painting seems soaked in blood, and its gory horror is heightened by the tumble of dead bodies in the foreground. Like machines, the faceless soldiers are aligned in identical poses, as they have been trained, carrying out orders and thus in no way individually responsible for the killing they are about to execute. The rebels, in irregular groupings to contrast with the uniformity of the French, are described with careful particularity in their defiance and despair.

It is surprising to consider the probable source for Goya's composition, so surprising that the likelihood has been overlooked. American art was not highly thought of, nor indeed was much of it known, except for works by West and Copley, who were associated with the English School, so that one would not expect a great European artist to find inspiration in an unknown American. But engravings traveled easily, and there can be no reasonable doubt that Goya knew Paul Revere's engraving *The Boston Massacre* (1770) (Brown *et al.*, fig. 110). With a church and government building in the background, the English soldiers are lined up in uniforms on the right side of the composition, all of them in identical positions, with their rifles pointed at the rebels. At the left, a motley crowd is irregularly arranged, contrasting with the uniformity of the English; an American stands with one arm raised as he faces the guns. The detail that reveals unmistakably the link between Revere's engraving and Goya's painting is the dead man lying in the foreground in a pool of blood, with a tumble of rebels, already shot, in the left-hand corner.

Like West's *Death of Wolfe* and other heroic death scenes that we have already considered, Goya's painting, too, evokes the crucifixion of Christ; in the shadowy background on the left there is even a mother and child to strengthen the association. Unlike the central figure in earlier scenes, however, this martyr is nameless. As a figure of courage, he is exceptional in Goya's depiction of the human race, which he most often represents in every kind of base act from utter folly to total depravity. Bitterly he had watched greed, vanity, stupidity, war, and revolution triumph over Reason. Disappointed, disillusioned, disheartened in his old age, he covered the walls of his house with paintings that leave no doubt about his despair, distilled in one dreadful image, *Saturn Devouring His Children* (1819–23) **(G 21.12; H&F 15.4)**.

# Eugène Delacroix

Eugène Delacroix (1798–1863) told a friend, "Géricault allowed me to come to see Medusa while he was working on it in a bizarre studio he had. . . . I was so overwhelmed by it that after leaving there I ran like a crazy man all the way home." The impact of the picture is reflected in the subject matter and color of the painting that brought Delacroix his first public attention at the Salon of 1822, *The Barque of Dante* (1822) (Pool clpl 6). Drawn from Dante's *Inferno* (Canto VIII), the painting depicts Dante and Virgil standing in a boat to which the damned are clinging with hellish frenzy. It is not surprising, of course, to find Michelangelo's *Last Judgment* quoted not only in some of the poses, but in the over-all image, which goes back to the bark of Caron in the lower right corner of the Sistine Chapel altarpiece **(G 17.35; H&F 11.29)**.

The Greek struggle for independence against the Turks was a burning issue in Europe during the 1820s. European liberals sympathized with the Greeks, and a shock of horror shot through the continent as the news of Turkish atrocities at Chios became known. In 1823 Delacroix met a Colonel Voutier who had just returned from Greece, and who told him how the oppressed Greeks would shout their defiance with the words "Zito Eleutheria" (Long Live Liberty). The artist began work immediately on his *Massacre at Chios*, and went about his new project the way Géricault had in preparing *Medusa*. He sought out people who had been in Greece, read every report, bought books such as *The Habits and Customs of the Turks* and *Letters on Greece and Egypt*, and acquired engravings of Turkish and Greek costumes. The finished painting was exhibited at the Salon of 1824, where, it is said, Delacroix saw Constable's *The Hay Wain* and repainted parts of *Massacre* as a result. Unfortunately the painting has suffered from deterioration and restoration.

The high-colored expression of exoticism, anguish, and pathos did not meet with unqualified admiration. Gros called it "the massacre of painting," which is ironic since according to Delacroix his first inspiration for *Massacre* came from Gros's *Pest House*. The young painters, however, rallied to him and he was forthwith recognized as the head of a new school of painting.

One of the greatest culture heroes of the period was George Gordon, Lord Byron, whose romantic persona was as stirring to his contemporaries, including Delacroix, as his poetry. His death at Missolonghi, where he went to support the Greek liberation movement, offered Delacroix an opportunity to pay homage to the legendary idol of European liberals and express his own tribute to the courage of the Greek defenders who blew up the walls of Missolonghi, destroying it and themselves.

Although the painting is an example of modern history painting, we see immediately that it is totally unlike the tradition that had been established for realism and accuracy. With a single female figure looming large against a dark, melancholy sky, the painting immediately suggests allegory. It is not presented as a record of an event so much as a group of abstract virtues: courage, love of liberty, willingness for self-sacrifice are all embodied in the face and figure of a beautiful woman. Her dramatic pose, bare breasted, with both arms extended palms forward, communicates defenselessness and resignation, but she is on one knee, as if she will rise again on these warm stone slabs—slabs that in themselves evoke the memory of ancient Greece and the tradition of soaring human achievement that has been so viciously attacked. Between the slabs the arm of a fallen defender is visible— an image, in its way, of dismemberment.

Byron also provided the theme for the painting that was a sensation at the Salon of 1828, *The Death of Sardanapalus*. Again Delacroix's work provoked heated controversy, although the majority opinion was hostile. One observer wrote that Delacroix would have to hire two vans to move the furniture of Sardanapalus, three hearses for the dead, and two buses for the living. The scene is related to Byron's play *Sardanapalus*, although Delacroix has invented the details of slaying the Assyrian monarch's wives as he faces defeat by the approaching Medes and Persians and has ordered his eunuchs and palace officers to destroy all of his treasures and set fire to his palace. The painting is like an old-fashioned Hollywood spectacular, and indeed Delacroix's description of it reads like a scenario: "The rebels beseige him in his palace. Reclining on a superb bed at the summit of an immense pyre, Sardanapalus gives the order to slay his pages, his women—even his horses and favorite dogs [*even* his horses and dogs!] so that nothing would survive him."

The strong influence of Rubens is evident in the poses of the women and in the color, which Delacroix sought to make even more intense with the use of distemper, pigments mixed with egg yolk or egg white and a sizing such as a thin glue, as an underpainting. This kind of medium, used for scene painting and wall decoration, is brittle and not suitable for canvas. As a result, *Sardanapalus* deteriorated severely and had to be restored.

Studying the art of Delacroix we must stress his color because it was this aspect of his work that had such enormous interest for the Impressionists and Post-Impressionists, leading directly to modern art. Although he saw both line and color as crucially important, he conceived of the realization of form as a function primarily of mass, and he made an analogy between painting and sculpture that reveals his thinking quite clearly: "The sculptor does not begin his work with a contour; with his material he builds up an appearance of an object which, rough at first

**175**

glance, immediately presents the chief characteristics of sculpture—actual relief and solidity. The colorists, men who unite all the phases of a painting, have to establish at once and from the beginning, everything that is proper to their art. They have to mass things in with color, even as the sculptor does with clay or marble or stone. . . . Contrary to the usual practice, the contour should come last, and only a highly trained eye can get it right." He also stated that to find a method of achieving correct contours is a lifetime study.

One of the severe criticisms made against *Sardana-palus* was its spatial treatments. It is, in fact, impossible to find one's way through this space. Is it a room? Where is the wall? What is the spatial relationship between the various pictorial elements? There are almost no horizontals and verticals to cue-in the viewer and it is impossible to account rationally for the perspective from any one point of view. This kind of playing with space is a feature, as we have seen, of Mannerism, as is also the odd juxtaposition of scale. The plunging and tilting of space towards the back recalls particularly Tintoretto (**J 645; G clpl 17.67**), and should be kept in mind when looking at such works as Van Gogh's *The Night Café* (**G 21.68; H&F 17.18**) and other Post-Impressionist painting, including an early Cézanne, *The Orgy*.

There is indeed an orgiastic aspect to this scene of slaughter. Typical of the period, the horror is interlarded with voluptuous sensuality, and the close proximity of the radiantly light-colored female figure with the dark brown male is tinged with the particular erotic perversity that appealed to the taste of the time, although it is noticeable that they are turned away from each other and do not touch. There is no blood in this violent scene. Nevertheless the prevalent red tonality strongly suggests the bloodiness of the horrible event.

## Liberty leading the people

Picking up the thread of French political history, we recall that Napoleon was finally defeated at Waterloo in 1815 and the Bourbons returned to the throne. Charles X attempted to restore the privileges of the aristocracy and to indemnify the returned émigrés for their property, confiscated during the Revolution. This aroused the hostility of the upper bourgeoisie since it resulted in a reduction of interest on government bonds. A coalition of rising capitalist forces and liberals was formed, whose opposition to Charles met with increasing repression. Finally, in 1830, the political conflict reached crisis stage. Repressive measures were taken by the government against the press, with the editors of two newspapers imprisoned and fined for open attacks on the king. In the June elections the opposition forces won a majority of two-thirds against the government and the king dissolved the new assembly, changed the electoral laws, and abrogated all laws guaranteeing freedom of the press. Fighting broke out and the three-day July Revolution began. A provincial

government formed by the liberals offered the Duke of Orleans, Louis Philippe, the Lieutenant Generalship, and within ten days Charles had fled to England and Louis Philippe was installed as king of the French (not king of France, an important difference suggesting a kind of democratic monarch with the king in the role of a citizen-king, carrying out the will of the people).

During the three days of fighting in the streets, Ingres was a volunteer guard in the galleries of the Louvre, protecting his beloved Italian paintings. Daumier participated in the street battles and was wounded by a saber cut on the forehead. Alexandre Dumas père encountered Delacroix when the fighting broke out and recorded his impression that the artist was alarmed at the sight of the angry mobs but became enthusiastic when he saw the tricolor flying over Notre Dame.

Shortly after order was restored and the new administration was in control, the government established a Ministry of Commerce and Public Works in a bid to win popular support by acknowledging the tradition of royal patronage of the arts. The minister announced that a number of commissions for paintings were being offered, and published a list of subjects for the commissioned paintings, including *His Royal Majesty the Duke of Orleans Receiving a Prize for a Theme at the College of Henry IV*, and similar ideas. Delacroix could not bring himself to the proper pitch of inspiration with the suggested subjects and decided to work on an idea he had had in mind before the commissions were announced. *Liberty Leading the People* (**G 21.19; H&F 15.17**) was exhibited at the 1831 Salon.

Delacroix's painting is a synthesis of the experience as he must have heard it from others. As in *Missolonghi* he departs from the reportage tradition that had been established for modern history painting in favor of combining factual appearance with allegory. The over-life-size figure of Liberty, draped in the characteristic manner of Greek *Amazon* statues, with one breast exposed (Delacroix, in fact, exposes a bit more), plunges forward with a rifle in her left hand, holding a flying tricolor in her right. She, too, seems almost to be flying slightly above street level, and the flag flutters behind her like a wing, emphasizing her heritage from the Hellenistic *Victory of Samothrace* (**J 206; G 5.76; H&F 5.10**). Liberty/Victory advances over the realistically rendered dead that have sacrificed themselves to her, and this interplay between the real and the allegorical is expressed formally in the brilliant composition in which a right-angle triangle (the hypotenuse of which starts in the right-hand corner and rises diagonally to the man with the cutlass) composed of naturalistic, "real" figures is played off against a pyramidal structure with the allegorical figure of Liberty as its central axis and apex.

*Liberty* was bought by the state but it was withdrawn from public view because it was considered too inflammatory. It was not exhibited again until the World Exposition in Paris in 1855, and did not enter the Louvre collection until 1874, shortly after the triumph of the Third Republic.

Themes involving physical anguish and violence continued to attract Delacroix through his forty years of professional life. Some of his most memorable scenes from North Africa, which he visited in the 1830s, are those of tiger and lion hunts such as *The Tiger Hunt* (1854) **(G clpl 21.20)**, full of wild savagery. "There is in me some black depth which must be appeased," Delacroix wrote of himself.

## Honoré Daumier

Seemingly at the opposite end of the aesthetic range from Delacroix in the first half of the nineteenth century is the art of Honoré Daumier (1808–1879). His significant work in the period from about 1830 to 1850 is represented by his lithographs, which deal with the contemporary political scene and appeared in periodicals, the most important of which was *La Caricature*. It was his work in this journal that brought him fame, starting with *Gargantua*, an attack on Louis Philippe which shows the pot-bellied king sitting on a throne that is actually a chamber pot. Officials of his regime are channeling food, the produce of the hard-working French people, up a ramp into the mouth of the monarch, whose royal waste in the form of benefits to the bourgeoisie is filling the chamber pot. This cost the artist five hundred francs fine and a six-month's sentence which he was not required to serve. However, six months later another political cartoon did land him in jail for two months.

Daumier's most severe blow against the constitutional monarchy of Louis Philippe came in April 1834, when he published his *Rue Transnonain* **(G 21.36)**. A strike of the silk weavers in Lyons, whose wages had sunk to ninety centimes per eighteen-hour day, led to street fighting. The barricades went up, and the government called out the National Guard. A shot was said to have been fired from an apartment in Rue Transnonain, an officer was said to have been wounded, and troops rushed into the building, shooting and stabbing with their bayonets indiscriminately.

Daumier's night-shirted victim is anonymous, like Goya's guerrilla fighter. The tragic dimensions of the event are given a particularly nineteenth-century inflection because of the peculiar pathos of the commonplace, ordinary setting that has become a terrible scene of death. Overturned furniture, the sheet dragged with the man from the bed, the visually dismembered bodies—we see the head of one man at the right margin, and the figure of a woman at the left margin drawn from a perspective that makes the head all but invisible—the child dead under its father's body, bloodstains on the floor are made even more horrible by the warm, everyday sunshine that lights up this massacre. Unlike West's *Wolfe*,

this man has no comrades' arms into which he can fall back; unlike Marat, he has no well-established iconographical identification with Christ. The scene is secular, and realistic.

One sees echoes of Géricault's *Medusa* in Daumier's lithograph, and very strong reminders of another street uprising, Delacroix's *Liberty Leading the People*, especially in the two figures in the foreground, the one on the right foreshortened, the one on the left sprawled half-naked with only the upper part of his body covered. Daumier thus belongs in his style and aesthetic sensibility to the first half of the century; he is a Romantic Realist. In his painting after 1850, however, the Realist current becomes uppermost. He is the first great modern artist to find monumental subject matter in the new social history created by the working class.

## Romantic Realism

The heightened attention to nature seen in the eighteenth century's infatuation with gardens, and in the increasing importance given in painting to landscape as a setting for human action, continued unabated into the nineteenth century. Just as the demand for greater accuracy in modern history painting had strengthened, so a similar demand for greater accuracy in landscape developed. The cosmeticized woodlands and gardens of the Rococo no longer satisfied the new taste for sensual reality. At the same time, nature's various aspects—sunny, dark, wild, cultivated, sheltering, threatening—began to be seen as reflections of human emotions, as has already been noted in connection with Géricault and the role of animals in nineteenth-century art. Nature painting of the first half of the nineteenth century thus mirrors this seeming anomaly, subjective objectivity, the perception of phenomenal reality expressed so as to externalize the private emotion of the artist.

A poet would externalize his emotions in words, as Wordsworth did:

> I wandered lonely as a cloud
> That floats on high o'er vales and hills,
> When all at once I saw a crowd,
> A host, of golden daffodils;
> Beside the lake, beneath the trees,
> Fluttering and dancing in the breeze.
>
> . . . . . . . . . . . . . . . .
>
> . . . oft, when on my couch I lie
> In vacant or in pensive mood,
> They flash upon that inward eye
> Which is the bliss of solitude;
> And then my heart with pleasure fills,
> And dances with the daffodils.

John Constable (1776–1837) is the Wordsworth of visual poetry. Just as Wordsworth invested the commonplaces of carefully observed nature with lyrical, or melancholy, or nostalgic emotion, so, too, did Constable see and record with attentive accuracy and the charged vision of deep feeling the familiar scenes of his rural life. Woods, millstreams, pastures, quiet ponds, rustic houses, plough horses, and weathered surfaces were his favorite subjects, portrayed in every kind of weather and under every kind of sky **(J 820, 821; G 21.30; H&F 15.11)**. His studies of clouds are meteorologically correct, and he noted on these outdoor sketches the exact time of day and weather conditions when he did them, just as, decades later, photographers would do. He devised a technique of separating his brush strokes, laying complementary colors next to each other, which gave his paintings the effects of light and freshness that he wanted, and enhanced the brilliance of their color. This technique had significant consequences, for it caught the eye of Eugène Delacroix when Constable sent *The Hay Wain* (1821) **(G 21.30)** to the French Salon of 1824. Delacroix adopted this technique of broken brush strokes, which was to become central to the painting of Monet and Renoir through Delacroix's influence on them.

Turning to Constable's great contemporary, Joseph Mallard William Turner (1775–1851), we may find the key to understanding the art of this radical innovator with the help of John Ruskin, one of the most powerful influences in nineteenth-century aesthetics, and Turner's first interpreter:

> The difference between ideas of truth and imitation lies chiefly in the following points: First, Imitation can only be of something material, but truth has reference to statements both of the qualities of material things, and of emotions, impressions, and thoughts. There is a moral as well as material truth—a truth of impression as well as of form—of thought as well as of matter; and the truth of impression and thought is a thousand times the more important of the two. Hence, truth is a term of universal application, but imitation is limited to that narrow field of art which takes cognizance only of material things. (Eitner, *Neo-Classicism and Romanticism*, pp. 73–74)

Turner's *The Slave Ship* (1840) **(J clpl 111; G clpl 21.29)**, based on a report that slaves had been thrown overboard when disease broke out on the ship, is one of his greatest works, and a consummate achievement of nineteenth-century painting. It may be taken as a paradigm of the artist's theory and practice of art. Characteristically, Turner is here totally uninterested in finding painted translations for natural experience—in making water look like water, or differentiating between one texture and another. Instead, he used paint to distill the meaning of an entire experience, as he imagined it from the reports, and at the same time, to retain the look of paint. The medium, the process of painting, and the image were fused by the power of his passionate pictorial imagination, which lifted experience into the realm of the elemental and transcendent.

Turner rarely painted from nature. He told a young painter that one must paint one's *impressions*, by which he meant quite the opposite of what the Impressionists were to mean: he did not seek, as they would do, to capture the *retinal* effect actually seen as one observed the motif, but the *remembered* impression, a concept analogous to Wordsworth's definition of poetry as "emotion recollected in tranquillity." He held in his mind his experience of the elements of nature—once he even had himself lashed to the mast of a ship, in order to experience a storm at sea *(Snow storm: Steam-boat off a Harbour's Mouth)* (1842) **(H&F 15.23)**—and these elements, water, earth, air, and fire, were his materials, illuminated, irradiated by light. No single touch of paint corresponds to any specific object. Objects are described, they emerge, or half-emerge, as floating existences in the process of becoming. Turner's turbulent sea, the air, the fiery sun suggest a primal state of the cosmos, when nothing was separated, everything belonged to a common flux.

The gruesome subject of *The Slave Ship* reminds one of Goya, and the period's perverse taste for the horrible. Arms and legs are seen helplessly struggling in the water, while in the right foreground small fish swirl around the body of a slave whose fettered foot sticks out of the water. The small fish are unaware that they will be cheated of their dinner by the huge leviathan bearing down only a short distance away. As if in retribution, a dark purple-and-green stormy mass at the left looms over the guilty ship, a mass that takes on the vague shape of a giant figure with one avenging arm raised.

The German artist Caspar David Friedrich (1774–1840) similarly reached for, and often attained, a cosmic vision. His first major work, *The Cross on the Mountain*, introduced religious painting into landscape, an innovation which was not universally welcomed since it suggested pantheism instead of true Christianity. In this painting, a crucifix standing atop a steeply rising mountain peak and silhouetted against the sky unites heaven and earth. The Corpus faces away from the viewer, towards the setting sun which represents death, while it is flanked by evergreen fir trees, symbols of eternal life. Friedrich's style is one of meticulous realism in a peculiarly airless, boundless space, which creates an eerie, surrealist effect. With his ruins of medieval abbeys and lonely wanderers in mountain mists **(G 21.33; H&F 15.9)**, he evokes a mood that is brooding, elegiac, and mysterious.

Like Turner's *Slave Ship* and Géricault's almost contemporary *Medusa*, one of Friedrich's most famous paintings, *The Polar Sea* (1824) **(J 823)**, was inspired by an actual contemporary event, a shipwreck during the arctic explorations of William Parry, and resonates with symbolic meaning. Once again we see the nineteenth century's perception of human affairs ending in disaster. Thomas Cole, the first great American landscapist, also reflects this pessimism in such a work as his *Course of Empire* series, which depicts in five paintings the beginning of civilization, its rise to greatness followed by war, and its final stage, *Desolation* (1836) **(G 21.31)**.

# Revivalist Architecture

The taste for history that arose in the eighteenth century flourished wildly in the first half of the nineteenth. In architecture it lasted into the twentieth. If the client saw himself as a noble Roman, one could give him classical columns and a pediment; if he yearned for the spirituality of the Middle Ages (the most typical yearning of this materialist, positivist period), he could have Gothic pointed arches and filigree work.

One of the knottiest problems for architecture in this period was—or should have been—how to build public buildings for democratic societies. As Nikolaus Pevsner points out in *An Outline of European Architecture* (p. 272), "To erect public buildings, specially designed as such, had been extremely rare before 1800 . . . if one takes the 19th century on the other hand . . . the best examples [of urban architecture] are Governmental, municipal, and later private buildings, museums, galleries, libraries, universities and schools, theatres and concert halls, banks and exchanges, railway stations, department stores, hotels and hospitals, i.e. all buildings erected not for worship or luxury, but for the benefit and the daily use of the people." However, it is demonstrable throughout history that style lags behind function and technology. The Greek temple retained features of wood construction even when the Greeks built in stone. In our time we have seen the automobile begin its stylistic life as a horseless carriage. In the nineteenth century, the style for bank buildings was classical, since Classicism was associated with rationality—and surely an institution devoted to the safekeeping of money had to be reasonable above all else. The style for universities was universally Gothic, associated with scholasticism. Both architects and clients held to the familiar forms, and even when iron technology made possible entirely new architectural forms, it was put to the service of support in the form of columns and vaults.

Henri Labrouste (1801–1875) was daring in his Renaissance design for the Reading Room of the Library of Ste. Geneviève (1843–50) **(J 811; G 21.85)** in making the iron columns extremely slim, so as to emphasize the strength of this new building material which could achieve great height with graceful lightness. Most daring was the fact that he left the iron construction unsheathed, so that the skeleton of the building was exposed. This is possibly the earliest example of the taste for exposure that will become the overriding value in modernist architecture of the twentieth century.

century found its image in the mixed marriage of the past, from Gothic through Classical revivals, with its present. The result was a romanticizing of both: the past had ridden through history embodied in the virtue and courage of its heroes; the present had produced its own hero in the great tradition—Napoleon—but in addition was creating a new kind of hero whose struggle was to be in the mind and in the laboratory, rather than on the battlefield. Scientific evidence became normative for knowing, and this kind of realism is reflected in the accuracy with which works of art depicted their motifs, but the eyes that gazed into the microscope were filmy with the romance of the past. The commonplace reality of life, let alone the seamy side, past or present, remained invisible until mid-century, with Daumier and Courbet.

The most compelling aesthetic demand of the period covered in this unit was for naturalism, and we have observed how the idea of nature was absorbed in and inflected the playful artifices of Rococo, the austere idealism of Neo-Classicism, the schematizing of what we may think of as Neo-Mannerism, and the romanticizing of Neo-Gothicism. We have also seen the ascendancy of subjectivity externalized in a range of expression from lyrical to utmost despair.

Differences in national temperaments appeared as we considered the art of contemporaries such as David, Goya, and Blake; of Constable and Friedrich. And yet, transcending those national differences, certain features such as the taste for the eerie, the erotic, the exotic, the horrible, the ecstatic appear throughout Western Europe, testifying to a "spirit of the times"—the German word *Zeitgeist* is sometimes used—that signals homogeneous elements within the cultural heterogeneity of the region.

The importance of the art academy as an institution, and the canonizing of classical theory through the academy system are features of the period that largely determined the subject matter and the style of the art that was publicly exhibited, and thus shaped the taste of the public. However, we have also seen how events beyond the art world contributed to the shaping of aesthetic expectations, bringing about such radical shifts as that from Rococo to Neo-Classicism.

It is against the background of the hegemony of the entrenched academic system and the revivalist sensibility, together dominating the art world in the first half of the nineteenth century, that we will view subsequent developments and understand the struggle to uproot the past and lead art toward the twentieth century.

## Summary

In this chapter we have witnessed the end of an era and the birth of the modern world. Knowing its heritage we cannot wonder at the child's dual nature, rational, responsive to reason, but also anti-rational, responsive to emotion. Never wholly one or the other, the nineteenth

## Textbook References

**J** Janson covers the Rococo as part of the chapter on the Baroque in France and England. In the section on France he touches on Georges de la Tour and Le Nain, describes the contributions of Poussin and Claude Lorraine, and surveys the palaces of Versailles and the Louvre. A brief glance at the sculpture of the Louis XIV period is followed by a short discussion of the founding of the French Royal Academy of Painting and Sculpture. Painters Watteau and Fragonard, sculptors Clodion and Falconet, and the architect Boffrand exemplify Rococo, with Chardin and Vigée-Lebrun also included. In England he begins with the Renaissance architecture of Inigo Jones, moves to Baroque with Sir Christopher Wren, and takes up the painting of Hogarth, Gainsborough, and Reynolds, and the sculpture of Roubillac.

In the following chapter Janson covers the period from about 1750 to 1850 under the heading "Neoclassicism and Romanticism." Starting with Palladianism in England, he turns to Soufflot and Boullée in "rationalist" France. Gothic, classic, and the beginning of industrial architecture are exemplified in England in the work of Walpole, John Nash, Benjamin Latrobe, Sir Charles Barry and A. Welby Pugin (designers of the Gothicizing Houses of Parliament in London); in France there is a brief glance at Charles Garnier's opera house, and Labrouste's library of Ste. Geneviève.

Painting of the period includes history painting by Americans in England, West and Copley, and various aspects of the romantic sensibility seen in England in George Stubbs, Fuseli, Blake, and landscapists Alexander Cozens, Constable, and Turner. Romanticism in Germany is represented by Freidrich and in America by George Caleb Bingham. The Neo-Classical style in France is taken up as a reform movement against Rococo, exemplified by Greuze and David, followed by Gros as the Neo-Baroque painter of Napoleon. Ingres as the upholder of the Davidian tradition is seen also with marked Romantic tendencies. In Spain, Goya is located in the Neo-Baroque tradition. Janson then turns to Romantic painting in France, with Géricault, Delacroix, and Daumier, and concludes the review of painting with a glance at landscape painting in France at mid-century. Sculptors included in this period are Jean-Antoine Houdon and Antonio Canova, Neo-Classicists, and Auguste Préault, François Rude, Antoine-Louis Barye, and Jean-Baptiste Carpeaux who are shown to exemplify Romanticism's range of formal styles which combine in various ways Neo-Classical, Baroque and Gothic tendencies.

**G** Gardner gives a good introduction to the eighteenth century, touching on new political, social, and economic factors that were forces for change. Beginning with the Baroque architecture of Filippo Juvara in Italy and John Vanbrugh in England, the authors move to Palladianism, and then to France, with the Rococo interior architecture of Boffrand, and its spread into Germany in the work of French architect François de Cuvilliés and the Italian-influenced Balthasar Neumann. The ceiling frescoes of Tiepolo and the sculpture of Quirin Asam are introduced as decorative accompaniments to this development in Germany.

Rococo painting is represented by Watteau, Boucher, Fragonard, and the pastelists Rosalba Carriera and Quentin de la Tour; Chardin's difference from his contemporaries is pointed out. The Rococo section ends with Hogarth, whose Englishness is emphasized.

Gardner sees the shift from reason to feeling occurring in the second half of the eighteenth century. The authors discuss the problem of defining "romantic" and conclude that the word with all of its broad range of meaning does convey a recognizable expression. The Gothic and Classical styles in architecture are seen in a selection of typical structures in England and France; also included are glimpses of Thomas Jefferson's Palladian-inspired home, Monticello, and his Roman-classical inspired designs for the State Capitol at Richmond, Virginia. Sculptors included for this period are Houdon and Clodion; painters are Gainsborough, Reynolds, and Benjamin West, in England, Vigée-Lebrun, Greuze, and David, in France. The discussion of the end of the century singles out Flaxman, Fuseli, Blake, Giovanni Battista Piranesi, and Goya.

**H & F** Honour and Fleming begin their chapter, "Enlightenment and Liberty," with an introduction to the intellectual background of the eighteenth century, citing Descartes, Locke, and Newton. Rococo painting is discussed with the work of Watteau, Boucher, Fragonard, Chardin, and a little-known artist, Jean-François De Troy; Boffrand's *Princess' Salon* in the Hôtel de Soubise is cited here as in the other two texts. A selection of buildings in Germany brings the Rococo beyond French influence alone, showing the inspiration of Italian Baroque.

The discussion of eighteenth-century painting in England focuses on the work of Hogarth, Gainsborough, Reynolds, and West. The chapter ends with David, Canova, and Boullée representing the rationalism of Neo-Classic art.

Romanticism is the subject of the first part of the next chapter in Honour and Fleming. An introduction discusses the political and economic issues that propelled western Europe into the modern era. In their view, Romanticism developed out of the fragmentation of Neo-Classicism as it issued from David's studio in his various pupils, exemplified by one of them, Gros.

A discussion of Goya introduces the new emphasis on pain and suffering, which is then taken up in the work of Géricault. Another aspect of the period is touched on in Ingres's erotic nudes. His opponent, Delacroix, is then discussed, with emphasis on the very real expressive difference between them. The link between Romanticism and philosophy is brought out in connection with the work of Caspar David Friedrich; and the mystical element, which is a prominent feature in his painting, is shown to be a characteristic also of William Blake. Romantic landscape painting is exemplified by the work of Constable and Turner in England and by Corot in France. The eclecticism of the period's architecture, with examples of classicizing and gothicizing buildings, brings the chapter to mid-century.

**Janson**, **Part III**, **Chapter 6, pp. 542–563.** France: Architecture—Francois Mansart, Colbert, Jules-Hardoin Mansart. Sculpture—Giraudon, Coysevox, Puget; The Royal Academy. Painting and sculpture—Watteau, Boffrand, Clodion, Falconet, Fragonard, Chardin, Vigée-Lebrun. England: Architecture—Wren. Painting—Gainsborough, Reynolds. Sculpture—Roubillac.

**Part IV, Chapter 1, pp. 574–617.** Architecture—Palladian England, Rationalist France: Boullée, Jefferson, Walpole, Hash, Latrobe, Barry and Pugin, Garnier, Labrouste. Painting—Copley, West, Stubbs, Fuseli, Blake, Cozens, Constable, Turner, Friedrich, Bingham, Greuze, David, Gros, Ingres, Goya, Géricault, Delacroix, Daumier, Millet, Bonheur, Corot. Sculpture—Houdon, Canova, Preault, Rude, Barye, Carpeaux. Photography—Nadar, O'Sullivan, Brady, Gardner.

**Gardner, Chapter 19, pp. 756–767.** Painting—Poussin. Architecture and sculpture—Le Vau, Perrault, Le Brun, Hardouin-Mansart, Le Nôtre, Coypel, Puget, Wren.

**Chapter 20, pp. 770–802.** Architecture—Juvarra, Vanbrugh, Kent, Boffrand, Cuvilliés, Neuman; Painting and Sculpture—Tiepolo, Asam, Watteau, Boucher, Fragonard, Carriera, Chardin, Hogarth; Romanticism: Architecture—Stuart, Walpole, Adam, Jefferson, Soufflot; Sculpture and Painting—Clodion, Houdon, Gainsborough, Reynolds, West, Greuze, Kauffmann, David, Flaxman, Blake, Piranesi, Goya.

**Chapter 21, pp. 808–835.** Architecture—Barry, Pugin, Morris. Sculpture—Canova, Greenough, Rude. Painting—Goya, Girodet, Gros, Géricault, Delacroix, Ingres, Chassériau, Couture, Gérome, Turner, Cole, Friedrich, Runge.

**Honour and Fleming, Chapter 14, pp. 459–479.** Watteau, De Troy, Boffrand, Chardin, Boucher, Fragonard, Pöppermann, Tiepolo, Hogarth, Reynolds, Adam, Guardi, Gainsborough, West, Houdon, David Ledoux, Boulée.

**Chapter 15, pp. 480–493.** Gros, Goya, Géricault, Ingres, Delacroix, Daumier, Friedrich, Blake, Constable, Turner.

## Study Questions

1. What are the formal characteristics of Rococo art?
2. How do Watteau, Boucher, and Fragonard differ from each other?
3. What is the difference between Classical and Neo-Classical?
4. Give one characteristic of Géricault's *Raft of the Medusa* that is Romantic and one that is Classical.
5. Looking back to artists of the sixteenth century who are classified as Mannerists, point out Mannerist features in Ingres.
6. Give two examples of the influence of religious iconography in secular art.
7. Explain how Goya's view of humankind is expressed in *The Third of May* and in *The Family of Charles IV*.
8. How is naturalism seen in the paintings of Delacroix? In what way is he anti-naturalistic?
9. How is naturalism seen in the paintings of Turner? In what way is he anti-naturalistic?
10. Compare the landscape painting of Constable and Caspar David Friedrich.
11. Who were two of the outstanding architectural designers of the Enlightenment period?
12. How does Gothic revivalism in architecture reflect the Romantic sensibility of the period? Give one painter whose work also reflects Gothic revivalism.

## Glossary

**academy**   a place of specialized study. In the fourth century B.C., Plato and his disciples met in a garden near Athens, named for the hero Academus. The first art academy was the Accademia di Disegno in Florence, organized by Giorgio Vasari in 1563.

**aesthetic**   as a noun, a theory or set of principles that pertains to the nature of beauty. The aesthetic of ugliness, for example, refers to the peculiar effect of pleasure that may be felt under certain circumstances by the perception of the ugly. As an adjective, *aesthetic* refers to the perception of beauty: an aesthetic experience involves the awareness of beauty.

**chinoiserie**   decorative motifs based on Chinese designs which became very popular in Europe in the eighteenth century. Used particularly for furniture, porcelain, and other household articles.

**empiricism**   the philosophic theory that holds experience to be the sole source of knowledge. The human mind is a *tabula rasa* at birth, a "smoothed tablet," an empty slate which registers information received by experience, perceived by the senses.

**façade**   in architecture, usually the front or "face" of a building; can sometimes also refer to the sides and back of a structure.

**foreshortening**   a method of presenting three-dimensional objects in two-dimensional space so that the visual illusion matches the real visual effect. A human face represented on a canvas in a three-quarter view is *foreshortened*.

**genre**   a category of subject matter in art that deals with the realistic representation of people in characteristic activities of everyday life, most often in leisure moments.

**hierarchical**   pertaining to the classification of persons, objects, or ideas (such as values) in accordance with their relative positions of importance or power. The hierarchy of medieval values would place chivalry at the top and hard work at the bottom.

**iconography**   the study of images in art in terms of their symbolic content. In a painting of the Virgin Mary, for example, lilies in a vase would symbolize purity.

**idealization**   in art, the representing of form so as to approach perfection according to an *idea* of what perfect form may be for any particular form: the absolutely perfect does not exist in the sensual world.

**isocephalic**   the arrangement of two or more human figures so that their heads are at the same level.

**linear**   refers to the method of representing forms as delimited by their contours, in contrast to the painterly methods, which represents form primarily in terms of mass.

**monumental**   the expression of grandeur, regardless of size.

**naturalism**   the faithful representation of phenomena so as to match their appearance as they are perceived in the  world of the senses. Implies a commitment to such representation.

**odalisque**   a female harem slave in Near-East cultures.

**painterly**   see linear.

**pastel**   composed of pigments ground and compressed into chalk-like sticks. Also refers to light, pale colors.

**picture plane**   the surface of the picture.

**phenomenon**   an object perceptible to the senses. Plural, *phenomena.*

**rationalism**   the philosophic theory that reason is the primary source of knowledge, independent of sense perception. For the opposing view, see above, *empiricism.*

**severe style**   used in connection with Greek classical sculpture in the fifth century B.C., in which the geometrical conception of the figure is apparent, contrasted with the more curvilinear "graceful" style of the following century.

**still life**   a painting representing an arrangement of inanimate objects such as flowers and fruits.

**trompe l'oeil**   literally, "fool the eye." A representation, usually of inanimate objects, painted with such verisimilitude as to trick the viewer into believing they are actually three dimensional.

## Artists, Patrons, and Important Personages

**Alembert, Jean le Rond d'** (1717–1783). French mathematician and philosopher.

**Bacon, Francis** (1561–1626). British philosopher and statesman. Father of the inductive method of modern science.

**Banks, Sir Joseph** (1743–1820). British naturalist. Accompanied Captain James Cook on his voyage around the world and made a large collection of biological specimens. Most of the plants were previously unclassified. Botany Bay, in Australia, was named on this voyage.

**Blake, William** (England, 1757–1827). Poet and painter. Except for *Poetical Sketches,* he published his own books from copper plates on which he engraved both the text (written backwards) and the drawings. They were then hand colored by himself or his wife.

**Boucher, François** (France, 1703–1770). A classicizing Rococo artist, he was the most fashionable painter of his day.

**Boullée, Etienne-Louis** (France, 1728–1799). Visionary architect. His designs were austerely geometrical, and were planned on a scale of such magnitude that they could not then be built.

**Bourbon.** French royal family with branches in Italy and Spain. Except for the Napoleonic era, the Bourbons ruled in France from Henry IV (1589) to Charles X (1830).

**Burlington, Earl of** (Richard Boyle) (1694–1753). Wealthy British amateur architect, most powerful supporter of Palladian architecture in eighteenth-century England.

**Byron, George Gordon, Lord** (1788–1824). British poet, social lion of London in 1811, social outcast in 1816. He died after a short illness in Missolonghi, where he had gone to work for Greek independence in the war against Turkey.

**Chardin, Jean-Baptiste** (France, 1699–1779). Best known for his still life and genre paintings, he is widely recognized as an outstanding colorist in the history of French art.

**Charles IV.** King of Spain, 1788–1808.

**Charles X.** King of France, 1824–1830.

**Cole, Thomas** (England, 1801–1848). Although born in England, Cole is properly classified as an American artist. He was the most accomplished of the "first generation" Hudson River School landscape painters, those artists who painted in the Hudson River Valley during the second quarter of the nineteenth century.

**Constable, John** (England, 1776–1837). One of England's greatest landscape painters.

**Cook, James** (1728–1879). British explorer and navigator. (See above, Joseph Banks).

**Copley, John Singleton** (America, 1738?–1815). The first great master of painting born in America. After a highly successful career in Boston as a portrait artist, he settled in England (1775), where in addition to portraiture he practiced modern history painting.

**Corday, Charlotte** (1768–1793). Stabbed to death Jean Paul Marat, leader of the most radical of the French revolutionary parties, the Jacobins, who had crushed the Girondists, the more moderate revolutionary party to which she adhered.

**Coypel, Antoine** (France, 1661–1722). Member of a French dynasty of painters.

**David, Jacques-Louis** (France, 1748–1825). The premier painter of the Neo-Classical movement.

**Delacroix, Eugène** (France, 1798–1863). Recognized in his own time and ever since as the standard-bearer of nineteenth-century Romanticism.

**Descartes, René** (1596–1650). French philosopher, scientist, and mathematician. Often called the father of modern philosophy, his influence on a wide range of intellectual subjects was immense. His name is almost synonymous with the idea of rationalism. He is associated with the formulation, "I think, therefore I am."

**Diderot, Denis** (1713–1784). French encyclopedist, he was one of the universal geniuses of the modern era. His reviews of art exhibitions at the Salon during the 1760s makes him the founder of modern art criticism.

**Du Barry, Jeanne Bécu, Comtesse** (1743–1793). Mistress of Louis XV of France from 1768 until his death in 1774, when she retired from court life. She was guillotined in 1793.

**Fielding, Henry** (1707–1754). One of the major figures in the emergence of the English novel as a significant literary form. A social and political satirist, his characteristic and most famous works are *Tom Jones* and *Joseph Andrews.*

**Flaxman, John** (England, 1755–1820). Sculptor and draftsman. Flaxman's drawings of subjects from *The Iliad* and *The Odyssey* were highly influential in the shift of taste from severe Classicism to the Mannerist revival. Professor of sculpture at the Royal Academy, in 1816 he was able to persuade the British government to purchase the sculpture fragments brought to England by Lord Elgin (known ever since as the Elgin marbles), which include parts of the Parthenon frieze.

**Fragonard, Jean Honoré** (France, 1732–1806). Rococo painter; a master of the loose, sketchy method of applying paint. Fragonard's works convey a peerless sense of gaiety and wit.

**Friedrich, Caspar David** (Germany, 1774–1804). Friedrich's fusion of minutely observed, realistic landscape with religious content created paintings that are the last convincing mystical images in Western art.

**Fuseli, Henry** (1741–1825). Although born in Zurich, Fuseli lived in England for almost fifty years and is properly classified as a British painter. His art belongs to the eerie and erotic current of his time.

**Gérard, François** (France, 1770–1837). Classicizing artist trained in the studio of David.

**Girodet, Anne-Louis** (France, 1757–1824). Trained in David's studio, he was one of the artists who shifted to a manneristic style in the 1790s.

**Goya, Francisco** (Spain, 1746–1828). The greatest painter of his time, his range included sympathetic portraits of intellectual contemporaries, and subject matter of peerless savagery.

**Greuze, Jean-Baptiste** (France, 1725–1805). Master of the melodramatic, his moralizing images seem quaint to modern eyes; some of his representations of young women attract prurient attention and were no doubt meant to do so.

**Gros, Antoine Jean** (France, 1771–1835). One of David's favorite pupils, Gros's move away from Classicism took him into the neo-Baroque style in which he produced his most memorable paintings.

**Herschel, Caroline** (1750–1848). British astronomer, born in Germany. Author of the *Index to Flamsteed's Observations of the Fixed Stars*, she was a close collaborator in the work of her brother, William.

**Herschel, William** (1738–1822). British astronomer, born in Germany. His discovery of the planet Uranus was only one of the enormous contributions he made to astronomical knowledge.

**Hogarth, William** (England, 1697–1764). One of the most famous graphic masters in Western art and a penetrating portraitist. *The Analysis of Beauty* (1753), in which he set forth his art theory, became one of the most widely read and influential books among artists of the eighteenth century.

**Ingres, Jean-Auguste** (France, 1780–1867). Widely considered the standard-bearer of nineteenth-century Neo-Classicism, he was one of the greatest draftsmen in Western art.

**Jovellanos, Don Gaspar Melchor de** (1744–1811). Spanish statesman and poet; an important patron of Goya, who painted his portrait in 1798.

**Kent, William** (England, 1684–1748). An important influence on eighteenth-century landscape gardening, Kent collaborated with Lord Burlington (see above) in designing his *Chiswick House*, and was thus an important figure in rooting Palladian architecture in England.

**Labrouste, Henri** (France, 1801–1875). Designer of the *Bibliothèque Ste. Geneviève*, one of the first architects to make effective use of iron construction.

**Largillière, Nicolas de** (France, 1654–1746). A transition figure between Poussinist Classicism and Rubenist-inspired Rococo.

**Le Brun, Charles** (France, 1619–1690). Organizer of the French Academy, he exerted immense influence in formulating and propagating academic theory, and in giving the Academy the power it more or less retained until the late nineteenth century.

**Ledoux, Claude Nicolas** (France, 1736–1806). Can be said to have "translated" Newton into architecture with his massive geometric structures.

**Linnaeus (Karl von Linne)** (1707–1778). Swedish botanist who founded the modern system of classification of plants.

**Locke, John** (1632–1704). English philosopher, founder of British empiricism (see Glossary). The influence of his *Essay on Human Understanding* is beyond measure, and his political theory provided the philosophical basis for republicanism in the eighteenth century. He both reflects and

further inspired the naturalist sensibility that emerged in his lifetime and is still flourishing.

**Louis Phillippe** (1773–1850). King of the French from 1830 to 1848. His reign is known as the "July Monarchy" because it began with the three-day revolution of July 1830.

**Marat, Jean Paul** (1743–1793). A leader of the Jacobins, the extreme left wing of the revolutionary movement in France, which had crushed the more moderate Girondists. See above, Charlotte Corday.

**Mengs, Anton Raphael** (Germany, 1728–1779). Prominent in Italy during the 1750s, he was called to Madrid where he became painter to Charles III and introduced an academic classicizing style into Spanish art which Goya eventually had to confront.

**Napoleon I** (1769–1821). Emperor of the French, 1804–1814. The greatest military genius of modern times, Napoleon was ruthless in suppressing opposition but promoted liberalism, introduced an admirable law code, and improved the economic conditions of the French. The Empire style in furniture and fashion, created during his reign, has some of the manneristic-classicizing features of contemporary painting.

**Newton, Sir Isaac** (1642–1727). British physicist and philosopher. One of the greatest scientists of his time, his influence on the thought of the eighteenth century was profound and far-reaching. His demonstration of the nature of light had important consequences for color theory in art.

**Pompadour, Marquise de** (1721–1764). Mistress of Louis XV. Born into the middle class, she was highly intelligent, very beautiful, and witty; she acquired immense power over the king and for a time became virtual ruler of France. She supported the work of the *Encyclopédie*, and was an active patron of the arts, especially of decorative painting for her residences.

**Pope, Alexander** (1688–1744). British poet. His *Essay on Criticism* accurately reflects the taste of his times.

**Revere, Paul** (1735–1818). Leading silversmith and engraver, and midnight rider of Longfellow's poem.

**Richardson, Samuel** (1689–1761). British novelist. His moralizing, sentimental style met with extraordinary success in *Pamela: or Virtue Rewarded* (1740) and *Clarissa: or the History of a Young Lady* (1748). The dates of his work indicate the rise of this sentimental mode, which is reflected in France in the following decades in the work of Greuze.

**Rousseau, Jean-Jacques** (1712–1778). French philosopher, social theorist, composer, and writer. The influence of his thought in politics, in literature, and in education is incalculable, and his sensitive response to nature, reflected in his writings, is widely held to have given rise to the romantic sensibility.

**Soufflot, Jacques Germain** (France, 1713–1780). Chiefly remembered as the architect of the building now called the Panthéon, originally constructed as the Church of Ste. Geneviève.

**Trumbull, John** (America, 1756–1843). A "founding father" of American art and follower of Benjamin West in the development of modern history painting. His most famous work is *The Declaration of Independence*.

**Turner, Joseph Mallard William** (England, 1775–1851). The greatest landscape and seascape artist in British art history. His cosmic vision transformed landscape and seascape into symbols of nature's mighty forces and metaphors for human passion. It is likely that he exerted posthumous influence on the development of Impressionism, especially in Monet.

**Vanbrugh, Sir John** (England, 1664–1726). Vanbrugh's masterpiece is Blenheim Palace, the most extravagant example of Baroque architecture in England.

**Vien, Maria Joseph** (France, 1716–1809). An early convert to Neo-Classicism, Vien retained some of the Rococo style in which he had been trained. He was a teacher of Jacques-Louis David.

**Voltaire (François Marie Arouet)** (1694–1778). French philosopher and author. One of the most productive intellectuals of his time, Voltaire maintained a massive correspondence with the most prominent men and women among his contemporaries. His novels and pamphlets, in which he attacked the prevalent values embodied in established institutions, found their anonymous way all over Europe. His most widely read novel in modern times is *Candide*, which scoffs at mindless optimism.

**Walpole, Horace** (1717–1797). British author, whose letters mirror Georgian England. His "Gothic castle" *Strawberry Hill* became a showplace in its time and exerted important influence on the rise of Gothic taste in architecture. His novel *The Castle of Otranto* also contributed to the Gothicizing taste of late eighteenth- and early nineteenth-century England.

**Watteau, Jean-Antoine** (Flanders [Belgium], 1684–1721). Painter; founder of Rococo art. He was highly influential in the shift from the classicizing Baroque art of Poussin and his followers, notably Charles Le Brun.

**West, Benjamin** (America, 1738–1820). His remarkable career took him from the backwoods of Pennsylvania to President of the British Royal Academy (1792). Influential in the development of Neo-Classicism in England, he also reintroduced contemporary history painting, and then moved ahead to anticipate Romanticism.

**Winckelmann, Johann** (1717–1768). German archaeologist and classical scholar. His *History of the Art of Antiquity* provided the basis for modern art historical methods.

# Bibliography

*Note:* The titles listed below are books (including exhibition catalogues) published in English, except for references to illustrations. For special aspects of an artist's work you should consult the *Art Index* and the *Répertoire Internationale de la Littérature de l'Art* (RILA), which will guide you to articles in periodicals.

### PICTORIAL REFERENCES *IN ADDITION TO* JANSON, GARDNER, AND HONOUR & FLEMING
Fleming, W. *Arts and Ideas.* 7th ed. New York, 1986.
Pool, P. *Delacroix.* London, 1969.
Rosenblum, R. and H.W. Jausou. *Nineteenth Century Art.* New York, 1984.
Rosenblum, R. *Ingres.* New York, 1967.

### SURVEYS IN THE PERIOD CA. 1700–1850
Brion, M. *Art of the Romantic Era: Romanticism, Classicism, Realism.* New York, 1966.
Braham, A. *The Architecture of the French Enlightenment.* Berkeley, 1980.
Clark, K. *The Gothic Revival.* New York, 1970.
———. *The Romantic Rebellion: Romantic versus Classical.* New York, 1974.

Conisbee, P. *Painting in Eighteenth-Century France.* Ithaca, N.Y., 1981.
Friedlaender, W. *From David to Delacroix.* New York, 1968.
Herrmann, L. *British Landscape Painting of the Eighteenth Century.* New York, 1974.
Honour, H. *Neo-Classicism.* New York, 1979.
———. *Romanticism.* New York, 1979.
Irwin, D. *English Neo-Classical Art.* London, 1966.
Kalnein, W. G., and Levey, M. *Art and Architecture of the Eighteenth Century in France.* New York, 1973.
Macaulay, J. *The Gothic Revival.* Glasgow, 1975.
Novotny, F. *Painting and Sculpture in Europe, 1780–1880,* 2nd ed. Harmondsworth, England, 1978.
*Rococo to Romanticism: Art and Architecture 1700–1850,* The Garland Library of the History of Art, vol. 10. New York, 1976.
Rosenblum, R. *Transformations in Late Eighteenth Century Art.* Princeton, 1967.
——— and Janson, H. W. *Nineteenth Century Art.* New York, 1984.
Waterhouse, E. K. *Painting in Britain, 1530–1790,* 4th ed. New York, 1978.
Wittkower, R. *Art and Architecture in Italy, 1600–1750.* New York, 1980.

### ARTISTS
**William Blake.** David Bindman. *Blake as an Artist.* Oxford, 1977.
**François Boucher.** Alexandre Amanoff. *François Boucher.* Lausanne, Paris, 1976.
**Jean-Baptiste Simeon Chardin.** Georges Wildenstein. *Chardin,* rev. ed. Trans. Stuart Gilbert. Oxford, 1969.
**John Constable.** Basil Taylor. *Constable: Paintings, Drawings and Watercolors,* 2nd ed. London, 1975.
**Jacques-Louis David.** Antoine Schnapper. *David.* Trans. Helga Harrison. New York, 1982.
———. David L. Dowd. *Pageant Master of the Republic: Jacques-Louis David and the French Revolution.* Lincoln, Nebr., 1948; reprint, 1969.
**Eugène Delacroix.** Frank Trapp. *The Attainment of Delacroix.* Baltimore, 1970.
**Jean-Honoré Fragonard.** David Wakefield. *Fragonard.* London, 1976.
**Caspar David Friedrich.** Traeger Jörg. *Caspar David Friedrich.* New York, 1976.
**Théodore Géricault.** Lorenz Eitner. *Géricault, His Life and Work.* London, 1983.
**Francisco Goya.** Pierre Gassier and Juliet Wilson. *The Life and Complete Works of Francisco Goya,* 2nd ed. New York, 1981.
———. José Gudiol. *Goya, 1746–1828.* Barcelona, 1971.
**Jean-Baptiste Greuze.** Anita Brookner. *Greuze: The Rise and Fall of an Eighteenth Century Phenomenon.* London, 1972.
**William Hogarth.** Ronald Paulson. *Hogarth: His Life, Art and Times.* New Haven, 1971.
**Jean-August Ingres.** Robert Rosenblum. *Ingres.* New York, 1967.
**Joseph Mallard William Turner.** Martin Butlin and Evelyn Joll. *The Paintings of J. M. W. Turner.* 2 vols. New Haven, 1977.
**Antoine Watteau.** Donald Posner. *Antoine Watteau.* London, 1984.
**Benjamin West.** Helmut von Erffa and Allen Staley. *The Paintings of Benjamin West.* New Haven, 1986.

# Realism, Impressionism, and Post-Impressionism

## Learning Objectives

This chapter surveys the foundations of modernism. You should note the three areas of emphasis in the treatment of this material, two of which are formal, dealing with style in the narrower sense of *how* a work of art is made—the kinds of color, line, space, brush stroke, or textural surface that are used, for example; the third is cultural, dealing with subject matter and expression. Thus emphasis is placed on the particular contributions to modernism made by each of the seminal artists, who will be considered—contributions that are both formal and cultural. Internal development of styles will also be explored, that is the connections between movements—how Courbet's Realism broke with the prevailing styles of the first half of the nineteenth century and thus prepared the ground for the further revolutionary aesthetics of Impressionism, and how Post-Impressionist painting built on the advances made by Impressionism while at the same time rejecting some of its basic principles.

Together with this internal development of styles, the program and texts will lay out some basic features of Western culture that shaped the sensibility and thus the aesthetic perceptions of the artists who played leading roles in creating the new art. You will discover how Realism, Impressionism, and Post-Impressionism reflect these factors of internal development and general cultural values both in their formal aspects and in their subject matter.

In dealing with each of the major artists, we have selected key works that trace the stylistic explorations of that artist's career and also call attention to shifts in subject matter at various times, where pertinent. You will understand, on the basis of style and subject matter, and in a broad, general way, not only how to identify these artists by recognizing their individual formal styles—the nature of their characteristic colors, shapes, textures, brush strokes, and spatial relationships— but also how to make a fairly reliable estimate of when the painting was executed. For example, knowing Renoir's style in the mid-1870s, when he painted *Le Moulin de la Galette* (a

scene of contemporary life in Paris) and his very different style in 1885, when he painted *The Bathers* (based on a seventeenth-century sculptural relief), you will be able to relate other works by Renoir to these, and thus be able to locate them generally in the context of his career.

Biographical information has been kept to a minimum, giving only those facts that entered directly into the artist's professional life. Since these facts are obviously significant, you should be comfortably familiar with them. Remember, you cannot have Mary Cassatt painting a picture influenced by Degas *before* she met Degas: therefore it is important to notice *when* she met him.

This unit will take you to the end of the nineteenth century. It is meant to prepare you step-by-step for the radical changes that occurred in the very first decade of the twentieth century. Each step in the advance of the vanguard toward the future must be carefully noted and integrated into the narrative flow of history.

In this unit, you will:

- Gain a working knowledge of the major styles and trends appearing in the visual arts during the second half of the nineteenth century;
- Understand the formal characteristics of innovative art movements in terms of new approaches to color, shapes, lines, light, space, or composition;
- Discover the critical linkages between an evolving notion of "modernism" as expressed by social, scientific, literary, and political currents and their expression in the visual arts;
- Appreciate how each experimental stage brought one set of aesthetic problems to a degree of resolution while opening new paths for further artistic issues and styles;
- Recognize which artists were celebrated as traditional exemplars of the Beaux Arts manner (i.e., Bouguereau, Repin, Sargent, Eakins) and which personalities (Manet, Monet, Lautrec, Van Gogh, Gauguin) successfully launched their avant-gardist assault upon academic art;
- Learn how to identify the characteristic styles and approaches of the leading visual artists in terms of techniques, subject matter, and point of view;

■ Enjoy the accelerating flow of movements and masters contributing to the visual arts and inevitably transforming the nineteenth century as the spanning bridge into the modern world.

## *Part 1* REALISM AND IMPRESSIONISM

## Historical Background

In 1829 George Stephenson demonstrated the practicality of the steam engine for locomotion with this famous (and prophetically named) locomotive, *Rocket*. In 1844 Samuel F. B. Morse demonstrated the practicality of his telegraph. In 1845 the practicality of the screw-propeller steamship was demonstrated in an Atlantic crossing. By mid-nineteenth century, practicality, demonstration, and speed were the terms that defined the modern Western world. No one living in Western culture was unaffected by the mind-set that assumed the priority of science in discovering truth, and of industrial technology in making truth useful. People communicated with each other faster by far than ever before in human history. They moved over the water faster than wind could blow them, and over the ground for the first time faster than a horse could carry them. This exponential leap in the human ability to control nature penetrated every human experience and inevitably created a new sensibility, for some—especially artists and intellectuals—more quickly than for others. The essence of modern sensibility was speed. The line from the locomotive to instant coffee is perfectly straight.

There were numerous other new factors that together contributed to the creation of the modern sensibility. Political movements of a socialist or communist nature that began to appear in the course of the nineteenth century, workers' protests that turned into violent uprisings, had raised consciousness with regard to lower classes of society—the proletariat was in itself a new class created by the industrial revolution—and people who had been socially invisible were emerging as socially significant. The poor, the humble, the uneducated became the nineteenth-century's noble savage, Europe's ever-present, waveringly effective corrective for its chauvinism.

In addition to the new proletarian class, there had also emerged the class of the "nouveau riche," the new rich who had made fortunes in developing the new industries brought into being by the industrial revolution, and their associates, the new financial manipulators who were creating the modern economic society. The values of the new entrepreneurs were necessarily different from those who had been born to wealth and privilege, and as the former gained political power commensurate with their

new economic power, their values, too, began to prevail. However, in achieving the status of those with ancestral wealth, many of the new rich took on their manners and tastes, and allied themselves with the traditional cultural institutions, such as the French Royal Academy, and upheld their values. Others—far fewer, of course—began to feel the need for cultural expression that more nearly harmonized with their values, and found themselves drawn into the orbit of those artists who were at odds with the Academy. Thus, a new market, a new patron class, appeared which contributed importantly to the development of modern art.

The heroic struggle of the artists who fought the Academy's power—and won—is the central myth of modernism. Nevertheless, it must be recognized that history was on their side, on the side of those who created the first modernist movement—Impressionism. No hierarchical institution, neither governmental, such as a nation, nor aesthetic, such as an art academy, could remain stable against the upward thrust of the democratic idea. But social movements are slow. It took half a century to destroy the power of the French Royal Academy.

The Academy had established standards, and ruled on all matters of art ever since its founding under Louis XIV in the seventeenth century, as absolutely as the king had reigned. Its chief instrument of control was the Salon, the exhibition where, during the period under discussion, the artists of France annually showed their work. Members of the Academy, many of them teachers in the Ecole des Beaux Arts, France's official school of art, constituted the jury of selection. They favored their own students in deciding on which works to accept, and favored their own styles, which they imparted to their students. This is what is meant by the "academic style"—work that was carefully composed so that there was a hierarchy of interest, the most important idea or figure emphasized by one or another means, with subsidiary ideas or figures arranged by the artist so that the viewer's eyes could be led from one area to another in accordance with the area's relative importance in the entire composition; figures were to be designed as ideal, classical forms; color was to be applied to canvases prepared with a ground (like a base coat) that was graded from dark to light, and laid on with blended brush strokes so that the surface presented a pleasant and elegant finish, with no harsh tones or sharp contrasts; subject matter was usually drawn from ancient history or mythology, with formally composed landscapes and still lifes also represented. The rules for choosing subject matter and executing works were wellknown, accepted practice, and the most successful and prominent artists were those who exhibited the most skill in applying the rules. It should be said that a great many fine paintings were produced by artists who, like Adolphe Bouguereau (1825–1905), for example, were able to push skill to the level of art. But by and large, the Academy system's stress on skill deadened imagination, and its self-perpetuating features inhibited change. The new forces for change in society decreed its doom long before anyone knew it.

Science, too, contributed to the new sensibility. Science had largely replaced religion as the key to knowledge. Purged of non-material elements, knowledge became identified with facticity. The assertion that the proper study of "Man" is "Man" had increasingly been interpreted to take in more and more of "Man's" environment, and microscopic investigations took a closer look in order to analyze the component parts. The taste, the need, the desire for analytical scrutiny brought the world into close-up view. What were things really—people, governments, microbes, and stars? The question led, in art, to Realism.

## Realism

Realism usually refers to a style that aims to achieve verisimilitude, the faithful imitation of natural appearance. It is closely linked to naturalism, but differs in that it often refers to subject matter that reveals the plight of the unfortunate, or social consciousness in a more general sense. Realism was social Truth—the demand was for those depicted to be portrayed so as to express physically their class position in society. (This usually meant the middle and lower classes. Fashionably dressed people in luxurious surroundings hardly ever counted for Realism, no matter how accurately they were portrayed, since an element of pathos usually adheres to the word.) Frederick Engels asserted that the artist's province was "all of men's existence . . . the artist must inform as to the inner workings and meanings of society." In style and subject matter Realism paralleled the dominant intellectual view of the period that what was real was physical, "out there," and thus accessible to investigation and demonstration, to discovery and improvement.

Realism has a time dimension. You cannot see, nor in your lifetime could you ever have seen, the Horatii brothers swearing loyalty to their father nor Vergil and Dante cruising through Hell. Gustave Courbet proclaimed that he would paint only what he could see and touch— no ancient history, no angels for *him*.

His was not a lone voice by any means. As the bracing air of modernity swept through studies and studios around 1850, Europe's century-long love affair with history began to sour. Historicity waned as a new sense of living in a truly modern world began to pervade the liberal sectors of the intellectual and artistic community. Realism was hailed (or condemned by conservatives) as the sign of the times. Out of Realism, modernism was born.

An "ism" by definition is a doctrine. When used as a suffix it often signals a commitment to the idea of the word to which it is appended. Just as the value-neutral, descriptive word "social" becomes ideological when "ism" is added, so with "modern": Modernism connotes a deliberate identification with those elements that most essentially define what is modern; for the modernist, to be up-to-date is an important value. The speed of social change began to accelerate at mid-century at an unprecedented rate, and, as Honoré Daumier said, "one had to be of one's time." While the majority of people were, as always, conservative, the pressures for change were irresistible, although the majority resisted. The new was fought on all fronts, and in art, modernism's battle was fought by artists who came to be known by a military term, the avant-garde.

The beginning was not earth-shaking, but it was earthy. Realism had its roots in naturalism. Although Delacroix and Ingres held their preeminent positions in the art world, young artists around mid-century were turning away from the grand, both Romantic and Classical. The naturalism of the earlier decades, granted that it produced a Constable and a Corot, and in the United States a Cole and a Church, had not represented the high style of the period; now naturalism began to win over large numbers of artists.

A specialized study of Western art at mid-century would reveal that a mood of quietude swept over European and American painting. In France, Camille Corot (1797–1875), who earlier had painted Poussinesque landscapes such as *Papigno* (1826) **(J 848)** structured by architecture but drenched in bright sunlight, now shifted to the filmy, twilight scenes like *Memory of Mortefontaine* (1864) (Rosenblum/Janson fig. 21) which brought him his greatest success. The shift coincides with his return from Italy in 1843, when he began to paint in the countryside around Barbizon, a small village in the forest of Fontainebleau. Here an artists' colony had been growing that eventually took on an identification as a movement—the Barbizon School—synonymous with a kind of landscape and figure painting that ennobled their humble subjects while remaining faithful to appearance.

The most famous of the Barbizon artists was Jean-François Millet (1814–1875), a painter of peasants who monumentalized his subjects in a figure style and in poses that transformed them into heros of the soil. Characteristic are his *Man with a Hoe* (1852–62) **(H&F 15.24)**; *The Gleaners* (1857) **(G 21.35)**; and *The Sower* (ca. 1850) **(J 846)**. The most important landscapists of the Barbizon School were Charles François Daubigny (1817–1878) and Theodore Rousseau (1812–1867), whose *Under the Birches* (1842–43) (Rosenblum/Janson clpl 30) reveals the importance of this movement in its influence on some of the artists who will develop the aesthetics of Impressionism. The Barbizon painters sketched on the spot the gnarled trees, the cows and sheep standing like still lifes near mirror-smooth and gleaming ponds, but they used these sketches as models for studio paintings, and were still more or less following the traditions of Dutch and English painting. Their innovation was in their insistence on capturing the look of nature as it is, without idealizing or romanticizing. That they did in fact idealize and romanticize reveals the strength of tradition and the difficulty of making sharp breaks, as well as that aspect of the sensibility of the period which we think of as Victorian.

Barbizon naturalism is assertive, urging the superior values of the country over the city, and country people over city people. These artists painted—created—in rural Barbizon; they only exhibited and sold their creations in Paris. It is here that we begin to see clearly the roots of the society-alienated artist, characteristic of modern times. The artists' life-style was going to be sharply different from that of their patrons, not *only* because of the difference in wealth, but even more important, because of the difference in values. In the early years of the twentieth century, Apollinaire, spokesman for the avant-garde, will speak of the artists' right and duty to "épater la bourgeoisie"—shock the middle class—as many had been doing ever since Gustave Courbet (1819–1877).

## Courbet

The middle and upper classes who frequented the Salon were indeed shocked at what seemed to them to be the gross ugliness of Courbet's painting. The boldness of his style and the matter-of-fact depiction of his clumsy country folk were not to their delicate and refined taste. The figures in his *Burial at Ornans* (1849) **(G 21.38; H&F 15.20)**, which was exhibited at the Salon in 1850–51, are life-size, which affronted people accustomed to associating large-scale figures with grand history paintings such as Thomas Couture's *Romans of the Decadence* (1847) **(G 21.27)**, a thinly disguised attack on the regime of Louis Philippe. The large scale conferred an importance on these country folk that Parisians found totally inappropriate. The critics, while admiring Courbet's power and vigor, and his obviously superior craftsmanship, were also put off by his "brutal" imagery. His good friend Félix Nadar, a pioneering photographer, addressed him directly in a Salon review in which he wrote, "Coarseness is not strength, any more than brutality is frankness." Jules-François Champfleury, a stanch defender, asked, "Is it the painter's fault if material interests, the life of a small town, sordid egotisms, provincial shabbiness leave their stamp on the face, quench the face, wrinkle the forehead, besot the mouth?" He anticipated that *Burial at Ornans* would be called a "masterpiece of the ugly." Some compared Courbet with Caravaggio, the seventeenth-century apostle of Realism; some spoke of him as a kind of rag-picker of art, "spearing the truth in the mud of the streets."

Truth to tell, Courbet was not all that committed to thoroughgoing Realism. The *Burial at Ornans*, in which the townspeople of Courbet's birthplace are gathered to pay their last respects to the dead, traditionally taken to be a paradigm of mid-century Realism, has recently been shown by Yvonne Korshak to incorporate a number of symbolic features, which of course compromises its Realism. The funeral turns out to be that of Courbet's grandfather Oudot, who is also represented *as if alive* at his own burial: he is at the left, just behind the coffin. Oudot was a longtime, deeply convinced Republican who had been a revolutionary partisan during the French Revolution. Courbet had absorbed from early childhood the political radicalism of his grandfather. Although profoundly disappointed by the defeat of the Second Republic which had triumphed over the monarchy of King Louis Philippe in the February Revolution of 1848 but which ended with the dictatorship in 1849 of Louis Napoleon (two years later, Emperor Napoleon III), the artist always remembered Grandfather Oudot's slogan, "Shout loudly and march straight ahead." Republicanism would never die, and thus Oudot, its symbol, as Korshak maintains, is represented as both dead and still living, a Realist impossibility, but a spiritual truth for a believer.

The two figures to the left of the grave were friends of Oudot and veterans of the French Revolution; they are dressed in the clothes of that period. They would have been quite elderly, but Courbet represents them as much younger, symbolizing the eternal youth of the revolutionary spirit.

The idea of the ageless, undying spirit linked to the eventual resurrection of the Republic is also stressed by the crucifix, which is raised high over the procession accompanying the coffin. Furthermore, the cemetery depicted is the *new* cemetery, where one would not find old, disinterred bones such as those in the foreground of *Burial*. The presence of the old bones symbolizes, once again, death and resurrection.

Korshak's final argument in dealing with the non-realist elements in *Burial* pertains to the transformation of religious imagery into secular imagery, the beginnings of which we have observed in eighteenth-century painting. In Courbet's painting, too, that transformation is evident. As Korshak writes, "Synthesizing his personal and political world, the death of his grandfather in 1848 with the failure of the Revolution of 1848, the artist mourns both. However, moving beyond despair, through a reinterpretation of funerary images that express faith in the ultimate triumph of life in the Christian sense, Courbet expresses his belief in the fundamental and continuing vitality of the idea of Revolution."

Probably the painting most written about in Courbet's oeuvre is *Interior of My Studio, A Real Allegory Summing Up Seven Years of My Life* (1854–55) **(J clpl 117)**. The painting was refused by the jury for the 1855 Salon exhibition, and the artist built a temporary gallery to exhibit it, together with the *Burial* and a number of other works. It puzzled its contemporaries—Delacroix found it ambiguous although superbly painted—and has stimulated a number of modern commentaries. The most intriguing among recent exegeses is that by Hélène Toussaint, which we will come to presently. First let us take in the scene.

At the center of the tripartite composition is Courbet

in the act of painting a landscape in his studio. In front of him stands a child who watches with innocent eye, symbol of perception unmediated by culturally absorbed assumptions and thus an allegorical figure of "truth." The Realist artist does indeed surround himself with truth, for behind him is his muse, the naked "Truth." On the back wall hang some of his paintings, which identify the locale as his studio. A group of well-dressed people are placed at the right, balanced by a motley assortment of people on the left.

Courbet described both groups: on the right is the art world peopled by his friends; prominent at the far right, reading, is Charles Baudelaire, one of the greatest of nineteenth-century French poets and a profoundly discerning art critic. His Salon criticism in 1846, titled "On the Heroism of Modern Life," exerted an important influence not only on Courbet but even more decisively on the young Edouard Manet. On the left is the other, commonplace world where misery, poverty, wealth, the exploiters and exploited are represented—characters to serve as models for his paintings.

Courbet's subtitle, "A Real Allegory," a contradiction in terms, does not seem justified on the basis of only the two allegorical figures of truth at the center. Writers have pondered Courbet's meaning, which they knew was deliberately obscured. "It is rather mysterious," Courbet wrote in a letter of 1854, while still working on the painting. "Let who will, guess!" Hélène Toussaint's research seems to have met the challenge. The mystery concerns the group on the left, she shows, each figure of which represents both a contemporary personnage and an allegory for either hypocrisy or heroism.

This is not the place to review the whole cast of characters but we can point out one of each category. In the center of the group is a man who is shown as a traveling salesman selling his wares. This represents Victor Fialin de Persigny, a Republican turncoat who helped engineer the coup d'état that made Louis Napoleon emperor. Rewarded with an appointment as Minister of the Interior, Persigny was tireless in "selling" the Second Empire to whoever would buy, such as the Turk and the Chinese to whom he is offering his "goods." On the other hand, the fourth standing figure from the left is one of Courbet's heroes, Garibaldi, in the costume of a hunter.

There is furthermore another level of meaning which Toussaint finds in *The Painter's Studio*. The painting, she claims with interesting evidence to support her, is a disguised symbol for Freemasonry, a still-flourishing secret society that has often been at odds with religious and government establishments. As for Courbet's Realism, Toussaint points out that the tumble of clothes to which the cat is reacting can be seen as a kind of animal creature with its head between its paws, snapping at the cat. Here Courbet seems to have invented a new kind of Realism that we may call Fantastic Realism, in addition to his once-mysterious Allegorical Realism!

On the easel in *The Painter's Studio* is a landscape, and we must not forget that Courbet was a landscape painter as well as a figure painter. What the *Studio* tells us, of course, is that while Courbet made sketches outdoors in nature, he actually painted his landscapes in the studio. Nevertheless, his cliffs have the hardness of tactile and visual experience, and scenes such as *The Shaded Stream* (1865) (Rosenblum/Janson fig. 218) completely capture the sense of presence and of unarranged nature. Unlike Barbizon painting where one finds overtones of moral sermonizing, in Courbet's nature the material world is reflected for itself.

## Manet

Where does modernism begin? Some would say with Courbet. Writing in 1876, well into the Impressionist years, Edmond Duranty, a leading critic, considered him to be one of the founders of modernism, while Théodore Duret, writing in 1922, called attention to Courbet's influence on Cézanne, by implication placing Courbet in the forefront of the aesthetic revolution. More, however, would say Edouard Manet (1832–1883), because his radical break with traditional techniques laid the groundwork for modernist painting methods, and also probably because Courbet was such a one-man show. He was not identified with a group movement, a feature that became characteristic of modernism. By contrast Manet was: more than that, Manet was seen as the leader of the group of young artists who were creating a new kind of art in the late sixties, only a few years after he had made his first impact.

The group took to meeting at the Café Guerbois most evenings, when daylight dimmed and it was no longer possible to work. There one would find Edgar Degas, Théodore Fantin-Latour, Camille Pissaro, sometimes Paul Cézanne, and beginning in 1869, Claude Monet, Pierre-Auguste Renoir, Frédéric Bazille, and Alfred Sisley, plus a few sympathetic critics. They gathered together regularly, and through their informal table talk, which sometimes became heated argument, they gradually clarified their ideas about the aesthetic issues of the day: what to paint and how to paint it.

They were not radical in confronting those issues. Even conservative critics complained about the boring, stale art produced by the Academy. The novelist and critic, Théophile Gautier, not conservative but at the center of French intellectual life, expressed the situation as so many saw it even in 1853: "Today art has at its disposal only dead ideas and formulas that no longer correspond to its needs. . . . It is well known that something must be done—but what?" What indeed. It was in their solution to the problem that the future Impressionists were radical.

Out of the countless discussions at the Café Guerbois, and the artists' constant thinking and experimenting in their studios, a set of ideas more or less loosely coalesced into a style that came to be known as Impressionism. Accepting the Realist principle that art must be about contemporary life, probably first and foremost among the new ideas they proposed was the notion that painting must reflect optical truth: the question they asked was, how does reality *present* itself to us? And their answer assumed the ever-changing nature of our light-, time-, and space-dependent perceptions. To communicate these constant changes on canvas, they saw, it would be necessary to create the sensation of fleeting time and changing light. They thus aimed at achieving spontaneity: to produce immediate, unrehearsed, uncalculated effects, as if catching life on the wing. To accomplish this, various methods were employed, including the technique of the broken brush strokes which look like hurried short dashes of broken-off thoughts—the artist rushing to put down exactly what he sees before him, without taking the time to blend the strokes into smooth, harmonious transitions.

Another method of achieving spontaneity had to do with the new feeling for the casual. The extreme informality of present-day life in the late twentieth century can be seen in its emergent stage in the second half of the nineteenth century, and Impressionist art reflected this in several ways, notably in the momentary poses and gestures of figures, and also in the generalized view in which individual figures and things merge into their surrounding: the result is a general "impression" of a scene casually happened upon rather than a clearly focused account of it. To heighten the effect of freshness, Impressionists used bright, clear colors, and painted on a white ground that reflected light. They worked outdoors, and made finished works on the actual site, instead of bringing sketches back to the studio for careful finishing.

Was Manet an Impressionist? Not exactly. Yet, at certain times and in limited ways, we shall see that his work exhibits important features of Impressionism. But he never participated in the Impressionist exhibitions which began in 1874, when he was very close in friendship to Monet and Renoir, with whom he painted that summer at Argenteuil, on the outskirts of Paris, and he was never committed to *plein-air* painting—executing a work outdoors from start to finish. Nevertheless, John Rewald, whose *History of Impressionism* is still the definitive study of the movement, includes Manet, and to my knowledge there is no book on Impressionism that does not.

Was he a radical? Yes, Manet was a radical in spite of himself. He did not intend to be an aesthetic rebel. He wanted his paintings to be accepted for exhibition at the annual Salons. But his vision and sensibility were modern. He rejected the academic way of constructing space in the framework of mathematical perspective which had dominated Western painting for four hundred years—of seeing with one eye. He rejected the traditional way of realizing plastic form by means of very gradual modula-

tion of light and dark, and of color. He rejected the method of blending brush strokes that gave a finished, polished look to a picture.

In view of all those rejections, it seems strange, now, that Manet was surprised at the scorn, even anger, that his paintings provoked among the majority of critics and the public. A few recognized Manet's genius, including Emile Zola, who would become a prominent, widely read Realist novelist (and defender of Alfred Dreyfus); Charles Baudelaire, the poet-critic portrayed in Courbet's *The Artist's Studio*; Jules Champfleury; and Stephane Mallarmé, among others. But most shared the negative opinion of Paul Mantz, critic for the *Gazette des Beaux Arts*, who in 1863 saw in the portrait of the Spanish dancer *Lola de Valence* (1862) (Philadelphia Museum of Art, *Manet*, pl. 44; Rouart/Orienti clpl XIV) a "caricature of color, not color itself." It was not that painting, however, that in 1863 called down the wrath of the Parisian public and critics on the head of Manet. The barbs of opprobrium and derision were mainly directed at the artist's *Luncheon on the Grass* (*Le Déjeuner sur l'herbe*, 1863) (**J 4; G clpl 21.39**) exhibited at the *Salon des Refusés*.

As explained earlier, the official Salon was the exhibition instrument of the French Academy. There had been a growing and increasingly rebellious resentment among French painters against the Academy, which every year refused more works. The situation came to a boil in 1863 when an unprecedented number of works was turned down. The painters protested to the Emperor. Napoleon III liked to present himself as a liberal and with a great show of concern for the protesters, instructed his Imperial Superintendent of Fine Arts, Count Nieuwerkerke, to arrange for them to exhibit their works in a gallery near the Salon, so that people visiting the official show could also take in the show of those who had been refused, called the Salon des Refusés. Napoleon probably acted with cunning calculation, anticipating the ridicule of the public and the critics who visited the Salon des Refusés. Laugh and sneer they did, giving full justification to the Academy for rejecting these amateurish daubs.

Most of the works exhibited, however, were not really of any interest, but the work that produced a storm of gale magnitude was Manet's *Luncheon on the Grass*, which turned out to be no picnic for the artist. The pun is particularly appropriate here since Manet himself, it seems, has incorporated a pun in his painting: in this period Spanish subjects were all the rage in Paris, and Manet's oeuvre in the 1860s includes many Spanish-inspired paintings. He was, in this period, Spanish-conscious. The word "merienda" in Spanish means a light afternoon meal, equivalent to lunch, and the name of Manet's favorite model at this time, who posed for the nude in *Luncheon*, was Victorine Meurend. Mlle Meurend is the "merienda" on the grass.

The painting is in the well-established tradition of the "fête champêtre," an outdoor gathering of aristocrats enjoying music and dancing in a cosmeticized nature setting.   Although Manet's painting obviously breaks radically from that tradition, it is difficult for viewers in our time to understand its shock effect.   Still, imagine a movie in which is shown a similar group of young people in our own day casually enjoying a picnic—the men in jeans and T-Shirts, and one of the girls naked.   That was *one* of the features to which the Parisian public objected.   Manet could have told the angry viewers that he appropriated the composition from a detail in a work by Raphael, *The Judgment of Paris* **(J 5)** (Manet probably had a pun on the word "Paris" in mind), but that would not have helped—Raphael was depicting gods and goddesses, and anyway they were *all* nude.   Or he could have pointed out that in the nearby Louvre Parisians could see *The Concert*, **(G clpl 17.60;   H&F clpl 11.20)**, a Venetian Renaissance work by Giorgione and/or Titian, in which two male figures, dressed in contemporary Renaissance style, were seated on the grass, making music with two nudes, one seen from the front, the other from the back, giving the viewer a fairly rounded picture of female form.   That would not have soothed anyone's feelings, either, since the Renaissance was long ago, and Italy was far away.   Manet's figures represented modern Parisians;   the scene was of here-and-now, and therefore intolerably vulgar.   Furthermore, the painting was unpleasant;   the bright colors were garish to contemporary eyes, accustomed to toned-down colors.

There is no record of complaint about the still life in the left foreground, although there might well have been.   The tradition of still life is rooted in the formal structural relationship of things that do not move, as Manet well knew.   Objects are displayed on a table in such a way as to stress their immobility and formality.   With wonderful wit, Manet upsets this tradition.   The basket of fruit and

rolls has been casually overturned, compromising its immobility as an object, and the food has spilled out;   one roll is actually on the ground.   The picnic cloth is untidily bunched up, and the entire formality of still life is gone with the new wind that is leveling hierarchies and blowing away old, restrictive social forms even in the southern United States where the Civil War was raging when Manet painted this work.

His own reluctant war of liberation from the past was just beginning.   The Salon des Refusés gave him a true *succès de scandal*;   *Luncheon* made him famous in the Parisian art world, and established his position of leadership among the young artists.   In 1865 he sent *Olympia* (1863) (Rosenblum/Janson clpl 46) to the Salon, where it was accepted—and provoked another scandalous success.   This time it was Titian's *Venus d'Urbino* **(G clpl 17.63;   H&F clpl 11.26)** that he appropriated, a painting he had actually copied when a student.   A comparison of the Titian with *Olympia* tells the whole story of Manet's revolution.

There are obvious similarities to make the visual quotation clear, such as the reclining pose of the two figures, the arrangement of their arms and hands, and the design of the bed sheet pulled up to expose the couch or bed.   These similarities and the double vision we get from seeing both the original and Manet's reinterpretation of it contribute a good deal to the impact of *Olympia*.   It is as if we were to see *Othello* in modern dress, spoken in modern language, with a black war hero marrying a white debutante.

Let us look at the double vision.   Titian's nude, though called "Venus," is actually a woman of the Renaissance period, contemporary with Titian, as Olympia is with Manet.   She seems to be a bride, about to be adorned by

Eduoard Manet, *Olympia,* 1863. Paris, Musée d'Orsay. (SCALA/ ART RESOURCE, NEW YORK)

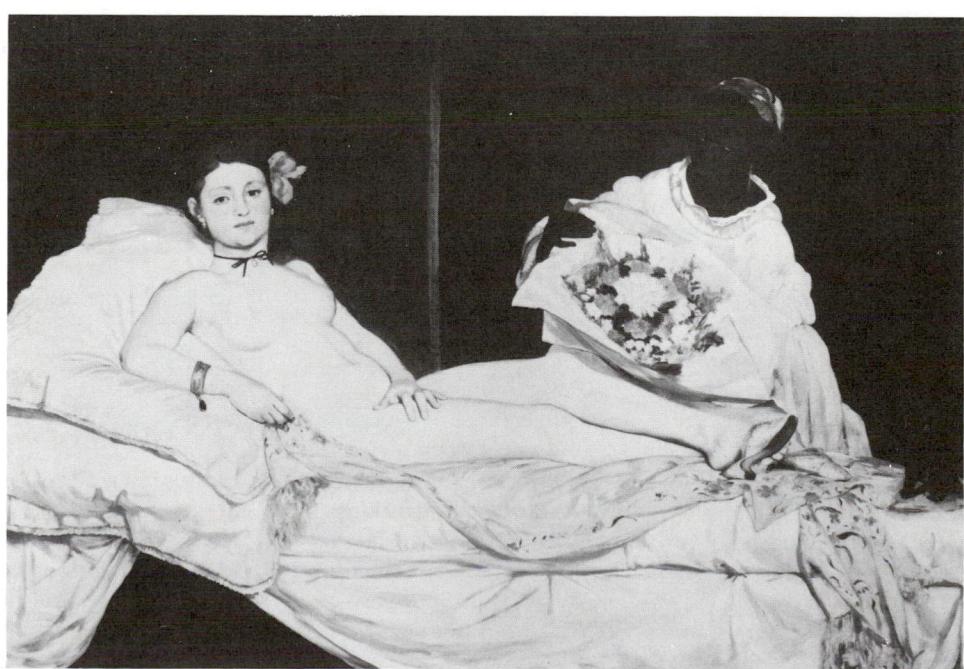

her servants who are busying themselves with the contents of a dowry chest. She wears a bracelet and holds a small bouquet of violets, the flower of shyness. At the foot of the bed a small dog, symbol of fidelity, is curled up. "Venus" sinks softly against the pillow and her gaze modestly avoids that of the viewer. One follows the gentle long curves of her figure and savors slowly the almost imperceptible changes of color tints that render her lovely contours and rounded forms. She is so enveloped in a veil of light-filled atmosphere that she hardly seems nude—and certainly does not look *naked*.

Manet's Olympia is not an upper-class woman, like Titian's "Venus"; she comes from the lower class but lives well as a courtesan, a woman supported by a wealthy man in return for her erotic companionship. Her boudoir and black maid convey her status quickly and baldly, and her name underlines it—Olympia is a courtesan in the younger Alexandre Dumas's novel *La Dame aux Camélias*, titled in English, *Camille*. Instead of a little dog, there is a black cat at the foot of the bed, a symbol of eroticism, in contrast to faithful love. She is receiving a huge bouquet of flowers from her gentleman friend, at the center of which is a large white camelia. The bracelet, neck ribbon, and bedroom slippers accentuate her *nakedness* and, going considerably beyond Courbet's *studio* nude, she looks out boldly at the viewers, coolly and directly challenging them with *her* "naked truth," anticipating by many years the candid sexuality that appears in twentieth-century art. She leans stiffly against a hardly yielding pillow (compare that of "Venus") and looks out boldly at the viewer. The image is aggressive in unmasking hypocrisy and in stating the truth of her type's pervasive presence in Parisian society, a truth that Parisian society found in bad taste to have flung in its face, especially so crudely. Reacting to the ridicule and jeering of the visitors, the directors moved it from its original place in the Salon gallery and hung it in a back room high on the wall where it was hard to see, but crowds kept coming.

Perhaps even more than what Olympia represented, *how the work was painted* was responsible for the scandalized attention it received. It was visually jarring. Instead of the gradual merging of tones as seen in the "Venus" (and accepted academic painting), *Olympia* is painted with abrupt and extreme contrasts so that the foreground with its figures stands out sharply against the back wall and curtain. The viewer's eyes have no time to adjust to the difference between the planes. Speedy transitions also characterize the handling of Olympia's figure: instead of the long sinuous curves of "Venus" over which the eyes can linger, her contours are rendered in relatively straight lines with abrupt, angular turnings; notice, for example, the sharp angle formed by the intersection of her left arm with her left thigh. The restful expression of "Venus" is countered by the impudence of Olympia. Rejecting the humanitarian and sermonizing social realism of the Barbizon School, Manet builds on

Courbet's straightforward, in a sense, flat-voiced, style, as if the subject is presented without comment. But to achieve his startling effects of contrast, he compressed his pictorial space, bringing the figures psychologically close-up to the viewer to enhance the impact. There is no mediating veil of atmosphere that invites the viewer to take time to savor the subtleties of the image; in this new kind of space the image is taken in directly and immediately. Through its formal language Manet's painting reflects the speeded-up sensibility of his time.

Nevertheless, for all of its innovations, Olympia is structured within the tradition of a vertical-horizontal grid that produces stable effects. The wall and curtain, emphasized by the bright vertical strip of red, are countered by the horizontal couch. Olympia, tilted away to the left of the vertical red stripe, is balanced by the maid whose pose tilts her away to the right of the stripe. This will remain the basic structure of Manet's compositions to the end of his life, and will be seen in his last great work, *The Bar at the Folies-Bergère* (**J 871; G 21.41; H&F 17.4;** Rosenblum/Janson clpl 62).

Among the masterpieces of the sixties, his appropriations of Goya's *Shootings of May 3* (**J clpl 114; G 21.10; H&F clpl 15.17**) for his *Execution of Emperor Maximilian* (**H&F clpl 15.26**) and the Spanish master's *Majas on a Balcony* for his *The Balcony* (Rewald, p. 221) reveal with utmost clarity the contrast between the charged expressionism of Romantic painting and the laconic cool objectivity that Manet introduced into modernism: evenly distributed cool blues and greens instead of bursts of hot reds and bright yellows, in the execution paintings; matter-of-fact daylight instead of cloak-and-dagger dusk, in the balcony pictures.

In the seventies Manet was partly won over to Monet's *plein-air* aesthetic, and at Argenteuil he began to paint outdoors. Previously it had been his practice to sketch in the open, when his subject called for it, but to finish such work in the studio. This was his most Impressionist period. He was never committed entirely to *plein-airism*, however, and in this last decade of his life he painted both outdoors and in his studio.

The final major work of his career, *The Bar at the Folies-Bergère*, is a masterpiece of "indoor Impressionism." A barmaid stands in front of a large mirror, the frame of which is parallel to the marble bar in front of her. Her upright pose, the architectural pillars reflected in the mirror, and the bottles establish the formal, vertical-horizontal structure of the composition, the stability of which is strongly reinforced by the isosceles triangle at the center, created by the barmaid with her arms slightly extended to each side. This is *not* an Impressionist design. It is indeed quite classical: recall Leonardo da Vinci's *Last Supper*, with Christ at center forming a similar triangle. But the scintillating chandelier and blur of figures reflected in the mirror, and the light sparkling on the bottles and glass objects, and the scene itself, the ambiance of theatre and night-life, are all characteristics of the Impressionist vision.  As we asked at the start, was Manet an Impressionist?  Not exactly.

Manet's immense contribution to modernist art consists in substantive, expressive, and formal features.  In the first category is his discovery of a completely new subject matter—urban bourgeois everyday life, usually at leisure moments, what we might call *urban genre*, since genre painting had traditionally taken country folk as its subject.  In the second, expressive, category is the cool, casual approach he introduced:  with subjects that had formerly been treated passionately or perhaps lyrically, Manet distanced himself, taking an objective, even, one may say, a scientific attitude.

In formal terms, it is in Manet's work that we begin to see the tendency to compress pictorial space which, together with his manner of applying color flatly, without gradual transitions, and his way of making abrupt color contrasts and sharp linear turns, has the effect of making a more direct impact on the viewer than could be achieved by traditional means.  This impact is *visual*, and Manet made his most important move in the development of modernist art when he set the aesthetics of painting in the direction of pure visibility, the most radical innovation to appear since the Renaissance.  At this juncture it will be useful to look back and then forward, in order to grasp where Manet stands in the history of art.

In the period of the Renaissance, Western culture came to terms with the phenomenal world, and art reflected that fact by learning how to depict the space we live in.  Mathematical perspective was a way of making that space illusionistically visible.  As the values of the phenomenal world rose, the taste for illusionistically represented phenomenal reality grew, and soon artists were appealing not only to the eyes that recognized space, but to the tactile sense that recognized how things felt.  From the seventeenth century on, the senses themselves, all five, were often the subject of painting.

As the taste for analysis developed in Western culture, however, the problem of the nature of things began to absorb primary attention, as we have said, with the result that interest began to be centered on things-in-themselves.  Eventually, philosophy became philosophy about philosophy, political science about political science, music about music, and the visual arts about art.  This meant dealing with the materials of the subject.  Just as music dealt with sound and appealed to hearing, the theory developed that since painting dealt with marks on a surface, it should appeal only to vision.  To achieve this it would be necessary to strip narrative or subject meaning from visual art, since such references gave art the secondary role of mediator, instead of the primary role of being itself.

In a picture that refers to something in the phenomenal world, one looks *through* the surface to its meaning, instead of *at* the surface to see the marks.  When we read a language we understand, we do not notice the printed surface of the page;  the printed words serve to mediate

meaning.  When, however, we are confronted with a book written in Chinese, let us say, when we do not know the characters, we see the marks on the page because we cannot see through them to their meaning—for us, it is as if they do not have meaning.  This is the crux of the modernist issue.

Modernist artists want us to look at their art;  to serve meaning, they hold, is the work of literature.  Thus modernist art has focused on appealing only to our eyes.  To do this it was necessary to emphasize the surface of the painting and, as a result, colors had to be bright, brush marks *noticeable*, and the pictorial space had to be compressed so that a viewer's eye was not allowed to wander into depth—it had to stay on the surface.  Step by step these features were developed by various artists in a number of ways:  that is the story we have to tell, the story of modernist art.  What seemed bright color in the 1860s became brighter color in the following decades;  what seemed individualistic in brush stroke in the early part of the period became much more individualistic as modernist ideas continued to develop;  what seemed flat, in Manet's *Luncheon on the Grass*, became much flatter as artist's wrestled with the problem of the nature of art as primarily marks on a flat surface.  It is worth repeating the key idea here:  the new conception of art was in its character as an object to be looked *at*, for itself, not to be looked *through*, as a mediator of an idea beyond itself.

If we think back to Manet's *Olympia* now, we are ready to consider the meaning of the lack of erotic appeal in the main figure.  The painting painfully wrenches sex out of what one had every right to suppose was a sexual subject.  It is here that we can pinpoint the very faint beginnings of pure visibility:  it is the painting as such, as an artistic composition, that Manet has brought forward, and it is doubtless that this in large measure can account for the anger and ridicule the painting aroused.  Not aware of why, viewers were nevertheless frustrated in their understandable expectations.  Nudes went back in Western art to the Praxitelean Aphrodite of Cnidus and her sculptural progeny **(J 197; G 5.67; H&F 5.4a, 5.4c)**, and were meant to celebrate the beauty of the female body.  This Olympia was no beauty and thus, this was no nude in any artistically familiar sense of the word.  But Manet had created something artistically unfamiliar, and from his time on, the attempt to achieve pure visibility has been a major effort of modernist art.  In the coming decades these features will be more developed:  Manet laid the groundwork.

## Degas

Edgar Degas (1834–1917) designed the most daring compositions of any artist of his time.  Whereas Manet remained in the horizontal-vertical grid structure dictated by the rectangular frame, Degas, from about 1873 to around 1890, up-tilted his pictorial space, and tilted away from the vertical and horizontal the figures and objects within it, so that the diagonals of his design played *against* the rectangle of the frame. The difference is crucially decisive in the expressive result attained by each: horizontals and verticals are absolutes, and convey formal stability; diagonals are relative slants vis-à-vis the horizontal and vertical, and imply movement. Degas's use of this expressive power of diagonals was one of the most important innovations to be made in the developing art of his time.

Although Degas's mature style was based on this inherently anti-classical approach to composition, the most important formative influence on his art was none other than the nineteenth century's standard-bearer of classicism, Ingres. Degas chose to study with Louis Lamothe, because Lamothe had been a pupil of Ingres, and he met the master himself around 1854, whose words to him he never forgot: "Draw lines, young man, and still more lines, both from life and from memory." Degas's early works, apart from portraits of family and friends, were on Ingresque historical themes such as his *Evils Befalling the City of Orleans*, which was accepted at the Salon of 1865.

However, Degas had already begun to turn to modern life for subjects, with paintings sketched at the race track, but finished in his studio. Although he maintained close ties to the Impressionists with whom he exhibited, in the years ahead he, like Manet, never adhered to their *plein-air* principle—painting finished works outdoors on the spot. "It's all very well to copy what you see," Degas said to a friend, "but how much better to draw what only the memory sees. Then you get a transformation, in which imagination works hand in hand with memory and you produce only . . . essentials." Nor was he interested in the momentary, changing effects of light on objects, a key feature of Impressionism. He did share with the Impressionists, however, their aim of creating spontaneous, unstudied effects, which he achieved not at all as they did, through spontaneous, hurried reactions to the motif. "No art is less spontaneous than mine," Degas asserted. "Everything I do is the result of long reflection, of my study of the masters . . . of dogged observation." And he shared, of course, the Impressionists' adherence to modern life as the only appropriate subject for modern art.

His painting *The Cotton Office at New Orleans* (1873) (Rewald, p. 276; Fosca, clpl p. 37) is the first work in which a business office provides the setting. It is basically a genre scene. However, *The Cotton Office* breaks with the leisure tradition of genre, though it is not the first to do so: in American art, William Sidney Mount painted in 1835 a genre scene of two farmers going about the business of bargaining over a horse. But big business, carried on in an urban setting by city dwellers, was new to art—as it was to life. Making it the subject of an important painting thus builds on Courbet's Realist-monumentalizing of the peasant class in *Burial at Ornans* and, also like *Burial*, *The Cotton Office* is totally lacking in romance and glamour.

But there is a further, almost unnoticeable seed germinating in *The Cotton Office*. By reducing the subject to mundane concerns and treating it with such cool matter-of-factness, *subject matter itself becomes less important*. This diminished role of subject matter, here seen in its incipient moment, will become increasingly evident as the role of formal matters—color, line, space—is enhanced. Thus, though with the *Cotton Office* we are still very far away, we are unexpectedly on the road towards the diminishment of subject matter that leads to abstraction and non-objectivity.

One of the vital new influences on the artists of the Café Guerbois group was the Japanese woodcut. In 1854 Commodore Perry had negotiated a treaty with Japan that reopened trade with the West and soon after, the West developed a taste for Japanese objects. According to an oft-repeated story which may well be true, Félix Braquemond, one of the group, came upon some Japanese woodcuts that had been used to wrap tea cups. Excited by this exotic art with its strange reversed perspective and decorative surface, he took a few of the woodcuts to show his friends at the Café.

Degas noticed in these Japanese compositions how the genre scenes offered a sharp sense of the momentary—not through the play of light, as we shall see in Monet, but by means of the momentary pose or gesture, and by the technique of cutting through figures at the picture's margins and by vertical objects within the design. As can be observed in his *Women on the Terrace* (ca. 1877) (**H&F 17.13**; Fosca, clpl p. 64), this gives an unplanned effect to the scene, such as *later* became popular with "candid camera" shots.

In this connection, it should be carefully noted that the widely accepted notion that photography channeled art into abstraction because the camera could better capture the look of the world, thereby pressing the artists to look for an alternative vision, is totally fallacious. One has only to consider how music—never imitative except for the kind that goes in for bird-calls and the like—broke away from its traditional tonal intervals, its regular time signatures and rhythms, and became structured on entirely new premises, exactly as did the visual arts. For example, traditional compositions were structured on an overriding tonal center; the twelve-tone system of Schoenberg rejects that tonal-centered system in favor of interrelated autonomous pitches. Traditional musical compositions were based on nature insofar as they employed the overtone series which is an actual phenomenon of nature; modernist music does not use the overtone series as the basis of its harmonic structure. Traditional metrical rhythms have been overturned in favor of irregular rhythms no longer dependent on body or verbal pulses. In sum, music was "liberated" from those aspects of its composition that were nature-based, exactly as visual art was "liberated" from those aspects of its composition that were nature-based. The urge toward anti-naturalism, the urge for art that was self-centered, was a cultural phenomenon that appeared in the nineteenth century, and probably is related to the scientific discoveries that contradicted the experience of the senses—that what in nature seems to be "solid," for instance, is really composed of empty spaces and a lattice of tiny vibrating atoms. In terms of lived reality, such a scientific truth is an abstraction. Whatever the myriad reasons for this turn in the history of thought, suffice it to say that the visual arts, like music, were reflecting this turn. It should be noted, too, that far from seeing photography as a rival, artists used photographs as inexpensive, convenient, and stationary models for their paintings.

Degas's amazing breakthrough to what amounts to a new view of the world can be seen in a series of three paintings of ballet scenes. In *The Dance Foyer at the Opera* (1872) (Fosca, clpl p. 47), he takes his view at eye level with the practice bar. Aside from the unusual amount of empty space in the central area, and the chair given the place of honor in the center foreground, the composition is fairly conventional. In *Prima Ballerina* (ca. 1876) (**J 875**), he has taken a high view looking down, so that the ballerina is seen sharply foreshortened on an equally foreshortened stage, making us aware of how things really look. Degas has not been consistent in his viewpoint, however, since the background figures are seen at the level of the dancing master's head.

He arrived at the full realization of his purpose finally in *At the Theatre* (1880) (Fosca, clpl p. 69), a painting of breathtaking innovation towards which we can see him moving during the previous seven years. The subject is a women seated in a theatre box watching a ballet in progress. The foreground is given to the large-scale diagonally outspread fan held by the woman whom we do not see, with the exact center of the composition marked with her large-scale right hand holding her opera glasses. The bright red plush upholstered rail of the box slashes diagonally across the scene, meeting the fan at an angle, cutting the foreground from the background which is so uptilted as we look down from the box that we share with the woman that it appears to rise vertically almost in the picture plane. Beyond the rail, then, our eye is astounded by figures rendered at a fraction of the scale of the foreground motifs, so that the entire figure of the ballerina at the right is the same size as the woman's white-gloved hand and arm. The dancers are on a stage below the level of the box, of course, but pictorially they are *above* it. The corps de ballet in the upper left corner is seen only from waist down so that their feet are dancing, so to speak, in the air.

Now all of this is intensely realistic. Things close to us look large, and become smaller with distance. We are accustomed to see this in paintings organized on the basis of mathematical perspective, although the illusion is such that, as in real life, we hardly notice the diminution. By taking a radical view from high up looking down and from close up looking at some distance, Degas has shown us the world as we see it without being

aware of how we see it, *without tactile and other sensual clues*. Impressionism's effort systematically to capture the effects of optical reality—achieved by Monet and Renoir by means of color-as-light, as we shall see—was achieved by Degas through line, the controlling factor of his composition. While the subject of *At the Theatre* is ostensibly the ballet, the real subject is the primary role of visibility in the visual arts. Degas has thus taken a giant step in the direction of pure visibility. Let us remember, however, that while making his crucial contribution to modernism, he has created a glorious work of art.

# Impressionism

## *Monet and Renoir*

*Impression—Sunrise* (1872) (**H&F 17.12;** Rewald, p. 317, titled *Impression Setting Sun . . .*) is the landmark painting by Claude Monet (1840–1926) that gave Impressionism its name in 1874 when the movement was about five years old. Monet's artistic education began at the age of seventeen, when he met Eugène Boudin, an older artist who lived in Le Havre where the Monet family had settled. Although Boudin had had a few years in Paris at the Ecole des Beaux Arts, his natural bent led him to paint directly from nature, outdoors. It was this direct confrontation with land and sea that gave Boudin's paintings the breezy, sun-filled look that started Monet on the path to Impressionism. In 1862, returning from Le Havre from military duty, he met Johann Jongkind, a Dutch painter who painted with stabbing strokes of bright color that further sent Monet along his way.

Monet had had a brief period of study in Paris in 1859, before his military duty, and in 1862 he returned, to enter the studio of Charles Gleyre. There he met several other new students, Pierre-Auguste Renoir (1841–1919), Alfred Sisley, a Belgian (1839–1899), and Frédéric Bazille (1841–1870), whose promising career ended tragically when he was killed in the Franco-Prussian War. These young artists soon found themselves to be kindred rebellious spirits and when Gleyre's studio closed in 1863, they maintained the close friendship they had formed. They painted together, shared studios, and those that could helped out the others financially, like Bazille, although he himself was often pawning his watch to tide him over. In 1869 Renoir wrote to Bazille from his parents' home near Bougival, where Monet was living, that he was spending almost every day with the Monets who were entirely without resources. "They don't eat every day." He often brought bread with him (from home) which was all the Monets ate that day. Renoir himself was not much better off, and yet, despite the absolute poverty in which they subsisted, they had the enormous emotional energy and aesthetic conviction they needed to continue to paint against prevailing taste, and in the face of merciless criticism. Monet credited their strength partly to the informal gatherings at the Café Guerbois that he and Renoir began to frequent in 1869; he told an interviewer years later, "Nothing could be more interesting than these *causeries* with their perpetual clash of opinions. They kept our wits sharpened, they encouraged us with stores of enthusiasm that for weeks and weeks kept us up, until the final shaping of the idea was accomplished. From them we emerged with a firmer will, with our thoughts clearer and more distinct" (Rewald, p. 197). Side by side, that very year, Monet and Renoir painted *La Grenouillère* (**H&F clpl 17.9;** Rosenblum/Janson clpls 50, 51; Rewald, p. 229) their first Impressionist paintings.

Literally "The Frog Pond," the scene depicts a recreation spot on the Seine. People are swimming, boating, and dining in the restaurant or simply enjoying the shade under the tree on the island at the enter of both compositions. The leisure setting will be a characteristic of Impressionism, as will be the choice of highly reflecting surfaces, above all, water, which seems to have been Monet's natural element. The similarities of the paintings underline the differences between Monet and Renoir that will characterize their careers.

Both paintings are handled with short, blunt, unblended brush strokes, now far more broken than the broken strokes of Constable or Delacroix, giving the impression of rapid execution. The effect of spontaneity is enhanced by the sketchiness of the image in contrast to the polished, finished look of traditional painting, which to contemporary critics was one of the most irritating features of the new art. The color is bright, and the shadows are not uniformly dark, as in traditional technique, but contain colors reflected from the surroundings: the effects of light, in nature, are "translated" in Impressionist painting, by color. The design tends to extend all over the picture plane, as in Manet's *Concert in the Tuileries Garden* (1862), (Rosenblum/Janson clpl 45; Rewald, p. 77), creating an "impression," instead of leading the viewer to focus on one motif. In this pair of paintings, Renoir is in advance of Monet in taking a closer, higher view, which tilts the background upward, and in coloring the water so that it merges with the screen of trees, all of which devices compress the pictorial space: remove the central island and one sees how background and foreground are *almost* compressed into a single flat plane, as will eventually happen in twentieth-century abstract and non-objective art. We are still a very long way from flatness, but with Impressionism we are on that path.

Among the most significant differences in the paintings is the treatment of the figures on the island. Monet does not see them as individuals. They do not interact. They are so little defined as to be almost abstractions of human forms, no more than spots of color like flowers in a flower bed. Renoir, on the other hand, singles out a number of figures to the right of the tree for visual interest, and one sees they are chatting with each other. There is even the anecdotal detail of the dog reaching for the

rowboat. Renoir was always to remain primarily a figure painter, Monet a landscapist.

In 1865 Monet had the satisfaction of seeing two of his seascapes hanging in the Salon, and the following year his portrait of Camille, soon to be his wife, was accepted and praised by Zola, who saw in it "a window thrown open to nature." But his resulting optimism was short lived. He had no money, he had married and Camille was pregnant, and the painting into which he had poured his greatest effort and hopes, *Women in the Garden* (1866–1867) (Rosenblum/Janson fig. 240; Rewald, p. 169), was rejected by the Salon of 1867. The glare of sunlight on white dresses blinded the jury to the more traditional Rococo garden aspects of the work.

The Salon jury was particularly fierce that year, and Cézanne and Renoir among others of the "young school," as Zola called the Café Guerbois group, were also rejected. From that time on it was Monet's dream to organize a group exhibition among themselves, and although Manet opposed the idea, Monet finally won over the others. What goes down in the annals of art as the First Impressionist Group Exhibition opened on 15 April 1874, an important date in Western cultural history.

That Renoir, like Manet and the others, was not rebelling against the past *per se*, but against the academic repetition of the past is clear in Renoir's life-long devotion to Gleyre's training in classical form, and in his love of Rococo art. One sees in *The Promenade* (1870) (White, clpl p. 35), where a young man is leading into the woods a backward-glancing young woman, a recall of a similar couple in Watteau's *Embarkation to Cythera* (**J clpl 106**). During the struggling days of Impressionism he was able to find acceptance at the Salon with figure paintings such as *Bather* (1870) (White, p. 37; Rewald, p. 238) based on the *Cnidian Aphrodite* of Praxiteles (**J 197; H&F 4.23c**).

Even when Renoir moved closer to Monet, this basic difference can be quickly observed. Comparing Renoir's 1867 cityscape *The Pont des Arts* (White, clpl p. 26) with his similar scene of 1872, *The Pont Neuf* (White, clpl pp. 42–43), one sees that the earlier work is painted in large patches of color. Space is deep, with the contours of figures and objects clearly delineated against contrasting backgrounds, very much like Monet's *Terrace at Sainte-Adresse* (ca. 1867) (Rewald, p. 153) painted about the same time, when both artists were under the influence of Manet. *The Pont Neuf* is seen from a slight height, the clarity of contours has been given up in favor of fuzzy edges, and the Manet-esque horizontal-vertical grid has been complicated with diagonals slicing into each other. These features are seen in Monet's painting of the same year, *Boulevard des Capucines* (1873) (Rewald, p. 320), but fuzziness and sketchiness are more advanced. Figures are simply dabs of paint while in Renoir they are still clearly figures.

During the seventies both artists continued to explore the implications of the allover composition, momentary effects of light, and to sharpen their perception of color—

Renoir in figure painting, Monet in landscape. They saw that no object can be seen as a single-colored solid, since color is reflected from the surfaces of everything surrounding it. Color, they discovered, was dependent on context not only in the way it changed in relationship to other colors, but in the way light stole color from the environment to dapple it onto bodies, buildings, gardens, boat sails, and rivers. In Renoir's *Moulin de la Galette* (1876) **(J clpl 120; G. clpl 21.57),** a garden in Montmartre is the setting for a large number of figures dancing and taking refreshments. The young women in their bright colored dresses and the young men in their dark suits are equally dappled with reflected color in the general flicker of light filtering through the trees. The impression of movement comes from this sweeping colored light far more than the pose of the dancers—the seated group in the foreground seems equally vibrant with motion. The repetition of colors and forms throughout the composition gives it the allover look characteristic of Renoir's painting in this period.

Monet's *Gare Saint-Lazare* (1877) (Rosenblum/Janson clpl 59) is a cityscape that is not more than a pretext for the study of steam, recalling Constable's clouds. The glass roof and the puffs of steam reflect colored light from the sky and earth, and give the scene the same kind of vivacity seen in Renoir's *Moulin*. It should be noted, however, that Monet is slower to adopt fully the allover design, although, in the end, he will carry it the furthest. It will lead, eventually, to the radically new concept that pictorial weight, that is, the heaviest pictorial elements such as earth, does not have to be represented in the lower section of the image, to match our ordinary view of the world. For the purposes of the composition, the weight can be at the top—reversing the traditional weight at the bottom, called ponderation.

The word "impression" had become current among the naturalists during the sixties, particularly in connection with the attempt, as the Barbizon painter Théodore Rousseau put it, to capture the "virgin impression of nature." But Manet, too, had expressed his intention, in indoor settings, to "convey his impression." By 1874, the method of naturalistic, direct observation had developed those tendencies in it that emphasized sketchiness, and Monet had gone further than the others in this direction. When a critic, Louis Leroy, reviewed the 1874 exhibition, he grabbed onto the word, repeating it over and over as a kind of motif for his satirical criticism, and thus, taking his cue from Monet's *Impression—Sunrise,* he inadvertently became the godfather of the first vanguard movement, Impressionism!

Toward the end of the seventies Renoir began to have misgivings about Impressionism. As a figure painter he was dissatisfied with its form-dissolving effects. His *Portrait of Mme. Charpentier and Her Children* (1879) (Rewald, p. 420) shows him turning away from the dappled skin surfaces in favor of the smooth porcelain effects of his pre-Impressionist style. Although the back-

ground of this sumptuous portrait is still handled in the sketchy technique, the composition puts the sitters in relief, and the seeming random arrangement of figures, as in *Moulin de la Galette,* is abandoned for a classical triangle with Mme. Charpentier's head as its apex. *Mme. Charpentier* brought Renoir his first great success and no doubt contributed to turning him away from Impressionism. His new tendencies can be fully appreciated in *Luncheon of the Boating Party* (1881) **(H&F clpl 17.3),** the last of his large group compositions of modern leisure life that began with *La Grenouillère*. While Renoir retains the Impressionist brush stroke for his foliage background, the figures are arranged along a strong diagonal rising from the lower left to the upper right, producing a stable right-angle triangle. Some areas of reflected color are still evident, but there is none of that sweeping color effect that enlivened *La Moulin de la Galette*.

Renoir's classicizing taste was reinforced by a trip to Italy late in 1881. He found himself thrilled with Raphael and fascinated with ancient Roman classicism, which he saw at Pompeii. By 1883 he declared, "I had wrung Impressionism dry and I finally came to the conclusion that I knew neither how to paint nor how to draw." He began to make copies after Ingres and to study the Renaissance masters.

It was far from easy to find a new direction without giving up the gains that had been made in freshness of color. Renoir's problem can be grasped in his *Bathers* (1887) (White, clpl fold-out pp. 69–70). Three monumental nudes form a classical triangle in the foreground of a watery, Rococo setting, with two others in the middle ground. The figures, appropriated from a seventeenth-century sculptural relief at Versailles by François Girardon, are indeed rendered with sculptural plasticity against the background of an Impressionist landscape. The composition thus falls into a foreground and background that are hardly related.

By the end of the decade Renoir recovered the unification of his compositions while retaining form through the use of dominant tonalities, tending to red, and the nineties brought him the success that had flirted with him so fitfully over the years. However, he had been a chronic sufferer from arthritis, and from the nineties on he was constantly going to doctors and constantly in pain. He was increasingly unable to handle a brush with any dexterity, and his style grew broader as his subjects grew more classical. By 1900 Impressionism had come completely to dominate the Establishment, and Renoir was a culture hero, appointed *chevalier* of the Légion d'Honneur in 1900 and *commandeur* in 1919, although he had abandoned many of the basic principles of Impressionism; his work from 1880 to 1885 is in transition to his late style, which from 1886 on belongs to the Post-Impressionist period.

Unlike Renoir, Cézanne, Pissaro, and others, Monet did not shrink from the form-dissolving implications of Impressionism. He studied the problem of colored light all of his life and arrived in the end at almost total abstraction. During the Franco-Prussian War he had gone with Pissarro to England, where they saw works by Turner. Although Monet denied Turner's influence, the visual resemblance to Turner's late works strongly suggests otherwise, especially in paintings such as *Impression—Sunrise* and others featuring the sun seen through fog and mist which he painted intermittently during his career. Compare Monet's painting with Turner's as seen in *The Slave Ship* **(J clpl 111; G clpl 21.29).**

In 1891 Monet undertook a series of paintings that confronted inadvertently the question of subject matter, a confrontation that had consequences as radical as any work theretofore produced. As we have seen, subject matter had been a key issue ever since Courbet. Then, with Manet, a second issue arose alongside the first: in addition to *what,* the artists faced the problem of *how* to paint. The latter was answered by Degas and by Impressionism, both of which led to compressed space and increased emphasis on the surface. The former was answered with paintings of modern life which finally won over the taste of the critics and public, along with landscape and still life.

When, in 1891, Monet began his *Haystacks* (Rewald, clpls pp. 562–563), he planned only two pictures, one for gray weather, one for sunshine. In the course of executing those two, he found that light conditions were constantly changing, and decided to enlarge his idea to capture many more effects of light on his motif. By the time of his exhibition later that year he had finished fifteen paintings of the same two haystacks, each one devoted to one "instant" effect. He kept several canvases ready so that when one effect disappeared, he was ready to start on the next. In this way Monet, always pursuing his goal of registering on canvas his perception of reality, had, with no intention of doing so, taken another giant step in the direction of abstract and non-objective art. He repeated his experiment in 1894 when he studied the façade of Rouen Cathedral **(G clpl 21.55).** The views are similar for each painting, and they are "different" paintings because of the variation in the color schemes due to changes in the light—from morning to evening. He referred to this method as "instantaneity."

He followed through the implications of this trend in paintings of his water garden at Giverny which he had been working on since 1890, and its development through high color and increasing alloverness can be traced through the series of *Water Lilies* **(J 877; H&F clpl 19.4)** and other pond and garden subjects from around 1903 to the end of his life. It became his intention to surround the walls of his studio with the water lily paintings, which would have been the first modern environmental work, a plan he was unable to complete due to serious eye trouble. In these late water garden works, Monet takes the high view which he had mostly avoided after the *Boulevard des Capucines,* and looking

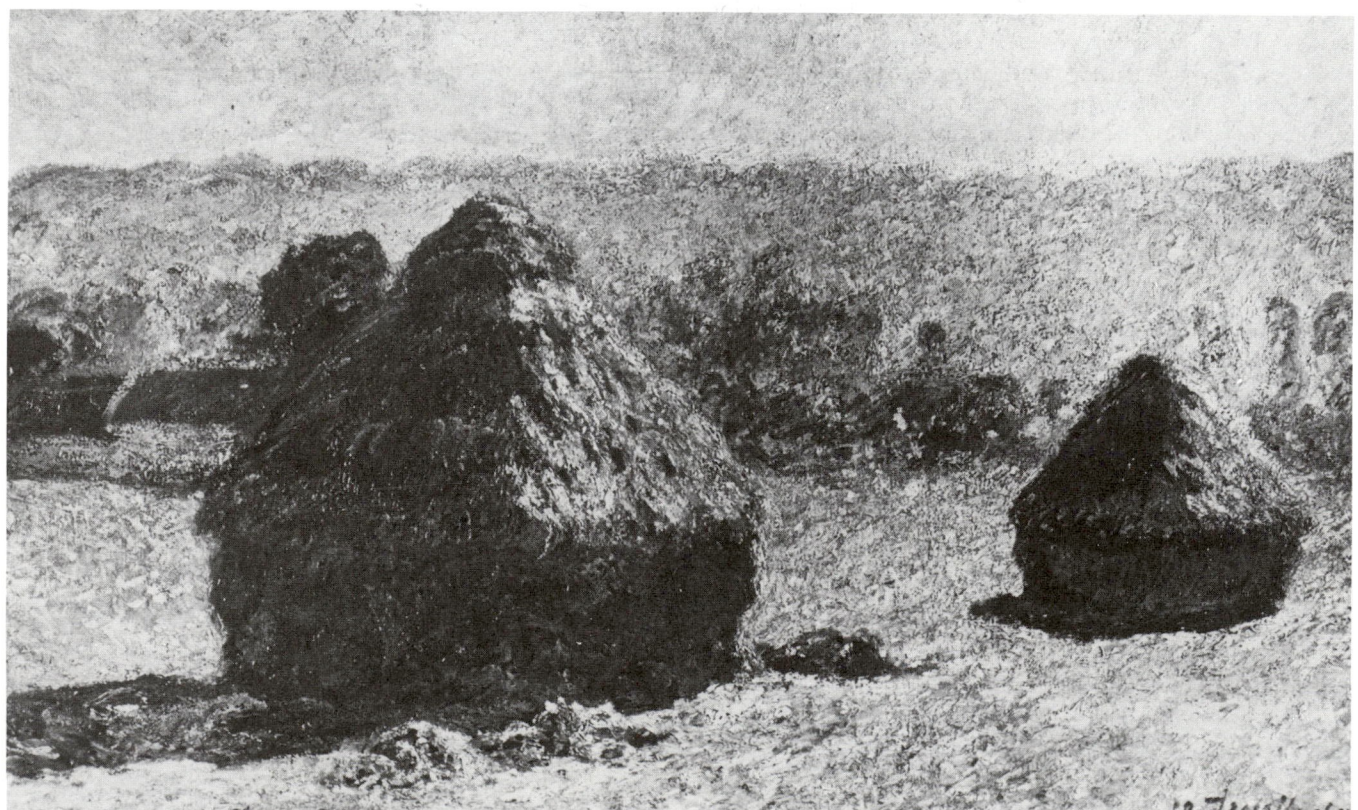

Claude Monet, *Haystacks,* 1891. Paris, Musée d'Orsay. (ART RESOURCE, NEW YORK)

down at the pond, he sees nothing but the surface of the water with its flowers and cloud reflections. The horizontal world becomes a vertical field of color and reality as elusive as water running through one's fingers.

Impressionism can be said to be a major style because from its earliest appearance in, say, the *La Grenouillère* paintings by Monet and Renoir, it contained the possibility of growth and development, like a fertile idea. But, just as ideas change in the course of their development, so styles, too, change. At what point in its evolutionary change does an idea, or a style, become something other than it was in its origins? We cannot look for the answer in Renoir's art, since Renoir *turned away* from Impressionism, as we have seen, and his paintings from the 1880s on are no longer Impressionist—they must be seen as Post-Impressionist, meaning quite literally, "after Impressionism."

Of all the Impressionists it was Monet alone who accepted the implications of the style as each stage implied a further development, and his late paintings can thus be called late Impressionism. As foreseen by Cézanne and Renoir, the development of Impressionism did lead step-by-step to the loss of form, if form is assumed to be an attribute of matter that divides it from chaos; a three-dimensional quality belonging to objects in the phenomenal world which in paintings are projected on a two-dimensional surface. But in the course of the twentieth century, form *in art* turned out to something different from the picturing of natural form; form in art came to be understood as referring only to itself, having nothing to do with the projection of natural forms on a two-dimensional surface. Understood thus, any mark or set of marks that an artist chooses to make, when making a work of art, can constitute form in art. Although Monet's paintings increasingly lost natural form, his water garden works always retained something of the natural forms that inspired them. Nevertheless, he came very close to the concept of form as non-representational in his last paintings at Giverny.

## The Impressionist circle

While Courbet, Corot, Manet, Degas, Monet, and Renoir must be accounted the seminal figures in the development of Realism and Impressionism, some of the artists who worked beside them produced paintings just as visually satisfying as theirs. Berthe Morisot (1841–1895), the daughter of a wealthy magistrate, had begun to paint seriously in her teens under an academic teacher, Joseph Guichard. She was drawn, however, to outdoor painting, and took friendly guidance for a while from Corot. In 1864 two of her landscapes were accepted by the Salon. She met Manet in 1868 and was soon drawn into the circle around him, although she did not attend the gatherings at the Café Guerbois—this would have been improper for a woman. Manet was attracted to her charming manner as well as her beauty, and asked her to pose for him, which

she did: she is the seated woman in Manet's *The Balcony*.

In her own work, the influence of Manet can be seen in the pose of the woman on the embankment in one of Morisot's early paintings, *The Harbor of Lorient* (1869) (Rewald, clpl p. 227). There is, however, already something of Monet in the coloring. Although she remained devoted in her admiration for Manet (and became his sister-in-law in 1874), she nevertheless opposed him when he tried to persuade her not to join Monet and his group in their 1874 exhibition. Her painting by that time was fully Impressionist, as it was during her entire career, and she exhibited in seven of the eight Impressionist shows between 1874 and 1886.

Mary Cassatt (1844–1926), born in Pennsylvania of a prominent, well-to-do family, settled in Paris in 1866, one of the famous triumvirate of American ex-patriates who won international success—the other two, of course, where James McNeil Whistler and John Singer Sargent. She began to exhibit at the Salon in 1872 when her painting *On the Balcony* was accepted, a work influenced by Manet's painting of the same subject, but in no way reflecting what Morisot called Manet's wild, slightly green fruit flavor. It does show, however, an accomplished painter able in a shallow space to give rounded form to her figures. Her style changed radically after she met Degas in 1877, and she abandoned the Salon to join the Impressionists, with whom she exhibited in four shows. Cassatt's compositions are clearly in the manner of Degas in her use of the radically cut-off figure, but in the viewpoint she takes, she is closer to Renoir, seeing her figures rather close up. *La Loge* (1879) (Rewald, p. 473) the title also of a Renoir work of 1874 (White, p. 51), exemplifies the way she combined the influences of both.

The impact of a great Japanese print exhibition in Paris in 1890 is reflected in one of her best-known mother-and-child paintings, *The Bath* (ca. 1892) **(J 887; G 21.63)**, where the Japanese taste for decorative patterns and strong outlines is much in evidence. While the momentary pose and tilted space of the composition retain the characteristics of her Impressionist style, the clear outlines and smooth treatment of skin and fabrics place the work in the Post-Impressionist period.

In 1893 she participated in the decorations for the World's Columbian Exposition in Chicago, and in 1904 she was appointed *chevalier* of the Légion d'Honneur. Toward the end of the century her eyes began to give her serious trouble, and she was able to do very little painting in the last twenty years of her life.

In addition to her achievement as an artist—she was the greatest woman artist America had as yet produced—Cassatt made an important contribution to American collecting. She persuaded her friend Louise Waldron Elder, later to become Mrs. H. O. Havemeyer, to buy a Degas pastel in 1873, and this became the first work in the peerless Havemeyer Collection, much of which is now in the Metropolitan Museum.

Camille Pissarro (1831–1903) is the author of some of the most splendid paintings made in the heroic years of Impressionism. His early style from the mid-fifties to about 1867 shows his first leanings toward Corot and the Barbizon painters, especially Daubigny. He was accepted at the Salon in 1865 and 1866. In 1867 he met Manet, whereupon he became a regular at the Café Guerbois and two years later painted with Monet at Louveciennes.

For the next fifteen years he was a convinced Impressionist, Monet's strongest supporter in organizing the first Impressionist exhibition, and an unfailing exhibitor in all eight of the Impressionist shows. His landscapes, however, are more structured than Monet's, and a comparison of the two artists' paintings of the same title, *The Road to Versailles at Louveciennes—Snow Effect* (Rewald, pp. 212–213), both painted in 1869, shows how close they were and yet reveals the differences. Monet's three-part design has few resting places for the eye, which takes in the scene as a whole. Pissarro has contrasted the two sides of the road, bares more of the houses to view, and stops the eye closer to the picture plane by placing a horse-drawn carriage in the path. Monet's figures are sketchily rendered, while Pissarro's have the bulk of a Millet peasant as if seen from a distance. These are the constant tendencies in Pissarro's Impressionist painting.

Toward the end of the seventies he began an important series of figure paintings recording peasant life. His palette is somewhat more brilliant, and in *Young Woman Washing Dishes* (1882) (Hayward Gallery, clpl p. 39) it becomes iridescent. Color is flecked on in a way that seems to anticipate Seurat's Neo-Impressionism. Pissarro, however, acknowledged Seurat's innovation when he himself undertook to explore the pointillist style in 1886.

Beyond his contributions to mainstream art as a painter, Pissarro was preeminent as a teacher. Morisot declared, "He was such a teacher he could have taught stones to draw." Cézanne, by 1900 the acknowledged master of avant-garde painting, declared, "Pissarro was like a father to me." He considered Pissarro to be the originator of Impressionism and underscored the debt he felt to "that humble and colossal Pissarro" by referring to himself in a catalogue of 1906 as his pupil.

The younger generation also recognized their debt to Pissarro. Van Gogh, writing to his brother about a self-portrait explained, "I have tried to make it simple," and added, "Show it to old Pissarro if you see him." A man of deeply serious political views and moral awareness, Pissarro reinforced these traits in Paul Gauguin. It was Gauguin who after Pissarro's death best summed up his place in the pantheon of Impressionist masters. "Examining Pissarro's role as a whole, despite its fluctuations, we find in it not only an overwhelming sense of purpose that never fails, but an essentially intuitive and highly distinguished artistic sense. . . . He paid attention to everyone, you may say—well, why not? Everyone paid attention to him, too."

## American alternatives to Impressionism

A parallel interest in the effects of light appeared in contemporary American art, especially in the work of Thomas Eakins and Winslow Homer. Winslow Homer (1836–1910) arrived at a vision similar to that of French artists around 1866, with as yet no European contacts behind him. He was gifted with a strong sense of design and a responsive eye, and his early genre scenes are surprisingly like those of Monet in the same years; compare, for example, Homer's *Croquet Scene* (1866) (Wilmerding, *Genius,* clpl p. 155) with Monet's *Women in the Garden* (1866–1867) (Rosenblum/Janson fig. 240; Rewald, p. 169). Both artists are interested in the pattern made by the contrasts of light and shadow, as well as what appears to be the casual effect of a scene happened upon. In *Long Branch, New Jersey* (1869) **(H&F clpl 15.27)** and other genre works painted after Homer's trip to Paris in 1866, we see essentially the same style, although his palette is lighter, showing that his interest in light effects owes nothing to French influence, which in 1866–67, the period of Homer's Paris sojourn, had not yet arrived at an equal blondness of palette. Homer, furthermore, preferred side-lighting instead of the sun-drenched and silhouette effects that the Impressionists arrived at in the seventies, so that his surfaces and contours remain crisp instead of dissolving in light.

In 1881 and 1882 Homer went to England where he painted for two seasons at Tynemouth, a fishing village on the North Sea. It is notable, again, that just when Impressionism was undergoing revisions, Homer's art, too, changed. The predominantly lighthearted genre paintings disappear permanently, and from this time on, Homer's art is about struggle—the human struggle with nature, as in *Life Line* (1886) (Wilmerding, *Genius,* p. 152) and the much later *The Gulf Stream* (1899) (Goodrich, *Homer,* clpl 86), one of the greatest paintings of the late nineteenth century anywhere; the struggle for survival among nature's creatures, as in *Fox Hunt* (1893) **(G clpl 21.47)**; and natural forces themselves, sea and land, in an everlasting struggle of attack and resistance, as in *Early Morning After a Storm at Sea* (1902) (Goodrich, *Homer,* fig. 71). Some of Homer's greatest achievements, such as *After the Tornado* (1899), were executed in watercolor (Goodrich, *Homer,* clpl 83).

Another American, Thomas Eakins (1843–1916), went to France in the same year as Homer but stayed away four yeas, acquiring a strong academic training that inhibited him not at all in finding his way into the great realist tradition of Velásquez and Rembrandt. His paintings reflect the scientific mind and aesthetic eye with which he confronted nature both indoors and outdoors. An early masterpiece, *Max Schmitt in a Single Scull* (1871) (Wilmerding, clpl p. 156), is a model of his interests and his genius: constructed on a grid system of horizontals and verticals, with space structured according to the laws of mathematical perspective, the painting's radiance utterly transcends the rules that govern its composition. Its theme is discipline and intelligence—central themes of Eakins' oeuvre. Whatever else an Eakins subject may be doing, he or she is either thinking and/or involved in a skill. See, for example, his Rembrandtesque *Gross Clinic* (1875) **(J 885, G clpl 21.42; H&F 15.29)**, *Miss Van Buren* (1889), *The Swimming Hole* (1883), *Between Rounds* (1899) (Goodrich, clpls pp. 31, 24, 34).

One may note in Eakins' *William Rush Carving the Allegorical Figure of the Skuylkill River* (1877) (Goodrich, clpl p. 18) another extremely odd similarity between an American and a French work, when, as with Homer and Monet, there seems to have been no opportunity for contact. Courbet's *Studio* was not exhibited publicly at any time when Eakins might have seen it, and yet we have in both cases an artist's studio, with an artist at work, a female nude, and a bundle of garments prominent at the center. Both pictures, moreover, deal with allegorical figures. *Coincidence?*

For his posthumous reputation, James McNeil Whistler (1834–1903) made the most serious mistake of his life when he left Paris in 1863 to settle in London. Paris was where modernism dug its strongest roots; it was to become the center of mainstream art and thus the center also of mainstream criticism. Whistler was already part of the circle that was to form the nucleus of the avant-garde; he had won Courbet's admiration and friendship, and he showed his famous Courbet-influenced *White Girl, Symphony in White no.1* (1862) (Wilmerding, *Genius,* p. 147) at the Salon des Refusés. His most famous painting, *Arrangement in Black and Gray: The Artist's Mother* (1871) **(J 882)** is a kind of elderly *Olympia,* with the curvilinear forms of the figure silhouetted against a wall and curtain in a compressed space, revealing the influence of Manet's early style.

When Whistler painted *Nocturne in Black and Gold: The Falling Rocket* (1875) **(J 883),** it was the most advanced painting in Europe. A night scene, it carries Impressionism to a new frontier, capturing the instantly evanescent colored sparks of fireworks which disappeared more rapidly than any fleeting play of sunlight on leaves. He was also in the front line of advance in his concept of creating painting effects that were analogous to musical effects: he deliberately called attention to the parallel in titling a number of his works *nocturne,* which was a new musical "free" form in the nineteenth century. It seems possible that, had he stayed in Paris, he would have been able to follow through with these advanced ideas, to become a major figure in art history. While it is true that Whistler developed a following, especially because of the influence of his moody, crepuscular style, and his etchings, this was so principally among American artists, and thus had no part to play in the ongoing evolution of modernism. Although Whistler is now much admired for works such as *Nocturne in Blue and Silver: Cremorne Lights* (1872) **(H&F clpl 17.7),** it is hardly realized that the work is spatially more advanced than

Monet's *Impressionism: Sunrise* of the same year, and that this and other *nocturnes* dating as early as 1865 are among the first Western paintings to absorb the spatial principles of Japanese art. Although he won recognition, was appointed chevalier of the Légion d'Honneur in 1889, and was highly successful in the last decade of his career, he rather quickly faded from view for some decades after his death. With the upsurge of interest in American art that began around the middle of the twentieth century, he is now recognized as an American master.

## English painting of the late nineteenth century

One of the curious stylistic zig-zags in art history is presented by British painting after Turner and Constable. Young artists who were embarking on their careers at mid-century showed not the slightest interest in the former's glowing, transparent veils of color nor the latter's earthy, loving naturalism. Their legacy had to cross the channel eventually to find legitimate heirs in the Impressionists, Constable's indirectly through the influence of Delacroix, Turner's directly, it would appear, when Monet and Pissarro saw his work in London during the Franco-Prussian War. William Holman Hunt (1827–1910), John Everett Millais (1829–1896), and Dante Gabriel Rossetti (1828–1882) formed the Pre-Raphaelite Brotherhood to convey their rejection of the prevailing Neo-Classical and academic art and their intention to bring painting back to honest and realistic expression; to go back beyond the sophistication of the High Renaissance to the "archaic" masters of the quattrocento, such as Piero della Francesca and Fra Angelico. They had grown up in a cultural atmosphere in which the dominant values centered on religiously inspired moral piety, earnestness, self-improvement, social responsibility, industriousness, the conscientious observation of facts, and chaste love. The sense of righteousness that one enjoyed who practiced these virtues led to the obligation to teach others to be equally virtuous, and to the pleasure of sentiment as one contemplated one's own goodness and sensitivity to the plight of others. Duty and sentiment were the primary colors of British Victorian culture. As Queen Victoria's husband, Prince Albert, saw it, art was somewhere between religion and hygiene.

Pre-Raphaelite paintings reflect those virtues and sentiments perfectly digested, and with the factual, detailed realism of the camera. However, knowing how Courbet's realism offended the taste of French art critics and connoisseurs, we are not surprised to learn that British critics were equally unprepared to see the realist values of their lives translated into art, and that they were equally hostile. When Millais exhibited his *Christ in the House of His Parents* (1850) (Rosenblum/Janson clpl 39) the *Times* found it "revolting." Why? Surely it was not the morally didactic subject that offended—the painting is a homily on Zechariah (13:6), "If anyone asks him, 'what are the wounds in your body?' he will reply, 'These I received in the house of my friends.'" Like the present-day film *The Last Temptation of Christ*, Millais's painting presented Jesus realistically in human terms. His painting was met with the same anger. "The attempt to associate the Holy Family with the meanest details of a carpenter's shop, with no omission of dirt, misery, of even disease, all finished with the same loathsome minuteness, is disgusting," said the critic for the *Times*. To Charles Dickens, Mary looked like "a monster in the vilest cabaret in France, or the lowest gin shop in England."

Hunt's *The Awakening Conscience* (1853) (Rosenblum/Janson clpl 40) suggests Northern rather than Italian fifteenth-century painting, with its domestic interiors, its love of surface variety and minute details, and its symbolic use of commonplace articles. Compare Hunt's painting, for example, with Jan van Eyck's *The Virgin with the Canon van der Paele* (G 18.10), or with the *Merode Altarpiece* by the Master of Flemalle (Robert Campin?) (J clpl 60). *The Awakening Conscience*, like Manet's *Olympia*, takes up the "kept woman" theme. The model, Annie Miller, had in fact been a prostitute with whom Hunt fell in love. He wanted to marry her—after first "improving" her—but it turned out that, unlike the character portrayed in the scene, Annie was not improvable. In the painting she has apparently looked out of the window and seen the beauty and purity of nature—reflected in the mirror in the background—and will presumably turn over a new leaf. Strewn through the room are the echoing symbols of her "depraved" ways—a bird has been destroyed by the cat; the strands of embroidery wool lie on the floor like an unravelled life; the lettering on the sheet music identifies the song as "Tears, Idle Tears," with lyrics by Tennyson, and so on.

Rossetti's *Beata Beatrix* (ca.1863) (Rosenblum/Janson clpl 41) also reflects a personal love relationship and moves aesthetically forward in the path of self-referential art which is increasingly evident in the twentieth century. His wife, Elizabeth Siddal, had died of an overdose of laudanum and, as Robert Rosenblum describes it, the painting is a memorial "inspired by his namesake Dante's interpretation of the death of his own beloved Beatrice in *La Vita Nuova*. Bearing the thickly voluptuous red hair and full, sensual features of Rossetti's dead wife, Beatrice appears in a state of trance. . . . A haloed bird . . . drops the poppy of sleep and death into her hands; a sundial points to nine, the hour of her passing; and in the filmy background, Dante and Love walk through the desolate streets of Florence." Such work belongs to that current of nineteenth-century expression that Mario Praz has characterized as the "Romantic Agony," with the featured roles taken by *femmes fatales*.

Although the Brotherhood as a coherent group lasted only a few years, the artists retained prominence and influenced the development of the Symbolist movement and of Art Nouveau through one of their members, William Morris, as we shall see.

In France, an era was coming to its close. Manet, the elder statesman of the once-rebel vanguard artists, finally realized his life-long goal of forcing the establishment to recognize him on his own terms when in 1882 he was made a chevalier of the Légion d'Honneur. The Impressionist dealer Paul Durand-Ruel was invited to organize an exhibition of Impressionist paintings in New York in 1886, and the movement quickly won international notice if not universal acclaim. People who had large investments in such academic stars as William Bouguereau and Ernest Meissonier were unenthusiastic about innovators, but new collectors were emerging. The Impressionist struggle was ending in triumph. Few realized that this had been only the first big battle in what was to be an on-going war of the avant-garde.

## Part 2
## POST-IMPRESSIONISM

Renoir was not alone in his rejection of the form-dissolving tendencies in Impressionism and in his anxiety that naturalism was not grand enough to compete with the achievements of the past. By 1880, a new current of sensibility had begun to flow into nineteenth-century positivism. As we have seen, an unquestioning faith in the world of sensual experience, governed by the rules of reason and factual evidence, had provided society with the confidence that everything was knowable. The Impressionists, for all the radical changes they had made, had indeed reinforced this perception of the world. They observed with an unprecedented intensity, as if the world had never been clearly seen before, and they gave a report of their observations with attention to the most minute details of how things really looked contingent on the circumstances at the time of observation. Implicit in positivist Impressionism is the assumption that one could give an objective account of the world-out-there. Nevertheless, it is perfectly obvious that sensations of color and form are *subjective*, and so, within Impressionism there is a subjective factor.

Realism and Impressionism had reacted against the subjectivity of Romanticism, which was seen in the earlier decades of the century as representing the new and modern. But, so complex is human culture that even while rejecting Romanticism, the Impressionists venerated Delacroix, Romanticism's standard-bearer. They studied his color, however, not for its expressionist function but for its formal method, in which they found clues to achieve the spontaneous effects they wanted. However, in so doing, they intensified the significance of formalism as a visual concern and contributed to the concept of art-for-art's sake which has been a dominant element in modernism. Unlike "Impressionism," "Post-Impressionism" is not a stylistic term. It refers to a period from about 1886 to about 1900 and is usually applied to the work of artists who reacted against Impressionism but who nevertheless incorporated Impressionist anti-traditionalist principles in their art. It rejects objectivity in favor of subjectivity, and confronts formalist problems as major issues. As exemplified in the work of the four most important Post-Impressionist artists—Paul Cézanne, Paul Gauguin, Vincent Van Gogh, and Georges Seurat—there were four major solutions to the problem set by Impressionism which we will take up in turn. Thus, there is no Post-Impressionist style *per se.*

Within scientific positivism itself, with its passion for investigating all phenomena and analyzing quantifiable data, it was recognized that there were areas of experience such as sentiment that were not measurable, and although such experience could not be dignified by the name of knowledge, still one had to acknowledge the existence of subjective feeling. This sentimentality was the content of that aspect of nineteenth-century sensibility to which Queen Victoria's name has been attached.

Subjectivity thus brought up the rear while Positivism led the vanguard under the banner of Realism. Moreover, subjectivity remained viable throughout the ascendancy of Positivism through the influence of Immanuel Kant and Transcendental philosophy, which allowed for the role of intuition that was based on the senses as a means of knowing. What is important for us here is the idea of the connection between intuition and artistic expression. According to one line of thought, intuitive knowledge of reality as given by sense experience is *verbally inexpressible.* Experience can be grasped only by reproducing it. For example, let us say that you know the reality of the taste of chocolate because you have experienced it in a chocolate bar. No description of the taste will communicate to an outer-space visitor what the experience is. Your knowledge remains locked up within your subjective intuition. Your flying-saucer friend will have to taste it to have that knowledge.

This, then, was the cultural situation around 1880. Objectivity had begun to wear out is red-carpet welcome. The feeling arose among artists that they wanted to give a more subjective account of the world than Impressionism had afforded. It is at this point that we begin to see artists consciously attempting to reach viewers directly in order to communicate to them, that is, *to reproduce for them* some verbally inexpressible perception. Cézanne called it his "sensation," and his aim, he said, was "réalizer ma petite sensation," that is, to give visual embodiment to his intuition of reality.

## Paul Cézanne

If Cézanne (1839–1906) had died at the age of thirty-one, as Georges Seurat did, we would have had no inkling of an important loss. His early Delacroix-inspired, Romantic,

erotic visions such as *The Orgy* (1864–1868) (Raynal, clpl p. 20) show the passionate brushwork one would expect from an artist so influenced, but surely nothing innovative. When, however, in the early seventies, he moved into the light palette of Impressionism after his contact with Pissarro, one sees an independence of approach that would *perhaps* lead one to make a mental note, "This is a painter worth watching." His *View of Auvers* (ca. 1874) (Raynal, clpl p. 40), which shows Pissarro's influence in its depth of view and general tone, nevertheless distributes blocky houses across the field that, with the benefit of hindsight, we can now see anticipates Cézanne's structural approach to landscape (and all other themes, for that matter). This approach culminates in such a work as *Mont Sainte-Victoire Seen from Les Lauves* (1902–1904) **(H&F clpl 17.24),** in which the topographical features have been abstracted into a composition that leads directly into Cubism.

Cézanne was born in the south of France, at Aix-en-Provence, where, as he grew up, his closest friend was Emile Zola. He seems always to have wanted challenges, and as a youth climbed the most dangerous mountain peaks around Aix and became an exceptionally strong swimmer. He began to draw at an early age but at school he won prizes in Greek and Latin, and in science, not in art. When he was seventeen, however, he enrolled in the Aix School of Drawing and there managed to win a second prize. By the time he was twenty he had made up his mind that he wanted to be an artist, winning over his successful banker-father with some difficulty. He made his first trip to Paris in 1861, and for the rest of his life he moved back and forth between city and country.

His friendship with Zola brought him into contact with the young rebels of the Salon des Refusés, but his art in the sixties does not reflect their interests. He was still full of erotic-religious visions, and his melodramatic paintings of this period include a *Vision of Saint Anthony, Murder, A Strangled Woman,* and a *Luncheon on the Grass* that looks more like a spiritualist seance waiting for the table to rise (Raynal, clpl p. 27). Despite the dark romantic brooding, however, the structural compulsion that ruled his compositional method is perfectly evident: every composition is divided symmetrically down the center, which is marked by some kind of more or less prominent feature. In the *Luncheon,* for example, it is the point where the outer edge of the elbow of the man in the white shirt meets the table; a central axis can be drawn through this point, reinforced by the apple on the right. In *A Modern Olympia* (ca. 1872–1873) (Raynal, clpl p. 34), the central axis passes through the opening between the nude's legs and the point where the visitor's cane touches the edge of his hand. The painting may well have been done as a tribute to mark the tenth anniversary of Manet's radical painting and as a comment on the vast changes that had occurred since Manet's *Olympia.* It is one of Cézanne's last overtly erotic paintings, but that kind of force does not disappear; one may see in the radiance of his mature visual meditations on form and color his successful sublimation of a powerful sexuality. As Meyer Schapiro has shown, in Cézanne's still lifes "there is a latent erotic sense, an unconscious symbolizing of a repressed desire."

After a few years' investigation of Impressionism under the guidance of Pissarro, whose influence is present in *The House of the Hanged Man* (1873) (Musée d'Orsay, p. 64), Cézanne arrived at one of the first landscapes of his early maturity, *The Pool at the Jas de Bouffan* (ca. 1878) (Raynal, clpl p. 51). Here he took the first step beyond Impressionism by synthesizing the light palette with a geometrical structure. There is no attempt here to create the shimmering effect of light on water, nor of fleeting time, or spontaneous movement. Cézanne takes Monet's motif of reflected forms, seen typically in *The Bridge at Argenteuil* (1874) (Musée d'Orsay, p. 88), rippling as a fresh breeze ruffles the surface of the water in which they are reflected, and transforms it into a compositional strategy governed by the vertical tree at the center and the horizontal pool edge.

Cézanne was essentially a still life painter. Still lifes deal with objects that have no will and no emotion; they are ideally suited to aesthetic manipulation and at the same time lend themselves as vehicles for symbolic meaning and emotional content. Possibly the most significant contribution that Cézanne made to modernist art was his innovation in treating all themes as still life, and draining from still life its traditional appeal to the senses, its evocation of a variety of remembered sensual experiences. As we saw in Ingres' *Odalisque* (**J clpl 113**), each sense—sight, touch, smell, hearing, taste—is meant to be stimulated by the nude and the objects that surround her. The painting mediates between what is represented and our remembered sensual experience of the represented object. In the great Dutch still lifes, the artists took delight in contrasting textures of things and appealing to taste: see, for example, Willem Kalf's *Still Life* (**G 19.56**) where highly reflecting glass is contrasted with thick, light-absorbing carpet, and the half-peeled lemon makes our mouths remember the sensation of tartness.

Cézanne's *Still Life with Onions* (ca. 1895) (Musée d'Orsay, clpl p. 77) is a masterly, mature, and typical composition (but see also **J 895; G 21.65**); there is only one sensual differentiation among the objects represented—the visual. The onions are arranged in a variety of views; the wine bottle, glass, knife, table, and bunched-up table cloth provide contrasts of shape; but no sensual experience other than the visual is evoked. It is like a musical composition in which no sensual experience other than the aural is evoked; we hear variations and contrasts on a theme. Cézanne's bathers (Rosenblum/Janson fig. 314), card players (**H&F 17.29**), portraits and figure studies (**G 21.67**), and landscapes (**J 896**) from about 1880 on are equally drained of all "naturalistic" attributes, and constitute variations and contrasts on a theme.

This said, a kind of contradiction must be acknowledged. It has been shown that there are hidden images in Cézanne's paintings, as indeed have also been discovered in Van Gogh and Gauguin, as well as other artists—we have seen how an alternative reading of the pile of garments in Courbet's *Studio* transforms them into a "creature." While we cannot go into this intriguing matter, interested readers will find references to articles on the subject in the bibliography for this unit. For one example, we may point out that in this Cézanne *Still Life with Onions,* one may read the tablecloth as a female figure standing at the side of the table, and draped over it, with another partially seen female figure behind. I believe such imagery is inadvertent and unconscious, and falls into place as another example of the well-founded interpretation of Cézanne's work as disguised or displaced eroticism. In its intention, Cézanne's art is essentially formal in the musical sense of building a composition on a structure of thematic material. This view is supported by the artist's remark that one must see in nature the cylinder, the sphere, and the cone—his "petite sensation" of the geometrical structure of nature.

Cézanne returned many times to his favorite motifs, such as the Bay of Marseilles seen from L'Estaque, and the Sainte-Victoire mountain, which he drew and painted more than sixty times. In *Mont Sainte-Victoire with a Great Pine Tree* (1885–87) (Raynal, clpl p. 66), we see a clear demonstration of his often-quoted remark that he wanted to "do Poussin over again from nature." Poussin's landscapes are classicizing Baroque compositions that are controlled by horizontals that recede from the picture plane linked by Baroque diagonals. They are inventions, not directly perceived observations. *Landscape with the Burial of Phocion* (**J 759; G 19.62**) is a characteristic example, the view studded with architectural blocks. A comparison of the Poussin with the Cézanne reveals how the latter structures his composition in a similar way, using the landscape features as orderly stabilizers. The difference, of course, is that Cézanne studied the view directly.

Further comparison shows how Poussin imagines a view from ground level, and stretches the space illusionistically into an infinite, distant plane. Cézanne takes the high view, which as we have seen, compresses the space by uptilting the ground, bringing the distant plane closer to the picture plane. But he also compresses space by the device of shaping the branches spread across the picture plane so as to be echoed by the mountain's profile, and this leads us to an important discovery. A visual oscillation results from the visual rhyme since, if you focus on the valley you see the mountain as distant; if you look at the upper section you see mountain and branches close together, bringing the distant plane into the foreground plane. With this formal device, pictorial movement becomes inherent in the formal structure of the work, not dependent on pose, gesture, or some other traditional device that is imitative of life and therefore extra-artistic. Cézanne takes modernism another giant step toward the

Paul Cézanne, *Mont St. Vict-oire,* 1898. London: Courtauld Institute. (GIRAUDON/ART RESOURCE, NEW YORK)

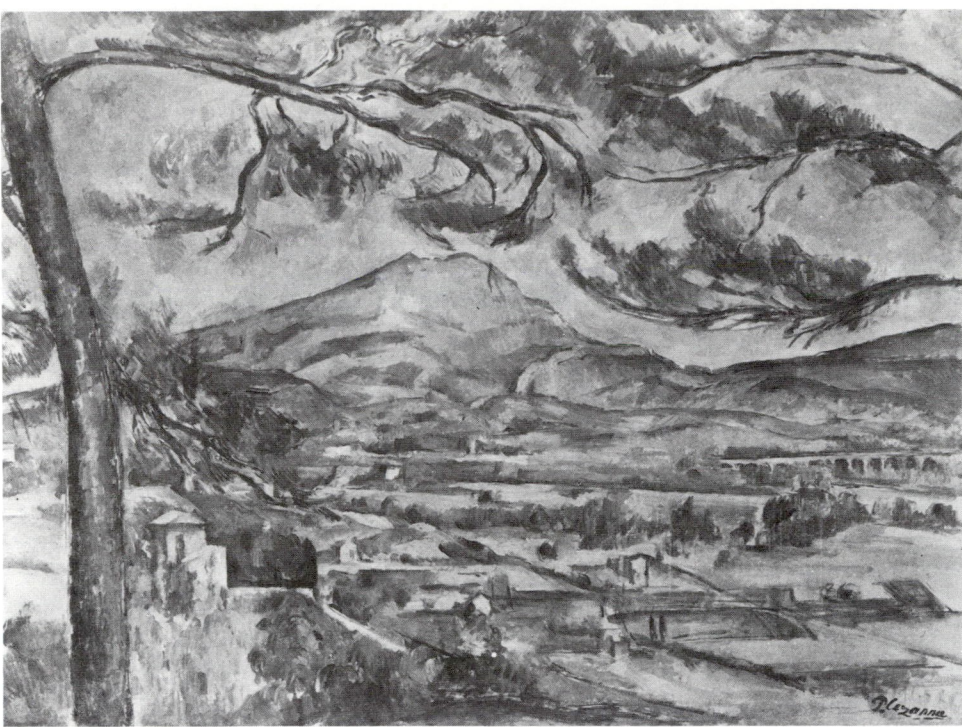

autonomy of the work of art, freed from the task of imitation of nature. This oscillation, the visual shifting of planes, not only continued to be a feature of Cézanne's work, but will become an important device in Cubism called *passage.*

A visual journey through one of Cézanne's greatest compositions, *The Great Bathers* (Raynal, clpl p. 115) reveals the elements of his style as we have seen them thus far: some rather small accent that marks the central axis of the composition; phenomena drained of their naturalistic attributes; figures treated like still-life objects; and space handled ambiguously. To these features must be added Cézanne's method of painting and drawing simultaneously, constructing his planes on the basis of the quality of color that makes warm colors (red) seem to come forward and cool colors (blue) seem to recede. In *The Great Bathers,* the alternation of cool blue and warm reddish-brown reinforces the oscillation that can be seen by following the main rhythmical lines of the composition. The tree trunk at the top left of center is on the picture plane but half way down it is in a recessed plane, with a bather in front of it. Loop through the directions indicated by arms and legs and buttocks, and you will eventually find yourself up the tree trunk on the right, back on the picture plane at the top margin, having gone through a number of planes in the process of making the round trip.

## Paul Gauguin

1848 was a revolutionary year in France. King Louis Philippe was overthrown in the February Revolution, which created the short-lived Second Republic; Marx and Engels published the *Communist Manifesto;* and Paul Gauguin (1848–1903) was born. Perhaps he came to feel that this circumstance obligated him to develop a fiery and rebellious personality. There was also the romantic glamor of his family background that doubtless influenced his self-perception: his great grandfather was said to have been a Spanish nobleman who lived in Peru, and his great uncle had been viceroy of Peru. His grandmother had been a writer, a socialist activist and radical, his father so seriously committed to liberal politics that he exiled himself and his family to Peru at the time of Louis-Napoleon's *coup d'état* (1851). Paul Gauguin's taste for the exotic was probably nurtured by the memories of his childhood years there, and he came to think of himself as a savage and a primitive, indifferent to the manners and morals of conventional society.

This self-perception, however, took a while to erupt—he started out as a successful stock broker in 1871. But three years later he began collecting paintings by the "rebels" (Cézanne, Manet, Monet, Pissarro, Renoir, and Sisley) and began to paint, himself; and that was the beginning of the end for his sober-spirited middle-class Danish wife. After a few years as a "Sunday painter," painting began to absorb more and more of his time, and by 1876 he was able successfully to submit a painting to the official Salon. However, he met Pissarro that year and moved into the Impressionists' circle, exhibiting with them in their last five shows in 1879, '80, '81, '82, and '86. By this time he had thrown up his job entirely and had begun to move beyond Impressionism with Pissarro, whose broken brush stroke had become coarser and whose color had turned to the orange-red range.

**205**

Partly because he was now reduced to poverty, and partly because he was drawn to the idea of living in a primitive society, Gauguin left Paris in 1886 to live for a few months (and thereafter intermittently for a few years) at Pont-Aven, in Brittany, possibly the most backward region of France. The peasants had hardly moved out of the Middle Ages in their religious devoutness, and Gauguin was prepared to see in them the humble children of God. It was thus he painted them in one of the first great masterpieces of his career, *The Vision After the Sermon* (1888) **(J clpl 127; H&F 17.17).** In this painting we see the fully developed Synthetism and Cloisonnism that Gauguin had worked out largely on the basis of theories formulated by Emile Bernard, a young painter-friend of Van Gogh who, at Vincent's suggestion, had gone to Pont-Aven to look up Gauguin.

Synthetism refers to what Gauguin called "the synthesis of form and color derived from the observation of the dominant element." The concept is fundamentally abstract, as Gauguin himself recognized, since it involves the rejection of observed, naturalistic relationships in favor of emphasizing those features that—to the artist—characterize the motif. Eliminating the incidentals of nature, Synthetism produced a simplified silhouette; stressing dominant color, it produced broad, flat areas of discrete hues. Cloisonnism is a system of painting in irregularly shaped color compartments that are closed off by line; its name derives from the medieval technique of making enamel jewelry by enclosing the colored enamel in bent wire fillets, giving the effect of stained-glass decoration in which the colored pieces of glass are enclosed in tracery.

It is no accident that this medievalizing technique arose in the atmosphere of backward Brittany, in a period that saw a peculiar upsurge of mysticism, occultism, and religion. These were the years that saw the rise of Theosophy, a European version of an Indian religio-philosophy that would prove of immense importance for modernist art, since both Wassily Kandinsky and Piet Mondrian became adherents.

The Pont-Aven artists were part of a larger cultural development which produced Symbolism. Largely a literary movement whose founder was Stéphane Mallarmé, Symbolism attempted through nuance and subtle suggestion to communicate ineffable experience. *The Vision After the Sermon* is the visual counterpart of literary Symbolism. Under the influence of the sermon they heard (the priest with Gauguin's features sits among them, cut off in Degas-fashion at the right margin), the women of the village, wearing their traditional coifs (each village in Brittany has its own style of coif) are shown in the thralldom of the mystical event of Jacob's struggle with the mysterious angel (Genesis 32). Beyond the power of speech to say what they *feel,* they are depicted *beyond a natural state of being,* in a transcendent realm of passionate faith, symbolized by the passionate red of the field of struggle. Degas' worldly *Au Théatre,* with its daring diago-

nal balcony rail and view onto the stage from up high, has been transformed into a visionary *experience*—like music, Gauguin explained, painting "acts on the soul through the intermediary of the senses: harmonious colors correspond to the harmonies of sound."

Brittany proved not far enough away from the Parisian world that Gauguin disdained, and in 1891, after a farewell banquet at the Café Voltaire, Gauguin sailed for Tahiti. Except for a stay in Paris, 1893–95, he lived for the rest of his life in the South Pacific, first in Tahiti, then in the Marquesas. He was desperately ill much of the time (Dr. William Feldman of the Mayo Clinic theorized that he suffered from leprosy, rife in Peru when Gauguin was there as a child), and Gauguin thus stands as a radiant example of the artist whose genius empowers him to rise above physical debilitation as well as tragic lack of recognition.

The brilliant color of his Pont-Aven days, and his Synthetist style, remained his signature style in Oceania, and can be seen in his great masterpiece, *Whence Come We? Where Are We? Whither Go We?* (1897) (Estienne, clpl p. 91), which has been rightly called his "spiritual testament." Working on it, he wrote to his closest friend, "I wanted to die, and full of despair I painted it at one go. I made haste to sign it and took a tremendous dose of arsenic" (Estienne, p. 91). The work is a kind of summa of Gauguin's personal beliefs, and of modernism's principles, especially that element in modernism that seeks to communicate perceptions, sensations, that elude words. When he finished this painting, "awakening" from it, as he wrote to a friend, he asked himself, "Whence do we come? Where are we? Where are we going?" and he went on to explain that the words were "a thought which has no longer anything to do with the canvas, expressed in words quite apart on the wall which surrounds it. Not a title but a signature. You see, although I understand very well the value of words—abstract and concrete—in the dictionary, I no longer grasp them in painting. I have tried to interpret my vision in an appropriate decor without recourse to literary means."

The ineffable experiences of birth, life, death, the enigma of human existence, are expressed in the representation of the stages of life from infancy to old age, and in the brooding, mysterious atmosphere created by the color—"blue and Veronese green from one end to the other," he wrote (Estienne p. 93). Left far behind are Impressionism's fleeting moment, its glancing light, its *naturalism.* "Have always before you the Persians, the Cambodians and a bit of the Egyptian," Gauguin wrote a friend. "The great mistake is the Greek one, however beautiful it may be" (Estienne p. 96).

## Vincent van Gogh

Linked by common social convictions and aesthetic perceptions, Paul Gauguin and Vincent van Gogh (1853–1890) are also indissolubly joined in the history of art by the tragic nature of their lives, and the tragic moment they shared. They met in 1886, in Paris, shortly after Van Gogh's arrival there, to begin his career as an artist in earnest—his third attempt to find a life work that suited the moral and religious demands of his spirit. Van Gogh was the last great religious artist in the history of Western art, although except for some copies after other artists that he admired, particularly Rembrandt and Delacroix, he never painted an overtly religious subject.

Born in Holland, he was the son of a minister and nephew of three art dealers associated with an important French firm, Goupil and Company. He worked for Goupil from 1873 to 1876, in The Hague, Brussels, London, and Paris, in all four of which cities he succeeded in alienating not only his fellow employees but the firm's clients. He was fired, of course, and decided wisely that business was not to be his metier. Deeply religious, he prepared to enter a theological school in Amsterdam but failed the entrance examination. In Brussels he took an evangelical training course, and managed to get himself sent to the Borinage, a coal mining district famous for the miserable conditions in which the miners lived. He gave away whatever small personal possessions he had, and chose to live more poorly than the poorest of his flock. The miners and his superiors found his zeal incomprehensible and once again he lost his job.

Vincent had been drawing from an early age, and now he determined that he could serve God through his art. He called himself a "painter of peasants," like Millet, whom he admired, and saw his new career as a vocation for which he had prepared. "It's not for nothing that I have spent so many evenings brooding before the fire in the homes of miners, turfcutters and weavers," he wrote in a letter. Indeed, so we see in the painting that climaxes his first period, 1880–1885, *The Potato Eaters* (1885) (**J 899;** Rosenblum/Janson clpl 72), a convincingly realistic scene of poor peasants at their evening meal—or so at first it seems. They are dour, unlovely people, lumpy as the potatoes they subsist on, of the earth, earthy. And yet, we are caught and held by a mysterious intensity that soon transforms the humble real into something more beautiful and more wonderful than the eye perceives. A single flame burns in this room—in traditional iconography, a symbol of the presence of God, as for example in Jan van Eyck's Arnolfini wedding portrait (**J clpl 62; G 18.12**) and in the central panel of the *Mérode Altarpiece* (**J clpl 60; G 18.6**), where this meaning is stressed as one candle is extinguished, leaving only one burning to signify the entrance of Christ into the world. To underline sacred associations, Van Gogh has arranged his figures in an oval, close to a circle, a symbol of eternity. One man, perhaps the grandfather/patriarch of what appears to be an extended family of three generations, holds out his cup in a pose that is both offering and receiving. On the wall at the left is a small picture of a Crucifixion. All of these features, together with the fact that the family *is* a sacred group, that eating one's daily bread *is* for such families an act of sacred thanksgiving, point, then, to the religious content of *The Potato Eaters*. The dark color, the deliberately crude-looking draftsmanship, the proportion of the figures to the cramped space, which makes them seem monumentally large, is the vocabulary Van Gogh uses to express his thought in non-religious, vernacular imagery.

Van Gogh had not only handled a great deal of art in his years as a dealer, he had also gone constantly to the museums where, in The Hague, in Brussels, in London, in Paris, he had seen many of the masterpieces of Western painting. When he arrived in Paris, he was no novice when it came to art. His brother Theo, moreover, was there to guide him into the most advanced circles, and he soon gave up the dark realism of his first style, quickly trying out the lessons to be learned from Impressionism and Post-Impressionism, including the pointillist style of Seurat, to which we will presently turn.

Even before Paris, he had been drawn to Japanese woodcuts, and now he found reinforcement among the vanguard painters for this taste, as reflected in his portrait of *Père Tanguy* (1887) (Rewald p. 45). The sitter was a dealer in artists' supplies, devoted to his struggling customers. His shop was a meeting place for Pissarro, Cézanne, Gauguin, and many others, and he accumulated a peerless collection of paintings that, when he took them in lieu of payment, few people cared about.

Van Gogh produces an amazing new flavor for the eyes by surrounding this heavy-bodied Breton peasant with the exotic elegance of Japanese woodcuts. *Tanguy* is portrayed with much of the stolid crudeness of the Belgian peasants of *The Potato Eaters,* his hands as thick and knobby as theirs. But the painting style is a world away from Van Gogh's recent past. The colors of the background are bright, setting off the more somber hue of Tanguy's bulky figure, which is presented with archaic frontality, his presence established like an icon. And we see now what becomes one of Van Gogh's constant formal means of expression; the varying of brush strokes—long, short, stumpy, curved, straight, often arranged parallel to each other—that creates a totally new kind of visual rhythm.

Van Gogh had conceived of the south of France as a kind of Japan. Just as Gauguin felt the need to get as far away as he could from what he saw as the over-civilized, over-conventionalized culture of Paris, so too, Van Gogh. He could not go to Japan, so he went south, to Arles, arriving in February 1888. Here he found his Japan in the flowering orchards of springtime, and here in Arles, the living energy of nature became Van Gogh's true subject, nature understood as the presence of God in the world.

It was his perception of nature and religion that led him to his idealized view of Japan. As he wrote to his brother with chilling prophecy, it was necessary to see "beyond the disasters that are all the same bound to strike the modern world and civilization like terrible lightning, through revolution or war, or the bankruptsy of worm-eaten states. . . . If we study Japanese art, we see an artist who is undoubtedly wise, philosophic, intelligent, who spends his time doing what? In studying the distance between the earth and the moon? No. In studying Bismarck's policy? No. He studies a single blade of grass. But this blade of grass leads him to draw every plant, and then the seasons, the wide aspects of the countryside, then animals, then the human figure. So he passes his life, and life is too short to do the whole. Come now, isn't it a true religion that these Japanese teach us . . . ?" The description of the Japanese philosopher-artist reveals, of course, Van Gogh's grasp of the interrelatedness of all of nature and his own artistic intentions.

Nature, religion, and Japanese influence combine in one of the great masterpieces of the Arles period, *The Sower* (Pickvance clpl 128), painted in the fall of 1888, inspired by Millet, whom Van Gogh highly esteemed, and by the Bible which Van Gogh knew from constant, devoted reading. With the quotation above in mind, forecasting the dire end of civilization, we should turn to Matthew 13, in which the parable of the sower is explained, and especially to Matthew 13:36, where Christ explains, "The field is the world; the good seed is the subjects of the kingdom, the weeds the subjects of the evil one . . . the harvest is the end of the world. At the end of time, the Son of Man will send his angels and they will gather out of his kingdom all things that provoke offenses and all who do evil, and throw them into the blazing furnace. . . . Then the virtuous will shine like the sun in the kingdom of their father. Listen, anyone who has ears!" We may be sure that Vincent had attentive ears.

*The Sower,* composed like Gauguin's *Vision after the Sermon,* and painted during Gauguin's stay with Van Gogh in Arles, makes even more explicit than *The Potato Eaters* Van Gogh's conviction that the humble of the earth are really its saints. He has adjusted the relationship of the sun to the head of the sower in such a way as to make it look like a halo. The tree sends out rapier branches that look as if they could pierce human flesh, but at the same time it bears blossoms, symbols of return to life. The sower is the re-awakener of life in mother earth, after her long winter dormancy; he is also the saved, the humble resurrected who shall inherit the earth after its destruction by the wars and revolutions that Van Gogh predicted.

It is not the least of Vincent's tragedy that he constantly sought love and peace, and just as constantly antagonized everyone around him. One of Van Gogh's hopes, in going south, was to establish an artists' colony, and he envisioned a community of artists all working happily together, sharing their problems and their discoveries. This was the reason for Gauguin's trip to Arles; he was to help Vincent prepare the ground for others. Waiting for Gauguin's arrival toward the end of October, 1888, Van Gogh was like a bridegroom, fixing up a room for his friend, and planning their future blissful artistic life. For a short time things apparently went well enough for them, but by December tensions between them were mounting. On Christmas Eve, according to Gauguin, he went out for

a walk, heard footsteps behind him, turned to find Van Gogh following him as if in a trance, holding a razor. What ever happened then, Van Gogh fled back to his house, slashed off part of his left ear, wrapped it up and took it to the local brothel that he visited—hating himself after each visit—and gave it to one of the women in the house. A strange Christmas gift. Its sexual connotations aside, surely there is more than coincidence in the date—the birth of Christ, whose wounds would eventually symbolize salvation—his self-wounding, and the gift to a "sinful woman," a Mary Magdalen.

Gauguin went back to Paris, Vincent spent two weeks in a hospital, but recognized in the spring of 1889 how desperately disturbed he was and had himself committed to an asylum at Saint-Rémy, not far from Arles. During 1889 he had three serious attacks of madness, but between them, he painted some of the greatest works of his career, including *Starry Night* (1889) **(G 21.69),** a work in which Meyer Schapiro found "apocalyptic fantasy" (*Van Gogh,* p. 100). In this painting, cosmic in its implications, the world is nevertheless closing in, as can be seen increasingly in all of his compositions from the Saint-Rémy period to the end of his life. There is no path for the eye to explore the landscape or look up to a distant sky. The heavens are as present as the cypress tree.

The whole universe heaves and swells in a cosmic drama that dwarfs humankind. And yet, humankind is not overwhelmed by the titanic forces of the universe. If the church cannot aspire to the heights of nature's cypress, it nevertheless reaches up to the heavens, and it stands protectingly over the small houses that nestle around it. It has been suggested that *Starry Night* was inspired by Genesis 37:9, where Joseph tells his brothers, "I have had another dream. I thought I saw the sun, the moon, and eleven stars bowing to me." If so, perhaps this unappreciated, unrecognized genius foresaw the day when, like Joseph, he too would command the esteem of the world, and *his* true worth would be discovered. As it did for Joseph of the many-colored coat, so indeed has that triumphant day come for this Joseph of the brilliant-colored canvas, on which he gestured his exalted vision of universal love.

## Georges Seurat

Destiny has strange ways of bringing people together, and it was surely extraordinary that Georges Seurat (1859–1891), an aspiring teen-age art student in the late 1870s, should have been brought to Piero della Francesca, in every way his spiritual ancestor. Piero was of a scientific turn of mind, deeply interested in applying the laws of mathematics to art. His geometric conception of form, in fact, produced images that—staggering to contemplate— anticipate Cubism by 450 years (see **J 568,** the upper left corner representing the City of Jerusalem, and compare it with a Georges Braque landscape with houses of 1908). Piero's was the ultimate rational mind among Early

Renaissance painters, and Georges Seurat inherited this mantle to wear among the French vanguard artists of the 1880s, thanks to Charles Blanc.

One of France's most influential critics and professors of art history in the nineteenth century, Blanc had commissioned a minor artist to make copies of Piero's famous fresco cycle in the Church of San Francesco at Arezzo **(J clpl 68; G 16.35)** for the Ecole des Beaux Arts. The impact of Piero on Seurat, who studied at the Ecole from 1877 to 1879, cannot be doubted. Translated into nineteenth-century terms, Seurat's first important painting, *Bathers, Asnières* (1883–1884) **(J 897; H&F clpl 17.10),** brings Piero's stately forms to modernism. In it one sees the two elements on which Seurat's art was based: scientific research, which gave him his formal language, and socialist ideology, which influenced his content.

Seurat was fascinated with the physics of color which showed that there were *laws* of color, just as there were *laws* of musical harmony. Most important of the laws of color was the law of simultaneous contrast as it had been expounded by Michel Eugène Chevreul, a noted French chemist, who showed that a color achieves its maximum intensity of effect when juxtaposed to its complementary color. This means, for example, that blue seems most intense when seen next to orange, red when seen next to green, yellow when seen next to violet, and so on, with every hue contrasted with its complementary. To this physical analysis of Chevreul on the nature of color, Seurat added the analyses of Charles Henry, a brilliantly gifted young scientist whose mind was equally excited by the arts. Henry held that color relationships and line relationships produced determined *expressive* effects— light emphasized over dark, and upward moving lines produced happy effects, the opposite combinations created the contrary effects—and the possibilities of combinations were almost infinite.

In the *Bathers,* whose monumental size together with several stylistic features suggests that Seurat was aiming to rival the immensely admired muralist of the period, Puvis de Chavannes **(G 21.51; H&F clpl 17.11),** he systematically, although not yet completely, brings into balance the various formal elements that an artist deals with—light and shade, color relationships, and linear directions—and expresses his socialist sympathies in three ways. He chose for his scene a recognizable spot on the Seine at Asnières, an industrial section of Paris—in the background are factories with smoke plumes issuing from the chimneys; he formally monumentalized his subjects who were *working-class young men;* and he presented his working-class subjects in an iconographical context associated with high classicism—*Bathers*. The work is executed in relatively large, flat, Impressionist-influenced broken strokes using pure colors and earth colors, which Seurat had observed in Delacroix. It was Paul Signac (1863–1935) who persuaded him to give up the earth colors, when they met in 1884 at the Society of Independ-

ents, which they co-founded with other artists rejected by the Salon. Together the two young painters worked out the complete theory of what has become known as Neo-Impressionism, Impressionism systematized. The term was invented by Félix Fénéon, a critic of the same age as the artists. He was the first and only one to recognize the importance of Seurat in 1884, when *Bathers* was exhibited at the Independents, and began to write about him in 1886 at the last Impressionist exhibition, where Seurat showed his monumental *Sunday Afternoon on the Island of La Grande Jatte* (1884–1886) **(G 21.64),** which was greeted by a chorus of abuse as loud and angry as any suffered by Manet and the Impressionists.

*La Grande Jatte* is the first fully realized work in which Seurat worked out the theories he had developed. It is executed in a technique using small dabs of color that soon was called pointillism or divisionism. He employed three pairs of complementary colors—red/green, yellow/violet, and blue/orange—and adjusted his lights and darks, and his horizontals and verticals, to achieve an effect of static balance. The rhythm is stately and has the ceremonial effect of Piero's majestic procession showing the Queen of Sheba with her entourage in the Arezzo fresco.

This is, indeed, a ceremonial procession. Sunday is a ceremonial day, when middle-class people follow the ritual of church and Sunday dinner and a walk in the park. One knows that the "same" people will be seen every Sunday, walking, sitting, in the sun or shade, as much a part of the scenery as the upright trees and the flat ground and the shimmering mirror-like river. They are dressed in the stiff, tightly corseted style of the Victorian period, and their movements match their clothes. With one prominent exception. In the foreground, in the left-hand corner, is the figure of a man who by his garb and slouching, relaxed posture is shown clearly not to belong to this upright middle-class society. He is the only one who is not entirely there, since the lower part of his left leg, and his right foot, are not in the picture. Wearing a cap, as opposed to the top hat worn by gentlemen, and a sleeveless shirt, and smoking a cheap pipe—not a fine Havana, which we can be sure the cigar-holding stroller is smoking—this worker on his day of rest is the first of his class to invade the precincts of the middle class. The implication that he will be followed by others seems inevitable, and the class resentment thus aroused is acted out by the aggressive little dog, wearing a collar, going after the unnoticing mongrel, enjoying his sniff at the grass.

With Seurat's interest in science, and his faith in its practical applications, it is not surprising to find that, unlike Gauguin and Van Gogh, he welcomed industrial technology. He was the only major artist of his time to respond artistically to the engineering marvel that was completed in 1889 for the Paris Exposition that year, the Eiffel Tower. Given his ideological bent, it is not surprising that when Seurat turned to entertainment for a theme, he chose the circus and the sideshow, attractions of a lower-class clientele than frequented the ballet at the opera or the Folies Bergère. *La Parade* (1878–88) **(G clpl 125)** depicts a street show meant to entice passersby to buy tickets for the circus performance on the inside. It offered the challenge of an urban night scene, illuminated not by nature, as in Impressionist painting, but by artificial means, and goes further than *La Grande Jatte* in adhering to mathematical order, since it is composed on the principle called the golden section, which since antiquity had been considered to produce ideal proportions.

Despite the rigid application of his theories and the manikin appearance of his figures, there is a strange poetry in Seurat's work. He is a founder of the structuralist current in modernism, but his sedate, orderly compositions have a luminosity that, while not in the least religious, makes them shine with a spiritual, expressive glow. His methods have been applied, and even the peculiar brooding atmosphere that permeates his compositions has been imitated. And yet, few Neo-Impressionist paintings have the lyrical power that Seurat achieved in the tragically few years of his career. Perhaps only Pissarro in his Neo-Impressionist period matched Seurat's mystery and intuition while painting according to rules.

## Summary

By mid-century, the cultural contours of the Western world were undergoing rapid changes. Imperialism had brought the non-Western world into closer view, world trade was accelerating, and soon the old tradition of local fairs expanded into the first World's Fair in London in 1851, followed by the Paris Exposition in 1855, which was the first to feature an international section devoted to the arts. The globalization of the world had begun. An important moment in this movement toward globalization occurred when in 1854 Matthew Perry succeeded in opening up Japan to Western trade, and soon Japanese-consciousness began to seep into advanced Western artistic circles. Japanese methods of design, attractive for exotic reasons, were also appealing because they offered alternatives to three-dimensional modeling and mathematical perspective; the resulting images made more immediate impact and were consequently more consonant with modern sensibility. Japanese art thus contributed to the compression of space which became a feature of modernism in its effort to liberate itself from serving narrative or didactic ends.

By mid-century, too, the features of modern life as we know it today were emerging. No one could have said then which features of contemporary life were significant, but looking back we see clearly that the class structure of Western culture was feeling deep and strong seismic shocks. The new working class and peasants were making bids for power in the body politic which, despite setbacks, show a steadily rising profile. At first this rise was reflected in the increased visibility of rural workers in works of art that monumentalized them while depicting the unadorned truth of their lives, and in the rural landscape. This was the field cultivated by Courbet, Millet, and the Barbizon painters.

The bourgeoisie had also gained in economic and political power and now had hours of leisure in which to enjoy entertainments. Public theatres, cabarets, and pleasure resorts mushroomed and flourished, and became the new subject matter for vanguard artists. Manet, Degas, and the Impressionists developed the painting of this aspect of modern life, especially in its urban environment.

The phenomenon of rapid change in every facet of human culture began its acceleration around the middle of the nineteenth century, and with it came the heightened values of speed and contemporaneity. In art these values were translated into the sketchy look, the spontaneous effect, the fleeting moment, and the momentary pose. A new vantage point revealed the world-out-there in a new light but, paradoxically, the effort to capture objective optical reality resulted in a shift of emphasis from the objective world to the artists' subjective world of the canvas: art gradually took itself as primary subject matter.

Around 1880 certain dissatisfactions with Impressionism began to appear. Not only did former Impressionists—Renoir, Pissarro, Cézanne—alter their styles, but younger artists at the beginning of their careers found Impressionism inadequate for their artistic intentions. The four seminal painters of the 1880s, the leaders of Post-Impressionism, were Cézanne, Gauguin, Van Gogh, and Seurat. These were the major artists who, through their works, taught the basic lessons of modernism. In the units on twentieth-century art it will be convenient to refer back to the following outline, so that the origins of modernist styles can be quickly seen.

Cézanne taught that

1. Form is created out of the relationship of color tones.

2. Surface and depth planes are interlocked by means of modulated color.

3. Space is understood as *pictorial space:* it is not illusionistic, meant to match the world-out-there as if seen through a window or on a stage. Pictorial space is a surface with spatial vibrations produced by color relationships.

4. Because of the nature of pictorial space, objects do not have a fixed relationship with the picture plane: an oscillation occurs as viewers move their eyes from one area to another of the picture.

Cézanne called himself the primitive of a new way. Essentially he saw art as the transformation of nature by the formative mind of the artist. Colored forms are *metaphors* for the world, not representations of it. Cézanne influenced both of the two main currents of twentieth-century style, constructivism and expressionism, but his immediate impact was made with the former, since it offered clues to Picasso and Braque that led them to the development of Cubism.

Gauguin sought to resolve the perceptions of the sensory world and the spiritual world and taught that

1. To express in painting is not the same as to describe.

2. Memory gives back what is important, thus the artist must create without direct observation of the model—which has been previously observed and is remembered in the act of creating. This is the method of Synthetism, the act of intensifying and concentrating the natural impression stored in memory.

3. Painting acts upon the soul, like music. Color harmonies are like sound harmonies. Color is not meant to describe the surface appearance of a thing but to convey the emotion evoked by the thing, which is the *raison d'être* of its presence in the painting.

4. The artist's truth is found in myth, destroyed in Europe by the rationalism of the Greek tradition, but still alive in distant lands—Tahiti, for example—where the natives lived in a state of nature and thus experienced reality more directly.

Gauguin's impact was made on the artists associated with the Fauve movement, Derain especially, and on the entire Expressionist development. He also prepared the way for primitivizing in modernist art.

Van Gogh taught that

1. Color can convey spiritual meaning and human passions.

2. Line may suggest the pulsating, dynamic rhythm of the universe. An object is not defined by or contained by lines: its inner vitality, struggling to be expressed, takes control of its contours.

3. The liberated, dynamic contours create an enlivened space that becomes a visual field of energy.

Van Gogh's impact on the Expressionist current of modernism is incalculable. The German Expressionists, the Italian Futurists, the American Abstract Expressionists all owe a direct debt to Van Gogh.

Georges Seurat taught that

1. The contrast of complementary colors is fundamental to the construction of a composition, and to its expressive effect.

2. Adjustments of color and line react on viewers with the effect of subject matter: it is not the gay or sad scene that communicates emotion, but the relationships produced by the formal language of color and line.

3. Scientific clarity of conception is not antithetical to poetic intuition.

Seurat's pointillism (also called divisionism, and referred to as Neo-Impressionism) was highly influential in the formative years of Fauvism, especially in the art of Matisse and Derain, and of Futurism. It was one of the earliest manifestations of the analytical spirit that has been an important feature of modernism. It was adopted momentarily by a number of twentieth-century artists, including Picasso, for a variety of effects, none of which had anything to do with Seurat's scientific intention.

Assessing the position of art at the end of the nineteenth century, we see that the nature of art had undergone radical re-definition since mid-century, and two aesthetic currents were flowing into mainstream Western art. The expressionist current saw that its prime responsibility was no longer to give a physical account of the perceived world, but to mediate for viewers the expressive reality of the world. Thus the representation of measurement, the glorious discovery of the Renaissance, became irrelevant; knowing was seen to be intuitive and subjective, not accessible therefore to rulers and clocks. Picturing the world as ordinarily perceived was no longer a task worthy of art; art was obliged to venture beyond perception to find a language of feeling.

The second current, geometric and constructive, was less noticeable, at century's end, but was soon to become significant in the hands of Picasso and Braque. Both expressionist and constructivist modes contained the impulse toward abstraction and non-objective art. Meanwhile, medievalism and modernism had made a stunning alliance in the world of decoration, creating the style known as Art Nouveau.

## Textbook References

**J** Janson covers the topics of Realism, Impressionism, and Post-Impressionism in two chapters. He begins with an extensive discussion of Courbet, followed by a summary of Manet's revolutionary achievements. A discussion of the Impressionist works by Morisot, Degas, Renoir, and Monet precedes a treatment of the English reaction to Realism, through the works of the Pre-Raphaelite artists, in particular Rossetti and Morris. American achievements in the same period are examined in works by Whistler and Eakins. A good summary of sculpture through the work of Rodin ends the discussion of Impressionism. Post-Impressionism is primarily studied through the works of Seurat, Cézanne, and Van Gogh. Gauguin is treated as part of the Symbolists, along with the Nabis group, Redon, Moreau, and the English artist Beardsley. This section leads directly into a discussion of the Viennese Secession. Maillol, Minne, Lehmbruck, and Barlach are used to focus on sculptural developments in the late nineteenth century. The chapter closes with a short but perceptive discussion on photography.

**G** Gardner begins her study of Realism and Impressionism with Corot, Millet, and Daumier, and examines their ideas on form and color value. With Courbet, she examines the search for new themes for the modern world, and the artist's simple, direct methods of expression, as well as his composition and technique. The impact of Courbet is examined mainly through the works of Manet, as well as those by the English painter Rossetti, the American Thomas Eakins, and the German Wilhelm Leibl, among others. The Romantic rejection of Realism is discussed through the works of English masters Millais and Burne-Jones, as well as academic painting in France as represented by Bouguereau. An extensive summary of Impressionism and the responses to the new style in the work of Seurat, Cézanne, Van Gogh, Gauguin, Moreau, and Redon follows. Sculpture and architecture are briefly addressed at the end of the chapter.

**H&F** Honour and Fleming give a highly abbreviated account of the Realist, Impressionist, and Post-Impressionist movements. Like Janson and Gardner, the emphasis of this text is on developments in France and on painting almost to the exclusion of architecture and sculpture. Honour and Fleming's treatment is more theoretical. They cite the essential aesthetic and philosophical premises at the core of modern art, as they also make an attempt to set the revolutionary developments within the context of late nineteenth-century society.

**Janson, Part IV, The Modern World, Chapter 2: Realism and Impressionism, pp. 618–636.** France: Courbet, Manet, Monet, Morisot, Renoir, Degas. England: the Pre-Raphaelites. America: Whistler, Homer, Eakins, Cassatt.

**Post-Impressionism, pp. 640–658.** Cézanne, Seurat, Van Gogh, Gauguin and Symbolism, Picasso's Blue Period.

**Gardner, Part V, The Modern World, Chapter 21, section 2: The Second Half of the Nineteenth Century: The Predominance of Realism, pp. 836–877.** Transition: Corot, Millet, Daumier. Realism: Courbet, Manet; Eakins, Homer. Romantic responses to Realism (the Pre-Raphaelites). Impressionism: Monet, Pissarro, Renoir, Degas, Cassatt. Post-Impressionism: Seurat, Cézanne, Van Gogh, Gauguin, Toulouse-Lautrec.

**Honour and Fleming, Part 4, Chapter 15: Romanticism to Realism, pp. 480–507.** Historicism and Realism; Courbet; Millet; Manet; Homer; Eakins.

**Chapter 17: Impressionism to Post-Impressionism, pp. 520–546.** Impressionism: Monet, Renoir, Manet, Degas. Japonisme, Whistler. Neo-Impressionism, Seurat; Symbolism, Gauguin; Van Gogh; Cézanne.

## Study Questions

1. What are the similarities and differences between the paintings of Courbet and the Barbizon artists?
2. If you had been a member of the jury selecting paintings for the Salon of 1863, would you have voted to accepted Manet's *Luncheon on the Grass?* Explain your answer.
3. What approximate date would you assign to a painting by Manet dealing with a Spanish subject?
4. Give one Impressionist characteristic exemplified in paintings by Degas; by Monet; by Renoir. Give different characteristics for each, citing a painting as an example.
5. Give two reasons for the dissatisfaction some artists felt with regard to Impressionism beginning around 1880.
6. What similarities are found in advanced painting in France and the United States in the middle of the 1860s?
7. What nineteenth-century values are reflected in Pre-Raphaelite painting?
8. What did Cézanne mean by saying that one must see in nature the cylinder, the sphere, and the cone?
9. Which artist is associated with Synthetism? Explain its meaning.
10. What features of Japanese art attracted Van Gogh?
11. Explain what is meant by complementary colors. What artist systematized the use of complementary colors and in what painting does the system first appear fully developed?
12. What is the central difference between Impressionism and Post-Impressionism?

## Glossary

**Art-for-Art's Sake** the nineteenth-century term for the theory that art should be primarily concerned with formal matters—basically color, line, texture, and space—rather than subject matter. The position is succinctly stated by Whistler, a proponent of the analogy between music and painting: "Art should be independent of all clap-trap—should stand alone, and appeal to the artistic sense of eye or ear, without confounding this with emotions entirely foreign to it, as devotion, pity, love, patriotism, and the like."

**allegory** in art, a metaphoric representation, often the personification of an abstract idea such as Truth, Beauty, or Goodness, or the personification of a feature of nature, such as the figure of a river god representing a river.

**Barbizon School** refers to painters loosely grouped together because they lived and worked (ca. 1830–1870) in Barbizon, a village near the Forest of Fontainebleau, and because they shared certain aesthetic aims, including naturalistic representation and the evocation of quietude and serenity.

**broken brush stroke** the technique of leaving individual brush strokes as independent marks on the canvas, instead of blending them with other strokes. A kind of calligraphic painting. Helps to produce the brilliant flicker effect of Impressionist art.

**cloisonnism** the technique associated with Gauguin and other Pont-Aven painters whereby irregular shapes of discrete color are enclosed in line.

**complementary color**    pertains to either of a pair of contrasting colors which, on a color wheel for example, occupy opposite places. Each of the pair has the property of creating an afterimage of its "complement." If you stare at something red, and then close your eyes, you will see an "afterimage" of green, red's complement.

**Divisionism**    the technique of applying complementary colors next to each other in very small broken brush strokes. Also called pointillism and Neo-Impressionism.

**Impressionism**    a style of painting that emerged in France about 1869 in the work of Monet and Renoir. It is characterized by the technique of broken brush strokes, makes use mainly of light, bright color, and gives a sketchy, spontaneous effect of dazzling, flickering, momentary light or movement caught in action. It is holistic in composition, that is, the painting is meant to be taken in as a whole image rather than examined part by part.

**Neo-Impressionism**    *see* Divisionism.

**pastel**    colored chalk. Degas was the first artist to use pastel as a major medium for subjects other than portraits.

**picture plane**    the surface of the image co-extensive with the support, usually canvas, or paper, or wood panel, or plastered wall. The nature of vision is such that, although all marks actually lie on the surface, some produce the illusion of being farther away, creating *pictorial* depth. The destruction of the illusion of pictorial space has been a major issue in modernist art, and can be seen to emerge in the work of Manet.

**plein-air**    refers to painting outdoors, and theoretically, at least, to making finished paintings "on the spot."

**Pointillism**    *see* Divisionism.

**Positivism**    a philosophical system associated with Auguste Comte (1798–1857) that affirms experience as given by the five senses as the only valid method of knowing reality.

**Post-Impressionism**    refers to several styles that grew out of a rejection of the form-dissolving features of Impressionism and its primary emphasis on optical experience. Cézanne, Gauguin, Van Gogh, and Seurat are the four artists mainly associated with Post-Impressionism.

**Pre-Raphaelite Brotherhood**    a group of British artists who formed a movement at mid-nineteenth century to reject both academic teaching and Neo-Classical style, which they considered products of the High Renaissance. Pre-Raphaelitism aimed stylistically for photographic clarity of image and detailed description; in content it tended to be piously moralistic.

**pure visibility**    the theory that visual art should appeal uniquely to the sense of sight. The argument for pure visibility rested largely on the analogy between painting and music, which appeals uniquely to the sense of hearing.

**Realism**    pertains to verisimilitude in form, and to class- or plight-consciousness in content.

**Symbolism**    in painting, the art of suggesting an idea by means of color, line, texture, and space. The Symbolist movement was primarily a literary development.

**Synthetism**    associated with Gauguin, who aimed to synthesize form and meaning by symbolic means.

**Transcendentalism**    associated with Emanuel Kant, this is a system of thought directly opposite to Positivism (see above). It conceives of space, time, and certain categories of knowledge as inaccessible to the senses and therefore not within the reach of experience but knowable through reason.

## Artists, Patrons, and Important Personages

**Baudelaire Charles**    (France, 1821–1867). Poet (*Flowers of Evil*) and highly influential critic.

**Bazille, Frédéric** (France, 1841–1870). One of the original group that formed the Impressionist movement.

**Blanc, Charles.** Founder of the *Gazette des Beaux-arts* (1859), still France's leading journal of art history. He was a foremost conservative critic and important art historian, author of *Histoire des peintres,* a multi-volume work completed in 1875.

**Boudin, Eugène** (France, 1824–1898). An early practitioner of outdoor painting and an important influence in forming Claude Monet's style.

**Bouguereau, Adolphe William** (France, 1825–1905). A leading academic painter in the second half of the nineteenth century.

**Cassatt, Mary** (United States, 1845–1926). The first American woman artist to win international recognition. Related to the Impressionists, in style, her work was influenced mainly by Degas and Renoir.

**Cézanne, Paul** (France, 1839–1906). The artist Matisse called "the father of us all." He imposed geometric, classical compositional methods on Impressionism, and is seen as the forerunner of Cubism.

**Champfleury, Jules** (France, 1828–1889). Novelist and art critic; the acknowledged leader of the Realist movement.

**Corot, Camille** (France, 1796–1875). Although a figure painter of considerable power, he won international acclaim for his lyrical landscapes, and was an important transition figure in the development of naturalism from the first half to the second half of the nineteenth century.

**Courbet, Gustave** (France, 1819–1877). Most brilliant painter of the Realist movement, to which he gave enormous impetus.

**Couture, Thomas** (France, 1815–1879). An outstanding academic painter and would-be teacher of Manet, who studied in his studio for several years.

**Degas, Edgar** (France, 1834–1917). One of the foremost masters of French nineteenth-century painting, and of the vanguard movement that formed in the 1860s. A daring composer, his contribution to Impressionism lay in his skewed view of phenomena which resulted in compressed pictorial space and unconventional shapes that led in the direction of abstraction. The first artist to employ pastel as a major medium for subjects other than portraits.

**Duranty, Edmond.** Journalist, novelist, and art critic who understood and admired Degas and the new art, which he defended in reviews.

**Duret, Théodore.** Journalist and art critic. Foremost among the defenders of Manet and the new art.

**Eakins, Thomas** (United States, 1844–1916). Widely acknowledged as the outstanding American realist painter of the nineteenth century.

**Fénéon, Félix.** Critic who coined the term Neo-Impressionism in connection with the pointillist style.

**Gauguin, Paul** (France, 1848–1903). One of the four seminal painters in the Post-Impressionist period. He developed, with Emile Bernard, a style which he called Synthetism and which is also referred to as cloisonnism (see Glossary for both terms).

**Gautier, Théophile.** French novelist; among the most prominent drama and art critics of his day.

**Homer, Winslow** (United States, 1836–1910). A master of genre painting in his first period, Homer's later works deal on a commanding level with the universal theme of struggle. Some of Homer's most majestic works were executed in watercolor, in which medium he has not been surpassed.

**Hunt, William Holman** (England, 1827–1910). One of the founders of the Pre-Raphaelite Brotherhood (see Glossary).

**Jongkind, Johann** (Holland, 1819–1891). A forerunner of Impressionism with his transparent, luminous effects of light, especially reflected on water, he was a major influence on Monet and a master in his own right.

**Leroy, Louis.** Critic who is responsible for attaching the term "Impressionist" to Monet, Pissarro, and their circle in his review of their exhibition in 1874.

**Mallarmé, Stéphane.** French poet; founder of the Symbolist movement in literature. His best-known poem, *Afternoon of a Faun,* inspired a composition by Debussy and a ballet made famous by Vaslav Nijinsky, one of the greatest dancers of all time.

**Manet, Edouard** (1832–1883). Widely considered the founder of modernist painting. Associated with Impressionism, he only partially shared Impressionist aesthetics. He never participated in an Impressionist exhibition.

**Millais, John Everett** (England, 1829–1896). A founder of the Pre-Raphaelite Brotherhood (see Glossary).

**Millet, Jean François** (France, 1814–1875). Major French genre painter of the nineteenth century, Millet's paintings of peasants were of some influence on Van Gogh.

**Meissonier, Ernest** (France, 1815–1890). Prominent academic painter.

**Monet, Claude** (France, 1840–1926). Leader of the Impressionist movement. The definition of Impressionism is based on Monet's style, and thus no other painter fits the description "Impressionist" quite as well.

**Morisot, Berthe** (France, 1841–1895). Member of the Impressionist group, she exhibited in seven of the eight Impressionist Exhibitions, missing only that of 1879.

**Nadar, Felix** (France, 1820–1910). One of the first masters of photography, whom, in a cartoon, Honoré Daumier accused of trying to raise photography to the heights of art. Nadar lent his studio to Monet and his friends for their first group exhibition in 1874, now known as the first Impressionist exhibition.

**Pissarro, Camille** (St. Thomas, W.I., 1831–1903). Theorist and teacher of Impressionism, the only artist to participate in all eight Impressionist exhibitions. Took up pointillism in 1886, which he practiced for several years.

**Renoir, Pierre-Auguste** (France, 1841–1919). Of the original Impressionists, Renoir was the most classically inclined and was therefore the first to search for a way of synthesizing Impressionism with traditional values.

**Rossetti, Dante Gabriel** (1828–1882). Painter and poet; one of the founders of the Pre-Raphaelite Brotherhood (see Glossary), and author of the famous poem *The Blessed Damozel.*

**Rousseau, Théodore** (France, 1812–1867). Foremost landscape painter of the Barbizon School (see Glossary).

**Whistler, James McNeil** (United States, 1834–1903). A strong exponent of Art-for Art's Sake (see Glossary), his theory of art anticipated the development of abstract painting. His etchings are among the most highly prized in the field of graphic art.

**Zola, Emile.** A contemporary and childhood friend of Cézanne, he was a leading French novelist of the naturalist school of literature, devoted to scientific accuracy in portraying in his fiction the class structure of France.

## Bibliography

This bibliography includes books and exhibition catalogues written in English, plus several citations including *catalogues raisonnés* in French when there is no English edition. Articles are not listed, except for those cited in the text.

### ILLUSTRATION REFERENCES *IN ADDITION TO JANSON, GARDNER, AND HONOUR AND FLEMING*

Estienne, Charles. *Gauguin.* The Taste of Our Times series. 1953.

Fernier, Robert. *La Vie et l'oeuvre de Gustave Courbet* (catalogue raisonné). 2 vols. Lausanne and Paris, 1977–78.

Fosca, François, *Degas.* The Taste of Our Time series. 1959.

Goodrich, Lloyd. *Thomas Eakins: Retrospective Exhibition.* New York, 1970.

———. *Winslow Homer.* New York, 1959.

Hayward Gallery, *Pissarro.* London, 1981.

Musée d'Orsay. *Impressionist and Post-Impressionist Masterpieces.* London, 1984.

Philadelphia Museum of Art. *Manet.* Philadelphia, 1966.

Pickvance, Ron. *Van Gogh in Arles.* New York, 1984.

Raynal, Maurice. *Cézanne.* The Taste of Our Time series. n.d.

Rewald, John. *The History of Impressionism.* 4th ed., rev. Greenwich, Conn., 1973.

Rosenblum, Robert, and Janson, H. W. *Nineteenth-Century Art.* Englewood Cliffs, N.J., and New York, 1984.

Rouart, Denis, and Orienti, Sandra. *Tout l'oeuvre peint d'Edouard Manet* (catalogue raisonné). Lausanne and Paris, 1970.

White, Barbara E. *Renoir, His Life, Art, and Letters.* New York, 1984.

Wilmerding, John, ed. *The Genius of American Painting.* New York, 1973.

### SPECIAL SUBJECTS

Boime, Albert. *The Academy and French Painting in the Nineteenth Century.* Oxford, 1971.

Broude, Norma, and Garland, Mary D., eds. *Feminism and Art History: Questioning the Litany.* New York, 1982.

Clark, Timothy J. *The Painting of Modern Life: Paris in the Art of Manet and His Followers.* Princeton, N.J., 1984.

———. *Image of the People: Gustave Courbet and the Second French Republic, 1848–1851.* London, Princeton, 1982.

Goldwater, Robert. *Symbolism.* London, 1981.

Herbert, Robert I. *Neo-Impressionism.* New York, 1968.

*Japanisme: Japanese Influence on French Art, 1854–1900.* Cleveland, Ohio, 1975.

Lockspeiser, Edward. *Music and Painting: A Study in Comparative Ideas from Turner to Schoenberg.* London, 1973.

Mayne, Jonathan, trans. and ed. *Art in Paris, 1845–1862: Salons and Other Exhibitions Reviewed by Charles Baudelaire.* London, New York, 1965.

Nochlin, Linda. *Realism.* Harmondsworth and Baltimore, 1971.

———, ed. *Realism and Tradition in Art, 1848–1900.* Sources and Documents in the History of Art series. Englewood Cliffs, N.J., 1966.

———, ed. *Impressionism and Post-Impressionism.* Sources and Documents in the History of Art series. Englewood Cliffs, N.J., 1966.

Novak, Barbara. *Nature and Culture: American Landscape Painting, 1825–1875.* New York, 1980.

Pincus-Witten, Robert. *Occult Symbolism in France: Josephin Peladan and the Salon de la Rose Croix.* Garland Diss. series. New York, 1976.

Schmutzler, Robert. *Art Nouveau.* New York, 1978.

Sloane, Joseph. *French Painting Between Past and Present: Artists, Critics, and Traditions, from 1848 to 1870.* Princeton, 1951.

Wilmerding, John, *et al. American Light: The Luminist Movement, 1850–1875.* Washington, D.C., 1980.

Wood, Christopher. *The Pre-Raphaelites.* London and New York, 1981.

## ARTICLES ON "HIDDEN IMAGERY"

Halasz, Piri. "Abstract Painting in General: Friedel Dzubas in Particular." *Arts* 58, no. 1 (September 1983): 76–83.

Jaffe, Irma B. "Religious Content in the Painting of John Steuart Curry." *Winterthur Portfolio* 22, no. 1 (Spring 1987), 23–45.

Korshak, Yvonne. "Realism and Transcendent Imagery: Van Gogh's 'Crows over the Wheatfield,'" *Pantheon* 43 (1985): 115–123.

Lesko, Diane. "Cézanne's 'Bather' and a Found Self-Portrait," *ArtForum* 15, no. 4 (December 1976): 52–57. Reply by John Rewald, *ArtForum* 15, no. 9 (May 1977): 10.

Roskill, Mark. "On the Recognition and Identification of Objects in Painting." *Critical Inquiry* 3 (Summer 1977): 677–707.

## INDIVIDUAL ARTISTS

Adelyn D. Breeskin. *Mary Cassatt: A Catalogue Raisonné of Oils, Pastels, Watercolors, and Drawings.* Washington, D.C., 1970.

Roger Fry. *Cézanne: A Study of His Development.* London, 1927.

William Rubin, ed. *Cézanne: The Late Work.* New York, 1977.

Meyer Schapiro. *Paul Cézanne.* New York and London, 1962.

(For additional entries on Cézanne, see above, under Illustration references.)

Jean Leymarie. *Corot.* Geneva and London, 1979.

Linda Nochlin. *Gustave Courbet: A Study of Style and Society.* Garland Diss. series. New York, 1976.

Petra Ten Doesschate Chu, ed. *Courbet in Perspective.* Englewood Cliffs, N.J., 1977.

Hélène Toussaint. "Le Dossier de *L'Atelier* de Courbet." In Grand Palais, *Gustave Courbet (1819–1877).* Paris, 1977–78.

Royal Academy of Arts. *Gustave Courbet.* London, 1978.

Yvonne Korshak. "Courbet's *Burial at Ornan:* The 'Passion' of an Idea." *Pantheon* 60 (Oct.–Dec. 1982): 275–281.

(For additional entries on Courbet, see above, under Illustration references.)

*Tout l'oeuvre peint de Degas* (catalogue raisonné). Paris, 1974.

Theodore Reff, *Degas: The Artist's Mind.* London, 1976.

Jeah Sutherland Boggs, et al. *Degas.* New York and Ottowa, Canada, 1988.

(For additional entries on Degas, see above, under Illustration references.)

Paul Gauguin. *Paul Gauguin's Intimate Journals.* Bloomington, Ind., 1958.

Wayne Andersen. *Gauguin's Paradise Lost.* New York and London, 1971.

Jaworska Wladyslava. *Gauguin and the Pont-Aven School.* New York and London, 1972.

Richard Bretell, *et al. The Art of Paul Gauguin.* Washington, D.C. and Chicago, 1988.

(For additional entries on Gauguin, see above, under Illustration references.)

John Wilmerding. *Winslow Homer.* New York, 1972.

George P. Landow. *William Holman Hunt and Typological Symbolism.* New Haven, Conn. and London, 1979.

George Heard Hamilton. *Manet and His Critics.* New York, 1969.

Beatrice Farwell. *Manet and the Nude: A Study of Iconography in the Second Empire.* Garland Diss. Series. New York, 1981.

The Metropolitan Museum of Art. *Manet, 1832–1883.* New York, 1983.

(For additional entries on Manet see above, under Illustration references.)

Walker Art Gallery. *John Everett Millais.* Liverpool, 1967.

Robert L. Herbert. *Jean-François Millet.* London, 1967.

William Seitz. *Claude Monet: Seasons and Moments.* New York, 1960.

Metropolitan Museum of Art. *Monet's Years at Giverny: Beyond Impressionism.* New York, 1978.

Robert Gordon and Andrew Forge. *Monet.* New York, ca. 1983.

Daniel Wildenstein. *Claude Monet: Biographie et Catalogue Raisonné.* 4 vols. Lausanne and Paris, 1974–85.

Ira Moskowitz, ed. *Berthe Morisot: Paintings, Drawings, Pastels, Watercolors.* New York, 1960.

Louis d'Argencourt, *et al. Puvis de Chavannes, 1824–1898.* Ottowa, 1977.

Virginia Surtees. *The Paintings and Drawings of Dante Gabriel Rossetti (1828–1882): A Catalogue Raisonné.* 2 vols. Oxford, 1971.

Musée du Louvre. *Théodore Rousseau.* Paris, 1967–68.

William I. Homer. *Seurat and the Science of Painting.* Cambridge, Mass., 1964.

Norma Broude, ed. *Seurat in Perspective.* Englewood Cliffs, N.J., 1978.

*Tout l'oeuvre peint de Seurat.* Paris, 1973.

Meyer Schapiro. *Vincent Van Gogh.* New York, 1950.

*The Complete Letters of van Gogh.* 3 vols. Greenwich, Conn., and London, 1958.

J.-B. de la Faille. *The Works of Vincent van Gogh.* Amsterdam and London, 1970.

Jan Hulsker. *The Complete van Gogh: Paintings, Drawings, Sketches.* New York, 1980.

Bogomila Welsh-Ovcharov, ed. *Van Gogh in Perspective.* Englewood Cliffs, N.J., 1974.

(For additional entries on Van Gogh, see above, under Illustration references.)

Andrew McLaren Young, Margaret McDonald, and Rubin Specer. *The Paintings of James McNeil Whistler.* 2 vols. New Haven and London, 1980.

## UNIT VIII

# Into the Twentieth Century

## Learning Objectives

Setting the cultural context for Unit 8, Part 1 begins with turn-of-the-century Vienna, where Art Nouveau, there called *Secessionstil,* created some of its most brilliant decorations. You should note how handicraft becomes an ideological issue as manufacturing becomes increasingly the standard mode of production. Also to be noted here is the new emphasis on psychic and sexual liberation, themes that will be shown to underly much of twentieth-century art. You should ask yourself whether this kind of personal liberation has anything to do with the growth of political liberation movements. Another aspect of European culture that surfaces importantly is the accent on youth, and another is the rejection of positivist values in favor of spiritual values.

The seminal *formal* movements of the twentieth century emerged between 1900 and 1920. These include Fauvism, Cubism, Futurism, German Expressionism, Neo-Plasticism, and Suprematism. All but the last are taken up in Part 1, and you should be able to discuss the connections between the styles and the salient contributions that differentiate them. For example, Mondrian developed his signature style of Neo-Plasticism out of Cubism. You should be able to explain the connections between Cubism and Neo-Plasticism, and the salient contributions Mondrian made that transformed Cubism into Neo-Plasticism. Close attention should be given to the stylistic and theoretical sources of influence for each of the major artists taken up in this section.

An important distinction is made between "abstract" art and "non-objective" art. You should note the difference and learn to apply the terms correctly.

In Part 2 of Unit VIII, the text takes up post–World War I German art (Neue Sachlichkeit), Dada, modernism in Russia around 1910–1920 (Suprematism and Constructivism), the Bauhaus, International Style, Brancusi, and Surrealism. There is an extended discussion of Picasso's *Guernica.* As usual, the leading artists are presented with illustration indications for their signature style works. Emphasis is given to the importance of socialist ideology among artists and intellectuals in shaping aesthetic theories, especially in developing the "machine aesthetic." You should note also the influence of Freud in connection with anti-art and anti-rationalist movements.

In the twentieth century, analysis of the nature of art and analysis of the nature of painting and sculpture (related but separate problems) have often been the *subject matter* of works of art. For this reason, you should give careful attention to all references to art theory given in Units VIII and IX. Modern art cannot be understood beyond a rudimentary level without some understanding of the theories behind it.

In this unit, you will learn to:

- Distinguish the major movements of the early modern period and understand how they presage developments in the visual arts for the entire century;
- Understand the formal and theoretical goals of each of the modern art movements, particularly how they are related to their essential plastic means;
- Appreciate the differences and similarities in the goals of modern art movements in Europe and America;
- Identify the technical and structural means, as well as new building materials, that allowed architects to realize the goals of modern architecture;
- Understand the impact of industrialization and urbanism, technology, as well as the cataclysm of World War I on the visual arts, and the variety of reactions to these phenomena as revealed in form, plastic means, as well as in narrative themes.

---

### Part 1
### THE EMERGENCE OF MODERN STYLES

---

## Historical Background

On December 31, 1899, facing the new century, the old one, if it had had a mind to, could have looked back on some fine achievements in western Europe. Discoveries in the sciences and inventions in every realm made life easier, at least for a good many; disease control reduced grief; political liberty had spread a bit, and deepened some; economic enterprise had raised the standard of living, at least statistically; the arts—all of them—had produced dazzling masterpieces. It might have seemed that the twentieth century was about to dawn on a beautiful morning. Progress, cult god of the nineteenth century, would endure forever. According to Hachette's Guide to the Paris Exposition of 1900, "The 1900 Exhibition, world-wide and universal, is the magnificent result, the extraordinary balance sheet of a century which has not only proved to be the most fertile in discovery and the most prodigious in scientific invention, but which has revolutionized the economic order of the Universe. . . . [The exhibition demonstrates] the forward march of progress from the mail-coach to the express train, from the messenger to wireless telegraphy and the telephone, from lithography to radiography, from the earliest burrowing for coal in the bowels of the earth to the aeroplanes now seeking to open up the highway of the sky. Our exhibition is that of the great century now drawing to its close and which ushers in a new era in the history of humanity" (Cassou *et al., Gateway to the Twentieth Century,* 1962, p. 8).

But Europe was not altogether well. Something seemed to be stuck in its soul. The Viennese playwright Arthur Schnitzler's metaphor in *La Ronde* (*Merry-Go-Around*), 1903, was the social disease that passed from one class to another mediated through irresponsibility and faithlessness. It almost seems possible to say that Dr. Sigmund Freud was invented in Vienna because society knew it needed psychoanalysis. Of course, so was the Viennese waltz invented there, a century before, and wasp-waisted Merry Widows still danced with gloriously uniformed Prince Danilos. In the late nineteenth century, they danced on the polished floors of the Ringstrasse private palaces while the band played on. The fissures that had been cracking the surface of aristocratic European society, held smooth in the Middle Ages by the outstretched arms of the Church and the seamless ordering of all things under the sun by Thomas Aquinas, were not uncomfortably perceptible, although now one also danced with new millionaires, and occasionally one had to acknowledge an introduction to a wealthy or brilliantly talented Jew. The rumble of revolution could hardly be heard above the music.

The Ringstrasse, a wide boulevard circling the inner city, was built up over a period of twenty years between the 1860s and 1880s. Lining it were public and private buildings in a variety of revival styles—a neo-Greek Parliament, a neo-Gothic City Hall, and neo-Baroque apartment "palaces." It was ironically a bulwark of façades that took their values from the past and had nothing to say for the present.

And yet, beyond the Ringstrasse, there were those who recognized the fin-de-siècle decadence, the tired forms, the exhausted ideas of the new boulevard that was old before it was finished. There were serious artists and intellectuals who knew that it was time to break out of the conventions of academic Vienna. A great cultural revival emerged abruptly in the midst of the fashionable wealthy burghers and successful bureaucrats enthralled by Habsburg imperial pomp. Suddenly in the city where Hayden, Mozart, and Beethoven had once flourished, there was an Arnold Schoenberg (1874–1951), whose creation of atonal music occurred almost simultaneously with Cubism, its visual arts analogue. There was Max Reinhardt (1873–1943), who became a foremost exponent of modernist experimental theatre; Hugo von Hofmannsthal (1874–1929), whose plays, poems, and opera libretti created suggestive moods, often of disappointment and resignation. They are closely related to the Symbolist movement which can be seen as anticipating the passive, helpless, nihilist mood in modern culture.

And there were Joseph Maria Olbrich (1867–1908), Josef Hoffmann (1870–1908), and Adolf Loos (1870–1933), who brought the modernist cultural revolution to Viennese architecture. All of them, like Schoenberg, Reinhardt, and von Hofmannsthal, were in their twenties in the last decade of the century. Of the innovators, only Otto Wagner (1841–1918), belonged to an earlier generation. Looming large in influence is the slightly older Gustav Klimt (1862–1918), the most important exponent of Art Nouveau in Austria, where it was known as *Secessionstil.* It is not the least of ironies that this cultural revival centered its interest on the lavish luxury of decadence, but that being so, it is not surprising that *Secessionstil* captured in a few brief years the patronage of the very class whose decadence it portrayed. The orientalizing splendor, the extravagant display of expensive materials, the *sensuality* of the style made it irresistible. By 1900 it had reached a triumphant peak, and at the Paris International Exposition that year the Austrian Pavilion, designed by Olbrich and Hoffmann—representing, of course, the imperial government of Austria—won international attention for its luxurious ornamentation. A reviewer commented that "Nowhere have the ideas of the new decoration been so favorably received as in Austria" (Selz, p. 150).

## Art Nouveau

Art Nouveau was an international phenomenon that was rooted in the convergence of Impressionism, Symbolism, and industrialization at a moment of economic prosperity and stability in the late years of the nineteenth century. It also owes a debt to late nineteenth-century socialist ideology. From Impressionism it drew the taste for movement expressed by the implication of change: the Impressionist painting catches the fleeting moment, as we have seen in Impressionist works. Essentially naturalistic, it avoids straight lines and sharp angles. It is ahistorical, concerned with the ever-shifting here-and-now. There is thus embedded in Impressionism a current of fashion, which is always of the moment.

From Symbolism, Art Nouveau drew its eroticism, with its related emphasis on Woman as the center of feeling—love, hate, envy, spirituality, and fertility, as seen in Gustave Moreau's *Jupiter and Semele* (ca. 1875) and Odilon Redon's *The Cyclops* (1898) **(G 21.72, 21.73).** In Art Nouveau decorations, it is always springtime. The *Secessionstil* journal was titled, in fact, *Ver Sacrum,* sacred springtime. Stravinsky's "scandalous" ballet, *The Rite of Spring,* performed in 1913 by Nijinsky, is a late Symbolist work that has crossed the border into Expressionism. Symbolism, is, like Impressionism, an art of the fleeting moment, but unlike Impressionism, it is subjective; its moments are those of interior experience, not optical perception. It is thus psychologically weighted. The Symbolist artist tended to stress the extremes of spirituality and sexuality.

Industrialization had produced a reaction against the machine-made product. A renewed sense of the value of craft, of *hand work,* appeared in the Arts and Crafts movement in England (*Arts et Métiers,* in France; *Kunsthandwerk* in Germany), inspired by William Morris, a writer, artist, printer—and socialist. He had faith in the ultimate achievement of the brotherhood of humankind, and linked to that idea was his conviction that beauty and utility were affinities: there was a moral obligation to integrate beauty with the objects of everyday life. On the other hand, industrialization had brought about advances in technology that made new materials available, most notably in architecture, and it was indeed in architecture that Art Nouveau made its most significant contributions. For the most part it was an art of fashion and decoration, which nevertheless had important consequences for "fine art" since, as decoration, it stressed the flat surface and freedom from mimetic interpretation that contributed to abstract art.

The success of Art Nouveau (Liberty style in England, *Jugendstil* in Germany) owed much to the fact that industrialization had created new wealth and the new bourgeoisie needed—wanted—a new style in which to express itself. The stylelessness of the Ringstrasse and other revival pastiches was boring, and boredom was just too—*boring*.

The first *Secessionstil* building in Vienna was the Secession Building designed by Olbrich, from a sketch by Klimt. These men, together with Hoffmann and Koloman Moser, a brilliant interior designer, had revolted against the Academy in 1897 and had formed the Vienna Secession. Their building, completed in 1898, suggests the exoticism of Egypt, with sloping walls like a mastaba, but is crowned with an extraordinary perforated metal dome simulating laurel—symbol of organic vitality, of Apollo the sun god, of creative fertility. The Secession exhibition of 1902, however, which centered on a huge statue of Beethoven, reveals the essentially nineteenth-century Romanticism of *Secessionstil.* Installed in a temple within

the building, the statue represents Beethoven as Prometheus, who has stolen the fire of creativity from the Gods. He is seated on a great throne, which is supported by a massive boulder. There is deeply folded drapery over the legs of the otherwise nude torso. He is leaning forward, one leg crossed over the knee of the other—a pose that seems to present-day eyes grotesquely casual and out of tune with the statue's baroque monumentality, although its casualness would have seemed new and "modern" to contemporary viewers. Beethoven is contemplating the eagle that has come to rest on the rock, preparing to carry out its daily task of gnawing out the liver of the thief who has stolen the fire of the gods. Cherub heads are carved in relief on the upper border of the throne, behind Beethoven, symbolizing the heavenly realm. On one wall of the "temple" a step-like relief suggested a mountain. Klimt designed an allegorical frieze in the "temple" which symbolized humankind's yearning from release from the compulsion to sin. The frieze was executed in mosaic.

The concept of the work thus combined architecture, painting, sculpture, mosaic, and scenography. It is Wagnerian opera in its expressive bombast, and its large, comprehensive pretensions suggest the contemporary mammoth productions of Gustav Mahler, with, alas, the same weakness—lack of a strong formal unity.

But Vienna was thrilled with this *gesamtkunstwerk,* this total work of art that demanded the skills of many kinds of workers. It was familiar in its mythological reference, it was modern-looking compared to contemporary academic work, and it was about their own Titan, Beethoven.

In 1899 Otto Wagner shocked conservative Vienna by joining the Secession. Wagner had had a distinguished academic career, had received State commissions, and became professor of architecture in the Academy of Fine Arts in Vienna in 1894. Officials who were responsible for his appointment soon regretted their action as it became apparent in his book, *Modern Architecture,* published in 1896, that Wagner's aesthetic sympathies were with the new tendencies. In this he may have been influenced by ideas of his students, Joseph Maria Olbrich and Josef Hoffmann, who had been studying the work of the Scotsman Charles Rennie Mackintosh (1868–1928). His designs had been published in the mid-nineties, in *The Studio,* and their curious combination of simplicity and unexpected decorative effects appealed to the young students, who were in any case ready for something new. Mackintosh's Glasgow School of Art building (1897–1910), designed in 1896, represents the functional current in Art Nouveau, straight-lined and angular, contrasting massive walls with large areas of glass. The characteristic looping, swinging lines of Art Nouveau appear in the metal ornamental work and other curvilinear decorative features on both the inside and outside of the building.

Responding, then, to the new ideas being widely disseminated throughout Europe, Wagner broke with his conservative past and in 1904 designed his masterwork, the Postal Savings Bank, which was built in two stages, 1904–1906 and 1910–1912.

Once again laurel leaves make their symbolic appearance, here along the horizontal roof, keeping company with winged Victories, their arms raised symbolically toward the heavens. The horizontal extension dominates the vertical height, and this insistent horizontal is reinforced over the entrance, with two levels of projecting overhangs. Wagner's building is sheathed with a thin "veil" of marble in modular panels that are attached to the wall with large aluminum bolts, clearly exposing the truth of the structure. As observed by one critic, Stanford Anderson, "The concept of an engineered building is revealed to us . . . through the building's own modernist symbols of exposed industrial materials, structure and equipment" (quoted in Frampton, *Modern Architecture,* p. 83). The lower stories are decorated with a covering of wave-shaped marble slabs, giving the effect of traditional rustication, but here clearly shown, by the exposing of the wall between the slabs, to be applied, worn like a garment. It is this feature of exposure that can be seen as central to the development of modernist architecture through the twentieth century, to climax in the Centre Pompidou. Exposure, not only in terms of engineering but also of openness to light, is also a feature of Wagner's design for his bank building. The interior public space was covered by a vault of glass and thus brilliantly lit from above, and the floor was inlaid with glass panels to allow the light to penetrate to the basement.

Gustav Klimt, as the outstanding exponent of Vienna *Secessionstil,* commands the interest of anyone concerned with modern art. As the creator of some of the most seductively beautiful images, he deserves the attention of everyone's eye; he also brought to modern art a unique exoticism. While avant-garde artists in France and Germany were widening their aesthetic horizons with Japanese, Oceanic, and African art, Klimt enriched his style with orientalizing effects. *The Kiss* (1908) **(J 658),** his best-known work, is as splendid as a Persian rug. Here, the two figures are side by side, so that the two-in-one shape functions as a design imposed as an aesthetic concept with no naturalistic interpretation possible. The motif may have come from the Norwegian Edvard Munch, but if so, it has been transported into the world of Arabian nights. It has the jewel-like quality of Byzantine art which Klimt developed further in subsequent paintings.

The period's new Freudian awareness, and its new sense of sexual freedom, experienced first by artists and other marginal groups in society, are reflected in Klimt's erotic work that dates from about 1910. He began to work with lesbian themes; his female nudes assume provocative poses, emphasizing the breasts, the hips, and not omitting the pubic hair. This is part of the legacy that he passed to his young compatriot, Egon Schiele (1890–1918).

Schiele was born in the town of Tulln and was sent to school in nearby Klosterneuberg, on the Danube about six miles from Vienna, which would be important for his development. Klosterneuberg is the seat of the oldest monastery in Austria, and its altar is famous for its engraved and enameled plaques by Nicholas of Verdun **(J 299).** Looking at Schiele's work from around 1915 to his death in 1918, exemplified by *Portrait of the Painter Paris von Gutershloh* (1918) (Hunter clpl 205), one is struck by the resemblance of his "tense, nervous patterns," as Alessandra Comini describes his drawing, to the patterns made by Nicholas, which might be described in similar terms. Schiele was considered a child prodigy when he entered the Vienna Academy in 1906; it seems plausible to guess that he had schooled himself as a very young child with the designs on the Klosterneuberg altar.

Schiele transformed Klimt's decorative eroticism into twentieth-century nightmares of sexual anxiety; Klimt's *neo*romanticism into what one is tempted to coin *neuro*-manticism, in view of works such as *Girl with Black Stockings* (1911) (Arnason fig. 174) and *Embrace* (1913) (Hunter fig. 206). In his hands, the *Secessionstil* line becomes emotionally charged with suffering. His self-absorption, depicted in many self-portraits, is that of a tortured soul for whom rest and peace are impossible. It is as if he is contemplating an eventual gruesome destiny in which he sees his fate as that of all humankind. He seems, however, to have found some pitiful glimpse of peace in the last years of his short life. There is tenderness and hope in his painting *The Family,* even though he depicts the wife's face with a sad expression, looking away, as if doubting perhaps that the moment of happiness can last.

The intimations of disaster are nowhere clearer than in the painting of Oskar Kokoschka (1886–1980) whose sometimes morbid, sometimes violent, always anxiety-ridden portraits of his first artistic maturity succeeded in outraging Vienna as no other work did. Although influenced by Klimt, Kokoschka's raw revelations of decay, derangement, and fear in the works he showed at the Vienna Kunstshaus in 1908, exemplified by his *Self-Portrait* (1908) (Selz clpl 60) had none of Klimt's beguiling seductiveness. He was expelled from the Arts and Crafts School in the wake of the scandal the works stirred, but the following year revealed him unbowed: his paintings at the Kunstshaus of 1909 were met with equal hostility and, with no need to cap this climax of perverse public relations he nevertheless did so with a performance of his sadistic play, *Murder, Hope of Women,* on the theme of the battle of the sexes. His closest friend, Adolf Loos, took him to Switzerland to give him a change of atmosphere. In addition to discovering landscape painting, which became important to him much later, he found in Loos's wife and other patients in a tuberculosis sanitarium ideal sitters for portraits that were metaphors of society's sickness and death.

In 1910 Kokoschka went to Berlin, where he found a more responsive audience. The city's leading art dealer, Paul Cassirer gave him an exhibition, and he began to contribute drawings and writings to *Der Sturm,* a journal of literature and criticism published by Herwath Walden, who was soon to become the leading sponsor of the German Expressionist movement, which we will take up presently. The title of his journal expresses the mood of radical art of the time in Germany, and storm was indeed the ruling emotional climate of Kokoschka's art. His *Bride of the Wind* **(G 22.5)** depicts two lovers cradled in a cloud with turbulent Wagnerian winds sweeping around them. The woman sleeps peacefully on the man's chest, while he lies on his back, his hands clasped across his waist, his eyes open, sleepless.

As Michael Wood observed in the program, modernism's principal themes appeared early in the century in Vienna and in other great European capitols, and they include a deliberate and *sweeping* break with the past. Unlike the period in France from about 1850 to 1886, when only the Realists Courbet and Daumier, the Impressionist painters, and one sculptor, Rodin, fought the first modernist battles—conservative Beaux-Arts architecture was not yet challenged—the years immediately preceding and following the turn of the century produced painters, sculptors, architects, and decorative artists who changed the look of Western civilization. Among the innovations were a new interest in techniques and materials made available through new scientific discoveries and technologies; a heightened value given to individualism, asserted through self-expression; and a powerful breaching of previously closed walls through which suppressed emotions poured into the open. The *Rite of Spring* celebrated the out-in-the-open crowning of art and sex as the reigning divinities of the new pantheism, the divinities who parented the spiritual in art.

## Expressionism

All art is "expressive." If a work is not expressive it isn't art. Expression*ism,* however, is something else. It is a stylistic term, and like all "isms," the word conveys a commitment"—in this case, a commitment to art that conveys and evokes strong, highly emotional states of being. Classical art is expressive of balance, order, rationality, stability, and harmony, what one may think of as calm moods, even though the feeling of calm may be intense. Expressionist art seeks the opposite qualities. Insofar as there are discernible national characteristics in styles of art—and there are—German art has always shown consistent expressionist tendencies, as is evident in such masters as Altdorfer, Grünewald, and Dürer. On the other hand, it is possible that, had Germany been less culturally oppressive than it was under Prussian hegemony, the German modernist movement might have been less violent in its break with the past, less barbaric in its expressionism.

Several strong currents, both artistic and cultural, were gathering force and came together into the rushing mainstream of German Expressionism at the beginning of the twentieth century. While French art developed step by step in a logically consistent way, almost like an ongoing Olympic race with runners handing on the torch from one to the other, German art reflected the events in Paris with time lags, fused with the restlessness that was stirring within German culture in the late nineteenth century. There was a strong sense of the need to break with the values that dominated society, to break rebelliously, aggressively, and in a sense, destructively, because the hold of the ruling class of Prussian aristocrats and their military establishment aligned with the newly powerful industrialists seemed so airtight that only its total destruction would free German culture.

A number of movements were formed by young artists and writers. All of them were deeply affected by Friedrich Nietzsche, who substituted for the Prussian Superman, the brilliantly gifted Genius, for whom there is no morality apart from the cultivation of his—for Nietzsche there was no "her"—gift, whatever that might entail. His insistence on the individuality of the self and the privileged position of self-awareness as a means of understanding the universe, his lofty vision of a new value system—anti-bourgeois, elite, rooted in the superiority of individual genius—his call to fearless adventure created a mood in Germany (and elsewhere, particularly Italy) to which youth, and especially young artists, responded with religious fervor. In his greatest work, *Thus Spake Zarathustra* (1883–1891), he challenged, "To you alone, you bold seekers, tempters, experimenters, and to all who ever went out on the terrible sea with cunning sails—to you alone, you who are riddle-drunk and twilight happy, whose souls are lured by flutes to any treacherous chasm—To you who do not like to grope for a clue with cowardly hands and who prefer not to deduce when you can intuit—To you alone I shall tell the riddle that I saw." Failing to take up such a challenge one would have to admit to being a bourgeois. Youth all over western Europe were led, or at least helped by Nietzsche into an anti-bourgeois mood.

This was the mood that created the German Youth Movement which, in its beginning, was a true reforming experience for German culture. Unfortunately, it was eventually co-opted by the very groups it had come into existence to resist, and the emphasis on virility became militaristic, the elitism of the individual genius became the superiority of the German genius, and the seedling liberalism of the movement was easily transformed into the sinister force that served Nazism. But at the turn of the century who could have foreseen the tragic failure of what appeared at the time to be a brave opening of doors and windows, a welcoming of the fresh breeze of nature?

Within the Youth Movement, young German artists were readied to embrace the risky future that they must explore not with the light of reason, according to

Nietzsche, but with the insight of intuition. To a young, gifted German artist, a radical break seemed the only road to the future, and it was in this mood that German nature-worship developed in opposition to middle-class, Victorian refinement with its artificial conventions of manner, its overstuffed furniture and tightly corseted, high-collared garments for men and women. To strip society of its artificiality became the dynamic motif of youth: to find genuine feeling, genuine actions, to find truth and honesty, one had to turn to nature, to landscape and animals, and learn from nature the secret of harmony. Thus love of nature was a *moral* recipe for living which transcended the mere aesthetic element in the contemplation of the natural world. One quickly sees an analogy between the mood of this German nature movement and the emotions that stirred Gauguin and Van Gogh. Both turn from Victorian conventionality. Gauguin and Van Gogh were moved by the conviction that only in simple people, in lowly places untouched by the refinements of Western civilization, could one find true Beauty. The German artists who were forerunners of German Expressionism also responded to the rural environment and its people, although, as we shall see, the artists who became the German Expressionist avant-garde were not interested in peasants—European or exotic. Gauguin and Van Gogh each searched for the "real" within the framework of his heritage, French rationalism and Dutch Calvinism. In Germany, an inherently subjective idealist tradition, with its emphasis on the expression of the human soul, gave to the new mood an impetus that had no bridle, no moderating restrictions, and the result produced an art that rended the atmosphere around it with shrieking color and harsh, hard, angular lines. Freedom did not ring, in Germany: it screeched like a shell piercing the air and exploded like shrapnel.

## Die Brücke (The Bridge)

In 1904, three young artists attending the Dresden Institute of Technology, Ernst Kirchner, Erich Heckel, and Karl Schmidt-Rottluff, discovered their shared interest in art as self-expression, their mutual distaste for both formal correctness, as taught in the academies, and the "new art," *Jugendstil,* which seemed fit for ornament but not for meaningful communication of feelings about life. The following year they established their association which they named *Die Brücke,* The Bridge, suggesting the passage from past to future, which they would mediate. They worked together in a studio, actually an empty butcher shop in the working-class district where they could feel themselves physically as well as ideologically free from their bourgeois backgrounds, and lived a bohemian existence in close communion with each other. In these early years of their artistic companionship in Dresden, and in Moritzburg during the summer, they created the first Brücke style, featuring harsh color, hard angles, crude drawing with raw canvas left showing

around the contours of figures and objects, and primitivizing frontality. They were influenced largely by Van Gogh, whose work they saw at the Van Gogh exhibition in Dresden the very year they formed their association, and Munch, whose work had been known in Dresden since his exhibition there in 1892. They were also excited by exotic art, African and particularly Oceanic. As Michael Wood pointed out, tribal societies symbolized, for early twentieth-century Europeans, human beings living in a state of nature, unfettered by artificial conventions, giving full play to their natural, particularly sexual instincts, innocent of materialistic ambitions. Anthropology has taught us how naive this view was, but for several decades around the turn of the century, it contributed immensely to the dismantling of the repressive Victorian culture. The Brücke artists at Moritzburg, in the countryside, immersed in nature, tried to live according to the eighteenth-century ideal of the noble savage.

Ernst Kirchner (1880–1938) is widely held to have been the most brilliant of the original Brücke artists. He seems to have played a major role in developing the group style, and his painting exhibits the stylistic characteristics noted above, seen in *Self-Portrait with Model* (1907) (Selz pl. 29). The figure of the artist looms large in the picture plane, and is cut off at the top, bottom, and left side, creating the explosive feeling that he does not fit into the space. The colors of his robe, bright orange with deep blue roughly painted stripes, are strident, and in extremely dissonant contrast to the delicate pale blue of the model's chemise. Both figures are painted with deliberate crudeness, symbolic of the rejection of bourgeois notions of refinement. The model's small scale creates an ambiguous picture space, which adds to the sensation of tension and crowdedness. The triangular shape of the faces is typical of Brücke style in this period. Crude drawing and crowdedness are also seen in *Street* (1907) **(J 933),** where the influence of Edvard Munch is very much in evidence.

## Fauvism

The cult of nature that helped to liberate Austrian and German art from moribund academicism and over-ripe Impressionism also emerged contemporaneously in France as a reaction against the decadence of Symbolism, the art of the dream. French pantheism, however, had very different content. Whereas the German Expressionists tended to see the new "natural" freedom as liberating formerly suppressed feelings of guilt, anxiety, anguish, and used the human body as a metaphor for such liberation, the French were uninterested in portraying psychic states, and took the direction of *aesthetic* freedom. Where the German artists reflected in their art inferences they made about tribal life and barbaric practices, the French, heirs of Cartesian rationalism and characteristically more restrained (except when driving their cars) appropriated non-Western art for its lessons in alternative ways of thinking about artistic form and expression. During the formative years of Die Brücke, the new movement in France was emerging that eventually bore the name Fauvism.

A group of young artists including André Derain, Maurice de Vlaminck, and Albert Marquet, among others, had formed around the leadership of Henri Matisse (1869–1954) who had come to art almost accidentally, to amuse himself while convalescing from appendicitis. His art education absorbed within a few years the academicism of Bouguereau, the symbolism of Gustave Moreau, the early Impressionism of Monet, and the post-Impressionism of Van Gogh, Gauguin, Seurat, and Cézanne. In the spring of 1905 he sent a very large composition to the exhibition of the Salon des Indépendants, *Luxe, Calme et Volupté* (1904–1905) (Hunter clpl 165), the title of which is drawn from Baudelaire's *Invitation au voyage,*

> Là, tout n'est qu'ordre et beauté,
> Luxe, calme et volupté.
>
> (There, there is only order and beauty,
> luxury, serenity, and voluptuousness.)

In this painting Matisse uses the pointillist brush technique, developed by Seurat and Paul Signac, without, however, using their scientific system of color juxtapositions. The suppression of sensuality in the figures brings us close to Cézanne, whom Matisse called "the father of us all." (Matisse had bought Cézanne's *Three Bathers* from the dealer Vollard in 1899, and kept it even when he desperately needed money; he eventually gave it to the Museum of the City of Paris in 1938.) But whereas Cézanne's bathers inhabit a kind of arcadian landscape, in Matisse's painting, the clothed woman wearing a plumed hat of 1904 style identifies the scene as modern, just as in Manet's *Luncheon on the Grass* the men in their dark suits set the stage as here-and-now.

By 1905 Matisse had effected a synthesis of the masters of modern art, and at the Autumn Salon that year, he exhibited paintings that proclaimed an entirely independent stylist. Either at this exhibition, or possibly the following year, according to an oft-repeated account, Matisse's work was hung in a gallery together with works by Derain, Vlaminck, Georges Rouault, and other young artists, deemed too radical to be shown with established artists. Such brilliant, saturated color and bold design had never been seen in Paris—it seemed barbaric, and some writers said so, calling the artists "invertebrates" and "incoherents." "Chromatic madness," one critic wrote. "Why put all these maniacs together? . . . What is the meaning of this new farce? . . . What have the daubs of Messrs. Matisse, Vlaminck, and Derain got to do with art?" At the center of this gallery with its savage colors on the walls was set a small Renaissance-style bronze by Albert Marquet. A witty critic, Louis Vaucelles, joked, when he visited this gallery, "Ah, Donatello au milieu des fauves!" (Donatello surrounded by wild beasts). His witticism was repeated, and the name caught on.

While Matisse responded principally to Cézanne, among modern masters, the other two major Fauves, André Derain (1880–1950) and Maurice de Vlaminck (1876–1958), acknowledged Gauguin and Van Gogh as inspiration for their first important modernist achievements. Derain had met both Matisse and Vlaminck in 1899, and introduced the two in 1901 when they visited the Van Gogh exhibition that year at the Bernheim-Jeune Gallery. Matisse recalled how overwhelmed Vlaminck was by the Van Goghs. "I saw Derain accompanied by an enormous and vociferous young man who was saying 'you see, you must paint with pure cobalts, pure vermillions, veronese greens! (Crespelle, 1962, p. 108)'" Vlaminck recalled his own reaction at that exhibition, "At that moment, I loved Van Gogh more than my own father."

Working closely together, and with Matisse, they gradually clarified their ideas, which Matisse summarized:

> Construction by means of colored surfaces. A desire for a greater intensity of color, and the actual quality of the paint being of minor interest. Reaction against representation of light by the diffusion of local colors. Light was not suppressed, rather it was expressed by a conjunction of intensely colored surfaces. Color was proportioned to form. Form was modified by the interplay of neighboring colored areas. The impact comes from the colored surface, which the spectator grasps in its entirety.

Two words in that description, "color" and "impact," convey the essence not only of Fauve painting, but of much of modernism. Of the two words, "impact" is the most thoroughly decisive. Modernist art has aimed at involving the viewer on the level of experiencing a work of art. The emphasis on the colored surface belongs to that felt need to make painting autonomous, like music, independent of subject matter. The importance of the Fauve movement beyond the extraordinary quality of the painting lies in its contribution toward pushing the frontiers of art forward along the path of pure visibility by its suppression of tactile values in favor of visual impact. Also to be credited to the Fauves is the "discovery" of African tribal sculpture, which has had a decisive influence in modernist art.

It is in the Fauve and Die Brücke movements that the issues implied in late nineteenth-century painting begin to clarify: as early as 1853 John Ruskin had commented in *Stones of Venice* "that the arrangement of colours and lines is an art analogous to the composition of music, and entirely independent of the representation of facts. Good colouring does not necessarily convey the image of anything but itself. It consists in certain proportions and arrangements of rays of light . . ." (quoted in Sypher, p. 144). Probably more influential for the development of painting in France was the theory of Maurice Denis, who was possibly echoing Ruskin when he asserted in his "Definition of Neo-traditionism" of 1890 that "a painting before being a cavalry horse, a nude woman, or any sort of anecdote, is essentially a plane surface covered with colors arranged in a certain order" (quoted in Hamilton,

p. 107). It is likely that his statement contributed to the direction art was to take little more than ten years later, although he denied that he meant to propose abstract or non-objective art. In this book, "abstract" art is that in which an object of the phenomenal world can be at least residually discerned; by non-objective is meant art with no object content.

In Germany, idealism had been developing philosophical notions that in retrospect can be seen to have pressed toward abstraction and non-objectivity insofar as artists were aware of them. Again the role of color is stressed, as in Adolf Hoelzel's *Die Kunst für alle* (Art for All) (1904), where he held that art was produced by the harmony of colored forms and that color in itself communicates to everyone, regardless of education; Hoelzel was reflecting the Utopian tendency in intellectual circles that would be the guiding principle behind the non-objective art of Mondrian, and would surface importantly in Russian Constructivism after the Revolution in the belief that art must function for "the masses" and be understood by them.

Equally important with new ideas about color were the new ideas about line. Theodor Lipp's work, for example, was well known to artists in the last decades of the nineteenth century; his lectures in Munich stressed the psychic effects of "organized lines," by which he meant that linear patterns create psychological reactions in accordance with their character—curving or angular, short or long, rising or falling, and so on. By 1899 writers on art were insisting on the *autonomy* of the line, its freedom from the traditional view that lines belonged to objects and must serve to represent them. It was the linear aspect of Art Nouveau that gave it its place in the evolution of modernism. The Belgian architect Henry van de Velde, a major figure in Art Nouveau architecture, founder of the Weimar School of Arts and Crafts, forerunner of the Bauhaus, claimed in his writing that referential lines weaken their expressive force; the line must be independent and speak for itself; it must echo not a natural form but an independent *force* that derives its energy from the energy of the person who drew it.

This conception of the nature and function of line introduces a highly subjective current into the movement toward abstraction and non-objectivity, although the seed was already there in Impressionism. Among the Impressionists, the concern was with the optical effect of the object on the eye of the artist. Despite the apparent objectivity of Impressionism, however, it depended ultimately on the subjective eye of the artist. The central question for the artist was, What do I really see? To place the emphasis not on the eye but on the energy of the artist as it is communicated in his/her pencil- or brush-drawn line is to give the expressive task to the hand instead of the eye. This shift is of great importance, for the eye as a medium that links phenomena with the artist's organizing mind is a non-tangible contacting medium. The hand, on the contrary, is a medium that physically, tangibly links

the mind and the psychic state of the artist to the work of the art. What is intriguing to note in this is that as the hand of the artist—his/her touch, his/her body language—became increasingly important, tactile and other sensual appeals to experience in the phenomenal world decreased: the image made its appeal to the eye alone. Hearing belonged to music; taste belonged to food; smell and touch belonged to the furniture of the world we live in. Visibility was possessed by art as its own unique sense. The two principal goals of modernism, the achievement of pure visibility and the exposure of the physical elements of art—its nature as a flat canvas, its pigments, its shape, its size, and the physical action of the artist—can thus be seen as in large measure rooted in late nineteenth-century theory and practice. These goals were reached mainly by means of a relentless effort to investigate the ultimate possibilities of color, and of line.

Color was the Expressionist spearhead—derived, in France, from Van Gogh and Gaugin, and, in Germany, from Van Gogh and Munch—toward abstraction and non-objectivity. Cézanne's immense influence on Matisse had more to do with his use of color to build pictorial *structure* than with expressionist aspects of his work. This does not mean that Matisse was a structuralist; he was an expressionist who thought of structure as a means of building a firm composition. It was left to Pablo Picasso (1881–1973) and Georges Braque (1882–1963) to lead the linear wing of the avant-garde to new principles of constructing form that had been suggested by Cézanne's late work.

## Cubism

By 1894, Picasso's artist father was so overwhelmed with his son's awesome talent that, according to legend, he gave the thirteen-year-old boy his own palette, his brushes and paints, and vowed he would give up painting. This in fact he did not do, for in 1895 he accepted a post at the School of Fine Arts in Barcelona, where Pablo was admitted to the advanced classes in classical art and still life after completing the entrance exam in one day. In the next ten years Picasso went through the stylistic developments of the nineteenth century from Realism to Symbolism, and had entirely caught up with the most advanced painting in France. In 1904 after several trips to Paris he settled there permanently.

His style in the first few years of the century was essentially Symbolist, pervaded by a melancholy mood that was expressed by a slow moving, sinuous, elongated linearity (owed to the strange synthesis of Art Nouveau and El Greco) and the color blue. Apart from his friends, he found his subjects mainly in the poor and handicapped such as *The Old Guitarist* (1903) **(J 912)**. Around the middle of 1904 he abandoned the "blue" paintings and by early in the spring of 1905 he had completed a series of rose-colored works on the theme of circus people, inspired by his frequent visits to the Medrano Circus with his artist friends. One of these "rose period" paintings is

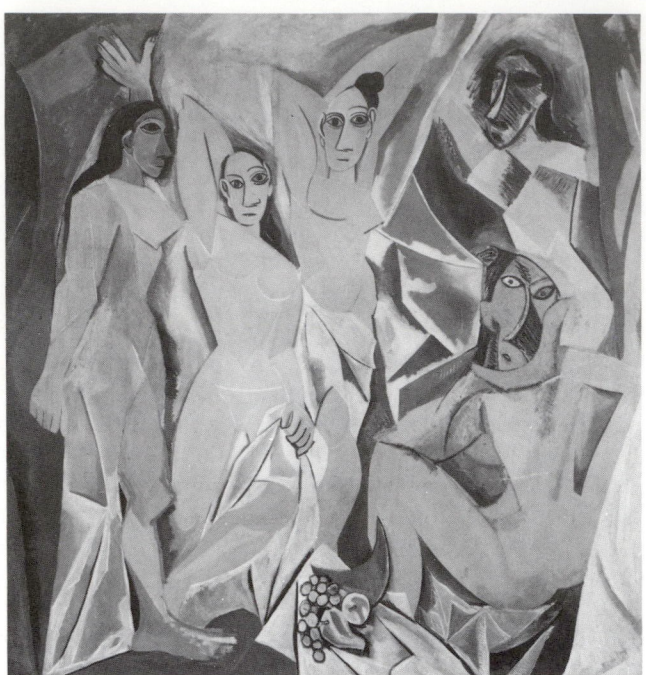

Pablo Picasso, *Les Demoiselles d'Avignon*, 1907. New York, Museum of Modern Art. (MUSEUM OF MODERN ART, NEW YORK. ACQUIRED THROUGH THE LILLIE P. BLISS BEQUEST)

*The Family of Saltimbanques* (1905) (Hunter clpl 223). One should note in this group of six figures that the standing man on the left is seen with his face in profile, while his back is given almost in full breadth; his right leg is in profile; he wears a traditional harlequin costume of colored diamond shapes and there are, aside from the small girl, three figures at the center and a seated figure at the right. This is basically, in the opinion of this writer, the composition of the watershed painting *Les Demoiselles d'Avignon* (1907) (**J 941; G 22.12;** Arnason clpl 63).

There are five female nudes in *Les Demoiselles*. At the left, the standing figure is seen in profile while the body, whose surface is rendered in a pattern of harlequin-like diamond shapes, is turned so as to be almost frontal; the legs are in profile. Of the two figures at the center, one is taller than the other, in reverse order to the two men in the *Saltimbanques*. In the lower right corner there is a seated figure, as in the earlier picture. What makes the similarity fascinating, however, is the vast stylistic distance between them, a distance that Picasso encompassed in two years. What happened?

For the first few years of the century, the advanced artists—those who were to become "Les Fauves"—were absorbed by the Expressionist work of Van Gogh and Gauguin, but in 1904, 1905, and 1906, there were important exhibitions of Cézanne's paintings, which began to change the aesthetic climate. 1907 saw the great triumph of Cézanne with a posthumous retrospective at the Autumn Salon, showing fifty-seven items, and a large show of seventy-nine watercolors at Bernheime-Jeune.

Furthermore, the art dealer Vollard, who was Cézanne's dealer, in 1904 became Picasso's dealer as well, and Picasso was therefore closely in touch with Cézanne's work. *Les Demoiselles* owes an important debt to Cézanne's monumental *Bathers* (Raynal, p. 98) in Philadelphia, with its strong architecture and compression of space. Cézanne's characteristic terracotta and blue tonality is also evident.

In 1905 the Autumn Salon included an Ingres retrospective in which *The Turkish Bath* was shown. This is a composition with many nude female figures in a great variety of poses including the raised arm "Venus" pose, with a small still life in the foreground. Early in 1906 Picasso began a series of works in which the flesh color of the figures is rendered in terracotta and the figure style and poses reflect his interest in Classical Greek sculpture. In the spring, he saw Matisse's large *Joy of Life* (**J 927**) at the Salon des Indépendants exhibition, and went to the Louvre to see an exhibition of Iberian sculptures carved by the pre-Celtic inhabitants of Spain. (The following year he bought two carved Iberian heads which had been stolen from the Louvre by the secretary of Apollinaire, the poet who became the leading spokesman for avant-garde art.) Also in the spring of 1906 he began the *Portrait of Gertrude Stein* (**G 22.11**) but dissatisfied with the head after she had posed for him more than eighty times, he painted it out before leaving for a summer vacation Spain. During that summer his painting began to reflect features of Iberian style, such as the large, almond-shaped eyes and high-domed forehead. When he returned to Paris he finished the Gertrude Stein portrait without further sittings, rendering her face in Iberian style. Iberian influence was strong during the rest of 1906.

In the spring of 1907, he visited the ethnographic museum where he was struck by the power of African sculpture.

Going back now to 1905 it is to be noted that Picasso and Matisse had met for the first time at the home of Gertrude and Leon Stein, patrons of both artists. There was both mutual admiration and competitiveness between them from the start, and when Picasso saw Matisse's large, important *Joy of Life* in 1906, he was spurred to create an equally monumental work on the theme of the female nude group. The result suggests the struggle in which Picasso pushed his imagination to its farthest reaches and called upon his already vast knowledge of art, called upon his intuition, called upon all the hard thinking he had done for years in his determination to rival the great masters of the Western tradition. The result—*Les Demoiselles*—is Picasso's answer to the artist that he perceived as his only living rival.

While Matisse's painting produces its hedonistic effect by means of its softly curvilinear style, and suggests deep space, and passive, seductive serenity, the curved contours of Picasso's nudes end in sharp pointed angles, and he has placed them in a space even more compressed than that of Cézanne's late work; the effect is aggressive and disturbing. *Joy of Life* invokes the far away and mythical long ago—the "golden age." Picasso, too, invokes the long ago with his "Egyptian" style figure at the left, his Iberian-headed nudes at the center, in poses associated with Classical Greece, but brings the image abruptly, brutally up-to-date with Western art's newest "discovery," African sculpture—his answer, the present writer is suggesting, to Matisse's "far away." If Matisse called on Ingres's *Golden Age* for his *Joy of Life*, Picasso could call on Ingres's more daring *Turkish Bath,* with its crowded display of luscious female sex objects, and, as pointed out above, *a small still life at the center foreground.*

The nudes in *Les Demoiselles,* like the fruit, are far from luscious, and have no sexual appeal. As with Matisse, the real-life sensuality of the objects represented is drained out of them, as is also the evocation of real-life three-dimensional space, and time. There is no ceiling, no wall, no floor—the oversize foot of the standing nude is planted on a level that cannot be read as floor, in relation to the other figures—and there is no way to account for how the drapery at the sides hangs. The table in the foreground is tilted upward so that the fruit, in real space, would slide off; the seated figure is seen from the back except for the scarified face, which is represented more or less frontally, and with the leg turned out to the left in a pose that Cézanne used in *Three Bathers,* the *very painting that Matisse owned and valued so highly* (Raynal, p. 60). Both artists, despite the wide stylistic differences between them, had learned the same lesson from Cézanne, who himself seems not to have been fully aware of the implications of his art: that it is the painting as such that must affect the viewer. *Les Demoiselles* communicates in much the same way that Stravinsky's *Rite of Spring* does: through dissonance and surprising, unpredictable rhythms. The pain and savagery as well as the ecstacy of initiation into nature's means of species-survival is conveyed by the music alone and in *Les Demoiselles,* the ferocity and pleasure of sex are expressed through painting alone. The lesson is worth repeating: it is the painting as such that must affect the viewer.

In the two years following *Les Demoiselles* Picasso's painting shows a constant probing of the problem of relating the figures or objects to space in such a way as to acknowledge the truth that the canvas is a two-dimensional surface and not a window onto nature, and the further truth that ordinary perception of objects in the phenomenal world is only partial, contingent on light and point of view. The *really* real is the sum total of all possible views, but how was this to be represented? Picasso undertook to find out.

In this enterprise he was joined by Georges Braque (1882–1963), who abandoned his early Fauve style under the impact of the Cézanne exhibitions of 1907, and then, taken by the poet Guillaume Apollinaire to Picasso's studio to see *Les Demoiselles,* was overwhelmed by the painting's revolutionary implications. Turning torsos and limbs, houses, or still life arrangements so that they were predominantly parallel to the picture plane helped to avoid somewhat the illusion of three-dimensional space. Restricting the palette to one main color, terracotta for the motifs, with various dark hues for ground, and contrasting lighter tones of terracotta with darker ones, or shading into brown, gave the two artists a pictorial metaphor for convexity and concavity, since the light would be interpreted as projecting planes, the dark, as receding planes. This planar organization of figures and objects gave them a vocabulary of form analogous to three-dimensional form while keeping illusionistic effects under close constraint. The light-dark pattern of planes geometrized the surface so that motifs began to look like amalgamations of fragments. But differentiating between motif and ground did produce the effect of relief, which compromised the truth of the flatness of the canvas. Gradually in painting after painting Picasso and Braque, working independently at first, increasingly interwove the motif with the ground by fragmenting and coloring both in the same way, and by 1909 arrived at the style that became known as Cubism—more precisely, analytic Cubism—which they developed working in close collaboration over the following three years. Many years later Braque recalled that period: "We were living in Montmartre, we saw each other every day and talked a lot. Things were said between us in those years that cannot be said again . . . that no one would understand now . . . that made us ever so happy. We were like two mountain climbers roped together." (Quoted in Leymarie, *Braque,* 1960.)

One of the earliest Cubist landscapes is Picasso's *Houses on the Hill, Horta de Ebro* (Rubin, *Picasso,* p. 130) painted in the summer of 1909. Houses and hill are recognizable as such, but details have been eliminated so that they are little more than blocks of various shapes, with the overall view rendered as if seen simultaneously from above, below, and from different sides—there is no central point of view. The house/blocks are piled up so that there is little space between the foreground houses and the background hills. In the same period Picasso subjected the human head to the same treatment, as in the bust portrait of his companion, Fernande, *Woman with Pears* (Rubin, *Picasso,* p. 133). Fernande is placed forward in the picture plane, her head rendered in geometric planes. A still life of pears and peaches, not fragmented into planes, is on a table recognizably behind her on the left, with a green drape behind her on the right: as in the landscape, although space is much compressed, there is still the illusion of a space that allows one to look into it and see objects in it.

By early 1910, Picasso had advanced to *Girl with Mandolin* (Rubin, *Picasso,* p. 136). Here the subject has been fully studied in terms of planes and is much more fully integrated with the background, which now comes forward, matching in color and block-like shapes the figure itself. Nevertheless, the figure still makes a hole in the center of the composition, and the mandolin is shaded so that it appears three-dimensional. In this painting one can observe the technique of *passage,* whereby one block shape merges into its neighbor by the elimination of a line delineating one of its sides. Notice in the sequence to the left of the mandolin player's arm how the blocks seem to recede in space on their right side, whereas along the picture margin there are no delineating lines, so that there is no recession. The picture plane becomes the plane of reference, behind which one still has the illusion of shallow space.

A few months later Picasso painted a portrait of the dealer Ambroise Vollard **(J 942).** Now the figure has been further fragmented and is further embedded in a fragmented and grayish surrounding that is only slightly differentiated from it. The head of Vollard, however, is still terracotta colored, and although fragmented is still legible—even recognizable. By summer 1911, in a work such as *The Accordionist* (Rubin, *Picasso,* p. 145), there are only a few legible clues left to identify as objects. Figure and ground are almost completely integrated, with only a slightly darkened triangular area covering the central part of the composition indicating the musician with his instrument.

The last feature to appear in fully developed Cubism, lettering, appeared in the summer of 1911. Its effect is further to emphasize the flat surface of the painting, and possibly to raise consciousness as to the abstract nature of art by associating it with familiar abstractions such as words. Moreover, while the motifs in Cubist painting, aside from landscapes and figures, were drawn from commonplace objects in the studio—tables, bottles, various kinds of dishes and bowls, cigarettes, pipes, fruit, and newspapers—as the work became increasingly abstract, musical instruments and references to music appear more often. This may possibly be linked to the ongoing association of music, an abstract, symbolic art, with the visual arts, although it is also true that music, played on guitar, mandolin, and accordion, was a staple among the artists, and it may be that there is no special significance in the presence of music imagery in Cubist painting. There was, however, special significance in Picasso's painting *Ma Jolie* in the winter of 1911–12 (Rubin, *Picasso* p. 155), since it was a tribute to his new lover, Eva Gouel, whom he called "ma jolie," referring to a popular song. The two words are lettered at the center, above the lower margin of the picture plane. A few identifiable fragments can be seen, but the image is essentially "hermetic," the term sometimes used to refer to this phase of analytic Cubism (1911–1912). The period is also referred to as the "musical" phase of Cubism.

Braque's development was similar, but in one way was in advance of Picasso. In the summer of 1908, at L'Estaque, he painted a series of landscapes in which the primary concern is structural, but in which recessive space is clearly evident, as in *Houses at L'Estaque* (1908) (Arnason clpl 64). However, the blocky, "cubic" look of

his painting that summer had not yet appeared in Picasso's work. In fact, it was in a review of Braque's exhibition at the gallery of the dealer Daniel-Henry Kahnweiler, in the fall of 1908, that the critic Louis Vauxcelles, inventor of the term "Fauve," mentioned for the first time the word "cubes." "M. Braques," he wrote, ". . . reduces everything to geometric patterns, to cubes." It was either late summer or early fall of 1908 when Picasso's landscapes began to show cubic volumes, as in his *Landscape* (Rubin, *Picasso,* p. 111). Cubic volumes disappeared from the work of both artists as the surface became dominated by planes. By 1911, Braque's images had become as "hermetic" as Picasso's, as is evident in *The Portuguese* (1911) (Hunter clpl 235).

We have seen that Renoir and other artists working in the Impressionist style around 1880 became aware that they were on a road that led to formlessness, and turned away in a different direction. Likewise Picasso and Braque, in 1912, could see that further development along the line they had taken would lead to total objectlessness and they, too, turned away from this step. The problem they faced was how to recover the object without going backward stylistically.

Braque had been trained in his father's business as a house painter. He was a skilled craftsman who knew how to imitate wood grain and marble with paint, and in 1909–10, in the midst of driving towards non-objectivity, in a painting in which still life objects are fragmented, he included an illusion of a nail painted as if driven into a wall and sticking out in space; to heighten this trompe l'oeil effect he painted a palette as if it were hanging from the protruding nail. In this work, *Violin and Palette* (Leymarie, *Braque,* p. 42), and several others, one sees Braque concerned with counteracting the abstract aspects of Cubist painting. The stenciled letters and numerals that Braque and then Picasso introduced in their painting also had the effect of objectifying the work of art, transforming it into an object among other objects in the phenomenal world. This move had crucial consequences for modernist art as we shall see in Unit IX.

When Braque then began to paint passages that imitated wood grain, the stage was set for the next stage of their work, a "way out" of the dilemma of not losing stylistic ground while not taking the step from abstraction into non-objectivity. In May, 1912, Picasso created the first collage (from the French word *coller,* to glue), *Still Life with Chair Caning* **(J 943; G 22.14),** in which extraneous material is pasted or glued into the work. In September Braque composed the first papier collé (pasted paper), in which colored and shaped papers are pasted.

*Still Life with Chair Caning* combines painted, Cubist-fractured objects, lettering ("Jou," the first three letters of "Journal," suggesting the emphemeral nature of news and newspapers, here made "concrete" in "real" lettering), and a piece of oilcloth printed to simulate chair caning, the whole framed by a real length of rope. Illusionism in art is made the subject of a kind of visual pun—analogous to the literary puns that James Joyce was working with to create interlocking levels of meaning.

Braque's first papier collé was *Fruit Dish and Glass* (1912) (Leymarie, *Braque,* p. 54), in which he pasted strips of wallpaper that imitated the look of wood grain; the paper is placed so that it suggests a wood table on which the Cubist fruit dish and glass are displayed. In 1960, when Braque was interviewed, he remarked with regard to papier collé, "With these works we succeeded in dissociating color from form, in putting it on a footing independent of form, for that was the crux of the matter. Color acts simultaneously with form, but has nothing to do with form." None at the time could have realized how extraordinary this observation was, for it is only recently, in the field of neurophysiology, that research has found indications that the perception of form is a function of a part of the brain that processes light and dark, and is distinct from the part that perceives color.

The invention of papier collé led to the reintroduction of color, and to a new method of Cubist composition known as synthetic Cubism. In papier collé, objects are made to lend themselves to a composition wherein recognizable fragments of their characteristic parts are assembled in an interlocking design. This design suggests a subject usually without representing any single object whole, although there are exceptions in works where a smoker's pipe, a bottle, a playing card, or some other object is clearly observable. In Picasso's *Guitar* (1913) (Rubin, *Picasso,* p. 168) all objects are fragmented; in *Glass, Guitar, and Bottle* (1913) (Rubin, *Picasso,* p. 170) a bottle is given in its whole shape. In Braque's *Clarinet* (1913) (Leymarie, *Braque,* p. 59) the musical instrument is seen as if whole, even though its stem is intersected by a strip of wood-grained wall paper.

Synthetic Cubist compositions can be described in a similar way, except that the interlocking fragments are *painted,* not pieces of paper pasted onto the support. The effect is decorative rather than formal. Picasso's *Three Musicians* (1921) **(J 945; G. 22.15)** is the climax of his synthetic Cubist period as well as of his series of *commedia dell'arte* paintings and drawings. Pierrot plays a clarinet, a Harlequin plays a guitar, and a third figure, a monk with open mouth, sings from the sheet of music he holds. A dog (fidelity?—the artist wedded to art?) sits under the table, its head protruding towards the left margin of the painting. The threesome suggests a kind of secular Trinity, awesomely frontal, represented as musician/artists depicted in their traditional garments, and, with the dog, stimulating in the viewer a myriad of art historical associations that interlock like the jigsaw puzzle shapes and colors of the composition itself.

The impact of Cubism on Western art cannot be overstated. It was the most radical development since the invention of mathematical perspective by Brunelleschi about 1420. Cubism spread throughout Western culture, influencing avant-garde artists in every country, and it continued to affect pictorial composition for fifty years.

## Cubist influence in Paris: *1911–1921*

Among the large number of artists who came under the direct influence of Cubism, Juan Gris (1887–1921) was probably the most intellectual. His Cubist work, begun around 1911, was inspired mostly by Picasso's, but differed from it in decisive ways. Gris never fractured the figures and objects that he painted to the same extent. He used brighter color, but combined it with black and white, and this yields a greater sense of volume, as can be seen in the masterly Cubist *Portrait of Picasso* (1912) (Soby, *Gris,* p. 18). The curvilinear arms, shoulders, and head are contrasted with the rectilinear wall, creating substantial relief. Throughout his short career (he died at the age of thirty-five) objects were rendered in larger fragments than Picasso and Braque used, and the sense of object construction is strong. As an intellectual, Gris's writings illuminate not only his own principles but also those of Braque and Picasso. "I consider that the architectural element in painting is mathematics, the abstract side; I want to humanize it. Cézanne turns a bottle into a cylinder, but I begin with a cylinder and create . . . a bottle. . . . [Georges Braque] has written, 'Nails are not made from nails but from iron.' . . . I believe exactly the opposite. Nails are made from nails, for if the idea of the possibility of a nail did not exist in advance, there would be a serious risk that the material might be used to make a hammer or a curling iron" (Soby, *Gris,* p. 110).

Cubist elements entered the work of Fernand Léger (1881–1955) as early as 1909. In the following years he increasingly fractured the appearance of things, in Cubist fashion, but used bright colors, from which fact one understands that he was less interested than the inventors of the style in examining the nature of form, as rendered on the two-dimensional surface. In his *Contrast of Forms* (1913) (Hunter clpl 252), what is contrasted, despite the title, are the colors, which are always surface aspects of things. Curiously, in the same year that Picasso painted his important *Three Musicians,* with three male figures, Léger painted one of his greatest works, *Three Women* (1921) (Hunter clpl 426). Looking as if they were metal cut-outs, or robots, as mechanical workers were soon to be called in Carl Capek's play of 1923, *R.U.R.,* the figures in this painting reflect Léger's association with the "machine aesthetic" of those years, as well as his political ideology.

With the success of the proletarian revolution in Russia, many artists and intellectuals were persuaded that world socialism was a real possibility, based on the working class and modern technology, which was symbolized by the machine. As a corollary, they were committed to the idea of the city, since it was the environment of the proletariat, where factories were established. Leger's *The City* (1919) **(J clpl 139; G. 22.18),** a monumental work like his *Three Women,* makes the city motifs slice across and into each other, as if they were parts of a machine, and the city itself were one great mechanism. We will observe the widespread influence of the "machine aesthetic" and its political inspiration when we see it at work at the Bauhaus, in Constructivism, and in the International Style in architecture.

# Futurism

Exactly what and how much the Futurists and Cubists owed each other was an issue of often bitter polemics between French and Italian artists. When, for example, Apollinaire referred in a review to Futurism in Delaunay's work, the latter wrote an indignant denial to the newspaper, and broke off his close and fruitful relationship with the poet. What is certainly true is that the contacts among European artists, even including the Russians, were in some degree enriching to all and mutually rewarding.

Futurism, like German Expressionism, erupted in a spirit of rebellion generated by the cult of youth and power; rebellion, youth, and power remained central to Futurist aesthetics. The movement (the "first" Futurist movement, to distinguish it from the subsequent movement that formed after the World War, with which we will not be concerned) was born in the revolutionary first decade of our century—those years when the European view of the exterior, physical universe and the interior, psychological universe was restructuring the cosmos and the psyche, just as political revolutions have been restructuring society ever since the Revolution of 1905 in Russia, right in the middle of the fateful decade. Physics and psychology have transformed our notions of reality, and thus our system of values.

In its beginnings Futurism was a literary invention, unlike its contemporary modernist styles, Fauvism, Cubism, and Expressionism. Its creator was a poet, Filippo Marinetti, Italian-born but for many years resident in France and close to the French literary Symbolists. Like almost all artists and intellectuals of his generation, he was deeply responsive to Henri Bergson's metaphysics and Nietzsche's ethics. In 1909 his "Futurist Manifesto," published first in France but known immediately in Italy, set the Nietzschean tone and defined the Dionysian philosophy of the Futurist movement. "We shall sing the love of danger," he began. "It is in Italy that we launch this manifesto of violence, destructive and incendiary . . . because we would deliver Italy from its canker of professors, archaeologists, cicerones, and antiquaries." Marinetti's call was to youth, and his appeal to youth was the traditional one—to destroy the past. "The oldest among us are thirty," he continued, "we have ten years to accomplish our task. When we are forty, let others, younger and more valiant, throw us into the basket like useless manuscripts. . . . Art can be nought but violence, cruelty, injustice." (Quoted in Taylor, p. 125.)

A year later the manifesto of Futurist painters, signed by Umberto Boccioni (1882–1916), Carlo Carrà (1881–1966), Luigi Russolo (1885–1947), Giacomo Balla (1871–1958), and Gino Severini (1883–1966) was read from the stage of the Teatro Chiarella in Turin by Boccioni. It began, "To the young artists of Italy." It stressed dynamism and originality as vital to artistic freedom. A few weeks later came the *Technical Manifesto* of Futurist art, in which one clearly discerns Bergsonian metaphysics. Bergson's description of reality as flux, of time experienced as a flowing, irreversible succession of states that melt into each other to form an indivisible *process*—time as duration—is expressed in this manifesto in terms of space perception: "A profile is never motionless before our eye but it constantly appears and reappears. . . . Moving objects constantly multiply themselves . . . space no longer exists. The street pavement, soaked by rain beneath the glare of electric lamps, becomes immensely deep and gapes to the very center of the earth" (Taylor, pp. 125–126). The Futurists invented what they termed "lines of force" and adapted the interpenetrating planes of Cubism in order to express psychological effects. They transformed the traditional, essentially mathematical function of line as a means of enclosing forms and of creating spatial relationships of size and distance implying the concept of time, to that of creating psychological relationships—creating space as *experienced* by a human perceiver. This reflects the Bergsonian view that any attempt to represent time by a spatial image such as line only generates abstract, mathematical time, devoid of human experience.

Bergson's notion of spontaneity as freedom of action that is directly experienced, as the gesture or response—the free act—in which total personality is expressed, is echoed in the manifesto's assertion that "The gesture which we would reproduce on canvas shall no longer be a fixed moment in Universal dynamism. It shall be dynamic sensation itself" (Taylor, p. 125). The stress on dynamism is also Bergsonian, for he held that the body-mind duality is resolved in the notion of real duration: perception is an *event* in the concrete present which is not a geometrical point or edge separating past from future but a flowing continuity in which past, present, and future overlap. As T. S. Eliot was to perceive it,

> Time present and time past
> Are both perhaps present in time future
> And time future contained in time past.

The cultivation of the non-rational faculty of intuition, an important element in Bergson's philosophic system, has its analogue in compositions that reject the rational space of mathematical perspective in favor of psychological space.

An analysis of Boccioni's *The Laugh* (1911) (Taylor, p. 40) reveals the presence of all of the foregoing features. Boccioni had gone to Paris for a short stay early in 1911, had come into contact with Cubism there, and in *The Laugh* he has adopted the technique of interpenetrating solids and voids by faceting their planes. However, he has employed the method not for the purpose of resolving the problem of representing three-dimensional forms on the two-dimensional surface but to convey the sensation of the mélange of color, form, and sound—to involve the viewer, that is, in the psycho-physical experience of simultaneous sensations.

The space of the composition is tipped forward as a further means of co-opting the viewer psychologically. The laugh emanating from the plump face of the woman pervades the entire space so that the brutal red, yellow, and blue hues seem saturated with raucous laughter. Lines of force are produced by the spears of light that interweave far and near, their perspective function flattened out and denied by their non-perspectival relationships, and by their relationship to the picture plane: *on* the picture plane at the upper margin, *going into depth* at various locations. The forms are all related, woven into the picture plane, denying both mathematical space and measured time. Everything happens at once in a kind of non-divisible duration. A strange and fascinating ambiguity pervades this café scene. The laughter seems harsh and joyless, and the fragmented faces that stud the space are glowering and sinister. There is a savage, animalistic quality that contrasts with the formal uniforms of the waiters and other guests, as if their faces are masks that conceal an explosive reality. The crowded café resounds with piercing, lonely laughter, and creates the effect of raw sensation locked into the dense, stifling, shallow pictorial space.

With the death of God, as proclaimed by Nietzsche, the Futurists placed their faith in modern science as the All-Knowing, and focused their worship on steel and electricity as the supreme power in the human world. They saw science mainly in its applications to the new technology. Marinetti declared, "A racing car, its frame adorned with great pipes, like snakes with explosive breath . . . a racing car . . . is more beautiful than the *Victory of Samothrace* **(J 206)**. . . . We shall sing of the man at the steering wheel, whose ideal stem transfixes the earth, rushing over the circuit of her orbit."

The Futurists were urban-oriented, of course, seeing in the city a symbol of the complex organization of modern society built on the foundations of science-generated technology. Marinetti proclaimed in his manifesto:

> We shall sing of the . . . multi-colored and polyphonic surge of revolution in modern capitalist cities; of the nocturnal vibrations of arsenals and workshops beneath their violent electric moons; of the greedy stations swallowing smoking snakes; of factories suspended from the clouds by their ropes of smoke; of bridges leaping like gymnasts over the diabolical cutlery of sunbathed rivers . . . of broad-chested locomotives prancing on the rails, like huge steel horses bridled with long tubes, and of the gliding flight of aeroplanes. (Taylor, p. 124)

Every one of Marinetti's poetic images can be found in Futurist painting. The aggressive force of Futurism embedded in his manifesto thoroughly pervades Boccioni's *The City Rises* (1910–11) (Taylor, p. 37), even though it is not yet fully Futurist in style, since the artist was still using the Divisionist method of his earlier years, before his contact with Cubism. At first it may seem curious that the central image is not a modern machine but a horse. Notice, however, that this horse is winged, and is thus to be identified as the mythological Pegasus, the horse of the muses and thus the flying steed of inspiration and imagination. It is also to be remembered that mechanical energy is measured in horse power. The design of the principal motif, a man with a rope pulled around the horse, literally "harnessing power," may have been derived, as I believe, from the strikingly similar motif of the capture of a bull on one of the famed Mycenean Vapheio cups **(G clpl 4.30)**. Nevertheless the overriding inspiration for the image comes from Marinetti, who had written a poem, "To My Pegasus," which begins, "Vehement god of a race of steel/ Automobile drunk with space . . . I let go your metal bridle and you thrust yourself drunkenly into the liberating infinite." *The City Rises* is thus an homage to Marinetti. It is about power and the modern world; it is the future that is rising, the new city that will be the spiritual home of the future civilization that is to replace Jerusalem, the spiritual home from which emanated the power of the old, Christian civilization.

Like Cubism, Futurism, too, became increasingly abstract, as in Boccioni's *Dynamism of a Cyclist* (1913) **(J 949)**. The figure is all but indiscernible in the faceted shapes, again rendered with Divisionist strokes to which he returned in 1913. Severini and Balla went all the way to non-objectivity, although in a sense their non-objective works were in fact representations, since Balla's *Iridescent Interpenetration* (1912) (Taylor, p. 62) and Severini's *Spherical Expansion of Light (Centrifugal)* (1914) (Taylor, p. 74.) both "represent" the dynamic energy of light.

Boccioni was the only one of the original Futurists who was a sculptor as well as painter. His masterpiece, *Unique Forms of Continuity in Space* (1913) **(J clpl 167; G 921)** may also be regarded as an homage to Marinetti, since it is a kind of modernist, male response to the classical female *Victory of Samothrace* who is alighting on the prow of a ship after her rushing flight through space. Boccioni's figure is a Nietzschean Superman, whose being is in perfect harmony with the cosmos. It is represented as if in successive phases of movement experienced simultaneously in the transcendent, non-Newtonian, non-Euclidean realm, the new scientific heaven which the superman of the future will inhabit.

Futurism (the "first" Futurist movement) began to disintegrate in 1914. Carrà began to search for a less hectic style; Severini was back in Paris, working in a style somewhat related to synthetic Cubism; and Boccioni had determined his need to "start over" from Cézanne. One of the last of his Futurist works is the painting/collage *The Charge of the Lancers* (1915) (Taylor, p. 114), in which horses with their riders charge across the picture plane, riding down the small figures of the helmeted enemy with fixed bayonets. Newspaper clippings pasted onto the cardboard support are news reports of the war, dated January 4, 1915.

There are two tragic ironies in Boccioni's death on August 17, 1916; he had been a vehement interventionist for Italy's entry into the war on the side of the Allies, and he had loved horses all his life. Italy did enter the war, and he was on military duty, not in battle but on a routine reconnoitering assignment when his horse suddenly reared. He was thrown, fell under the horse's hoof, and his skull was crushed. By that time Futurism, too, was dead.

## Mondrian: Neo-Plasticism

Although the originators of Cubism did not take the step into non-objective art, Piet Mondrian (1872–1944) did. The evolution of this artist's aesthetic ideas through representational Dutch landscapes featuring houses reflected in water so that the lower half of the painting echoes and balances the upper half, trees with widespread branches so that the left and right sides of the composition echo and balance each other, dunes asymmetrically balanced with the sky above them reveals a consistent devotion to the idea of balance and unity that in fact reflects a spiritual conviction. Indeed, Mondrian joined the Theosophist Society in 1909 because the tenets of this religio-philosophical system, in harmony with his own, proposed balance and unity as the ultimate nature of good in the universe. Late nineteenth-century Theosophy was heavily influenced by Indian sources which held that the universe exists on seven levels, and human action ascends through those levels from gross physicality to the pure Universal Self. To understand Mondrian's mature art it is obviously necessary to know that the absence of physical phenomena is a metaphor for pure spirituality and the designs of his paintings express good, through the perfect equilibrium of the elements of color and line.

He arrived at his signature style, Neo-Plasticism—the grid of black lines enclosing primary colors—over a period of about ten years: from his first contact with Cubism in 1911 to his *Composition with Red, Yellow, Blue* of 1921, the first of a long series of variations on the theme **(J clpl 140).** The adjustments in the size and color of the rectangles are dictated not by any scientific system such as the golden section, but by what the artist sensed as "the balance of unequal but equivalent oppositions."

Mondrian's first Cubist works were still lifes in which, as in Braque's and Picasso's still lifes, objects were reduced to essential shapes in a horizontal-vertical grid, and integrated with their surroundings. He returned to landscape features, and trees were now rendered in terms of the vertical trunk and the horizontal branches. Through a number of experiments with very short horizontal and vertical lines arranged in a rhythmic pattern, he arrived at the "plus-and-minus" style, based on the image of a pier jutting out into the ocean: the rhythmic pattern in this series is meant to suggest the rhythm of ocean waves. Next, the plus-and-minus signs became short black rectangles accenting a field of colored squares. Then the black disappeared, leaving the field to colored squares against a neutral grey ground, to reappear as frames around the colored squares. Working out several more variations of the idea, Mondrian at last came to the familiar red, yellow, blue rectangles enclosed in black frames.

Mondrian believed in the universality of the right angle and the primary colors. He believed his was a truly democratic art, since it required no education, no sophistication—all human beings understood these basic elements and could and would respond to them. That his designs influenced several generations of taste is doubtless. That the vast majority had no suspicion of the ideas behind the designs is also doubtless. But perhaps Mondrian would say that the designs spoke of balance, and order, and goodness, and that's what people liked, even if they did not realize that that's what they were all about.

## German Expressionism: Blaue Reiter

*Man is crying out for his soul, the whole period becomes a single urgent cry. And Art cries, too, into the deep darkness, crying for help, crying for the spirit. That is Expressionism.* Hermann Bahr, author of *Expressionismus* (1916).

Theosophy made a convert of one other major modernist artist, Wassily Kandinsky (1866–1944). Kandinsky also shares with Mondrian credit for taking the first plunge into non-objectivity. This staggering development was as crucial a move for modernism as Picasso and Braque made in creating Cubism. It is no accident that the two creators of non-objective art were Theosophists. They were led into non-objectivity· by their spiritual convictions, as we have already seen with Mondrian.

Born in Moscow, trained for law, Kandinsky had from childhood responded with peculiar excitement to color, and on a trip to the hinterlands, his most vivid experience was the extraordinary brilliance of the folk art he saw. He was thirty years old when he decided to take up painting as a profession after seeing an exhibition of Impressionist painting. Later, he recalled how he had been unable, at first, to recognize what he was looking at, and had responded to Monet's *Haystacks* as *painting* before he realized he was looking at haystacks. He moved to Munich, and his career unfolded in Germany; for this reason he is usually studied in the context of German Expressionism. Well traveled in Europe, he was aware of the modernist developments, and in 1911 he and his new friend, Franz Marc, founded the Blaue Reiter (Blue Rider) group in Munich, taking the name from the design on the cover of the almanac they published under the same name. Marc loved horses, Kandinsky loved the horse and rider design, they both loved blue, hence the title. Others in the group included August Macke, Heinrich Campendonk, and Gabriele Munter.

Although high-colored like the Expressionist artists in Die Brücke, the Blaue Reiter artists have none of the savagery and deliberate crudeness of execution that marks the style of the earlier group. While there are few stylistic characteristics that the Blaue Reiter artists share, they were committed to color as a prime expressive force, and to the fundamental idea that the nature of art is essentially non-materialist and has as its goal the spiritual enrichment of the viewer. These ideas were articulated fully by Kandinsky in his book *Concerning the Spiritual in Art,* probably the most influential book on modernist art of the first half of the twentieth century, finished in 1910, published in 1912. In it, he can be seen linked to Munch and the symbolist movement with its belief in the power of abstract symbols to evoke material things. The book also links him, although not German-born, to the German idealist tradition. "For the will . . . is ultimately nothing new, but the same urge as has always been valid in the Germanic world," wrote Paul Fechter, a critic and associate of Hermann Bahr. "It is the old Gothic soul which . . . despite all rationalism and materialism, again and again raises its head (quoted in Willett, p. 100).

The book gives the most extensive argument with regard to the color-music analogy, arguing that because music is the least *material* of arts it is the most effective vehicle for the expression of inner feeling. Some writers (Janson, for example, p. 672) have wondered why the "musical" content of non-objective art should be held to be more desirable than, for instance, literary content. The reason is that music is nothing but the medium of which it is composed—sound. Literature, on the contrary, is a vehicle for meaning: (as pointed out in Unit VII) when we read, we hardly notice the printed word; we penetrate beyond the words—the medium—to their meaning. With music the medium is all. Music has rhythm, mathematical construction, repeated notes that are expressive *because* they are repeated, like incantations. Kandinsky sought to make color and composition function like musical sound, although he recognized that there are characteristics in each art form that are peculiar to itself and not transferable or applicable. Music is at a disadvantage compared to painting, Kandinsky thought, because it requires the passage of time, while painting can make a direct, immediate effect. Music, on the other hand, is by its nature free from the need to imitate nature, while painting has traditionally been tied to the visible world. Kandinsky wanted to liberate painting from this responsibility.

He found the means to achieve this one day in 1910 when returning to his studio he saw a painting that struck him as very beautiful. "Bewildered," he wrote, "I stared at it. The painting lacked all subject, depicted no recognizable object and was entirely composed of bright patches of color. Finally, I recognized it—my own painting, standing on its side on the easel." From this moment,

Kandinsky became convinced that objects were irrelevant to painting. He executed a series of increasingly abstract paintings based on the theme of the Last Judgment, which symbolized for him the end of materialism, the scourge of the modern world, after which apocalyptic calamity, the world would be renewed spiritually. In *Composition IV* (1911) (Hunter fig. 193) one can see certain landscape features, a "mountain" with towers at the center, an abstracted horse leaping upward on the left, over the rainbow, and two figures rising as if from the grave, on the right. In 1913 he moved to total non-objectivity with paintings such as the *Sketch for "Composition VII"* **(J clpl 136).**

Kandinsky's transcendent vision should be understood in the context of the apocalyptic, visionary spirit that was widespread in Germany at the outbreak of the War. For many artists this was to be the Great Destruction that heralded the Last Judgment and the New Era of Peace under Socialism. According to Julius Bab, a German literary critic, "The German people's hour of destiny has found, and is finding, a lyrical echo in thousands and thousands of poetically excited hearts." Within a year, the romance with the War was over, at least for many of the artists and intellectuals. Max Beckmann had enjoyed the experience, but by May, 1915, after the second battle at Ypres, where the Germans first used poison gas, he wrote, "for the first time I've had enough." Tragically, Franz Marc (1880–1916) had not "had enough."

Marc's painting is marked by an intensity that grew ever more ecstatic over the few years in which his career unfolded. He projected onto animals his rapturous feeling for nature. In a series of paintings of horses, he worked out his path toward abstraction—he never became non-objective—integrating the curved shapes of the animals with the curves of the hilly landscape as in *Blue Horses* (1911) (Hunter fig. 196). Marc's horses are free. Unlike the horses of Manet, Degas, Gauguin, Boccioni, even Kandinsky, there is no human domination by a rider in Marc's horses. They are grouped together, and they are in harmony with each other and with their environment, as shown by the repetition of forms and color. That harmony, metaphor for peace and world brotherhood, is forcefully disrupted in his *Animals' Fate* (1913) (Hunter fig. 197), in which he synthesized Cubist fracturing of planes, Futurist lines of force, and Blaue Reiter color to create an image of apocalyptic prophecy. A blue deer, symbolizing hope, is about to be crushed by a falling tree, itself a symbol of destruction. The whole world seems to be on fire, with flames shooting diagonally across the picture planes as if issuing from cannon. Marc was killed in the war in 1916.

*Animals' Fate* was not the only picture of world conflagration painted on the eve of the World War. Equally apocalyptic was *Burning City,* by Ludwig Meidner (1884–1966), painted in 1913. This is no wilderness but a modern city, with apartment buildings lighted by fire and teetering as the bombed ground beneath them heaves, while people in the foreground watch the destruction of their homes. The end was near. German artists were ready for the new Utopia.

## Part 2
## ART BETWEEN THE WORLD WARS

If Europe was ailing at the turn of the century, by 1918 it was severely crippled. Apart from the lives lost, literally thousands of young men had lost limbs in the war, and it is not trivializing their tragedy to think of them as life imitating art. The partial figure, which perhaps expresses the modern human being's new sense of impotence in the face of overwhelming forces, had made its appearance in the work of Auguste Rodin, and was soon part of the modernist sculptural vocabulary. It is at least arguable that the fragmentation and mechanization of the figure in early twentieth-century modernist painting was also generated in part by the same infrastructure of perception. Abstraction is the realm of the mind, where things have no sensual reality, where things (including humans) are ideas to be structured, arranged, manipulated by metaminds to fit some over-all composition in which the wholeness of any of its parts is irrelevant. Curiously, humans *as* ideas *have* no ideas and thus no will. They are things like other things. In 1925 José Ortega y Gassett articulated the view held by others as well, that abstract and non-objective painting and sculpture dehumanized art, but perhaps it can be argued more forcefully that it is not art, but *humans* that have been dehumanized in the twentieth century. Such was the message of many artists, none more savagely delivered than that by George Grosz (1893–1959). His *Funeral of the Poet Panizza* (1917–1918) (Arnason clpl 107) is a recall of James Ensor's bitter *Christ's Entry into Brussels* (1888) **(G 107)** seen through the Futurist eyes of Boccioni and Carrà in the former's *Riot in the Galleria* (1910) (Taylor, p. 33) and the latter's *Funeral of the Anarchist Galli* (1910–1911) (Taylor, p. 31).

During the war, and for a few years following the Armistice, modernism in Europe and America underwent a revision that brought objects back into clear focus. Picasso turned to an archaicizing Classicism with paintings such as *Three Women at the Spring* (1921), *Mother and Child* (1921–1922) **(J 946),** and *Women Running on the Beach* (1922). Matisse's painting also became more representational, bold in color, and in some works is marked by sketchiness, as in *L'Artiste et son Modele* (ca. 1919), with an amazing control of a variety of patterns that rivals the Flemish painter Jan van Eyck. Even more daring in its combination of patterns is *The Moorish Screen* of 1921, a major work of this period that Matisse painted while he lived in Nice. In Italy Carrà and other former Futurists

turned their interest to the early stage of pre-Renaissance Classicism, with the influence of Giotto pre-eminent (*Pine Tree by the Sea*, 1921) (Haftmann II, fig. 416).

In Germany, the first two waves of modernist Expressionism were spent; the art that arose in the Weimar Republic, called the Neue Sachlichkeit (New Objectivity) rejected Expressionism's subjective *angst*. Still expressionist in terms of emotional content, and still as rebellious against bourgeois society as their Expressionist predecessors, the artists of the Neue Sachlichkeit attacked directly, in terms of subject matter, rather than indirectly, in aesthetic terms, as the Brücke and Blaue Reiter artists had done. Modernist compression of pictorial space and Cubist intersecting of planes are made to serve representational painting.

## Dada

The period's radicalism was expressed aesthetically in the anti-aesthetic movement known as Dada. The horror of World War I, the staggering loss of life as armies gained, lost, regained, lost again a few hundred yards of battleground made grotesquely meaningless the optimistic claims and assumptions on which European values had been based since the Enlightenment. Above all, the secular god, Rationality and its genius child, Science, which were to solve all human problems and answer all questions, had been revealed as, at best, powerless to prevent the war, and in some ways even as the cause of making that war the most hideous in the history of the world. If this was the work of Rationality and Science, let us worship at the altar of Irrationality and Accident, proclaimed Jean (Hans) Arp, sculptor, Hugo Ball, poet, Richard Hulsenbeck, writer, Marcel Janco, painter, and Tristan Tzara, poet. In Zurich, in 1916, as refugees from the war, they founded the Café Voltaire, named for the great author whose *Candide* is synonymous with willful self-delusion that this is the "best of all possible worlds." One evening, so the story goes, the group decided to found a new art movement—anti-art—that would hold up to ridicule the cherished bourgeois devotion to the fine art tradition. To find a name for their movement, one of them opened a dictionary at random and placed his finger on the page. The word under his finger turned out to be dada, a child's hobbyhorse. Since bourgeois truth was as much a target of ridicule as any other bourgeois value, there is little reason to believe this fairy tale told by Dadas except that one wants to. It is one of the movement's greatest works of art, bringing together the innocent world of childhood with the innocent world of archaic Greece. As Gauguin had put it: "We must go back beyond the horses of the Parthenon, back to the dada of our childhood."

The Dada movement sprang up all over Europe and the United States. Marcel Duchamp, however, had been making Dada art *avant la lettre*. He was in the United States during the war and had coined the term "ready-made" in 1915 for commonplace objects that he began to exhibit in 1916 at the Bourgeois Gallery in New York—a snow shovel (*In Advance of a Broken Arm*), a bottle rack—and in 1917, probably to test the aesthetic limits of the jury of the *First Annual Exhibition of the Society of Independent Artists,* who advertised their complete openness to all innovation, he sent his *Fountain,* a urinal signed R. Mutt, possibly a pun on the German word *armut,* poverty, and also possibly a reference to a German ceramic maker by the name of Richard Armutt. The jury refused to exhibit it.

Anti-art, like the anti-hero of modern fiction, was meant to assert the priority of reality in art, and to destroy the last vestiges of idealism and Romanticism. It affirmed cynicism and skepticism as the thinking person's guide to dealing with life and art. More positively, it also affirmed the priority of the human mind in making art. This had been a more or less prominent issue ever since Leonardo had asserted that sculpture, dependent on manual labor, was less intellectual than painting. The dynamic thrust in the development of art academies to supplant guilds was indeed the artists' determination to associate art with philosophy, which was institutionalized in academies. Duchamp's gesture in turning a snow shovel into art is the logical conclusion of this current of thought; his act states that the significance of the artist's artistic *act* lies not in its physical execution but in the power of the imagination, an intellectual power, to transform phenomena. It has now become commonplace to pick up a piece of driftwood from a beach or a stone from the floor of a woods and place it on display in one's home. Doing so, we discover, gives us the pleasure of possession of a thing worthless in itself but valuable because we have given it its new meaning. If today we are all artists, then it is Duchamp who is "the father of us all." He is, indeed, a seminal figure for much of late twentieth-century art.

The rise of Dada, with its emphasis on accident probably inspired by Freudian theory, paralleled the maturing of Mondrian's Neo-Plasticism and as we shall see, Kasimir Malevich's Suprematism, both of which relied on precision in relationships. It also paralleled the development of Constructivism in Russia, and overlapped the founding of the Bauhaus in Weimar, Germany. Each factor of the nineteenth-century duality expressed in terms of Romanticism and Classicism became intensified in the twentieth century in the opposing directions of chaos and order, the dialectic terms of twentieth-century sensibility. Throughout our century this dialectic has produced a sequence of styles based on the aesthetics of free form, on one hand, and geometric form on the other, or, in another pair of terms, Expressionism and Constructivism.

## Modernist Art in the Soviet Union

There is perhaps no greater irony in modernist culture than the defeat of the avant-garde in the aftermath of the Russian Revolution of 1917. The overthrow of the Czarist regime was welcomed by the intellectual and artistic community as heralding a new world emancipated from all the old constricting political and social forms. Freedom to write, to paint, as well as to construct a new society would create works of unprecedented power for the enrichment of the mind and soul of the newly created Soviet citizen, so it was fervently believed. Radical art was to be the partner of a radical new beginning for human society. So it was, for about three years. Some Russian artists who had left the country—Kandinsky, Naum Gabo, Antoine Pevsner, Marc Chagall—returned to participate in building this new world. They served in the ministry of culture and held other prestigious positions. By 1921 official Soviet doctrine took control of the arts along with everything else, and art became increasingly a handmaiden to the Communist party line. Kandinsky, Gabo, Pevsner, and Chagall left for western Europe; those that remained conformed with the demands of the regime, and eventually Socialist Realism, propagandist in imagery and intention, prevailed. The Utopian dream was dead.

One of the first mediators of western European modernism in Russia was Serge Diaghilev, who published a magazine, *World of Art* (1898–1904), and arranged art exhibitions. A Cézannesque group, the Knave of Diamonds, was formed in 1910, which helped to develop an audience for modernism. Natalia Goncharova (1881–1962) and Mikhail Larionov (1882–1964) began working with folk art, but after Boccioni's trip to Russia in 1911 they created Rayonism, which fused Cubist and Futurist formal ideas. Among the most accomplished of Russian Cubist painters was Liubov Popova (1889–1924), whose work bears a close resemblance to Juan Gris and Fernand Léger. Going beyond Cubism, as Mondrian had in Paris, Vladimir Tatlin (1889–1953) began making non-objective constructions possibly as early as 1912, and Kasimir Malevitch (1878–1935) evolved the non-objective style that he called Suprematism in the same year.

By Suprematism, Malevitch meant the supremacy of pure feeling in creative art. His first Suprematist work, a black square on a white field, antagonized even Larionov and Goncharova. The critics were appalled. "Everything we love is lost. We are in a desert," declared Alexander Benois, Diaghilev's close associate in bringing modernism to Russia. Malevitch's theory and practice did not rest on a philosophical or religious system, like Kandinsky's or Mondrian's. His obsession, however, was similar to theirs: a burning hatred of materialism. With this as a fundamental element in his view of the world, he arrived at the perception that, since materialism is evil, the representation of matter was inappropriate in art, since art was spiritual in nature. He opposed all ideas of functionalism, which was to be the primary force in Soviet thinking, and held that "a chair, a bed, and table are not matters of utility but rather, the forms taken by plastic sensations" (Chipp, p. 346). Although in appearance Malevitch's work such as *White on White* (1917) (Arnason fig. 271) looks like a startling anticipation of 1960s Minimalism, from the foregoing it can be seen that it was in fact created as a search for absolutes, for pure feeling, while the later movement developed out of the modernist exploration of the problem of the nature of art.

Tatlin journeyed to Berlin and Paris in 1913, and was able to visit Picasso's studio at the time when Picasso was concentrating his attention on collage and constructions made of sheet metal or wood such as *Guitar* (1912) (Rubin, p. 148). When he returned to Russia he began working out the ideas stimulated by his trip and created a series of reliefs constructed of wood, metal, and cardboard. These have not survived and are known only by some poor illustrations that appeared in contemporary catalogues.

Tatlin soon became a leader among the young Russians who were convinced that art must serve the people and thus identified architecture, sculpture, and painting with engineering. His greatest conception was a sculptural architectural structure, *The Monument to the Third International* **(J 1004; G 22.47),** that revealed its engineering like a bridge. Planned as a monument of glass and iron, it was, alas, a monument of irony: projected as an exemplar of functional building, it was never built. It was to have been a metal spiral, tilted away from the vertical, in which were to be constructed a glass cylinder surmounted by a glass cube, topped by a glass cone. The three units were to revolve, each at a different rate of speed, so that the cylinder would make its complete turn once a year, the cube once a month, and the cone once a day. The various units were to be used for conferences and other official business. The tower was to be 1,300 feet high, taller than the Eiffel Tower, and it was meant to symbolize the rise of humanity. The only realization of this splendid idea is the large-scale model that the artist constructed; a banner hung above it proclaiming, "Engineers create new forms."

Alexander Rodchenko (1891–1956), closely associated with Tatlin and Malevitch, made the first sculptures in which there is actual movement. Furthermore, he broke radically with sculptural tradition by hanging it instead of supporting it from the bottom. His *Suspended Construction in Space* (1920) (Hunter fig. 270), a forerunner of kinetic sculpture, which we will take up in the context of art of the 1960s, is an organization of intersecting circles that move with the surrounding air currents. It is wholly non-objective, a style that Rodchenko gave up when official government policy hardened against the "merely" aesthetic; he turned to photography, film, and stage design, in all of which he achieved notable success.

The aim and meaning of Constructivist art were formulated in 1920 by Naum Gabo (1890–1900) who, in his essay "The Realist Manifesto," explained the need for rethinking the purpose of art in order to make art reflect the essence of real life. This essence, according to the Constructivists, was constituted by space and time, and the work of art was thus the formal realization of this perception of ultimate reality. The Constructivists placed necessity at the head of their moral value system and effectiveness at the head of their aesthetic system. They held that the ordinary objects of our everyday life all have their essential reality, and that the labels given to things— chairs, tables and so on—are irrelevant to their essential being, which is the rhythm of the forces in them. This functionalist neo-Platonism required the rejection of all contingent attributes such as color and decoration. Constructivists renounced all descriptive elements, so that line, for example, would never be used to depict the outer shape of objects, but to indicate the direction of static forces and their rhythms *in* objects.

The sweeping radicalism of Constructivist theory and practice lies in their attack on the fundamental characteristics of traditional sculpture, mass and stability. Constructivism rejected the concept of mass as a sculptural element, replaced mass with *space* as the only possible expression of pictorial and plastic depth, and aimed at the expression of kinetic energy rather than static energy.

Ultimately the Constructivists meant to make "art for the people" that would in fact be an integral part of the peoples' lives. They emphasized the demand for immediacy: art was for the present and had to serve the needs of the present. In his manifesto Gabo asserted, "Today we proclaim our words to you people. In the squares and on the streets we are placing our work convinced that art must not remain a sanctuary for the idle, a consolation for the weary, and a justification for the lazy. Art should attend us everywhere that life flows and acts . . . at home and on the road, in order that the ardent passion to live should not be extinguished in mankind." Curiously, Gabo seems to have overlooked the fact that public art had existed from the most remote periods of civilization, and always expressed the prevailing values of its culture.

According to Constructivist thought, the value of art lay in its double capacity to communicate the emotions of the artist and to inspire similar emotions in the viewer. This is not exactly as simple or superficial an idea as it may at first appear. The emotion these artists were concerned with was the aesthetic emotion, which they conceived of as embodied in matter. The human being, they argued, by virtue of *being* matter, feels some deep, psychological bond with all of matter, and therefore the material of which a sculpture is created communicates naturally with the viewer: non-objective a work may be, but it is nevertheless natural because it is made of nature's matter.

In light of this basic tenet of Constructivist theory—the shared nature of all matter—it is interesting to observe that the Constructivists welcomed the invention of synthetic materials. Gabo's *Linear Construction* (1950) **(G 22.48),** for example, is constructed of plastic and nylon thread. They did, however, continue to work with natural materials such as Gabo's bronze wire and steel of *Construction for the Bijenkorf Department Store* (1954–57) (Hunter clpl 411).

# Bauhaus

Léger's socialist convictions and his combination of decorative surface and metallic looking objects that seem, even the figures, to be machine-made, as in *Three Women*, coincide with the social and aesthetic principles of the Bauhaus. This was an enormously influential institution in Weimar, Germany, established in 1919, that brought together artists and craftsmen who worked in almost every conceivable plastic art form—architecture, painting, sculpture, ceramics, metal work, and so on. The moving spirit of the Bauhaus, Walter Gropius, was himself an architect who was committed to the idea of functionalism as an aesthetic principle, and the idea of art as a social necessity. In the nineteenth century, the Arts and Crafts movement had sought to counteract the dullness and characterless quality of late Victorian manufactured designs by going back to the Gothic *hand*-made object. The hand-made, reflecting the presence of the human craftsman with its slight irregularities, was held to be not only aesthetically superior but to have moral content, since the value of human form-making was identified with individualism, which had become increasingly the secular society's supreme moral value. Individualism, however, was beginning to collide with the economic realities of modern western society, and the Arts and Craft movement could never be more than a small, isolated phenomenon, serving the aesthetic taste of an elite class.

The Bauhaus, to the contrary, became the most influential center in the western world for the development of modernist design. It should be remembered, however, that Frank Lloyd Wright's *Collected Works* was published in Germany in 1910, and his great influence in Germany brought elements of *Japanese* design into modernism. Furthermore, his concept of a work of architecture as the totality of a building and everything in it must be taken into account in assigning credit for the achievements of the Bauhaus.

Like William Morris and other Arts and Crafts leaders in England, like the Vienna artists of the Secession who formed the *Wiener Werkstatte,* and like Wright, Gropius saw the need to unite the arts, and to locate them in a "workshop." His inspiration came from the medieval *Bauhutten,* the lodgings for the workmen that clustered around a cathedral site while building was in progress. In this connection it is worth noting that the most prominent features of the Gothic cathedral are exactly the most prominent features of modernist architecture—the passion for glass, and the passion for height. The Bauhaus indeed "was founded with visions of erecting the cathedral of socialism," according to Okcar Schelemmer, a Bauhaus artist, and the woodcut by Lionel Feininger that decorated the Bauhaus Proclamation of 1919 was in fact a picture of a cathedral rising into a star-studded night sky. Although the goals differ, both the medieval period and our own have in common nature-defiant aspirations.

It is of great interest, however, that medieval architects *created* their innovative technology in order to achieve their aesthetic ends, while modern architects adapted already existing industrial technology.

For Gropius art was not different from craft. Like so many European artists after the Russian Revolution, he rejected ideas that reflected "upper-class" assumptions and expectations. His views were articulated in the Bauhaus Proclamation: "Let us create a new guild of craftsmen, without the class distinctions which raise an arrogant barrier between craftsman and artist. Together let us conceive and create the new building of the future, which will embrace architecture and sculpture and painting in one unity and which will rise one day toward heaven from the hands of a million workers like the crystal symbol of a new faith" (Frampton, p. 123).

The word "hands" should not be overlooked. In the beginning, the Bauhaus was not committed to state-of-the-art technology. Then partly, perhaps even largely, for economic reasons—the inflation disaster of 1921–22 in Germany—it became desirable to make things as cheaply as possible, and this meant to mass-produce them by factory methods. Gropius organized an exhibition under the title of "Art and Technology—A New Unity" in 1923 which decisively turned the direction of modernist aesthetics toward the machine. The Bauhaus principle held that all objects used by humans not only could be beautiful, but *must* be, and again, aesthetics was linked to morality, but reversed from the "capitalist" values of the Arts and Crafts movement: now it was the moral health of the working class that was at stake.

# International Style

The underlying aesthetic of Bauhaus design was functionalism. This became the aesthetic of International Style, the term given to avant-garde architecture by Henry Russell Hitchcock and Philip Johnson in their influential exhibition catalogue for the Museum of Modern Art's exhibition in 1932 which was called *International Style.* But it was a queer kind of functionalism that apparently confused workers with their machines. The objects made or inspired by Bauhaus design were uncurved and uncushioned, hard to handle or sit on, except for robots.

The triumph of the stripped down, geometrical form in architecture belongs in large measure to Charles-Edouard Jeanneret, known as Le Corbusier (1887–1965). Like Mondrian, he was that seeming paradox, the intellectual absolutist and the emotional poet for whom mathematics was the true realm of beauty. Formal relationships, he wrote, had no reference to the practical or descriptive: "they are a mathematical creation of your mind. They are the language of Architecture" (Frampton, p. 149). Although Le Corbusier studied briefly in 1907 with Josef Hoffmann in Vienna—famed as the designer, with Josef Maria Olbrich, of the brilliant Art Nouveau Austrian Pavilion at the Paris International Exposition in 1900—Art

Nouveau never interested him; from youth he had absorbed the Utopian-socialist tendencies of the period's intellectuals and artists, and his mature projects show the influence of this ideology, as seen in his *Pavillon de l'Esprit Nouveau,* which was designed in the spirit of engineering for mass production. Another compelling and enduring influence was Classicism, in which he *mistakenly* saw the precision of machinery. Writing of the Parthenon, he observed, "All this plastic machinery is realized in marble with the rigour that we have learnt to apply in the machine. The impression is of naked, polished steel." By the beginning of the twentieth century the refinements of the Parthenon—those subtle, life-giving *departures* from mathematical exactitude—were known among Classical scholars. Le Corbusier apparently had not come into contact with this information, and wrote his paean to the Parthenon on the basis of a nineteenth-century model, such as now can be seen in the Metropolitan Museum, which is constructed without the refinements. One can only wonder what effect a true knowledge of the Parthenon would have had on Le Corbusier's architecture—and the modernist architecture of the twentieth century.

Le Corbusier moved to Paris in 1916 from La Chaux-de-Fonds, the watch-making town in Switzerland where he was born. In Paris he met Amédée Ozenfant, the painter with whom he created the style of Purism. As suggested by its name, Purism was a classicizing style based on absolutist ideas of perfect form. The founders saw it as embracing all the visual arts of design, imparting to painting, sculpture, architecture, and the decorative arts cerebral content and practical function. The Purist image conveyed the sense of essential form from which

all contingency has been expunged, as seen in Le Corbusier's *Still Life* (1922) (Hunter fig. 254). Objects are reduced to simple forms of solid geometry while retaining their recognizability. It was the reductive nature of Purism that La Corbusier developed for his architecture: he conceived of houses as "machines for living," seeing the modern machine as the paradigm of functional design, with no extraneous decorative elements, although not yet "streamlined," but it seems likely that his early experience of watch-making was crucially important in forming his taste for precision and functionalism. The clock-work universe conceived by the eighteenth century was finally to be realized in twentieth-century technology.

One of the most famous of Le Corbusier's machines for living is the Villa Savoie (1929–31), located outside of Paris, which embraces the main elements of his architectural theory. The mass is elevated above ground on slender vertical piers called *pilotis,* recessed from the plane of the wall; the walls are not load-bearing and serve only to divide the spaces; the façades vary from symmetry to open form, which is echoed in the free-flowing interior spaces; light is provided by long horizontal sliding windows forming a strip of glass that contrasts with the opaque, white-painted concrete wall; the roof is used as a garden and leisure open area that is also intentionally like the bridge of an ocean liner. The Villa Savoie is like a Purist painting in three dimensions, composed of cubes, cylinders, ramps, and tubular hand rails, with the band of windows committing the interior spaces to a see-through transparency. It was one of the seminal structures that established the language of what became known from 1932 on as International Style.

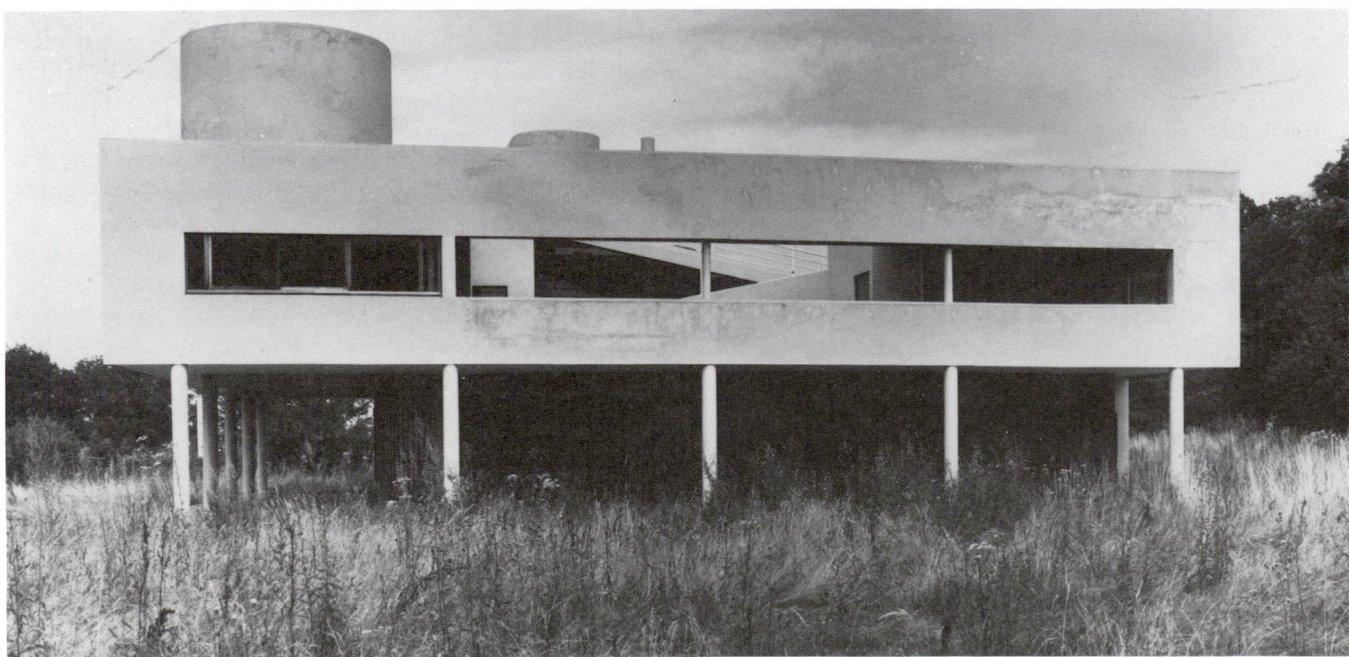

Edouard Jeanneret (Le Corbusier), *Villa Savoie,* 1925. Roissy-sur-Seine. (WAYNE ANDREWS/ESTO)

While Ludwig Mies van der Rohe (1886–1969) was also committed to functionalism—it was he who invented the oft-quoted phrase "less is more"—he differed from Le Corbusier in his feeling for rich materials. In his German State Pavilion at the Barcelona World Exhibition in 1929, where his mature aesthetic first emerged, the variety of materials created a sumptuous medley of textures and colors: glass, marble, and chromium each gleamed in its special way, climaxed by a reflecting pool which mirrored the building in such a way that its surface became not only fluid, but flickering, as the image was agitated by breezes that ruffled the water. Mies's background was in the artisan class, like that of Georges Braque, and one can indeed think of Mies's more decorative style compared to Le Corbusier's as similar to Braque's more decorative Cubism, as compared with Picasso's.

## Brancusi

Reductive form, free of object description, was not only a feature of functionalism. It was also a means of expressing the idea of essence, the pure state of being. The central formal theme of Constantin Brancusi (1876–1957), the curved volume, is informed with this content. "They are imbeciles who call my work abstract," Brancusi stated, "that which they call abstract is the most realist, because what is real is not the exterior form but the idea, the essence of things" (Chipp, p. 365). Brancusi, a Romanian who settled in Paris from 1904 on, absorbed many of the new ideas that comprised the rich cultural ambience of the city. Like Kandinsky and Mondrian, he was particularly responsive to Theosophy, and especially to its concept of sex as a life force. Sexual imagery, in Theosophic terms, is a visual metaphor for the generative impulse of the universe, expressed in an upward-pointing equilateral triangle for the male factor, a downward-pointing one for the female. The generative impulse is unmistakably present in Brancusi's work and can be credited in part to the influence of this Indian religion/philosophy. *The Kiss* (1908) (Arnason fig. 199) takes up the theme of two interlocked figures that we have seen in Munch and in Klimt. Here in Brancusi's stone, however, the essence of human interdependence, of love made explicitly sexual by the minimal but all the more telling differentiations of the two figures, the strange phenomenon that one and one does not make two, but one, is more profoundly conveyed.

Although the term "streamlined" is usually associated with industrial design, inspired by aviation, the principle of streamlining, as we have seen, appeared in architecture and art many years before it emerged in product design around 1930. Brancusi's *Bird in Space,* first designed in 1925, perfectly conveys the essence not so much of a bird, but of flight and speed, which became the essence of the streamlined aesthetic of the thirties, applied even to refrigerators.

*Bird in Space,* soaring as if Brancusi's typical egg forms (Arnason, figs. 194, 195) had hatched a bird out of its inherent form, not only made aesthetic history, but legal history in the United States. When it was brought here by a collector, Customs refused to admit it as a work of art and charged the collector in accordance with the duty on imported metal. The case was taken to court and decided in the collector's favor, thereby winning a battle for modernist art which at that time had little public sympathy.

## Surrealism

The decade that saw the creation of *Bird in Space,* with its sleek, rational poetry, also witnessed the birth of Surrealism. Dada paved the way and merged almost imperceptibly into Surrealism, which as a movement began in 1924. The chief figure in its creation was André Breton, something of high priest, commissar, and cult leader. Dramatically handsome, Byronic in features, intense, he fascinated a whole generation of his contemporaries. "I believe in the coming fusion of those two states, seemingly so incompatible, *Reality* and *the Dream,*" he wrote. "I believe in a sort of Absolute reality—a super-reality." It was Apollinaire, however, indefatigable spokesman for the avant-garde, who invented the word Surrealism.

The word took on tangible reality in 1927 when a gallery devoted to Surrealist art opened in Paris. The artists who exhibited there in the next few years, the core of the Surrealist movement, included Jean (Hans) Arp, Salvador Dali, Giorgio de Chirico, Marcel Duchamp, Max Ernst, Paul Klee, Man Ray, André Masson, René Magritte (whose *Le Double Secret* you saw on the program), Francis Picabia, Picasso, Pierre Roy, and Yves Tanguy.

Breton and the Surrealists around him were deeply influenced by the work of Freud, who provided the scientific authority for their art, which was based on the conviction that Truth and Reality exist in the substratum of consciousness called the unconscious. To externalize the unconscious, the Surrealists employed the method of *automatism,* which required the effort of putting oneself in a hallucinatory state and allowing the unconscious to guide the hand that held the brush. They encouraged *accident,* which Freud had shown to mask meaning that was suppressed by consciousness. The anti-rationalist tenor of Surrealism links the movement to Dada, and some of the Surrealists had been in fact associated with the Dada movement.

Surrealism projected trance-like states in which consciousness was suspended and ordinary objects were irrationally juxtaposed like "the chance meeting of a sewing machine and an umbrella on a dissecting table," according to the famous image of Isidore Ducasse, the Comte de Lautréamont, in a poem written in the 1860s. The visionary, dream-like nature of Surrealism was anticipated in Symbolist poetry, and indeed appeared in twentieth-century art much before Breton's movement or

Dada. Henri Rousseau's *The Dream* (1910) **(J clpl 129)** can be taken as a forerunner of Surrealism. *The Dream* brings together the contemporary Victorian world (the sofa) and the uncivilized jungle with such self-confidence that we are persuaded that the impossibility makes sense in a world where the rules of making sense have been changed. Marc Chagall (1887–1985) is another artist whose lyrical, floating worlds of fantasy and unrealistic scale relationships anticipate Surrealism, as seen in his *I and the Village* (1911) **(J clpl 142).**

The most directly influential painter for the Surrealists was Giorgio de Chirico (1888–1978), who spent the years 1911–1915 in Paris and was well known in the Parisian art world. In 1925 he participated in the first group exhibition of Surrealist painters, together with the former Dada, Jean Arp, Max Ernst, Paul Klee, Man Ray, André Masson, Joan Miró, Picasso, and Pierre Roy.

De Chirico was born of an Italian family living in Greece, where his father was a construction engineer for the railroads. It is reasonable to suppose that the artist's memories of his childhood, in which railroads and draftsman's instruments figured prominently, played an important role in his choice of those objects in many of his pre–World War I paintings. He was drawn to the works of the German Romantics and like many young people of his generation was significantly affected by Nietzsche. His work derives its impact from the sterilized hardness of his surfaces and the sharp-edged, always looming shadows, seen characteristically in *Mystery and Melancholy of a Street* (1914) **(J clpl 141 and p. 690).** The objects he depicts are given a mysterious portent due to the emptiness of the vast space he constructs. There is often the suggestion of something sinister, some unnameable threat that challenges our imaginations. De Chirico's pictorial space is unsettling because it *seems* to be constructed according to the rational rules of mathematical perspective but is manifestly not rational. We feel the tension in this contradiction. His subject is often the enigmatic nature of time (classical statues) and space (emphasized by emptiness), depicted as if suspended in an airless void.

There are basically two Surrealist styles, very different from each other, but linked because the artists identified with the Surrealist movement. One style is abstract—one sees enigmatic, suggestively identifiable objects, or objects that belong to a fantasy world of forms. Miró's work from about 1923–1924 on exemplifies this kind of Surrealism. The other is figurative, with easily recognized objects more or less distorted, or perfectly natural objects placed in a context impossible in the phenomenal world. Salvadore Dali's painting exemplifies this style.

Miró's first Surrealist painting was *Catalan Landscape* (1923–1924) (Hunter, fig. 307), which is rather hermetic to one who sees it without knowing the artist's earlier, realistic work. There, in farm scenes of Montroig in his native Basque region of Spain, many of the elements that make up *Catalan Landscape* are present. A tree in the new work is rendered as a circle, with a branch shooting out of it ending in a leaf. The horizon line is drawn, bisecting an eye—referring, of course, to the vanishing point in Renaissance perspective. A bearded, mustached peasant wearing a beret and smoking a pipe stands to the left, his head a triangle ending in a coil for the beret, his body and legs given as straight lines. Dotted lines suggest a running creature, perhaps a rabbit that the peasant is out hunting (the painting is subtitled *The Hunter*). The configuration at the upper left, with flags, represents an airplane that had been put into service between Toulouse and Rabat, and flew over Montroig. A fish, its body also rendered as a straight line, stretches across the lower area of the work, with the letters SARD written in the lower left corner. Most writers have assumed the letters refer to Sardana, the Basque folk dance; Jacques Dupin, who had the cooperation of the artist in writing his comprehensive book on Miró, learned from him that the letters meant sardine, referring to the fish.

In 1925, the year in which he painted *The Birth of the World* (Dupin, p. 217), Miró was immersed in the fantastic poetry of the writers who had become his friends in Paris, the literary surrealists. "As a result of this reading," Miró recalled later, "I began to work away from the realism I had practiced . . . until, in 1925, I was drawing almost entirely from hallucinations. At the time I was living on a few dried figs a day. I was too proud to ask my colleagues for help. Hunger was a great source of these hallucinations. I would sit for long periods looking at the bare walls of my studio trying to capture these [hallucinatory] shapes on paper or burlap." The critic Michel Leiris has connected Miró's "exercise" of staring at the blank wall with the Tibetan practice of gazing at something in the world, a garden, perhaps, and after fixing it perfectly in the mind, down to every detail, beginning the process of removing the details, one by one. The mind is stripped until nothing is left; it can now contemplate the void. The description of seeking to attain the condition of contemplating the void seems apposite to *The Birth of the World*, which Dupin considers the "greatest and perhaps the most beautiful, most mysterious of all the canvases in this manner."

The painting's title calls to mind Brancusi's *The Beginning of the World* (Arnason, fig. 195), which was cast in bronze in 1924, and which it is likely Miró had an opportunity to see. It is illuminating to note the contrast between the two "conceptions," one a sculptor's, the other a painter's. Whereas Brancusi imagines the "beginning" as an egg, a single self-contained form, Miró imagines it as a kind of watery birth, without clearly defined forms. The sculpture suggests the oneness of creation; the painting suggests a mythic time when form was just beginning to create itself out of chaos.

Salvador Dali (1904–1989) has been the most publicly visible figure among the Surrealists. His antics, his appearance, with his famous waxed mustache, his public utterances—for their shock value, it seems—have be-

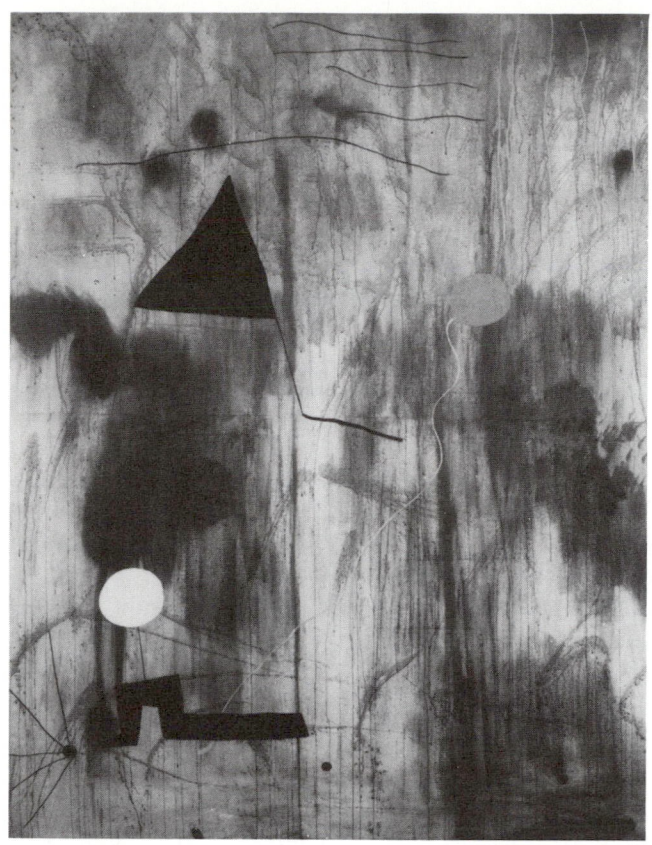

Joan Miró, *The Birth of the World,* 1925. Paris, Private Collection. (ART RESOURCE, NEW YORK)

leadership, expelling those whom he found less than perfectly loyal.

To Surrealism can be credited two innovations: the invention of biomorphic abstract forms as found in Arp and Miró—forms that suggest some kind of living creatures—and the invention of *frottage* by Max Ernst (1891–1976). *Frottage* is a technique of rubbing colored pencils or crayons on paper placed over a surface such as wood so as to reproduce on the paper the texture pattern; the artist then accentuates certain areas that accidentally suggest to him a figure or object, as seen in *Gray Forest* (1927) (Hunter clpl 310).

Although not remotely connected to the Surrealist group, and very likely unaware of Surrealist painting, the American painter Edward Hopper (1882–1967) nevertheless can usefully be seen in the light of that expressive mode. Light is important here, for it is Hopper's very strange, cold light that gives his pictures their hallucinatory realism. His scenes of American life seem caught in an airless realm where the figures he depicts are lost within themselves, alone, lonely, and anxious. Much admired for the strong abstract structure of his representational painting, Hopper has often been invoked as a predecessor of Pop Art, which flourished in the 1960s.

Dada, formed in response to World War I, had its tragic justification in World War II, a Dada event on a scale beyond anything conceived by Duchamp, Tzara, and the others. The magnitude of the irrationality to which service science and all human intellect was put is indeed beyond the conceptual powers of anyone not at home with cosmic measurement. From the Paris World Exposition of 1900 to the outbreak of World War II, the climate of the human world had shifted steadily from fair to hurricane. The Dadaists and their Surrealist heirs must have been appalled to witness the truth of their prophecy. Many of them witnessed that truth from a new vantage point, New York.

In 1936 the Museum of Modern art held two landmark exhibitions, *Cubism and Abstract Art* and *Fantastic Art, Dada, Surrealism.* Albert Gallatin's Museum of Living Art, housed at New York University, had made European avant-garde available to American artists since 1927, and in the last years of the thirties, the Museum of Non-Objective Painting (precursor of The Solomon R. Guggenheim Museum) added to the city's modernist resources. American artists were thus familiar with advanced European art, but it was not until Paris fell in 1940, and a good number of leading artists escaped to America, joining some who had already arrived, that a consciousness of New York as a new art center evolved. Breton, Chagall, Dali, Max Ernst, Fernand Léger could be met, here and there in the galleries, and American artists began to feel as if they were participants in the fabled School of Paris. The importance of art was underlined for them by the Europeans, who expressed their sense of significance *as artists* in a way of life that centered on themselves *as*

come legendary. He was, in fact, an extremist who wanted to push every experience and every thought to its irrational conclusion. Brilliantly gifted, he collaborated with his friend Luis Buñuel on the films *Un Chien Andalou* and *L'Age d'Or,* wrote poetry, libretti, designed jewelry, dresses, and window displays. He was a calculating clown. He invented what he called the "paranoiac-critical method," which called for simulating mental illness in which state the artist would be able to interpret irrational knowledge. His iconography uses physical abnormalities as metaphors for social disaster, as seen in his *Soft Construction with Boiled Beans* and *Premonition of Civil War* (1936), and for psychological aberrations, as in *The Persistence of Memory* (1931), in which the regularity of time and the measurability of space are both destroyed, an idea probably derived from de Chirico. His "soft" watches and other soft constructions anticipate and possibly inspired Claes Oldenburg, more than thirty years later.

Dali's political views were increasingly at odds with those of Breton, and eventually Breton, early on his admirer and friend, expelled him from the Surrealist movement, which Breton ran somewhat like a Communist cell; he exercized dictatorship rights over the members, welcoming new ones who paid proper respect to his

**239**

*artists,* even in the face of the calamity that had forced them to leave their homes. The Surrealists, above all, conveyed the sense of group identity. It may well have been their model for an art/life style that inspired the idea of cohesiveness that was to characterize the early years of the Abstract Expressionist movement. It was surely Surrealism and its psychoanalytical content that brought into being the American movement that for a few short years conquered and ruled the world of art.

## Sculpture and architecture of the inter-war period

The tumultuous creativity of the first three decades of the twentieth century settled down during the thirties, as if radicalism had to pause to catch its breath. In the process of consolidating its gains, however, modernism did produce some of its greatest art.

Henry Moore (1898–1986) is widely recognized as one of the great sculptors of our century. During the twenties he acquired a sophisticated knowledge not only of the Western tradition but also of non-Western art (African and pre-Columbian) and the advanced art of his own time. This insured that in these formative years he was exposed to the dominant aesthetics of Surrealism and stylizations based on Classical, archaic, and "primitive" art. Moore's mature art is a successful synthesis of these influences, with one or another more or less evident in various periods.

Moore came to world attention in the 1930s with a number of works on two themes—the reclining figure and, closely related, the mother-and-child, highly abstracted. They were characterized by soft, undulating contours, and, most startling at the time, pierced form. These themes, and the monumental expression with which he treated them, have remained hallmarks of Moore's style.

We may take as an example his magisterial *Family Group* (1948–49) (*The Museum of Modern Art,* 1984, fig. 169). To the mother-and-child theme has been added the father. The parents form a kind of protective parenthesis for the child, expressed in curving contours that are repeated throughout the work, reinforcing the idea of protective enclosure. The "wall" created by the backs of the parents, and the play of concavity and convexity of the forms (a characteristic of tribal African sculpture—particularly Fang—reflected in the hatching lines on the faces of the two right-hand figures of Picasso's *Demoiselles d'Avignon*) create a scooped-out space for the child—stimulating associations with womb and tomb, birth and death, and ultimately, the idea of continuity. Furthermore, in Western art, a family group inevitably suggests a Holy Family, with its connotations of birth, death, and resurrection (spiritual continuity). As in much of modern secular art, beneath the surface of Moore's work there is often to be found an element that belongs to the Christian religious tradition.

An architectural masterpiece of the thirties is the Kaufmann House (*Falling Water*) (1936) (Arnason fig. 446) by Frank Lloyd Wright (1867–1959), unquestionably his most dazzling achievement. Wright's fundamental conception of domestic architectural design rested on the relationship of house to environment. The design of his low-gabled, almost flat-roofed, horizontally extending Prairie Houses built in the midwest was imposed by the flatness of the terrain. The prime example of this Prairie style was the Robie House (1909) (Arnason fig. 290). Broad, cantilevered upper roofs cover the interior space but also project over the roofs of the lower floor, creating exterior space that rhymes with the interior and acts as a transition from house to environment.

These features are extravagantly expressed in *Falling Water* on a more monumental scale. It is immediately perceived that the site was a prime consideration in the dramatic design. The core of the house is built of local, unpolished stone, which is contrasted with light-tan concrete. The great terraces seem to float above the waterfall and pool. As Arnason has succinctly summarized it (p. 311), "the plan combines openness, efficient flow, and containment of individual areas, with the integration of exterior and interior." Although the shapes are rectilinear, the house harmonizes with the forest that surrounds it. With its cantilevered terraces it suggests a bird perched with widespread wings, ready to fly off into space.

It was in the thirties that Alexander Calder (1898–1976) invented the art form, *mobiles,* by which he is best known, and one that has become a staple in domestic furnishings; it is amusing that mobiles are used for entertaining babies in their cribs, but it is not at all an incongruous idea, since Calder had first come to attention in the Paris art world as a kind of toy maker. He had conceived and fashioned a miniature circus peopled with wire-and-wood marionettes that delighted his friends, particularly Mondrian and Miró, who, in turn, greatly influenced his sculpture.

We have seen in the work of the Constructivists the move toward turning sculpture inside-out, that is, using solid materials, metal or wood, as contours that shape space. Recall Tatlin's *Monument to the Third International* and Rodchenko's *Hanging Construction.* Space itself becomes an equal partner in creating the image. No artist has been more successful working in this aesthetic mode than Calder. By the time of his *Lobster Trap and Fish Tail* (1939) (Hunter, fig. 469), he had moved totally into non-objectivity, with Mondrian's primary colors and shapes reminiscent of Miró and Brancusi.

But he had gone even further. Rodchenko, we remember, had conceived a moving and hanging sculpture in 1920, but abandoned sculpture for other media. His sculpture was unknown in western Europe. What was known of Russian Constructivism was disseminated by Gabo and Pevsner. Therefore, while we acknowledge the priority of Rodchenko in this invention, it was to all intents and purposes irrelevant for the history of Western art.

Calder was living in Paris, the hub of the art world. His close friends were influential leaders of modernism. His central position in the mainstream thus justifies seeing him as the originator of hanging-and-moving sculpture. We can say that with his works in this mode, it was Calder who took the final step in the reversal of ponderation, or gravitational direction, that had begun in painting with the alloverness of the Impressionists and in sculpture with Rodin. As I pointed out earlier, painted and sculptural images traditionally had their weight at the bottom, which corresponds to our ordinary perception of the world: strength and mass support what is less strong and less massive. The solid earth is below the weightless sky. The invisible law of gravity that governs our perception of the universe was visually repealed when the Impressionists began to tilt the image forward by taking a high viewpoint, thus wrenching the earth from its horizontal extension. Step by step the relationship between up and down became increasingly problematic. Calder made the decisive break for Western art by hanging his sculpture from above instead of supporting it from below. It is fascinating that Frank Lloyd Wright achieved an analogous breakthrough in the same decade with his "hanging-in-the-air" *Falling Water*.

Dominating much of the design thinking in the thirties was the style that only much later—around 1960—came to be called Art Deco. Itself a revival of Art Nouveau, sleek and chic-looking, the style was as flexible as its predecessor, lending itself to all manner of object. Indeed, in the thirties, there was a close family resemblance between a belt buckle, an armchair, and the Chrysler Tower in New York, the paradigm of Art Deco skyscrapers. Although usually seen as regressive, Art Deco has shown unexpected strength with its appropriation in the sixties by Roy Lichtenstein, as we shall see, and into the 1980s in work by (among others) Charles Moore for the *Piazza d'Italia* (1975–80); Robert Stern for the *Pool House, Llewelyn, New Jersey* (1981–82); and Michael Graves for his *Portland Public Services Building* (Arnason clpls 316, 317, 318).

## Picasso's *Guernica*

Before we turn to developments in the post-war era, we must consider the painting which for many people is the greatest masterpiece created in the twentieth century. That painting is *Guernica* (1937) **(J 948; G 22.16).** There is a vast literature on this work and in this book we cannot review all that has been said about it. But in tribute to the painting that for many years riveted visitors standing before it at the Museum of Modern Art, the painting by the greatest master of modern art that deals with one of the greatest disasters of modern history—there are many who believe that Allied intervention on the side of the Loyalists to defeat Generalissimo Franco, leader of the rebellion,

would have aborted World War II—we must give a few moments to *Guernica*.

The painting memorializes one of the first great tragedies that our century's wars have visited on civilian populations—a bitter innovation of our culture. The destruction of that town by German bombers, and Picasso's painting of the event, became a symbol of the Spanish Civil War, which ended for forty years whatever possibilities had existed for the development of democracy in Spain. Its surface is black and grey, like a newspaper, evoking something of the immediacy of the news in those long-ago days when newsmen went through the streets yelling EXTRA! EXTRA!—Read all about it! "Guernica, the most ancient town of the Basques and the center of their cultural tradition," ran the *New York Times* account, "was completely destroyed yesterday afternoon by insurgent air raiders. . . . A powerful fleet of . . . Junkers and Heinkel fighters, did not cease unloading [bombs and incendiary projectiles] on the town. The fighters, meanwhile, plunged low from above the center of the town to machine-gun those of the civil population who had taken refuge in the fields. The whole of Guernica was soon in flames, except the historical Casa de Juntas, with its rich archives of the Basque race."

The bombing occurred on 26 April 1937. Earlier that year the Spanish government had asked Picasso to paint a mural for their pavilion in the International Exhibition to be held in Paris in 1938. He had not begun work, however. Three days after the bombing he began making sketches, and he finished the painting on 4 June. Many interpretations of its meaning have been offered—apocalyptic, political, psychological, and others. Given Picasso's mastery of Western imagery, his immense intelligence and emotional intensity, his Catholic Spanish roots and his positivist French culture, his left-wing tendencies (he joined the Communist party after World War II), and furthermore the importance of the picture to him, it appears that every seriously intended approach has some validity. There are two, however, that have especially rich possibilities, and brought together they add to our understanding of this visual epic: *Guernica* as autobiographical and as biblical.

For a Spaniard such as Picasso, the bullfight is far more than a national sport. Its roots go far back into Mediterranean culture, and from remote times the bull has symbolized creativity, fertility, and rebirth, sacred power, and sacrifice. In ancient times it was frequently a cult image, a bull of heaven, as in the Gilgamesh epic—a power to which humans paid homage. But it was also the creature that had to be subdued by the saviour. The bull is central to the ritualistic aspects of the bullfight which are evident in the person of the torero in the way he makes his appearance—like a priest, it has been said—like a hero, a saviour, whose victory over the bull, if indeed he is victorious, is a victory of good over evil. In his *traje de luces* (suit of lights), his brilliantly decorated garment, he personifies light, struggling with the black bull. If he dies, his death is seen as an act of sacrifice. Unamuno wrote,

> Blood runs for martyrdom
> of blackamoor or bull
> —joined in their doom—
> and the chorus full
> echoes the vaunt
> Spain! Spain is triumphant!

(Vincente Marrero,<br>Picasso and the Bull)

The passes made by the torero are sometimes said to be "the mocker mocking death."

The specifically Christian associations with the bullfight are widely recognized. Every kind of rite—canonization, a transfer of the Blessed Sacrament, the first Mass of a new priest—was accompanied by a corrida. When St. Theresa was canonized, every convent founded by her gave a corrida. After the canonization of St. Ignatius, the Jesuits petitioned that a bullfight be held in celebration after the ceremonies.

For Picasso, then, the bull and the horse were vital symbols in both the myth and religion of his culture. He would have been particularly sensitive to that aspect of the corrida that was heavy with dramatic ritual and infused with the spirit of tragedy. Inevitably, these were the symbols he chose to carry his rage and grief over the suffering of his native land. But what of the warrior who, under a radiant burst of light, has fallen from his horse, and lies so prominently along the lower margin of the painting? It has been suggested more than once that in this figure one sees the traditional iconography of St. Paul, but the evidence presented here is new.

Saul, persecutor of Christians, was on his way to Damascus when he was suddenly struck by a dazzling white light with such force that he fell to the ground, blinded. Scripture does not mention a horse, but painters have traditionally assumed Saul was riding to Damascus, and show him under or near a horse. Later (Acts 9:10–18), Ananias says, "Brother Saul, I have been sent by the Lord Jesus who appeared to you on your way here so that you may recover your sight and be filled with the Holy Spirit."

In *Guernica,* there is the horse, and the fallen warrior. There is a bird form on the table just below and to the left of the light. It is in deep shadow, except for one wing brightly lit. Is this "the Holy Spirit"?

In *Guernica,* the warrior's eyes are especially prominent, and are the only pair of eyes misaligned, one horizontal, the other vertical. They are wide open, but one eye is looking in one direction the other in another, so that it would be impossible to see with ordinary vision. This feature seems to suggest blindness.

On the prominent horseshoe under the warrior's neck there are seven nails. One of the roles of Mary is that of the Virgin of the Seven Sorrows, the first of which is prophesied by Simeon (Luke 2:34–35). "You see this child: he is destined for the *fall* [italics added] and for the rising of many in Israel, destined to be a sign that is rejected. . . . "

The criss-cross marks on the warrior's left hand form a Star of David, one, moreover, that is open at two points, as if it is about to come apart, and thus disappear, while on the right forearm of the hand that holds the broken sword (St. Paul's traditional attribute) is a very large cross. Both the nails and the marks suggest the fall of Israel and the rise of Christianity.

Moving to an apparently frivolous level, we look now at a drawing by Picasso (1917) (Rubin, *Picasso,* p. 197), in which Picasso has depicted himself with his new love, Olga Koklova, sitting at a café table. Olga's face is averted, and her right arm is pushing against him in a restraining pose that suggests she is resisting him, forcing him into the unwanted role of "saint": he has lettered the name St. Paul next to himself. His own name, Pablo, is, of course, the Spanish version of Paul, and we have this one occasion, at least, on which he identified himself with St. Paul.

Along with all of the other meanings *Guernica* contains, it thus seems to be about light and dark, about seeing and blindness, about the inner vision of a saint—or an artist, Picasso himself.

The painting was made to be seen at an International Exposition, by a multitude of people from all over the world. Perhaps Pablo Picasso knew the words of the saint for whom he was named. "We are made a spectacle unto the world, and to angels and to men (1 Cor. 4:9)." *Guernica has* been a spectacle to all humankind, and possibly to the angels.

## Summary

Both the threats and the promises of the nineteenth century were fully realized in the twentieth. War and revolution, unprecedented advances in science and human welfare marked our century almost from its birth. Momentous discoveries in every field of human endeavor were made in the very first decade, not the least of these in the field of the arts.

In this unit we have seen the century open in Vienna where the waltzing lilt of its culture made the most of the swinging arabesques of Art Nouveau. The new decor was opulent but svelte, as we saw in the work of the new architects, and the painter Gustav Klimt. But the unmistakable symptoms of sickness were evident in the deeply disturbed and disturbing images of Schiele and Kokoshka. Turn-of-the-century Vienna, then, becomes a prophetic metaphor for the modern condition—powerful, rich, enormously gifted but unable to shake off a chronic, debilitating nervous disorder that flares up every so often into fits of wild delirium.

In Germany the artists of *Die Brücke* responded to the mythic Nietzschean challenge to youth. Kirchner, Heckel, and Schmidt-Rottluff found in primitive Oceanic art clues to a high-keyed expressiveness that helped them bring German art boldly into the modernist mainstream while—willy-nilly—continuing the long tradition of German Expressionism in art.

Parallel in time with the creation of *Die Brücke* in 1905, the Fauve movement appeared in Paris. From the beginning it was clear that Matisse was the guiding genius of the new, brilliantly colored art. It was also clear that another genius had arrived in Paris—Pablo Picasso. Together with Georges Braque, these were the seminal leaders of early modernism. Cubism was the joint creation of Braque and Picasso, and following their lead, Robert Delaunay, Fernand Léger, and other artists in Paris worked out their individual perceptions of Cubist potentialities. In Italy, the Futurists absorbed just enough of Cubist method to solve the formal problems they confronted in creating their dynamic, psychologically expressive works. In Russia, the innovative spirit appeared in the first decade, and following contacts with Cubism and Futurism, the Constructivist and Suprematist movements evolved.

Meanwhile, a number of theoretical currents were flowing together that eventually liberated art from its task of describing schematically or naturalistically the furniture of the world. The seminal artists in the development of non-objectivity were Mondrian and Malevich, in the calculated, geometrizing style, and Kandinsky in the free-flowing, expressionistic style.

It is interesting to note that Picasso, who went through more style changes than any other artist in the Western tradition, never painted a non-objective work. Nor did Braque. When they saw themselves only a step away, they veered sharply, and invented collage and synthetic Cubism, which solved the problem of going forward without going into non-objectivity.

The notion that, just as music employed sound and appealed only to the sense of hearing, the visual arts, too, employing visible material, should appeal only to the sense of sight, led to the attempt to achieve pure visibility. This became a compelling feature of modernist aesthetics. In the realm of cultural ideology, socialism was a dynamic force in the creation of the "machine aesthetic," which developed with significant consequences at the Bauhaus, where the influence of Frank Lloyd Wright also was felt. Not the least of these consequences was the creation of the functionalist aesthetic which was the basis of the International Style in architecture as practiced by its originators, Le Corbusier and Mies van der Rohe. The flowering of International Style architecture paralleled that of Art Deco architecture, which pervaded design thinking in the decorative arts as well.

Among the most intriguing developments were the anti-art and anti-rationalist movements, both based in large part on disillusionment. The humanist tradition that associated art with beauty, and beauty with good, also associated reason with good—and that tradition had failed to continue upward and onward with the arts and sciences. The World War had intervened. The spread of Dada was in large measure a direct result of the war. Closely related to the nihilism of Dada, although different in method and spirit, was the bitter Neue Sachlichkeit style of George Grosz and Otto Dix, which appeared in Germany after the war. Although the ground of surrealist art had been long prepared, the emergence of Surrealism as a movement was probably accelerated because of the anti-rationalist sensibility that arose in some circles following World War I. The contributions of Miró and Dali to Surrealism represent the two branches of the style.

## Textbook References

J Janson takes up twentieth-century painting and sculpture in Chapter 4, and architecture in Chapter 5. He defines three currents, which he calls Expression, Abstraction, and Fantasy. Expression starts with the Fauve movement touching on Matisse, Rouault, Chaim Soutine, and Bacon, followed by Expressionism with mention of Die Brücke, plus Nolde, Kokoschka, Max Beckmann, and Kandinsky, in Germany, Arthus Dove and Georgia O'Keeffe in the United States, and José Clemente Orozco in Mexico. He then goes on to Cubism, starting with *Les Demoiselles d'Avignon,* mentions "Facet Cubism," and follows with "Collage Cubism," developed with Braque. For what in this book is called Synthetic Cubism, he uses the term "cut-paper style," and concludes his section on Picasso with a discussion of *Guernica.* In "Variants of Cubism" Janson mentions Boccioni as the "most original" of the Futurists, and sees Joseph Stella's *Brooklyn Bridge* as an echo of Futurism, with Grosz also representing a "dynamized form" of Cubism, contrasted with Léger whose *The City* is "stable without being static." Cubo-Futurism and Suprematism in Russia and de Stijl in Holland complete the section on variations of Cubism. Under Fantasy are included Henri Rousseau, De Chirico, Paul Klee, as well as the Dadaists Duchamp, Ernist, and Arp. The section (not the chapter) concludes with Surrealism, represented by Ernst, Dali, and Miró. In Chapter 5 there is a summary of late nineteenth-century architecture, leading into Frank Lloyd Wright. The Bauhaus is touched on, followed by International-style architects Le Corbusier, whose later style is also mentioned, and Mies van der Rohe. The problems of modern urban planning are presented, with Moshe Safdie's Habitat complex in Montreal shown as one possible solution. The chapter concludes with a note on Post-Modern architecture, exemplified by the Pompidou Arts Center in Paris and the Neue Staatsgalerie by James Stirling in Stuttgart.

Gardner's introduction to the modern period stresses the role of science in changing our view of reality and sees the science enterprise of our times as opposite to that of our art. This duality underlies the discussion of Fauvism represented by Matisse, Derain, and Rouault and German Expressionism, covered with Kokoschka, Nolde, Max Beckmann, Grosz, Käthe Kollwitz, and Kandinsky. Cézanne's importance is stressed as the prime influence in the development of Cubism by Picasso and Braque, with Einstein's relativity theory also seen as related in the sense of its affinity of thought. A good summary of analytic Cubism is followed by a section on synthetic Cubism, and Picasso's career is summarized up to and including *Guernica*. The spread of Cubism in France is represented by Léger's *The City*, and Duchamp's *Nude Descending a Staircase #2;* beyond France in Futurist work by Boccioni, abstraction by Georgia O'Keeffe and in non-objective painting by Mondrian, Kandinsky, and Malevich. After explaining the background of Dada, Gardner introduces Kurt Schwitters' collages and a painted glass work by Duchamp as examples. The ideas behind Surrealism and the art of fantasy are then taken up, and these tendencies are represented by De Chirico, Ernst, Marc Chagall, and Paul Klee. A section on Social Realism including Orozco, Edward Hopper, and Ben Shahn is followed by a section on sculpture ranging through a variety of styles and artists including classicist Aristide Maillol, expressionists Wilhelm Lehmbruck and Gaston Lachaise, symbolist Ernst Bartlach, Matisse (as a Cubist-related sculptor), Cubists Jacques Lipchitz and Alexander Archipenko, Boccioni (as a Futurist sculptor) abstractionist Brancusi, welder Julio Gonzalez, and Constructivists Tatlin, Gabo, and Pevsner. Calder as inventor of mobiles leads into Dada and fantastic sculpture by Duchamp, Picasso, and Man Ray. The section ends with brief comments on Henry Moore and Alberto Giacometti. The architecture of the period begins with examples of Art Nouveau by Victor Horta and Antonio Gaudi, moves on to Frank Lloyd Wright and then into the International Style with examples by Le Corbusier, Gerrit Rietveldt, Walter Gropius, and Ludwig Mies van der Rohe, with Wright's *Falling Water* seen as related.

Honour and Fleming cover this period in two chapters. Art from 1900 to 1919 is introduced with commentary that brings in Henri Bergson, Benedetto Croce, and Sigmund Freud, to set the stage intellectually, and the importance of Negro sculpture as a significant aesthetic influence. In this context the authors present Rousseau, Picasso's *Demoiselles,* and Emile Nolde. With a reminder that Monet was still painting in these years, they then take up the Fauve movement, concentrating on Matisse, and the German Expressionists of Die Brücke and Der Blaue Reiter, and include a passage on Expressionist architecture. Cézanne's influence on Braque and Picasso in developing Analytical Cubism is considered predomi-

nant. They suggest Art-for-Art's Sake and Symbolist affinities to explain the "autonomous nature" of Cubist painting—they consider Cubist shapes to be independent of the phenomena they stand for, which differs from the view put forth in this study guide. They draw attention to differences between Picasso and Braque in this period of their close working association. After a discussion of Collage, Picasso's Cubist sculpture is taken up and asserted to be even more radical than the painting. The spread of Cubism in France is described with work of Delaunay, Marcel Duchamp, Léger, and Francis Picabia. The Futurists are seen as formally dependent on the Cubists, although Boccioni's "Technical Manifesto of Futurist Sculpture" is acknowledged as parallel or antecedent to Picasso's sculptural breakthrough as is Futurism's long-lasting and widespread influence. Even early work by Brancusi is held to have some echoes of Futurism. The Russian response to Cubism is taken up, and its non-representational development is represented by Malevich, and the section on painting and sculpture concludes with Mondrian and De Stijl movement in Holland. In architecture, Louis Sullivan's important contribution to early modernism leads into Frank Lloyd Wright and his theory of "organic architecture." Finally, the pre-Bauhaus work of Walter Gropius and Adolph Meyer ends the chapter.

**Janson, Part IV, The Modern World, Chapter 4: Twentieth-Century Painting and Sculpture.** Painting Before World War II, pp. 666–695. The Fauves; Expressionism: Matisse, *The Joy of Life, Harmony in Red (Red Room);* Bacon; Die Brücke: Kirschner, *The Street;* Kokoschka; Non-Objective Painting: Kandinsky. Abstraction: Picasso, *Demoiselles D'Avignon;* Facet Cubism; Collage Cubism; Post-Cubist Picasso, *Guernica;* Variants of Cubism: Futurism and Dynamism: Boccioni; Stella, *Brooklyn Bridge;* Grosz; Suprematism: Malevich; De Stijl: Mondrian, *Composition with Red, Blue, Yellow.* Fantasy: De Chirico; Chagall; DADA: Duchamp, *Nude Descending a Staircase, No. 2, The Bride;* Surrealism: Dali; Miró. Sculpture (pp. 727–740): Brancusi; *Bird in Space;* Moore; Kinetic Sculpture: Boccioni, *Unique Forms of Continuity in Space.* Constructivism: Tatlin *Monument to the Third International.* Surrealism: Giacometti. Mobiles: Calder. Twentieth-Century Architecture, pp. 746–767. Art Nouveau: Mackintosh, Glasgow School of Art; Wright, Robie House.

**Gardner, Part V: The Modern World, Chapter 22: The Twentieth Century, pp. 886–975.** *Painting Before World War II,* pp. 890–917. Symbolism and Art Nouveau: Klimt; The Fauves and Expressionism: Derain; Matisse, *Red Room (Harmony in Red);* Die Brücke. Der Blaue Reiter. Kokoschka, *Bride of the Wind;* Nolde, *St. Mary of Egypt Among Sinners;* Grosz; Kandinsky. Cubism and its Derivatives: Picasso, *Demoiselles d'Avignon; Still life* *with Chair Caning;* Synthetic Cubism: *Three Musicians;* Braque; Léger, *The City;* Futurism: Duchamp, *Nude Descending a Staircase, No. 2.* De Stijl: Mondrian. [Russian Modernism] Malevich, *White on White.* DADA to Surrealism: Duchamp; De Chirico; Ernst; Miró; Dali, *Persistence of Memory;* Chagall; Sculpture Before World War II, pp. 918–926: Boccioni, *Unique Forms of Continuity in Space;* Brancusi, *Bird in Space;* Tatlin, *Monument to the Third International.* Architecture Before World War II, pp. 927–936: Gaudi; Wright, *Kaufman House (Falling Water).* The International Style: Le Corbusier, *Villa Savoye;* Mies, *German Pavilion, Barcelona International Exhibition.*

**Honour and Fleming, Part 5, Twentieth-Century Art, pp. 564–621. Chapter 19, Art from 1900 to 1919, pp. 564–587.** Revolt against naturalism; effect of primitive art. The Fauves and Expressionism: Matisse, *Joy of Life, Red Room (Harmony in Red);* Derain; Vlaminck. The German Expressionists: Nolde; Die Brücke; der Blaue Reiter: Kandinsky, *Improvisations;* Marc. Cubism: Picasso, *Desmoiselles d'Avignon;* Braque; Cubist sculpture: Picasso, *Guitar;* Synthetic Cubism; Orphism: Delaunay; Léger. Futurism: Marinetti; Boccioni, *Unique Forms of Continuity in Space;* Joseph Stella; Brancusi. Abstract or Non-Objective Art: Suprematism, Malevich. De Stijl: Mondrian. Architecture: Wright; Gropius.

**Chapter 20, Between the Two World Wars: 1920–1940, pp. 588–603.** DADA and Surrealism: Duchamp, *Fountain;* De Chirico; Dali. Constructivism, De Stijl, and the International Style: Tatlin; Mondrian; Le Corbusier, *Villa Savoye;* Mies, Brancusi, *Bird in Space;* Art Deco; Picasso, *Guernica.*

## Study Questions

1. People who belong to the same generation tend to share certain sensibilities. How many artists can you name who were born between 1880 and 1885? Do you see "shared sensibilities" among them?
2. Discuss the sources of influence that created Art Nouveau.
3. Explain the function of color in German Expressionism and French Fauvism. How is it similar, and how does it differ, in these two styles?
4. What is meant by pure visibility and tactility? How do these qualities become an issue in modern art?
5. What were the steps by which Braque and Picasso arrived at Cubism? What impasse did they meet? How did they find a way out of it?
6. Compare the style and theory of Cubism with that of Futurism.
7. Discuss the influence of socialism in art in the period ca. 1900–ca. 1930.
8. Which movements were affected by Freudian thought? Explain how, with examples of works of art.
9. There were two routes to non-objective art. What were they? Trace the steps that led to the creation of both styles of non-objectivity.
10. What is meant by "collage"? How does Constructivism relate to collage.

## Glossary

**abstract**   art in which imagery from the phenomenal world is rendered in a summary form, often so reduced in recognizable details that the image itself is unrecognizable, as in some analytic Cubist paintings of 1911–1912.

**anthropomorphize**   to confer human attributes on non-human entities.

**arcadian**   pertaining to Arcadia, a rural, pastoral region in ancient Greece, hence, ideally simple, rustic, and pleasureable.

**Art Deco**   term coined in 1960, at the time of its revival, derived from *L' Exposition Internationale des Arts Décoratifs et Industriel Moderne,* held in Paris in 1925. Outstanding examples of Art Deco architecture are the Chrysler Building and Radio City Music Hall. Characterized by geometric stylization.

**Art Nouveau**   an international style prominent in domestic and architectural decoration ca. 1895–1910.

**Bauhaus**   name of the school of architecture, art, and design in Weimar Germany, established in 1919.

**collage**   from French, *papier collé* (pasted paper). A composition created with a variety of pieces of paper pasted together on a flat surface.

**Constructivism**   the non-objective, three-dimensional style developed in Russia ca. 1914 by Tatlin and Rodchenko. It stressed the techniques and materials of which a work was made.

**Cubism (analytic)** the abstract style developed by Picasso and Braque between 1908 and 1912. Rejects perceptual reality. Organizes phenomena in terms of flat planes, thus acknowledging the flatness of the painting surface. Almost monochromatic.

**(synthetic)** the abstract style developed by Picasso and Braque between 1913 and 1921. Organizes recognizable fragments of phenomena into a composition; similar to organizing motifs in music into a composition. Reintroduces color.

**Dada**   a movement that developed ca. 1916 in response to the failure of reason to guide human events. It stressed the creative power of irrationality and completely redefined the nature of art: "Art is what an artist says it is."

**De Stijl**   (neo-plasticism) the non-objective style developed by Mondrian and Theo van Doesburg ca. 1916. In Mondrian's version, only primary colors are permitted, plus black and white, and all lines must be straight and meet at right angles. Seeks to achieve perfect balance of all elements, as a metaphor for perfect balance in human affairs, in harmony with perfect balance in the cosmos.

**Die Brücke**   (The Bridge) a movement founded by three young German painters, Kirchner, Heckel, and Karl Schmidt-Rottluff in 1905 to break with the established groups whose styles derived from nineteenth-century art. Characterized by high color and deliberately crude drawing. A representational style, but with figures and objects sometimes so broadly rendered that in those instances Brücke style verges on abstraction.

**Der Blaue Reiter** a movement developed by Kandinsky, Marc, and August Macke starting in 1911. It stressed the spiritual nature of art. The name refers to a group, not to a style, since the images created by the various artists who exhibited together under this name ranged from representational to non-objective.

**Expressionism** this word covers a wide range of style in art. For specific use in Program 8, see *Die Brücke* and *Der Blaue Reiter*.

**exotic** (here) pertaining to non-Western cultures.

**found object** an object selected from the world of objects, displayed as a work of art, in itself, or, in combination with other objects, to create an aesthetic composition.

**Futurism** a style developed by Balla, Boccioni, Carrà, Russolo, and Severini between 1911 and 1914. Rejects perceptual reality. Organizes phenomena according to psychological effects on a human perceiver, stressing interrelationships in space and time.

**golden section** a geometric relationship in which the smaller part is to the larger part as the larger part is to the whole. Believed to be the ideal proportion for achieving perfect balance and harmony of effect.

**International Style** an architectural style rooted in Bauhaus theory. Formally it displays a cubic, asymmetrical plan, with flat roof and large glass windows, the "glass curtain wall." The exterior surface is smooth, and without ornamentation. In New York City, the Lever House represents the style at its best.

**medium** the material of which a work of art is made.

**monochromatic** pertaining to a work executed in a more or less single color, including variations.

**Neue Sachlichkeit** (New Thing-like-ness) difficult to translate, the style stressed the object quality of things. Prominent in the movement were Grosz and Dix. Neue Sachlichkeit painting is characteristically bitter in depicting post–World War I German society.

**non-objective** non-representational; not representing any object

**orientalizing** (as an adjective) pertains to an effect that suggests the Near or Far East without adopting authentic Oriental methods.

**primitive** refers to a variety of styles in which non-Western methods of organizing form and creating expressive effects are employed. African and Oceanic art have been most useful in contributing in this way to Western art.

**Secessionstil** Viennese term for Art Nouveau (see above).

**signature style** the style that identifies the artist. Some artists change styles; Picasso went through many such changes. The signature style is then the identifying style for an artist in a particular period, e.g., Picasso's "Blue Period" style, 1901–1904.

**Suprematism** the non-objective style developed by Malevich around 1913. Rooted in spiritual concepts, like the styles of Kandinsky and Mondrian, the term reflects the artist's conviction that feeling is supreme in art.

**Surrealism** a movement (rather than a style) that attempted to project the artist's unconscious in either abstract or representational images. Its Freudian roots are evident. The term was invented by Apollinaire in 1917; the term and movement were defined by Breton in 1924.

**veronese green** yellow-green, or emerald green.

**Wiener Werkstatte** a workshop in Vienna founded by Josef Hoffmann in 1903. It produced Art Nouveau jewelry and domestic decoration such as tableware.

## Artists, Patrons, and Important Personages

**Apollinaire, Guillaume.** Art critic, poet, spokesman for the avant-garde. Author, *The Cubist Painters: Aesthetic Meditations* (1913; Eng. trans. 1914), and other works.

**Barr, Alfred H., Jr.** Art historian, museologist, a founder of the Museum of Modern Art and its first director. Author, *Cubism and Abstract Art,* 1936, and other books.

**Boccioni, Umberto** (Italy, 1882–1916). A founder of the Futurist movement. Painter and sculptor, and theoretician of the movement, author of *Technical Manifesto of Futurism* (1912), with contributions by Balla, Carrà, Russolo, and Severini.

**Brancusi, Constantin** (Rumania, 1876–1957). The earliest artist to approach non-objectivity in sculpture.

**Braque, Georges** (France, 1882–1963). With Picasso, creator of Cubism.

**Breton, André.** Writer, theoretician of Surrealism.

**Calder, Alexander.** (United States, 1898–1976). Originator of mobiles. (See below, Rodchenko.)

**Corbusier, Le (Charles-Edouard Jeanneret)** (France, 1887–1965). Played a seminal role in developing International Style architecture. His influence was worldwide in establishing the International Style's impact on twentieth-century building design.

**Duchamp, Marcel** (France, 1887–1968). One of the most influential of modernist artists. Invented the concept of "Readymades" which eventually forced a redefinition of the nature of art. Prefigured Dadaism. His direct influence extended well into the post–World War II period, and the effect of his work can still be discerned in art of the 1980s.

**Fry, Roger.** English artist and critic. Curator of paintings at the Metropolitan Museum, 1905–1910. Author, *Vision and Design* (1920), among other books.

**Gropius, Walter** (Germany, 1883–1969). Forerunner of the International Style. Founder of the Bauhaus, the most famous school of architecture and design of the twentieth century; director from 1919 to 1928.

**Kahnweiler, Daniel-Henry.** German art dealer settled in Paris until World War I. Enthusiastic supporter of Cubism.

**Kandinsky, Vasily** (Russia, 1866–1944). The first artist to practice non-objective art in the expressionist vein. His influence extended throughout western Europe and the United States not only because of the authority of his painting but also because of the persuasiveness of his book, *Concerning the Spiritual in Art.*

**Kirchner, Ernst** (Germany, 1880–1938). Founder, with Heckel and Schmidt-Rottluff, of *Die Brücke,* and its most gifted artist.

**Klimt, Gustav** (Austria, 1862–1918). The leading artist of the Vienna *Secession,* and the most eminent of Art Nouveau (*Secessionstil*) painters.

**Malevich, Kasimir** (Russia, 1878–1935). In 1913 Malevich made a drawing of a black square on a white field and thus became one of the two creators of geometric non-objectivity (the other being Mondrian), which he called Suprematism.

**Marinetti, Filippo.** Italian poet, creator of Futurism.

**Matisse, Henri** (France, 1869–1954). A pioneer of modernism and one of the most influential artists of the twentieth century. He was the recognized leader of the group that became known in 1905 as the Fauves.

**Mies van der Rohe, Ludwig** (Germany, 1886–1969). With Le Corbusier, a major figure in the development of International Style architecture. Director of the Bauhaus, 1930–1933.

**Miró, Joan** (Spain, 1893–1983). The greatest of the Surrealist painters, and one of the most internationally influential.

**Mondrian, Piet** (Holland, 1872–1944). Shares with Malevich the radical move into geometric non-objectivity, although it should be remembered that his first non-objective *looking* paintings actually referred to objects in nature and were technically abstract rather than non-objective.

**Moore, Henry** (England, 1898–1985). The first artist to pierce wood or marble carved sculpture.

**Picasso, Pablo** (Spain, 1881–1973). Shares with Georges Braque the creation of Cubism. The most famous and probably the single most influential painter in the twentieth century, in terms of the numbers affected by his art, and the widespread impact of Cubism.

**Rodchenko, Alexander** (Russia, 1891–1956). Created the first moving-and-hanging sculpture, thus breaking entirely with the tradition of support from the bottom.

**Stein, Gertrude.** Radically innovative writer, art collector, one of the earliest patrons of Matisse and Picasso. Began acquiring their works in 1905. Author of several books of criticism, poetry, and essays, as well as *The Autobiography of Alice B. Toklas* (1933), which became a best-seller.

**Tatlin, Vladimir** (Russia, 1895–1956). Founder of Constructivism. Created some of the first non-objective sculptures, ca. 1913.

**Wright, Frank Lloyd** (United States, 1867–1959). Transformed design of American domestic architecture. A pioneer of modern architecture, Wright can be counted as the first world figure among American architects.

**Vauxcelles, Louis.** Critic. Credited with using the terms "Fauves" and "Cubes" in his writing, which resulted in giving Fauvism and Cubism critical and public currency as stylistic names.

# Bibliography

*Note:* For art of the twentieth century (the subject of programs 8 and 9), art magazines and exhibition catalogues with color illustrations provide excellent information and criticism on very recent art and artists. Recommended magazines include *Art Forum, Art in America, ARTnews,* and *Arts Magazine.*

## SURVEYS OF MODERN ART

Arnason, H. H. *History of Modern Art: Painting, Sculpture, Architecture, Photography.* 3rd edition. Englewood Cliffs, N.J., 1986.

Haftmann, W. *Painting in the Twentieth Century.* 2 vols. New York, 1965.

Hamilton, G. H. *Painting and Sculpture in Europe 1880–1940.* Rev. and repr., New York, 1978.

Hughes, R. *The Shock of the New.* New York, 1986.

Hunter, S., and Jacobus, J. *Modern Art: Painting, Sculpture Architecture.* New York, 1985.

———. *American Art of the Twentieth Century.* New York, 1973.

Russell, J. *The Meanings of Modern Art.* New York, 1974, 1975, and 1981.

## PICTORIAL REFERENCES *IN ADDITION TO* JANSON, GARDNER, HONOUR AND FLEMING, **AND** THE ABOVE

Barr, A. H. *Matisse: His Art and His Public.* New York, 1951.

Crespelle, J.-P. *The Fauves.* Greenwich, Conn., 1962.

Dupin, J. *Joan Miró: Life and Work.* New York, n.d.

Leymarie, J. *Braque.* Paris, 1961. (Also see Leymarie, *Georges Braque, Museum of Modern Art.* New York, 1984. New York, 1988.)

Ritchie, A. C., ed. *German Art of the Twentieth Century.* New York, 1957.

Raynal, M. *Cézanne.* n.d.

Rubin, W., ed. *Pablo Picasso: A Retrospective.* New York, 1980.

Selz, P. *German Expressionist Painting.* Berkeley, Calif. n.d. [ca. 1954].

Soby, J. T. *Juan Gris.* New York, 1958.

Taylor, J. C. *Futurism.* New York, 1961.

Vriesen, G., and Imdahl, M. *Robert Delaunay: Light and Color.* New York, 1967.

## SPECIAL SUBJECTS

Ashton, D. *Twentieth-Century Artists on Art.* New York, 1985. Statements by artists.

Brown, M. W. *The Story of the Armory Show.* [Greenwich, Conn.], n.d. [1963].

Cassou *et al. Gateway to the Twentieth Century.* New York, 1962.

Chipp, H. B. *Theories of Modern Art.* Berkeley, Los Angeles, and London, 1971. Writings and statements by artists and critics.

Focillon, H. *The Life of Forms in Art.* New York, 1958. A study of style.

Fry, R. *Vision and Design.* Harmondsworth, 1961. Art criticism.

Goldwater, R. *Primitivism in Modern Art.* New York, 1967.

Harris, A. S., and Nochlin, L. *Women Artists: 1550–1950.* New York, 1978.

Hess, T. B., and Nocklin, L., eds., *Woman as Sex Object: Studies in Erotic Art, 1730–1970.* New York, 1972.

Henderson, L. D. *The Fourth Dimension and Non-Euclidean Geometry in Modern Art.* Princeton, 1983.

Herbert, R. L., ed. *Modern Artists on Art.* Englewood Cliffs, N.J., 1964. Statements by artists.

Kramer, H. *The Age of the Avant-garde.* New York, 1976. Art criticism.

Lemaitre, G. *From Cubism to Surrealism in French Literature.* Cambridge, Mass., 1947.

Marrero, V. *Picasso and the Bull* (tr. Anthony Kerrigan). Chicago, 1956.

Ortega y Gassett, J. *Velásquez, Goya and the Dehumanization of Art and Other Essays.* New York, 1972.

Raven, A., Langer, C. L., Frueh, J., eds. *Feminist Art Criticism: An Anthology.* Ann Arbor, Mich., 1988.

Rose, B. *Readings in American Art.* New York, 1975. Statements by artists.

Rosenberg, H. *The Tradition of the New.* New York, 1959. Art criticism.

Rosenblum, R. *Modern Painting and the Northern Romantic Tradition: Friedrich to Rothko.* New York, 1975.

Rubin, W., ed. *"Primitivism" in Twentieth-Century Art: Affinity of the Tribal and the Modern.* New York, 1984.

Steinberg, L. *Other Criteria: Confrontations with Twentieth-Century Art.* New York, 1972. Art criticism.

Sypher, W. *Rococo to Cubism in Art and Literature.* New York, 1960.

Venturi, L. *History of Art Criticism.* New York, 1964. (Chapter 11, "Art Criticism and Pure Visibility.")

## MAJOR MOVEMENTS

### Art Nouveau
Solomon R. Guggenheim Museum. *Klimt/Schiele*. New York, 1965.

Madsen, S. T. *Sources of Art Nouveau*. New York, 1956.

Varnedoe, K. *Vienna 1900: Art, Architecture, and Design*. New York, 1986.

Selz, P., and Constantine, M., eds. *Art Nouveau: Art and Design at the Turn of the Century*. New York, 1959.

Vergo, P. *Art in Vienna, 1898–1919: Klimt, Kokoschka, Schiele, and Their Contemporaries*. New York, 1975.

### German Expressionism: Die Brücke (The Bridge); Der Blaue Reiter (The Blue Rider); Neue Sachlichkeit (New Objectivity)
Joachimides, C. M., Rosenthal, N., and Schmied, W., eds., *German Art in the Twentieth Century: Painting and Sculpture, 1905–1985*. London, 1985.

Lincoln, L., ed. *German Realism of the Twenties: The Artist as Social Critic*. Minneapolis, 1980.

Selz, P. *German Expressionist Painting*. Berkeley, Calif., 1957.

Willett, J. *Art and Politics in the Weimar Period*. New York, 1978.

———. *Expressionism*. New York and Toronto, 1970.

### Fauvism
Crespelle, J. P. *The Fauves*. Greenwich, Conn., 1962.

Elderfield, J. *The "Wild Beasts": Fauvism and Its Affinities*. New York, 1976.

### Cubism
Apollinaire, G. *The Cubist Painters*. New York, 1949.

Barr, A. H. *Cubism and Abstract Art*. New York, 1936.

Buckberrough, S. A. *Robert Delaunay: The Discovery of Simultaneity*. Ann Arbor, 1982.

Fry, E. *Cubism*. New York, 1966.

Golding, J. *Cubism: A History and an Analysis, 1907–1914*, 2nd ed. London, 1968.

Gray, C. *Cubist Aesthetic Theories*. Baltimore, 1953.

Rosenblum, R. *Cubism and Twentieth-Century Art*, rev. ed. New York, 1976.

Spate, V. *Orphism: The Evolution of Non-Figurative Painting in Paris, 1910–1914*. Oxford, 1979.

### Futurism
D'Harnoncourt, A. *Futurism and the International Avant-garde*. Philadelphia, 1980.

Martin, M. *Futurist Art and Theory, 1909–1915*. Oxford, 1968.

Taylor, J. C. *Futurism*. New York, 1961.

### Dada and Surrealism
D'Harnoncourt, A., and McShine, K. *Marcel Duchamp*. New York, 1973.

Lippard, L. R., ed. *Surrealists on Art*. Englewood Cliffs, N.J., 1970.

Motherwell, R., gen. ed. *The Dada Painters and Poets: An Anthology*. New York, 1951.

Picon, G. *Surrealists and Surrealism*. New York, 1978.

Rubin, W. S. *Dada, Surrealism, and Their Heritage*. New York, 1968.

### Suprematism and Constructivism
Gray, C. *The Great Experiment: Russian Art, 1863–1922*. New York, 1962.

Bowlt, J., ed. and trans. *Russian Art of the Avant-Garde: Theory and Criticism, 1902–1934*.

Rickey, G. *Constructivism: Origins and Evolution*. New York 1967.

### Bauhaus
Itten, J. *Design and Form: The Basic Course at the Bauhaus*, rev. ed. New York, 1975.

Whitford, F. *Bauhaus*. London, 1984.

Wolfe, T. *From Bauhaus to Our House*. New York, 1981.

### Architecture: The International Style
Frampton, K. *Modern Architecture: A Critical History*. New York, 1980.

Hitchcock, H. R. and Johnson, P. *The International Style*, 2nd ed. New York, 1966.

# World War II and Beyond

## Learning Objectives

This unit begins with a description of the New York art scene as many of the leading figures of modern art, fleeing from the Nazification of Europe, arrive in the city. It then goes on to cover the development of art styles of the past five decades, including the present one. As in the film, the unit is divided into two parts. The first part is a study of styles and major artists of the forties, fifties, and sixties. The second part deals with art of the seventies and eighties. Each section begins with a brief setting of the socio-cultural context in which the style emerged, and this context, underlying the entire discussion in the section, is seen to be composed of the following phenomena: World War II, the atom bomb, the political reaction that arose in the post-war years, the influence of Freudian and Jungian thought, the impact of nihilist disenchantment due to the commodification of art, on one hand, and the tragic involvement of the United States in Vietnam, on the other, and, finally, the advanced development of Internationalism. These general conditions are shown to have contributed to the inner logic of formal stylistic evolution, and you are expected to grasp their salient relationships.

Of utmost importance for the understanding of modernist art is the body of critical thought that has constructed a sophisticated theoretical framework for each of the modernist styles of the period. You should be alert to passages in which aesthetic aims and other theoretical matters are discussed. Note the particular contribution of each of the artists on the "cutting edge" who first and foremost define the various styles with which this unit is concerned.

Paradigm works for each artist are discussed in formal and iconographical terms. These discussions should serve as guides for how to look at and think about a work of art, so that you may have a helpful context of reference to apply to your own experience in museums and galleries.

Pictorial references to Janson, Gardner, and Honour and Fleming have been given wherever possible. For this period, however, Arnason provides more illustrations, and discusses modern art more fully than the other texts, of course, since it is a survey of twentieth-century art only. It has also been necessary to refer to several other books, for illustrations.

It should be noted that there is some variation in terminology among writers on modern art. To give one example, Gardner refers to Abstract Formalism and includes under this term Barnett Newman. In this book, Newman is included in the section headed Abstract Expressionism: The New York School, and is classified as an Abstract-Imagist.

In this unit, you will:

- Learn to respect and value the ongoing redefinition of the visual arts even as they evolve into stranger, deviating, and more bizarre styles and formats;
- Understand how technological advances creating a "global village" through electronic mass media have been incorporated into the language of the fine arts;
- Appreciate the primacy of the expressive act and the creative process in art movements more concerned with cerebral and psychic gestures rather than the actual physical objects shaped or images painted;
- Comprehend the newly expanded meanings of visual expression as popular culture is mirrored by the artistic acquisition of elements taken from consumer products, film, television, trendy fashions, street graffiti, kitsch, rock & roll, and other fragments of international credit-card economies—modern art develops from Manet to the post-modern attitude of MTV;
- Become better acquainted with the major styles and critical skills necessary to decipher, translate, and interpret examples of avant-gardist trends such as Abstract Expressionism, Color Field, Hard Edge, Minimal, Pop, Op, Performance, Conceptual, Earthwork, Assemblage, Earth, Photo-Realism, Neo Expressionism, and even the yet unnamed movement of tomorrow;
- Enjoy visiting museums, galleries, and site installations featuring modern, post-modern, contemporary arts, and multi-media events with the attitude that every person can become an active participant instead of a passive observer.

## *Part 1*
## ART IN THE POST-WAR ERA

## Historical Background

As the twentieth century approached its midpoint, the basic premises of modernism had been given shape in painting, sculpture, and architecture. The groundwork for its future development had been completed. The reversal of values that clearly emerged among vanguardists during the nineteenth century, in competition with earlier values—the thrust toward egalitarianism, the distaste for standardization, the preference for the casual, the unpolished, the immediate—accelerated and penetrated every segment of society. More evident in America, where the struggle to achieve national identity naturally harbored resentment against European values anchored in hierarchical concepts, the new values that fueled the populist, social, and personal liberationist movement nevertheless made strong inroads in western Europe. World War II was a powerful force for strengthening the new values, and the tone of post-war culture was cacophonous with the clash of old and new voices aggressively proclaiming their intention to control the newly enlarged world, in shambles though much of it was.

In the first few years after the war the atom bomb was the central new fact in the world. Some people were optimistic, believing that the bomb meant no more war, since everyone knew a nuclear war would destroy the earth. Most, however, were pessimistic, believing that conflict among nations was inevitable. Nevertheless, a baby boom occurred, as if an explosion of virility might assert the species' determination to survive. Eventually that baby boom would produce a substantial new audience and patron group.

On the whole, the years immediately after the war constitute a passionate period. In intellectual, academic, and aesthetic circles one constantly heard the echoes of Jean-Paul Sartre and Albert Camus: Existentialism, holding the *engagement* of the individual acting in the world as the definition of Being, reinforced the already highly developed value of subjectivity. Influenced largely by the French thinkers, the political left, from liberal to communist, struggled in various ways to realize what Henry Wallace in the United States called "the century of the common man," until the political right was captured for a few years by its reactionary wing in the person of Senator Joseph McCarthy. Rising quickly to power as the cold war froze Soviet-American relations, McCarthy persuaded vast numbers of Americans that the whole liberal-to-extreme-left spectrum was one huge Communist conspiracy. Suffering or threatened with loss of employment, and even prison, most political activists were silenced or lost their nerve. Few voices of protest were heard in the land. Passion was drained by fear, and unleavened by dissent, the mood of the fifties turned apathetic.

Indifference is an uneasy state of unfocused attention. The mind and eye wander. One is immersed in a chaos of undifferentiated experiences, where one value is no better or worse than another and everything within our perception is reduced to the commonplace. The world seems wrapped in banality; even evil seems unexceptional, Hannah Arendt argued in her 1963 book, *The Banality of Evil*. Such, however, is the buoyancy of the human spirit that is it able to make use not only of the useless, discarded junk of civilization, but of the trite. The sixties saw the phenomenon of pop culture put the things of everyday life into a strange new light. It reshaped the taste of the rich, to whom it appealed the way "slumming" had in the twenties or the way visiting a madhouse had, in the early nineteenth century. It flourished also within and alongside the counter-cultural but essentially amorphous student movement until the issues imbedded in the Vietnam War brought the cultural scene into sharp focus once again. The buzz word of the sixties was "cool," siphoned out of Marshall McLuhan's influential writings, and cool was Minimal Art, flourishing alongside Pop.

The arts flourish best in very rich soil. Money is the great cultivator. The newest blooms of art appear where the soil is the richest, and so it was in the United States, the richest nation in the world after World War II, that the most influential developments occurred in painting and sculpture. Nevertheless, the older European masters—Picasso, Matisse, Miró—continued to create vital works, while a younger generation emerged with ideas radically different from their predecessors, in many ways similar to the new art of the New York School. Important modernists appeared among French, Netherlandish, German, Italian, and British artists, as we shall see, after considering the "triumph of American painting."

## Abstract Expressionism: The New York School

Fleeing from Hitlerized Europe in the thirties, many artists and intellectuals found shelter in America. Here the art scene was dominated by figurative painters and sculptors, Social Realists who were responsive to Communist ideology, which held that art must be a social weapon, and Regionalists who were committed to grass-roots nationalism. Artists in both groups had been enabled to go on as artists, during the Depression, through the establishment of the Works Federal Arts Project, a branch of the Works Progress Administration (WPA), which paid them a monthly stipend of 95 dollars in return for 96 hours per month for the Project, as it was called. As Irving Sandler has pointed out in his study of Abstract Expressionism, one of the effects of the Project in New York was to bring artists together frequently, on jobs, and out of these meetings a camaraderie developed that had lasting results in creating a vigorous New York art community that came to dominate American art.

Abstract and non-objective art was not totally absent, however, from American painting at this time. The American Abstract Artists was organized in 1936, and held successful exhibitions during the rest of the decade, making New York aware of modernist painting particularly in the non-objective tradition of Mondrian. Other groups began to form, with various modernist tendencies, largely influenced by Picasso and by Kandinsky, with whose writings they were acquainted. By 1940, with Paris about to fall to the German invaders, America possessed a small but influential group of knowledgeable artists, museum curators, dealers, and patrons whose interests were engaged by modernism.

Surrealism and Neo-plasticism provided the springboard for American art in the following decades, with Surrealism by far the leading influence in the early stages of the development of what became known as the New York School. The first stylistic movement identified with the New York School was Abstract Expressionism and during the forties and fifties the power of this style created an aesthetic imperialism that spread irresistibly through Europe and eventually to the Orient.

Abstract Expressionism is the richly endowed child of extremely complex parentage. One way to deal with its origins is through Arshile Gorky (1904–1948). Gorky went through a prolonged period of absorbing European modernism, especially as represented in the painting of Picasso and Miró, at first, and then in the enigmatic work of the abstract Surrealists. Among the latter, his encounter with Roberto Matta (1912–  ) seems to have been the most liberating—he was less in awe of his contemporary than he was of the great modernist masters of earlier generations. He found in Matta a kind of biomorphic landscape—the canvas a field of atmospheric colors implanted with small areas of suggestive shapes as in *Disasters of Mysticism* (1942) (Arnason clpl 135)—and equally important, he saw the possibilities in Matta's emphasis on abstract automatism, the method of the Surrealists that (in theory, anyway) by-passed rationality and consciousness by opening a direct channel between the unconscious and the brush of the artist.

In *The Liver Is the Cock's Comb* (1944) (**J 966;** Arnason clpl 177) we see at last Gorky's full synthesis of all he had learned from modernism. The space is as shallow as Cubist space or Kandinsky's; there is no horizon line; the composition tends to general dispersal of pictorial elements; color is free from all descriptive function; shapes are vaguely figurative without being surely identifiable. The title can perhaps be seen as an assertion of Gorky's deliberate embrace of Surrealism as it calls on the viewer's associations with the cock's comb as a symbol of virility. As we have already seen, Freud, with his sexual interpretation of life, was a critical figure in the development of Surrealist theory.

No account of the origins of the New York School and Abstract Expressionism can slight the immense contribution made by Hans Hofmann. Having lived in Paris during the radical years of modernism, he saw the discoveries of Cubism and Fauvism. Having established an internationally successful art school in Munich, he was already famous as a teacher when he arrived in the United States in 1932 and opened an art school in New York. Hofmann had the authority of one who had actually known the great masters of the age. He had strong theoretical tendencies, and was able to explain the principles of Picasso, of Matisse, of Kandinsky, and to familiarize the young artists with notions of the interaction of planes of color on the flat surface of the canvas. He stressed, as did Kandinsky, the spiritual content of art, which was achieved as an effect produced dialectically by "the relation of two given realities." In his work as well as his teaching he showed how two juxtaposed colors may visually oscillate, producing pictorial movement from the "push-pull" tensions created by the nature of color itself and in this way achieving the essence of life itself—movement.

Through Matta, Gorky, and Hofmann, then, the entire theory and practice of European art from Cézanne to the present became accessible to American artists on the threshold of artistic maturity in 1945. In addition there were two intellectual systems that came to dominate the thinking and the mood of the artists at this time: Jungian psychology and Existentialism. The appeal of both, at least in part, was due to the reaction against the political activism that dominated the thinking of the thirties, greatly influenced by Marxism. This implied to painters and sculptors, even those—the great majority—who were not card-carrying Communists, an obligation to make art that was meaningful to the public. The Nazi-Soviet pact disillusioned many artists about the Utopian nature of the Marxist state, but their disillusionment left them intellectually homeless. From the political, public stage they turned for shelter to the psychological, private realm. Jungianism provided an ideal resort: the shared obligations of the artist-as-citizen to build a better world were replaced by the personal ministrations of the artist-as-shaman to evoke the shared heritage of the past. The key notion in Jung was the concept of archetypes, commonly shared primordial images which lay in the unconscious cultural memory. It was the task of the artist to give expression to these images through an act of psychological archaeology, bringing them to the surface of consciousness in the process of painting. The notion of myth as cultural memory and dream served importantly as subject matter for Abstract Expressionist painting, indicated often by the evocative titles of the works.

The appeal of Existentialism, too, was psychological, since it called for action based on self-expression—for artists this meant painting as self-realization. As a moral system it shifted priority of value from public obligations to private, personal freedom. Both Jungianism and Exis-

**251**

tentialism stressed the importance of the self, and reinforced the already dominant note of "me" in the modernist cultural scale, which had grown increasingly louder since the twin notions of individualism and self-consciousness had emerged as important values in the late eighteenth century. The rise of these values can be graphed from 1900 to 1988 on the basis of the number of autobiographies published, proportionate to the population. The graph would show a dip in the thirties, but would rise again in the forties. Still climbing. And along with individualism and self-consciousness rose uniqueness and innovation.

Given the Abstract Expressionists' fundamental reinterpretation of the nature of art as *self*-expression, and of its purpose as *self*-realization, it is not surprising that Abstract Expressionism reveals a great diversity of styles. These styles fall into one of the other of the two wings of "gesture" and "Color Field," in each of which there are many subdivisions. What united them was the conviction that shared imagery was imitative, imposed from outside, like language. Art had to "say" something innovative, and such a statement could only come from deep within the unique psyche of the individual artist. Furthermore, like the Futurists who had determined to break with their own grand but burdensome tradition, the Americans of the forties felt stifled by the aesthetic wealth they had inherited. "The Armory Show," Clyfford Still wrote in 1959, "dumped on us the combined and sterile conclusions of Western European decadence." By 1948, when the artists had dropped their earlier adherence to Surrealism, Barnett Newman asserted that "we are freeing ourselves of the impediments of memory, association, nostalgia, legend, myth, or what have you, that have been the devices of Western European painting. Instead of making *cathedrals* out of Christ, man, or 'life,' we are making it out of ourselves . . . the image we produce is . . . one of revelation . . . that can be understood by anyone who will look at it without the nostalgic glasses of history" (Rose, p. 135). Nationalistic though these statements and many similar ones may appear, the desire to reject the European tradition was less rooted in nationalism than it was in the American artists' need to rid themselves of the nettlesome sense of aesthetic provincialism. Ironically, perhaps, Jackson Pollock (1912–1956), the American artist who most completely synthesized the theories, practices, and intellectual currents traced above, was indifferent to anti-Europeanism as an issue: "I accept the fact that the important painting of the last hundred years was done in France," he wrote in 1944 (Rose, p. 122). "An American is an American and his painting would naturally be qualified by that fact, whether he wills it or not."

We have seen the search for essence, for purity, for impact as driving forces in the history of modernist style. We have also watched the disappearance of pictorial emphases in favor of an all-over composition, as we have followed the will to achieve pure visibility. With Pollock these tendencies reached a new intensity. Expressionism seems to have been an innate feature of his temperament, since it was that element that emerges as dominant in his early work with Thomas Hart Benton. When Pollock studied with him, Benton had adopted an energetic, mannerist, figurative style through which he mythologized the American agricultural West. Pollock was also strongly attracted by the powerful expressionism of the Mexican painters, José Clemente Orozco and David Siqueiros, and to the generalizations of Albert Pinkham Ryder, who abstracted the essence of shape and movement from nature. National consciousness in the thirties had created a new awareness of and taste for American Indian culture, and Pollock's receptiveness to Indian art was doubtless enhanced by his friend John Graham's view of American Indians as a primitive people and therefore more closely in touch with the wellsprings of feeling. "The art of primitive races," Graham wrote in the *Magazine of Art,* April 1937, "has a highly evocative quality which allows it to bring to our consciousness the clarities of the unconscious mind, stored with all the individual and collective wisdom of past generations and forms . . . an evocative art is the means and the result of getting in touch with the powers of our unconscious." That Graham had absorbed Jungian and Freudian thought is evident here and elsewhere in his writing. It is thought that the Navajo technique of dripping colored earth to form ritual-based designs may have had something to do with Pollock's adoption of the drip technique. Pollock himself called attention to the similarity of his technique of painting from all four sides, with his canvas on the floor so that he could walk around it, with that of Indian sand painters (Pollock, *Possibilities* 1, winter 1947–48).

With its principal totemic figure, Pollock's *The She-Wolf* (1943) brings many of the foregoing elements together. Its power arises from the dynamic, surging rhythms that swirl across the pictorial field.

Pollock's greatest works were created between 1946 and 1950. Using industrial paints and sometimes extraneous materials to add variety to the surface, he poured and dripped his colors over the canvas, making them participants in a great ritual dance that reaches frenzy as it increases in emotion. *Number One* (1949) exemplifies the best of this period and style. A web of white lines entangles the jewel-like dripped splotches. Here and there one seems to see the suggestion, by design or accident, of a figure or fragment, but the eye is compelled to keep moving, directed by the force of the artist's will to create and possess a world of his own making, and absorbed by the spectacle of a feeling so intense that despair and exaltation are undifferentiated. The planar unity of figure and ground is almost complete, matching the singleness of the emotional expression. It is as if the scream of Munch's anguished figure and the flaming universe it engendered had been fused on a transcendent and unified cosmic plane. Not since Van Gogh had such intensity of feeling been so successfully externalized in paint. That he was able to sustain such intensity in a body of work that includes *Enchanted Forest* (1947), *Lavender Mist* (1950) (Arnason clpl 180) and *One* (#31, 1950) **(J clpl 146)** testifies to his genius. Pollock's painting can be thought of as the expression of the soul of the artist by means of body language.

It is perhaps not too far-fetched an analogy to compare his balletic execution of a painting to the performance of a dancer who leaps and twirls with perfect freedom, able to defy, it seems, even gravity, because what has been learned is under such perfect control that it appears to be effortless. If we had some way of tracing every contact of the dancer's feet with the ground over which they moved, would we not be able to discern some pattern in the web of marks, some clue that would tell us that the marks were made within the context of controlled choices? In championship tennis, the players move this way and that, instantaneously responding to the demands of the ball and the situation within the rules of the game. If, again, we could trace on the court each movement made by feet and ball so that great skeins of interwoven lines would become visible, how would that pattern compare with one made by ordinary players? Would we not see far more control in the pattern drawn by the champions than by the others, with their false starts, their helpless rushing, their indecisive, irregular strides?

Art as its own subject matter, a theme we have been watching closely since Impressionism, was never more forcefully dramatized than by Willem de Kooning (1904–   )—dramatic because he did not entirely give up figurative imagery with its inevitable iconographic associations and yet managed to achieve a painterliness that is insistently medium-conscious. His fully mature, wholly individual style was realized in a series of works based on the female figure, the most venerated form of classical art since Praxiteles, held to be the perfect motif for the expression of harmony, grace, and wholeness—which he subjected to a painterly handling that totally subverted those qualities *in the figure* but celebrated them in the *painting*. Cézanne had moved in this direction with his *Bathers*, Matisse with his *Blue Nude* (1907) (Arnason clpl. 36), Picasso in *Les demoiselles d'Avignon*, and other artists had followed, but none so fully reversed the content-value as De Kooning was to do—excepting Jean Dubuffet, who just a few years earlier had begun his *Corps de Dame* series.

De Kooning had moved decisively into modernism in the thirties with a series of male figures that showed compressed space and simplified forms, and in the early forties modernist, fragmented biomorphism appears in his work, soon elaborated with scrawled lettering and becoming more geometrized with Cubist-style shifting and interpenetrating planes. De Kooning added to this vocabulary of modernism by adopting the sweeping brush action that stressed the artist's presence, physically and emotionally, in his work. By 1950 he had assembled his means and began the *Woman* series that provoked criticism as ferocious as the images themselves. Typical

are *Woman I* **(G 22.72)** and *Woman II* **(J clpl 147),** where compressed space, anatomical fragmentation, and shifting, quasi-geometric, quasi-biomorphic shapes are realized through what appears to be a wildly slashing action of laying on color with a brush. Harking back "beyond the horses of the Parthenon" to prehistoric fertility idols such as the *Venus of Willendorf* **(J 19; G 1.13),** De Kooning's frontal, iconic images of the early fifties are nature-powers that confront and overwhelm the viewer. In the three decades following this series he has sometimes equaled but never surpassed its magisterial achievement.

The impact of paintings by Pollock and De Kooning is achieved in large measure by the visible evidence in the works of the artist's presence and bodily activity. The viewer's involvement is dependent on muscular empathy with the work's rhythmic movement, which is more or less linear. As our eyes travel along the swaths of brush strokes, the artist's action in making them evokes a similar sense of engaged action. Nevertheless, despite these physical features, the images do not communicate to our tactile sense even though they heighten our physical sense of participating in the work. We do not feel that we can reach out to touch them, like three-dimensional objects.

## The Abstract-Imagists

Closely associated with Pollock and De Kooning in developing the New York School, yet quite different in method, were artists who depended not on gesture but mainly on color to convey their meaning. Sometimes classified as Color-Field painters, in this book we will call them Abstract-Imagists. Both groups, the gestural and the

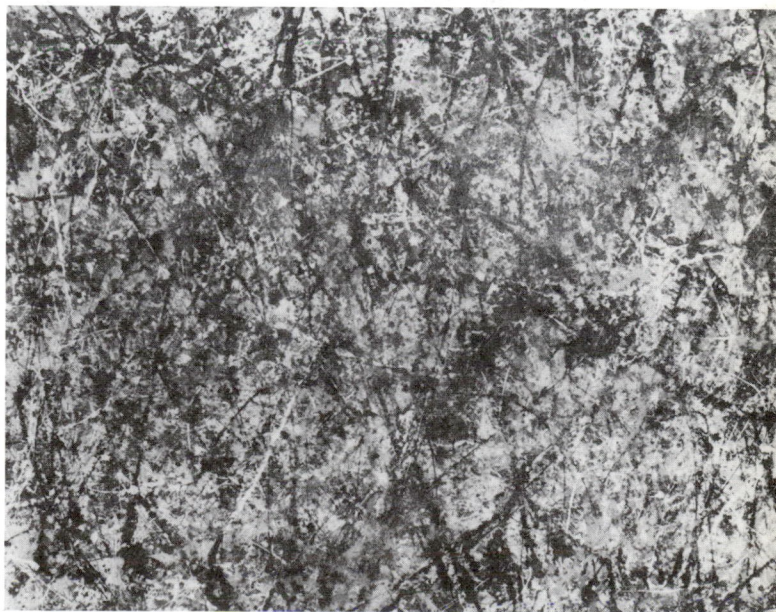

Jackson Pollack, *One* (#31, 1950). Washington, National Gallery of Art. (NATIONAL GALLERY OF ART, WASHINGTON, D. C.)

Imagists, were concerned with art as the visible expression of inward, subjective perception; both have their roots in the western Romantic tradition which preferred passion to reason, drama to exposition, aspiration to accomplishment. Both saw art as an existential demand for action, and considered the canvas as the artist's world in which to act meaningfully, and to communicate meaning without recourse to signs or symbols that could have verbal equivalents.

In their early phases—as among the gestural painters—Jungian associations with the mythic past tended to be explicit, but eventually this essentially narrative element disappeared from their painting as their aesthetic aims were clarified. They were determined to make art totally inward, totally subjective. To achieve this, these artists had somehow to avoid *outsideness,* to separate meaning from language, so that meaning was no longer anchored to words but became as if free-floating, existing in a universe inhabited only by the creator-artist and the viewer, moving between the two in a wordless interplay of pure experience.

Prominent among those who worked in the more serene vein of Abstract Expressionism—the Abstract-Imagists—were Clyfford Still, Mark Rothko, and Barnett Newman. As we have noted before, one of the recurring problems of modernism has been the threat of formlessness, and this danger was a significant feature in the development of the kind of area painting that emerged in the work of Still, Rothko, and Newman by about 1947. Still (1904– ) began as a loosely figurative artist in the 1930s. In the early 1940s certain figurative images can yet be discerned in his work, although the non-objective dominates the expanding field with its residually suggestive, ragged-edged, irregularly shaped areas of color that lend themselves to figure-ground interpretation. As he refined his thinking, his painting became increasingly more cosmic in effect, as if the artist had intuited a transcendent landscape in the limitless reaches of his mind, as in *Number 2* (1949) (Arnason clpl 193). For a few years at the end of the forties and into the next decade, Still worked with severely restricted color, just as Pollock and De Kooning had shifted at about the same period to black and white. Then, like them, he returned to high color and with this shift achieved a more complete integration of color areas so that the figure-ground relationship became more ambiguous. The threat of formlessness was turned back by the holistic image thus created.

The sexuality inherent in psychological archaeology (as if penetrating the depths of time, uncovering lost worlds, was a metaphor for the struggling and liberating experience of the sexual act), was visualized in biomorphic imagery, which links Mark Rothko's work of the early forties to that of Matta and Gorky. Rothko (1903–1970) turned from naturalistic figuration in the 1930s to Surrealist biomorphism in the early 1940s. Like so many artists of his generation, he too was looking for a way out of rationalism, materialism, and dealing with prosaic facts.

Like others, he found in ancient myth the archetypal passions that energize human life, and going back even further he seemed to imagine a paleozoic underwater world of creatures evolving their being-shapes, as in *Geologic Reverie* (1946) (Sandler fig. 13.1). By 1947 Rothko began to find that his aspiration for the universal, the transcendent, was shackled by this nature-anchored imagery. He purified his painting by eliminating the evocative shapes, allowing color alone, luminous, glowing, throbbing color, to convey his sense of the sublime. Color, so physical in essence, so metaphysical in effect, was the vessel he offered those willing to join him in his adventure into the unknown. Repudiating decoration, Rothko spread veils of color across his canvas and conjured luminous rectangles of light that seems to become more intense as one gazes, inducing in the viewer a sense of weightlessness, as if the gravity-free world of the artist's creation were the real atmosphere into which one might enter. In the work of the 1950s one sees the *Calme, Luxe et Volupté* of Matisse translated into non-objective terms. Even the canvas support disappears, leaving one with the great apparition before one's eyes: disembodied floating rectangles of transparent, vibrating color. In the last years of his life his color darkened. Joyous or tragic, Rothko's paintings command awe.

Abstract-Imagist painting was carried to its most extreme by Barnett Newman (1905–1970). Compared to Still, whose irregularly shaped, interrelated color areas imply a kind of lava-like movement, or to Rothko, whose light-drenched color produces a throbbing sensation, Newman's painting field seems mysteriously quiet. The vertical stripes, although cut by the upper and lower margins of the picture plane, do not suggest movement beyond. They do, however, produce "movement" in two subtle ways. They create vertical sections within the overall field, thus setting up a tension between narrower and wider that produces a sensation of movement. In addition, the stripes contain the rectangles they create, so that the huge expanse of color seems to press against them, as if against walls. This double action is most evident in horizontal formats such as *Vir Heroicus Sublimus* (1950–51) **(G 22.76),** but is also present in vertical formats such as the fourteen-part work *The Stations of the Cross.* As with the other artists of his generation, Newman's ambitions were heroic. He aimed to create a sublime art; he took as his subject the transcendent themes of human agony, despair, and ultimate triumph, which was life itself. He scorned the idea of design as serious art. He held shape to be a living thing, as it was, he wrote, with the Kwakiutl Indian artist, "a vehicle for an abstract thought-complex, a carrier of the awesome feelings he felt before the terror of the unknowable" (Rose, p. 113). What Newman aspired to was the visualization of an "idea-complex that makes contact with mystery—of life, of men, of nature, of the hard, black chaos that is death, or the grayer, softer chaos that is tragedy," as seen in *The Stations of the Cross: The Twelfth Station* (1965) (Arnason fig. 596). Was he correct in believing that his subject would be understood by anyone looking at it with fresh eyes—"without the nostalgic glasses of history" (Rose, p. 135)?

One could construct a genealogy for the color black in modernist painting that might start with Goya (not only the late "black paintings"), and include Turner, Manet, Whistler, and Picasso. All of these artists knew how to make black a powerful vehicle to convey an extraordinary range of feeling, from tragedy (obviously) to eroticism. Franz Kline (1910–1962) built his career with black, which he discovered in 1949. His huge, thrusting signature works composed of broadly brushed swaths of black paint "have the impact of a sledge hammer" (Goodrich-Baur, p. 220). They suggest the powerful movements of modern industrial machinery, or of sex. Robert Motherwell (1915–  ) evokes echoes of Goya and Picasso in his most famous and most masterly series of paintings, those inspired by the Spanish Civil War. *The Elegies,* as they are known collectively, comprise more than one hundred works and in them he combines both the gestural and the Abstract-Imagist methods of painting, as in *Elegy to the Spanish Republic No. 34* (1953–54) (Arnason clpl 190). Although he sometimes executed works in small format, his important paintings are immense, like those of all the other Abstract Expressionists who seemed to have shared Rothko's insight that the large painting places the viewer within it; it inhibits the distancing that results from contemplation, from *looking at,* transforming the viewer into a participant. One may be reminded of seventeenth-century Baroque art that also aimed at viewer participation, especially the great ceiling paintings that "opened up" as if inviting the viewer below to be absorbed into the heavenly realm above.

It is tempting to speculate about the development of American art had there been no World War II. It is evident from the foregoing that modernism was astir in New York even in the mid-thirties, yet, virtually every observer agrees that the presence in New York of so many important European modernists was crucial in shaping the direction of the New York School. On one hand it is impossible to imagine that the towering genius of Pollock or of De Kooning could have remained unrealized to the full extent by which we know their art; on the other hand, the entire history of art teaches us the importance of cutting-edge sophistication in the creative process. In the opinion of the present writer, New York's time had come. Like Florence at the beginning of the fifteenth century, where economic, social, political, and intellectual factors made possible the miracle of the Renaissance, so in New York those factors had coalesced to create another miraculous flowering of art.

The central issue, *the subject matter,* one might almost say, of Abstract Expressionism was freedom. The marks that covered the canvas of the radical painter, the shapes formed by the radical sculptor, were expressions of personal choice, brought into being by the demands of the work itself, undictated by any formulas for making art,

or academies for judging art. But the issue of freedom went far beyond aesthetics. "Modern art is related to the problem of the modern individual," Robert Motherwell wrote in 1944, with the memory of the thirties and its social commitment still vivid. Freedom, in modern terms is unalterably linked to individualism. For two centuries Western civilization has been debating the question of the correct balance between the proper demands of the State on its citizens, and the civil rights of the individual citizen vis-à-vis the State. In the United States, the balance achieved by the American Revolution has been gradually upset, with more and more weight added to the individualist side. President John F. Kennedy had this history clearly in mind when he enjoined the American people to "ask not what your country can do for you, but what you can do for your country." Just as the pre-Revolutionary weight of the British government's rights over the individual had become intolerable, so now does it seem that our modern individualistic society is verging on the unwieldy, gridlocking what should be the easy, controlled flow of social life into an immense traffic jam, each horn honking loudly but of course ironically lost in the cacophonous chaos of the me-first-last-and-only symphony in no movements.

## Painting in Post-War Europe

Until recently, the dazzling achievement of American painting in the forties and fifties obscured the impressive work of European artists in the post-war period. With several decades behind us now, we are better able to see the accomplishments of the ongoing modernist movements, especially in England, France, Italy, and the Netherlands. At approximately the same time that Abstract Expressionism was developing in America, a group of artists in Copenhagen, Brussels, and Amsterdam came together to form the CoBrA movement. Perhaps the exhibitions of Peggy Guggenheim's collection, which included several important paintings by Pollock, contributed to the direction taken by the CoBrA artists—the collection was shown in Venice, Florence, Milan, Amsterdam, Brussels, and Zurich. It is certainly likely that Asger Jorn, Karel Appel, Pierre Alechinsky, and Corneille Guillaume van Betterloo (Arnason clpls 210–211; figs. 683–686) went to see the Guggenheim exhibition. Their paintings have a surface resemblance to Abstract Expressionism, but in retaining figuration they were less innovative than the New York group. They were also less influential, since as a movement CoBrA was short-lived (1948–50) and lacked the organizational backing that the Americans found in galleries such as Peggy Guggenheim's Art of This Century Gallery, the Kootz Gallery, the Egan Gallery, and the Betty Parsons Gallery.

In England, the sensibility which in the United States produced Abstract Expressionism was realized in the figurative painting of Francis Bacon (1909–  ) the greatest British painter since Turner. For him, as for the Americans, the image was paint, and the paint was the image. "Every movement of the brush on the canvas alters the shape and implications of the image," he wrote, sounding like Pollock. "I think that painting today is pure intuition and luck and taking advantage of what happens when you splash the stuff down" (Chipp, p. 620). In the 1950s Bacon painted a series of works based on the portrait by Velázquez of *Innocent X*. These *Popes*, mouths wide open in a hideous scream, seated as if they are strapped into an electric chair, are analogous to De Kooning's *Women* in the violence of their conception **(J 670 & clpl 133; G 938)** and in the immediacy of their impact. Does this suggest that De Kooning, too, is dealing with intolerable fear? Bacon's male nudes of subsequent years are among the most shocking, the most intensely horror-provoking images in all of Western art, not excepting Goya's *Disasters of War* **(G 21.11; H&F 15.3, 15.4).** Boneless, contorted, putrified in color and sometimes splattered as if bloody, these figures are eloquent with the misery of the human condition in the aftermath of the most destructive war in history.

In France, too, expressionism triumphed. Called "Art Autre," "Tachisme," "L'Art Informel," it was an art that, like Abstract Expressionism, aimed at *looking* different from all past art; an art that practiced psychic improvisation and flirted dangerously with formlessness. Unlike the new American painting, however (except for Still), the post-war School of Paris stressed the tactile surface and used admixtures of coarse substances. Among the most innovative and influential artists of this post-war School of Paris were Jean Fautrier (1898– ), Jean Dubuffet (1901–1985), and Wolfgang Schulze, known as Wols (1913–1951)—this last a German-born artist who went to Paris in 1932 and should be considered as a School of Paris painter. Their works have in common a crusty tactility of surface. In post-war Italy artists tended to adhere to one or the other of what had become the two leading styles of modernism, hard-edged formalism and art informel. Lucio Fontana (1899– ), however, introduced a new concept to which he gave the name Spatialism (Arnason fig. 758; clpl 231), which called for the end of the traditional categories of painting, sculpture, and architecture in favor of their integration. In 1949 Fontana began to work out his concept with the creation of spatial environments which he continued to explore in the fifties with the architect Luciano Baldessari. They designed large-scale, free-flowing, sculptural spaces, using ultra-violet light to effect transformations of the architectural-spatial environment. Fontana also attacked the foundation of painting as essentially a two-dimensional art by slashing the canvas—this in the very period when two-dimensionalism of painting was becoming canonized. Trained initially as a sculptor in Argentina, where he was born, his theory of Spatialism aimed to subsume the differences between painting and sculpture by absorbing both in a space-and-time continuity. His signature image is a curious mixture—cool, ethereal,

pristine, remote and yet warmed by shadows and mystery-evoking light effects (Arnason fig. 758).

A second major modernist to emerge in Italy in this period is Alberto Burri, whose sensibility combines art informel with something of Dubuffet's love of texture. Burri was a doctor who began to paint when he was interned in the United States as a prisoner of war. Using available materials, burlap sacking and cheap, thin wood from fruit and vegetable crates, he splashed paint on their rough-textured surfaces, creating effects reminiscent of blood-stained bandages and discolored, festering wounds (Arnason clpl 201).

In general, one can observe that the aesthetic sensibility of the post-war period in Europe responded, as in the United States, to expressionist and informal art. While on both sides of the Atlantic some important artists remained figurative—De Kooning in America, Bacon in England, Dubuffet in France, Guttuso in Italy—the taste of the times favored non-objectivity.

It is a striking fact that no prominent painters took for their themes the war itself, or its consequences. If one had to rely on mainstream art alone for information or understanding, one would never even guess that there had been a war. How is one to interpret this? Escapism comes to mind, of course, but the history of art teaches us differently: Few major artists have treated the theme of war. In the Renaissance there was Uccello **(J clpl 69)** and in the modern era there were Goya **(G 21.10, 21.11)** and Picasso **(J 948; G 22.16).** War scenes were traditionally celebratory, like John Trumbull's paintings of the American Revolution; unlike Trumbull's, they were usually commissioned by rulers to commemorate their victories, from the despots of the ancient Near East and the Pharaohs of Egypt, to Louis XIV, and the seventeenth century can show a large inventory of such paintings. In modern times, heads of state no longer command artists. Moreover, the hideous truth of war has displaced the traditional romantic, glamorous view, and has made celebration impossible; a serious painting of war would have to show its terror. Terror, however, is not an attractive subject *to look at*; it is hard enough to read vivid descriptions of physical torment, but at least one can put down the book. A picture on the wall is *there,* and an artist must usually consider the salability of his work.

Furthermore, throughout the twentieth century topical, narrative subjects have been disdained as "literary," inappropriate to the medium of visual art. (Even Surrealism was attacked on the grounds that it was a literary style.) Artists who *have* painted horror pictures of topical subjects have suffered almost total neglect, until recently, as we shall see at the end of this unit.

## Color Field Painting

The geometric, reductionist tendency in American painting exemplified in the work of Barnett Newman and Ad Reinhardt, which is closely related to Color Field, can be seen as related to the pre-war Mondrian tradition. In this view it is analogous to European post-war painting that continued working in the vein of Concrete Art, the term current in the thirties for geometric non-objectivity. Both in the United States and Europe, however, this cerebral art was transformed by the infusion of sensations of irrationality into its measured rationality. Whatever geometry might control the spaces in paintings by Newman and Reinhardt, the demands that the paintings make compromise their mathematics. Evoking the infinite, they cross the classical border into Romanticism.

Since the development of Impressionism the entire enterprise of painting, step by step, feature by feature, had come under examination. Gradually the decision had been made to give to nature what was nature's and to art what was art's. But exactly what, indeed, was art's? As color, form, space were liberated from their traditional tasks of natural description and shifted to the domain of the artist, their new capabilities had to be discovered. The history of modernism is the tracing of those discoveries, with every element of art becoming the object of experimentation. An early step was taken by Seurat when he painted the frame of his painting with dots, so as to make a transition between the space of the painting and that of the viewer. This gave to the painting a quality of objecthood, as part of the furniture of the real world and, paradoxically, led to the revelation that the less art imitated nature, the more it became a part of the natural world. Josef Albers brought to a climax the first phase of this experimental spirit in art in the 1950s when he embarked on his long series of paintings titled *Homage to the Square* in which he explored color relationships within the strict limits of one absolute form—the square (Arnason clpl 149). This led directly into the next investigation, Color Field painting, which, with its heightened support-consciousness, that is, awareness of the canvas (or whatever the support might be) as a physical, integral element of the painting, inevitably demanded the final experiment, the investigation of the one element in traditional art that had remained unchanged, the support itself. With what seems now foreseeable logic, the 1960s saw the development of the shaped canvas, which authenticated the objecthood of the work of art, the achievement of the painting as a thing-in-the-world.

In this book, Color Field painters are distinguished from Abstract-Imagists on the basis of separating those artists who developed within the Abstract Expressionist movement from those who did not. A salient fact about Color Field (also called Hard-Edge Abstraction and Post-Painterly Abstraction), is its deliberately experimental nature, a feature that links it to Josef Albers. It is as if artists such as Morris Louis, Kenneth Noland, and Jules Olitski were *testing* the frontiers of painting, going beyond Albers' experiments with relationships of color held strictly to the square by confronting problems of the nature, the size, proportions, shapes, and relationships of all of the constituent elements of a work of art. Although

Color Field embraces a wide variety of styles, the name implies a group of characteristics found in various combinations in the work of a considerable number of artists active in the 1950s and 1960s who participated in a number of significant group exhibitions held during the sixties. Differences aside, these works were non-objective, extremely large, flatly painted yet optically illusionistic. Purged of all physical signs of the artistic process, they frequently showed raw canvas or canvas so thinly painted or stained that the weave became part of the visual field. Typically, the design was open, that is, it implied continuity beyond the edge, and holistic—it offered an all-over coverage of a surface either uninflected, or articulated with subtle variations of hue, or with a single dominating shape. The concentrated visual energy—like a strange presence—derived from the repetition of motifs (stripes, repeated or echoing shapes, or swathes of color, for example), or from the outward pressure of the shape against the picture margins **(J 971, 974, clpl 148; G 22.73, 22.76, 22.77).**

A key figure in the rise of Color Field painting in competition to Abstract Impressionism is Helen Frankenthaler (1928– ), who began in the 1950s to dilute her colors so that they soaked into the weave of the canvas. This method of staining the color into the linen material produced an airy effect, causing the shapes to lose their materiality, and become transparent, as in *Interior Landscape* (1964) and *Elberta* (1975) (Arnason clpls 233, 234). Staining also advanced the century-long struggle to achieve a totally anti-illusionistic composition, which demanded absolute flatness. Stained into the support, colors fused with the canvas itself—they were not marks *on* the canvas but *in* the canvas.

While Frankenthaler's imagery owed something to Gorky, perhaps, in her early years, her innovative technique and the sheer beauty of her painting had important consequences. When Morris Louis (1912–1962) and Kenneth Noland (1924– ) came up to New York from Washington, D.C., in 1953 to visit the galleries, and see at first hand what was happening in the studios of New York artists, they discovered Frankenthaler's work.

Louis reacted immediately, and after some months of experimentation he achieved a new look in modernist art. Using unsized, unprimed cotton duck canvas, he spilled out his thin paint, color into color, sometimes scrubbing it in, so that the colors bled into each other and into the canvas, allowing the weave to show through. The resulting diaphanous effect of such work *Beth Feh* (1958), for example **(J clpl 150),** led critics to refer to these works as Morris's "veils." Later he worked out a series of paintings called *Unfurled,* with wavering-edged stripes forming right-angle triangles at the sides, leaving most of the canvas untouched.

By his own account, Kenneth Noland's breakthrough came when he discovered the center of the canvas. He began a series of paintings of concentric bands of color, inscribed in a square canvas, the center of which was identical with the center of the circular image as in *A Warm Sound in a Gray Field* (1961) (Arnason clpl 244). The tension between circle and square was only mildly interesting, but it did raise the question of the relationship between the real canvas (square) and the painted image (circle). Noland then investigated the possibility of the chevron as a shape, placing a series of chevrons of different, carefully juxtaposed hues one inside the other so that their points lay along a straight line forming a central axis. The relationship between image and canvas was more complex, but was still static. The artist then shifted the point of the bottom chevron away from the center, arranged the design so that points of convergence within the chevron deliberately lay to one side of the center, and achieved a dynamic result that could appear to move down, up, outward, or inward, depending on however the viewer happened to see it, from moment to moment. Moving from Frankenthaler in a different direction, Jules Olitski sprayed layers of paint over the field, varying the intensity of color so that it seemed as if light were coming from behind in uneven waves or beams. The works suggest the feel of air, and come dangerously close to atmospheric formlessness. To counteract this Olitski began to run contrasting ribbons of color along or near one or two borders of the principal color area. In all of these works one discerns a growing support-consciousness. Enter Frank Stella (1936– ), the most influential painter to explore the possibilities of the shaped canvas as a means of extending modernism's expressive affects.

Stella's stylistic development during the sixties constitutes a history of many of the issues of the decade. Continuing, like the Abstract Expressionists, to work on canvases of huge dimensions, sixties art ironically drained them of their heroic aspirations and faced them with impassivity. Typical are Robert Ryman (1930– ), *Classico III* (1968) (Arnason fig. 796), and Brice Marden (1938– ), *The Dylan Painting* (1966) (Arnason clpl 258). "Touch" was rejected in favor of the smooth look of metallic, factory-made products, reviving and updating the machine aesthetic that had triumphed at the Bauhaus without, however, the social philosophy that had been an integral part of its development there. Artists learned to dazzle the eye with higher color brilliance and/or optical effects that produce sometimes fascinating ambiguities and induce the sense of movement through manipulation of color and line. Victor Vasarely (1908– ), with his *Vega Per* (1969) (Arnason clpl 253), and Bridget Riley (1931– ), with her *Drift 2* (1966) (Arnason fig. 780), are characteristic Op artists. In Op art, pure visibility becomes self-referring; the subject of the painting is the act of perceiving. Art rooted in pure visibility reflected, in the sixties, a laboratory orderliness and hygiene, mathematical precision, and total control of the means of production. It constituted, in short, a critique of the fifties, a reaction from the personal to the impersonal, and Frank Stella stands to Pollock as Minimal, Hard Edge,

Post-Painterly Abstraction, and Op art stand to gestural Abstract Expressionism; there are elements of all of these styles in Stella's art.

Stella came to dramatic notice in 1959 when four of his black pin-stripe paintings were exhibited in the Museum of Modern Art's *Sixteen Americans* show: great rectangles seeming to contain nothing but monotonously repeated, precisely measured black painted stripes separated by thin stripes of the white canvas. Apart from a perfectly white, unpainted canvas, Stella had reached the edge of the cliff as far as reductive imagery could go. But as for pure visibility, there was one more step to be taken, and Stella took this step the following year when he notched the support, and painted stripes that repeated the shape of the notch, thereby unifying the image more tightly than ever before. By shaping the canvas, and allowing it to determine his design, Stella demonstrated that it could no longer be thought of as a field separate from the image on it. The free, existentialist world that had been the Abstract Expressionist canvas was supplanted by the dictatorship of the frame. Or so at first it seemed. But in the following years the artist proceeded to exhibit with amazing virtuosity the variations that could be rung on the theme of the shaped canvas (Installation view of three paintings (1962) **[J 976]**; *Empress of India* (1965) **[J clpl 152]**), introducing bright primary and complementary color as in *Jasper's Dilemma* (1962–63) (Arnason clpl 249), and moving eventually from the rectilinear to the curvilinear, using the 360-degree circle, with arcs and quadrants, as his unit of form, always with geometrical precision, as in *Agbatana III* (1968) (Arnason clpl 250). One gained insight into the possibility of another kind of freedom, different from the freedom of Abstract Expressionism—one controlled by endlessly inventive, rational thought, rather than pure emotion.

Stella was familiar with Islamic art, and seems to have taken his aesthetic cue from a passage referring to it in the widely known and highly influential book, *The Life of Forms* by Henri Focillon. Discussing Moslem ornament, Focillon argued that the very rigorousness of its rules challenged artists to make countless ingenious variations. Based on mathematical reasoning and cold calculation, nevertheless, he wrote, "deep within them, a sort of fever seems to goad on and to multiply the shapes; some mysterious genius of complication interlocks, enfolds, disorganizes, and reorganizes the entire labyrinth." Each shape, he concludes, "both withholds the secret and exposes the reality of an immense number of possibilities." His book was published in 1928.

One could hardly find a better description of Stella's paintings and the kind of aesthetic reward they offer. Their large size precludes the viewer from taking them in holistically, and the resulting forced shifting of the eyes produces fascinating visual effects that fulfill the nineteenth-century insight that painting reaches beyond the senses "to that region of the imagination which is supposed to be under the exclusive dominion of music."

# Minimalism

Stella's black pin-stripe paintings with their interior rectangles repeating the shape of the frame as they diminished in size were essentially structural in concept. They lead directly into Minimalism, the logical conclusion of the reductivist tendencies of modernist art which step by step stripped from the work of art all of its traditional features. This stringent, stripped-bare art has its roots in the constructivist current of modernism. As the name implies, Minimalism refers to art that approaches zero-content and zero pictorialism.

The Minimalist image is holistic, avoids the illusionism of movement across its surface or into depth, and has been called "cool." The use of the term highlights a sensibility of the sixties that gives insight into the relationship of high-culture Minimalist art to a dominant feature of the most popular of the popular arts, television. The anti-elitist pressure of the past quarter-century has been a significant influence among some modernist artists, but did not surface as an important issue in Minimalism. It should be recognized, now, however, that Minimalism's "cool" sensibility relates it to the popular art of television, therefore relating it also to the very different but contemporary movement, Pop art, which also is related to popular art: things related to the same thing are related to each other. Furthermore, not only does the "cool" sensibility act as a bridge between Minimalism and Pop art but reductiveness, too, serves as a bridge between these very different kinds of art: reductiveness, we have said, is a feature of Minimalism; Pop art, as we shall see, is also reductive in the sense that in appropriating images and objects from everyday life—images and objects that are integral and familiar to popular culture—it makes, apparently, only minimum changes in them. However unwittingly, Minimalism's sensibility had moved high art closer to popular art. One can now see that a phenomenon of the sixties was the narrowing of the gap between high and popular art.

The term "cool" comes from the writings of Marshall McLuhan, one of the most influential thinkers of the decade of the sixties, and thus contemporary with Minimalist art. McLuhan observed that a medium that gives relatively little information, like cartoons or television, is "cool." Such a medium forces close attention because the viewer or listener must fill in what is not given. A medium such as radio, according to McLuhan, is "hot" because it is full of data. The latter allows a passive attitude, the former requires active participation. The question of McLuhan's possible influence on the visual arts of the sixties is problematic; at the very least, however, he did provide insights useful to art criticism at the time and that now allow the perception of the cultural link of Minimalism to television, as well as to other manifestations of popular culture.

Minimalism as a medium can be said to give very little information, and thus demands from the viewer the utmost attention to its every nuance if communication is to be effected. Thus it is, like television, a "cool" medium. Minimalist art furthermore *looks* cool. It is serene, classically well-balanced, emotionally restrained, and lacking in expressionistic evidence of process, the reverse of gestural Abstract Expressionism.

With Minimalism, pure visibility arrived at its farthest point, challenged from all sides by work such as Reinhardt's, with its image almost invisible, and Newman's, with color so vast in expanse and intensity that viewing it, one could feel one's self turning the same color as the canvas, suggesting if the whole world were red, or blue, or yellow, its forms would become invisible, leaving us only with the perception of surface color—if, indeed we could see anything. Perhaps if visibility were perfectly purified the effect would be invisibility.

It is in the work of Agnes Martin (1912– ) that visibility is seen in its most purified state. No longer a young artist when she arrived in New York in the early sixties, she had a body of more or less conventional modernist works behind her. In New York she began the process of reduction that eventually led to the creation of her signature style—images of geometric grids of all-over, nuanced color, with differentiations so finely tuned as to be nearly imperceptible. Characteristic is her *Night Sea* (1963) (Arnason clpl 257), in which the surface appears to emit an aura of light. Although nature seems to be her inspiration, it is nature dematerialized as feeling and further refined as concept, to judge from what she has said about her work. "My paintings have neither objects, nor space, nor time, not anything—no forms. They are light, lightness, about merging, about formlessness breaking down form. . . . You wouldn't think of form by the ocean." Martin's poetic perception has profound philosophical echoes. While it is true that the ocean has boundaries, and surface, this is not the way one perceives it, nor thinks about it, nor remembers it. It is "formless," as all of nature is, without a human perceiver and knower to interpret it. Martin's grids impose form on formlessness, which is to say, she transforms nature into art—in a way that is both minimal and yet unequivocal. The image she offers of orderliness is not confined to what we see but clearly implies an orderly system that continues beyond the picture plane.

Orderliness as one of the characteristics of Minimalism is seen in a different version, called Systemic Art by Lawrence Alloway, where a single color field carries a simple motif of a different color, not too brilliant in contrast, which, like a module, is repeated, and is repeatable serially in a potentially infinite extension, as in Paul Feeley's *Minoa* (Alloway, *Topics,* fig. 23). One may be reminded of the infinitely expansive universe implied in the star-studded sky of the fifth-century Mausoleum of Galla Placidia at Ravenna (Gardner, p. 267).

Sculpture is three-dimensional and cannot in fact literally disappear. Aethestically, however, it can be said to disappear, *as sculpture,* when its three-dimensional nature is compromised to the point that it does not make its appeal to the viewer's tactile sense, or sense of experiential space, as happens with Donald Judd's series of identical, light-reflecting box shapes. This is evident in the work of Sol Lewitt (1928– ) whose rigidly controlled grids are like three-dimensional Agnes Martins. Although, like *Sculpture Series "A"* (1967) (Arnason fig. 825), they are sometimes executed in very large size so that they cover large spaces, their tactile value is minimal.

One of the most intellectually exciting and visually provoking of artists who came to the attention of the art world in the sixties is Robert Morris (1931– ), whose art at that time was Minimalist; Michael Wood exhibited his mirrored cubes and other works in the program. Morris has explored many avenues of modernism, as you saw, and has worked with materials that do call on our tactile responses, such as his pieces made of felt. Charged with philosophical wit, Morris's work challenges the authority of the scientific conception of the world as objective in a number of images as penetrating as they are plain funny. In his *I-Box,* he confounds object and subject: The box is a kind of closet designed with the capital letter I on the door, facing the viewer—the symbol, that is, for the person as subject, as in "I think, therefore I am." When the door is open one sees the photograph of the "real" I, that is, the nude artist, as the object inside the box. But the letter I is also a "real" I, and the object of the viewer's attention, while the photograph is not "real" since it is only a representation of the subject. Understanding both realities depends on the context in which they are seen. In another work, Morris hangs three rulers, each marked off with "thirty inches," but each differing from the others in length. Objective standards, as commonly understood, are human artifacts, variable, therefore, as such. In his *Corner Piece,* Morris again faces the viewer with the problem of contextual perception: the three-dimensional form is placed in the right-angled intersection of two walls so that the intersection is hidden; the three-dimensional form appears flat, and the "absolute" right-angle corner disappears, thus demonstrating that the shape of the room is dependent on the viewer's subjective perception, with its changing mental and optical focus—a lesson adumbrated, it seems, by Matisse in his *Red Studio* (1911) (Arnason clpl 42), in which one sees that the upper part of the back wall appears straight across, while on the floor level at the left a corner is implied.

## Pop Art

At the opposite end of the sensibility spectrum, up popped Pop and "Junk art," somewhat alike in their mockery of consumer-society values. A term invented by Lawrence Alloway, "Junk art" referred to objects made from castaway, factory-made objects that were once useful, bright, and shiny. Retrieving them from the junkpile of broken, useless, unwanted things, the artist reassembled them or reformed them into works of art. As

such, they acquired a new value—possibly higher, in money value, than they had ever previously had—while retaining their *uselessness,* thus ironically making uselessness valuable. The vast cemeteries of abandoned, cannibalized, crushed autos that do not beautify the American landscape were the inexhaustible "quarries" that provided John Chamberlain (1927– ) with the raw material of his sculpture. He assembled ragged-edged, torn pieces of rusted, discolored metal, and painted them so that the pieces looked like large gestural brushstrokes. His sculpture suggested Abstract Expressionist painting that had somehow been inflated into three dimensions, as seen in *Essex* (1960) (Arnason clpl 169). Junk material lent itself, surprisingly, to monumental treatment in the work of Louise Nevelson (1900–1988). Using old boxes, crates, furniture parts and other discarded materials, Nevelson built wall-size constructions which in the late fifties and sixties she painted black. *Black Cord* (1964) **(J 1014)** demonstrates the dizzingly variety of sizes and shapes which she was able to orchestrate into a unified whole. Her masterful control of this material is achieved through her method of using a basic grid of repeated verticals and horizontals, as in Analytical Cubism, which she seems to have married happily to Mondrian's Neo-Plasticism. Each construction is a virtuoso performance of playing sizes and shapes against each other, and embodies much of modernist art history; in addition to Cubism and Neo-Plasticism one perceives her links to Abstract Expressionism (wall-size, all-over composition), Color Field (optically illusionistic, flatly painted, open, holistic design) and Pop (use of discarded material). In subsequent years, Nevelson painted her works in all-over gold, and all-over white, the latter of which is most spectacularly exemplified in the magnificent *Chapel of the Good Shepherd* in the church of St. Peter's in the City Corp building in New York, where in 1977 she created a total environment (Arnason fig. 737). Wood was unsuitable for outdoor sculpture, and Nevelson has successfully worked with various metals to execute her numerous commissions for monumental public works. *Dawn Shadows* (1982) (Arnason fig. 736), in Chicago, is thirty feet high, made of steel, and painted black. This, like all of her later work, is no longer in the Junk or Pop mode.

Leading the way in America into Pop art were two artists whose turn away from Abstract Expressionism contributed to the revival of tactility and figurative imagery, each in different ways: Robert Rauschenberg (1925– ) through an extension of collage, and Jasper Johns (1930– ) through his adoption of commonplace images, targets, flags, and maps whose inherent noncommital content and flatness he compromised by a sensual handling of the paint surface and/or the incorporation of three-dimensional elements.

The crucial experience in Rauschenberg's formation as an artist was his attendance at Black Mountain College in North Carolina and his coming into contact there with John Cage. Black Mountain College itself was a liberating experience: there were no requirements, no exams, the curriculum was centered on the arts, and the faculty included the Director, Josef Albers, and, coming and going, such innovative artists as Merce Cunningham and John Cage with both of whom Rauschenberg has had an ongoing professional relationship. Along with a very small but growing number of artists and theorists who found precedents in the Futurist Manifestoes, Cage believed that all of life was material for art. It was art's task to heighten the everyday awareness of the commonplace, to make one conscious of one's experiences and senses—to live, that is, on a higher plane of consciousness. He was, therefore, opposed to the contemporary aesthetic attitude of the Abstract Expressionists whose effort was to delve below consciousness to find the unique truth in the unlearned, the untaught perceptions that furnished the psyche. Curiously, both attitudes end up in the same place—in the person of the individual, who is the "discoverer" and "maker" of his/her own world—the "me" of the modernist value scale. Cage's aesthetics of heterogeneity, reflecting the wide-angle vision of modern experience which allows us to take in the whole world, the important and the trivial almost simultaneously, can be seen embodied in the work of Robert Rauschenberg.

Rauschenberg's significance was established in the fifties with such works as *The Bed* (1955), *Monogram* (1959) (Arnason figs. 696, 697) and *Odalisk* (1955–58) (**J clpl 159).** It is immediately evident that his art historical place is in the Dada tradition, and works by Duchamp, Miró, and Schwitters come to mind. What is also evident is the drip and gestural brushwork of Abstract Expressionism, which gives his work an entirely different look from that of his earlier predecessors. He called these assemblages of paper, fabric, paint, plus a large inventory of objects, "combines." *Monogram* is a wildly improbable combination of an angora goat with a tire around its middle, mounted on a platform that is collaged, and painted somewhat like an Abstract Expressionist work. The platform serves as a grazing pasture for the goat. Rauschenberg stresses the unreadability of his work, and surely the images are puzzling and resist interpretation. However, it has been pointed out that as a child he kept pets, including a rooster and a goat, and possibly his choice of objects reflects an autobiographical element in his work. One wonders if, in the manner of Duchamp, Rauschenberg is punning with his *Monogram,* as he did with *Odalisk,* a pun which pairs odalisque, a female harem slave, with obelisk, a four-sided pillar with slightly tapering sides, and with *Lake Placid Glori-Fried Yarns from New England* (1971) (Arnason fig. 698). A number of writers have indeed called the angora goat a ram (which is a male sheep), and a monogram is a design of two elements combined, e.g., monog/ram; furthermore, monogamy is a zoological term that refers to pairing with a single mate—two elements *combined*.

Interpretations aside, Rauschenberg's combines bring together unrelated objects—mostly junk—as if they had appeared at random from among the infinite objects in the phenomenal world. Within the work of art they both retain and loose their original identity, in the manner of "readymades" or "found" art, and as a group they defy general classifications of any kind. They differ in textures, both real and as represented in the collaged reproductions; they differ in category as things made of organic and inorganic materials; they differ in the part of the world to which they belonged, nature or art. They are unified only by the artistic will of the artist. Their incongruity serves to sharpen the viewer's awareness of everything about them, their physical, psychological, intellectual nature of being-in-the-world. This is the aesthetics of heterogeneity carried to a new level of randomness. Rauschenberg's work forced new critical questioning of the nature of art and its problematic frontier with phenomenal reality.

Jasper Johns's work came to public attention at the same time as Rauschenberg's, his close friend and studio neighbor. His carefully painted and composed representations of flags and targets, such as *Flag* (1954) and *Target with Plaster Casts* (1955) (Arnason figs. 699, 700) caused as much consternation as Rauschenberg's messy and dilapidated looking objects. For many centuries people had been accustomed to think of the imitation of natural or man-made objects as the primary goal of art: Gainsborough's superb translations of silks and satins and Copley's near-miraculous differentiations of wood, leather, and metal are only two among the most skillful of legions of artists. What was it about Johns's targets and flags that was so uncomfortably new? First in importance of annoyance, most likely, was the subject. A flag, all by itself, just the banner, did not seem to be an appropriate object to "imitate." The manner of painting was probably equally disturbing. *Flag* gives the viewer what the title announces, and even more; it is an accurate representation of the *American* flag. And yet, it does not *look* like a *painting* of a flag: the image is co-extensive with the canvas, and its rigidity seems unnatural. Johns has said that the flag as a motif came to him in a dream, and possibly that helps to explain the unreality of the apparently real. The image is abstracted from life, like a dream image.

Johns has denied being a Pop artist, although some of his imagery doubtless falls into the definition of Pop art, which, according to Lawrence Alloway "deals with material that already exists as signs [in popular culture]: photographs, brand goods, comics—that is to say, with precoded material. The subject of Pop art, at one level, is known to the spectator in advance of seeing the use the artist makes of it. Andy Warhol's Campbell's soup cans, Roy Lichtenstein's comic strips are known either by name or by type, and their source remains legible in the work of art." Pop art, moreover, has "a deadpan" look, as if its factual, objective, and impersonal appearance is presented without comment, although it is often loaded with irony (Alloway, *American Pop Art,* 1974, p. 7ff.). The balance between sociological statement and artistic concerns differs from artist to artist, but every one of them has been concerned primarily with the formal properties of art—space, color, line, form, texture—and with the issue of just how far one can go in manipulating these properties and still remain in the realm of art.

Pop art broke with traditional ideas of picture-making and sculpture by incorporating three-dimensional or free-standing objects within a painting or within its presumed space, or by applying paint to three-dimensional objects; by using industrial materials and techniques, including having works manufactured by machine; by "imitating" man-made objects in the popular environment; and by denying the value of any person or thing as superior to any other person or thing as material for a work of art. We see, then, that the commitment to art-for-art's sake led through pure visibility to the gradual, but eventually complete, disappearance of objects. Finally, by reacting against pure visibility, it led to the revival of the object, but now with the complete democratizing of all objects as appropriate aesthetic subjects.

By these criteria, Johns's Flag, Map, and Number paintings can be classified only tangentially, if at all, as Pop art. Some of his work, however, such as *Painted Bronze* (1960) **(G 22.87),** does fit the definition requirements. Johns explained how he happened on this motif: he had heard that Willem De Kooning had remarked about the prominent modern art dealer Leo Castelli that "you could give him two beer cans and he could sell them." Johns, seeing the connection with motifs that he was using—flashlights and light bulbs—made the beer can casts and indeed, Castelli did sell them. One has only to think of the kings and popes who have been made immortal in bronze to realize how closely our culture's leveling process is reflected in its art.

Pop art appeared first in England, where Richard Hamilton (1922–  ) made one of its earliest images, the small collage *Just What Is It that Makes Today's Homes So Different, So Appealing?* **(G 22.87; H&F 21.13).** Packed with popular consumer items, the work is composed of the ingredients listed by Hamilton in his recipe for the new, as yet unnamed art: "popularity, transcience, expendability, wit, sexiness, gimmickry and glamor" (Hunter, p. 333). It has been pointed out that the contemporary Beatles phenomenon was composed of similar material. The term Pop art was invented in 1958 in an article by Lawrence Alloway, at that time an English critic (now American). He used it "to refer approvingly to the products of the mass media," seeing those products as art, as "part of an expansionist aesthetic with a place for both abstract expressionism and Hollywood, the Bauhaus and Detroit styling" (Alloway, *American Pop,* p. 1). In the United States, however, as the American Pop artists began to emerge at the beginning of the sixties, the term excluded commercial products and was used to refer only to high art. It signified the critical recognition that the commonplace signs and objects of everyday experience had been absorbed into subject matter by artists who were

as serious about their aesthetic purpose as Cézanne—only the aesthetic sensibility had changed.

An important aspect of Pop art is its mockery of middle-class values. Modern artists have represented a counter-culture—with values allied both to socioeconomic have-nots and with a section of the very rich; both classes have in common a total indifference to middle-class values. The all-pervasive permissiveness of the period of the thirties and forties, however, led the art-viewing public to an attitude of acceptance (even, rather quickly, of Abstract Expressionism) so that artists found it difficult to exercise their historically given right to "épater le bourgoisie"—shock the middle-class—the stated goal of modernists for more than a half-century. It was becoming increasingly hard to shock anybody. Patently low-brow art successfully, although only briefly, of course, achieved this goal—comic strips and soup cans, so it seemed at first, *could not be a subject for art;* art had to be beautiful and highminded, as, it had now become clear, Abstract Expressionism was. For a while the artists could enjoy their great joke, but soon the middle-class public learned that Pop art only *appeared* to be slick—easy to do, satisfied with clichés and banality—and learned that *subject matter* was irrelevant for art. All important was the *concept* and *how* the concept was executed. The attempt to shock once again petered out into acceptance, to the vexation of artists like Robert Morris, who wrote with rueful irony in 1969, "At the present time the culture is engaged in the hostile and deadly act of immediate acceptance of all new perceptual art moves, absorbing through institutionized recognition every art act" (Rose, p. 214). Meanwhile, new patrons appeared, in tune with this aspect of sixties art, and the artists went on with their work, which was, as Lichtenstein shows us, to compose formal compositions, or, as Rauschenberg shows us, to make non-relational works that achieved unity through the power of the artistic will.

Roy Lichtenstein (1923–  ) classically elegant, intellectually composed paintings have the pictorial power of works by Ingres. They are also penetrating demonstrations—lectures in paint—that illuminate a number of the fundamental issues of modern art. From the early comic-strip paintings, which dealt with the most low-brow of subjects, through the images of classical architecture, and copies of masterpieces by the greatest artists in the Western tradition, he has been concerned, for example, with the organization of perception, the problem of "building a unified pattern of seeing" (Russell/Gablik, p. 92). In *Girl at Piano* (1963) **(J 984),** the supposed objects—girl, piano fragment, back wall—are all cut by the picture plane, into which they are thus subsumed. The curvilinear shapes that echo each other with variations here and there—piano, shadow, dress folds, necklace, lips, eyes, brows, hair—are regularized as the frame of the balloon of lettering (printed words) which since Cubism we have been able to understand as a means of assimilating an image to its ground. *Lettering implies a flat surface,* a surface on which one can write or print. We see the tension between the "objects" and the "background" with startling clarity.

Optical flatness is demonstrated in a new way, in Lichtenstein's painting: whereas Johns had "imitated" flat *objects;* Lichtenstein "imitated" flat *images.* Comic strips were printed matter, and so were many of the other motifs he used—prints of the Parthenon, prints after Matisse, Picasso, Monet, and others. Examples include *Whaam!* (1963) (Arnason fig. 707) and *Artist's Studio: The Dance* (1974) (Arnason clpl 220), the latter based on Matisse's *Still Life with the "Dance."* His sense of humor is expressed with exquisite grace in *Big Painting* (1965) (**H&F 21.12;** Arnason fig. 708), a comment on the all-important brushstroke of Abstract Expressionism.

Lichtenstein has also made use of the essentially two-dimensional Art Deco architectural motifs of the thirties. Using previously invented designs (turning upside down the formerly prized value of originality of invention), Lichtenstein subjected them to *stylistic* re-invention and in so doing puns aesthetically on the nature of originals and prints: He transforms a Picasso print after a Picasso painting into a Lichtenstein painting so that his source, the Picasso print, becomes the "original" image; he transforms a comic-strip print that was only one frame in a series of actions into a single painting, a stop-action act that drains the image of its original context and, therefore, drains it of its meaning, since meaning is always context-dependent. Lichtenstein demonstrates how both iconography and style are thus re-formed. Moreover, although use of a known image constitutes a cliché, its *deliberate* choice and stylization estranges it from banality and ends by conferring on the commonplace the flavor of the exotic.

Also classicizing in form and spirit is the painting and sculpture of Robert Indiana (1928– ). Indeed, he referred to his early constructions as "Herms," a fact worth some consideration. A "herm" was a vertical pillar surmounted by a head of Hermes, the Olympian messenger god who was also guardian of boundaries and roads. Indiana has been a "messenger artist," using words to extend his visual expression, and his desire to communicate through language is explicit in his remark, "I really would like to communicate with everyone on the face of the world." His imagery, moreover, has dealt insistently with roads, through such roadside "signs" as *The Demuth Five* (1963) **(J 982),** and with boundaries, depicted as maps of states. Given the pervasiveness of autobiographical content in his art, one may guess that ultimately the artist identifies himself with the ancient Olympian god of messages, roads, and boundaries.

*The Demuth Five,* an homage to Charles Demuth, whose *I Saw the Figure 5 in Gold* was, in 1963, Indiana's favorite American painting in the Metropolitan Museum. As is characteristic of Indiana's work in the 1960s, this work is classically symmetrical around a central axis. The five squares each contain a five-point (American) star

inscribed symmetrically in a circle, recalling Leonardo da Vinci's famous *Study of the Human Body,* the paradigm image of rational order, measure, and balance, the hallmarks of Classicism. Even the color, despite the vivid red, is classically restrained in effect, controlled by the grey background. The cruciform shape confers monumentality on the image, and possibly recapitulates Indiana's early *Crucifixion,* a mural inspired by his early job at the Cathedral of St. John the Divine, composed of forty-four joined pieces of paper. It is notable that modernists have seldom turned their back on the traditions of Western art. Indiana's *Crucifixion* is a case in point; the Futurists are the only important exception, and Italian art, following them, turned back to Giotto and the fifteenth-century masters. An outstanding characteristic of the 1980s, as we shall presently see, has been "appropriation" of past styles and even particular artists. Intimate knowledge of art history has always been a significant element in the personal development of an artist.

Indiana produced one of the two most famous images produced by Pop art, *Love,* the other being Andy Warhol's *Campbell Soup* (1965) (Russell/Gablick fig. 96). With *Love,* the artist's aspiration "to communicate with everyone on the face of the world" seems, to his surprise, to have been realized. Hard-edged, spare, like the work of his friend Ellsworth Kelly, who exerted the most influence on his art (Kelly, *Red, Blue, Green* (1963) **[G 22.77]**), Indiana is close to being a Minimalist with a message.

If Lichtenstein and Indiana represent classicizing tendencies in Pop art, one is tempted to say that Claes Oldenburg (1926– ) is a master in the baroque tradition. The appeal to the senses, the involvement of the viewer in the work of art, the irregularity of contours, the use of illusionistic devices, the creation of public monumental sculpture that characterize the work of Bernini are equally attributes of Oldenburg's art. There is an important difference, however: Bernini made images that perfectly harmonized with the values of his society, as exemplified by the iconography of such public works as his *Four Rivers Fountain* at the center of Piazza Navona, or his *Barcaccia Fountain* at the foot of the Spanish Steps. Oldenberg made images that were meant to shock, or even antagonize his society by proposing antithetical values. In his environmental work *Street* (1960), he offered figures and objects made of paper, wood, and wire, broken and dun-colored, which projected from the wall, hung from the ceiling, lay on the floor, and in every way interacted with the space of the gallery and with the viewer, whose presence immersed him/her in the shabby yet colorful street scene of lower eastside Manhattan, inhabited by society's disenfranchised—bums, drunks, prostitutes, and the like. The creation of total environments did not emerge in the sixties for the first time in the history of art: in the Villa of Mysteries at Pompeii **(J clpl 24; G 6.28),** images of Dionysian ritual wrapped the walls to surround believers in the cult; in Early Christian and Medieval art, church mosaics and stained glass such as at

Chartres represented depictions of the heavenly environment into which the Christian believer could enter temporarily and eventually, they could hope, eternally. These environments were reverent and religious, of course, in keeping with the dominant mind-set of the time. Sixties environments by contrast were irreverent and secular. Looking back to the eighteenth-century secularization of art, we see how that trend, which emotionally *echoed* religious art while retaining its forms, has, in our time, arrived at emotionally rejecting or spoofing it. Admittedly, this would not be apparent to one who was not familiar with the art historical reference any more than, say, the prison scene in Tom Wolfe's best-seller *The Bonfire of the Vanities* would call up Dante's *Inferno* to one who was not familiar with it.

Oldenburg has said that he believes eroticism is the basis of art, and he tends to think of form in terms of male/female. It is thus not by accident that most of his sculptures suggest sexual images, as a glance through any Oldenburg exhibition catalogue would confirm. His Chaplinesque humour, baggy and monumental, is sensationally realized in his "urban monuments." His proposals for these public enhancements, few of which, understandably, have been constructed, include a toilet-ball float for the Thames River, a Good-Humor bar for New York's Park Avenue, Scissors for Washington, D.C., "to replace the Washington Obelisk"—all built at colossal scale like the actual monument in Philadelphia, *Clothespin* (1976) **(G 22.100)**, a wildly funny, stately parody of Brancusi's *The Kiss* (Arnason fig. 199), and the *Swiss Army Knife* installed in the courtyard at the Musée Nationale d'Art Moderne Centre Pompidou in Paris. Classical in form, these works are pure baroque in their exaggerations.

One of the most impressive of Pop art paintings, in concept as well as size, is *F-111* (1965) (Arnason fig. 709; Hughes pl. 235) by James Rosenquist (1933–  ). Ten feet high by eighty-six feet in length, the painting derives from the artist's commercial work as a billboard painter of advertisements that had to scream loudly to catch the attention of the crowds that hurried on their way across New York's Times Square. The figures had to be gigantically enlarged in order to be seen from the street level far below, and the artist had to grasp mentally the entire image while painting one section of curving red lips that stretched perhaps twenty feet across the board. Painting fragments became his daily experience.

*F-111*—the title is the name of a fighter jet plane—is a series of fragments in psychedelic color on fifty-one interlocking pieces. Garishly bright Day-Glo pink and vulgar chartreuse make the artist's statement about the nature of our consumer culture generally, and the imagery specifically was meant to protest against the huge military spending and the Vietnam War. The mélange of unrelated objects—unrelated except as they add up to his single, coherent, sardonic view—includes the plane's fuselage, a field of orange-colored spaghetti that looks like human guts, an acid-colored beach umbrella (mushroom-shaped) surrounded by the bubbling red residue from an atomic blast, and the painting's most disturbing image, the cloyingly cute face of a little girl with a saccharine red-lipped smile beneath a metal hairdryer that resembles a bullet or the nose of a jet. Installed in its entirety, the painting was meant to surround the viewer and thus belongs to the development of environmental art.

Irreverence is often colored with black humor in Pop art. Amusing as the "double-takes" may be, outright funny as are the wild associations that impact on our perceptions, the message that the modern consumer society has trivialized life by reducing human relationships to the comic strip (or soap opera) level by reducing communication to one-syllable words, by flattening all natural and human-made phenomena onto one plane of significance, by aggrandizing the commonplace, is essentially sinister. This anti-humanist nature of our mechanized society was the major subject matter of Andy Warhol's row upon row of soup cans and Coca-Cola bottles and Marilyn Monroes. See, for example, *200 Soup Cans* (1962) (Huges pl. 230); *Green Coca-Cola Bottles* (1962) (Hunter fig. 558); and *Marilyn Monroe Diptych* (1962) (Hughes pl. 232). (The student should consider that Edward Hopper's name has often been invoked as an ancestor of Pop art, and in this light look at Hopper's *Early Sunday Morning* (1930) **(J 154.)** Warhol's cans and bottles are not situated on shelves in a supermarket; they have no environment and have thus been converted into symbols; the image of Marilyn Monroe is similarly abstracted, as the sex symbol she was, but here rendered without the famous body. The sexual symbolism is thus undermined and replaced by machine symbolism; like the machine-made cans and bottles, Marilyn, too is packaged, contained in a series of frames that recall a camera strip. By making his image coextensive with the canvas, like Jasper Johns' flags, Warhol, too, subverts the notion of "imitation" in art.

Warhol drew much of his imagery from daily life, as reported sensationally in the press. His irony is in transforming violence and sensationalism into boring repetition, banality, and cliché, thereby draining from the "commonplace" tragedies of everyday life—car crashes, and other violent deaths—their real human anguish, as he does in *Suicide* (1963) (Hughes pl. 231).

At the opposite end of the emotional scale are the tableaux of Edward Kienholtz (1927–  ) which nevertheless share with Warhol a sense of the sinister in modern life. His subjects include abortion, insanity, quirky sexuality, and death. Like the Oldenburg of *Bedroom Ensemble,* to be viewed from the outside (unlike audience-participatory environments), Kienholtz invents a set in which a narrative is implied, but he includes figures in his brutal scenes. His grisly *The State Hospital* **(J clpl 160)** shows an emaciated old man strapped to the lower level of a double-decker banged-up cot. His head is a fish bowl, containing live goldfish. On the upper level of the cot lies his duplicate, surrounded, however, by a comic strip balloon stemming from the "head" below, as if the old man is telling us what he has been reduced to. The bed pan alludes to bodily functions, suggesting that the dying man is lying between bodily and mental activity. *The Wait* (1964–65) (Whitney Museum) offers a skeleton of a woman who has waited "forever," sitting in her "living room" surrounded by the memorabilia of her life. The commonplace objects of this lower-middle-class, emphatically American home, and the satiric comment they make about American values—marital fidelity (husband's oval portrait), patriotism (son's photo in uniform), womanly activities (sewing basket), responsibility (canary in a birdcage), sentimentality (roses in the wallpaper)—gives Keinholtz the position of bridging Pop art and environment art. He exemplifies the movement "off the wall," which comprises Pop, Environment, Assemblage, Happenings (also called performance art), and Earthworks.

In 1958 Allan Kaprow invented Happenings, which had roots in Futurist and Dada manifestations. Its vintage years in the United States lie between 1959 and 1961 and its emergence at that time signals an important shift in aesthetic aims. The dominating flatness aesthetic of modernism began to be countered by artists who started to project images into space, which led eventually to creating total environments, and ultimately to Happenings, to performing the process of making art—not privately, like Pollock, but publicly.

In Happenings, the breakdown between art space and viewer space was complete. The viewer became a full participant, and was expected to enter the environment, to move around in it, and to move things in it from one place to another, thereby changing the composition. In addition to their artistic genealogy, Happenings should be considered in the light of the modernist theatre, particularly the Theatre of the Absurd, which developed in Paris after World War II in the plays of Samuel Beckett, Jean Genet, and Eugene Ionescu, among others. Linked to the existentialist philosophy of Albert Camus and Jean-Paul Sartre, which held that the universe was not rational but "absurd," thus placing on humans the obligation to put meaning into life through intentional actions, Happenings can be seen in this light to be related to Abstract Expressionism; both assumed the importance of human interaction with the work of art. On the other hand, Happenings look back to Dada, whereas Abstract Expressionism was created within the Surrealist mode. A number of Pop artists have been involved in performance art—Rauschenberg, Oldenburg, Jim Dine, and Warhol among them.

In Europe, Happenings tended to express extreme violence and degradation. Yves Klein (1928–1962) produced one of the more memorable of events when he directed the performance in which naked women were smeared with "International Klein blue," his trademark, then pulled and rolled around on a canvas on the floor.

Human bodily functions were the subject of a number of other events by various artists in Germany. The most influential of the European Performance-Assemblage artists is Joseph Beuys (1921– ), a Luftwaffe pilot in World War II who was in his forties when he began his career in art. *The Pack* (Hughes pl. 245) is an autobiographical image that celebrates his survival after his plane had been shot down over the Crimea in the dead of winter during the war and he had been given up for lost. As it turned out, he had been rescued and pulled on a sled to safety by Tartar nomads, who wrapped him half-frozen, more dead than alive, in felt, and fed him on fat. *The Pack* comprises twenty sleds attached to a Volkswagen bus, each sled equipped with a roll of felt blanket, pieces of fat, and a flashlight. Felt and fat have remained, for Beuys, prime symbols of the will to survive: With appalling effect he created a glass coffin-shaped "reliquary" which contains a random arrangement of blocks of fat on a beat-up hot plate, putrified sausage, a stuffed rat, and an engraving of the concentration camp at Auschwitz with its baleful rows of blockhouses.

## Earthworks

In terms of style, Earthwork art can be seen as the logical extension of the move off the wall and out of the studio. Liberated from the constraints of studio, gallery, or even museum space, an artist's imaginative power might be matched by the near-boundlessness of the great outdoors; concepts could be infinitely enlarged. There were, in addition, cultural factors that entered into its emergence. The materialism surrounding the gallery and museum complex antagonized some artists who found distasteful the transformation of the art object into a commodity. (Indeed, one wonders why there did not develop some Pop version of the stock market, with artists as "stock." Those would-be collectors who could not afford to buy the artists' works could at least buy a share in the artists' market value.) Making Earthworks, or site-specific works (compositions that manipulated some feature of the place where it was located, such as outcroppings of rock, or foundations of an abandoned structure), seemed to offer the possibility of thwarting the private gallery-museum exhibition system. If there was no art object to exhibit and sell there would be an end of art as furniture, art as a pawn in the financial ambitions of dealers and the career ambitions of museum curators. Furthermore to account for the appearance of Earthwork art at this time, it should be remembered that popular scientific writing began to penetrate into the public consciousness with its warnings of spoiling and despoiling. People who had never thought much about it got the appalling message that human beings were plundering and polluting the earth. Watchdog environment groups accelerated their activities. The sixties began to register a heightened awareness of the earth, sea, and sky in the public generally, and most sharply in the artists' community.

Earthworks can be thought of as going back in time to Egypt and the rock-cut tombs of the provincial nobility in the late Old Kingdom and early Middle Kingdom period (ca. 2300–1800 B.C.). These burial sites were carved out of the mountain cliffs that embrace the wide fertile Nile valley. Possibly the most overwhelming of earthworks is that of the temple at Kailasa, in India, cut into a mountain from the *top down*. In a sense, all necropolises and cemeteries are "earthworks." Manipulating earth to make gardens is another aspect of earthworks. Twentieth-century Earthworks, however, are *works of art* because they involve form-making for its own sake by an artist whose intention it was to make a work of art. They have no function. They are sculptures, with the earth as medium, or, to link them with painting, they are landscapes made literal.

One of the most beautiful of Earthworks was *Spiral Jetty* (1970) by Robert Smithson (1938–1970) **(J clpl 170; G 22.84)**. Made of boulders and earth dug out at the site, this 1,500-foot-long, fifteen-foot-wide coil snakes into the Great Salt Lake (Utah) from its north shore. Visible in its entirety only from above, in a plane or helicopter, relatively few people have seen it at first hand, or ever will. Like Happenings, the fact of its existence is recorded in photography, not only as a finished work, but in the process of being built. The eons of time in which geologic earth movements take place, and natural forms are made, are evoked in the film in close-up shots of huge dinosaur-like machines chewing great rocks out of the natural site, to be loaded into trucks that will dump them into place in the artificial jetty. Thus the human artist competed with nature, and seemed to beat nature at is own earth-building game—but not for long. The great snake is eroding, as Smithson himself knew it would, and will eventually disappear as nature transforms what he formed.

Smithson had begun in the early sixties as a Minimalist, and his *Spiral Jetty* retains the holistic and spare nature of his earlier style. A more flamboyant Earthworks artist is Christo (Christo Javacheff, 1935–   ), who interprets the modern world, not implausibly, in terms of packaging and megalomania. Putting the two cultural phenomena together, he arrived at the concept of megalo-packaging, and has wrapped enormous extents of earth and water into packages. In 1968–69 he wrapped one mile of the coastline at Little Bay, Australia, in woven polypropylene, tied with rope. Between 1980 and 1983 he worked on *Surrounded Islands* **(J clpl 171,** preparatory drawing; Hunter fig. 695). Using a small army of workers and specialists in various fields of nature studies, he surrounded eleven small islands in Biscayne Bay, off of Miami, Florida, with six million square feet of polypropylene, dyed the characteristic Florida flamingo pink. Spectators were taken up in helicopters to view the finished work, and were thrilled with the effect of these giant blossoms floating on the water, comparing them to Monet's waterlily paintings, which, indeed, the artist has acknowledged as his inspiration.

## The Figurative Tradition in Post-War Art

Modernist art has reflected a kind of dialogue among artists, and between art generations. It is as if one proposal has evoked a counter proposal, or further comment, as, for example, Pop art, brash and irreverent, gave answer to Abstract Expressionism, passionate and dedicated, or Environmental art explored the implications of Pop, and Earthworks the implications of Environment. There were, moreover, in the sixties, artists intent on finding a synthesis of modernism with tradition, in dialogue, that is, with a pre-abstraction past. Among such can be numbered George Segal, Philip Pearlstein, Leon Golub, and Leonard Baskin, each of whom effected this synthesis in a different way.

George Segal (1924–   ) can be situated in the realist, genre tradition, closer to the painter Edward Hopper than to a sculptor predecessor. Marginally related to Pop art, Segal's work differs from it in tone, casting an aura of intense concentration around itself. It also differs from Environmental art, although his years of association with Allan Kaprow and Kaprow's theatrical Happenings probably contributed to his thinking of sculpture in pictorial terms as a *scene*. The power of Segal's images derives from the extraordinary tension created by the contrast between their ghostly, abstract whiteness, and the recognizable, familiar environment in which he places them as realistic human forms, and from his breathtaking mastery of the telling pose. *Cinema* (1963) **(J 986)** shows a man apparently taking down the last letter on a theatre marquee. Cast in plaster from a living person (Segal usually used his friends for models) the man stands somewhat awkwardly, his right arm and leg stretched forward, his left arm and leg keeping his balance as counterweights. An ordinary man. "If you saw him on the street you'd never turn around," as Helen Morgan once sang in *Show Boat,* "not the kind that you would find in a statue." Yet, the statue is there; turn the figure around and you will recognize the figure's remote ancestor, *Augustus of Primaporta* **(J 256; H&F clpl 5.25).** But the twentieth century is not interested in its Caesars as works of art, although in literature they still attract millions of readers—a fact worth pondering, although beyond the scope of this book. We find ourselves aesthetically engaged by the relatively powerless, like Segal's lonely unskilled man who works at night after the last show has begun. There is always a narrative implied in Segal's images—something has happened, something *will* happen—because despite their abstract whiteness, the always lonely figures with their momentary poses and gestures are imbedded in a life situation, as in the Hopperesque *The Diner* (1964–66); *Girl Putting on Scarab Necklace* (1975) (Arnason pl. 225 and fig. 726); and *The Restaurant* (1976) (Hunter fig. 700).

When Philip Pearlstein (1924–   ) left his native Pittsburgh and arrived in New York in 1949 he found

Abstract Expressionism dominating the art scene. Until 1961 he worked as a gestural painter but with clearly recognizable landscape motifs. Curiously, his figural painting since that time has retained something of the landscape mode: his figures, like some Greek sculpture, suggest allegorical images of mountain or river gods and goddesses, naturalized in America. Sometimes he seems to come very close to Hellenistic figures such as the late third-century *Dying Gaul* and *Barbarini Faun* **(J 201, 202).** Contemporary with the emergence of Minimalism, Pearlstein's compositions with nude figures in interiors reveal an analogous spareness and geometrization. Almost always cropping the figures, tipping and compressing the pictorial space, the artist has emphasized his sympathy with modernism. Although some critics speak of the sexuality of his figures, the present writer sees them more as still life objects, inert and arranged for compositional purposes. In his later work, in which he includes furniture and fabric with the nudes, as in *Two Female Models with Regency Sofa* (1974), he seems to be marrying modernism with some of the great masters of nineteenth-century painting, particularly Ingres and Gauguin. Pearlstein, however, calls attention to his art as *art* by stressing the studio environment, and the figure in the character of a model, no more titillating sensually than a Cézanne apple, whereas the nineteenth-century artists—even Gauguin—placed their figures in a lived-in environment, retaining their ties to the tradition of art as a reflection, if not imitation, of nature.

Leon Golub (1922–  ) has also looked long and hard at Classical and Hellenistic Greek sculpture; seeing his *Gigantomachy* one thinks of the metopes of the Parthenon **(G 5.50; H&F 4.19),** although his work more often recalls the mighty struggle of the gods and giants depicted on the *Altar of Zeus at Pergamum* **(J 205; H&F 4.19).** The comparison with sculpture is not arbitrary; the artist has described his method to the critic Donald Kuspit (*Leon Golub,* 1985) as "reminiscent of carving techniques, the removal and chipping away or carving out of surfaces, rebuilding (repainting) and then carving into the surfaces again. This effect is achieved by heavy overlays of paint which are then reduced by solvents, and carved by sculpture tools. What remains is a "sculptural image of man, ravaged and eroded but still retaining its essential existential structure." Golub's paintings, gargantuan in size, are figural analogues of both Jackson Pollock's Abstract Expressionist work and Color Field Painting. In spirit, however, they are closer to Goya and his perception of the brutality of which human beings are capable. Our modern, savaged world is pitilessly depicted in such works as Golub's *Mercenaries* (1980) **(G 22.96),** *Interrogation,* in which the torturers laugh at the victim, and *White Squad IV. El Salvador* (1983).

This had been a moment of caesura in the history of modern art, it now seems, looking back to 1959; a moment in which modernist energy seemed spent, and no one knew exactly what direction would prove fruitful.

### *Part 2*
### 1968 TO THE PRESENT

Nationalism is a modern concept. Unknown in the Middle Ages, nationalism put up its first shoots in the period of the Renaissance, and began to flower when France became a unified cultural and political entity in the course of the reign of Louis XIV. The organization of the western world into nations was Europe's main political business in the following century-and-a-half or so. Nations consolidated and expanded their dominion through the techniques of capitalism. The rise of socialism with its international goals challenged the nationalist capitalist structure which has, particularly since World War II, steadily itself been developing into internationalist capitalism—what some observers call "late capitalism." The political and cultural unification of the world has begun, we can surmise now, as clues to the future synthesis of socialism and capitalism on the international level have made their certain appearance. As so often (perhaps always) in the past, artists have been the first to sense the human future. The widely observed pluralism of art in the last, post-modernist twenty years—no one style has dominated, as Abstract Expressionism did in the forties and fifties—signifies the internationalization of art, as well as the art market. Post-modernism is the cultural vanguard of post-nationalism.

## Transitions

The parallel tendencies of constructivism and expressionism, and of abstraction and representation, have continued their sometimes fugal, sometimes harmonious relationship, with neither one nor the other dominating the art scene. The career of Richard Diebenkorn (1922–  ) has been unusual in that he has produced masterful works at both ends of the stylistic scales. His representational paintings are informed with his full control of the formal language of art; his abstractions convey the sense of landscape. Inherent in both is the aesthetic presence of Matisse, surely the single most important influence in his art. An artist with Diebenkorn's intellectual probing and artistic will finds affinities with, and learns from, many kinds of art and artists. Persian miniatures taught him the difference between scale and size—that one can convey the sense of vast space even on a small surface. He learned from his teachers, Daniel Mendelowitz, Erle Loran, David Park; he learned from Cézanne, and Picasso, and from Arthur Dove, and Edward Hopper, from Mark Rothko, and Clyfford Still and perhaps Milton Avery. But above all it was Matisse who gave him the artistic grasp that pervades his painting. His figurative work of the fifties and early sixties often takes up the theme of interior-exterior spaces juxtaposed, and one can compare his *Man and Woman in a Large Room* (1957) (Arnason fig. 765) with Matisses's interior-exterior compositions, such as *The Piano Lesson* (1916) (Arnason clpl 113). Another "lesson" from Matisse seems to have been how to make the repeated horizontals and verticals of the composition rhyme harmoniously as well as structurally with its framing edge. This is apparent in his figurative work as well as in the abstractions to which he turned in the mid-sixties.

Diebenkorn has lived and painted most of his life in California, and the luminous blues, golds, and greens of his painting are translations from nature. These are the colors that dominate his famous and justly admired *Ocean Park* series (Arnason clpl 241). Here one must recall Cézanne, whom Matisse called "the father of us all," and the tireless way in which he studied his "motif," Mont Ste. Victoire, finding in it endless structural relationships that inflected his emotional response, which he recorded in color and form. Also as with Cézanne, the *Ocean Park* series constitutes a kind of *summa* of years of reflection on the problems of making art. By means of their often subtle changes in composition within their almost invariable vertical format (the earlier, figurative paintings are almost always horizontal), they record the repetition and nuanced variations of emotional experience that the artist felt almost daily, driving along the California coastline, down the wide stretch of Santa Monica beachfront, to his studio.

Also California-based since 1968 is the English-born artist David Hockney (1937–  ), whose successful career dates back to London and the Pop art movement of the early sixties. His Pop imagery quickly moved from the appropriation of commercial products for his subject matter, as in his *Typhoo Tea* of 1962 (Russell/Gablik pl. XVI)—a shaped canvas "imitating" a box of tea—to the commonplaces of his own life and circle of family and friends. He has increasingly used photography in a variety of ways, notably for Cubist-inspired collages in which his Polaroid prints are fragmented and re-composed so that space slips back and forth, negating rational relationships. While his work demonstrates his ongoing awareness of contemporary styles and techniques, he has maintained a steady concern with subject matter, as exemplified in his well-known series of swimming pool paintings such as the early *A Bigger Splash* (1967) (Arnason clpl 213), which is typical of their brilliant, Matisse-like color. Also influential have been Japanese prints and Chinese scrolls, an influence reflected in a greater decorativeness, as in his great *Mulholland Drive* (1980), with its shifting perspectives.

Artists who, like Diebenkorn and Hockney, rose to prominence in the fifties, and stardom in the sixties, have held their preeminent status in the seventies and eighties. Thus the styles that emerged successively in the former period have co-existed in the latter, contributing to the pluralistic look of the contemporary art scene. Some artists have taken their imagery through radical changes, none more so than Frank Stella and Robert Morris who have both moved from their early minimalism to an explosive baroque (Stella, *Shards V*, 1983, Arnason clpl 251; Morris, *Untitled*, 1984, Arnason fig. 1057—a large series based on Holocaust imagery). Environmental and site-specific or installation art has continued to interest Christo, as we have seen, along with younger artists including, notably, Mary Miss (1944–  ) and Alice Aycock (1946–  ) (Arnason figs. 942, 943). Peter Shelton's *Floating Deadman* (1985–86) is an elaborate installation piece consisting of a lightweight building suspended two feet off the ground in the exhibition gallery. It sways and grates as one moves through it, counterbalanced by the weight of the "dead man," a figure cast in concrete, and a dozen or so other hanging objects, playing up the theme of vertigo and balance. Among those who have remained close to their early signature style is Claes Oldenburg, whose *Swiss Army Knife* (1972–77) intrigues visitors to the Museé D'Art Moderne Centre Georges Pompidou.

## New Museum Architecture

The increased public interest in art plus enormous private wealth that in former times would have gone into building private palaces have resulted in the construction of an astonishing number of new museums and museum wings during the past two decades. The Centre Pompidou, located in an area called the Beaubourg, in the heart of Paris, is one of the major monuments of modernist architecture, and climaxes modernism's obsession with openness—a phenomenon of our culture that is expressed in the exteriorization of formerly interior, private, or hidden elements or concerns: people speak openly now about matters that were once whispered—sex and sexuality, terminal disease, the imprisonment for fraud of a personal friend. The superior value of the open society over the closed society is taken for granted, with the corollary that freedom of the media means the right to total exposure of no matter what, or at what possible cost. Our glass-curtained cathedrals of finance assure the public that everything inside is open and above board. Once more it is Duchamp who, in painting, led the way with his *Passage of the Virgin to the Bride* (1912) (Arnason clpl 103), an image in which human and mechanical plumbing merge. Values have been turned inside-out.

The Centre Pompidou (**J clpl 175; G 22.117;** Arnason fig. 845), designed by Renzo Piano and Richard Rogers, is a huge glass-curtained shed, which makes it psychologically accessible—like our modern banks. Going beyond the glass-curtained skyscrapers, however, this transparent building has its functional parts turned, notice, like Duchamps' *Virgin,* inside-out—tubular structural frame, pipes, conduits, service ducts of various kinds, the escalator, all here do double duty on the exterior as function and decoration.

A second imperative of modernism in architecture has been the notion of flexibility: Since one cannot foresee all future possibilities, it is necessary to allow for changing needs and uses. At Beaubourg, while some of the original ideas directed toward achieving maximum flexibility of interior spaces have had to be curtailed, versatility is still inherent in the design. There are few spaces of fixed dimension and shape; works are not exhibited within compartmentalized galleries; the emphasis is on spatial flow, with no attempt to direct the viewer's steps one way or another, reflecting the modernist value of freedom—or permissiveness, depending on one's point of view.

In addition to transparency and flexibility, architectural functionalism, interpreted formally as the rejection of all non-structural elements, all ornamentation, has dominated Western architecture as an aesthetic obligation throughout the modern period. A second aspect of functionalism, however, its specific responsibility to *express* its function, has been more or less ignored. Ludwig Mies van der Rohe's designs were structural grids sheathed in glass, no matter what purpose the building was to serve, and this influential conception of architecture is the base on which the Centre Pompidou is structured. As some of its critics have observed (Alan Colquhoun, in *Centre Pompidou*), it is impossible to say what kind of objects it is meant to display. It is a kind of machine for exhibiting things, but its break with the traditional vocabulary of museum architecture is so complete that its function has been reduced to being a "container, and a servicing mechanism which recedes into the background when animated by people." Although some of its critics hold that the Centre Pompidou gives no message, has no ideology, the present writer differs: Centre Pompidou is ideologically committed to demystification—another feature of modernism. What you see is what you get. There is nothing mysterious about a museum or its contents, which are things like other things. Such is the message. It cannot be accepted on its simple terms any more than the similar message of a glass-walled Park Avenue bank. Money and art really are both quite mysterious, as everybody really knows.

During the decades when Mies's International Style provided the thesis for museum architecture beginning with the Mies-influenced 1939 Museum of Modern Art (New York) by Edward Durrell Stone and Philip Goodwin, the antithesis surfaced here and there, most prominently, perhaps in the Guggenheim Museum by Frank Lloyd Wright, designed in the 1940s although not completed until 1959. Wright went to the heart of museum architectural tradition, the rotunda, and conceived his building as a vast dome structure enclosed within walls. Nevertheless, he did not reject the modernist principle of spatial continuity; the great ramp flows downward through space like a young powerful river. Marcel Breuer's Whitney Museum of American Art, built between 1963 and 1966, is also a walled structure, its rich dark exterior looming with impressive strength among its commercial and domestic neighbors. Here, too, partitions give the vertically stacked galleries flexibility that allows for the installation of many kinds and sizes of exhibitions.

The buildings by Wright and Breuer were signals that the International Style era was coming to an end. Two events of the sixties heralded the advent of post-Modernism, one a building, the other a book. Philip Johnson's Sheldon Memorial Art Gallery at the University of Nebraska (Lincoln, Nebraska) (1963) set the stage for a viable alternative to the glass-enclosed loft type epitomized by the Centre Pompidou. Going back for inspiration to the beginnings of public museum architecture—the early masterpiece is Karl Friedrich Schinkel's Alte Museum in Berlin (1823–30)—Johnson designed a walled building with open and blind arcades, an axial plan, a central hall with galleries off to the sides, and a staircase and sculptural court. This is an early example of "appropriation," a term not then in use but which has, in the eighties, become a buzz word of art criticism. The term refers to the recycling of images and styles of the past, incorporating them into a new work of art, like quotations, calling up associations that are often witty and expressively effective. How this works will become clear as we get further into the art of the eighties.

The book that laid the theoretical foundations for post-Modernism was Robert Venturi and Denise Scott Browne's polemical *Complexity and Contradiction in Architecture* (1966), in which they attacked the reductive principles of Le Corbusier and especially those of Mies van der Rohe with his slogan, "less is more." Venturi and Browne's second book, *Learning from Las Vegas* (1972), argued for vernacularism in contemporary architecture. As had occurred in Happenings and other art forms where accident and the commonplace were invited to participate in the making of art, in architecture, too, the new sensibility demanded a way of letting contemporary life enter art.

The features of post-Modernist architecture can be seen in a number of recent museum buildings, an important example of which is the Museum of Contemporary Art in Los Angeles, designed by Arata Isozaki. This up-beat looking building is a composition of cylinders, cubes, and pyramids jumbled together and colored to give a buoyant and animated atmosphere to a kind of structure that traditionally wore a high-serious expression on its façade.

Very different from the Los Angeles buildings is the Getty Museum in Malibu, designed by Richard Meier, a neo-classicizing architect whose imposing compositions express that very high-seriousness that Isozaki rejected. The Getty, as everyone is very much aware, is one of the richest institutions in the art world. Post-modernist with its design based on a classic Pompeiian villa, it has been given an embodiment that communicates the grandeur and stateliness that old wealth wears easily.

As in the United States, museum building has been booming in West Germany during the past decade, with a number of exuberant structures including the innovative Stadtisches Museum Abteiberg in Monchengladbach, West Germany. Rising on a series of terraces, Hans Hollein's Monchengladbach is a kind of "assemblage" of irregularly shaped structures, reflecting the implausible alliance of Las Vegas and Austrian *Secessionstil.* This curious mix is owed, of course, partly to Venturi and Browne's *Learning from Las Vegas,* which made it possible for Hollein to synthesize his youthful experience in America during the psychedelic Pop years with his taste for the decorative art of the turn of the century, which he "appropriated" and "recycled." Recycling the elegant *Secessionstil* with the brash and vulgar Las Vegas style is a witty and daring example of "appropriation."

Another example of post-Modernist appropriation is seen in James Stirling's stunning amalgamation of art historical styles in the Stuttgart Museum (1977–83). The massive sloping walls of an Egyptian mastaba **(J 56; G 3.5);** the series of ramps leading to the holy-of-holies of the Temple of Queen Hatshepsut **(J 74; G 3.23);** the rotunda shape of the ancient Roman Colosseum **(J 235; G 6.45);** the contrasting, alternating colors of the stone columns in the nave at Durham Cathedral in Stirling's native England **(J 391; G 9.17),** or the striped marble quoins of the Florence Baptistery **(J clpl 44)**—these are only some of the associations called up by the Stuttgart Museum. Like Hollein's Monchengladbach museum, Stirling's building, too, is an "assemblage" of structures of various shapes and sizes which are reached by ziggurat-like, zig-zagging ramps **(J 89; G 2.10).** High-color accents give a high-tech expression to the complex and are the final jazzy note of Stirling's rejection of International Style.

## New Image Art and the Triumph of the Camera

In addition to the "old masters" who have continued to hold their place on the contemporary stage, new names with new concerns have come forward, rejecting so much of what had been established as modernism that it became evident that a new post-Modernist sensibility had emerged in painting, sculpture, and photography as well as architecture. The most dramatic visual change was the reappearance of phenomenal reality as the dominant aesthetic vehicle. As a result, even artists who had won some recognition and a great deal of admiration, but who had nevertheless seemed peripheral to mainstream art— Pearlstein, Segal, Golub, among others—are now accorded major interest. Along with the visual shift from formal to figurative, iconographical values have reemerged, with the emphasis on political and social issues. Pop art had, of course, dealt with the figure, and with political and social content, but its imagery had been largely inflected by its Minimalist twin—it tended to be hard-edged and cool. The literalist art of the seventies and eighties, even some that can be interpreted as late Pop, is warmed by expressionism that is often savage.

It is not helpful to think of this development as a revival, or return to the figure, since the new elements far outweigh whatever reference to tradition is apparent. New Image art frequently employs the camera as a tool and a medium, alongside traditional tools and media such as brushes, paint, chisel, and clay. Perhaps the ubiquitous presence of television in the early life of artists who have won recognition in the past two decades, the consciousness of film as a medium of expression, and of the furniture of the world, including the human figure, as a vehicle of content, have contributed significantly to the rejection of abstraction. Richard Estes, who won recognition before New Image Art developed as a movement, has been one of the most successful of the Photorealists, with urban street scenes that constitute a virtual triumph of Pop art warmed by a vision that takes delight in whatever it sees. His compositions are designed with masterly control of abstract principles, but their geometry is infused with the visual drama of a great city as in *Bus Reflections, Ansonia* (1972) (Arnason clpl 272). Duane Hanson, who also anticipated New Image Art, and might be classified as a Pop artist, has translated the images of life's helpless but enthusiastic *Tourists* as caught by the camera (1970) (Arnason clpl 274) into compelling sculptures that show us, just as Duchamp's snow shovel did, that the commonplace and mundane are transformed when seen in the context of art.

Photography penetrated the spaces of "Fine Art" in the sixties as a kind of ancillary to Earthworks, discharging its traditional responsibility as documenter of "facts." The problematic nature of "fact," however, is exactly the point of entry for some artists who have been using the camera as an instrument of interpretation. Cindy Sherman (1954–   ) has projected in immense blow-ups, like Pollock-size canvases, the fantasies she shared with most teen-age girls culturally raised on Hollywood movies. Her exposures, in both senses of the word, are about the hollowness of cosmeticized illusions. Lampooning herself as an actress—the femme fatale, the housewife, the girl-next-door (Arnason figs. 1042–43)—her early work in the seventies also celebrated herself as an artist who had freed herself from illusions. In the early eighties Sherman gave up the pose of exposed illusions, and sought curious, surrealist effects. Her recent work has dealt with disease, deformity, and death—as far away emotionally, as well as aesthetically, as one could get from the "real" illusions of a decade ago. Yet, despite the radical shift, the presence-of-Cindy-Sherman-in-her-work is always the *subject* and the cut between exposure and concealment is as unsettled, and unsettling, as ever.

One of the characteristics found frequently in contemporary art is ambiguity of form and/or content. The surface of a canvas (or photographic paper) is no longer the battlefield of the artist's struggle for self-expression, nor the cool pool of ironic or deadpan comment. It is a lens reflecting a lens reflecting a lens, art about ways of seeing. Jennifer Bartlett (1941–  ) uses the technique of juxtaposing multiple film frames, thus jogging the eye to adjust to multiple points of view, as in *Yellow and Black Boats* (1985) (Arnason fig. 1008). She thwarts the camera's illusionistic way with space, forcing it to lend ambiguity to her imaginative vision.

Along with ambiguity, the phenomena of "appropriation" has made its appearance in post-Modernist painting as in architecture. A number of critics have linked the present broad practice of appropriation to the rejection of originality as the compelling value it had had for post–World War II artists. Sherrie Levine recalled when interviewed in December 1987, when she was doing photographs after Rodchenko and a suite of photolithographs after Degas, that "this usage [of appropriation] coincided with the general proliferation of audio and video casettes. Reproduction of imagery became a question of property: what is original? what can we own? You don't need a philosophical or art-historical background to think about these issues. . . . Since 1980, my work has been an exploration of the notion of originality. I continue to think about ambiguity and the improbability of certainty" (*Art in America,* December 1987, p. 114).

Despite Levine's demur, it seems likely that an "art-historical background" has considerable relevance in throwing light on the appropriation issue. Although art history has been an academic discipline for almost two hundred years, until recently it had relatively few professional practitioners, compared with, say, philosophy, theology, history, or literature, its closest humanist sisters. Not many years ago, if, answering a query, one identified oneself as an "art historian," one had to pronounce the two words slowly and clearly, and even then would most likely be met with a somewhat puzzled "Oh?" Today, art history has gained almost glamorous status. One finds art historians as characters in the movies, figuring in multi-million-dollar stock-market frauds, and posing as taste mentors to the public in full-page color clothing ads in the Sunday *Times.* Art history has arrived, and having been taught by now to several generations of college undergraduates, is largely responsible for the huge crowds that patronize museum and gallery exhibitions: People not only know what they like but like what they know.

Appropriation is nothing new, of course. Sometimes artists made close copies, in the style of the original, usually for study purposes; more interesting are the "copies" in their own style, sometimes of entire compositions, sometimes of sections or motifs: Poussin quoted from classical sculpture for the poses and gestures that he gave his figures; Manet helped himself to the three river gods in the foreground of Marcantonio Raimondi's engraving after a Raphael design for his *Luncheon on the Grass,* and to Titian's *Venus of Urbino* for his *Olympia.* Picasso re-styled Velásquez (*Las Meninas*) and other masters. Countless examples can be found, and it is not at all a bad exercise for training one's eyes to go "motif hunting" or "composition hunting."

Artists such as Carlo Mariani and others who are taking possession of past styles and past imagery for making their art of the eighties, can count on a large pool of art-historically hip viewers for recognition and enjoyment. The references are usually clear enough for identification but recycled, they make a viewer feel, on the most trivial level, rather clever for detecting them, on a more rewarding level, engaged in the artist's own problem of the nature of originality.

Appropriation can raise the problem of ambiguity, however, when the artist's attitude to his work is unclear. Viewing Carlo Mariani's copies of Baroque and neo-Classical works, one is uncertain about the artist's intention. He at once appears to be paying homage to masters of the past and seems to be commenting on the hollowness of skill by demonstrating how it can be duplicated. He treats the old master paintings like theatrical dialogue, faithfully repeated in performance after performance, and yet, as has been suggested, he seems to be commenting on the relationship between the "copy" and the "imitation," a favorite distinction of eighteenth-century art theory: Sir Joshua Reynolds, President of the British Royal Academy, reflected contemporary thought when he advised students in his "Sixth Discourse" to learn by imitating the great masters, but, he explains, "it is not to be understood that I advise any endeavor to copy the exact colour and complexion of another man's mind." Nevertheless, he concludes, "Study . . . the great works of the masters . . . consider them as models which you are to imitate, and . . . as rivals with whom you are to contend" (Joshua Reynolds, *Discourses on Art,* 1965, pp. 79, 91).

Mariani (like Sherrie Levine with the camera, and others) is pushing those questions of copying and rivaling, of the nature of originality, of innovation, to their ultimate frontiers. By deliberately making inauthentic works—they are not forgeries, since there is no intention to deceive—he is, after all, making authentic works—his own. This is his paradoxical innovation, the particular space that he wishes to carve out for himself in the world of modern art.

But the aesthetic space in which artists have been able to move since the late sixties has been somewhat maze-like, with all roads apparently open but with no certain best way to turn. When one overriding style prevails, it pre-empts the imagination, the ambition, the aesthetic sensibility of the art community around it. This is possibly easiest to grasp if one takes as an example the Italian Renaissance in Florence: at a certain point, around 1440 or so, if one wanted to be a recognized artist and win commissions, one *had* to paint according to the new system of perspective. There was no stylistic alternative; that was the way to go. Throughout the centuries one finds similar situations, although with increasing latitude. As society became more socially complex, the patron class became more diversified. More options opened for artists in terms of style and subject matter. Finally, at the present time, there are countless options for all artists;

patrons can be found for every style and subject. Artists must ask themselves, What kind of artist do I want to be? How do I move forward, as an artist? It is not surprising that a feature of some post-Modernist art has been ambivalence as well as ambiguity.

What *is* surprising is that one finds no double-edged questioning in the work of Gilbert and George, where one might reasonably expect ambivalence and ambiguity to be built into the collaborative conditions of its creation: Two artists acting as if they were one. Furthermore, Gilbert and George constitute one work of art. They are in fact their first creation. They began their collaboration in the late sixties with a "performance" in which they stood motionless as statues, side by side, wearing neat business suits and ties, with their faces and hands covered by metallic, bronze-colored paint, while a scratchy phonograph played popular, sentimental songs (Arnason fig. 916). It was a comic and profound inversion of the tradition-laden Pygmalion myth of art becoming life. The work implied as sweeping an attack on art market practices as any earthwork executed a thousand miles from nowhere: physically identical with their art, they were "not for sale." It furthermore closed the remaining crack between art and life. They made one symbol (abstraction) of their two selves (reality), paradoxically transforming life into art by being both at one and the same time.

Their major effort subsequent to the "living sculpture" has gone into photo-pieces, which they define as sculpture, thereby calling attention to the tactile quality of their images. Hand-colored blown-up photo frames are juxtaposed to form immense murals, so that the result is a gridded image of figures (most often themselves, but often with other young males), reminiscent of medieval leaded stained-glass windows. Religion is an important theme in their work (along with sex), and the repeated grids should be seen, it seems, as joined crosses. Their commitment to social themes is expressed in formal as well as iconographic terms. In *Red Morning* (1977), for example, the grid form suggests the regularity and orderliness of life. But the images of young men overlap the grids, which thus states in formal terms their critique of orderliness which becomes dull, routine, and commonplace, and their commitment to interrelatedness.

Camera-generated art tends to present smooth surfaces. New Image artists, who have relied principally on paint (with various additives), have tended to work up their surfaces. Both, however, have been absorbed in the kind of emotional imagery that links them to the Expressionist tradition.

In the United States Julian Schnabel (1951–   ) has gained stardom for his particular mix of currently attractive selections from the menu of twentieth-century art history. One recognizes the legacy of Futurism, with the figure embedded in an energy field which, as with the Futurists, is meant as a metaphor for an emotional state, "a state that people can literally walk into and let

themselves be engulfed by," the artist has said. Schnabel is also heir to the Expressionist tradition, both German and Abstract, which in him reaches Wagnerian heights. He piles his work with objects such as deer antlers, tree roots and branches, and works on densely colored surfaces as smooth as velvet or as cluttered as a bombed-out building. On a visit to Barcelona he "discovered" Antonio Gaudi's tiled mosaic work which inspired his now famous broken crockery paintings. Ceramic fragments project from the picture plane and catch light so that the flickering effect is somewhat like pointillist painting in which the figure emerges from the dots of color. Schnabel draws his subject matter from a broad culture that is literary as well as visual. *Geography Lesson* (1980) (Arnason clpl 299) is part of a series of four paintings titled *Huge Wall Symbolizing the Fate's Inaccessibility* and has the apocalyptic look of Franz Marc's *Animals' Fates* (Hunter fig. 197) with possibly similar portentous meaning.

The internationalism of the art world is evident in the shared familiarity of European and American audiences with the work of artists on both sides of the Atlantic. The American Schnabel is seen in exhibitions in Germany and London. The Italians Sandro Chia (1946–   ) and Francesco Clemente (1952–   ), the Germans George Baselwitz (1938–   ) and Anselm Kiefer (1945–   ) are as much at home in New York as they are in their native lands. These were among the artists featured in the tour of the Pompidou Center in the last program of this series.

Chia and Clemente are leaders of the Neo-Expressionist movement in Italy, winning international attention at the Venice Biennale of 1980. Chia's art is an up-dated Futurism, on the surface, without the Futurists' interest in finding visual symbols for the psychological experience of movement in space. He comes close to Boccioni in a work such as *Melancholic Drinker* (1981), with a light palette and faceted planes in the manner of Boccioni's *Dynamism of a Cyclist,* and makes a witty reference to Marinetti in his *Very Courageous Boys,* with a bright yellow automobile embedded in a crackling ground of Futurist-derived zig-zag grafitti exploding like fire-crackers, a blue-suited and bow-tied young man standing beside the car in the pose of the Victory of Samothrace— visually quoting Marinetti's famous line from his 1909 Futurist Manifesto (quoted in Program 8, section 1), Chia is more interested, however, in imagery that conflates heroic figures in the classical tradition with peasant/proletariat types, as in his huge *Boys on a Raft* (1983).

Francesco Clemente's art, like Julian Schnabel's, carries a heavy burden of hidden meanings. On the surface his paintings are about the human body, and often focus on the body's openings—eyes, nose, mouth, and anus, as in *Two Painters* (1980) (Arnason clpl 297). Clemente seems to be not two but three painters, in terms of style, as if he changes persona when he changes his abode. As H. H. Arnason has pointed out, he divides his time between India, Italy, and the United States, and has made paintings that stylistically suggest those three cultures. There are, furthermore, myriad erudite references to esoteric sciences such as alchemy and astrology in Clemente's work, which resist interpretation and yet, like his stylistic transformations, imply autobiographical content.

The Expressionist tradition, always strong in Germany, has produced some of the most interesting painters identified with the Neo-Expressionism of the eighties. Possibly the largest talent to emerge has been Anselm Kiefer who, in the view of many critics, is the contemporary artist who has done most to interrogate, who has pressed farthest to understand, through art, the horrific destiny of the German nation in the middle of the twentieth century, which culminated in the depravities and destructions of World War II. Born into a generation that was not paralyzed by closeness or complicity with the national trauma, Kiefer has been able to marshall his powerful expressive resources to his purpose: to recover the symbols and the obnoxious atmosphere, the very texture, of the recent German past. By means of his coarse or coarse-looking media—often pigment mixed with sand and straw—he has forced the actuality of horror as he has imaginatively relived it into images that make it seem palpable. Exceptional among expressionists, Kiefer does not externalize a subjective anguish but seems to grieve over something much larger, the self-betrayed culture in which he is immersed. His dark, heavy-hearted architectural and landscape compositions convey a sense of tragedy, as in *Sulamith* (1983) (Arnason fig. 1026), which refers to the beloved Shulammite of the *Song of Songs,* and *Departure from Egypt* (1984) (Arnason fig. 1027), a deep landscape of scorched and rutted earth; a lead rod representing the staff of Moses or Aaron (as in Exodus) is attached to the surface. Kiefer has grand ambitions, and the artistic resources to realize them.

When George Kern moved away from his native, Soviet-occupied village of Deutschbaselwitz, he took his village with him, in a manner of speaking, adopting its name for his own. It is as Baselwitz that he has become one of the most prominent of the new German painters. New, that is, to the international scene. Baselwitz's career goes back to the sixties when his struggle to reintroduce the figure into modernist art began. It was not until he turned his figures upside down, as in *Orangeater* (1981) (Arnason clpl 291), transforming them into abstractions by wrenching them from the reality of gravity, that he caught the attention of the mainstream art world. The abstraction, it should be noticed, turns back on itself, as the upside-down figures irresistibly become metaphors for a real, topsy-turvy society gone mad.

Three unrelated but important recently "arrived" artists seen briefly at the Pompidou are the Conceptualist Daniel Buren, the sculptor Anthony Gormley, and the painter Howard Hodgkin. Conceptualist Art, which flourished mainly in the late sixties and early seventies, is rooted in the idea of art as concept. We have seen this idea most firmly and tangibly proposed by Marcel Duchamp. Updated, it was elegantly demonstrated by Joseph Kosuth in 1965 with his *Three Chairs,* a real chair, a photograph of a chair, and a dictionary definition typed and pasted to the gallery wall. The notion of Conceptual Art is wholly contained in Donald Judd's comment, "If someone says it's art, it's art." Buren's signature motif is a series of uniform, evenly spaced stripes which he exhibits on billboards amid advertisements, on placards which he parades in the streets, as well as in galleries. *The stripes never change.* The *context* in which they are seen changes. The concept, of course, is the philosophical one that all reality is context-dependent, like words which can only render meaning when arranged in a recognizable syntax. Anthony Gormley is a member of the celebrated generation of British sculptors who have been largely responsible for the rejuvenation of contemporary sculpture. Gormley's figures are often modeled from his own nude body, and through posture and their environment seem to act out some of the sensual and anxious dramas of human existence. Also British is Howard Hodgkin, awarded first prize at the 1984 Venice Biennale. He is a tasteful colorist who has successfully revitalized narrative content in contemporary painting.

Among the many manifestations of value-reversal that art has produced in the past century, none is more revealing of the dialectics of our culture than the concern for images of *im*permanence. The irony of "Look at my works, ye mighty, and despair" (P. B. Shelley, "Ozymandias") governs much of the twentieth-century sensibility that accepts as normal the built-in obsolescence of consumer goods. The Pharaoh might not have known it, then, but everybody knows now that nothing lasts. This is the spirit behind Process Art, the aestheticizing of the ephemeral. Process artists use structureless materials like soft cloth, pebbles, sawdust, steam and smoke, to create their evanescent works. These are often necessarily temporary gallery installations, such as the exhibition arranged in a gallery in Rome by Jannis Kounellis (1936–   ), where he stabled a dozen horses. As is often the case in Process Art, Kounellis's statement had to do with the relationship between nature and the human-structured object. There is also frequently a more or less overt attack on the socio-political system to which the artist feels alien.

Art as a social weapon has been highly visible in the past decade or so. Artists like Leon Golub and Nancy Spero have put their art to the service of attacking the social-political order that is responsible for the ultimate in human degradation—war and torture. Red Grooms's wild imaginings of the urban scene, the rodeo, and most recently the New York artists' world, satirize the megalopolis with its historical monuments, its churches of religion and its churches of finance, its motley crowd of subway riders, all jumbled in a hilarious commotion; joke at Western fadism's fake machoism in what was once a genuine folk event; make fun of the posturing of his contemporaries, and, quoting their styles in their portraits, kid the trend of appropriation.

Punning and joking are frequently present in modernist art, as we have seen. Playfulness and whimsy, however, characteristic of eighteenth-century rococo art, have been rare in modern times, but even these light-hearted attitudes are present, as in George Rhoads's sculpture in the New York City Port Authority Bus Terminal. Rhoads's kinetic sculpture should be associated with the kinetic movement of the sixties which we considered in Part 1 of this unit. However, his work is inflected by the irreverent spirit of neo-Dada. His humorous mechanical devices are not concerned with the effects of slow or fast motion, or changing patterns, as in the work of Len Lye, Pol Bury, and George Rickey; instead, he engages the viewer in the aesthetic pleasure of rhythmic movement—and sound—for their own sake.

## Women in Art

The issue of women in art has generated some heat. Many women in the art world—artists, critics, art historians—are not in sympathy, for example, with the establishment of the National Museum of Women in the Arts in Washington, D.C. On the other hand, there are many who do support it. It appears to be true that the artistic concerns of most women artists are not gender motivated and it is evident that the range of styles and subject matter is as broad among women as among men. It is also true that some of the most prominent women artists have made gender their subject.

Barbara Kruger stands as one of the most convincing artists of the younger generation. She overlays large

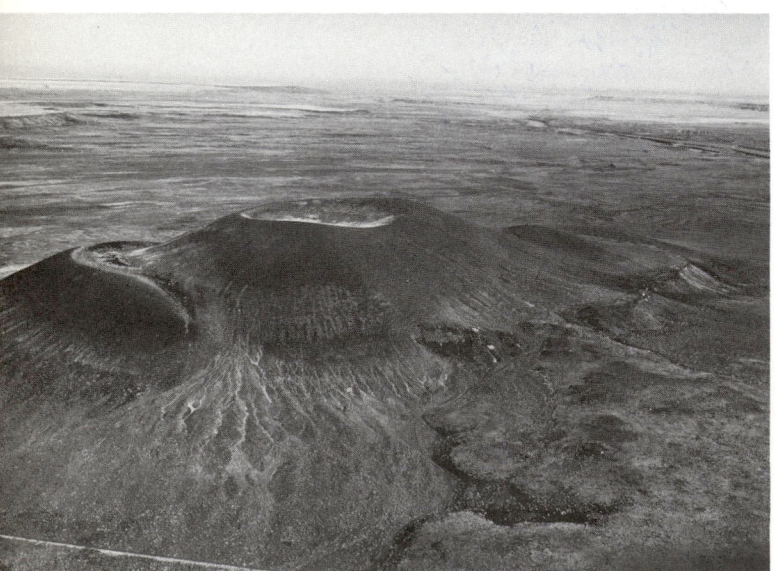

James Turrell, *Crater*. (COPYRIGHT © DICK WISER)

photographic images with challenging, declamatory texts such as "We won't play NATURE to your CULTURE; We will no longer be seen and not heard" (1985), highlighting the power of language and image to shape our social perceptions.

Judy Chicago's *Dinner Party* is a stupendous homage to womankind, celebrating the deeds of historical and mythological women in media traditionally associated with women's work—china decorating and cloth embroidery. On a triangular floor forty-eight feet on each side, made up of nine-hundred-ninety-nine tiles, each carrying the name of a historical woman, a slightly smaller triangular table stands with thirty-nine place settings, thirteen on each side. Each setting represents a particularly significant woman, identified symbolically by the design on the porcelain plate, and by name, which is embroidered on a cloth runner on which the plate lies. An enormous team of women and men craft artists worked for three years to produce this installation work, which was the concept of Chicago. Miriam Schapiro (1923– ), who with Judy Chicago was co-director of the Feminist Art Program, also chooses to stress gender in her work. She uses sewing materials in the manner of collage, to make highly decorative wall panels, as in *I'm Dancing as Fast as I Can* (1985) (Arnason clpl 278). While it is true that the content of the art of these women is gender-laden, it is equally true that the power of their aesthetic language is gender-neutral.

Gender-neutral also are Susan Rothenberg's lyrical expressionist paintings. Rothenberg (1945– ) came to notice in the seventies as a New Imagist. For several years her signature motif was the horse, which she insists has no special meaning for her: she is concerned with form, as is evident in *Pontiac* (1979) (Arnason fig. 997). Her figurative, light-filled, scraped and scrubbed surfaces attain a translucent effect which has become more marked in her work of the eighties, such as *Bucket of Water* (1983–84) (Arnason clpl 285), and which are no more "feminine" than Rothko's abstract epiphanies. Rebecca Horn is another among countless women artists whose sex is irrelevant to their art. As is shown in the television discussion of her work, *Das Gegenlaufige Konzert,* she is an installation or environment artist, often concerned with the nature of human experience in terms of time, space, and order which she dramatizes by creating situations in which they are held in tension by their opposites.

## Site-Specific Art

Since environment and installation art have been the most dramatic of the innovations of contemporary art, it is fitting to end this series with a glimpse of the work of James Turrell, an outstanding master of this category of art-making. Since 1974 he has been preoccupied with his *Roden Crater Project*. He did not actually buy the site—

a gigantic volcanic basin in Arizona near the Painted Desert—until 1977, and construction began in 1979. The work is due to be completed in the 1990s. The artist conceives of this titanic work as a kind of cosmic observatory, and as we listen to him talk about it, thoughts of Stonehenge come to mind. Stonehenge, however, was meant to chart the movement of the sun and planets. The *Roden Crater* has far different aims, and perhaps philosophical observatory would be an appropriate description of it: Turrell is concerned with perception, and the experience of the perceiver in extraordinary circumstances. As Michael Wood has remarked while lying in the bowl of the crater, "We are in the presence of an absolute sublimity, and our stillness, our isolation, and our receptivity are fundamental to it. Art is not in front of your eyes. It is within them." We are reminded of Ralph Waldo Emerson, who expressed a similar experience of transcendence in his essay, *Nature,* written in 1836: "Standing on the bare ground—my head bathed by the blithe air, and uplifted into infinite space—all mean egotism vanishes. I become a transparent eyeball; I am nothing; I see all; the currents of the Universal Being circulate through me; I am part or parcel of God."

## Summary

A decade rich in innovation, the sixties saw the implications of modernism carried out in seemingly all of their consequences. All modernist styles were available for combining and recombining; sculpture and painting were no longer distinct modes of art-making; the nature of color, the nature of form, the nature of line, the nature of pictorial space, the nature of the canvas support, had been thoroughly revealed. Finally, the last factor in the art equation to be revealed, the artist came on stage, and soon was at its center. It was in the sixties that the artist achieved the status of stardom.

Rooted in the premises of gestural Abstract Expressionism, the significance of the artist *per se* developed in several ways. Some artists participated bodily in their work, like Bruce Nauman (1941–  ) in his *Self-Portrait as a Fountain* (1966–70) (Arnason fig. 914), or Lucas Samaras (1936–  ), who photographed himself in outrageous poses, turning himself into a Dracula in *Photo-Transformation* (1973–74) (Arnason, p. 263). Some made artworks of their persona, like Warhol. The artist who appears to be the most profound thinker of his generation is Robert Morris (1931–  ) whose art critical writings explain his own art, and contemporary art theory. As we have seen, in his early *I-Box*, Morris raises philosophical questions about being and representation, subject and object: a box with the capital letter "I" cut into the front of it opens to reveal a nude photograph of the artist. The "I," upright like
a standing person, is a symbol that "stands" for the actual person, whose standing photographic image is inside the "I." Here Morris is the "Hamlet" of modernism.

How do these self-portrayals differ from traditional self-portraits so that they invite special comment?

When Bernini made a self-portrait grimacing in a mirror, his aim was to study how emotions affected the muscles of the human face. When Samaras does the same, his intention is to portray himself in a role, as an actor. He thus transforms himself into a work of art, just as all actors do when they take on the persona of a character: Olivier's *Hamlet* was not Olivier, but a creation, a work of art, which he simply embodied, as does Cindy Sherman. Among the significant artists of the past one can think only of Rembrandt who liked to play roles, and dressed himself up in costume, for some self-portraits—and those belong to his youthful period. Self-dramatization was rare until recently, and possibly owes something to the theatricality of Happenings. In any case it surely is a consequence of the galloping "me-ism" to which we have referred.

The artist as media personality is another aspect of this phenomenon of artistic stardom. Artists have been the subjects not of only films meant to be shown in the context of educational and art institutions, but of documentaries targeted for the public. In these films, the artists as personalities are at least as important as the glimpses shown of their art. The reticent Jasper Johns, whose image appears only as a shadow in his important series of paintings titled *The Seasons* (1987), nevertheless was featured in color on the front page of the *New York Times Magazine,* 19 June 88, together with the punning title of the issue's main article, "The Unflagging Artistry of Jasper Johns."

Thus, one of the most intriguing developments of Post-War art has been this transformation of the artists into celebrities. By the end of the seventies there were already many waiting in the wings for their chance. Some became the stars of the eighties.

As we near the end of our own century, it is time to look back to where we have come from in order to get a perspective on where we are. There are many ways this long story can be told. I propose here to tell it in terms of values. This, in my view (which I share with many), is what art has always primarily been about.

Taking a long view of Western art we can discern a spiral pattern that has moved from stylization of some kind to representation of some kind, in response to the values of the culture in which stylization or representation appeared. Greek art was the first to arrive at a more or less close match between the humanly observed world and the humanly pictured world, reflecting the value that Greek culture placed on humankind *per se*. Despite great differences between Greek and Roman culture, human deeds and events, human needs and desires, the human environment, remained uppermost in Roman concerns as they had been among the Greeks, and were accordingly served in Roman art and architecture.

With the triumph of Christianity, pagan values were rejected and a new vocabulary of art was required to express Christian values. These values were heaven-oriented; the material world of human experience became the temporary abode of the soul which would find its eternal glory or damnation in heaven or hell. Medieval art speaks unequivocally in its visualization of the glories to be enjoyed in the former, the pain to be endured in the latter. In any case, in a system of thought that deals with the infinite and the eternal, there is no need to represent worldly space and time, and none is represented.

Many factors contributed to the fall of the Classical world, and many factors contributed to the emergence of the period we call the Renaissance. The rebirth of Classical antiquity included, of course, humanist values. This required a method of representing human interests in the human environment. The laws of mathematical perspective were discovered about 1420, and thus the means of depicting the three-dimensional, humanly observed world on a two-dimensional surface were placed in the hands of artists in the course of the fifteenth century. The triumph of representation lasted four hundred years, along with the fundamental belief in the rightness, the moral superiority of Western humanism.

There were enormous ongoing socio-economic and political changes, of course, during those four centuries. With hindsight we can see that they tended in the direction of broadening the social base and widening the cultural horizon to include non-Western peoples. There were also profound intellectual changes, and again with hindsight we can see that humanism, with its emphasis on the individual, began to give way to socialism, with its emphasis on the group or mass.

It is not a coincidence that painting and sculpture reflect substantial and compositional broadening and leveling: formerly overlooked or disdained subject matter was admitted into mainstream art; former hierarchical methods of composition gave way first to relative and eventually to perfect equality of interest over the entire surface—what we have seen as all-over or random composition.

Every movement produces a counter-movement. The socializing of Western culture which tends to make an abstraction of human beings, has been countered by individualizing—but an individualizing that focuses not on the Classical notion of person, but on the basically Freudian notion of personality. The aesthetic vocabularies of the twentieth century have been created to express these values—of socialization on one hand, interiorization on the other.

These values are far from neatly compartmentalized in any one person's mind. The most convinced socialist may also accept the value of psychological insight. It is headline news, these days, that Freud has at last been accepted in the Soviet Union, and psychoanalysis has won respectability there. Capitalism has long ago made its peace with social welfare. The entire range of attitudes is open for inspection, all values competing in the socio-economic Olympics. We live in a global pluralism.

This has meant, for art, an unprecedented variety of styles flourishing in the twentieth century. In the capitalist West, the artists' need for markets has resulted in raising the value of innovation to first-rank aesthetic importance, but innovation is not for everyone. Conservative collectors bid in the same auction houses that are patronized by adventurous ones—but not at the same auction sale. There are galleries to suit every taste, to meet every set of values.

Yet, it is true that the more innovative artists give us the latest news. We have seen the turn away from the human-centered humanist society in various kinds of figurative, abstract and non-objective art. Does this not reflect—with brilliance and profundity—the artists' insight into that element in modern culture that makes us feel anonymous and helpless? We have also seen the struggle to express, in figurative, abstract, and non-objective art, a new spiritual level of feeling. Does that not tell us with equal brilliance and profundity something about the human discontents with the materialist, consumer world created by the "industrial revolution?" We have seen the calm assurance of functionalism asserting the value of precision and control flourishing alongside hectic, deliberate irrationalism, asserting the value of freedom and the creative power of accident. Is there any way of bringing these values together so as to say, "this is the underlying character of modern times"?

As we look back over the past one hundred years or more of aesthetic and intellectual endeavor, it becomes apparent that the prevailing trend has been analytical. Western culture has been absorbed with the problem of learning the nature of things—in physics, the nature of elements that comprise the cosmos, in political science, the nature of the elements that comprise the state, in the science of human beings, the nature of the mind and body. In art, as we have seen, each element that goes into constituting a painting or sculpture—color, line, space, medium, the artist—has come under analysis. The nature of analysis, however, is to *denature* the thing it analyzes, breaking it down into its constituent parts so that it is no longer the thing-in-itself. Thus, things—the cosmos, the state, the person—become abstractions. Under analysis they are taken out of their particularity as space-time objects and are studied in terms of relationships that are abstract and general. Abstract and non-objective art can thus be seen, from this point of view, as phenomena that arose out of and flourished in the intellectual and aesthetic climate of analysis.

The turn way from analysis—in the sciences and the humanities, as well as in the visual arts—began to be noticeable in the sixties, emerged as a recognizable shift in the seventies, and is now in full bloom. In place of analysis we are getting, and can expect to see develop further, the descriptive mode. While the terms of description as it will go on to develop are unpredictable, it seems certain that in art new solutions to the problem of representation will appear and that photography will continue to play an important role in the period ahead: it has proven to be the medium of choice for many of the most progressive artists in the major art centers of Europe and America. What can we expect for content?

Increasingly, through the seventies and eighties, world anguish has held the stage, challenging Western civilization to solve the crises that daily erupt, at the peril of its own demise. Those solutions have demanded and will inevitably continue to demand the jettisoning of some values, to be replaced by others. Some of the new values that enter the Western world will arise from the dialectics at work within it, others will penetrate from non-Western cultures, continuing a social phenomenon that began to be significant in the second half of the nineteenth century. The twenty-first century will be as different from the twentieth, as the twentieth is from the nineteenth. Values change with time; art changes with values.

## Textbook References

**J** Janson continues his discussion of painting, sculpture, and architecture of the twentieth century and does not make a division between that produced before and after World War II. The section on painting deals with the most important examples of Abstract Expressionism, Pop, Minimalism, and ends with Neo-Expressionism and the reappearance of the figure in painting in the works of the 1980s. Sculpture is studied through works by Calder, Gonzalez, and David Smith, each serving as a point of focus for the new goals of sculptors in the modern period as they experiment with abstract form in space and kinetics. The environmental works of Smithson and Christo are also included, along with the monumental works of Claes Oldenburg and the tautly minimal creations of Ellsworth Kelly and Barnett Newman. A short, but thorough summary of modern architecture beginning in the late nineteenth century is followed by a fine survey of photography.

**G** Gardner's discussion of art in the post-war period almost exclusively focuses on painting and architecture. Abstract Expressionism is the subject of a fairly long and good discussion, although Gardner also includes material on figurative art of the same period. The 1960s are shown to be a period in which a number of different styles coexisted; and carefully selected examples of works by Johns and Rauschenberg, Nevelson, Christo, Smithson, Kienholz, and Estes give a good idea of the extent of variation possible at this time. The discussion of painting and sculpture ends with works created in the early 1980s, and is then followed by a

treatment of post-war architecture, ending with post-modernist works of the 1980s.

**H&F** Honour and Fleming set off art created after World War II in a separate chapter devoted exclusively to contemporary art. The major concepts that guided painters, sculptors, and architects are defined, and works in all three mediums are treated simultaneously and compared. As in Janson and Gardner, the sections on painting and sculpture deal primarily with American works of the Abstract Expressionist and Pop schools; however, Honour and Fleming do not bring the student in contact with works created after the 1970s. The discussion of architecture is extremely brief and gives pertinent examples of the international modernist style of the 1950s and 1960s as well as the early post-modernist designs of Venturi, Graves, and Izosaki.

**Janson, Part IV, Chapter 4, Section 2: Painting Since World War II, pp. 695–783.** Abstract Expressionism: Gorky; Rothko; Pollock, *one;* De Kooning, *Woman II;* Frankenthaler; Dubuffet; CoBrA; Color Field, Stella; Pop Art; Johns, *Three Flags;* Indiana, *The Demuth Five, Love;* Lichtenstein, *Girl at the Piano.* Environment, Assemblages, and Installations; Rauschenberg, *Odalisk;* Segal, *Cinema;* Kienholz; Conceptual Art, Joseph Kosuth, *One of Three Chairs;* Photo Realism; Op; paintings in the 1980s; Clemente, Kiefer. Sculpture: Kinetic Sculpture; Constructivism; Surrealism (Primary Structures); Goeritz; Bladen, *The X;* Smithson, *Spiral Jetty;* Christo, *Surrounded Islands;* Nevelson; Oldenburg; Architecture: International Style; The Bauhaus; Le Corbusier, *Villa Savoye;* Mies van der Rohe; Post Modern; James Stirling, *Neue Stattsgalerie, Stuttgart;* Rogers and Piano, *Georges Pompidou National Arts and Culture Center.*

**Gardner, Part V, Chapter 22: The Twentieth Century, pp. 886–975; Painting and Sculpture After World War II, pp. 936–962.** Expressionism: Figural and Abstract; Pollock; Kline; De Kooning, *Woman I;* Rothko. Painting: Abstract Formalism; Barnett Newman, *Vir Heroicus Sublimus;* Bridget Riley. Sculpture: Nevelson; Judd; Bladen, *The X;* Smithson, *Spiral Jetty;* Bury. Pop Art; Hamilton, *Just What Is It That Makes Todays Homes so Different, So Appealing?;* Rauschenberg; Johns, *Painted Bronze;* Lichtenstein, Oldenburg; Kienholz. New Realism: Estes. Process; Conceptual Art; Christo, *Running Fence.* Post-Modernism: Schnabel; Golub; Oldenburg, *Clothespin.* Architecture: Mies van der Rohe; Le Corbusier; Rogers and Piano, *Georges Pompidou National Arts and Culture Center;* Johnson; Venturi.

**Honour and Fleming, Part V, Chapter 21: Contemporary Art, pp. 604–621.** Abstract Expressionism; Hofmann; Gorky; Pollock; De Kooning; Kline; Still; Rothko; Newman; Pop Art; Lichtenstein; Hamilton, *Just*

*What Is It That Makes Today's Homes So Different, So Appealing?;* Rauschenberg; Johns; Oldenburg; Warhol; Bacon. Minimal and Conceptual Art to Photo-Realism; Robert Morris; Yves Klein; Christo; Photo-Realism, Estes; Modernism and Post-Modernism; LeWitt; Mies van der Rohe; Le Corbusier; Venturi and Scott Browne; Isozaki; Beuys.

## Study Questions

1. Discuss the influence of salient features of psychoanalytic thought on Abstract Expressionist style as seen in the work of three artists identified with the movement.
2. Compare New York School painting, ca. 1945–ca. 1955, to various developments in European painting.
3. In what styles does human figuration appear, in this period? Compare the treatment of the human figure in each of these styles.
4. Explain what is meant by "the dialogue among artists, and between art generations," by giving specific examples of certain artists and their works.
5. What stylistic movements supplanted "pure visibility"? Explain in what way spatial perception and tactility re-entered Western art.
6. Discuss the phenomenon of "openness" in painting and architecture. Give specific examples of works that express this feature.
7. Define "post-Modernism" and give specific examples in painting and architecture.
8. Give two examples of value-reversal and demonstrate your examples with works of art.

## Glossary

**Abstract Expressionism**   (1) *gestural:* a style of painting that arose ca. 1945 in New York. Chief figure in the movement was Jackson Pollock. Relied for its effect on brushwork that implied the action of the artist, and apparently accidental effects such as produced by the drip technique. Rooted in esthetics of spontaneity that emerged with Impressionism. (See below, "first generation.") (2) *Imagist:* a style of painting in which the body language of Abstract Expressionism is rejected in favor of large fields of pulsating color.

**affect**   (noun; accent on first syllable) inherent feeling, emotion in a work of art that is evident, expressive, and capable of influencing a viewer's feeling.

**appropriation**   the incorporation in a modern work of some feature associated with a work of the past. Similar to a quotation in literature. Appeared prominently in the 1980s, along with the widespread critical use of the term.

**archetype**   the original model of a thing or idea of which all later representations are copies, either literally or metaphorically. (Venus is the archetype of female beauty.)

**Art Brut**   an anti-aesthetic style, stressing rough textures. Also refers sometimes to art of the insane. Jean Dubuffet is an important exponent of *Art Brut.* Emerged as an important aesthetic position in the 1950s.

**Assemblage**   a three-dimensional work of art composed of a variety of materials and objects. The work is rooted in Picasso's early constructions, and has had a long life; the term became current, however, in the 1960s.

**automatism**   the psycho-philosophical theory, adopted by the Surrealists, that consciousness does not control action. The Surrealists attempted by various means to *suppress* consciousness, to allow the *un*conscious to assume automatic control.

**biomorphic**   referring to shapes that suggest living organisms.

**CoBrA**   an expressionist movement that flourished immediately after World War II, founded by Karel Appel with Asger Jorn and Pierre Alechinsky. The letters stand for Copenhagen, Brussels, and Amsterdam.

**Color Field**   also called Hard-Edge Abstraction and Post-Painterly Abstraction. Embraces a range of styles; characteristics are large size, non-objective, flatly painted, often with sharp-edged shapes, but also can be soft-edged, as in Helen Frankenthaler's work. Appeared in the 1950s, but became prominent in the sixties. Some authors classify Abstract-Imagists in the Color Field category.

**Earthworks**   usually large-scale manipulations of land, often temporary, sometimes intended to be permanent. Appeared in·the late 1960s.

**Environmental Art**   the term is used in two contexts. (1) First used in connection with artists who created scenes similar to theatrical sets, into which the "viewer" entered, to interact with the objects in the "set." Important development in the 1950s. (2) Also used in connection with Earthworks that shape the environment.

**field**   the flat surface on which an artist paints or otherwise makes marks in order to create a work of art.

**"first generation"**   a term frequently used in connection with the artists who created Abstract Expressionism in the 1940s; Adolph Gottlieb, Willem de Kooning, Franz Kline, Robert Motherwell, Jackson Pollock, Mark Rothko, and Clyfford Still were among the most prominent. The style continued to be influential among painters who turned to it in the fifties and sixties.

**Happening**   an event similar to a performance; planned but spontaneous in practice. Prominent in the early 1950s.

**iconic**   in art, an image that represents the figure frontally.

**iconography**   see Glossary, Unit I.

**Junk Art**   art composed of discarded objects, usually broken, rusted, or in some other state of disrepair. Associated with assemblage, the term gained currency in the 1960s.

**Kinetic Art**   sculpture that moves either by mechanical means or by air currents. Appeared early, in Russian Constructivism and in the work of Alexander Calder, but was given its terminology in the 1960s.

**Kunsthalle**   art gallery (*Kunst,* German for "art").

**Minimalism**   an application to painting and sculpture of the principle "less is more." Characterized by geometric precision and impersonal, "cool," expression. Appeared in the 1960s.

**mode**   a particular manner; related to the word "style," but less formal in connotation.

**myth**   a narrative the truth of which is symbolic rather than literal.

**Neo-Expressionism**   figurative expressionism that appeared early in the 1980s.

**Op Art**   non-objective painting of patterns in such a way as to create optical ambiguities and the illusion of movement. Appeared in the sixties, the two-dimensional analogue of Kinetic sculpture.

**paradigm**   a model or pattern, usually with the meaning of essence of, or perfect example of. *Number One* is a paradigm of Abstract Expressionist style.

**phenomenon**   a fact or event observable by the senses (sight, hearing, smell, taste, touch), susceptible of scientific description and explanation.

**Performance Art**   a performance by an artist in an art environment, usually a gallery or museum. Appeared in the sixties but flourished in the seventies.

**Pop Art**   the appropriation by fine art of objects and images of popular culture.

**positivism**   a system of philosophy originated by August Comte (1798–1857) which holds as real only natural phenomena or properties of knowable things. According to positivist thinking, spiritual reality is a contradiction in terms.

**post-Modernism**   a term that began frequently to appear in modernist criticism of the 1980s. Refers to the reinterpretation of past styles in the context of contemporary taste in painting, sculpture, and architecture. Modernist revivalism.

**Primary structures**   a term for Minimalism in sculpture.

**Process Art**   based on the aesthetics of anti-structure. Involves the use of material which by its nature is relatively formless and disintegrative, subject to the effects of natural forces. Suggests the ultimate condition of all phenomena.

**rationalism**   in philosophy, the theory that reason is a source of knowledge in itself, independent of the senses. In practice, acting or believing in accordance to what appears to be reasonable, recognizing cause-and-effect relationships. In art, painting and sculpture that express reason in the method of handling materials, and in its imagery. See *automatism*, for contrast.

**Systemic Art**   related to Color Field, with similar hard-edge characteristics.

**tactile**   pertaining to the sense of touch. In painting, the effect of calling up in the viewer the memory of how depicted objects actually feel. Since objects exist in space, tactility is related to the experience of three-dimensionality.

**totemic**   in art, representation that suggests the primitive style of people whose cultural organization is based on totemic relationships. Frontal. Similar to iconic (see above).

## Artists Patrons, and Important Personages

This list comprises pertinent publications and activities cited for the period 1940 to 1955 only.

**Bacon, Francis** (England, 1909–   ). Figurative expressionist, and appropriator of past art (see Glossary, *appropriation*), Bacon's grotesque imagery constitutes a powerful statement on the age of anxiety.

**Baur, John I. H.** Associate director in this period (later, Director) of the Whitney Museum of American Art. Author, *Revolution and Tradition in Modern Art* (1951).

**Beuys, Joseph** (Germany, 1921–1986). Highly influential in developing Performance and Process art, and in using these modes of expression as statements of political ideology.

**Cage, John.** Composer; decisive intellectual and aesthetic influence on many modernists, especially Rauschenberg.

**Castelli, Leo.** Gallery owner; first important supporter of Johns and Rauschenberg.

**Christo (Christo Javachef)** (Bulgaria, 1935). Associated with wrapping architecture and with variations of Earthworks.

**De Kooning, Willem** (Holland, 1904–   ). One of the "first generation" Abstract Expressionists. Played a major role in winning world-wide influence for modernist American art.

**Dubuffet, Jean** (France, 1901–1985). The greatest painter to appear in post-World War II France. Exponent of **Art Brut** (see Glossary).

**Egan, Charles.** Gallery owner. Supported avant-garde art in the 1940s.

**Estes, Richard** (United States, 1936–   ). Master of illusionism, one of the most important painters in the revival of realistic imagery.

**Frankenthaler, Helen** (United States, 1928–   ). Her systematic use of staining color into raw canvas was highly influential in the development of Color Field painting.

**Fuller, Buckminster** (1895–1983). The most radical architect-engineer of the twentieth century. He is associated with his invention of the Dymaxion House in 1929, the most advanced functional structure in the world, a veritable machine for living that makes Le Corbusier look conservative. His famous geodesic dome design, based on the structure of crystals, has been used by the American Army for living units, and the dome has served a variety of industrial uses.

**Goldwater, Robert.** Critic; editor of the *Magazine of Art,* first journal to pay critical attention to Abstract Expressionism (1940s).

**Greenberg, Clement.** The single most important critic supporting Abstract Expressionism in the 1940s. His writing appeared in *The Nation* and *Partisan Review.*

**Grooms, Red** (United States, 1937–   ). Creator of the most extensive environment pieces, which comment on American life on an antic level. (See Glossary, environment (1).)

**Guggenheim, Peggy.** Opened her Art of This Century gallery in 1942. Designed by sculptor Frederick Kiesler as a Surrealist environment, this gallery became the meeting place for European and American artists.

**Hess, Thomas B.** Managing Editor, *Art News,* beginning 1948, which gave strong support to Abstract Expressionism under his leadership.

**Hockney, David** (England, 1937–   ). Exponent of English Pop Art in the 1960s, Hockney has won recognition as one of the leading artists of this period.

**Hunter, Sam.** Art critic, *New York Times,* 1947–1949.

**Janis, Sidney.** Critic; gallery owner. Author, *Abstract and Surrealist Art in America* (1944).

**Johns, Jasper** (United States, 1930). Radical innovator of the fifties, forerunner of Pop Art. Widely recognized as a major contemporary American artist.

**Johnson, Philip** (United States, 1906–   ). As director of the architectural department of the Museum of Modern Art he organized, with Henry-Russell Hitchcock the exhibition *The International Style: Architecture Since 1922,* a watershed exhibition that canonized International Style and gave it its name. Has been a major force in American architecture.

**Judd, Donald** (United States, 1928–   ). A major figure of Minimalism, Judd's puristic interpretation raised basic issues about the nature of a work of art—not a new question in the twentieth century, but constantly renewed as definitions have been forced to retreat in the face of innovations.

**Kaprow, Allen** (United States, 1927–   ). Inventor of Happenings.

**Kieffer, Anselm** (Germany, 1945–   ). Leading figure in the Neo-Expressionist movement in the 1980s.

**Kienholz, Edward** (United States, 1927– ). Broadened the range of American expressionism in three-dimensional art with the savagery of his social comment.

**Kootz, Samuel M.** Gallery owner; author, *New Frontiers in American Painting* (1943).

**Lichtenstein, Roy** (United States, 1923– ). One of the creators of Pop art.

**Martin, Agnes** (United States, 1912– ). Pioneer American Minimalist painter.

**Miller, Dorothy.** Curator of Painting and Sculpture, Museum of Modern Art, 1943–47; curator of museum collections, 1947–67; exhibition organizer for *14 Americans* (1946), the first exhibition at the Museum of Modern Art that included Abstract Expressionists.

**Morris, Robert** (United States, 1931– ). A major figure associated with Minimalism, Process Art, and Neo-Expressionism.

**Motherwell, Robert** (United States, 1915– ). The most important artist-theoretician of the early post–World War II period. Master of monumental collage (originally conceived as a small-form mode) and an outstanding "first-generation" Abstract-Expressionist.

**Nevelson, Louise** (United States, 1900–1988). Foremost pioneer in American monumental Assemblage and Junk Art.

**Newman, Barnett** (1905–1970). Associated with the Abstract-Imagist branch of Abstract Expressionism, and forerunner of Minimalism.

**Oldenburg, Claes** (Sweden, 1926). An early participant in the creation of Happenings and a creator of Pop Art, which he transformed into a monumental mode. Originator of "soft sculptures" in the Dada tradition of non-functioning functional objects.

**Parsons, Betty.** Gallery owner; strong supporter of avant-garde art in the fifties.

**Pearlstein, Philip** (United States, 1924– ). Outstanding for his successful adaptation of minimalist spareness to illusionistic realism. Famed for his studio nudes.

**Pollock, Jackson** (United States, 1912–1956). Most widely known of the Abstract Expressionists and symbol of the movement.

**Putzel, Howard.** Friend of prominent artists of the American avant-garde, including Jackson Pollock, Hans Hofmann, Adolph Gottlieb, Mark Rothko, among others. Assistant 1942–1944 to Peggy Guggenheim, he introduced her to American modernists, some of whom subsequently had solo exhibitions at her Art of This Century Gallery.

**Rauschenberg, Robert** (United States, 1925– ). Creator of "combines," the most important advance in the development of assemblage since the Dada period. Forerunner of Pop Art.

**Reinhardt, Ad** (United States, 1913–1967). A stylistic purist, closely related to the Abstract Imagists, he became a leading influence on Minimalism.

**Rosenberg, Harold.** Highly influential critic; invented the term "action painting."

**Rothko, Mark** (United States, 1903–1980). One of the "first generation" Abstract Expressionists, in the Abstract Imagist wing.

**Schnabel, Julian** (United States, 1951– ). Major influence in the emergence of Neo-Expressionism in the 1980s.

**Schapiro, Meyer.** Eminent art historian. Author, "Rebellion in Art," in *America in Crisis,* ed. Daniel Aaron (1952). Advised and inspired many avant-garde artists.

**Segal, George.** Created an innovative synthesis of extreme realism with abstraction by casting figures from life and placing them in life-like environments while keeping them in an obviously artificial state of white plaster, which emphasizes the medium.

**Smith, David** (United States, 1906–1965). The most influential American sculptor in the field of welded metal sculpture constructions.

**Smithson, Robert** (United States, 1938–1973). Creator of the most famous of Earthworks, *Spiral Jetty* (1969–70).

**Soby, James Thrall.** Author, *Contemporary Painters* (1948).

**Stella, Frank** (United States, 1936– ). Since 1960, the most influential American artist. From the bare, geometric, Minimalist, shaped canvases of the sixties, through a series of stylistic shifts to the dramatic wall reliefs of the eighties, every move has made an impact on Modernist world art.

**Stirling, James** (England, 1926). One of the leading influential figures of post-Modernist architecture.

**Sweeney, James J.** Museologist; writer. Director of Painting and Sculpture, Museum of Modern Art, 1945–46; Director, Guggenheim Museum, 1952–60. Wrote introduction to the catalogue of Jackson Pollock's first solo show, 1943, at the Art of This Century gallery.

**Venturi, Robert** (United States, 1925). The most influential figure in the creation of post-Modernism in architecture.

**Warhol, Andy** (United States, 1930–1987). The public symbol of Pop Art.

## Bibliography

**ILLUSTRATION REFERENCES IN ADDITION TO THE ABOVE**

Alloway, L. *Topics in American Art Since 1945.* New York, 1975.

Arnason, H. H. *History of Modern Art: Painting, Sculpture, Architecture, Photography.* 3rd ed. Englewood Cliffs, N.J., and New York, 1986.

Hughes, R. *The Shock of the New.* New York, 1981.

Hunter, S., and Jacobus, J. *Modern Art: Painting, Sculpture, Architecture, Photography.* 3rd ed. New Jersey/New York, 1986.

Russell, J., and Gablik, S. *Pop Art Redefined.* New York, 1969.

**ARCHITECTURE**

Searing, H. *New American Art Museums.* New York, 1982.

Stephens, S., ed. *Building the New Museum.* Princeton, N.J., 1986.

**SPECIAL SUBJECTS**

Ashton, D. *Twentieth-Century Artists on Art.* New York, 1985. Statements by artists.

Chipp, H. *Theories of Modern Art.* Berkeley, Los Angeles, and London, 1971.

Harris, A. S., and Nochlin, L. *Women Artists: 1550–1950.* New York, 1978.

Hess, T. B., and Nochlin, L., eds. *Woman as Sex Object: Studies in Erotic Art, 1730–1970.* New York, 1972.

Kramer, H. *The Age of the Avant-garde.* New York, 1976. Art criticism.

Raven, A.; Langer, C. L.; Frueh, J., eds. *Feminist Art Criticism: An Anthology.* Ann Arbor, Mich. 1988.

Rose, B. *Readings in American Art: 1900–1975.* New York, 1975. Statements by artists.

Rubin, W., ed. *"Primitivism" in Twentieth-Century Art: Affinity of the Tribal and the Modern*. New York, 1984.

Steinberg, L. *Other Criteria: Confrontations with Twentieth-Century Art*. New York, 1972. Art criticism.

## MAJOR MOVEMENTS

### Abstract Expressionism

Ashton, D. *The New York School: A Cultural Reckoning*. New York, 1973.

Geldzahler, H. *New York Painting and Sculpture: 1940–1970*. New York, 1969.

Greenberg, C. *Art and Culture: Critical Essays*. Boston, 1961.

Rosenberg, H. *The Tradition of the New*. New York, 1959.

Sandler, I. *The Triumph of American Painting: A History of Abstract Expressionism*. New York, 1970.

### European Painting in the Forties and Fifties

Lucie-Smith, E. *Late Modern*. New York, 1976.

Leymarie, J. *Art Since Mid-Century: The New Internationalism*. 2 vols. Greenwich, Conn., 1971.

### Minimalism and Op Art

Alloway, L. *Systemic Painting*. New York, 1966.

Barrett, C. *Op Art*. New York, 1970.

Battcock, G. *Minimal Art: A Critical Anthology*. New York, 1968.

Foster, S. *The Critics of Abstract Expressionism*. Ann Arbor, Mich., 1980.

Greenberg, C. *Post-Painterly Abstraction*. Los Angeles, 1964.

Popper, F. *Origins and Development of Kinetic Art*. Greenwich, Conn., 1968.

Seitz, W. C. *The Responsive Eye*. New York, 1959.

Tuchman, M. *American Sculpture of the Sixties*. Los Angeles, 1965.

### POP ART, ASSEMBLAGE, PERFORMANCE, AND EARTHWORKS

Alloway, L. *American Pop Art*. New York, 1974.

Beardsley, J. *Earthworks and Beyond: Contemporary Art in the Landscape*. New York, 1984.

Goldberg, R. *Performance: Live Art 1909 to the Present*. New York, 1979.

Haskell, B. *Blam! The Explosion of Pop, Minimalism, and Performance: 1958–1964*. New York, 1984.

Henri, A. *Total Art: Environments, Happenings, and Performance*. London, 1974.

Kaprow, A. *Assemblage, Environments, and Happenings*. New York, 1966.

Lippard, L. *Pop Art*. New York, 1966.

Lucie-Smith, E. *Art in the Seventies*. Ithaca, N.Y., 1980.

Mahsun, C. A. *Pop Art and the Critics*. Ann Arbor, Mich., 1987.

Pincus-Witten, R. *Postminimalism: American Art of the Decade*. New York, 1977.

Russell, J., and Gablik, S. *Pop Art Redefined*. New York, 1969.

Seitz, W. C. *The Art of Assemblage*. New York, 1961.

Sonfist, A., ed. *Art in the Land: A Critical Anthology of Environmental Art*. New York, 1983.

### Representation

Arthur, J. *Realism/Photorealism*. Tulsa, Ok., 1980.

Goodyear, Jr., F. H. *Contemporary Realism Since 1960*. Boston, 1981.

Wallis, B. *Art After Modernism: Rethinking Representation*. New York, 1984.

### Art of the Eighties

Cowart, J. *Expressions: New Art from Germany, George Baselwitz, Jorg Immendorff, Anselm Kiefer, Markus Lupertz, A. R. Penck*. St. Louis, 1983.

Kramer, H. *The Revenge of the Philistines: Art and Culture, 1972–1984*. New York, 1985.

Kraus, R. *The Originality of the Avant-Garde and Other Modernist Myths*. Cambridge, Mass., 1985.

Krauthammer, C. *Cutting Edges: Making Sense of the Eighties*. New York, 1985.

Kuspit, D. *The New Subjectivism: Art in the 1980s*. Ann Arbor, Mich., 1988.

Pincus-Witten, R. *Postminimalism into Maximalism: American Art, 1966–1986*. Ann Arbor, Mich., 1986.